Principles and Methods of Adapted Physical Education and Recreation

Principles and Methods of Adapted Physical Education and Recreation

David Auxter, Ed.D.
Senior Scientist
Research Institute for Independent Living
Edgewater, Maryland

Jean Pyfer, P.E.D.
Chair of Kinesiology
Texas Woman's University
Denton, Texas

Carol Huettig, Ph.D.
Instructional Specialist
Preschool Program for Children with Disabilities
Dallas Independent School District
Dallas, Texas

EIGHTH EDITION

with 265 illustrations

 Mosby

St. Louis Baltimore Boston Carlsbad Chicago Naples New York Philadelphia Portland
London Madrid Mexico City Singapore Sydney Tokyo Toronto Wiesbaden

Dedicated to Publishing Excellence

A Times Mirror
Company

Vice President and Publisher: James M. Smith
Senior Acquisitions Editor: Vicki Malinee
Developmental Editor: Brian Morovitz
Project Manager: Deborah L. Vogel
Production Editor: Judith Bange
Layout Artist: Jeanne E. Genz
Designer: Pati Pye/E. Rohne Rudder
Manufacturing Supervisor: Linda Ierardi
Cover Design: E. Rohne Rudder

EIGHTH EDITION

Printed in the United States of America
Composition by Clarinda Company
Lithography by Clarinda Company
Printing/binding by R.R. Donnelley & Sons Company

Mosby-Year Book, Inc.
11830 Westline Industrial Drive
St. Louis, Missouri 63146

Library of Congress Cataloging in Publication Data

Auxter, David.
     Principles and methods of adapted physical education and
  recreation / David Auxter, Jean Pyfer, Carol Huettig. -- 8th ed.
       p.   cm.
     Includes bibliographical references and index.
     ISBN 0-8151-0891-5
     1. Physical education for handicapped children--Study and
  teaching--United States.   2. Handicapped children--Recreation-
  -United States.   I. Pyfer, Jean.   II. Huettig, Carol.   III. Title.
  GV445.A94   1996
  371.9'04486--dc20   96-16198
                                                  CIP

96 97 98 99 00 / 9 8 7 6 5 4 3 2 1

To our families, students, and friends who understand and support our need to enable individuals with disabilities to take their rightful place in the mainstream of society

Preface

We approached the eighth edition of the text with excitement and with several questions. Professionals have committed their lives, or are planning to commit their energy, to enhancing the lives of infants, toddlers, youngsters, teenagers, young adults, and adults with disabilities by improving their ability to participate in play, games, leisure, recreation, sports, and physical fitness activities

There are many fine doctoral, master's, and undergraduate programs throughout the country training professional adapted physical educators, therapeutic recreators, and physical educators to serve individuals with disabilities. Medical and assistive technology exists that can significantly improve the quality of life of individuals with disabilities. More individuals with disabilities have the opportunity to participate in play, games, leisure, recreation, sports, and physical fitness activities than ever before in history.

However, adapted physical education specialists, physical educators, and therapeutic recreators face, perhaps, their greatest challenge since Section 504 of the Rehabilitation Act of 1973 and Public Law 94-142 (1975) became law. Almost 25 years after the "right" to a free and appropriate public education for *all* children and youth was affirmed, educators and recreators will be challenged with broad and systemic societal and educational changes that place in question the very existence of programs designed to meet the unique and specific needs of all individuals with disabilities, particularly those programs some deem nonessential, such as physical education and recreation. These systemic changes include economic policies that:

- Place in question the future of programs for infants and children with disabilities who are in need of a jump start in life if they are going to succeed in school and society.
- Place in question equal access to quality education, social services, and medical and health care programs.
- Place increased emphasis on local control of education policy and reduction of state and federal standards regarding the education of all children and young adults, including those with disabilities (fine within a humanistic community—devastating in one that is not).
- Emphasize "inclusion" programs that may be a result of administrative expediency and misperception regarding the reduced cost of those programs, rather than being designed with a child in mind.
- Increase focus on academic activities—"ABCs" and "readin', writin' and 'rithmetic"—as opposed to quality-of-life issues essential to the lives of all children and adults, particularly those with disabilities—physical education, leisure and recreation, sex education, creative arts, music, and drama. Such an approach disregards entirely Gardner's potent and significant notion that there are eight diverse types of intelligence that should be taught and fostered in our country's schools.

We have tried to address these issues, and others, as honestly as possible and have suggested strategies for adapted physical education specialists, physical educators, and therapeutic recreators to deal with "real-world" issues that confront children and adults with disabilities and those who hope to serve them. It is vital that professionals committed to quality, individually designed, developmentally appropriate physical education and recreation programs for children and adults with disabilities rally and mobilize to ensure that those we serve receive the services they deserve.

Content Features

Content throughout the book has again been thoroughly researched, referenced, and updated. Two new chapters address contemporary issues in physical education and recreation programs for individuals with disabilities: Chapter 5, Delivering Services in the Most Inclusive Environment (including a matrix that considers seven components involved in decisions regarding the least restrictive environment); and Chapter 10, Infants, Toddlers, and Preschoolers.

> PART ONE: THE SCOPE provides updated information regarding the law and litigation as it impacts the lives of individuals with disabilities.
>
> PART TWO: KEY TECHNIQUES includes an updated chapter addressing developmentally appropriate assessment in the psychomotor domain, with a classic explanation of the sensory-motor integrative process and the role of the adapted physical educator in intervention. In addition, the development of appropriate individual education programs is considered, which includes specific information on the individual transition plan and the "futures planning" process.
>
> PART THREE: GENERIC EDUCATIONAL NEEDS addresses educational needs that can effectively be addressed in physical education settings and include motor, physical fitness, and psychosocial development. Strategies to determine developmental levels and intervention strategies to overcome delays are presented.
>
> PART FOUR: NEEDS OF SPECIFIC POPULATIONS has been completely reworked so that in addition to new, "state of the art" information, it boasts a consistent framework that is easy to follow. Each chapter follows the same format and, as such, becomes a useful reference for the adapted physical educator, as well as the regular physical educator.
>
> PART FIVE: ORGANIZATION AND ADMINISTRATION has been completely revised and includes information key to contemporary school reform, including site-based management, multiculturalism, and family involvement.

Inclusive Coverage of Dynamic Issues

We have addressed specific issues of vital importance to the adapted physical education specialist, physical educator, and therapeutic recreator, including:

- Recent laws and litigation that affect programs for individuals with disabilities
- Strategies for interacting effectively with parents and their advocates
- Practical suggestions for providing quality physical education and recreation services for children and adults with disabilities and their families in the most inclusive environment
- The nature of the consultancy and the consultant's responsibilities in adapted physical education
- Strategies for dealing with professional, paraprofessional, and volunteer personnel in the schools
- The role of the professional in site-based management and in response to educational change (e.g., total quality management and multiculturalism)
- The educator/recreator as an advocate for children and adults with disabilities
- Assessment and the development of the IEP, with a new section dealing with portfolio assessments for young children with disabilities
- The individual family service plan and transition plan
- Strategies for using computer technology to enhance instruction

New to This Edition

- Chapter 5, Delivering Services in the Most Inclusive Environment, helps the regular physical educator serve the student with disabilities in the regular classroom setting. This chapter also serves as a valuable reference for the adapted physical educator to assist the regular physical educator with inclusion.
- Chapter 10, Infants, Toddlers, and Preschoolers, offers information that physical educators need to provide quality intervention for infants, toddlers, and preschoolers.
- A real example of the relationship between comprehensive assessment and intervention (a *real* child with a made-up name—Billy Bogg) is followed throughout the chapters that address "key techniques" and "generic educational needs" (i.e., Chapters 2 through 9).
- Scenarios describe *real* children and young adults at the beginning of each of the chapters that describe specific disabilities (i.e., Chapters 11 through 17). The reader is encouraged to consider material with the *real* student in mind. Reader tasks and activities refer to these scenarios.

- Chapters on specific disabilities are consistently organized to allow the student to find distinct information and identify the magnitude of severity.
- Key terms are in boldface type in the text and are defined in the expanded Glossary in the back of the book.
- New graphics and a more effective photo program enhance the visual appeal of the text.
- Appendix C, Sports Organizations for Persons with Disabilities, lists contact information for a number of national and international organizations offering unique activity opportunities.

Pedagogical Aids

- **Scenarios** open applicable chapters and guide the students to a real-world application of content.
- **Tasks** at the start of applicable chapters help students read the text from the perspective of how it can be directly applied to their future teaching experience.
- **Key terms** are printed in boldface type within each chapter and can be found in the expanded **Glossary.**
- **Review Questions** and **Student Activities** assist in fostering class discussion and introduce advanced topics for exploration.
- **References** and **Suggested Readings** have been thoroughly revised to include the most up-to-date documentation for students who wish to further research topics being discussed.

Ancillaries
Instructor's Manual

Extensively revised for this edition, this manual provides instructors with lecture outlines, teaching suggestions, new test questions, an alphabetical resource list of organizations that serve individuals with disabilities, and new transparency masters.

Computerized Test Bank

ESATEST Computerized Test Bank, with over 300 matching, true/false, listing, and essay questions, is available in IBM Windows and Macintosh formats to qualified adopters.

Gross Motor Activities for Young Children with Special Needs

With your purchase of this new textbook you will receive this excellent resource for students and instructors looking for activities to use in the classroom. This pocket guide includes 210 games and activities designed to promote equilibrium, sensory stimulation/discrimination, body image, locomotor skills, cross-lateral integration, aerobic fitness, and relaxation, as well as entertaining cooperative and "animal action" games.

Acknowledgments

Many contributed their efforts, wisdom, and support in the preparation of this eighth edition of the text. We wish to acknowledge their contributions. In particular, we would like to acknowledge Cole and Molly, who gave up many camping trips and "ball at the lake" days to allow their moms time to work on this edition.

We would like to thank the following individuals for their exceptional commitment to individuals with disabilities and for their willingness to share photographs and program information with us.

- Maureen Dowd, Director, Manitoba (Canada) Special Olympics
- Ron Davis, Associate Professor, Adapted Physical Education, Ball State University, Muncie, Indiana
- The Achilles Track Club, New York City
- The San Diego Parks and Recreation Department
- Wilderness Inquiry
- Barbara Brandis, President, Research Institute for Independent Living
- George Smith, Director of Unified Sports, Special Olympics International
- Tom Songster, Sports Director, Special Olympics International
- Joe Natale, Texas Woman's University, with special thanks for his comprehensive, creative, computer-assisted library searches . . . he saved us hours in the library

We would also like to express our thanks to the following individuals in the Dallas Public Schools for their support and assistance:

- Alberta Pingel, the "constant" leadership within the Special Education Program
- Angela Pittman, Specialist, Birth-to-Five, for her innovative leadership in programs designed to serve infants and young children and their families
- Judy Achilles, Specialist, Speech and Language, for honoring and respecting the essential relationship between language, movement, and play development

- Carol Powell, Instructional Specialist, Preschool Programs for Children with Disabilities, who knows more about gently facilitating the learning of young children than anyone we know
- Virginia Nelson, Specialist, Autism, for her continued dedication to students with autism and their families
- Arlene Stein and Diane Garner, for their incredible personal and professional commitment to the deaf and hearing impaired
- Joanne Hughes, Principal, Walnut Hill Elementary School, and Dick Knox, Principal, Seagoville Middle School, for their vision and leadership in the development of quality inclusion/developmentally appropriate educational programs for preschoolers

Comments and criticisms from users of the seventh edition were carefully considered for this edition. A panel of reviewers currently teaching adapted physical education courses in colleges and universities was selected to assist with the revised manuscript to meet the needs of the instructors and their students. There was close scrutiny of the book to verify that content was ex-

cellent and usable. To these colleagues, we would like to express our sincere appreciation:

Robert W. Arnhold, Ph.D., Slippery Rock University, Slippery Rock, Pennsylvania

Martin E. Block, Ph.D., University of Virginia, Charlottesville, Virginia

William B. Karper, Ed.D., University of North Carolina at Greensboro, Greensboro, North Carolina

Christine Stopka, Ph.D., and David George Suro, M.S., University of Florida, Gainesville, Florida

Finally, at Mosby we would like to thank Judi Bange, our production editor, for her assistance in streamlining and improving the text. And, perhaps most important, we would like to extend our thanks and appreciation to Brian Morovitz, our developmental editor, for his zeal, enthusiasm, and excitement. His interest in our work helped us respond with zeal, enthusiasm, and excitement—the mark of a great editor.

David Auxter
Jean Pyfer
Carol Huettig

Contents

Part Three   Generic Educational Needs

Part Four   Needs of Specific Populations

Part Five   Organization and Administration

Appendixes

Principles and Methods of Adapted Physical Education and Recreation

part *one*

The Scope

In this section we provide a historical overview of societal attitudes toward individuals with disabilities. In the 1990s the United States is still attempting to implement the commitment to protecting individual and civil rights of persons with disabilities mandated by legislation of the 1970s. The mandates and detailed procedures to follow for compliance with the laws are presented in this section. Effective teaching methods and types of assessment to meet specific needs are discussed.

Educating People with Disabilities

Objectives

Describe the nature and prevalence of disabling conditions.

Explain the history of services to persons with disabilities.

Cite the impact of legislation for provision of physical education services to individuals with disabilities.

Describe the effects of disabling conditions as they relate to social forces during school and postschool years.

Explain the role of the physical education teacher within the context of a generic human delivery system.

Cite the significance of labeling on physical education programming for individuals with disabling conditions.

Trace the status of implementing physical education programs for individuals with disabling conditions with respect to conformance to federal legislation.

Courtesy Dr. Ron Davis, Ball State University, Muncie, Ind.

A ssumptions about how persons with disabilities are to be physically educated are changing. To meet the needs of students with disabling conditions, physical educators must be prepared for the changing service patterns. When the Education of the Handicapped Act of 1975 (P.L. 94-142)[63] (originally known as the Education for All Handicapped Children Act) was enacted, physical education was the only educational curriculum specifically named. This singular identification has placed unique opportunities and responsibilities on the physical education profession to serve persons with disabilities.

Physical education teachers instruct children with a variety of disabling conditions in many different instructional settings. The mission of the physical education teacher is to promote the development of motor skills and abilities so that children can live healthful and productive lives and engage in independent leisure, physical, and sport activities of their choosing. This chapter is concerned with the nature of disabling conditions, the legal mandates pertaining to the rights of persons with disabilities, and benefits that can be derived from appropriate physical education programs for these populations.

Prevalence

The number of children with disabling conditions is fundamental to knowledge of personnel demands and other resources needed to serve this population. Prevalence refers to the number of people in a given category in a population group during a specific time interval (i.e., the number of mentally retarded children who are of school

age this year). The prevalence of school enrollment of children by disabling conditions during the 1992-1993 school year is shown in Figure 1-1. Each year the U.S. Department of Education, Office of Special Education and Rehabilitation Services (OSERS), reports to Congress pertinent facts about disabled populations. Some of the most recent facts are as follows: (1) there are over 4.4 million children 6 to 21 years of age with disabilities who receive special education services; (2) children with disabilities in special education represent approximately 11% of the entire school-age population; (3) about twice as many males as females receive special education; (4) approximately 90% of school-age children who receive special education services are mildly handicapped[29]; and (5) the three largest categories of children

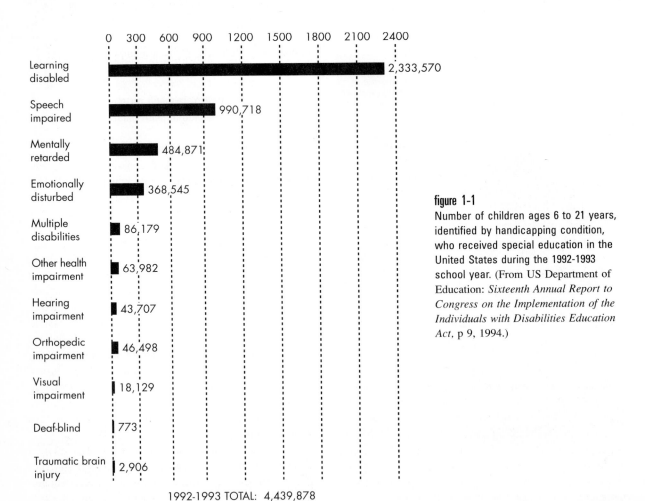

figure 1-1
Number of children ages 6 to 21 years, identified by handicapping condition, who received special education in the United States during the 1992-1993 school year. (From US Department of Education: *Sixteenth Annual Report to Congress on the Implementation of the Individuals with Disabilities Education Act*, p 9, 1994.)

with disabilities are those with learning disabilities, those with speech and language impairment, and those with mental retardation.

The incidence of children with disabilities in the public schools does not represent the magnitude of the need of persons who can benefit from special physical activity designed to accommodate the needs of individuals. In addition to those conditions outlined in the Individuals with Disabilities Education Act (IDEA), other special needs may qualify a child for special physical education considerations.

The number of individuals with multiple disabilities also is increasing. The reasons are many, but the primary ones seem to be the growing numbers of infants affected by drug use and inadequate prenatal care of the mother during the pregnancy, the higher rate of survival among infants born prematurely, advanced techniques of medical science that are keeping children with one or more disabilities alive, and increasing poverty, as well as child abuse and neglect.

Historical Implications
Early History

In highly developed countries the current level of concern for the well-being of the individual has evolved gradually over thousands of years. One characteristic of the typical early primitive cultures was their preoccupation with survival. Historians speculate that members of many early primitive societies who were unable to contribute to their own care were either put to death, allowed to succumb in a hostile environment, or forced to suffer a low social status. In some societies, persons displaying obvious behavioral deviations were considered from converse points of view—either filled with evil or touched by divine powers.

Humanitarianism

Great social and cultural progress occurred during the Renaissance. The seed of social consciousness had been planted. From this time on, a genuine concern for the individual developed, giving each person dignity. With a desire for social reform came a multitude of movements to improve life. Reforms dealing with peace, prison conditions, poverty, and insanity were organized, and many social and moral problems were attacked in the first decade of the nineteenth century.

Pinel unchains the insane. (Courtesy Parke, Davis, & Co, Detroit.)

During the latter part of the nineteenth century and the early part of the twentieth century, emphasis was placed on the development of instructional methodology to educate individuals with intellectual disabilities. This work had a significant impact on modern pedagogy. The Montessori approach was developed during the early part of the twentieth century for use with children with mental retardation. This was a didactic system in which learners used sequential materials consistent with their developmental level. The Montessori approach was a forerunner of individualized instructional programming, which is widely used at present.

Medical Approach to Disabling Conditions

World War I was a period that greatly advanced medical and surgical techniques designed to ameliorate many physically disabling conditions. In addition, individuals were restored to usefulness by vocational and workshop programs. During the interim between World War I and World War II, state and federal legislation was enacted to promote vocational rehabilitation for both civilians and the military disabled. The Smith-Sears Act of 1918 and the National Civilian Vocational Rehabilitation Act of 1920 were the forerunners of the Social Security Act of 1935 and the Vocational Rehabilitation Act of 1943, which provided individuals with disabilities with both physical and vocational rehabilitation.

With World War II came thousands of ill and incapacitated service personnel. Means were employed to restore them to function as useful and productive members of society. Physical medicine became a new medical specialty. Many services heretofore considered hospital services became autonomous ancillary medical fields. The paramedical specialties of physical therapy, occupational therapy, and corrective therapy considerably decreased the recovery time of many patients.

However, the main impetus for aiding individuals with disabilities did not occur until early in the twentieth century and as late as the early 1960s for persons with mental retardation or emotional disturbance. The contributions of figures such as President Franklin D. Roosevelt, supporting the fight against crippling diseases such as poliomyelitis, and the Kennedy family, working to help individuals with mental retardation, can hardly be overlooked when discussing the humanitarian concerns in the United States.

During the 1960s, instructional techniques such as task analysis, which had been developed during World War II, were tried with individuals with mental retardation and found to be successful. Studies carried out in that decade demonstrated that when a task could be reduced to its component parts, with those parts taught in sequence, even individuals with profound retardation could learn relatively complex tasks.[25] When behavior management techniques were used to focus the learner's attention on a specific task, productivity was greatly enhanced. The value of combining task analysis with behavioral management strategies to enable persons with mental retardation to learn coincided with a growing national sensitivity to the rights of all persons with disabilities.

Federal Legislation and the Rights of Persons with Disabilities

The rights of persons with disabilities became a central concern during the 1970s when landmark court cases ruled that children with disabilities had a right to a free and appropriate education and training, and that persons in institutions had a right to rehabilitation. These court decisions paralleled the enactment of education and re-

habilitation legislation, such as the Rehabilitation Act of 1973 and the Education of the Handicapped Act of 1975 (P.L. 94-142).

During the 1980s the education and training of persons with disabilities was transformed by the implementation of P.L. 94-142.[37] The laws guaranteed parents a central role in decisions about the education of their children. Preschool programs and voluntary programs for infants and toddlers were addressed in legislation (P.L. 99-457). The requirement that secondary programs focus on transition skills that would facilitate independent life in the community began to be emphasized.

At the beginning of the 1990s the passage of the Americans with Disabilities Act (ADA) and the Individuals with Disabilities Education Act (IDEA) further addressed the rights of persons with disabilities. At this writing the U.S. Congress is once again restructuring the federal laws that pertain to rights of individuals with disabilities. Legislation will no doubt reflect the growing practice of including all children, regardless of ability level, in the regular classroom and place more educational decision making at the state and local levels.

Challenge of the Future

The challenge of the future will be to provide appropriate and adequate educational programs for increasing numbers of children with disabilities. It has been projected that the number of children living in poverty will continue to rise dramatically in this country.[17] Because the concomitants to poverty (poor health care, inadequate nutrition, less schooling) contribute to the incidence of disability,[49] an increase in the need for special educational provisions is anticipated. In addition to delivering educational programs, schools will be pressed to assume the responsibilities for providing social and health services, nutritional programs, and prevention and health promotion programs. Because of the value of physical fitness and motor skills to a healthy and functional lifestyle, the physical educator has a central and critical role in contributing to the education of persons with disabilities.

Physical Activity and Functional Development

The relationship of physical activity to functional development and well-being has long been valued. In 460 BC Hippocrates used exercise to strengthen muscles and aid rehabilitation. Galen (30 BC) recommended specific ex-

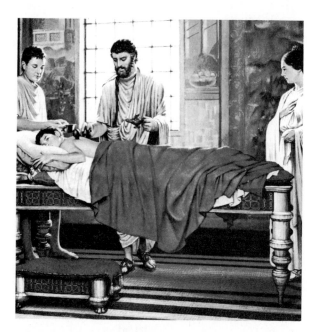

Galen treating an ill child by cupping. (Courtesy Parke, Davis, & Co, Detroit.)

ercises for muscle tonus, and Erasistratus advocated walking for dropsy. The fundamental value of the exercise was the physical well-being of the individual achieved through specific exercise regimens.

After World War II an emerging philosophy was social participation in sports and games. Such activity provided an opportunity to meet social and recreational needs, as well as promote physical and organic development. In 1952 the Committee on Adapted Physical Education adopted a resolution to accommodate children with disabilities in physical education programs of diversified developmental activities designed to specifically meet their needs.[1]

The commitment to this population was strengthened in the early 1970s when a group of adapted physical educators dedicated to providing appropriate programs for students with disabilities met in Washington, D.C. The purposes of their meeting were to define what constituted appropriate physical education for persons with disabilities and develop a strategy for ensuring that physical education was identified in P.L. 94-142. They were successful in their efforts, and that led to a national thrust to prepare physical educators with specialized training in providing programs for persons with disabilities. The definition they agreed on for physical education for persons with disabilities appears later in this chapter.

Since 1975 thousands of school-age children and youth with disabilities have been educated in the public and private schools in this country. The most fortunate of those students were taught by highly qualified physical education professionals. Those less fortunate were relegated to keeping score, were excused from physical activity, or were assigned to a regular physical education class taught by an educator with little or no background in providing for their needs.

To counter the trend of providing less than appropriate physical education experiences to students with disabilities, in 1994 the National Consortium for Physical Education and Recreation for Individuals with Disabilities published national standards for adapted physical education.[42] A certification examination to accompany the standards is now under development. It is hoped that the standards will provide state directors of physical education an understanding of what quality adapted physical education is and create a process for validating that the teacher is competent to deliver those services.

Definitions of Disabling Conditions

The term **developmental disabilities** in the Rehabilitation Act of 1973 refers to all disabilities collectively. Although each state or authority may have differing definitions of developmental disability or specific disabilities, this text is concerned with current federal definitions.

Section 504 of the Rehabilitation Act of 1973 (P.L. 93-112) defines a school-age person with a disability as anyone who has a physical or mental impairment that substantially limits one or more major life activities, such as:

- Caring for one's self
- Performing manual tasks
- Walking
- Seeing
- Hearing
- Speaking
- Breathing
- Learning
- Working

Students who do not qualify for special education services under the Individuals with Disabilities Education Act (IDEA) of 1996 but who might be eligible under Section 504 of the Rehabilitation Act (if their impairments substantially limit one or more of their major life activities) include those with the following conditions:

- Drug or alcohol dependency
- Attention deficit disorder or attention deficit–hyperactivity disorder
- Other health needs, such as insulin-dependent diabetes, severe allergies, arthritis, epilepsy, or temporary disabilities
- Communicable diseases, such as the human immunodeficiency virus (HIV)
- Social maladjustment
- Learning disabilities without a severe discrepancy between ability and achievement
- Removal from special education because the student no longer meets eligibility criteria under IDEA[46]

The scope of special education for the exceptional child is broad. Programs of instruction can be offered in a number of places, depending on the needs of the child. Special education is available in hospitals, special residential and day schools, and special classes for children with disabilities within the regular schools, as well as in-home instruction. However, the majority of students with disabilities attend regular schools.

The concern of all persons is that every individual with disabilities should have the opportunity to reach full potential through an individualized education program.

Physical Education for Persons with Disabilities

Persons with disabilities engage in physical activity that is administered by many different types of personnel and carried out in a variety of settings. The following terms are associated with physical activity for persons with disabilities:

adapted physical education Modification of traditional physical activities to enable the child with disabilities to participate safely, successfully, and with satisfaction.
corrective physical education Activity designed to habilitate or rehabilitate deficiencies in posture or mechanical alignment of the body.
disability A limitation that is imposed on the individual by environmental demands and that is related to the individual's ability to adapt to environmental demands.[34]
disabled Describes an individual who has lost physical, social, or psychological functioning that significantly interferes with normal growth and development.[34]
disorder General mental, physical, or psychological malfunction of the processes.[34]
habilitation An educational term that indicates that the person with a disability is to be taught basic skills needed for independence.[34]
remedial physical education Activity designed to habilitate or rehabilitate functional motor movements and develop physical and motor prerequisites for functional skills.[34]
special physical education Another term used to describe adapted physical education.

An obstacle course facilitates the development of wheelchair mobility. (Courtesy Adapted Physical Education Department, Jefferson Parish Public School System, New Orleans, La.)

Definition of Physical Education

There is and has been a traditional curriculum common to most physical education programs. For the most part, physical education activities include participation in sports and the development of sufficient physical fitness to accomplish the activities of daily living and maintenance of health.

Traditionally, good teaching implies accommodation of the individual needs of the learner to enable successful participation. Special accommodations are made in the teaching of skills, and adaptations are made to include children in sport activities and group games. Physical education for individuals with disabilities was specifically defined in P.L. 94-142, and that definition was also used in IDEA. It included all of the previous definitions mentioned but was simply stated. We have accepted that definition for use in this textbook[63]:

1. The term means the development of:
   a. Physical and motor fitness
   b. Fundamental motor skills and patterns
   c. Skills in aquatics, dance, and individual and group games and sports (including intramural and lifetime sports)
2. The term includes special physical education, adapted physical education, movement education, and motor development.

The two essential components of physical education for persons with disabilities are teaching the defined curricula of physical education and conducting an individualized program for the child.

Benefits of Physical Education for Students with Disabilities

When a child is identified as having a disability, it serves notice to educators and parents that the child risks becoming dependent on others for leisure physical activity and social living skills. The physical educator can make a major contribution to reduce this risk and facilitate independent living through physical activity in the following ways:

- Develop recreational motor skills for independent functioning in the community.
- Develop physical fitness for maintenance of health.
- Develop **ambulatory skills** to master mobility in domestic and community environments.
- Develop physical and motor prerequisites to self-help skills required for independent living.
- Develop physical and motor prerequisites to vocational skills required for independent living.
- Develop prerequisite motor skills necessary for participation in self-fulfilling leisure, physical, and social activity.

The physical education program is a vital part of the total education program, which is designed to maximize the potential for self-sufficient living in the community.

It has long been argued that participation in sports develops the social characteristics of participants. Participation alone may not benefit individuals with disabilities; however, when the conditions of participation are well controlled (e.g., appropriate activities are offered at the ability level of the learner) and environments are designed that include a carefully structured modeling process, social development can be fostered through physical and sport activity.[12] To ensure that social benefits occur to all persons, the social environment should be constructed so that there is a match between the environmental demands of the sport or physical activity and the social capabilities of the participants. Furthermore, the participants without disabilities must be supportive of the socialization process.

Scope of Physical Education for Students with Disabilities

Public policy requires that children with disabilities be provided with physical education. The incorporation of physical education into the Education of the Handicapped Act of 1975 and the subsequent IDEA acts has led to many opportunities for offering appropriate services to students with disabilities, such as the following:

- Teaching motor skills to all children with disabilities, who will use these skills in recreational environments in the community
- Teaching the person with disabilities to generalize skills obtained in instructional settings into the community[8]
- Helping develop the fundamental motor skills, such as walking for persons with impaired ambulation
- Developing prerequisite physical and motor fitness for persons with severe involvement so that they

may develop self-help skills, such as feeding and dressing

▪ Being involved directly and meaningfully with persons who are severely and profoundly disabled, for whom the primary education program is motor

Clearly, the physical education program is vital to every person with a disability. Often the need for physical education bears a direct relationship to the severity of the disabling condition. Persons with profound mental retardation often have an educational program of development of ambulation skills, self-care skills, and communication. The physical education profession is needed to develop the fundamental skills of ambulation and the physical and motor prerequisites for the self-help skills. Persons who are mentally retarded often rely on recreational motor skills for their leisure.

Physical Education and Individualized Instruction

The content and purposes of individualized instructional procedures for physical education were well known long before IDEA. However, focus on individualized formats of instruction have added new meaning to the physical education profession. The focus of individualized physical education for persons with disabilities has had the following benefits for the profession:

▪ It has enabled an identifiable body of content that is the physical education curriculum (defined by federal law), developed out of a substantial history and tradition.

▪ It now has unique integrity with the recognized procedure and products associated with special education (specially designed instruction to meet unique needs as set forth in the individualized education program).

▪ The integrated disciplines of special and physical education rely on accurate language to meet public policy demands.

Parents often mediate for children with the school and community. For them to maximize opportunities for their children, they need to know specifically the benefits and the skills that are developed in school physical education programs and opportunities in the community where these acquired skills can be expressed. Therefore physical education teachers and parents of children with disabilities should meet frequently to ensure that the

school programs meet the child's needs for participation in the community.

Each child with a disability should have an **individualized physical education program.** The activities of the program should promote the acquisition of a skill, and each activity should begin at the child's present level of ability and progress in a sequence of small steps. It also is expected that aids will be introduced and the environment modified to enable successful participation. Tasks that meet the needs of the specific learner should be selected, and the length of participation in the tasks should be commensurate with the amount of self-sufficiency the child needs to develop.

The mission of physical education for persons with disabilities is to improve their quality of life. However, for physical education programs to be of greatest benefit, they must be carried over into daily leisure physical activities in the community after school. This requires coordination of services and resources in the home, school, and other community recreation agencies.

Recreational Sport Opportunities for Persons with Disabilities

Recreational sport opportunities for persons with disabilities vary at differing stages of life. In infant and preschool programs for children with disabilities, the focus is on motor development that is prerequisite to a wide variety of physical activities. When the individual enters the public school, there are three opportunities for participation in recreational sport activities. One is the physical education instructional program, which teaches the student the physical skills and knowledge necessary to play games and then actually generalizes the skills into play. A second environment that may be available in some schools is an intramural program. Here the student with disabilities has an opportunity to express the skills learned in physical education class in recreational play activity within the schools. A third source of opportunity for the child with a disability is community-based recreation programs that may take the form of integrated activity with other children in the community (YMCAs, YWCAs, and Little Leagues). Family participation in these activities is an outstanding motivator for the child. In addition, organizations that advocate for specific disabling conditions may organize physical activity to enable participation for specific groups (e.g.,

Special Olympics for mentally retarded individuals and wheelchair sports for orthopedically impaired persons).

When individuals with disabilities are postschool age, there are basically two options for recreational sports participation: (1) generic community recreation services that are available to other citizens and (2) a disabled-only program that has been developed for a specific categorically disabled group (e.g., blind, orthopedically impaired, mentally retarded). A third avenue of sports participation entitled Unified Sports League has been developed through Special Olympics International. In this program, equal numbers of individuals with and without disabilities form teams in a league and engage in meaningful sport activities in the community. The eventual objective is the transition of the individual with disabilities from mixed play to independent, integrated recreational sport activities in the community.

Three barriers that prevent individuals with disabilities from participation in community recreation pro-

Competitive tennis provides opportunities for challenge and personal growth. (Courtesy National Foundation of Wheelchair Tennis.)

grams are lack of information on the existence of such services, physical barriers that prevent access, and inadequate transportation.

Legislation for Individuals with Disabilities

There has been a steady history of government and social policy supporting the development of individuals with disabilities so that they may have greater opportunities to participate in independent life in the community. The most recent legislation is the Individuals with Disabilities Education Act (IDEA) of 1996. This act expands on the Education of the Handicapped Act of 1975 (P.L. 94-142) and the 1983 (P.L. 98-199) and 1986 (P.L. 99-457) amendments to the act, as well as the 1990 version of IDEA (P.L. 101-476). Each of these federal laws mandated more extensive services to a broader range of individuals and is discussed in more detail later in this section. Briefly:

- P.L. 98-199 provided incentives to states to identify and provide services to handicapped infants and preschool children ages 3 to 5 years.
- P.L. 99-457 expanded the definition of handicapped to include children from birth through 2 years of age who are diagnosed with a physical or mental condition and/or who are highly likely to experience developmental delays.

The laws provide funding to assist states with planning, developing, and implementing a statewide comprehensive multidisciplinary program for children with disabilities and those at risk for developing disabling conditions who qualify for services.

Services to be included in the state plan are family training, counseling, and home visits; special instruction; speech pathology and audiology; occupational therapy; physical therapy; psychological services; medical services; early identification, screening, and assessment services; and health services.[41]

Concepts from Legislation

Three primary concepts that have emerged from legislation have implications for the conduction of physical education for students with disabilities: (1) school personnel must spell out achievable objectives in detail and be held accountable for subsequent evaluation; (2) parents must be fully informed of the nature of the programs in which their children participate; and (3) the education should take place in the most integrated setting, with children without disabilities in regular classes, if possible. Each of these components of the educational delivery system requires the focus to be on the individual needs and learning of children with specific disabilities.

Implications for Intramurals and Interscholastic Sports

Children with disabilities need the same opportunities as all other children for participation in intramural and interscholastic sports activities. Furthermore, these opportunities ideally should be provided in the most integrated setting. However, provisions should be made to separate students with disabilities from other children during participation "when it is necessary to ensure the health and safety of the students, or to take into account their interest," and only if no qualified student with a disability is denied the opportunity to compete for teams that are not separate or different. The central theme of the provision of equal opportunity in intramural and interscholastic participation for persons with disabilities is that of "reasonable accommodation" for these learners (Section 84:37).[62] Figure 1-2 details the percent of class time that children with disabilities spend in regular academic classes.

Due Process

When a person's civil rights are violated, that person is entitled to **due process** (the right to be heard in a formal hearing). Due process complaints under IDEA are usually filed to resolve the content or procedures employed in development or conduct of the individual education program (IEP) or placement in an appropriate setting. A hearing also may be possible through an Office of Civil Rights (OCR) complaint under Section 504 of the Rehabilitation Act of 1973. Lack of opportunity for participation in intramural and interscholastic activities would most likely be addressed through the OCR forum. Due process is a safeguard for achieving the goal of quality and equal educational opportunities for all children with disabling conditions.

Major Legislation

The rights of individuals who are developmentally disabled have been enhanced through four major pieces of federal legislation. This legislation includes the Rehabilitation Act of 1973, the Education of the Handicapped

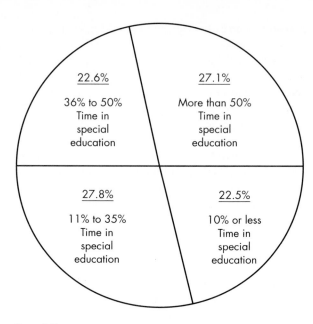

figure 1-2

Percent of class time in regular academic class by percent of children with disabilities as reported by the U.S. Department of Education (Office of Special Education Programs). Placements from the least percent of time in special education to the most are as follows: (1) placement in special education for more than 50% of the time, 27.9%; (2) placement in special education between 36% and 50% of the time, 22.6%; (3) placement in special education between 11% and 35% of the time, 27%; (4) placement in special education 10% of the time or less, 22.5%. (From US Department of Education: *Sixteenth Annual Report to Congress on the Implementation of the Individuals with Disabilities Education Act,* p 22, 1994.)

Act of 1975, the Americans with Disabilities Act (ADA) of 1990, and the Individuals with Disabilities Education Act (IDEA) of 1990. These four pieces of legislation have similarities, as well as differences.

The purpose of all the acts was to provide equal opportunity for individuals with developmental disabilities. The similarities are (1) equity of services for individuals with disabilities when compared with those without disabilities, (2) accessibility to environments so there is equal opportunity to derive benefits from services, (3) accommodation for the disabling condition for the provision of equal opportunity, and (4) encouragement of integration of individuals with and without disabilities.

All of the acts apply these basic principles but focus on different contexts.

The Rehabilitation Act of 1973 is general civil rights legislation that applies to social services within the community, as well as within the public schools. Its enforcement is restricted to those agencies that receive federal assistance. The ADA of 1990,[65] however, widens civil rights protections for the disabled to *all* public accommodations and addresses private discrimination.

The Education of the Handicapped Act of 1975 (P.L. 94-142) focuses on educational settings and is designed to provide equal educational opportunity for individuals with disabilities. The primary accommodation is the IEP. This act has been amended and retitled the Individuals with Disabilities Education Act.

The ADA went into effect in January 1992. As President George Bush said at the signing ceremony, "This historic act is the world's first comprehensive declaration of equality for people with disability. . . . Legally, it will provide our disabled community with a powerful expansion of protections and basic civil rights." The act was recommended to Congress in a report called, "Toward Independence," produced by the National Council on Disability. The act builds on and expands on rights created by the Rehabilitation Act of 1973.

Basically, the law prohibits discrimination by places of public accommodation against those with disabilities. More important, the act declares that our society will provide equal opportunity to citizens with disabilities in all aspects of American life, including recreation. This philosophy, reflected in a public law, should heighten social awareness of the recreational rights and needs of individuals with disabilities.[68]

The 1990 version of IDEA (P.L. 101-476)[66] replaced the term *handicapped* with *disability* and expanded on the types of services that must be offered and conditions that qualify children for services. Additional services that must be made available are transition, assistive technology, recreation therapy, and social work. Transition services that will promote movement from school to postschool activities must be included in the IEP of all students with disabilities by age 14 years. Assistive technology services that are now required include evaluating students' needs for equipment that will maintain, improve, or increase their functional capabilities; purchasing the equipment; customizing it; and training students, their families, and school personnel in the use

of the equipment. The law also requires schools to include the related services of recreation therapy and social work in each student's IEP.[46]

IDEA expands eligibility for all services to children with autism and children with traumatic brain injury. These conditions and physical education programming concerns are discussed in later chapters of this book. Table 1-1 depicts legislation ensuring the rights of individuals with disabilities.

Implications for Physical Education and Recreation

Before the ADA there was a lack of federal legislation to prevent private enterprise from discriminating against disabled individuals. However, the ADA mandated that operators of establishments offering services to the public cannot discriminate because of a person's disability and, subsequently, prevent "full and equal" enjoyment of services or accommodations offered by the establishment. Community recreational facilities, as well as most health and physical fitness facilities, are included under this law.

To ensure the inclusion of persons with disabilities to the maximum extent possible, the ADA requires that services of public accommodations be provided to permit use of facilities by all individuals, regardless of capability. The main instrument for greater inclusion of the disabled in society is the application of the principle of **reasonable accommodation** in applied settings. This may require modification of policies, practices, and/or procedures, including provision of auxiliary aids or services, or both. However, when accommodations for inclusion alter the nature of the service or result in an undue hardship to the operators, such accommodations are exempt from implementation.[35]

The ADA vastly enlarges the rights of people with disabilities, freeing them from discrimination in community recreation environments and enabling them to use nearly every recreational facility and service common to life in the United States. These rights will create many new opportunities for disabled persons to achieve recreational independence in the community. In this respect, the ADA will greatly enhance the educational and rehabilitation process by creating real opportunities for recreational freedom. Not only does the ADA facilitate recreational independence for persons with disabilities, but also it makes a major contribution to the fundamental

Federal Legislation Impacting Individuals with Disabilities

1961   P.L. 87-276 Special Education Act

Designed to train professionals to prepare teachers of deaf children.

1965   P.L. 89-10 Elementary and Secondary Education Act

Enabled the states and local school districts through provision of monies from the federal government to develop programs for economically disadvantaged children.

1966   P.L. 89-750 Amendments to the Elementary and Secondary Act

Created the Bureau of Education for the Handicapped.

1973   P.L. 93-112, Section 504 of the Rehabilitation Act

Actually adopted and declared that handicapped people cannot be excluded from any program or activity receiving federal funds on the basis of being handicapped alone.

1974   P.L. 93-247 Child Abuse and Prevention Act

Created systems to protect children from abuse. Mandated that a person who suspects child abuse must report it.

1975   P.L. 94-142 Education for All Handicapped Children Act

Created a free appropriate public education for all handicapped children between the ages of 3 and 21 years. Required that an individual education program (IEP) be developed for each handicapped child and that students with disabilities pursue their programs in the least restrictive environment. Physical education was identified as a direct service to be provided to these students with disabilities. Intramural and interscholastic competition is to be provided to the same extent as for nonhandicapped students.

1983   P.L. 98-199 Amendments to the Education for All Handicapped Children Act

States were required to collect data to determine the anticipated service needs for children with disabilities. It provided incentives to the states to provide services to handicapped infants and preschool children.

1986   P.L. 99-372 Handicapped Children's Protection Act

Attorney's fees were reimbursed to parents who were forced to go to court to secure an appropriate education for their child. Parents who prevailed in a hearing or a court case could recover the cost incurred for lawyers to represent them.

1986   P.L. 99-457 Education for All Handicapped Children Amendments of 1986

States were to develop comprehensive interdisciplinary services for handicapped infants and toddlers, birth through age 2 years, and to expand services for preschool children ages 3 through 5 years.

1987   Reauthorization of the Child Abuse Prevention and Treatment Act

The National Center on Child Abuse and Neglect was directed to study the incidence of abuse of children with disabilities and the incidence of disabilities that result from abuse.

1988   The Technology-Related Assistance for Individuals with Disabilities Act

Made technical amendments to the Education of the Handicapped Act P.L. 100-407 to develop technology-related assistance for individuals with disabilities.

1990   P.L. 101-476 Individuals with Disabilities Education Act

Replaced the term *handicapped* with *disability* and expanded on the types of services offered and conditions covered.

1990   P.L. 101-336 Americans with Disabilities Act

Widened civil rights protections for the disabled to all public accommodations and addressed private discrimination.

1996   Individuals with Disabilities Education Act Amendment

Amends and reauthorizes discretionary programs, strengthening services to at-risk children (legislation pending as of this writing).

---

outcomes of physical education for children and youth with disabilities. The "transition" clause of IDEA should ensure that skills attained in physical education will be generalized from school to independent community recreation settings. Thus physical education programs that incorporate community-based assessment of physical education needs of students with disabilities will have increased opportunities to conduct effective programs that link skills learned in school with meaningful recreational experiences within the community.

Least Restrictive Environment

The **Regular Education Initiative (REI),** the placement of all children with disabilities in regular classes, has stimulated considerable controversy in special education. Advocates of full inclusion argue that the current special education delivery model should be eliminated and that regular education and special education should be merged into one system.[45] Others argue for the retention and improvement of the current special education delivery system.[24] As we enter the last few years of this decade, every state in the nation is in the process of implementing inclusion for the vast majority of students with disabilities.

Legal precedents

Traditionally, persons with disabilities have been segregated in isolated settings. These segregated settings have hospital-like characteristics and are removed from the daily activities of the normal community. At one time it was believed that if sufficient numbers of persons who had special problems were in one place, they could be better served because management would be easier. However, beginning in the early part of the twentieth century, legal precedents were set for what is known as the doctrine of the **least restrictive environment.** Confinement to an institution massively curtails one's liberty, which also occurs when decisions about one's welfare are made by others. Such infringements exist when others decide when one will arise in the morning, when one goes to bed in the evening, when and what one will eat, where one will live, where one will toilet and wash, if and where one can work, when one can work, and what one will do. It is decided what health services will be provided and when and where, and what the extent of those provisions will be. There often is little recreation; when there is, the restrictions surrounding it are extensive. Clearly, institutionalized living is, in many instances, incarceration with no crime committed by the incarcerated.

Legal background

Equal educational opportunity for children with disabilities in the public schools did not come about by chance. Rather, many laws and court cases important to the education of children who had special needs made their education a fluid and dynamic process. The concept of educating children with disabilities in regular public schools had its roots in the *Brown v. Board of Education of Topeka* decision that established the right of all children to an equal educational opportunity. The court wrote[9]:

> [Education] is required in the performance of our most basic responsibilities. . . . It is the very foundation of good citizenship. Today it is a principle in preparing him [sic] for later . . . training, and in helping him adjust normally to his environment. In these days, it is doubtful that any child may reasonably be expected to succeed in life if he is denied the opportunity of an education. Such an opportunity, where the state has undertaken to provide it, is a right which must be made available *to all on equal terms* [italics added].

Brown v. Board of Education of Topeka set the precedent for the legal influences of education for individuals with disabilities. Additional court decisions that had an impact on the education of individuals with disabilities are delineated in Table 1-2.

Courts have conducted an extensive investigation of denial of unconditional inclusion of a child with disabilities in regular classes and concluded the following[30]:

> There are a great number of other spina bifida children throughout the State of West Virginia who are attending public schools in the regular classroom situation, the great majority of which have more severe disabilities than the plaintiff child Trina Hairston, including children having body braces, shunts, Cunningham clips, and ostomies, and requiring the use of walkers and confinement to wheelchairs. The needless exclusion of these children and other children who are able to function adequately from the regular classroom situation would be a great disservice to these children. . . . A major goal of the educational process is the socialization process that takes place in the regular classroom, with the resulting capability to interact in a social way with one's peers. It is therefore imperative that every child receive an education with his or her peers insofar as it is at all possible. This conclusion is further enforced by the critical importance of education in this society.

Each of the four major pieces of legislation focuses on the integration, or inclusion, of individuals with disabilities. Testimony by social scientists, which indicated that segregation and restriction of children from culturally relevant social learning experiences was undesirable, convinced Congress of such worth. Senator Stafford of Vermont made the following points before Congress[54]:

> For far too long children with disabilities have been denied access to the regular school system because of an inability to climb the steps to the schoolhouse door, and not for any other reason. This has led to segregated classes for those

Court Decisions That Impacted Education of Handicapped Persons

1954   Brown v. Board of Education (Kansas)

Segregated education in public schools was ruled unconstitutional.

1970   Diana v. State Board of Education (California)

Children cannot be placed in special education on the basis of culturally biased tests.

1972   Mills v. Board of Education of the District of Columbia

Every child has a right to equal opportunity for education.

Emotionally disturbed children cannot be excluded from school, and lack of funds is not an acceptable excuse for lack of educational opportunity.

1972   Larry B. v. Riles (California)

IQ tests cannot be used as a sole basis for placing children in special classes.

1979   Armstrong v. Kline (Pennsylvania)

Children with disabilities who regress and cannot recoup their gains over extended layoffs from school are entitled to an extended school year through the summer.

1982   Rowley v. Hendrik (Hudson, New York School District)

Declared a handicapped child's right to a personalized program of instruction and necessary supportive services and required that the IEP be reasonably calculated so the child may benefit from it.

1984   Irving Independent School District v. Tatro (Texas)

Ruled that services needed to enable a child to reach, enter, exit, or remain in school were required.

1986   Doe v. Maher (California)

Children with disabilities cannot be excluded from school for misbehavior that is handicap related. Educational services can be stopped if the misbehavior is not related to the handicapping condition.

1988   Polk v. Central Susquehanna Intermediate Unit (Ohio)

A school district cannot have a blanket policy that no child will get one-to-one physical therapy by a licensed physical therapist if that is what is needed.

1990   Chester County Intermediate Unit v. Pennsylvania Blue Shield

If a doctor states that a service (in this case, physical therapy) is necessary to enable the child to benefit from education, the school district, not the insurance company, should pay for the service.

1990   Cordrey v. Euckert (Ohio)

A child is entitled to an extended school year if it would be not merely beneficial but a necessary component of an appropriate education for the child. Empirical regression data are not the only permissible evidence of need.

1991   Greer v. Rome City

Allowed a child with Down syndrome to enroll in a regular kindergarten program instead of a "substantially separate" special education class. Ruled that the child's IEP was inappropriate because (1) it failed to accommodate the child with supplementary aids and services in the regular class, (2) no attempts were made to modify the kindergarten curriculum, and (3) the school developed the IEP before the meeting and failed to inform the parents of the range of options available.[27]

1993   Oberti v. Board of Education of Clementon School District

Ruled that a school district could not segregate a student who demonstrated disruptive behavior because the district failed to provide supplementary aids and services to reduce the child's disruptive behavior.

1994   Sacramento City Unified School District v. Rachel

Developed a four-factor standard for educational placement in the least restrictive environment based on (1) the educational benefits of a full-time regular class, (2) the nonacademic benefits of a regular class, (3) the effects a student has on the teacher and children in the regular class, and (4) the cost of placement in a regular class.

1994   Clyde K. and Sheila K. v. Puyallup School District

Ruled that if children with emotional and behavioral disorders adversely affect the learning of other children and the educational environment, they may be removed and placed in a more restrictive educational environment.[16]

children with physical handicaps. This is an isolation that is in many cases unnecessary. It is an isolation for the handicapped child and for the "normal" child as well. The sooner we are able to bring the two together, the more likely that the attitudes of each toward one another will change for the better. . . . I firmly believe that if we are to teach all of our children to love and understand each other, we must give them every opportunity to see what "different" children are like. . . . If we allow and, indeed, encourage children with disabilities and children without disabilities to be educated together as early as possible, their attitudes toward each other in later life will not be such obstacles to overcome. A child who goes to school every day with another child who is confined to a wheelchair will understand far better in later life the limitations and abilities of such an individual when he or she is asked to work with, or is in a position to hire, such an individual.

Social integration of individuals with disabilities is a matter of public policy. Procedures should be taken to ensure that to the maximum extent appropriate, children with disabilities are educated with children who do not have disabilities[54] and that they be moved to special classes and programs only when a regular class cannot meet their needs. The fundamental premise of integration, or inclusion, in the schools is that it prepares all individuals for life in a world in which they must live and work with one another.

Brown and co-workers[10] addressed the reasons surrounding improved learning that schooling severely disabled children with nondisabled children provides. For the most part, these benefits reflect those of the integration concept proposed by Congress. They maintain the following position[10]:

Long-term heterogeneous interactions between severely disabled and nondisabled students facilitate the development of the skills, attitudes, and values that will prepare both groups to be sharing, participating, contributing members of complex, postschool communities. Stated another way, separate education is not equal education. . . . Segregated service delivery models have at least the following disadvantages:
1. Exposure to student models without disabilities is absent or minimal.
2. Students with severe disabilities tend to learn "handicapped" skills, attitudes, and values.
3. Teachers tend to strive for the resolution of problems related to the child's disability at the expense of developing functional community-referenced skills.
4. Most comparisons between students are made in relation to degrees of disability rather than to standards of performance for individuals without disabilities.

5. Lack of exposure to severely involved students with disabilities limits the probability that the skills, attitudes, and values of students without disabilities will become more constructive, tolerant, and appropriate.

Certainly, it is possible that interaction may not take place even if students with severe disabilities are in the physical presence of students without disabilities. However, unless these students occupy the same space, interaction is impossible. . . . In the future, students with severe disabilities, upon the completion of formal schooling, will live in public, minimally segregated, heterogeneous communities, where they will constantly interact with other citizens. Thus, the educational experience should be representative and help prepare both students with severe disabilities and students without disabilities to function adaptively in integrated communities.

Continuum of lesser restrictive environments

There are continua of lesser restrictive environments in educational settings and in the community. The lesser restrictive environment in the community where the individual will live as an adult is very important, but

A parent is a child's first teacher.

frequently not very well defined. In the school setting the lesser restrictive environments are fairly well defined with respect to matching the severity of a problem of an individual with the setting in which the individual with a disability will be placed.

One purpose of the Education of the Handicapped Act was to provide education in the least restrictive environment. Thus implementation procedures require first an IEP and then placement in the least restrictive environment. There has recently been considerable discussion in the literature of different models of least restrictive environment in physical education.[2,23,40] Options range from full-time regular physical education to full-time adapted physical education in a special school or facility, with various placement options in between. Some special education professionals advocate placing all students with disabilities in regular education.[56,57]

Although least restrictive environment is an essential component of IDEA, there have been misconceptions regarding how it should be implemented.[2,58] Concepts that are related to, but different from, least restrictive environment are mainstreaming, integration, normalization or inclusion, and the regular education initiative.[28,52] **Mainstreaming** is placing a child with a disability into a "regular" class, even if this may not be the child's least restrictive environment. **Integration,** on the other hand, is descriptive of educational placement of students with disabilities in environments with nondisabled students; in these environments the individual with a disability is considered a full member of the social group and is an active participant in all activities of the group.

The **principle of normalization** refers to routines of life that are typical for individuals without disabilities. Normalization should apply to all aspects of the least restrictive environment. The U.S. Department of Education, Office of Special Education and Rehabilitation Services, is required to report least restrictive environment placements.

The regular education initiative is a "trend" toward wholesale inclusion of children with disabilities into regular education. The regular education initiative is discussed further throughout the text.

If we expect students with disabilities to live and work in society, we must prepare them by first integrating them in school. The school, in a sense, becomes a microcosm of the society.[4] Thus the least restrictive environment is considered to be the setting that most closely resembles regular class; the most restrictive is a setting that is removed from the local school that non-disabled students attend.

Effects of labeling on placement

The wisdom of placing individuals with disabilities into specific categories such as "mentally retarded" or "specific learning disability" has been argued for many years. Stainback and Stainback[55] believe that the classification of exceptional children by category of disabling condition may actually interfere with assessment and instructional planning that is directed toward the real learning needs of each student. According to these authors[55]:

> These categories often do not reflect the specific educational needs and interests of students in relation to such services. For example, some students categorized as behavioral disordered may need self-control training, while some students not so labeled may need self-control training as part of their educational experience. Such categories . . . actually interfere with providing some students with the services they require to progress toward their individual educational goals. Eligibility for educational and related services . . . should be based on the abilities, interests, and needs of each student as they relate to instructional options, rather than on the student's inclusion in a categorical group.

With the recent advances in instructional technology for individualization of instruction, tailoring instruction to the needs of each student irrespective of disabling condition is possible.[50,69] Whenever possible, this instruction should be provided in the regular class, since the regular class has been found to be effective at age levels ranging from preschool[21,38] to high school[70] with exceptional children whose disabilities have ranged from mild[60] to severe.[8,18] However, these successes have been primarily in academic areas.

The research describing benefits of integration of students with disabilities with nondisabled students in physical education settings is less clear. Watkinson and Titus[71] report that the value of integration in physical activities cannot realistically be determined, because little research has been done in this area. However, the findings from Special Olympics mixed teams indicate that planned interventions with appropriately trained and committed personnel can yield great benefits to all players in community-based sport activity.[11] While the benefits of inclusion in physical education at present are at best mixed, Heward and Orlansky[36] identify six variables that need to be considered and controlled before the process may be successful. These are (1) knowledge of the student, (2) knowledge of the regular class teacher, (3) knowledge of the nondisabled peer, (4) knowledge of the parents of students with disabilities, (5) knowledge of the parents of children without disabilities, and (6) knowledge of the school administrator. As Taylor, Viklen, and Searl[59] observed, decisions concerning the educational program of a students with a disability are based on that child's needs and the environment. Not all children with the same disability should be placed in the same setting. The goal, instead, is to find an appropriate least restrictive environment for each child. Reynolds, Wang, and Walberg[50] call for the joining of demonstrably effective practices from special education to establish a general education system that better serves all students, particularly those who require greater than usual educational support. Implementing such programs would require many changes in our present school systems. Change in most school systems does not occur very rapidly; however, if we are to serve all students to the best of our ability, changes are needed and necessary.

Community-based lesser restrictive environments

Special Olympics International has designed a model of lesser restrictive environments to promote integration of mentally retarded individuals into independent recreational activity in the community.[53] The continuum of services is as follows: (1) Special Olympics training with mentally retarded individuals only; (2) mixed participation with a one-to-one ratio of nondisabled peers and mentally retarded players; and (3) individualized participation in generic recreational sport services in the community. This continuum applies to specific sport activities because, while an individual may be capable of participating in unrestricted recreation in some sport skills (e.g., bowling and distance running or weight lifting), this may not be the case for that individual in games such as softball, basketball, or volleyball.

Fundamental concepts of least restrictive environment

Despite legal support for the principle of least restrictive environment, school placement of children with specific disabilities will be argued in informal discussions and formal hearings. The following points are critical to the concepts of least restrictive environment:

- The placement of children with disabilities must be flexible and reevaluated. Appropriate action should be taken on reevaluation.
- The desirable placement goal is movement of the child to less restrictive environments where it is possible to participate in normal community and school activities with nondisabled children.
- The placement of children with disabilities occurs after development of the IEP.
- Eventual placement of students with disabilities into less restrictive, more normalizing environments requires individual programs so that they can develop the motor and social skills necessary for participation with nondisabled children in a variety of settings.

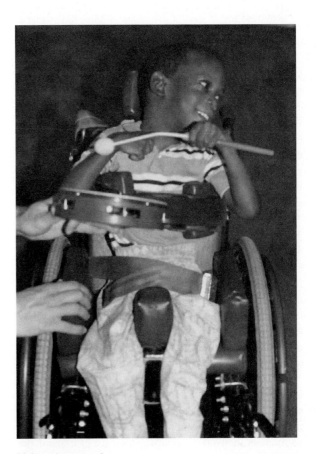

Make a joyous noise.

Transition

In the broadest sense, **transition** means changing from one situation to another.[31] Transition within the context of IDEA is not an event but a process that includes preparation, implementation, and follow-up. The process should ensure generalization of knowledge and physical skills learned in physical education settings to other school and community physical activity settings. When students actively participate in the planning and selection of activities they will engage in in the community, the transition process aids in helping them take responsibilities required of adulthood.

Transition was first introduced in 1984 in the reauthorization of the Education of the Handicapped Act (P.L. 98-199), and in 1990 it was clearly defined in IDEA. The legal definition of **transition services** in the 1996 legislation follows[67]:

> The term "transition services" means a coordinated set of activities for a student, designed within an outcome-oriented process, which promotes movement from school to post-school activities including adult education, adult services, independent living, or community participation. The coordinated set of activities shall be based on the student's needs, taking into account the student's preferences and interests, and shall include instruction, community experiences and other postschool adult living objectives.

The effective transition of skills learned in physical education to skills needed for effective integration in the community is a challenge to the 16,000 local school districts in the United States.

Transition and Functional Secondary Curriculum

Transition from school to community life begins at age 14, when most students are in high school. For effective transition, the curriculum must consist of functional activities that can be generalized to community-based settings. In addition to activities that can be accessed in the community, the physical education curriculum should also consist of taking students into the community and teaching them how to interact in that environment.

The extent of a school's transition program is influenced by the size of the district, the location of the school, and the available resources.[22] To facilitate the transition process, school districts should (1) develop community networks among agencies, (2) expand the range of community-based opportunities, (3) encourage the community to support integrated activities, (4) support efforts to develop long-range strategies to increase interaction in community activities, and (5) train more professionals who have skills to facilitate successful transition.[51]

An individual transition plan (ITP) is a component to the IEP for students 14 years and older. Ideally the ITP requires collaboration among professionals from a variety of settings, with the family of the student being the key facilitator.[32] The family should be involved in helping to identify activities their child would be interested in participating in and ensure that the skills that need to be developed are included in the youth's ITP. The teacher who provides instruction to the youth should systematically evaluate the student to determine the extent to which the student's transition skills have been developed.[33]

Transition Problems

The transition of individuals with disabilities from school-based physical education programs to community opportunities for physical activity is a formidable challenge. Some problems that confront adapted physical educators and parents who want their child to be active in the community are:

- Some educators believe that transition from school to community settings will occur without special intervention strategies.
- There is a lack of personnel trained to implement the transition process.[73]
- Physical educators who teach regular classes may not have the capabilities or resources to meet the functional requirements of transition.
- Adapted physical educators, parents, and staff may not be familiar with the community professionals, services, and agencies that provide physical activity programs.

Assistive Technology

The Technology-Related Assistance for Individuals with Disabilities Act of 1988 defined **assistive technology** as "any item, piece of equipment or product system . . . that is used to increase, maintain, or improve functional capabilities of children with disabilities."[64] IDEA defined **assistive technology service** as "any service that directly assists a child with a disability in the selection, acquisition, or use of an assistive technology device."[67]

Assistive technology has many applications that directly impact movement capabilities. These include:

- Personal mobility devices (e.g., powered wheelchairs)[44]
- Microcomputers and adapted switches for toys for young children with disabilities[43]
- Implants that enhance spatial visualization[47]
- Single- and multichannel internal neuromuscular electrical stimulation for dropped foot, paralyzed legs, and gait relearning[5]

In addition, the newest technology can be used to assist in training and monitoring the performance of teachers. Examples include interactive video systems to train adapted physical educators,[7] portable computers to facilitate gathering observational data,[26] and video-based microcomputers to assess social skills.[39]

Emerging technology shows great promise for benefiting both individuals with disabilities and their teachers.

Accommodating the Student with Disabilities in Integrated Settings

Many argue that teaching children with heterogeneous learning characteristics is impractical; however, growing numbers of educators take exception to that position. Initiatives were taken by the U.S. Office of Education in the 1960s and 1970s to encourage innovative ways to accommodate individual differences. Programmed instruction had proved to be extremely productive in the development of knowledge and skills for all persons, individuals with disabilities included. With considerable federal investment, learning research laboratories developed systems for individualization of *all* children. Materials are now available that enable all children to participate at their current level of educational performance.[72,74]

Prerequisite to the conduct of physical education skills with individualized formats are (1) prearranged written physical education skills with written objectives and (2) a training system that enables learners to direct and evaluate their own learning. Learners with disabilities at mental age 6 are usually able to convert stick figures into objective performance.[74] We want to emphasize that such individualized instruction for accommodation of individual differences applies only to the de-

velopment of skills for each individual. Play in group games requires procedures for modification of tasks, rules, and the environment to enable accommodation in group play. Descriptions of procedures for modification of specific disabling conditions for specific types of tasks are included in subsequent chapters.

Successful teaching of individuals with disabilities in regular classes requires teaching skills that enable the accommodation of heterogeneous groups through individualization of instruction. Adequate **support personnel** are frequently necessary when instruction is individualized. In addition, it requires teachers who can modify rules, environments, and tasks to promote meaningful play among students with and without disabilities.

Progress of children advancing on a continuum of least restrictive environments requires (1) periodic review of educational progress, (2) frequent assessment of what least restrictive environment means for a particular child at a particular time, and (3) possible modifications in the type of delivery of services that may produce optimum progress in the future.[19]

Most Appropriate Placement

Children with disabilities should be placed in settings that most appropriately meet their physical education needs. Clearly, these children should not be placed in regular classes if it is not in their best interest. Appropriate placement requires consideration of several variables, such as the type of curriculum in the regular program, characteristics of the regular class teacher, the nature of the activity the child is to perform, and available support services. The full range of variables to consider when placing a student in the least restrictive environment is discussed in detail in Chapter 5.

Needs of the Child

Children with disabilities have physical, social, and emotional needs that are to be met in physical education class. To accomplish this, the following four conditions should be met:

1. The instructional level of activity should be commensurate with the ability level of the child. Some form of individualized instruction should be provided.
2. Activities should be modified to accommodate individual differences in group games.

3. The social environment should be such that it can promote interaction (see Chapter 9).
4. Activities should enable participation rather than spectatorship.

Teacher Qualities

The characteristics of classes that restrict individual liberties for free association with peers vary. Teachers may possess different skills for accommodation of individual differences when teaching specific content. Teachers' attitudes toward acceptance of all children in their class, their ability to accommodate children with disabilities, their knowledge of behavior management techniques, and the teaching style they use are considerations for appropriate placement.

Curriculum

Some activities enable accommodation of differences to a greater extent than others. Individual sport skills such as tumbling and gymnastics do not depend on the performance or ability of others. Skill development in sports is not particularly difficult to individualize in a regular physical education class. The application of these sport skills in competition is much more difficult. The nature of the activity and the ability of the teacher to modify activities to include students with a wide range of ability levels are important variables to consider. All children are entitled to a learning environment where they may participate successfully and safely.

Role of the Adapted Physical Educator

The function of the adapted physical education teacher is clear in IDEA. The physical educator is to develop physical and motor fitness, fundamental motor skills and patterns, team sport skills, and knowledge of rules and strategies that go with participation in physical activity. However, over the past decade the actual duties of physical education teachers who serve students with disabilities have become clouded. Factors contributing to this confusion include (1) lack of certification standards for adapted physical educators in most states, (2) failure by the states to enforce the physical education requirement, and (3) willingness on the part of states and individual school districts to permit inadequately prepared individuals and professionals to deliver physical education to students with disabilities.

Since the enactment of the Education of the Handicapped Act, only 9 states have developed certification, endorsement, or approval in adapted physical education.[18] Furthermore, in a review of state plans conducted by Bundschuh,[13] 30 states indicated a need for adapted physical education teachers, whereas 18 states did not indicate adapted physical education as a needed area. Of the 18 that reported no need, only 2 states had either endorsements or approval in adapted physical education. State departments of education apparently have not enforced or provided the necessary information of needs assessment in federal surveys to clarify the role of the adapted physical education teacher. As a result, many other professionals have become involved in the motor planning for students with disabilities. Most of these are adjunctive services of the medical profession (e.g., occupational therapy, corrective therapy, physical therapy).

Preparation and subsequent employment of adapted physical educators is perhaps the key factor in ensuring that children with disabilities receive appropriate physical education services.[15] There is evidence of a significant reduction in the number of adapted physical education teachers being trained and placed in the school systems of this country. As a result, the needs of children with disabilities relative to adapted physical education continue to go unfulfilled.[6] There is a need for teachers to be trained so that they can provide quality assurances in physical education to individuals with disabilities.

Community-Based Programming

A relationship should be established between skills learned by students in instructional environments and the application of those skills to natural environments in the community. Such programming in physical education starts with the needs of the student for successful participation in physical activity in neighborhood and recreation centers, and in opportunities in the community. This requires mutual relationships between students with disabilities and the total community environment, both physical and social.

Community-Based Physical Education Programs

The major goal of IDEA was to provide an education so that individuals with disabilities could become independent adults in the community. Prerequisite to independent living is the acquisition of the physical and motor skills that will enable these individuals to participate in domestic, recreational, and vocational life in the community. The physical and motor skills attained in instructional settings in the schools should be generalized to physical activity in the community. For the most part, individuals with disabilities can make the adaptation to community recreational life. However, many such individuals, particularly those with severe involvement, may find it difficult to generalize what was taught in the public schools to community sport and physical activity. To overcome this problem, one of the recent initiatives in education for persons with disabilities is community-based assessment and programming, which is a system that provides specific curriculum content for an individual. The school curriculum focuses on behaviors and skills that an adult will be able to use in the community environment.[38] This system requires that the relationship between the curriculum for children with disabilities and the physical, sport, and recreational skills learned permits participation in independent recreation in the community. Thus to maximize opportunity for independent recreational programming for persons with disabilities, matches must be made on two levels.

Recreation and leisure activities provide opportunities for joy throughout the life span. (Courtesy Recreation Services, Division Care and Treatment Facilities, Department of Health and Social Services, Northern Wisconsin Center for the Developmentally Delayed.)

Community-based assessment and programming ensure the linkage between the community, school curricula, and the needs of the child. The key to the curriculum process is generalization. For the instructional content to have value, the student must learn skills that can be generalized from the instructional setting to independent recreational, physical, and sport activities in the community.

Normalization

Normalization means making available to individuals with disabilities everyday life opportunities that are as close as possible to the opportunities persons without disabilities enjoy. For this to occur, society's view of persons with disabilities must be consistent with the following conditions:

- They must be perceived by society as human beings, not as subhuman (vegetables, animals, etc.).
- They must be perceived by society as possessing a legal and constitutional identity (due process of law for involuntary institutionalization, as well as equal opportunity in education, housing, and employment).
- They must be viewed as persons who can adapt to their environment and acquire skills for as long as they live.
- They must be provided an opportunity by society to take full advantage of their culture.
- Services must be provided by trained personnel with technical competence in education and habilitation.
- The human services that care for persons with disabilities and provide opportunity for skill development must be valued and well understood by society.
- Persons with disabilities must be provided opportunities to play valued roles and lead valued lives in our culture.

In the past, many persons with disabilities were considered socially deviant. Wolfensberger[75] indicates that a person may be regarded as deviant if some characteristic or attribute is judged different by others who consider the characteristic or attribute important and who value this difference negatively. An overt and negatively valued characteristic that is associated with deviance is a *stigma*. For instance, members of ethnic minorities, persons with cosmetic disfigurements, dwarfs, and children with disabling conditions have, unfortunately, been considered deviant.

Deviance is a social perception. It is not characteristic of a person but rather of an observer's values as they pertain to social norms.[75] When a person is perceived as deviant or is stereotyped, as is the case with many children with disabilities, he or she is prescribed to a role that carries great expectancies by the person without disabilities. Furthermore, most of these social perceptions clearly reflect prejudices that have little relationship to reality. As Wolfensberger indicates, the lack of objective verification is not a crucial element in the shaping of a social judgment or social policy.

Educational Accountability

When applied to the teaching process, the concept of accountability means that a particular program, method, or intervention can be demonstrated to cause a significant positive change in one or more behaviors.[58] It is accepted policy that written records be maintained on each student with a disability to document specific progress toward preestablished goals and objectives. Technical procedures for the appropriate selection of objectives for specific learners have been developed.[3,25] Once these specific meaningful behaviors have been defined, it is then possible to apply accepted behavioral principles to develop them with this sophisticated technology.

Coordination of Delivery of Services

There has been considerable emphasis on the belief that programs for persons with disabilities should be of an interdisciplinary nature. However, because of a lack of coordination of services, problems may exist in the delivery of services within the system. Professionals within the system have taken on the roles, functions, and goals of each other. This has happened because of inadequate planning or coordination and without consideration of the effectiveness of the various professionals in their new roles. As a result, we have homogenized professionals who no longer have defined expertise and programs that are less than desirable. Role confusion can lead to duplication of services in some programs and voids in others, which results in a lack of comprehensive programming for children with disabilities.

Public policymakers have assigned educational functions to those who provide **direct services** and those who provide **indirect services.** Direct services are those, such as physical education, that teach curricula sanctioned by school boards. Related (indirect) services help children with disabilities gain benefits from the intended outcomes of the direct services (e.g., physical therapy, occupational therapy, and recreational therapy).

Concept of Related Services

Before a **related service** such as physical therapy, occupational therapy, or recreational therapy can be implemented in the curriculum, it should be determined whether the limitations of that particular child are such that direct services (physical education) cannot effectively deal with the child's educational problem. A related service should be provided when a child cannot make the expected progress in skill development in physical education. For instance, if it is decided that a child with a disability does not have the prerequisite

The joy of success. (Photo by Jo Arms, Courtesy Texas Special Olympics.)

strength of a specific muscle group to acquire a sport skill and that the physical educator cannot rectify the problem, a physical therapist may be called on to provide a related service. The physical therapist designs a program for the specific muscle group to establish prerequisite strength; then the child can acquire the skills to be taught by the physical educator. The physical therapist's plan should include measurement of developmental progress in terms of the strength of the specific muscle group. In addition, the physical therapist and those who plan for the related service should indicate the dates of initiation of services, the dates of termination of services, and the duration of the training. However, the development of the skill to be taught in the physical education class is the responsibility of the physical educator. The development of the physical prerequisites (of a pathological nature) to a skill is the responsibility of the related service provider. Such a procedure streamlines services, with greater emphasis on the education of the child, and upgrades the quality of instruction.

Current Status of Adapted Physical Education

From a national perspective, physical education for students with disabilities is still inadequate. Studies done in different states indicate that physical education for students with disabilities remains a woefully neglected and underdeveloped area of public school programming.[14,20,48] One reason students with disabilities are not receiving adequate instruction in physical education is because they are inappropriately placed. By law, children with disabilities should be placed in the most appropriate, least restrictive setting that meets their needs. The regular class is the desirable setting; yet it does not constitute the least restrictive environment for all individuals with disabilities. Frequently students with disabilities are inappropriately placed in the regular physical education class. **De facto integration** of students with disabilities into regular physical education classes is almost exclusively by administrative decree. Efforts must be made to ensure that these students are provided an appropriate physical education that will promote their eventual ability to perform as independently as is humanly possible. Parents and educators must insist that students with disabilities be appropriately placed in physical education on the basis of individual test results and that qualified adapted physical educators provide appropriate programming. This may ensure skills and attitudes that provide the prerequisites for self-sufficient, healthful leisure lifestyles in the community during and after the formal schooling years.

SUMMARY

Concern for the needs of individuals with disabilities surfaced during the Renaissance; however, social reforms directed toward improving the quality of life for the disabled did not begin until the nineteenth century. World Wars I and II provided the impetus to develop rehabilitation programs to improve the function of persons with disabilities. The focus on upgrading the opportunities for individuals with mental retardation became a reality in the 1960s. A national effort to provide school and community services for all persons with disabilities began with the Rehabilitation Act of 1973 and the Education of the Handicapped Act of 1975. These two pieces of legislation mandated appropriate physical education programs and opportunities to participate in intramural and interscholastic sports for school-age citizens with disabilities. The Individuals with Disabilities Education Acts (IDEA) of 1990 and 1996, and the Americans with Disabilities Act (ADA) of 1990 extended the provisions of earlier legislation.

Physical education for students with disabilities is a comprehensive service delivery system designed to identify problems of children in physical and motor fitness, fundamental motor patterns and skills, and sport skills and games. Services include assessment, individualized education programming, and coordination of activities with related resources and services. These services may be delivered by specialists who possess skills to conduct instruction for students with disabilities in regular or segregated classes. Special physical education may serve both children with disabilities and those without disabilities. Specially designed physical education also may occur in any setting on the least restrictive alternative continuum.

An estimated 10% to 20% of the total school-age population will perform inadequately on physical education tasks at some time during their education. Many of these children have disabilities and require an individual education program (IEP) in physical education.

The physical education program should develop physical and motor fitness, fundamental motor patterns and skills, and skill development that enables participation in team and lifetime sports. The physical education curriculum and teachers must be able to service children with sensory, physical, mental, and social-emotional disabilities. The services for children with disabilities should be provided in environments where the children have an opportunity to engage in culturally relevant learning experiences with their peers. This is the regular class if possible. However, each child with a disability must be placed in the school environment that is most appropriate for that child. The physical educator must coordinate services with the special education teacher, related service personnel, school administrators, and parents. All parties are cooperatively involved with the physical education program for the special child.

By age 14 years, each child's IEP should include an individual transition plan (ITP) that clearly delineates community-based activities the student should be taught. In addition to learning functional activities that can be accessed in the community, students should be taught the social interaction skills necessary to participate fully in integrated settings.

Review Questions

1. What are the three most prevalent disabling conditions?
2. What is a historical theme in services for persons with disabilities?
3. What is a legal definition of physical education?
4. What are some benefits of a quality physical education program for children with disabilities?
5. Describe the purposes of the Rehabilitation Act of 1973, the Education of the Handicapped Act, the Individuals with Disabilities Education Act, and the Americans with Disabilities Act.
6. What are the entitlements of students with disabilities for intramural and interscholastic sports under federal legislation?
7. What is the difference between least restrictive environment and least restrictive alternative?
8. What is community-based physical education programming?
9. Describe some principles of normalization.
10. What is a related service? What is the relationship of a related service to a direct service?
11. Why is physical education an integral part of special education?

12. What are some of the roles and tasks of physical education teachers of students with disabilities?
13. What are some opportunities for individuals with disabilities to participate in sports and physical activities?
14. What is the present status of physical education for individuals with disabilities as compared with the legislative entitlements of these children?

Student Activities

1. Interview a person with a disability or the teacher or parent of a child with a disability to determine enjoyable physical activities.
2. Provide physical activity for a child with a specific disabling condition. Indicate your feelings before and after the teaching experience.
3. Select two environments where services for persons with disabilities are delivered. One environment should be more restrictive than the other. Describe the differences between the two environments.
4. Identify two or three skills of a child with disabilities that would assist self-sufficient living in the community where the child lives.
5. Visit and interview a physical education teacher of students with disabilities. Survey the tasks that are performed while the teacher conducts the class.
6. Interview some students with disabilities who are of different ages to determine their interests.
7. Discuss the view of another professional on the impact that labeling has on subsequent conduction of physical education programs for individuals with disabilities.
8. Interview an adapted physical education teacher, the parents of a child with a disability, or a student with a disability to determine what types of programs have benefitted the social and physical development of the individual with a disability.

References

1. American Association of Health, Physical Education, and Recreation: Guiding principles for adapted physical education, *J Health Phys Educ Rec,* p 15, April 1952.
2. Aufsesser PM: Mainstreaming and the least restrictive environment: how do they differ? *Palaestra* 7:31-34, 1991.
3. Bellamy T, Peterson L, Close D: Habilitation of the severely and profoundly retarded: illustrations of competence, *Educ Train Ment Retard* 10:174-186, 1975.
4. Bliton G, Schroeder HJ: *The new future for children with substantial handicaps: the second wave of LRE,* Bloomington, 1986, Indiana University Developmental Training Center.
5. Bogataj U et al: The rehabilitation of gait in patients with hemiplegia: a comparison between conventional therapy

and multichannel functional electrical stimulation therapy, *Phys Ther* 75:490-502, 1995.

6. Bokee M: *Adapted physical education, therapeutic recreation, and arts for the handicapped,* Washington, DC, 1994, US Department of Education.

7. Bowers L, Klesius S: *Technology and training adapted physical education teachers.* Paper presented at the annual meeting of the National Consortium of Physical Education and Recreation of Individuals with Disabilities, Old Town, Va, July 15, 1995.

8. Brinker RP: Interactions between severely mentally retarded students and other students in integrated and segregated public school settings, *Am J Ment Defic* 11:587-594, 1985.

9. *Brown v The Board of Education,* 347 US, 483, 1954.

10. Brown L et al: *Toward the realization of the least restrictive educational environments for handicapped students,* Position paper, University of Wisconsin–Madison, Grant No OEG 0-73-6137, 1977, US Department of Education, Office of Special Education.

11. Brown L et al: A strategy for developing chronological age appropriate and functional curricular content for severely handicapped adolescents and young adults, *J Spec Educ* 13:81-90, 1979.

12. Budoff M: *Massachusetts mixed softball: a final report,* Washington, DC, 1987, Special Olympics International.

13. Bundschuh E: *Needs assessment in special education,* CSPD-PE project, Athens, 1985, University of Georgia.

14. Chandler JP, Greene JL: A state-wide survey of adapted physical education service delivery and teacher in-service training, *Adapt Phys Act Q* 12(3):262-274, 1995.

15. Churton MW: Addressing personnel preparation needs to meet the challenges of the future, *Adapt Phys Act Q* 3:118-123, 1986.

16. *Clyde K, Sheila K v Puyallup School District,* 21 IDELR 664 (9th Cir, 1994).

17. Cohen DL: Despite widespread income growth, study finds increase in child poverty, *Educ Week* 24:11-14, Aug 5, 1992.

18. Cowden J, Tymeson G: *Certification in adapted/special physical education: national status update,* Dekalb, 1984, Northern Illinois University.

19. Cratty BJ: *Adapted physical education for handicapped children and youth,* Denver, 1980, Love Publishing.

20. Decker J, Jansma P: Identifying least restrictive environment options in physical education, *Phys Educator* 62(2):69-70, 1991.

21. Esposito BG, Reed TM: The effects of contact with handicapped persons on young children's attitudes, *Except Child* 54:224-229, 1986.

22. Fairweather JS, Stearns MS, Wagner MM: Resources available in school districts serving secondary special education students: implications for transition, *J Spec Educ* 22:419-432, 1990.

23. French R: *Serving the handicapped: least restrictive environment (LRE): usage in physical education.* Presentation at the Preconvention Symposium at the National Convention of the American Alliance for Health, Physical Education, Recreation and Dance, New Orleans, April 1990.

24. Fuchs D, Fuchs LS: Inclusive schools movement and the radicalization of special education reform, *Except Child* 60:294-309, 1994.

25. Gold M: *Task analysis: a statement and example using acquisition and production of complex assembly task by the retarded blind,* Champaign, 1975, Institute for Child Behavior and Development, University of Illinois at Urbana-Champaign.

26. Greenwood CR et al: Development and validation of standard classroom observation systems for school practitioners: ecobehavioral assessment systems software (EBASS), *Except Child* 61:197-210, 1994.

27. *Greer v Rome City School District,* 950 F 2d 688 (11th Cir, 1991).

28. Grosse S: Is the mainstream always a better place to be? *Palaestra* 7:40-49, 1991.

29. Hagerty GJ, Abramson M: Impediments for implementing national policy change for mildly handicapped students, *Except Child* 53:315-323, 1987.

30. *Hairston v Drosick,* 423 F Suppl 180 (SD W Va, 1976).

31. Hallahan DP, Kaufman JM: *Exceptional children: introduction to special education,* Boston, 1994, Allyn & Bacon.

32. Halloran WD: Transition services requirement: issues, implications, and challenge. In Eaves RC, McLaughlin PJ, editors: *Recent advances in special education and rehabilitation,* Boston, 1993, Andover Medical Publishers.

33. Halpern A: A methodological review of follow-up and follow-along studies tracking school leavers in special education, *Career Dev Spec Educ* 13:13-28, 1990.

34. Hardman ML, Drew CJ, Egan MW: *Human exceptionality, society, school and family,* Boston, 1987, Allyn & Bacon.

35. Herbert HL: The Americans with Disabilities Act, *Fitness Management,* March 1991.

36. Heward WL, Orlansky MD: *Exceptional children,* Columbus, Ohio, 1988, Merrill Publishing.

37. Hickson L, Blackman LS, Reis EM: *Mental retardation,* Boston, 1995, Allyn & Bacon.

38. Howell K, Moorehead MK: *Curriculum based evaluation in special and remedial education,* Columbus, Ohio, 1987, Merrill Publishing.

39. Irvin LK, Walker HM: Assessing children's social skills using video-based microcomputer technology, *Except Child* 61:182-196, 1994.

40. Jansma P, Decker J: *Project LRE/PE: least restrictive environment usage in physical education,* Washington, DC, 1990, US Department of Education, Office of Special Education.

41. Kelly L: Problematic issues for adapted physical education—implementation of PL 99-457, *J Health Phys Educ Rec*, pp 44-48, 1991.

42. Kelly LE: *National standards for adapted physical education*, Washington, DC, 1994, US Department of Education, Office of Special Education Programs.

43. Kinsley TC, Langone J: Application of technology for infants, toddlers, and preschoolers with disabilities, *J Spec Educ Technol* 12:312-324, 1995.

44. Lewis RB: *Special education technology*, Pacific Grove, Ca, 1994, Brooks/Cole Publishing.

45. Lipsky DK, Gartner A: Achieving full inclusion: placing the student at the center of educational reform. In Stainback W, Stainback S, editors: *Controversial issues facing special education: divergent perspectives*, Boston, 1992, Allyn & Bacon.

46. Martin R: *Special education law: changes for the nineties*, Urbana, Ill, 1991, Carle Center for Health Law and Ethics.

47. Normam KL: Spatial visualization—a gateway to computer-based technology, *J Spec Educ Technol* 12:195-201, 1995.

48. Pyfer J et al: *Status of physical education services for students with disabilities in Texas*, Unpublished paper, Denton, 1995, Texas Woman's University.

49. Reynolds MC: Child disabilities: who's in, who's out, *J Sch Health* 64(6):238-242, 1994.

50. Reynolds MC, Wang MC, Walberg HJ: The necessary restructuring of special and regular education, *Except Child* 53:391-398, 1987.

51. Snell ME: *Instruction of students with severe disability*, New York, 1993, Macmillan Publishing.

52. Snell ME, Eichner SJ: Integration for students with profound disabilities. In Brown F, Lehr DH, editors: *Persons with profound disabilities: issues and practices*, Baltimore, 1989, Paul H Brookes.

53. Songster T: *Integration technology in recreational sports for the mentally retarded, a proposal for the office of special education and rehabilitation services*, Washington, DC, 1987, Special Olympics International.

54. Stafford J: *Congress Rec* 121:10961, 1975.

55. Stainback W, Stainback S: A rationale for the merger of special and regular education, *Except Child* 51:102-111, 1984.

56. Stainback W, Stainback S: *Support networks for inclusive schooling: interdependent integrated education*, Baltimore, 1990, Paul H Brookes Publishing.

57. Stainback S, Stainback W, Forest M: *Educating all students in the mainstream of regular education*, Baltimore, 1989, Paul H Brookes Publishing.

58. Taylor SJ: Caught in the continuum: a critical analysis of the principle of the least restrictive environment, *J Assoc Persons Severe Handicaps* 13:41-53, 1988.

59. Taylor SJ, Viklen D, Searl SJ: *Preparing for life: a manual for parents on least restrictive environment*, Boston, 1986, Federation for Children with Special Needs.

60. Thomas G, Jackson G: The whole school approach to integration, *Br J Spec Educ* 13:27-29, 1986.

61. US Department of Education: *Sixteenth Annual Report to Congress on the Implementation of the Individuals with Disabilities Education Act, 1994*. Washington, DC, 1994.

62. US Department of Health, Education, and Welfare: 504 Regulations for the Rehabilitation Act of 1973, Rehabilitation Act Amendments of 1974, and Education of the Handicapped Act, *Fed Reg* 45:339-395, 1990.

63. US 94th Congress: Public Law 94-142, Nov 29, 1975.

64. US 99th Congress: The Technology Related Assistance for Individuals with Disabilities Act of 1988.

65. US 101st Congress: Public Law 101-336, Aug 9, 1990.

66. US 101st Congress: Public Law 101-476, Oct 30, 1990.

67. US 103rd Congress: Individuals with Disabilities Education Act, 1995.

68. Verville RE: The Americans with Disabilities Act, *Arch Phys Med Rehabil* 71:1010-1013, 1990.

69. Wang MC, Reynolds MC: Avoiding the "catch 22" in special education reform, *Except Child* 51:497-502, 1985.

70. Warger CL, Aldinger LE, Okun KA: *Mainstreaming in the secondary school: the role of the regular teacher*, Bloomington, Ind, 1983, Phi Delta Kappa Educational Foundation.

71. Watkinson EJ, Titus JA: Integrating the mentally handicapped in physical activity: a review and discussion, *Can J Except Child* 2:48-53, 1985.

72. Wessel J: *Fundamental skills*, Northbrook, Ill, 1976, Hubbard Press.

73. Wheman P: Transition from school to adulthood for young people with disabilities: critical issues and policies. In Eaves RC, McLaughlin PJ, editors: *Recent advances in special education and rehabilitation*, Boston, 1993, Andover Medical Publishers.

74. White C: *Acquisition of lateral balance between trainable mentally retarded children and kindergarten children in an individually prescribed instructional program*, Unpublished master's thesis, Slippery Rock, Pa, 1972, Slippery Rock State College.

75. Wolfensberger W: *Principles of normalization*, Toronto, 1972, National Institute on Mental Retardation.

Suggested Readings

Eaves RC, McLaughlin PJ, editors: *Recent advances in special education and rehabilitation*, Boston, 1993, Andover Medical Publishers.

Eichstaedt CB, Kalakian LH: *Developmental/adapted physical education*, New York, 1993, Macmillan Publishing.

part two

Key Techniques

The types of physical and motor problems that learners demonstrate are common to many children; however, each child has a unique profile that must be identified before appropriate programming can be determined. In this section, specific clues for determining each individual's present level of functioning, regardless of disability, and precise programming techniques are described.

chapter t w o

Determining Educational Needs Through Assessment

Objectives

List the different types of assessment.

Explain the different purposes of assessment.

Provide examples of each of the different types of assessment.

Describe how to use the different types of assessment to achieve a specific outcome.

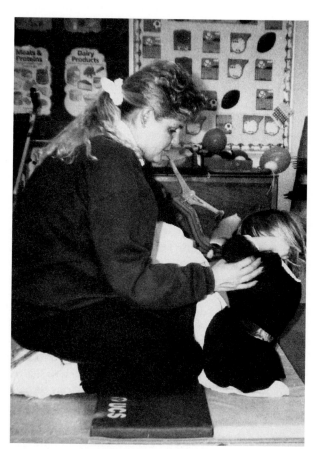

Courtesy Dallas Independent School District.

As we approach the end of the twentieth century, it is becoming increasingly clear that traditional educational practices that have served our society well in the past must be modified to keep pace with changing societal demands, as well as with the growing diversity of students being educated in our schools. It is becoming apparent that for our society to survive and grow, all students, regardless of gender, ethnicity, and functional capacity, must be adequately prepared to participate successfully in a multicultural society that is becoming increasingly dependent on advanced technology.[4] School curricula must be designed to provide students with information, skills, and problem-solving capabilities that will enable them to function fully in the career and community of their choice. A critical component of an effective curriculum is a means for determining at what levels students are functioning, the types of interventions needed to gain full benefits from their school experiences, their progress toward mastery of the school curriculum, and validation that what has been learned has application in the society. Appropriate assessment techniques can provide this information.

In this chapter a broad range of assessment information is presented. The purposes of assessment, types of instruments available to meet those purposes, ways to evaluate specific instruments to determine their appropriateness, and tips on administering tests are included. Recommendations of instruments that can be used with students who have specific types of disabilities, as well as ways to modify the testing situation to meet their needs, are included in each of the chapters that address those populations.

Purposes of Assessment

Assessment is a problem-solving process that involves a variety of ways of gathering information. Testing is the administration of specific instruments that are used to gather assessment data.[7] Motor assessment instruments provide different types of information. It is important to match the selection of the instrument with the purpose of the assessment. Just as a teacher should select activities that will contribute to students' learning and growth, so, too, must an assessment instrument provide the type of information that will give direction to establishing a program of benefit to the students. Assessment is an inseparable part of the student's ongoing educational program, and it is particularly critical for students with disabilities.

Assessment of students in educational settings has at least five purposes[7]:

1. To identify those who might be experiencing developmental delays
2. To diagnose the nature of the student's problem or delay
3. To provide information to use in developing the **individual education program (IEP)** and in determining appropriate placement
4. To develop instruction specific to the student's special needs
5. To evaluate student progress

Matching Type of Assessment to Purpose

Both formal and informal tests serve important functions in the educational process. The purpose of the assessment will dictate the type of instrument selected and the standards the instrument must meet. The more critical the decisions that are made from the assessment, the more rigorous the requirements for the instrument the evaluator will use.

Instruments that are used for screening groups to determine whether any individuals are experiencing significant delays can be very informal. Teachers can use published checklists or their own selection of activities, or they can simply observe students during the students' regular physical education class or during recess to try to identify students experiencing difficulty with movement. Whatever the method used, it is recommended that the information be recorded in some form so that documentation is available for the permanent record file. An example of an observational checklist that was developed for use in the Denton, Texas, Independent School District appears in Figure 2-1. When a student appears to be having problems performing to the level of classmates, more rigorous testing is necessary to determine the extent of the child's delay. Parental approval must be received before more in-depth testing is done.

Diagnostic instruments that are used to determine the nature and extent of a student's problem must, by law, meet certain standards. They must be formal tests that are validated for the specific purpose for which they are being used (e.g., be valid, reliable, and objective) and must not discriminate against students because of their race, culture, or disability (e.g., a child who is nonambulatory cannot be expected to jump or skip). The evaluation must be administered in the child's primary language or mode of communication by a person trained to use the test. Once the extent of a student's movement difficulties is determined, decisions must be made about the type of physical education program needed. This type of information can be gathered in several different ways.

Assessment information used for developing a student's IEP and for selecting appropriate activities can be gathered from a variety of sources, including observation, informal testing procedures, and formal tests. For example, if a student is unable to execute a sit-up on a standardized test, the teacher may wish to use informal probes to determine whether lack of understanding about how to perform the task, poor abdominal strength, or the presence of a persisting **primitive reflex** is interfering with the child's ability to move into a flexed position. Clearly, the underlying cause of the problem needs to be determined before an appropriate exercise program can be selected. Once the cause of the movement difficulty is pinpointed, long-range goals and short-term objectives that lead to those goals are selected and included on the student's IEP. Carefully written goals and objectives greatly facilitate the monitoring of student progress.

A well-designed IEP includes behavioral objectives and goals. Evaluation of student progress can be done by determining the extent to which the student is progressing toward the short-term objectives and long-range goals that have been included on the IEP.

Test Selection Criteria

As indicated in the previous section, depending on the purpose for the assessment, both standardized tests and less formal instruments are useful when working with students with disabilities. Once the purpose of the assessment has been decided, an appropriate assessment instrument is selected. Factors that must be considered in selecting the right test are (1) the need for, and adequacy of, **test standardization;** (2) **administrative feasibility;** and (3) the student's type of disability. Each of these factors is discussed here.

Standardization

To standardize a test means to give the test to a large group of persons under the same conditions to determine whether or not the test discriminates among ages and populations. When a test is going to be used for diagnostic purposes, adequacy of the standardized process must be verified. Questions that must be answered include:

1. Were the appropriate procedures used to select the population used to standardize the instrument?
2. Did the author(s) demonstrate an appropriate type and level of validity?
3. Did the author(s) establish an appropriate type and level of reliability?
4. Did the author(s) verify the objectivity of the instrument?

Selecting the standardization sample

Ideally, the sample that is used for the standardization of an instrument should include the same percentage of individuals in the same socioeconomic groups, geographic locations (South, East, North, Northeast, etc.), age groups, gender breakdown, and racial groups as those represented in the general population according to the latest population census. Hence, if the 1990 U.S. census reported that 52% of the population is female and 48% is male, those percentages should be duplicated in the test sample. If, in the same census, it is reported that the U.S. population is 40% African-American, 34% Angelo, 18% Hispanic, 3% American Indian, 2% Asian, and 3% other, then those percentages should be used to select the makeup of the sample to be tested. In addition, the test sample should include the ages of the persons with whom the test will be used, selected at random from

all areas of the country. Because few, if any, motor tests meet these stringent criteria, tests should be selected that come as close to the ideal as possible.

Establishing validity

Test validity is a measure of how truthful an instrument is. A valid instrument measures what the authors claim it measures. There are three acceptable types of validity: (1) content-related, (2) criterion-related, and (3) construct validity.

Content (sometimes called curriculum)–related validity refers to the degree to which the contents of the test represent an identified domain or body of knowledge. This type of validity is often determined by verifying that experts in the field agree about the components of the domain. To demonstrate content validity, the author must first provide a clear definition of what is being measured. Then, literature that supports the content is identified or the test is examined by the panel of judges who have been selected according to a predetermined set of criteria (i.e., five or more publications in the field, recommended by three or more professionals as an authority in the field, etc.). The panel members independently review each of the items in the test to determine whether they are appropriate, complete, and representative.

Appropriateness means that most knowledgeable professionals would agree that items measure what it is claimed they measure. For example, if the test designer claimed the test measured cardiovascular endurance and the only item included was a 50-yard walk, few professionals would agree that the test content was appropriate.

Completeness is determined by whether there is a wide range of items or only a select few. To be complete, a test that is purported to measure physical fitness would be expected to sample cardiovascular endurance, upper body strength, abdominal strength, leg power, lower back and hip flexibility, and percentage of body fat. If only one measure of strength and one measure of cardiovascular endurance were included, the test would be deemed incomplete.

For a test to be declared representative of a given domain, several levels of performance would be sampled. This is accomplished by including a range of items from simple to complex or allowing a set amount

Denton Independent School District
Adapted Physical Education Prereferral/Referral Form

Dates Received: Sp. Ed. Sup.   Area Dir.   APE Teacher
Please Initial   ___ ___   ___ ___   ___ ___
Student _____ ID _____ DOB _____
School _____ Type of Class (Unit) _____
Evaluation Request by _____ Medical Concerns: _____
Educational Implications _____
Area of Difficulty in Physical Education _____
School Contact for APE Teacher _____
Method of Ambulation: _____ Form of Communication: _____
Dear Teacher,

   Below are some behaviors that indicate a student's ability to move efficiently and interact effectively with others. Please check the appropriate response.

Psychomotor Development	Yes		Sometimes		No	
	RE	APE	RE	APE	RE	APE
Moves without bumping into others						
Stands on one foot for 5 seconds						
Jumps in place for 5 consecutive times (two feet)						
Hops (one foot) for 5 consecutive times						
Skips 10 feet						
Kicks stationary ball						
Throws a softball 15 feet						
Bounces and catches a playground ball to self						
Turns own jump rope 5 consecutive times						
Uses free time for active play						
Awkward and clumsy when moving						
Performs tasks more slowly than others						
Falls excessively						
Body Mechanics/Postural Orientation						
❏ Posture						
❏ Muscular/Skeletal/Neuro Impairment						
❏ Underweight /Overweight						
Mobility Skills (Nonambulatory)						
❏ Transfer ❏ Reverse						
❏ Range of Motion ❏ Brake						
❏ Doorways ❏ Pivot						
❏ Ramps/Curbs ❏ Wheelie						
❏ Stairs ❏						
Cognitive Development						
Can remember visual or auditory information						
Exhibits appropriate on-task behavior						
Participates in team activities						
Communicates with others while participating in group activities						
Can follow directions						
Dependent on others to accomplish tasks						
Impulsive responses to difficult tasks						

figure 2-1
Denton Independent School District adapted physical education prereferral/referral form. (Courtesy Denton, Texas, Independent School District.)

Adapted Physical Education Prereferral/Referral Form—Page 2

Student _____

Affective Development	Yes		Sometimes		No	
	RE	APE	RE	APE	RE	APE
Has indicated a dislike for physical education						
Clinging/demanding attention from others						
Loneliness—Prefers solo play						
Self-destructive acts						
Low frustration tolerance, cries easily						
Tends to be impulsive, accident prone						
Verbal aggression toward others						
Physical aggression toward others						
Short attention span						
Distracts others						
Lying/cheating						
Temper tantrums						

Thank you for your time. Please return this completed form to the Special Education Diagnostician in your school.

- -

To be filled out by the APE teacher

Date of Classroom Visit(s): _____ _____ _____ _____ _____ _____

Recommendations:

❑ The student is functioning within acceptable limits and does not need any further evaluation at this time.

❑ The student appears to be experiencing difficulty in the area(s) indicated above and will need further screening/evaluation.

❑ The student is able to be mainstreamed in regular Physical Education class with appropriate modifications as determined by the Adapted Physical Education Specialist.

❑ The student is experiencing difficulty in the area(s) indicated above and is recommended for evaluation by Adapted Physical Education teacher.

Comments: _____
_____
_____
_____
_____
_____
_____

_____   _____   _____
        Signed   Date   Area

figure 2-1, cont'd
Denton Independent School District adapted physical education prereferral form.

of time to complete as many of the same tasks as possible. In motor tests the representative requirement is frequently met by allowing students to perform to the best of their ability within a given period of time. That is, the number of sit-ups executed in 30 seconds is counted. Students with well-developed abdominal muscles will perform more sit-ups than those whose abdominal muscles are less well developed. The content validity of a test is frequently as strong as the literature cited and/or the knowledge base of the judges selected to evaluate the test. The broader the literature base and the more knowledgeable and critical the judges, the stronger the content validity.

Criterion-related validity indicates that the test has been compared with another acceptable standard, such as a valid test that measures the same components. There are two types of criterion-related validity: concurrent and predictive. Concurrent validity means that the test scores on one test accurately reflect what a person would score on another test at this point in time. For instance, if a student performed strongly on a 2-mile run, a strong performance on a bicycle ergometer test would be expected. Predictive validity means that the test scores can be used to accurately predict how well a student will perform in the future. Thus if a student performed well on a motor ability test, the student would be predicted to do well in a variety of sport activities.

Construct validity refers to the degree to which a test does what an author claims it will do. To establish this type of validity, the author sets out to develop a test that will discriminate between two or more populations. After identifying which populations the test should discriminate among, a series of studies are completed measuring each of the identified groups with the test. For example, an author might claim that students with learning disabilities will do significantly more poorly on their test than will students with no learning problems. After the test is designed, it is administered to two groups of students who have been matched on age and gender. One group has verified learning disabilities; the other does not. Each group's scores are compared to determine whether they are significantly different. If the group with learning disabilities scores significantly lower than the group with no learning disabilities, construct validity is claimed.

Different statistical techniques are used to evaluate validity. In the case of content validity, the percentage of agreement among the judges on the panel is reported. Acceptable content validity can be declared when the group of judges agree on the appropriateness of items included in the test at least 90% of the time. Criterion validity is usually reported as a coefficient that is derived from correlating the sets of scores from the two tests being compared. A correlation coefficient of $+0.80$ to 1.00 is the ideal. However, few motor tests reach this level of agreement. Construct validity is generally demonstrated by using a statistic that measures differences between the mean scores of each group. Thus when construct validity is claimed at the 0.05 level of significance, it means that it is expected that the test will accurately classify an individual as belonging to one group rather than another 95 times out of 100.

Determining reliability

Test reliability is a measure of an instrument's consistency. A reliable test can be depended on to produce the same scores at different times if no intervention, learning, or growth has occurred between test sessions. Three techniques for estimating reliability are test-retest, alternate forms, and split-half.

The **test-retest** technique is the most frequently used method for demonstrating reliability of physical and motor performance instruments. To establish test-retest reliability, the same test is administered to the same group of people twice in succession, and then the scores are correlated to determine the amount of agreement between them. The interval between administrations of the tests should be carefully controlled. A period of more than 2 weeks should never elapse between test administrations.

The **alternate-form reliability** technique is also referred to as equivalent-form reliability. When two tests that are believed to measure the same trait or skill to the same extent have been standardized on the same population, they can be used to determine alternate-form reliability. To estimate the degree to which both forms correlate, the tests are administered to the same population. Half of the group is tested by using test A first and test B second. The other half of the group is tested with test B first and then with test A. The scores from test A are correlated with the scores from test B to determine the amount of consistency (equivalency) between the tests.

To determine **split-half reliability,** a test is divided in half and both halves are administered to the same group. The two sets of scores are then correlated to determine their level of agreement. The most common way to determine split-half reliability with written tests is to divide the test by odd and even numbers. This type of reliability is seldom used with physical fitness tests because multiple items that measure the same factor are usually not included in the same test (e.g., a test would not usually include two items for measuring abdominal strength or for measuring cardiovascular endurance).

Determining the extent to which sets of scores achieved during the testing sessions correlate is the most frequently used statistical method for estimating reliability. The stronger the correlation coefficient, the more reliable the test. A reliability coefficient at or beyond $+0.90$ is considered strong; however, the larger the sample tested, the smaller the coefficient that is acceptable.

Determining objectivity

Objectivity means freedom from bias and subjectivity. The clearer and more concise the instructions, the more objective the instrument. **Test objectivity** is determined by having two or more scorers independently evaluate the performance of a subject being tested. The scorers' results are then correlated to determine the amount of agreement. The greater the amount of agreement between the scores, the higher the correlation coefficient. An objectivity coefficient beyond $+0.90$ would be considered an acceptable level of objectivity.

Administrative Feasibility

Administrative feasibility refers to how practical and realistic the test is. Several factors must be considered when one is attempting to determine whether a given test is administratively feasible to use for a given purpose. These factors include:

- *Cost:* Resources available to purchase test manuals and equipment must be carefully considered. Costs of tests continue to increase; it is not uncommon for motor tests to range in cost from $250 to $1000. To conserve resources, needed tests may be stored at a central source and made available for individuals to check out for brief periods of time.
- *Equipment:* The amount and kind of equipment needed to administer tests vary widely. Frequently it is possible to build, rather than purchase, equipment; however, some items, such as bicycle er-

gometers, may be clearly out of the practitioner's price range.
- *Level of training to administer the test:* Some tests require extensive training for accurate administration; indeed, some tests require evidence of professional training and certification of capability before the test can be used. Other tests simply require practice and familiarity with the items. Professionals familiar with test administration, such as university professors who teach assessment courses, can be contacted to provide workshops for practitioners who are responsible for testing.
- *Level of training to interpret the test:* Professional training in interpretation of test results is required for most tests. Educators should select tests they understand and can accurately interpret. Again, professionals can be retained to provide workshops in test interpretation.
- *Purpose of the test:* How a test is to be used will determine which test to select. As indicated earlier, different types of tests are used for screening, diagnosing, and programming purposes. For a test to be useful, it must provide the needed information.
- *Length of time to administer:* Limited time is available in school settings for test administration. However, too frequently a test selected because it can be administered in a short period of time yields little usable information to the educator. On the other hand, tests that require an administration time of more than 30 minutes are unrealistic for school settings. Tests need to be selected that provide the needed information yet require a minimum of time to administer.
- *Personnel needs:* Some tests can be used if adequate personnel are available to administer and score them. When paraprofessionals and/or volunteers are available, they must be carefully trained, particularly if they do not have a strong background in motor and physical development.
- *Standardization population:* If the test information is going to be used to diagnose a student's movement problems to determine whether special services are required, the test must be standardized on a population the same age as the student being tested. Sometimes practitioners avoid using the appropriate standardized test because they are aware that their student cannot adequately perform the

table 2-1

Selected Motor Tests Appropriate for Use with Individuals with Disabilities

Test/Description	Source	Population	Components	Type
Bruininks-Oseretsky Test of Motor Proficiency (1978) A standardized test composed of subtests that can be administered individually to determine underlying sensory input and ability level delays	American Guidance Services Publishers' Building Circle Pines, MN 55014	Normal, mentally retarded, learning disabled, ages 4½-14½ yr	Speed and agility, balance, bilateral coordination, strength, fine-motor, response speed, hand-eye coordination, upper limb speed and dexterity	Norm-referenced
I CAN (1978) A task-analyzed curriculum-imbedded program for moderate- to low-functioning individuals	Hubbard Scientific Co. P.O. Box 104 Northbrook, IL 60062	Ambulatory individuals of any age	Preprimary motor and play skills; primary skills; sport, leisure, and recreation skills	Criterion- and content-referenced
Mobility Opportunities via Education (MOVE) (1990) A task-analyzed curriculum-imbedded program to promote head, trunk, and limb control of severely and profoundly involved individuals	Kern County Superintendent of Schools 5801 Sundale Avenue Bakersfield, CA 93309-2924	Nonambulatory, severely and profoundly involved of any age	A sequence of motor skills that lead to independent self-management	Content- and criterion-referenced
Movement Assessment Battery for Children (Movement ABC) (1992) A standardized, updated version of the Stott-Henderson Test of Motor Impairment; designed to detect, quantify, and correct motor development delays	The Psychological Corp. Foots Cray High Street Sidecup, Kent DA145HP England	Motor developmentally delayed, ages 4-12 yr	Balance, fine-motor, object-control, locomotor	Norm- and content-referenced
Ohio State University Scale of Intra Gross Motor Assessment (OSU-SIGMA) (1979) A test to identify critical components of basic locomotor, climbing, and object control skills	Mohican Publishing Co. P.O. Box 295 Loundonville, OH 44842	Normal, ages 2½-14 yr	Basic locomotor skills, ladder and stair climbing, throwing, catching	Content- and criterion-referenced

table 2-1

Selected Motor Tests Appropriate for Use with Individuals with Disabilities—cont'd

Test/Description	Source	Population	Components	Type
Oregon Data-Based Gymnasium (1985) A task analysis of discrete movement behaviors of individuals with severe and profound involvement	PRO-ED Publishing Co. 8700 Shoal Creek Blvd. Austin, TX 78758	Severely disabled, any age	Movement concepts, elementary games, physical fitness, lifetime leisure skills	Criterion-referenced
Physical Best and Individuals with Disabilities: A Handbook for Inclusion in Fitness Programs (1995) A standardized test for measuring and developing the physical fitness levels of persons with disabilities	AAHPERD 1900 Association Drive Reston, VA 22091	Mildly to moderately retarded, Down syndrome, nonambulatory, cerebral palsy, visually impaired, 5-17 yr	Aerobic capacity, body composition, flexibility, upper and lower body strength and endurance	Criterion- and norm-referenced
Physical Fitness and Motor Skill Levels of Individuals with Mental Retardation (1991) A standardized physical fitness test with norms for persons with mental retardation	Illinois State Printing Service Illinois State University Normal, IL 61761-6901	Mildly to moderately retarded, Down syndrome, ages 6-21 yr	Balance, body composition, muscular strength and endurance, power, flexibility, cardiorespiratory endurance, hand-eye coordination	Norm-referenced
PROJECT ACTIVE Basic Motor Ability Test (1976) A task analysis of locomotor, nonlocomotor, and object control skills	Dr. Tom Vodola Township of Ocean School District 163 Monmouth Road Oakhurst, NJ 07755	Normal, mentally retarded, learning disabled, emotionally disturbed, ages preschool through adult	Balance/posture, gross body coordination, hand-eye coordination and accuracy, foot-eye accuracy	Norm- and criterion-referenced
Project M.O.B.I.L.T.E.E. Curriculum Imbedded Assessment (1981) A task-analyzed, curriculum-imbedded program for ambulatory and nonambulatory individuals (available at no charge from address provided)	Hopewell Special Education Regional Resource Center 5799 West New Market Road Hillsboro, Ohio 45133	Moderately and low functioning, ambulatory and nonambulatory, any age	Cardiovascular, speed, agility, power, strength and endurance, locomotor, object control skills, posture, skills for participation in games/sports, fundamental motor patterns for low-functioning individuals	Content- and criterion-referenced

Continued.

table 2-1

Selected Motor Tests Appropriate for Use with Individuals with Disabilities—cont'd

Test/Description	Source	Population	Components	Type
Project UNIQUE (1985) Presently being updated to a criterion-referenced instrument	Human Kinetics Publishers Box 5076 Champaign, IL 61820	Visually impaired, auditory impaired, orthopedically impaired, ages 10-17 yr	Body composition, muscular strength and endurance, speed, power, flexibility, coordination, cardiorespiratory endurance	Norm-referenced
Purdue Perceptual Motor Survey (1966) A survey designed to identify perceptual-motor delays	Charles E. Merrill 936 Eastwind Drive Westerville, OH 43081	Normal, learning disabled, mildly retarded, emotionally disturbed, ages 6-10 yr	Balance and posture, body image and differentiation, perceptual-motor match, ocular control, form perception	Criterion-referenced
Test of Gross Motor Development (TGMD) (1985) A standardized test of critical components of basic locomotor and object control skills	PRO-ED Publishing Co. 8700 Shoal Creek Blvd. Austin, TX 78758	Normal, ages 3-10 yr	Run, gallop, hop, leap, jump, skip, slide, two-handed strike, bounce, catch, kick, throw	Content- and criterion-referenced

items on the test. Recall that the purpose of using a standardized test is to establish that the student is performing significantly below same-age peers.

Type of Disability

The type of disability a student has greatly impacts the assessment process. Some tests are available that have been developed for use with individuals with specific types of disabilities. These tests obviously should be used for diagnostic purposes to determine whether a student qualifies for special services. Other tests, both formal and informal, can be used with minor modifications to provide information needed for developing the IEP and determining intervention programs. An overview of tests appropriate for use with individuals with disabilities is presented in Table 2-1. More information about tests that are appropriate for use with specific types of disabilities, as well as suggestions about how they might best be used, are presented in the chapters where distinctive populations are discussed.

Care must be exercised to select the assessment tool that is most appropriate and administratively feasible. The following section provides an overview of different types of assessment instruments, their characteristics, and the advantages and disadvantages of each.

Assessment Tools

There are several forms of assessment. Each can contribute in some way to enhancing the selection of appropriate educational environments and instructional procedures for the individual with a disability. For ease of understanding, forms of assessment have been grouped into three categories: measurement against a standard, measurement of content, and combination types. The most common forms of assessment against a standard are normative-referenced tests and criterion-referenced tests.

Assessment Against a Standard

Normative-referenced tests

Definition. **Normative-referenced tests** measure an individual's performance in comparison with others of

chapter **two** ▪ Determining Educational Needs Through Assessment 41

table 2-2

Fifty-Yard Dash (Seconds): Percentile Table for Boys and Girls Who Are Blind (Assisted)

Percentile	Age			
	M 10-13 (n = 15)	F 10-13 (n = 26)	M 14-17 (n = 43)	F 14-17 (n = 30)
95	7.2	6.5	6.3	7.6
90	7.2	8.7	6.6	7.7
85	7.7	9.0	6.6	8.0
80	8.5	9.5	7.0	8.1
75	8.8	10.1	7.2	9.2
70	8.8	10.5	7.7	9.5
65	9.5	10.7	8.0	9.6
60	10.5	11.1	8.3	9.6
55	11.0	11.6	8.3	9.6
50	11.0	12.2	8.5	10.0
45	13.0	12.3	8.7	10.7
40	14.3	13.3	8.8	11.0
35	14.5	13.5	9.2	11.3
30	14.5	13.7	9.5	11.3
25	15.0	14.1	9.8	11.5
20	15.5	14.3	10.0	11.6
15	19.2	14.6	10.7	13.0
10	19.2	15.0	11.8	13.5
5	26.0	15.7	13.3	15.0
M	14.1	12.1	9.0	10.7
SD	6.8	2.5	2.2	2.5

From Winnick JP, Short FX: *Physical fitness testing of the disabled—Project Unique,* Champaign, Ill, 1985, Human Kinetics.

the same age and gender. The scores (norms) achieved by the sampling population are placed on a continuum from high to low and are classified according to percentiles, age equivalencies, and/or stanines. Scores of individuals who later use the test are compared with the norms to determine which percentile, age, or stanine level the scores match (Tables 2-2 and 2-3). Usually, normative-referenced tests have been standardized using both sexes and a variety of races and socioeconomic groups from all geographic areas of the United States.[8]

Purpose. The purpose of the normative-referenced test is to permit comparison of an individual's performance level with the performance of the sampling population. Federal law requires that one criterion for determining whether an individual with a disability requires special services is below-average performance on a standardized test that has been validated for the specific purpose for which it is being used. A student qualifies as requiring special services when his or her scores fall significantly below the mean of the test or more than 1 year below performance standards for the child's age group.

Advantages
▪ If a child's test results show the learner to be below average, the child must be provided with appropriate intervention.
▪ Normative-referenced test results used in conjunction with other forms of test results can provide an overall profile of a child's developmental level, which enables more accurate selection of an appropriate intervention strategy.

Disadvantages
▪ The test results do not recommend or reflect a scope and sequence of behaviors to be trained.[5]

table 2-3

Norms for the Standing Long Jump in the AAHPERD Physical Fitness Test

Percentile Rank	Test Scores (Meters)*			Percentile Rank
	11 Years	12 Years	13 Years	
100th	2.56	2.26	2.59	100th
95th	1.87	1.98	2.15	95th
90th	1.82	1.90	2.08	90th
85th	1.77	1.85	2.03	85th
80th	1.75	1.82	1.95	80th
75th	1.70	1.80	1.90	75th
70th	1.67	1.75	1.87	70th
65th	1.67	1.72	1.82	65th
60th	1.65	1.70	1.82	60th
55th	1.62	1.67	1.77	55th
50th	1.57	1.65	1.75	50th
45th	1.57	1.62	1.70	45th
40th	1.52	1.60	1.67	40th
35th	1.49	1.57	1.65	35th
30th	1.47	1.54	1.60	30th
25th	1.42	1.52	1.57	25th
20th	1.39	1.47	1.52	20th
15th	1.34	1.44	1.47	15th
10th	1.29	1.37	1.39	10th
5th	1.21	1.26	1.32	5th
0	0.91	0.96	0.99	0

From the American Alliance for Health, Physical Education, Recreation and Dance, Reston, Va.
*To convert to centimeters, move the decimal point two places to the right (1.95 m = 195 cm).

- Results of the tests cannot be easily translated into instructional objectives.[5]
- Results are not always adaptable for individuals with disabilities.
- The tests measure the status quo (what is, rather than what ought to be).[6]

Criterion-referenced tests

Definition. **Criterion-referenced tests** are designed to provide information about a person's mastery of a specific skill or behavior. The criterion selected is an arbitrarily established level of mastery that has been deemed to be acceptable. The score indicates whether an individual has demonstrated performance above, at, or below the criterion level. How far away from the goal a person performed is not considered relevant.

Criteria used may reflect acceptable levels of performance as measured by percentage of successful attempts or level of accomplishment within a set time period. The following are examples of criterion-referenced statements:

1. Throw a 4-inch ball a distance of 20 feet so that it hits a 2 × 2 foot target 5 out of 5 times.
2. Run a mile in 6 minutes and 15 seconds.
3. Play 30 minutes of volleyball without a rule violation.

These tests are derived for the most part from arbitrary judgments concerning what each instructor or school district wants to teach or what students are to learn; however, in recent years, more standardized, published criterion tests have become available.

When criterion standards are being developed for use in an educational setting, care should be taken to select criteria that match demands in the natural environment. For instance, if one is teaching throwing so that a child can play softball, a logical criterion-referenced test item might be to accurately throw a ball a distance equal to that between third and first base after fielding the ball. When one is selecting a published criterion-referenced test, it is important to choose the type of test that best reflects the curriculum.

During the 1990s, in an effort to identify and reward fitness levels that represent a desirable level of "wellness," several tests were developed, standardized, and placed on the market. The validity of the items was established by a panel of experts (content validity), reliability and objectivity levels were determined, and testing procedures were standardized.

Purpose. Criterion-referenced tests are used to determine whether an "acceptable" level of performance in a given domain can be demonstrated.[6]

Advantages
- Test items can be custom designed to reflect a given school or district-wide curriculum, or a national goal.
- Test items provide goals and objectives that are already written in behavioral terms.
- When imbedded into the day-to-day curriculum, the testing can take place in the natural environment and is not perceived by the student as being artificial.

Disadvantages
- One student's performance is not compared with

another's; thus parents are not provided information about how their child is performing in relation to others.

- The test items are limited to those behaviors selected by a few individuals.
- The tests provide information about what the student can and cannot do, but fail to provide sufficient information about how the instruction should be altered to improve learning.
- It is not always possible to identify a valid criterion.[1]
- Locally developed tests have not been standardized; thus their validity, reliability, and objectivity have not been demonstrated.

Content-Referenced Assessment

Thus far, we have discussed normative-referenced and criterion-referenced test assessments that are used to measure an individual's performance against a standard. Each has a different purpose. Normative-referenced assessment determines deficiencies according to normal groups. Criterion-referenced assessments, for the most part, determine what "acceptable" behaviors a pupil can and cannot demonstrate. Neither normative-referenced nor criterion-referenced tests provide information about how to design the learning environment to facilitate learning. Content-referenced assessment that measures the components of desirable movements and tasks attempts to remedy this.

Definition. **Content-referenced assessment** is the process of determining which components of a task or steps in a sequence of tasks have and have not been mastered. There are three types of content analyses: (1) analysis of the discrete components of a movement pattern, such as running (see box above); (2) analysis of the sequence of movements that contribute to the success of a skill or task; and (3) analysis of a series of tasks that contribute to successful functioning in a given environment (see box on p. 44). Content-referenced assessment instruments that measure these sequences include formal and informal inventories (including checklists) and standardized tests.

Checklists are frequently developed and used to delineate critical aspects of motor coordination and sport skills. A specific motor pattern or skill is task analyzed into observable components, and content assessment is accomplished by observing performance of the skill. An

Content Task Analysis of a Locomotor Pattern: Running

1. There is a brief period when both feet are off the ground.
2. Arms move in opposition to legs with the elbows bent.
3. Foot placement is near or on a line (not flat-footed).
4. Nonsupport leg is bent approximately 90 degrees.

Modified from Ulrich DA: *Test of gross motor development,* Austin, Tex, 1985, PRO-ED.

example of a content task analysis of a softball throw is illustrated in the box on p. 45. The teacher checks off which components of the skill the performer demonstrates. That information then provides both an accurate picture of the present level of performance and a list of the components not yet mastered.

Checklists of this type can also include errors in movement or behaviors that interfere with movements. The anatomical functional content-referenced checklist for walking and the motor development checklist (see boxes on pp. 46-48) are examples. An advantage to including errors and/or deviations in the checklist is that the teacher is provided with clues as to why the movement inefficiency is occurring.

Such checklists are useful for screening one student or a whole class of students before beginning a unit of instruction. Through the use of the checklist the teacher can determine which tasks a student can already execute and which tasks need to be taught. Hyde[2] developed an instrument for screening kindergarten children for developmental delays (see box on p. 48).

Ecological inventories are a form of content-referenced assessment. The term *ecological* refers to the relationship between a person and his or her environment. Ecological inventories are developed as a means of identifying the behavioral contents (demands) of an environment. A **community-based assessment** is an ecological inventory that identifies the physical, motor, and sport skills needed to function independently in a specific community setting (see the content analysis for bowling in the box on p. 44). Once the inventory has been developed, a student's skills can be matched against

Content Task Analysis of a Series of Tasks Needed to Bowl Independently

1. Can determine when bowling lanes are available.
   a. Finds the number of the bowling establishment in the phone book.
   b. Calls the bowling establishment to determine when open bowling is available.
2. Can get from home to the bowling establishment.
   a. Knows which bus to take to the bowling establishment.
   b. Walks to the nearest bus stop.
   c. Waits at the bus stop until the bus arrives.
   d. Checks the bus sign to make sure it is the correct bus.
   e. Gets on the bus.
   f. Checks with the bus driver to be sure the bus goes to the bowling establishment.
   g. Drops the fare into the box.
   h. Asks the driver to let him or her know where to get off.
   i. Moves to an empty seat and sits down.
   j. Listens for the driver's announcement of the correct stop.
   k. Pulls the cord to alert the driver that he or she wants to get off at the next stop.
   l. After the bus stops, departs from the bus.
   m. Checks to determine where the bus stop is for the return trip home.
3. Can reserve a lane, rent shoes, and select the appropriate ball.
   a. Goes to the counter and tells the clerk how many games he or she wants to bowl and asks for the correct-size bowling shoes.
   b. Pays for the games and shoes and receives the correct change.
   c. Takes a seat behind the lane that has been assigned and changes from street to bowling shoes.
   d. Searches for a ball that fits his or her hand span and is the correct weight.
   e. Selects a ball that fits and is not too heavy.
   f. Places the ball on the ball-return rack of the correct lane.

4. Can correctly deliver the ball.
   a. Picks up the ball with both hands.
   b. Cradles the ball in the nondominant arm while placing his or her fingers in the ball.
   c. Positions self in the center of the approach approximately 15 feet from the foul line.
   d. Holds the ball in both hands and aims.
   e. Walks to the line, coordinating the swing of the dominant arm and the walking pattern of the feet.
   f. Releases the ball from behind the foul line.
   g. Follows through with the dominant arm.
   h. Watches the ball move down the lane and strike pins.
5. Can retrieve the ball and continue bowling.
   a. Walks back to the ball-return rack.
   b. Awaits the ball's return.
   c. Continues to aim and deliver the ball, being careful not to throw the ball while the pins are being reset.
6. Stops bowling when the electronic scoring device indicates that three games have been completed.
   a. Returns the ball to the storage rack.
   b. Changes back into street shoes.
   c. Returns the rented shoes to the counter.
   d. Exits the bowling establishment.
7. Can return home from the bowling establishment.
   a. Goes to the bus stop and awaits the bus.
   b. Checks the bus sign to verify it is the correct bus.
   c. Gets on the bus.
   d. Asks the bus driver if the bus goes to the street he or she is seeking.
   e. Drops the fare into the box.
   f. Asks the driver to let him or her know where to get off.
   g. Moves to an empty seat and sits down.
   h. Listens for the driver's announcement of the correct stop.
   i. Pulls the cord to alert the driver that he or she wants to get off at the next stop.
   j. Waits for the bus to stop before rising from the seat and departing the bus.
   k. Walks home.

Content Task Analysis of a Softball Throw

1. Demonstrate the correct grip 100% of the time.
   a. Select a softball.
   b. Hold the ball with the first and second fingers spread on top, thumb under the ball and the third and fourth fingers on the side.
   c. Grasp the ball with the fingertips.
2. Demonstrate the proper step pattern for throwing the softball 3 out of 5 times.
   a. Identify the restraining line.
   b. Take a side step with the left foot.
   c. Follow with a shorter side step with the right foot.
3. Demonstrate the proper throwing technique and form 3 out of 5 times.
   a. Grip ball correctly.
   b. Bend rear knee.
   c. Rotate hips and pivot left foot, turning body to the right.
   d. Bring right arm back with the ball behind the right ear and bent right elbow leading (in front of) hand.
   e. Bend left elbow and point it at a 45-degree angle.
   f. Step straight ahead with the left foot.
   g. Keep the right hip back and low and the right arm bent with the ball behind the ear and the elbow leading.

   h. Start the throwing motion by pushing down hard with the right foot.
   i. Straighten the right knee and rotate the hips, shifting the weight to the left foot.
   j. Keep the upper body in line with the direction of throw and the eyes focused on the target.
   k. Whip the left arm to the rear, increasing the speed of the right arm.
   l. Extend the right arm fully forward, completing the release by snapping the wrist and releasing the ball at a 45-degree angle.
   m. Follow through by bringing the hand completely down and the right foot forward to the front restraining line.
4. Throw a softball on command 3 out of 5 times.
   a. Assume READY position between the front and back restraining lines with feet apart.
   b. Point the shoulder of the nonthrowing arm towards the restraining line.
   c. Focus eyes in the direction of the throw.
   d. Remain behind the front restraining line.
   e. Throw the softball on command.
   f. Execute smooth integration of skill sequence.

Permission for the Special Olympics Sports Skills Instructional Program provided by Special Olympics, created by The Joseph P. Kennedy, Jr., Foundation. Authorized and accredited by Special Olympics, Inc., for the Benefit of Mentally Retarded Citizens.

those in the inventory to determine which components have been mastered and which are lacking. Once the missing components are identified, an educational program to develop those skills is designed. The more sequential the arrangement of the items included in the content-referenced assessment, the easier the task of designing an educational intervention strategy that addresses the skills to be developed.

Purpose. Content-referenced testing is used to determine which components of a task or series of tasks a student can and cannot perform. It does not compare individuals with others; rather, it ascertains what aspects of a movement or skill or series of skills a student is able to demonstrate. Content-referenced testing can be used to assess critical motor development patterns, specific sports skills, and mastery of activities needed to

participate fully in home, school, and community settings. Those aspects that are not demonstrated become the focus of the educational program.

Advantages
- Each component can be treated as a test of competence.
- When the components of the task have been placed in a hierarchy, the process enables the physical educator to provide a pupil with instructional activity based on the first short-range objective (in a sequence) the pupil was not able to demonstrate.[3]
- The pupil's ability to perform each component of the task or sequence successfully eventually leads to the acquisition of a major or terminal motor skill.
- The items can provide a qualitative, as well as a quantitative, analysis of what needs to be learned.

Anatomical Functional Content-Referenced Checklist for Walking

Directions: (1) Study the four phases of the walk (heel strike, midstance, push-off, and midswing). Study the child to see if the walking pattern fits in column I (normal and mature). (2) Determine behaviorally the deficit related to a specific phase at a specific anatomical location. (3) When a behavioral deficit has been determined anatomically and in a specific phase of the pattern, pair it with column III to determine potential weak muscles, which may contribute to deficient walking. The initial survey to determine specific muscles that need programmed instructional objectives is complete. Integrated programming would involve (a) matching the activity with the muscles to be developed, (b) constructing a sequence of objectives that develop the activity, and (c) matching the task differently to the ability level of the learner. This assessment system assesses *only* strength deficits related to walking.

I: Mature, Normal Walking Pattern	II: Immature, Pathological Walking Pattern	III: Weak Muscles That May Contribute to Deficit
Phase 1: Heel strike		
1. Pelvis has slight anterior rotation.	Pelvis has posterior rotation.	Back extensors and flexors
2. Heel strike knee is extended.	Knee is locked in hyperextension.	Knee extensors and flexors
3. Heel strike foot is at right angle to the leg.	Heel strike foot is placed flat on floor with slapping.	Ankle dorsiflexors
4. Heel strike leg is in vertical alignment with the pelvis.	Heel strike leg is in abduction at the hip.	Hip abductors
5. Plantar surface of the forefoot of the heel strike leg is visible.	Plantar surface of the heel strike leg is not visible.	Ankle dorsiflexors
6. Head and trunk are vertical.	Head and trunk tip to support leg; pelvis tilts upward on the swing leg side.	Hip abductors of the support leg side
Phase 2: Midstance		
7. Pelvis is tilted slightly downward on the side of the swing leg.	Pelvis has exaggerated downward tilt on the swing leg side.	Hip abductors of the support side
8. Support leg is in slight lateral rotation.	There is exaggerated outward rotation of the hip on the support leg side.	Hip abductors, medial rotators, knee extensors, and foot evertors of the support side leg
9. Toes of the support foot are in the direction of travel.	Toes of the support foot turn out; toes of the support foot turn in.	Foot invertors and evertors
Phase 3: Push-off		
10. Support leg is slightly rotated laterally.	Support leg is in exaggerated lateral rotation.	Hip and knee extensors of the support leg
11. Pelvis has slight anterior rotation.	Pelvis has exaggerated anterior rotation.	Abdominals and hip extensors
12. Push-off ankle is plantar flexed.	Push-off ankle has limited plantar flexion.	Ankle plantar flexors
13. Toes of the push-off ankle are hyperextended.	Toes are straight.	Ankle plantar flexors

Anatomical Functional Content-Referenced Checklist for Walking—cont'd

I: Mature, Normal Walking Pattern	II: Immature, Pathological Walking Pattern	III: Weak Muscles That May Contribute to Deficit
Phase 3: Push-off		
14. Plantar surface of foot at mid-push-off is visible.	Plantar surface of the foot at mid-push-off is not visible.	Ankle plantar flexors, hip and knee extensors
Phase 4: Midswing		
15. Swing foot is at right angle to the leg.	Toes of the swing foot drag on the floor.	Hip and knee flexors and ankle dorsiflexors
16. Hip and knees of the swing foot are flexed (toes clear floor).	Exaggerated hip and knee flexion of the forefoot of the swing leg is dropped.	Ankle dorsiflexors
17. Pelvis has very slight anterior rotation.	Pelvis has posterior rotation.	Back extensors and hip flexors
18. Head and trunk are vertical.	Trunk is displaced to support the leg; pelvis is lifted on the swing leg side.	Hip and knee flexors and ankle dorsiflexors
19. Swing leg is in vertical alignment with the pelvis and has slight medial rotation at the hip.	Swing leg is laterally rotated at the hip.	Hip medial rotators
20. Swing foot is at right angle to the leg with slight eversion.	Forefoot of the swing leg is dropped (eversion is not available).	Ankle dorsiflexors and foot evertors

- Sequences identify what skills learners do and do not perform and what skills are to be taught next.
- The teacher never waits for a learner to be ready to learn a given skill but begins to teach the prerequisite skills specified in the skill sequence.
- Skill sequences make individualization of instruction easier.
- The items can reflect behaviors critical for independent functioning in the home, school, or community setting.

Disadvantages

- One student's performance cannot be readily compared with another student's.
- Individuals who select and analyze the items must be familiar with essential motor components (e.g., the parts of a mature throwing pattern), the steps included in a skill sequence (e.g., how to execute a layup in basketball), and the hierarchy of tasks required to successfully participate in a variety of activities (e.g., the skills needed to participate in recreational activities in the community).
- Individuals who develop checklists and inventories must be adept at the task analysis procedure.

Combinations of Different Types of Assessment

Not all assessment instruments represent a distinct category. Some instruments combine characteristics of different types of testing. The I CAN and Special Olympics Sport Skill Guides are examples of combining content- and criterion-referenced assessments. Both include task analyses of activities, as well as criteria for different levels of mastery.

I CAN

The I CAN[9] series includes task analyses of several different types of tasks that address proper form, as well as a sequence of incremental skill levels for each task. The sit-up and balance tasks focus on a sequence

Motor Development Checklist

Name_____　　　　　　　　　　　　　　Examiner_____

Birthdate_____Sex_____　　　　　　　　　　　Date_____

Category	Special Notes and Remarks		
Static balance	___does not attempt tasks	___heel-toe stand, 5 sec ___balance on preferred foot, arms hung relaxed at sides 　___5 sec 　___10 sec	___heel-toe stand, eyes closed, 5 sec ___balance on preferred foot, arms hung relaxed at sides, eyes closed 　___5 sec 　___10 sec
Hopping reflex	___no response ___no righting of head ___trunk no step in direction of push 　___right___left 　___forward___backward	___head and body right themselves ___step or hop in direction of push 　___right___left 　___forward___backward	
Running pattern	___loses balance___almost ___twists trunk ___leans excessively ___jerky, uneven rhythm	___elbows away from body in arm swing ___limited arm swing ___short strides	___full arm swing in opposition with legs ___elbows near body in swing ___even flow and rhythm
Jumping pattern	___loses balance on landing ___no use of arms ___twists or bends sideways	___arms at side for balance ___legs bent throughout jump	___arms back as legs bend ___arms swing up as legs extend ___lands softly with control
Throwing pattern	___pushing or shoving object ___loss of balance ___almost	___body shifts weight from back to front without stepping	___steps forward with same foot as throwing arm ___steps forward with foot opposite throwing arm
Catching pattern	___loses balance___almost ___shies away ___traps or scoops	___arms stiff in front of body	___arms bent at sides of body ___arms "give" as catch ___uses hands
Kicking pattern	___misses ___off center	___arms at sides or out to sides ___uses from knee down to kick	___kicks "through" ball ___arm opposition ___uses full leg to kick ___can kick with either foot

Courtesy Beverly Hyde.

I CAN

PERFORMANCE OBJECTIVE:
TO DEMONSTRATE A FUNCTIONAL LEVEL OF
ABDOMINAL STRENGTH AND ENDURANCE

SKILL LEVELS	FOCAL POINTS FOR ACTIVITY
1. To perform a bent leg sit-up with assistance.	Given a verbal request, a demonstration, and physical assistance (complete assistance through entire movement), the student can perform a bent leg sit-up 2 out of 3 times, without resistance, in this manner: a. Starting position on back with knees flexed 90 degrees, feet flat on floor, arms clasped behind neck, partner holding ankles b. Curl up by tucking chin and lifting trunk, touching elbows to knees c. Return to starting position by uncurling trunk and lowering head in a controlled movement.
2. To perform a bent leg sit-up with partial assistance.	Given a verbal request, a demonstration, and partial assistance (support student's trunk as he sits up), the student can perform a bent leg sit-up 2 out of 3 times in this manner: a. Independently assume starting position on back with knees flexed 90 degrees, feet flat on floor, arms clasped behind neck, partner holding ankles b. Initiate curl-up by tucking chin and lifting trunk; complete curl-up by touching elbows to knees c. Independently return to starting position by uncurling trunk and lowering head in a controlled movement.

I CAN

PERFORMANCE OBJECTIVE:
TO DEMONSTRATE A FUNCTIONAL LEVEL OF
ABDOMINAL STRENGTH AND ENDURANCE

SKILL LEVELS	FOCAL POINTS FOR ACTIVITY
3. To perform a bent leg sit-up without assistance.	Given a verbal request and a demonstration, the student can perform two consecutive bent leg sit-ups without assistance by curling up and lifting the trunk, touching the elbows to the knees, and returning in a controlled fashion to the starting position.
4. To demonstrate an appropriate level of abdominal endurance and strength.	Given a verbal request, a demonstration, and a command to "start" and "stop," the student can demonstrate consecutive bent leg sit-ups in this manner: a. Start and stop on command b. Meet the minimal performance criteria for individual's age and sex. (See table 1.)
5. To maintain an appropriate level of abdominal endurance and strength through activity participation.	Given the ability to perform the bent leg sit-up at the appropriate age and sex criteria (see Table 1), the student can maintain that criteria over a 12-week period.

figure 2-2
The I CAN program provides a task analysis (focal points for activity) and appropriate age and sex criteria for test performance. (From Wessell J: *I CAN Skills,* Glenview, Ill, 1979, Hubbard Press.)

that is inherent in the task being assessed. That is, the balancing task focuses on different aspects of balancing on one foot, and the sit-up task includes graduated sit-ups (Figure 2-2). In each of these examples it is assumed that the learner possesses all of the prerequisite components necessary to achieve at least the simplest step in the sequence. It should be pointed out that this is not always true when one is dealing with learners who have disabilities.

In some cases individuals with developmental delays have not developed underlying prerequisites to movement efficiency, such as development of their **vestibular sense** or **depth perception**. If a student is having difficulty realizing success with sequential steps in a hierarchy, the teacher may want to determine whether lower-level components are functioning satisfactorily. This type of probing is another form of content-referenced testing. For example, if the task is to balance on one foot with eyes open, hands on hips, and the free leg bent 90 degrees for 5 seconds, and if the learner cannot execute the task according to the criteria, the teacher can either (1) administer a balance test to determine whether the learner demonstrates a vestibular delay or (2) administer a cover test to determine whether **orthoptic visual** problems (depth perception difficulties) could be interfering with the learner's ability to use the eyes to help maintain balance (see Chapter 7). This can be considered a deep, probing content-referenced assessment. If a vestibular development delay or an orthoptic problem is found, these prerequisite components need to be corrected by knowledgeable professionals before the learner can be expected to perform the task according to standard. Techniques that can be used to probe for suspected underlying deficiencies are discussed in Chapter 7.

Special Olympics Sport Skill Guides

The Special Olympics Sport Skill Guides also use different forms of assessment. These include content (task analysis and performance) and criterion (mastery of all parts of the content task analysis) assessments. The guides include a checklist of performance of skills that require assessment as they are performed in competition. The items included in the checklists are behavioral outcomes of either the component parts of the task or the measure of performance. The task analyses for the Spe-

cial Olympics sports curriculum are examples of breaking a skill into teachable components. While the specific skill is taught, assessments can be made to determine which specific components can and cannot be done by a learner. In the softball throw, 19 observable components are listed. Using the task analysis of the throw to teach from involves content-referenced assessment because there is a direct relationship between assessment and the end result of the instruction. This also might be considered criterion-referenced testing because a standard of mastery could be set for all 19 components of the task.

Posture evaluation

Postural screening is an example of an assessment technique that measures deviations from a standard. The objective of the postural survey is to identify postural misalignments. A widely used postural survey chart is presented in Figure 2-3.

This specific survey is a form of criterion-referenced assessment because the figures in the left-hand column of the score sheet represent desired posture that a group of experts agreed on at some point in time. The figures in the middle and right columns represent deviations from the desirable standard. Because a person's posture can be compared with those standards, the instrument can also be classified as normative-referenced assessment.

Once appropriate assessment instruments have been selected, it is critical that the administration, interpretation, and recommendations from the tests produce the type of information that can be used to design a physical education program that will contribute to the growth and independence of students, particularly those with disabling conditions. General guidelines for ensuring that the procedure results in appropriate educational programming are presented in the next section.

The Testing Process

Whereas selecting an appropriate test is a critical step in gathering meaningful assessment information, the most important phase of the process is to ensure that the information gathered is truly representative of the student's capability. The effective evaluator fully prepares for the testing session, conducts the testing with care, and analyzes the information gathered as soon after the session as possible.

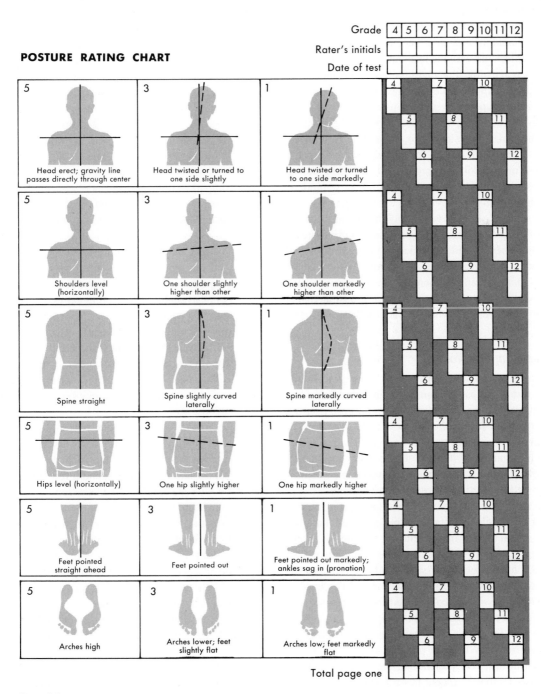

figure 2-3
New York State postural survey. (Courtesy New York State Education Department.)

Preparations for Testing

After an appropriate instrument has been selected, it is important to give careful thought to the testing process. Not only should the evaluator become thoroughly familiar and comfortable with the test, but so, too, should others who are assisting. Practice sessions in advance with peers and/or children who do not have disabilities or observing a videotape of the correct procedure to use followed by discussion of the critical aspects of each item can be helpful. To avoid having to constantly refer to the test instructions during the actual testing session, evaluators may choose to prepare and use "crib" notes while testing. These notes can be used as reminders about what positions are required, time limitations, and unique cues that can be given during the testing session. When other personnel are going to assist with the testing session, they should be trained to the point where it is evident that they are clear about how the test items are to be administered and scored. Once everyone is confident about the test procedures, decisions must be made about how, where, and when the test will be administered.

Administering the Test

Tests can be administered individually or in groups. Diagnostic tests are most frequently administered individually; however, screening and programming tests can be given to groups during the physical education period. When groups are being tested, the gymnasium can be divided into stations, with each station being designated for a particular test item, or the movements to be evaluated can be built into the lesson for the day.

Regardless of the procedure being used, it is important that a well-lighted, comfortably cool, uncluttered area be selected. The more removed the area is from noisy events and traffic zones, the better. Equipment that is required for the testing session should be arranged in close proximity to the location where it will be needed. Needed materials should be arranged so that they are accessible but not distracting to the students.

The best times to administer tests are midmorning and midafternoon. Whenever possible, one should avoid administering tests early or late in the day, just before or after lunch, after a student has been ill, or before or just after an exciting event. Regardless of the time of day the tests are administered, the attitude of the evaluators toward the students is a critical factor in obtaining optimum performance efforts.

Whenever possible, the test situation should be a positive experience for the students. Students who feel encouraged and valued will be motivated to try harder than will students who feel threatened and demoralized by the testing situation. Evaluators should be instructed to show interest in each child, offer words of encouragement, and reward every honest effort with praise. Unusual behaviors and ways of executing movements demonstrated during the session should be noted on the score sheet. Evaluators should avoid rushing the students, verbally comparing their performance with that of others, and providing clues not permitted by the test. Some practical considerations to keep in mind include the following:

1. The test should be administered by an individual who can communicate in the child's preferred language and/or form of communication. If an adult is not available, use a bilingual peer to interpret the instructions.
2. How a child performs a task often can be more informative than whether the child is successful with the movement. Watch for extraneous arm, trunk, or leg movements and unusual head positioning as the child performs. Record these observations.
3. Keep the testing conditions as comfortable as possible. Children perform better when the surroundings are free of distractions and the evaluator is relaxed and unhurried. Spend a few minutes talking with the child to establish rapport and convey your interest in the child.
4. Keep the number of observers to a minimum. Children with disabilities are often hesitant about performing in front of peers or parents. When they are insecure about their ability to perform, they will try too hard or fail to give their best effort if people are watching them.
5. Repeat trials when you think the child might be able to perform adequately if he or she is given more time or is less tense. If a child is having difficulty with a given task, go on to easier tasks until he or she regains some confidence. Then go back to a task that was failed earlier and have the child try again.

6. Observe the child on different days if possible. Children are like adults—they have their good days and their bad days. If the testing can be spread over 2 or 3 days, the child will have the opportunity to show different performance levels.

7. Limit testing time to reasonable periods. Children perform best for a period of 30 to 60 minutes. If the time is too brief, the child does not have time to get warmed up and into the procedure. If you go beyond 1 hour of testing time, fatigue and distractibility often interfere with performance.

A sensitive evaluator keeps the child's best interest in mind at all times. Focusing on the test rather than the child distorts test results and gives an inaccurate picture of the child's true capabilities. On completion of the testing session, observations and scores must be recorded, organized, and interpreted.

Organizing and Interpreting the Test Results

It is important to analyze the test results as soon as possible. The shorter the time lapse between administration and interpretation of the results, the easier it is to remember how the student performed individual tasks on the test. To facilitate reporting and interpreting of the data, the test results should be arranged in some organized fashion. There are several different ways to organize test results. Test performance can be charted, grouped according to strengths and weaknesses, or reported according to subset or subtest scores. Examples of each of these organizational techniques are presented with the case of Billy Bogg, depicted in Figures 2-4 through 2-6. As will be seen by studying these examples, there are advantages and disadvantages to each.

Charted data provide a simple visual record of how the student performed in comparison with established normative standards. This form of reporting can be accomplished in a brief period of time; however, little information from which to establish goals and objectives and develop an intervention program is available (see Figure 2-4). Readers are left to draw their own conclusions about the type of strength that is lacking and the extent to which the student is at risk. This form of reporting test results can be very helpful when large numbers of students are being tested with the same instrument more than once. The student's performance can be recorded in a different color each time so that quick comparisons from one test period to the next can be made.

Highlighting the student's strengths and weaknesses without providing subtest scores provides more information than simply charting the test results. Grouping test information according to strengths and weaknesses provides ready reference to areas of concern while also acknowledging the student's stronger points (see Figure 2-5). However, the evaluator must be trusted to accurately determine what constitutes a strength and a weakness. With this form of reporting, it is possible to determine what the student can and cannot do, but the child's performance cannot be compared with that of others the same age.

Reporting test results according to subtest scores, as well as including a narrative describing performance on tasks within the subtests, gives the reader the greatest amount of information (see Figure 2-6). Subtest scores reported in percentiles or age equivalency provide both the parent and the teacher with a comparative picture of how the student is performing in relation to his or her age group. The narrative report gives the reader insight into what parts of the domain the student is having difficulty with, which is very helpful in setting goals and objectives, as well as in designing the intervention program. Reporting of this sort facilitates communication between the evaluator and others who will read and use the information; however, it is very time consuming. If there are designated professionals whose major responsibility is testing students in a district, they may wish to use this form of reporting at least once every 3 years and just provide progress reports during the intermittent years.

When the test results are going to be used to determine whether a student's performance is significantly delayed to require special services, comparison with age-expected results is necessary and required by law. Usually any total or subtest score that falls beyond 1 standard deviation below the mean or below the 25th percentile or 1 year below the performance expected for the age of the child is considered a deficit area. But the evaluator should not rely on those scores alone. Poor performance on individual tasks is a clue to deficit areas. If a child does well on sit-ups but poorly on push-ups, one cannot conclude that strength is adequate. Rather, one notes that improvement of shoulder girdle strength is a very definite, unique need.

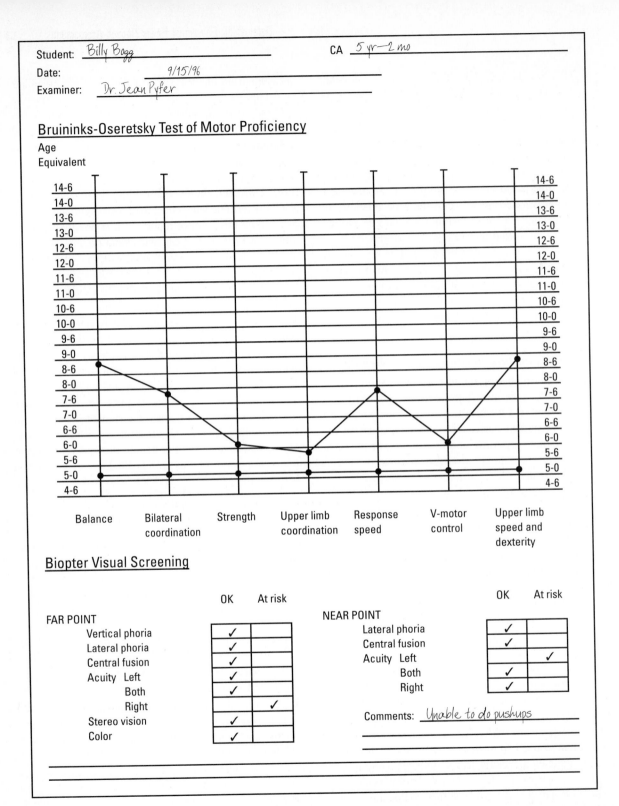

figure 2-4
Billy Bogg's adapted physical education summary—motor performance and visual screening.

Adapted Physical Education Evaluation

Name: Billy Bogg   DOB: 7/10/91   CA: 5 yr, 2 mo

Examiner: Dr. Jean Pyfer, Adapted Physical Education Specialist   Date: 9/15/96

Billy Bogg was referred to the TWU Institute of Clinical Services and Applied Research by his mother because she was concerned that his motor development was lagging behind his cognitive development. The Bruininks-Oseretsky Test of Motor Proficiency and visual screening tests were administered to Billy in MCL 908 at Texas Woman's University at 2:00 PM in the afternoon. There were no observers present in the room.

Strengths

1. Walking on a line on floor and on beam.
2. Balancing on one foot on floor and on balance beam with eyes open and closed.
3. Execution of tasks requiring coordination of limbs on same side of body.
4. Executed 15 sit-ups.
5. Response speed.
6. Tracing straight mazes.
7. Copying geometric figures.
8. Sorting cards, peg placing, bead stringing, drawing vertical lines, and making dots.
9. Eye alignment, central fusion, and acuity with both eyes at near and far point.

Weaknesses

1. Inability to execute push-ups.
2. Catching a thrown tennis ball with one hand.
3. Catching a thrown tennis ball with both hands.
4. Tracing curved mazes.
5. Cutting around a circle.
6. Acuity of each eye independently at far point.
7. Acuity of right eye at near point.

General Observations

During the testing session, Billy read large words from the score sheet (e.g., "examiner") and counted in multiples of 5. When completing writing tasks, he tilted his head to the left, held his head about 6 inches from the paper, and pursed his lips. After refusing to participate in the initial test (visual cover test), he willingly attempted all tasks requested of him. He sometimes hurried through tasks and constantly inquired about his success level. He kept saying he wanted to score high so that he could earn a prize; however, the evaluator had not promised him a prize.

Anecdotal Information

Billy is the youngest of two boys. His brother is 7 years old. His parents have been divorced for 3 years; however, the father takes a strong interest in his sons, and they spend every other weekend and holiday with him. Mr. Bogg is a computer expert and has taught his sons to operate the computer. In recent months Billy changed his father's computer password to "Billy." When asked why he did that, he replied that he wanted his father to think about him whenever he turned his computer on. Billy's mother enrolled in college 2 years ago and is studying toward a nursing degree. She reports that he has a growing problem of becoming angry when he does not get his way and striking out at her and his brother. She is concerned because Billy has no close friends and prefers solitary play.

Conclusions

1. The strengths Billy demonstrated with his performance of static and dynamic balance tasks, coordination of limbs on the same side of the body, abdominal strength, response speed, and most eye-hand coordination tasks while seated at a desk, as well as his eye alignment, central fusion, and acuity of both eyes at near and far point, indicate he is performing at or above his age level in these areas.

figure 2-5
Billy Bogg's adapted physical education evaluation—motor test results arranged according to strengths and weaknesses.

Continued.

Adapted Physical Education Evaluation—cont'd

2. Inability to execute push-ups indicates below-average shoulder girdle strength or lack of knowledge about how to perform the task.
3. His difficulties with catching a thrown ball, tracing curved mazes, and cutting around a circle could be a result of his acuity problems at far and near point, a result of his not having had a chance to practice these tasks, or a result of his not attending to the tasks.
4. Billy's persistent off-task behavior could be an indication of attention deficit–hyperactivity disorder (ADHD), fear of failure, or the fact that he has not been taught to persist at tasks.
5. Billy's constant focus on level of success and preference for solitary play strongly suggest an inadequate self-concept.

Recommendations

1. A visual acuity examination.
2. Screening for ADHD, self-concept problems, and compliance behavior.
3. A program of activities to promote bilateral integration (swimming and tumbling), shoulder girdle strength (tumbling, rope climbing, animal walks), and catching skills.
4. Opportunities to play with other children his age.
5. Billy's parents need to be provided information about how to establish and maintain a consistent behavior management program to be used with their son to enhance his self-concept and improve his attending behavior. This program should be used in school settings as well.

---

figure 2-5, cont'd
Billy Bogg's adapted physical education evaluation—motor test results arranged according to strengths and weaknesses.

When the information is going to be used to develop an IEP, determine goals and objectives, and/or design educational programs, descriptive rather than comparative information is needed. In addition, information about how a movement was performed will provide clues needed to determine what the underlying problem is and where to focus the intervention program. Billy Bogg's test results (see Figures 2-4 through 2-6) are used in Chapters 3 through 9 to demonstrate how actual data are used to generate intervention programs for students with disabilities. A behavior modification program addressing Billy's needs is included in Chapter 6.

Using Assessment for Classification

Assessment is sometimes used to classify performers so that competition between individuals is as equal as possible. To classify competitors, performance in the skill is observed to determine what the athlete is capable of doing. Once the abilities of the performers are determined, those with similar capabilities compete against one another. A running classification for physically disabled performers follows:

1. Move a wheelchair forward continuously a distance of 10 yards.
2. Move a wheelchair forward continuously a distance of 30 yards.
3. Move a wheelchair continuously up a 10-degree incline that is 10 yards in length.
4. Move a walker continuously a distance of 10 yards.
5. Move a walker continuously a distance of 30 yards.
6. Move with crutches a distance of 10 yards.
7. Move with crutches a distance of 25 yards.
8. Move with a cane continuously a distance of 15 yards.
9. Move with a cane continuously a distance of 30 yards.

Adapted Physical Education Evaluation

Name: Billy Bogg   DOB: 7/10/91   CA: 5 yr, 2 mo

Examiner: Dr. Jean Pyfer, Adapted Physical Education Specialist   Date: 9/15/96

Billy Bogg was referred to the TWU Institute of Clinical Services and Applied Research by his mother because she was concerned that his motor development was lagging behind his cognitive development. The Bruininks-Oseretsky Test of Motor Proficiency and visual screening tests were administered to Billy in room 908 of the MCL building at Texas Woman's University at 2:00 PM in the afternoon. There were no observers present in the room.

	Age Equivalency (Years-Months)
Motor Proficiency	
1. Gross motor subtest	
a. Running speed and agility—Did not administer	
b. Balance—Billy executed all tasks to maximum except balancing on one foot 10 seconds (6 seconds) and walking heel to toe on the floor and on the beam for six consecutive steps (four steps).	8-11
c. Bilateral coordination—Billy demonstrated the ability to make circles and tap simultaneously, and simultaneously tap fingers and toes on the same side of the body. He did not execute tasks requiring coordination of limbs across the body; however, that is age appropriate. He did jump and touch his heels and jump and clap his hands one time.	7-11
d. Strength—He long jumped 22 inches, executed 15 sit-ups, and was not able to complete any push-ups correctly.	6-2
2. Upper-limb coordination subtest	
a. Upper-limb coordination—Billy bounced and caught three balls with both hands, and 1 out of 5 with one hand. When the tennis ball was tossed to him a total of 10 times, he caught one with both hands and none with one hand. He hit a target with a thrown ball 3 out of 5 times and touched a swinging ball 3 out of 5 times. He touched his finger to his nose several times in succession and touched his thumb to each of his fingers with his eyes closed. He did not demonstrate the ability to pivot thumb and index finger.	5-11
3. Fine motor subtest	
a. Response speed—He stopped the response speed stick 7 out of 7 trials; his median score was 7.	7-11
b. Visual-motor control—Using his left hand he made 1 error when tracing a crooked maze and while tracing a straight-line maze; he made 9 errors when tracing a curved maze. While cutting around a circle with his right hand, he made 13 errors. He copied a triangle and a horizontal diamond with no errors; he copied a circle and overlapping pencils with 2 errors.	6-2
c. Upper-limb speed and dexterity—Billy completed all sorting, peg-placing, bead-stringing, vertical line–drawing, and dot-making tasks.	8-11

Visual Screening

1. Cover test—Billy shut his eyes and did not participate in the cover test.
2. Biopter test
   a. Far-point tests—Billy scored above average on the phoria, central fusion, stereo, and color tests. He scored average on acuity using both eyes, but below average on acuity using each eye independently of the other.
   b. Near-point tests—Billy scored above average on the phoria and central fusion tests and acuity tests using both eyes and when using the right eye only. He scored below average on acuity using the left eye only.

figure 2-6

Billy Bogg's adapted physical education evaluation—motor test results arranged according to subtest performance.

Continued.

Adapted Physical Education Evaluation—cont'd

General Observations

Billy read large words from the score sheet (e.g., "examiner") and counted in multiples of 5 during the testing session. During writing tasks he tilted his head to the left, held his head about 6 inches from the paper, and pursed his lips. After refusing to participate in the initial test (cover test), he willingly attempted all tasks requested of him. He sometimes hurried through tasks and constantly inquired about his success level. He kept saying he wanted to score high so that he could earn a prize; however, the evaluator had not promised him a prize.

Anecdotal Information

Billy is the youngest of two boys. His brother is 7 years old. His parents have been divorced for 3 years; however, the father takes a strong interest in his sons, and they spend every other weekend and holiday with him. Mr. Bogg is a computer expert and has taught his sons to operate the computer. In recent months Billy changed his father's computer password to "Billy." When asked why he did that, he replied that he wanted his father to think about him whenever he turned his computer on. Billy's mother enrolled in college 2 years ago and is studying toward a nursing degree. She reports that he has an increasing problem of becoming angry when he does not get his way. When that occurs, he strikes out at his mother and brother. She is concerned because Billy has no close friends and prefers solitary play.

Conclusions

1. Billy's ability to score at or above age level on the balance, coordination tasks requiring use of limbs on the same side of the body, response speed, sit-ups, long jump, visual motor control, and upper limb speed and dexterity indicate that his development in those areas is within or beyond expectations for a child of his age.
2. His inability to execute push-ups suggests that his shoulder girdle strength is lacking or he did not understand how to perform the task.
3. His below-average far-point acuity with each eye and with his left eye at near point could be causing his difficulty with catching tasks.
4. His use of different hands for different tasks plus his inability to execute activities requiring control of limbs on opposite sides of the body indicates that bilateral coordination has not yet occurred. (NOTE:: This development stage usually occurs between the ages of 5 and 8 years.)
5. His persistent off-task behavior could be an indication of attention deficit–hyperactivity disorder (ADHD), the fact that he has not consistently been required to persist at tasks, or an attempt to avoid tasks he believes he will not be successful with.
6. Billy's constant focus on his level of success strongly suggests an inadequate self-concept.

Recommendations

1. A visual acuity examination.
2. Screening for ADHD.
3. A program of activities to promote bilateral integration (swimming, tumbling), shoulder girdle strength (tumbling, rope climbing, animal walks), and catching skills.
4. Billy's parents need to be provided information about how to establish and maintain a consistent behavior management program to be used with their son. This program should be used in school settings as well.

figure 2-6, cont'd
Billy Bogg's adapted physical education evaluation—motor test results arranged according to subtest performance.

10. Move independently a distance of 10 yards.
11. Move independently a distance of 30 yards.
12. Run a distance of 30 yards (flight phase).

SUMMARY

Assessment is rapidly becoming an integral part of the educational process. Students are evaluated for the purpose of (1) comparing their performance with a set of standards to determine the present level of performance, (2) selecting appropriate intervention strategies, and (3) adapting instruction to the ability level of the individual learner. Evaluation instruments can be classified as comparative or content related. Comparative assessment instruments such as normative-referenced tests and criterion-referenced tests measure performance in relation to a standard that has either been determined by evaluating a large group of people or established by agreement of authorities in the field.

These types of tests, when properly standardized, can be used to determine whether an individual's performance differs significantly enough to require special services. Content-referenced instruments can be used to evaluate discrete aspects of a movement, individual components of a task involving several movements, or a series of tasks necessary for functioning in a given environment. Content-related assessment is most frequently used to facilitate selecting appropriate intervention strategies that match the ability level of the individual learner. Not all assessment instruments can be classified into single categories. Some instruments, such as I CAN and the Special Olympics Sport Skill Guides, include characteristics of more than one type of assessment strategy.

Which instrument is selected depends on whether standardization is required, its administrative feasibility, and the type of disability of the student. A variety of tests have been developed in the past 20 years that are very useful for fitness and motor programming for students with disabilities. Evaluators should be trained in test administration and interpretation.

Information gathered from assessment must be organized, interpreted, and reported in ways that facilitate communication and program development.

Review Questions

1. What is the difference between a content-referenced test and a normative-referenced test?
2. When would one use a normative-referenced test? A content-referenced test?
3. What are some potential problems of normative-referenced tests?
4. What advantages do content-referenced tests have for direct instruction?
5. What is a community-based assessment?
6. What are the purposes of assessment?
7. Give two examples of each of the following: (a) standardized normative-referenced tests, (b) criterion-referenced tests, and (c) content-referenced tests.
8. When is it appropriate to use each of the following: (a) standardized normative-referenced tests, (b) criterion-referenced tests, and (c) content-referenced tests?

Student Activities

1. Identify 10 assessment tools. Analyze each one and try to classify it according to type.
2. Set up a physical fitness program. Explain how you would incorporate standardized normative-referenced tests, criterion-referenced assessment, and content-referenced assessment.
3. Study some databases of children with disabilities (hypothetical if need be) and indicate the types of assessments that were used to gather the data.
4. Observe teachers assessing learners. Indicate the types of assessment used.
5. Assess a child or another student using a normative-referenced test, a criterion-referenced test, or a content-referenced test.
6. Interview a teacher of adapted physical education. Find out what types of tests the person uses to evaluate students with disabilities and why these tests are used. Ask to see a copy of these tests. Determine what type of test (normative-referenced, criterion-referenced, and/or content-referenced) each is.
7. Compare and contrast normative- and criterion-referenced tests. How are they similar? How do they differ?
8. Make a list of behaviors a person with disabilities would need in order to successfully use a fitness center in your community.

References

1. Baumgartner TA, Jackson AS: *Measurement for evaluation in physical education and exercise science*, Dubuque, Iowa, 1991, Wm C Brown.

2. Hyde BJ: *A motor development checklist of selected categories for kindergarten children,* Unpublished thesis, Lawrence, 1980, University of Kansas.

3. Jansma P, French R: *Special physical education,* Englewood Cliffs, NJ, 1994, Prentice Hall.

4. Meisels SJ: Designing meaningful measurements for early childhood. In Mallory BL, New RS, editors: *Diversity and developmentally appropriate practices,* New York, 1994, Teachers College, Columbia University.

5. Reichle J et al: Curricula for the severely handicapped: components and evaluation criteria. In Wilcox B, York R, editors: *Quality education for the severely handicapped,* Washington, DC, 1980, US Department of Education, Office of Special Education.

6. Safrit MJ: *Evaluation in physical education,* Englewood Cliffs, NJ, 1981, Prentice Hall.

7. Waterman BB: Assessing children for the presence of a disability, National Information Center for Children and Youth with Disabilities (NICHCY), *News Digest* 4:1-24, 1994.

8. Werder JK, Kalakian, LH: *Assessment in adapted physical education,* Minneapolis, 1985, Burgess Publishing.

9. Wessell J: *I CAN skills,* Glenview, Ill, 1979, Hubbard Press.

Suggested Reading

Seaman JA, editor: *Physical best and individuals with disabilities: a handbook for inclusion in fitness programs,* Reston, Va, 1995, American Association for Active Lifestyles and Fitness.

chapter three

Developing the Individual Education Program

Objectives

Explain educational accountability.

List the components of the individual education program (IEP).

Write a measurable annual goal and three specific behavioral objectives leading to that goal.

List the individuals who should attend the IEP meeting.

Discuss the agenda of the IEP meeting.

Explain some strategies a professional can use to make the parents an active partner in the IEP meeting.

Task

Turn to Figure 3-1 in this chapter (Billy Bogg's IEP) and read the goals and objectives that have been included. As you read through this chapter, think about Billy Bogg's upcoming IEP meeting. Make a list of the types of information that must be provided to his parents before the IEP meeting and list the persons who must attend the meeting. Also, think about the types of questions Billy's parents might raise during the meeting, and how you would answer them.

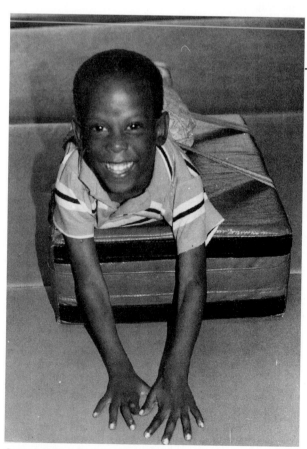

Courtesy Dallas Independent School District.

Twenty-one years after the passage of the Education of the Handicapped Act (1975), the educational needs of children and young adults with disabilities are still not being met. *Every* child in the United States is entitled to a free, public education. This is true of every child with a disability, as well. However, each child with a disability has unique abilities and unique needs. The very nature of a disability simply enhances the uniqueness and requires that the child be more carefully taught.

To ensure that every child with a disability receives an appropriate education, the Education of the Handicapped Act mandated that an individual education program (IEP) be developed for each student with a disability. The IEP should be the cornerstone of the student's education. It should be a living, breathing, and working document that the teacher and parents use as the basis for the instructional process. Again, the IEP is not a piece of paper; the IEP is a process in which parents, educators, and the student work together to ensure that the student is able to achieve his or her designated goals.

The IEP requires, by its very nature, that educators and administrators be accountable for the education of the child with a disability. The **IEP process,** by and through which a child's education is planned and executed, requires a specific education plan to be developed for each child with a disability. The federal mandates regarding the development of the IEP and the content of the IEP necessitate accountability. Educators and administrators must be able to document the child's need, based on a comprehensive assessment and evaluation, and outline specifically the methods, techniques, and procedures that will be used to educate the child, while keeping in mind the child's specific and unique needs.

Content of the IEP

The Individuals with Disabilities Education Act (IDEA) of 1990 explains the IEP and describes its required content as follows[12]:

> The term "individualized education program" means a written statement for each child with a disability developed in any meeting by a representative of the local education agency or an intermediate educational unit who shall be qualified to provide, or supervise the provision of, specially designed instruction to meet the unique needs of children with disabilities, the teacher, the parents or guardian of such child, and, whenever appropriate, such child, which statement shall include—(A) a statement of the present level of educational performance of such child, (B) a statement of annual goals, including short-term instructional objectives, (C) a statement of the specific educational services to be provided to such child, and the extent to which such child will be able to participate in regular educational programs, (D) a statement of the needed transition services for students beginning no later than age 14 and annually thereafter, including, when appropriate, a statement of interagency responsibilities or linkages (or both) before a student leaves the school setting, (E) the projected date for initiation and anticipated duration of such services, and (F) appropriate

objective criteria and evaluation procedures and schedules for determining, on at least an annual basis, whether instructional objectives are being achieved. (Sect. 1401.20.)

Description of Each Component of the IEP
Present Level of Educational Performance

Each IEP must include a specific description of the student's **present level of educational performance.** This may include a description of the student's need for related services in order to function within the educational environment. The statement describing the student's present level of performance must be based on the results of more than one assessment instrument. This is particularly vital, since placement decisions are made on the basis of this assessment.

The comprehensive determination of a student's present level of educational performance may include the following:

1. Intellectual assessment
2. Educational assessment
3. Developmental and sociological information
4. Emotional/behavior assessment
5. Physical examination or health update
6. Speech and language assessment
7. Language dominance assessment
8. Motor and play assessment
9. Vocational assessment
10. Related services assessment(s)

The statement describing the learner's present level of performance in physical education must always be based on the results of more than one assessment instrument, one of which must be standardized. A comprehensive statement of the student's present level of performance in physical education may include a description of:

1. Motor output that may cause one to suspect a **sensory-input system dysfunction**
   a. **Inappropriate reflex behavior**
   b. **Equilibrium dysfunction**
   c. **Sensory integration deficit**
   d. **Motor-planning deficit**
2. The learner's locomotor and nonlocomotor competency
3. The learner's fitness level
4. The learner's ability to participate in a variety of play, games, and sports activities

5. The learner's ability to participate in a variety of rhythms, dance, and aquatic activities
6. The learner's ability to engage in leisure and recreation activities
7. The learner's ability to use **community-based resources** to fulfill movement and participation needs

Annual Goals

Annual goals are statements that describe what a learner with a disability should be able to accomplish during a given year. There should be a direct relationship between the present level of educational performance (written in measurable objective terms), the goals, and the **short-term instructional objectives.**

The criterion for mastery of a task, whether it is an annual goal or a short-term instructional objective, is the standard at which the task should be performed. Being able to perform the task to criterion level indicates mastery of the task and hence pupil progress. Reaching a criterion serves notice that one prerequisite in a series has been mastered and that the student is ready to begin working toward the next step. Measures for task mastery can take several forms:

- Number of repetitions (10 repetitions)
- Number of repetitions over time (20 repetitions in 15 seconds)
- Distance traveled (8 feet on a balance beam without stepping off)
- Distance traveled over time (200 yards in 25 seconds)
- Number of successive trials without a miss (4 times in a row)
- Specified number of successful responses in a block of trials (3 out of 5)
- Number of degrees of movement (flexibility in degrees of movement from starting to ending positions)
- Mastery of all the stated conditions of the task

Edelen-Smith[8] has suggested that only if a service provider (teacher or related service personnel) can perceive a goal on an IEP as being valid and meaningful will that individual make a concerted effort to help the student achieve that goal. She suggests eight elements that are vital if the goals are to be perceived as being valid by professionals, parents, and the student. A listing of these elements is provided in the box at right.

Edelen-Smith's Criteria for Establishing Valid Goals

1. *Conceivable:* If all parties can conceive of the *outcome* that will result if these particular goals are met, the goals will have particular value for the student.
2. *Believable:* The student, parent, and professionals must believe the goal can be met. To be believable, the goal must also be consistent with family, cultural, and societal value systems.
3. *Achievable:* The comprehensive assessment, if done well, will provide data that make it possible to suggest goals that will be challenging, but achievable. "Setting goals at levels of expectation or performance that are too low is as much a disservice to the student as setting goals at unattainable levels. When IEP goals are set too high or too low, both teacher and student are negatively affected."
4. *Controllable:* The student must feel as if he or she has had input in decisions regarding personal goals; if the student has had no control, the student will feel unempowered.
5. *Measurable:* The goal must be written so it can be measured.
6. *Desirable:* Kaplan[14] has suggested that "every goal must pass the 'so what' test . . . that consists of asking yourself if there is any evidence that either the presence or lack of a particular skill, knowledge, or behavior is currently or potentially harmful to the social, physical, emotional, or academic well-being of the student. If the answer is 'yes,' then a goal . . . is desirable; if the answer is 'no,' then move on to another goal."
7. *Stated with no alternative:* In order for a student, parent, or teacher to take a goal seriously, it must be perceived as a significant target, not one that will be adjusted without demonstrated effort.
8. *Growth facilitating:* The goals must seek desirable behaviors instead of seeking to eliminate undesirable behaviors.

Data from Edelen-Smith P: *Intervent School Clin* 30(5):297-301, 1995.

Short-Term Instructional Objectives

Short-term instructional objectives are measurable intermediate steps between present levels of educational performance and the annual goals. The sum of all of the short-term instructional objectives should equal one goal. Because the present levels of performance are observable and measurable and all components of the IEP instructional process are related, the goals and objectives also should be observable and measurable. They are "the cornerstone of the individual education program."[26]

The short-term objectives represent increasingly difficult steps leading from the present level of performance to each annual goal. It is necessary to keep detailed records on each learner to monitor where the child is performing in the learning sequence. The mastery of one objective is prerequisite to the next complex or more difficult objective.

In addition to the hierarchical linkage between the present level of performance, the annual goals, and each of the short-term objectives, the annual goals and short-term objectives must incorporate four concepts: (1) possess an action (what?), (2) establish conditions under which the action should occur (how?), (3) establish a **criterion for mastery** of a specific task (at what level?), and (4) lie outside the child's present level of educational performance.

The action concept

The action portion of the instructional objective indicates *what* the learner will do when performing the task. It is important that the action be stated in verb form, such as "throw," "strike," "kick," "sit up," or "serve a volleyball."

Conditions

The **conditions** under which the action should occur describe *how* the learner is to perform at the task. It is important to be explicit. Changing the conditions makes a task easy or more difficult, inefficient or efficient, simple or more complex. Examples of conditions are: "With eyes closed and nonsupporting leg bent to 90 degrees, the student will . . ." "From a prone position the learner will . . ." "Keeping the back straight and arms at the side of the body, the student will . . ."

Statements of conditions are particularly necessary to ensure appropriate *levels* of difficulty in developmental sequences that lead to long-range goals. If the conditions are not specified, it is impossible to determine what the true capability of a student is and what activities are needed to advance the developmental level. If the conditions are not precise, it is unclear how the student is to perform the task, and once again the *value* of the objective is lost. The conditions for performing a push-up and the rationales for specifying these conditions are presented in the box below.

Acceptable and Unacceptable Instructional Objectives

There are three essential features to sound instructional objectives: (1) There must be justification that the objectives are relevant to the learner; (2) objectives must possess the capability of being reproduced when imple-

---

General Objective: Develop the Elbow Extensors and Arm Flexors with Push-Up Activity

Specification of Conditions	Rationale
1. Straighten back and hips to 180 degrees.	Bending either part of body reduces length of resistance arm and decreases degree of difficulty of task.
2. Place hands shoulder width apart on floor.	Spreading hands wider than shoulder width increases difficulty of task.
3. Tuck chin against sternum.	Raising head while performing tends to bend the back and shorten resistance arm.
4. Touch forehead to floor.	Touching forehead indicates starting and ending position of push-up.
5. Straighten arms to 180 degrees.	Straightening arms indicates degree of movement of arms (will count as one repetition).
6. Support weight on hyperextended toes, which rest on floor.	Supporting weight indicates point of fulcrum to control length of resistance arm.

mented by independent instructors; and (3) there must be agreement on what is to be taught and when it has been mastered by the student. When behaviors are stated in the form of objectives, behavioral principles for facilitating learning can be applied (see Chapter 4). Examples of acceptable and unacceptable objectives are presented in Table 3-1.

Acceptable objectives include what, how, and at what level the behaviors are to be performed. Unacceptable objectives fail for several reasons, as discussed here:

1. Run as fast as you can. *Conditions:* The condition, distance, or environmental arrangements, such as hurdles or nature of the course, are not specified. *Criterion:* Neither an objective, measurable distance nor specified time has been included in the objective. "As fast as you can" is subjective. The students may believe they are running as fast as they can, but the teacher may have a different opinion.
2. Walk on a balance beam without falling off. *Conditions:* The width of the balance beam, the position of the arms, and where the eyes are positioned make the task more or less difficult. None of these is specified. *Criterion:* The distance to be traveled or distance over time is not specified.
3. Swim to the end of the pool. *Conditions:* The type

of stroke is not specified. *Criterion:* Swimming pools are different lengths. It is unclear what exact distance the student is to swim.

Specific Educational Services

In the broadest sense, the "specific educational services to be rendered" means what professional services (e.g., remedial reading, speech therapy) will be made available to the student. In a stricter sense, "specific educational services" has been interpreted to mean what activities (e.g., aerobic activities, weight lifting) the student will engage in. This latter example relates directly to the instructional plan that will be used to achieve the goals and objectives included on the IEP. Every activity selected should contribute toward reaching specific objectives.

Related Services

Related services help the child with disabilities benefit from the educational process. The goals and objectives of related service personnel may be a vital part of the child's IEP and should be consistent with those of direct service personnel. If there are gross or fine motor goals on the IEP that the physical educator cannot fulfill, related service personnel (occupational and physical therapists) may be called on for assistance. These services should focus on offsetting or reducing the problems resulting from the child's disability that interfere with learning and physical education performance in school.[26]

Extent to Which the Student Will Participate in Regular Education

The IEP for each child with a disability must include a statement of "the extent to which the child will be able to participate in regular education programs."[11] One way of meeting this requirement is to indicate the percentage of time the child will be spending in the regular education program with nondisabled students. Another is to list the specific regular education classes the child will be attending[27] and/or the types of regular education experiences the learner will have (e.g., shared centers, field trips, art and music experiences, etc.).

Statement of Needed Transition Services

A statement that describes the process by which a child with a disability will make the transition into

table 3-1

Acceptable and Unacceptable Goals and Objectives Through Evaluation of Appropriate Criteria and Conditions

Action	Condition	Criterion
Acceptable Objectives		
Run	1 mile	In 5 minutes 30 seconds
Walk	A balance beam 4 inches wide, heel to toe, eyes closed, and hands on hips	For 8 feet
Swim	Using the American crawl in a 25-yard pool for 50 yards	In 35 seconds
Unacceptable Objectives		
Run		As fast as you can
Walk	On a balance beam	Without falling off
Swim		The length of the pool

community-based living must be included on the IEP of each child no later than age 14 years. In some cases it may be determined that the needs of the child justify inclusion of **transition services** earlier in the child's educational career.

Projected Dates for Initiation and Termination of Services

The projected dates for beginning and terminating educational and related services must be included on the IEP. This is just one more technique intended to ensure accountability. All IEPs must include a date when services should begin and an anticipated date when goals will be reached.

Appropriate Objective Criteria and Evaluation Procedures

Each IEP must also include a description of the techniques that were used to determine the child's present level of performance and to determine whether the child accomplishes each of the goals/objectives stipulated on the IEP. These must include specific evaluation/assessment instruments that allow each participant in the IEP staffing process to determine whether the student accomplished the goals/objectives in a clear and nonbiased way.

Figure 3-1 depicts an IEP that was developed from Billy Bogg's test results (see Chapter 2). The goals that have been included were, in the adapted physical educator's opinion, the most critical areas needing immediate attention. All objectives lead directly from the present level of performance to the goals.

Additional Components of Most School-Based IEP Documents

The physical educator is responsible for each of the components of the IEP discussed here. It is important, however, for the physical educator to be aware that there are many other pieces of information that are included in most school-based documents. Because the IEP document has often become the basis of litigation by parents and/or advocacy groups and is highly scrutinized by review teams from the state department of public instruction and/or federal grant agencies, the actual document has become increasingly complex. It is not unusual for this document to be 15 pages long. In fact, many educators find the documents to be prohibi-

tively complex and, most certainly, anything but user-friendly.

Additional information on most school-based IEP documents includes:

1. Information about the student
   a. Name
   b. Identification number
   c. Birth date
   d. Native language/mode of communication
2. Information about the parent or guardian
   a. Address
   b. Phone numbers (work, home, emergency)
   c. Contact person/phone for parent without access
   d. Native language/mode of communication
3. Determination of eligibility statement (i.e., does the child have a disability as determined by federal mandates)
4. Determination of placement or placement options along the service delivery continuum
5. Assurance of placement close to home and/or home school and a specific explanation if the child must receive services in a different setting
6. Amount of time per day or week spent in regular and special education by content area
7. Amount of time per day or week served by related service personnel
8. Waiver/nonwaiver status for state education agency–mandated examinations
9. Specific modifications in instructional strategies to ensure learning throughout placement continuum
10. Goals/objectives for extended-year services (summer school) if it is feared that regression may occur without such service
11. Modified standards for participation in extracurricular activities, if necessary
12. Specific strategies for management of behavior
13. Assurances that:
    a. Placement in special education is not a function of national origin, minority status, or linguistic differences
    b. Placement in special education is not directly attributable to a different culture or lifestyle, or to lack of educational opportunity
    c. Education will be provided in the student's least restrictive environment

Individual Education Plan

Name: Billy Bogg   **Date of Birth:** 7/10/91
School: Wilson Elementary   **Age When Tested:** 5 yr, 2 mo
Evaluator: Dr. Jean Pyfer, Adapted Physical Education Specialist
Date Tested: 9/15/96
Tests Administered: Bruininks-Oseretsky Test of Motor Proficiency, and biopter visual test (acuity, color, and central fusion).

Present Level of Performance

Gross motor, behavioral, and visual strengths: Balance in held positions and while moving, coordinating limbs on same side of the body, long jump, abdominal strength, response speed, paper pencil tasks, willingness to try when reinforced, eye alignment, central fusion of eyes, acuity with both eyes.

Gross motor, visual, and behavioral weaknesses: Inability to execute push-ups, catch a thrown ball with one or both hands, attend for more than 6 seconds, or play with other children, and reduced acuity of each eye independently at far point and with right eye at near point.

Long-Range Goal: By May 15 Billy will execute 20 modified (bent knee) push-ups in 20 seconds.
　Short-Term Objective 1. By November 15 Billy will execute 5 modified push-ups in 20 seconds.
　Short-Term Objective 2. By January 15 Billy will execute 10 modified push-ups in 20 seconds.
　Short-Term Objective 3. By March 15 Billy will execute 15 modified push-ups in 20 seconds.

Long-Range Goal: By May 15, using both hands, Billy will catch a tennis ball thrown underhand from a distance of 10 feet, 4 out of 5 times.
　Short-Term Objective 1. By November 15, using both hands, Billy will catch an 8-inch playground ball thrown underhand from a distance of 5 feet, 4 out of 5 times.
　Short-Term Objective 2. By January 15, using both hands, Billy will catch an 8-inch playground ball thrown underhand from a distance of 10 feet, 4 out of 5 times.
　Short-Term Objective 3. By March 15, using both hands, Billy will catch a tennis ball thrown underhand from a distance of 5 feet, 4 out of 5 times.

Long-Range Goal: By May 15 Billy will sit and listen to group instructions with minimal fidgeting for 1 minute.
　Short-Term Objective 1. By November 15 Billy will sit and listen to group instructions for 20 seconds.
　Short-Term Objective 2. By January 15 Billy will sit and listen to group instructions for 40 seconds.
　Short-Term Objective 3. By March 15 Billy will sit and listen to group instructions with minimal fidgeting for 45 seconds.

Long-Range Goal: By May 15 Billy will participate with the whole class in a low-organized game.
　Short-Term Objective 1. By November 15 Billy will complete individual activities at three stations without being reminded to stay on task.
　Short-Term Objective 2. By January 15 Billy will participate in parallel activity with a classmate for a minimum of 3 minutes.
　Short-Term Objective 3. By March 15 Billy will participate in a small group activity for a minimum of 3 minutes.

Physical Education Placement: Regular kindergarten physical education class with consultation with an adapted physical educator about strategies for improving attending and play behaviors.

Modifications/Adaptations: Whenever possible, avoid including relays and other competitive type activities in this class. Instead, use stations and movement education instruction for the first 2 months of class; add small-group activities during the next 2 months, and low-organized games in April. Assign specific places for children to sit during instruction (e.g., scattered dots on the floor). Reinforce Billy's attempts to attend at tasks and give him permission to leave large-group activity and go to a quiet space as needed.

Duration of Services: From October 1, 1996 to May 15, 1997
Date of Annual Review: May 20, 1997
Referral Recommendations: Contact the local YMCA about swimming and/or tumbling classes.

figure 3-1
Billy Bogg's IEP.

Parent/Guardian Rights

The often cumbersome IEP document is but one way in which school districts meet federal and state regulations regarding the rights of the child. In addition, there are specific mandated parent/guardian rights that must be made clear to the parent(s) or guardian(s) before a child is evaluated and either dismissed or admitted to a special education program.

Most school districts distribute a parent rights manual developed by their state education agency when the child is first referred by the parent or guardian, members of the extended family, classroom teachers, physical education teachers, social workers, day care personnel, medical personnel, child protective services personnel, and/or workers in homeless shelters. Usually the parent rights manual is given to the parent by a case manager or transition specialist.

Because children need to be evaluated in their native language or mode of communication, parents and guardians need to be advised of their rights in their native language or mode of communication. While most state education agencies have parent rights manuals developed in at least two languages (English and Spanish), translators must be used to explain parent rights to those parents who use another language. In addition, the law is clear in its intent—it is not enough to simply hand parents a booklet explaining rights that they may or may not be able to read, much less understand; it is crucial that they really do understand, and a professional must use parent-friendly language to make these rights clear.

In the comprehensive assessment process, the parent or guardian has the right to:

- Receive written notice (in native language) before the school assesses the child.
- Receive information about the abilities, skills, and knowledge that are to be assessed.
- Give or refuse consent for that assessment.
- Inspect and review all assessment records before the **IEP meeting.**
- Expect that the assessment information will be considered at the IEP meeting.
- Expect that tests and other assessment materials will be in the child's native language or mode of communication.
- Expect that no single procedure will be used as the sole basis for **admission, placement,** or IEP decisions.

- Seek an external assessment, an independent educational evaluation, within reason, at the school district's expense, if the parent or guardian disagrees with the results of the evaluation.
- Request mediation or a due process hearing if agreement on assessment procedures or results cannot be reached.

In regard to the IEP meeting, the parent or guardian also has the right to:

- Receive written notice of the IEP meeting before the meeting that explains the purpose, time, and location of the meeting and who will attend.
- Receive written notice of what the school proposes for the child as a result of the meeting.
- Have the IEP meeting scheduled at a time that is convenient for the parent or guardian and the school. (If the parent or guardian is unable to attend, the school must contact the parent or guardian via a visiting teacher or personal conference.)
- Have an interpreter present if the parent or guardian is deaf and/or uses a native language other than English.
- Bring others to the meeting for support or advocacy.
- Be an active and important participant in the IEP meeting and discuss any service the parent or guardian thinks the student needs.
- Have the meeting reconvened at a later date if the parent or guardian disagrees with the recommendations of the committee.
- Seek judicial intervention (due process) if the parent or guardian and school continue to disagree regarding the student's assessment, placement, or services.

Participants of the IEP Meeting

The IEP meeting must be attended by the following individuals:

1. The student, when appropriate
2. The parent(s) or guardian(s), or designated representative
3. A representative of the school administration, other than the child's teacher, who is qualified to provide or supervise the provision of special education (In most school districts the principal or principal's designee fills this role in the meeting.)
4. The student's special educator

5. A member of the evaluation team or a professional able to interpret assessment data (In many school districts this is the educational diagnostician, but individual state departments of education specify personnel who may fulfill this requirement.)

In addition, the following personnel should be part of this IEP meeting:

1. Any "regular" educator who will be working with the student, including the physical educator
2. Any direct or related service personnel who have assessed the student (adapted physical education specialist, occupational therapist, speech-language pathologist, etc.)
3. The school nurse, particularly if the student has a chronic and/or serious medical condition (e.g., asthma, AIDS, cancer) and/or requires special medical procedures (e.g., tube feeding, catheterization) in order to function in the school environment
4. An interpreter, as required

Difficult and occasionally adversarial relationships between parents and school districts have created situations wherein a parent may bring an advocate or a lawyer to an IEP meeting. If a student or parent advocate is present, the meeting should continue as scheduled; the advocate is representing the best interests of the student and/or parent and usually represents a nonprofit agency devoted to ensuring rights for children and adults with disabilities. The advocate may often be helpful to the parent and other members of the IEP committee as strategies for developing and implementing the best possible IEP are discussed.

If the parent brings a lawyer without providing appropriate prior notice to the school district so that the district's counsel may also attend, the meeting must be terminated and rescheduled so that both sides (the student and/or parent and the school district) are represented.

The intent of the IEP meeting is that every individual with important information about the child should meet with every other individual with important information about the child and share this information so that, in the end, the child receives the best possible education. Unfortunately, in the real world this is not always possible. For example, the adapted physical education specialist may be serving as a consultant for over 200 children. There may be only one physical therapist serving an entire district. As a result, not all the people who actually tested the child or who may ultimately be serving the student can attend every meeting.

The argument is made that it is neither expedient nor necessary for all evaluators and teachers to be present if those who do attend can interpret the test results and are qualified to develop an appropriate IEP. Adapted physical education teachers who find themselves in this situation should be certain that the person making the physical education report understands the evaluation results and why it is important to follow the physical education recommendations.

Discipline Concerns

The increase in violence and disruptive behavior in the schools has caused many school districts to adopt **zero tolerance** statements that indicate that a student will be expelled or removed to an alternative school for the following kinds of behavior:

- Hitting a teacher or another student
- Selling or otherwise distributing drugs
- Bringing a weapon into the school building or near school grounds
- Continued verbal aggression toward a teacher or another student

A student served by special education is subject to the district or school's student code of conduct unless specific exceptions are noted on the student's IEP. The parent has a right to expect that his or her child's IEP will include, if necessary, a behavior management plan that outlines disciplinary options to be used in addition to, or instead of, certain parts of the district code. This is to protect a student with a disability from being expelled, or seriously reprimanded, for behavior that is a direct result of his or her disability.

This is an increasingly serious issue in the schools. Escalating violence, murders, and assaults within the schools have caused many administrators and educators to endorse this zero-tolerance stance. Students with severe emotional/behavior disturbances may, for example, exhibit behaviors that are inconsistent with school conduct codes and may, certainly, be unable to control that behavior. Nevertheless, violent and aggressive behavior cannot be tolerated in a learning environment, much less in the larger society, and strategies must be developed to address the issue without discriminating against students with severe behavior disorders.

The IEP Meeting Agenda

A productive IEP meeting proceeds as follows:

1. The principal or meeting leader welcomes all participants and thanks them for attending. This sets the tone for a cooperative effort.
2. Individuals attending the meeting either are introduced by the meeting leader or introduce themselves.
3. Meeting participants review the agenda for the meeting. Although an agenda is not required by federal mandates, it has proved very useful in keeping on task. In addition, it helps create the proper mind-set in the minds of the participants; the IEP meeting is, in a very real sense, a business meeting and should be treated as such. At this point the committee members should also agree on an individual who will take minutes of the meeting. These minutes are invaluable in the IEP process and in the maintenance of records. In IEP meetings that may last 3 to 4 hours it is almost impossible to remember what was said and by whom, and while the **IEP document** should reflect committee concensus, it often does not address important concerns regarding the student's education. In addition, in the event that a professional serving the student was unable to attend, the minutes will bring that person "up to speed" about the committee's decisions. These minutes should become a valuable part of the student's comprehensive educational record and an attachment to the IEP.
4. The principal or meeting leader should begin the meeting by expressing a personal interest in the student and commenting on at least one of the student's strengths.
5. The principal or meeting leader should explain the reason for the meeting. This may include:
   a. Admission to special education
      (1) Initial assessment/evaluation
   b. Review of assessment and/or the program
      (1) **Three-year comprehensive reevaluation**
      (2) Annual review
      (3) Parent's request to reconsider *any* component of the existing IEP for *any* reason
      (4) A **disciplinary review**
   c. Dismissal from special education
6. If the IEP meeting has been called to discuss the 3-year comprehensive reevaluation or the annual review, each participant then addresses the student's present level of educational performance. It is vital that the parents be encouraged to begin that discussion and to provide their insight into their child's progress. This validates the parents and increases the likelihood that they will be active participants in the meeting. Then each professional reports on the student's present level of performance within that person's area of expertise. This includes a concise report that includes the names of the tests administered, the results of the testing (including strengths and deficits demonstrated by the child), and the goals and objectives that should be set for the child.

   Whenever possible, the physical educator should relate findings to results found by other professionals (e.g., poor balance often can be tied to fine motor delays; visual problems can be tied to reading difficulties; poor self-concept can be associated with motivational problems in the classroom).

   If the meeting has been called at the parent's request or is a result of an ongoing disciplinary problem, the involved participants should indicate specific behaviors that have necessitated the meeting.
7. An open discussion among the people present at the meeting usually is the next step. During this discussion all the needs of the child and alternative methods for meeting these needs are explored. At this point the true multidisciplinary nature of the meeting should surface. Each person must be willing to recognize the value of the services that other persons, particularly the parents, have to offer, as well as the value of his or her own expertise. The knowledgeable physical educator will understand and appreciate services that can be provided by the various therapies; however, he or she must also recognize that many activities in physical education can accomplish the physical and motor goals of the child in an interesting, novel fashion unique to the discipline.

   In some school districts a meeting of school personnel, both on-staff and consultant personnel involved with the comprehensive assessment, is held *before* the IEP meeting with the child's parents or guardians. This is often done so that school district personnel can approach the parents or guardians with a concensus. That is, however, not the intent of the law. Ideally, the parents or guardians should meet with all professionals involved in the assessment of the child and have access to their information, their insight, and their thoughts regarding the child's performance and subsequent education before a decision is made concerning services and placement.

It is important to note that in some instances a prestaffing meeting may be prudent because of the nature of the child's parents or guardians. This is true when dealing, for example, with the mentally retarded parents of a mentally retarded child or when dealing with the alcoholic mother of a child with fetal alcohol syndrome. This may also be the case when the child in question recently suffered a **traumatic brain injury** and the parent is in a state of denial, one of the stages of grieving. A prestaffing meeting may be held to discuss the best possible strategy for sharing information with a parent or guardian with unique needs.

8. The committee must then determine the annual goals and short-term objectives that are appropriate. Agreement must be reached among the participants about which of the child's needs are most pressing and which goals and objectives take precedence over others.

   Most states have determined specific expectations for their students at given age levels and within specific content areas. Whenever possible, the annual goals and objectives developed for the student with a disability should be similar to those expected by state department of education policies.

9. After determining appropriate annual goals and objectives, the committee must consider the **educational services** that will be required for the student to meet goals and objectives. When contributing to these decisions, the physical educator should focus on the present level of educational performance evidenced by the child in the physical and motor areas. If, through testing, the child is found to have basic-level deficits such as reflex abnormalities, vestibular delays, or range-of-motion limitations the physical educator does not believe can be included in the physical education program activities, referral to a related therapy may be the best recommendation. Such a recommendation does not mean the child should not or cannot participate in some type of physical education class. It simply means that the related therapies should focus on the immediate low-level deficits while the child continues to participate in a physical education program that is designed to reinforce the intervention programs provided by the other services. None of the related therapies should replace physical education; however, they could be used to help the student take a more active role in the physical education class.

10. The committee must then consider the extent to which the student will be educated in the **regular education program.** Given increased emphasis on inclusion, this is often one of the most difficult and potentially confrontative parts of the IEP meeting.

    Once again, physical educators should remember that their services are valuable, regardless of the child's demonstrated functioning levels. Under no circumstances should the physical educator agree that the child should automatically be "included" in a regular physical education class. Unfortunately, some parents and school personnel continue to perceive physical education as supervised "free play." Their perception that physical education is a non-academic experience causes them to devalue physical education. Careful consideration should be given to the decision regarding placement.

11. Transition must be considered in three situations:
    a. If the child has just turned 3 years of age and is entering a public school preschool program
    b. If the child is turning 6 and will be leaving preschool for a school program
    c. If the student is approaching his or her fourteenth birthday and decisions need to be made to prepare the student for community transition when leaving school

12. The committee must agree on dates for initiation and review of services.

13. The members of the committee must discuss and agree on the criteria for evaluating the student's progress toward IEP goals and objectives.

14. The meeting leader should briefly summarize the meeting and ask if any member of the committee has any additional questions or comments. All participants should sign the IEP document.

    If, after every attempt has been made to include the parent or guardian, the IEP meeting is held without this person, a representative of the school must contact him or her to explain the results of the meeting and secure a signature indicating agreement or disagreement with the findings of the committee.

Encouraging and Maximizing Parent Participation in the IEP Process

During congressional consideration of reauthorization of IDEA, one of the major educational thrusts addressed

Ebenstein's Strategies for Parents to Ensure the Educational Rights of Children with Disabilities

1. Maintain "business" records of your interaction with district personnel. Communicate only in writing and save a copy of *everything.* Do not rely on regular mail—hand deliver or send important materials certified mail.
2. Get support letters from your child's pediatrician, therapist, or other professional if you believe your child's needs are not being met.
3. Reevaluate your child's **educational classification.** Some services are available to a child with certain classifications that are not available to others.
4. Cooperate with the school district's *reasonable* evaluation system. If you disagree with an evaluation, review it carefully. Was your child sick that day? Was the child in transition from one medication to another? Was the evaluator trained to complete the evaluation? If you disagree with the district's evaluation, your child is entitled to an independent evaluation at district expense.
5. Demand IEP accountability. Make sure every professional who actually works with the student reads and understands the IEP. Make sure you know who is responsible for follow-up.
6. Try to settle major problems before the IEP meeting.
7. Don't hesitate to negotiate.
8. Be wary of proposals regarding inclusion. "Sometimes, a school district will include a child without providing needed services. Too often, this is a cost-cutting maneuver which sabotages the child's placement . . ."
9. "Treat the annual review as your most important business meeting of the year." Insist the child's other parent be included.

Data from Ebenstein B: *Except Parent,* pp 62-63, April 1995.

was increasing parents' involvement in their child's education. There are several strategies that can be used to increase the likelihood that parents will participate in the IEP process and in the IEP meeting.

First, consider some of the advice that a parent of a student with a disability gives to other parents of students with disabilities. As a lawyer representing parents in "special education matters," Ebenstein[7] has provided strategies for parents of students with disabilities to use when dealing with a school district in order to guarantee the learner's rights and maximize his or her educational opportunities. Her suggestions are listed in the box at left.

Second, consider some of the reasons why parents of a student may not attend or participate in the IEP meeting. Understanding these reasons helps to identify strategies for increasing the likelihood the parents will participate. Parents of a learner with a disability may miss the IEP meeting, or fail to participate actively if present, because of a number of factors, which are detailed in the box on p. 73.

To enhance parent participation in the IEP meeting, the climate of the meeting must be parent-friendly. The following are some specific strategies for ensuring this:

1. The professionals should:
   a. Use parent-friendly language. Explain assessment results and discuss goals and objectives without professional jargon or acronyms. The parents will be better able to make good judgments if they understand what is said.
   b. Use a parent's exact words, describing IEP goals and objectives. There is nothing more enabling for parents than having their thoughts and words embraced. The other bonus is that the parents will be much more likely to encourage the child to accomplish a goal they have understood and articulated.
   c. If possible, use audiovisual technology to share information with parents about their child. If it is true that a picture is worth a thousand words, a videotape of the child performing a movement activity may be worth a million words.
   d. Relate to common experiences whenever possible to enhance communication. The physical educator is in a particularly good position to develop rapport with the parent because most parents can identify with movement, play, leisure,

and recreation experiences more readily than with a specific academic curriculum.

e. Emphasize the positive. All parents want to hear good reports about their child; it is difficult for any parent to be bombarded by what the child cannot do.

f. Talk directly to the parent and not to the other professionals at the meeting. This is particularly important if there is an interpreter. Look at the parent and not at the interpreter.

g. Listen to the parents. Body language and facial expressions must reflect an openness to

---

Obstacles to Parental Attendance or Participation in the IEP Meeting

▪ The parent is overwhelmed by the educational system and chooses to avoid interacting with professionals involved with the child. This is common, particularly when the parent has not been treated at previous IEP meetings as a valuable member of the team of individuals seeking to educate the child.

▪ The parent, despite repeated attempts at notification, is unaware of the meeting. Difficulty notifying parents is typical in non-English-speaking families. It is also typical if parents are illiterate. Difficulty with notification is a particular issue with homeless families; as a rule, they are so transient it is difficult to maintain contact over the period of time required to complete the evaluation and/or paperwork.

▪ The parent is unable to attend the IEP meeting at the time it is scheduled. A constantly changing work schedule may be one reason for this problem. This is particularly true of migrant farm workers and other members of a temporary workforce.

▪ The parent cannot find transportation to the meeting site.

▪ The parent is unable to find a babysitter and is hesitant to bring other, younger children to the meeting.

▪ The parent's cultural background is such that he or she feels obligated to accept the decisions of the professionals involved; as such, the parent feels as if he or she has no input of value.

▪ The parent may have serious personal problems, developmental disabilities, or emotional disturbances, drug related or otherwise, that preclude participation, without careful assistance, in the IEP process.

---

their thoughts and feelings. This is often easier said than done. Sitting in an IEP meeting with parents you suspect of abusing their child and trying to validate them as human beings may be the most difficult experience an educator experiences. Extending your work day for an evening IEP meeting that a parent attends intoxicated makes this very difficult. Enabling a parent who is being verbally abusive to you is almost impossible, but it is an indicator of professional maturity.

2. Before the meeting, the meeting leader should:

a. Use every possible contact to ensure that a parent is informed of the IEP meeting, including visiting teachers, a parent who lives nearby to remind him or her, phone calls from a community service provider known to the parent, a network of professionals serving the homeless, etc.

b. Schedule the meeting at a time that is convenient for the parent(s). This is seldom during regularly scheduled school hours.

c. Help the parent with transportation difficulties by scheduling two meetings back-to-back and helping the parent carpool with a neighbor who does have transportation.

3. Immediately before the meeting, the meeting leader should:

a. Have a professional the parent already knows and likes greet the parent at the school office and escort the parent to the meeting room. There is nothing more intimidating for a parent than to enter a roomful of strangers alone.

b. Ensure that the meeting table is round so that all participants are given equal value; specifically, there is no "head of the table."

c. Ask if the parent cares for a cup of coffee or a soft drink. Although it may be costly to provide refreshments at every meeting, this may be particularly valuable if it believed that the meeting may be long.

d. Have name tags and use first names. Titles are confusing and intimidating to most parents.

Encouraging and Maximizing Student Participation in the IEP Process

If at all possible, the student should be involved in the IEP meeting. In actuality, only the most severely and profoundly challenged students would have difficulty participating in some way. After all, it is the student's performance that is being reviewed and the student's plan that is being discussed and developed. Lovitt, Cushing, and Stump[18] interviewed 29 students from two diverse high schools. The researchers found that ". . . student opinions concerning IEPs reflected confusion, ambivalence, distance or a lack of interest." Few participated in the IEP process or saw a meaning to the process. One student they interviewed regarding the significance of annual goals said, "It really is pretty stupid because . . . I do my work and everything in school. I did everything that was on my list. . . . And each year the objectives are exactly the same. So, it's . . . just basically learning the same stuff over and over every year. And it's been like that since about eighth grade."

Many of the strategies for making the parent feel like a vital part of the IEP process can also make the student feel like a vital part of the IEP process. For example, professionals must make eye contact with the student while talking, instead of looking at other professionals in the room. In addition, the following are strategies for getting students' input concerning their goals and objectives. Before the IEP meeting:

1. Ask the middle or high school student to meet with his or her teachers and therapists to discuss and write goals/objectives that the student believes will be challenging but attainable. If writing is difficult, the student can record his or her goals and objectives on a tape recorder. Then the student will be prepared with input for the IEP meeting.

2. Ask the elementary school student to express his or her desires regarding goals or objectives in the following ways:

   a. Tell what he or she would like to learn to do.

   b. Draw a hero and describe the qualities he or she likes in that hero.

   c. Describe the things a friend does that he or she would like to be able to do. Use a tape recorder or allow the student to make a magazine collage representing particular skills and abilities.

   d. Tell a story about his or her favorite character (e.g., Pocahontas, John Smith, Snow White, Thomas the Truck, Barney) and describe the things the character does that he or she would like to do.

   e. Make a list of the things he or she "does best."

   f. Describe the things he or she wants to do when he or she grows up.

Finally, and perhaps most important, professionals cannot hesitate to include goals and objectives in the child's language on the IEP. It will help to create a situation in which the child is involved in the process.

Concerns Regarding the IEP Process

The IEP has become, in some school districts, a paper chase that is unrelated to the actual process of educating the child with a disability. Care and concern for the student ends up being buried underneath mounds of paperwork. Indeed, school personnel are asked, "Are you done with Juan's IEP?" or "Have you written the IEP for Demetric?" The IEP is seen as an end product rather than an ongoing process of evaluation, review, and adaptation of the program to meet the child's unique educational needs.

Smith[25] has criticized the IEP process:

. . . despite overwhelming evidence that IEPs have failed to accomplish their mission, little has been done to rectify the situation . . . the IEP should be an essential component of instructional design and delivery that enhances and accounts for students' learning and teachers' teaching. Yet, data support the contention that IEPs are not functioning as designed, including being inept at structuring "specially designed instruction."

Indeed, Gerardi et al.[10] have suggested that the IEP may well be the "single most critical detriment to appropriate programming" for children in need of special education services. The researchers suggested that the IEP process has created a huge, ineffective bureaucracy. It has been viewed as superfluous to the ongoing educational process and an educational burden from which many special educators would like to escape.[19] It has been perceived as being troublesome and expensive to implement.[17]

While the potential for maximizing educational benefits for children with disabilities through the IEP process is great, there have been problems with IEP implementation. Specific problems and suggested solutions follow:

1. School district personnel write IEPs with goals and objectives that bear little relation to the teacher's instructional plans.[26] On the other hand, and perhaps more potentially devastating, teachers write goals and objectives that bear little relation to the learner's IEP.

Some teachers, including physical education teachers, cannot make an instructional plan and implement it so that it relates to the goals of the IEP. The problem can be partially resolved by ensuring that everyone involved in implementing the IEP, including the regular physical educator, is part of the IEP process and attends the IEP meeting. In addition, in-service training to teach personnel to write clearer goals and develop the instructional plans that support the goals is crucial.

The good teacher embraces the notion that he or she can and must be able to carefully document the child's progress and, more important, be able to design an instructional environment so that the child can accomplish the specific goals and objectives.

2. Educators fear they will be held accountable if the child fails to achieve the goals of the IEP. The IEP is not a performance contract.[26]
3. The campus leader, the principal, fails to recognize his or her responsibility to ensure that the IEP is implemented. Perhaps this will happen only when a principal's performance is measured by student performance on state-mandated standardized tests *and* by student accomplishment of IEP objectives.

It appears that the IEP process can be used to hide ineffectual and inappropriate education for children with disabilities. The IEP process can, however, be used to carefully plan and monitor the education of children with special needs.

The Individual Transition Plan

A process of lifestyle planning is needed to coordinate the formal instruction of the public schools and the informal services in the community so that the skills gained in physical education instruction may generalize into adult lifestyles that emphasize and embrace physically active leisure, recreation, and fitness activities. Thus a part of the planning process might well be directed toward the generalization of skills acquired in the physical education program to community-based activities or intramural programs that accommodate the needs of individuals with disabilities within the school setting. IDEA addresses this need, specifically, in the mandate that an **individual transition plan (ITP)** be included as part of the IEP. Each child, no later than his or her four-

teenth birthday must have a transition plan that addresses specifically the instructional strategies that will be used to prepare the student for the transition from school to community and work environments.

The Louisiana Department of Education has developed an excellent ITP that targets the following areas for holistic adult lifestyle transition planning (see box on pp. 76-77). These include (1) postsecondary education, (2) employment, (3) living arrangements, (4) homemaking activities, (5) financial/income needs, (6) community resources, (7) recreation and leisure, (8) transportation, (9) medical services, (10) relationships, and (11) advocacy/legal needs.

The Louisiana plan addresses each of these issues and designates the desired adult outcome for each of the areas (Figure 3-2). This plan then defines the process required to ensure that the individual meets the goals or desired adult outcomes by stipulating the responsibilities of the school, the family, and adult agencies in meeting these outcomes. Included for each desired adult outcome are "school action steps," "family action steps," and "adult agency action steps."

Personal Futures Planning

Personal futures planning (PFP) is a process not unlike the IEP process; in fact, if the IEP and ITP process had evolved as its designers and creators had hoped, there would have been no need for PFP in the education of individuals with disabilities. The intent of the PFP process is to *really* examine the capabilities, strengths, and interests of the learner with a disability in interaction with family members, neighbors, and friends, and in the context of the community in which the learner lives. Given this matrix, the individuals involved in the planning process help the learner and his or her family dream about the future, immediate and long-term.

This is a voluntary process, usually initiated at the request of a parent, and involves dedicated individuals willing to make a long-term commitment to the well-being and growth of the learner who is the focus of the plan. This is an extended commitment to the learner and the family of the learner and may require meetings several times a year.

Leatherby[16] suggested that at least the following persons should be included in the initial future planning meeting:

1. Learner

Target Areas for Holistic Adult Lifestyle Transition Planning

1. Postsecondary Education (Choose One)

___1.1 College
___1.2 Junior college
___1.3 Adult education
___1.4 Vocational/technical training school
___1.5 GED program
___1.6 Other_____

2. Employment (Choose One)

___2.1 Competitive employment—no support
___2.2 Competitive employment—transition support
___2.3 Supported employment—at or above minimum wage, individual placement
___2.4 Supported employment—subminimum wage, individual placement
___2.5 Enclave—small group in business setting, ongoing support
___2.6 Mobile crew—small group in a variety of businesses, ongoing support
___2.7 Sheltered workshop
___2.8 Day activity center
___2.9 Other_____

3. Living Arrangements (Choose One)

___3.1 Living on own—no support
___3.2 Living on own—with support
___3.3 With family or relative
___3.4 Adult foster care
___3.5 Group home—specialized training
___3.6 ICF-MR—training, ongoing support
___3.7 Adult nursing home
___3.8 Other_____

4. Homemaking Activities (Choose All That Apply)

___4.1 Independent—needs no services
___4.2 Needs personal care assistance
___4.3 Needs housekeeping, laundry assistance
___4.4 Needs meal preparation assistance
___4.5 Needs menu planning, budgeting assistance
___4.6 Other_____

5. Financial/Income Needs (Choose All That Apply)

___5.1 Earned wages
___5.2 SSI
___5.3 SSDI
___5.4 SSI/SSDI and earned wages
___5.5 Unearned income—gifts, family support
___5.6 Trust/will
___5.7 Food stamps
___5.8 Other_____

6. Community Resources (Choose All That Apply)

___6.1 Independent—needs no services
___6.2 Needs banking assistance
___6.3 Needs shopping assistance
___6.4 Needs assistance with identifying and using some resources (day care, voting, etc.)
___6.5 Needs assistance to use all or most community activities
___6.6 Other_____

7. Recreation and Leisure (Choose All That Apply)

___7.1 Independent—needs no services
___7.2 Needs assistance—needs support to participate in all or almost all activities
___7.3 Participates in family activities
___7.4 Attends community recreation activities with disabled peers
___7.5 Attends community recreation activities with disabled and nondisabled peers
___7.6 Participates in church groups, clubs
___7.7 Other_____

8. Transportation (Choose All That Apply)

___8.1 Independent—needs no services
___8.2 Needs assistance—uses public transportation
___8.3 Needs assistance—uses specialized transportation
___8.4 Uses family transportation
___8.5 Uses car pool
___8.6 Uses group home or residential transportation
___8.7 Other_____

Data from Louisiana Department of Education.

Target Areas for Holistic Adult Lifestyle Transition Planning—cont'd

9. Medical Services (Choose All That Apply)

___9.1 Covered by group insurance—Blue Cross, Medicaid, etc., and needs no assistance

___9.2 Covered by group insurance but needs assistance—monitoring medical needs, appointments, etc.

___9.3 Needs extensive medical services and support—regular tests and/or daily monitoring of medicine and/or therapy

___9.4 Other_____

10. Relationships (Choose All That Apply)

___10.1 Independent—needs no services

___10.2 Desires family-planning assistance

___10.3 Desires support group

___10.4 Desires counseling assistance

___10.5 Desires family respite or family support services

___10.6 Desires peer or "buddy" friendship network

___10.7 Other_____

11. Advocacy/Legal (Choose All That Apply)

___11.1 Independent—needs no services

___11.2 Desires some assistance—estate planning, will, etc.

___11.3 Desires extensive assistance—guardianship, etc.

___11.4 Other_____

---

2. Parent(s) and at least one other family member, particularly a sibling
3. At least one friend of the learner
4. At least one community representative who is not a service provider
5. At least one human service agency representative or provider
6. At least one school representative who knows the learner well

The first step of the process is to identify in a drawing the individuals who are part of the learner's circle. This maps, in a real way, the relationships of the learner. Like a sociogram, it gives pictorial evidence of those relationships that the learner would like to emphasize and maintain and indicates problem areas if they exist. (See Figure 3-3 for an example.)

The second step is to identify those places in which the learner can use strengths and potentials. (See Figure 3-4 for an example.)

The third step is to develop an action plan that identifies the steps that must be taken to maximize the learner's interaction within the context of his or her greater community. In addition, the action plan identifies a tentative time line for completion of these tasks. (See Figure 3-5 for an example.)

The PFP process is an ongoing, lifelong commitment to the quality of life of the targeted learner and in a real way contributes to the quality of life of the learner's family and friends as well.[22] It is a proactive process in which, after the learner's abilities, interests, and skills are targeted, a specific plan is developed to maximize the learner's opportunities to use the skills within the community.

Professional Personnel Who May Be Involved in the IEP, ITP, or PFP Process

The variety of personnel who provide both direct and related services and who may be involved in the initial evaluation and in the child's subsequent individually designed education program are described in this section.

IDEA stipulates those services that are to be "direct" and those that are to be "related." **Direct services** are those to be provided as part of the child's special education. These include (1) instruction conducted in the classroom, in the home, in hospitals and institutions, and in other settings, as well as (2) instruction in physical education. The personnel involved in the provision of these services are described here.

INDIVIDUALIZED TRANSITION PLAN

LOUISIANA DEPARTMENT OF EDUCATION   Page___ of___

Comprehensive transition planning should consider each of the following areas.
Check each area that was addressed for this student in this year's plan.

1. ___ Postsecondary Education   4. ___ Homemaking Needs   7. ___ Recreation and Leisure   10. ___ Relationships
2. ___ Employment   5. ___ Financial/Income Needs 8. ___ Transportation Needs   11. ___ Advocacy/Legal Needs
3. ___ Living Arrangements   6. ___ Community Resources   9. ___ Medical Services   12. ___ Other _____

We, the undersigned, have participated in this transition plan and support its intent and recommendations.

STUDENT	STATE ID #	SCHOOL SYSTEM	DATE
PARENT/GUARDIAN		RELATED SERVICE PROVIDER(S)	
TEACHER			
ITP COORDINATOR		ADULT AGENCY SERVICE PROVIDER(S)	
ODR			

DATE	DESIRED ADULT OUTCOMES	SCHOOL ACTION STEPS	DATE	FAMILY ACTION STEPS	DATE	ADULT AGENCY ACTION STEPS	DATE

figure 3-2
Individualized transition plan form. (Courtesy Louisiana Department of Education.)

Direct Service Providers

Special educators

Special educators are professional personnel who have received specific training in the techniques and methodology of educating children with disabilities. In the past, special educators were trained primarily to provide instruction to children with one particular disability. For example, special educators received training and subsequent certification in "mental retardation," "emotional disturbance," or "deaf education." Today, most professional preparation programs provide training that leads to a generic (general) special education certification. This general training and certification better prepares educators to serve disabled children in the public schools, who frequently have more than one disability. For example, one child may be diagnosed as learning

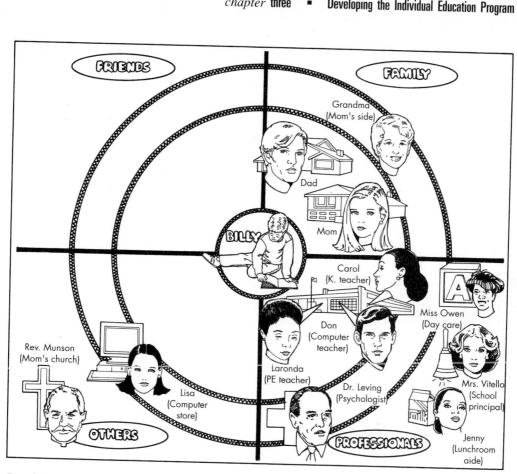

figure 3-3
Billy Bogg's circle of friends.

disabled, emotionally disturbed, and as having attention deficit–hyperactivity disorder. Each disabling condition must be considered when the learning environment is being designed.

The level and type of instruction provided to children with disabilities depend on the child's present level of performance and expectations for future performance. For example, special educators working with profoundly mentally retarded, multidisabled, medically fragile children provide sensory stimulation experiences and health care. Special educators working with autistic, developmentally delayed children provide a very structured prevocational, self-care program. Those teachers working with severely emotionally disturbed, abused children may present a preacademic or academic curriculum

within the framework of a structured behavior management program. The special educator, a classroom teacher, has primary responsibility for the child with disabilities.

Generally, as the child's primary teacher, the child's special educator is responsible for the implementation and monitoring of the IEP. The special educator should work closely with other professionals, including the physical educator and the adapted physical educator, to ensure that the child acquires developmentally appropriate motor skills. The physical educator should regularly communicate with the classroom teacher.

Hospital/homebound instructors

Hospital/homebound instructors are trained professionals who provide special education instruction to chil-

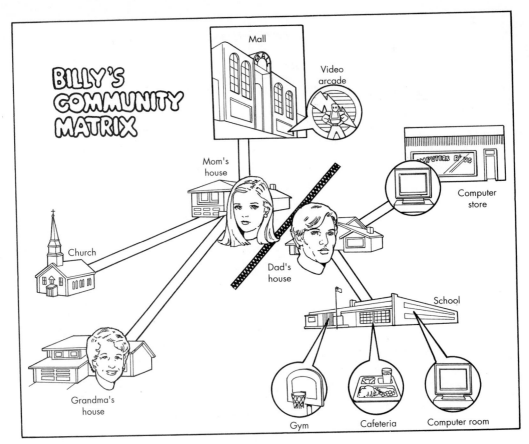

figure 3-4
Billy Bogg's community matrix.

dren who are hospitalized or who, because of severe medical disabilities, cannot be educated within the typical school setting. The education is the same; only the setting is different.

Instructors in institutions and other settings

For a variety of reasons, some children, often the profoundly, multiply disabled, receive their education within an institutional setting. Within recent years, court mandates have significantly improved the quality of both instruction and care within these facilities.

Adapted physical educators

The art, the science, and the profession of adapted physical education is described throughout the entire text. The role of the **adapted physical educator,** as part of the multidisciplinary team, is summarized here.

Adapted physical educators are physical educators with specialized training; the extent of required training is determined on a state-by-state basis. Specifically, these professionals have training in the assessment and evaluation of motor behavior and physical fitness, the development of the child's individual physical education program (IPEP), the implementation of the child's IPEP, and the processes of teaching and managing the behavior of children with disabilities. Their services are required by law.

The Education of the Handicapped Act mandated that physical education was to be a vital part of each child's special education program. In fact, physical edu-

Action Plan for Billy Bogg's Personal Futures Planning Group

Action	Time Line	PFP Person Responsible
Contact a local sport team and ask if they could use a computer wizard to help with statistics, programs, etc.	Before next meeting	Don, computer teacher
Gail will demonstrate sport-based CD-Rom technology to PFP team.	At next meeting	Gail, local Apple sales representative
Purchase and teach Billy to use sport-based computer software.	Within a month of next meeting	Dad
Contact first grade teacher to see if Billy can help tutor a peer or kindergartner in computer skills.	Within the month	Don, computer teacher
Arrange a time during school day so Billy can help make computer-generated "Personal Best" certificates.	Within the month	Laronda, PE teacher
Take Billy to the park to play.	Once a week for 1 hour	Jimmy, 7-year-old brother
Contact YMCA re swimming and tumbling programs.	Within 2 weeks	Mom
Expand play therapy time with Billy to 2 hours/week.	Beginning next week	Susan, child psychologist

figure 3-5
Billy Bogg's PFP action plan.

cation was the only curricular area designated specifically as a required, direct service. The intent of the law was that specially trained, adapted physical educators would provide quality, direct, "hands-on," daily physical education instruction to children with disabilities. A lack of financial and personnel resources, as well as a lack of commitment to physical education in general, has made this scenario a dream, rather than a reality, in most school districts.

Vision specialists

Historically, a severely visually impaired child received educational services within a segregated environment. Typically, educational services were delivered in a separate residential school facility or within a self-contained room in a given school building. In that setting the child's primary teacher was a **vision specialist,** a teacher specially trained to meet the educational needs of the blind child.

The **Regular Education Initiative (REI),** the federally supported concept that suggests that children with special needs should be educated within the "regular" education program, has had a significant impact on the education of the visually impaired. Specifically, the visually impaired child, whenever possible, is educated in his or her home school with support from vision specialists and orientation and mobility specialists. Children who are totally blind, legally blind, partially sighted, or multiply handicapped (whose visual loss is only one of their impairments) may be educated with support within the regular education classroom in school districts embracing the concept of the REI.

Vision specialists, and orientation and mobility specialists have the skills necessary to complete a visual evaluation and educational assessment to determine the extent of visual disability and the types and kinds of intervention that will make possible a successful educational experience. The vision therapist/teacher focuses

...odification of instruction, which may include spe-
...ic visual, tactile, and/or auditory learning techniques.
Other modifications also may be required for the child
to learn in the designated education setting. The therapist may suggest augmentative aids, such as a Braille
typewriter, an abacus, or a text enlarger, to meet the
unique needs of the child.

The orientation and mobility specialist will work
with the child and his or her regular or special educators to help develop the skills necessary, for example, to
use a cane or to successfully ascend and descend school
bus stairs.

Related Service Providers

The law also specifies and defines **related services.** As
indicated earlier in the chapter, these are services that
must be provided to the child with disabilities so that
the child can benefit from instruction. The related service providers are described here.

Audiologists

Audiologists are trained to complete a comprehensive evaluation of a child's hearing capabilities. This includes an evaluation of the child's response to the qualities of sound—intensity, pitch, frequency, and timbre.
Based on the results of the evaluation, the audiologist
makes recommendations to school personnel. The audiologist may suggest, for example, simple modifications
in the educational environment of the mildly hearing impaired child to facilitate learning; specifically, the child
may be placed close to the teacher for instructional purposes. The audiologist may recommend that a hearing
aid be provided for the more severely hearing impaired
child and may work closely with trained special educators who will help the child develop total communication skills, including sign language, speech reading, and
oral language.

Counselors

Counseling services are becoming increasingly important in the total education process for all children,
particularly children with disabilities. The school-based
counselor may serve children with disabilities by implementing programs designed to enhance self-esteem, to
teach children to identify and avoid sexual abuse, to
share techniques for values identification and clarification, or to teach techniques and methods for dealing with
grief.

Children with disabilities living within dysfunc-
tional families may need a more comprehensive intervention. These children may need individual counseling
services in order to benefit from educational services.
Because the family unit must be addressed if counseling
is to be of value and have long-lasting effects, the most
effective programs involve each member of the family
in the counseling process.

Medical diagnostic service personnel

IDEA indicates that medical diagnostic services
must be provided for a child who needs these services
in order to benefit from his or her education. Many
school districts have working partnerships with a hospital or rehabilitation facility so that children who require
medical diagnostic services can be referred to **medical
diagnostic service personnel** at that hospital or center.
It is important to note, however, that the law does not
mandate medical services, just medical diagnostics.

To be eligible for special education services, a child
with an orthopedic impairment or other health impairment must be diagnosed as having a disability; this diagnosis must be made by a licensed physician. For a
child to be identified as "emotionally disturbed," a licensed psychologist or psychiatrist must confirm the diagnosis.

Occupational therapists

The Education of the Handicapped Act mandated
that occupational therapy must be made available to a
child with a disability who requires this service in order
to allow the child to be successful in the educational environment. Before passage of this act, the pediatric **occupational therapist** functioned primarily within hospitals, community-based agencies, home health care
agencies, and rehabilitation facilities. Now pediatric occupational therapists are a vital part of the total educational process and can be an integral part of a motor development team.

The American Occupational Therapy Association
has adopted occupational therapy performance areas[4]
that are the focus of occupational therapists in all settings (see box on p. 83).

Occupational therapists working within the educa-

Occupational Therapy Performance Areas as Defined by the American Occupational Therapy Association

1. Activities of daily living
   a. Grooming
   b. Oral hygiene
   c. Bathing
   d. Toilet hygiene
   e. Dressing
   f. Feeding and eating
   g. Medication routine
   h. Socialization
   i. Functional communication
   j. Functional mobility
   k. Sexual expression

2. Work activities
   a. Home management
   b. Care of others
   c. Educational activities
   d. Vocational activities

3. Play or leisure activities
   a. Play or leisure exploration
   b. Play or leisure performance

Data from American Occupational Therapy Association: *Uniform terminology for occupational therapy,* ed 2, Rockville, Md, 1989, The Association.

tional setting have had to define their role and focus in relationship to special education. As a result, the school-based therapist has had to develop a strategy to function within the educational model rather than the medical model. The American Occupational Therapy Association has described the occupational therapist serving in the schools in the following way[3]:

> Registered occupational therapists in education systems are considered to be related service personnel. The occupational therapist is responsible for assessment, planning, and goal development and for providing appropriate intervention services designed to enhance the student's potential for learning, to assist the student in acquiring those functional performance skills needed to participate in and benefit from the educational environment, and to help the student function independently.

According to Orr, Gott, and Kainer,[24] the occupational therapist in the school setting must focus on the student role. Within the schools, these professionals concentrate on activities of daily living that are part and parcel of the process of going to school. In addition, the school-based occupational therapist defines "school" as a child's "work." The occupational therapist is responsible for ensuring that the student with a disability can assume the role of student and benefit from instruction within the school setting. They define behaviors and activities that constitute the role of the student and then develop strategies to allow the child to be successful in the student role.

The school-based occupational therapist might contribute to the child's school success in a number of ways. The therapist may help wheelchair-enabled students move independently within the school by teaching them to carry a lunch tray on their lap, manage a ramp to and from the playground, and move through crowded halls without running into classmates. The therapist may assist a learning-disabled student by providing sensorimotor training to ready the child to receive instruction. The therapist may help the autistic child develop basic play skills.

The occupational therapist will often work in cooperation with the physical educator, particularly to ensure student success in managing travel around the gymnasium or playground, in developing strategies to maximize the development of appropriate social skills and play behavior, and to contribute to the physical education individual exercise plan.

Parent counselors and trainers

IDEA affirmed the fact that the parent is the child's first and primary teacher. This echoes mandates in P.L. 99-457 (Education for All Handicapped Children Amendments of 1986) for parental involvement in early intervention.

The services provided by **parent counselors and trainers** are vital to those facing the reality of raising a child with a disability. This counseling and training is even more crucial for a single parent raising a disabled child. The financial struggles, the loneliness, and the fears are overwhelming.

Parent counseling and training focuses, as well, on helping the parent(s) develop appropriate expectations regarding the child's growth and development. The parent must be helped to develop realistic, yet hopeful, goals for the child.

Physical therapists

The **physical therapist** is trained to provide services that address range of motion, maintenance and development of muscle tone, gait therapy, and mobility assistance with and without physical aids or equipment. The physical therapist can be a vital and integral part of the motor development team. The therapist brings to the child with disabilities a vast wealth of information regarding human motion.

One of the major problems facing the public schools that are attempting to meet the mandates of the federal law is that it is increasingly difficult to hire a physical therapist to work within the schools. The services of physical therapists are sought by hospitals, rehabilitation facilities, and nursing homes; generally, the public schools cannot compete financially to hire and retain physical therapists.

Psychologists

Psychological services for children with disabilities, and if necessary for their parent(s), have been designated as a related service. Many school districts provide these services by hiring a **psychologist** or **psychiatrist** as a consultant or on a per-child basis. Larger school districts may hire school-based psychologists as part of the assessment and intervention team.

These professionals are involved in the assessment of children with disabilities referred because of emotional disturbance, aggressive behavior toward other children or their parent(s), severe depression, suicidal tendencies or attempted suicides, or because of reports of sexual or physical abuse or serious neglect.

Recreation therapists

The school-based **recreation therapist** provides instruction so that individuals with disabilities will be able to make wise choices in the use of leisure time. The intent is to provide instruction so that students will be able to participate in community-based leisure activities. Because of the commitment of recreation therapists to community-based, lifetime activity development, these professionals play a vital role in the development of the child's ITP. The child's IEP in middle school and high school must include specific goals and objectives related to community-based leisure and recreation activities.

Rehabilitation counselor

The **rehabilitation counselor** focuses on helping the learner with a disability gain the confidence and learn the skills necessary to function as normally as possible. Most rehabilitation counseling and rehabilitation ser-

vices address the needs of the learner with adventitious injuries or disabilities; these are injuries or disabilities that occur after the child has already experienced "normal" development.

Rehabilitation counseling addresses grief; specifically, the child with a new injury or disability must grieve the loss of function or ability before he or she can get on with life. It also addresses strategies for the reestablishment of self-esteem. Techniques are taught so that the child can adapt or compensate for the injury or disability and live a full life.

Play, games, and sports have been found to be effective tools in the rehabilitation process. Indeed, most major rehabilitation facilities encourage participation in these activities to facilitate recovery and development.

Assistive technology service personnel

Legislative initiatives such as P.L. 100-407—The Technology-Related Assistance for Individuals with Disabilities Act of 1988 (Tech Act)—and IDEA illustrate the importance the federal government has placed on assistive technology service personnel. Congress defined **assistive technology service** as:

> Any service that directly assists an individual with a disability in the selection, acquisition, or use of an assistive technology device. Such term includes—(A) the evaluation of the needs of an individual with a disability, including a functional evaluation of the individual in the individual's customary environment; (B) purchasing, leasing, or otherwise providing for the acquisition of assistive technology devices by individuals with disabilities; (C) selecting, designing, fitting, customizing, adapting, applying, maintaining, repairing or replacing of assistive technology devices; (D) coordinating and using other therapies, interventions, or services with assistive technology devices, such as those associated with existing education and rehabilitation plans and programs; (E) training or technical assistance for an individual with disabilities, or, where appropriate, the family of an individual with disabilities; and (F) training or technical assistance for professionals (including individuals providing education and rehabilitation services), employers, or other individuals who provide services to, employ, or are otherwise substantially involved in the major life functions of individuals with disabilities.[12]

The Tech Act and IDEA focused on the fact that an individual living in the twenty-first century must be comfortable with technology in order to thrive, in order to survive. Assistive technology services is a related service that must be provided to a child who needs such services in order to benefit from the educational experience. The technologies that must be made available to a child with disabilities include low-tech assistive technology, such as (1) note-taking cassette recorders, (2) simple switches, (3) head pointers, and (4) picture boards. High-tech assistance includes (1) optical character recognition, (2) speech synthesizers, (3) augmentative communication devices, (4) alternative keyboards, and (5) word processors with spelling- and grammar-checking capabilities.[5]

Lavine[15] suggested, "Personal computers may offer their greatest benefits to still another group of people—those who, for one reason or another, have limited abilities to influence and interact with the outside world . . . For them, personal computers can help bridge the barriers imposed by their handicaps." A statement of the Instruction Systems Technology Division of the Dallas Independent School District[9] included, "The population of students who stand to gain the most from microcomputer technology are those who have physical, sensory, emotional and/or cognitive limitations which have caused them to be isolated from their 'regular' peers."

Cain[6] suggested six reasons why computer technology must be included within special education programs. They are:

1. Computer technology is a vital component of "regular" education, so it should be a vital component of special education to ensure program equity.
2. These technologies prepare individuals with disabilities for the most productive life possible.
3. Computers can serve as a vital tool for compensatory, expressive, and receptive language.
4. Computers provide the opportunity for children with disabilities to experience the real world through simulation activities.
5. Computers serve as a prosthetic communication device for dyslexics, the deaf, the hard of hearing, the visually impaired, and the language disordered.
6. Computers can provide a recreational alternative for children to enable them to "play" soccer, golf, football, or Ping-Pong via computer.

School health service personnel

School health services must be provided to students with disabilities. In most school districts, the **school health service personnel** are nurses. These health ser-

vices include monitoring immunization records and monitoring and/or completing health procedures such as catheterization or tracheostomy tube suction. In Irving Independent School District v. Tatro (1984), the U.S. Supreme Court decided that health services needed to enable a child to reach, enter, exit, or remain in school during the day were required.[13]

School health services for children with disabilities become more complex as more medically fragile children pursue their right to a free, appropriate public education as mandated by IDEA and Section 504 of the Rehabilitation Act.

Social workers

Social work services, which include group and individual counseling with children and their families (home-centered where possible), are a vital part of related services required by law. The licensed **social worker** intervenes within the family, seen as part of the total community, and helps the child with disabilities and his or her family deal with issues that directly relate to the disability—discrimination, fear, guilt, substance abuse, child abuse, medical expenses, and the intrusion of well-meaning professionals into their lives.

The social worker is trained to assist the family in coping with the vast and often complex system designed to provide support for families in trouble. The social worker can, for example, help a parent apply for Aid for Dependent Children or, if necessary, unemployment compensation.

In some large school districts community social service agencies have opened offices within the schools to improve access to needed social services. This strategy has proved valuable in providing assistance to non-English-speaking children and their families.

Speech therapists

Speech and language therapy has as its goal the improvement of communication behaviors of students whose speech and/or language deficits affect educational performance. Haynes[11] has identified four separate speech and language components that must be addressed by the **speech therapist:** (1) semantics (language content or meaning), (2) syntax (language structure or grammar), (3) pragmatics (language use or function), and (4) phonology (the sound system of language).

Service delivery in speech and language programs

was historically based on a medical model in which the speech therapist provided therapy to children with speech and language deficits in a clinical, isolated setting. That is, the clinician provided speech and language programming in a setting removed from the child's regular education or special education classroom. That practice is changing.

Current, innovative practice in speech and language programs is based on the notion that speech and language is a basic and integral part of the child's total life experience. As Achilles, Yates, and Freese have suggested,[1] the child uses speech and language throughout the day, in a variety of environments, in response to a variety of stimuli, and in interaction with many different people; and as such, it is an ongoing process. Therefore speech and language therapy must be embedded within the total academic and nonacademic curriculum.

To allow classroom-based therapy to occur, the speech therapist functions collaboratively with the child's regular educator and/or special educator.[21] The therapist is often willing to collaborate with the physical educator or the adapted physical educator because the advantages identified in classroom-based language instruction pertain to the physical education "classroom," or adapted physical education "classroom" as well. In fact, the very nature of physical education makes it an exciting, language-rich opportunity. Children involved in dance, play, or games are functioning within their most natural environment; this environment demands communication in a variety of forms—gestures, signs, expressive facial behaviors, or expressive/receptive speech.

In addition, the therapist collaborates with the physical educator or adapted physical educator because of the obvious relationship between gross and fine motor development and the development of speech and language. Indeed, movement is speech; speech is movement.

Transportation specialists

In *Alamo Heights v. State Board of Education* (1986), the court mandated that transportation, like other related services, must be included on the child's IEP.[2] The Office of Civil Rights has decreed that a child with a disability should not have to ride the school bus longer than other children. The Office of Civil Rights has also indicated it is a violation of civil rights if a child with a

disability has a shorter instructional day than other children because of the school bus schedule. In addition, the child with a disability should have the same access to extracurricular, before-school or after-school, programs as any other child.[23]

If the child needs an aide (**transportation specialist**) on the bus during transportation to and from school, litigation indicates it should be included on the IEP as well. In *Macomb County Intermediate School District v. Joshua S.* (1989), the court mandated that the school district must provide an aide to help a multiply handicapped student who needed positioning in a wheelchair and a tracheostomy tube suctioned during the ride to and from school.[20]

Transition service personnel

One of the major transition services offered by **transition service personnel** is vocational education. A quality vocational education program includes a comprehensive assessment of vocational potential and capabilities. The student with a disability is given the opportunity to demonstrate his or her unique skills and talents so that appropriate job training can be provided. As the student enters middle school and high school, the focus of the education provided is vocational, if appropriate. Special education instruction focuses on the skills necessary to function within a workplace. Actual work-related opportunities are provided in "work production" or "work simulation" classes. Some progressive school districts have job placement opportunities for children with disabilities in the last years of their special education career. In fact, some provide "job coaches" to work "shoulder to shoulder" with a student with a disability at the actual job site to assist the student with the technical aspects, as well as the social nuances, of the job. For example, if the student is being trained as a maid for a major hotel chain, the job coach accompanies the student to the hotel, both wearing the same uniform as every other employee, and helps the student learn the day-to-day routine and processes involved in being a successful employee.

▪ ▪ ▪

Each of these professionals brings a special expertise to the child with a disability. Seldom does one child require the services of all these specialized professionals. However, the intent of the law is that these personnel must be made available, if necessary, for the child to benefit from the educational process.

Seldom are all these professionals on-staff personnel within a given district. Small school districts may rely on a special education center to provide such services. These centers are called by different names in different states. In Kansas, the term *cooperative special education center* is used. In Michigan, the title *intermediate school district* is given to centers that provide specialized services. In Texas, *regional special education service centers* work in close cooperation with local school districts. When this type of special education center is not available, school districts hire their own specialized personnel on a contractual basis or refer children to private practitioners and/or hospitals or rehabilitation centers for assessment/evaluation services and/or programming.

SUMMARY

The process of designing individual education programs (IEPs) in physical education for the student with a disability is a basic component of effective programming. The type of physical education program developed for each student will depend on the identified needs. After a student has been assessed to determine needs, annual goals and short-term objectives leading to each goal are selected. That information plus the types of related services needed, the extent to which the student will participate in the regular physical education class, and the projected dates for initiation and duration of services must appear on the student's IEP. Also, no later than age 14, an individual transition plan (ITP) must be developed that ensures the student's ability to function in a community when leaving the school setting. This information is shared with parents at a formal IEP meeting.

Federal law stipulates that the following individuals participate in the IEP meeting: a parent or guardian, the principal or principal's designee, an educational diagnostician, the student's classroom teacher, and, when appropriate, the student. In addition, it is helpful if others who will work with the student attend, including regular educators and all individuals who tested the student, as well as, when necessary, an interpreter, the school nurse, counselors, assistive technology service personnel, and transportation specialists.

During the IEP meeting, information about the student is shared with the parents, and potential services and placements are discussed. The professionals in attendance should make every effort to help the parents feel comfortable and understand their child's present level of performance, specific needs, and potential for learning and eventually functioning in a community setting. By law, the parents must agree to their child's educational program and the setting in which it will be delivered. In addition, parents may be given the opportunity to participate in a Personal Futures Planning (PFP) process with individuals willing to make a long-term commitment to the future of the child.

In large, urban school districts many direct and related service personnel are on staff and available to contribute to the assessment and programming process. Smaller school districts frequently contract with individuals to assess and program for their students with disabilities, or they rely on educational service centers that provide specialized services to a number of school districts.

Review Questions

1. Explain the difference between IEP, ITP, and PFP.
2. Explain the role of the adapted physical educator and physical educator in each.
3. Compare and contrast the role of the adapted physical educator with that of the occupational therapist.

Student Activities

1. Assume that Billy Bogg surprised everyone and accomplished all of his IEP goals in January, rather than May. Rewrite his annual physical education goals and specific behavioral objectives (see Figure 3-1) to present at an IEP meeting called for February 1 at his parents' request.
2. Billy's father has asked you for a home program so he can work with Billy during his visitation periods. Develop a home program to supplement Billy's spring physical education program.
3. Billy does continue to struggle, however, in the process of making friends. What could you do, as the physical educator, to help him with this sometimes difficult skill?
4. Picture Billy (Bill) as an adolescent. Develop a theoretical PFP, including a circle of friends, community matrix, and action plan for the PFP meeting to be held for Bill just before his twenty-first birthday.
5. Have the class break into small groups and share their lists of persons they believe should attend Billy's IEP

meeting and the possible questions the parents may raise. Also ask them to give their rationale for their selections.

References

1. Achilles J, Yates R, Freese J: Perspectives from the field: collaborative consultation in the speech and language program of the Dallas Independent School District, *Lang Speech Hearing Schools* 22:154-155, 1991.
2. *Alamo Heights v State Board of Education,* 790 F 2d 1153 (5th Cir 1986).
3. American Occupational Therapy Association: *Guidelines for occupational therapy services in school systems,* Rockville, Md, 1989, The Association.
4. American Occupational Therapy Association: *Uniform terminology for occupational therapy, ed 2,* Rockville, Md, 1989, The Association.
5. Behrmann M: Assistive technology for students with mild disabilities, *Intervent School Clin* 30(2):70-83, 1994.
6. Cain EJ: The role of the computer in special education: some philosophical considerations, *Pointer* 28:6-11, 1984.
7. Ebenstein B: IEP strategies: getting what your child needs from IEP meetings and annual reviews, *Except Parent,* pp 62-63, April 1995.
8. Edelen-Smith P: Eight elements to guide goal determination for IEPs, *Intervent School Clin* 30(5):297-301, 1995.
9. *A four-year plan to systematically integrate microcomputers, videodiscs, and other state-of-the-art technology into special education administration, management and classroom instruction.* Dallas Independent School District, January 1987, Instruction Systems Technology Division, Department of Special Education.
10. Gerardi RJ et al: IEP—more paperwork and wasted time, *Contemp Educ* 56:39-42, 1984.
11. Haynes C: Language development in the school years—what can go wrong? In Mogford K, Sadler J, editors: *Child language disability,* Clevedon, UK, 1989, Multilingual Matters.
12. Individuals with Disabilities Education Act, Public Law 101-476, US Congress, Oct 30, 1990.
13. *Irving Independent School District v Tatro,* 1984, 468 US 883.
14. Kaplan J: *Beyond behavior modification: a cognitive-behavioral approach to behavior management in the school,* Austin, Tex, 1991, PRO-ED.
15. Lavine RA: *Personal computers serving people: a guide to human service applications,* Washington, DC, 1980, Hawkins & Associates.
16. Leatherby J: *Reach for the stars—planning for the future: personal futures planning for young children.* Paper presented at the Ninth Annual Statewide Conference on Deaf-Blindness and Multiple Disabilities, Austin, Tex, Feb 1994.
17. Lewis A: Churning up the waters in special education, *Phi Delta Kappan* 73:100-101, 1991.
18. Lovitt T, Cushing S, Stump C: High school students rate their IEPs: low opinions and lack of ownership, *Intervent School Clin* 30:34-37, 1994.
19. Lynch E, Beare P: The quality of IEP objectives and their relevance to instruction for students with mental retardation and behavioral disorders, *Remed Spec Educ* 11(2):48-55, 1990.
20. *Macomb County Intermediate School District v Joshua S.,* 715 F Suppl 824 (ED Mich 1989).
21. Marvin CA: Consultation services: changing roles for SLP's, *J Child Commun Dis* 11:1-16, 1987.
22. Mount B: *Dare to dream,* Manchester, Conn, 1991, Communitas.
23. Office of Civil Rights, 1989, EHLR 326.
24. Orr C, Gott C, Kainer M: *Model of student role adaptation: merging the values of occupational therapy and special education,* Dallas, 1990, Dallas Independent School District.
25. Smith SW: Individualized education programs (IEPs) in special education—from intent to acquiescence, *Except Child,* pp 6-13, Sept 1990.
26. US Department of Education: Assistance to states for education of handicapped children: interpretation of the individual education program, *Fed Reg,* Jan 19, 1981.
27. *US General Accounting Office: Report to Congress,* Feb 5, 1981.

Suggested Reading

Mount B, Zwernik K: *Making futures happen: a manual for facilitators of personal futures planning,* St Paul, Minn, 1990, Metropolitan Council.

chapter four

Selecting an Intervention Strategy

Objectives

Describe the purpose of making a functional adaptation to a specific skill.

Explain the appropriate application of developmental and task-specific approaches and their differences.

Explain the programmed instruction process.

Describe a technique for integrating players with and without disabilities on a team.

Task

Review Billy Bogg's individual education program (IEP) in Chapter 3 (see Figure 3-1). Note the modifications/adaptations suggested for his physical education class. As you read this chapter, make a list of how you could use the bottom, up approach and the top, down approach in his class.

The Camden, NJ, Courier-Post, *Courtesy National Amputee Golf Association.*

Physical educators who teach individuals with disabilities agree that their primary goal is to facilitate development of purposeful skills for each student. There are, however, a variety of different approaches to programming from which physical educators can select. They range from general physical education activities believed to benefit all children, regardless of degree of function, to developmentally sequenced activities that serve as building blocks of motor development, to activities that enhance very specific skills.

Which approach a physical educator selects depends on the age of the students, the teacher's knowledge of motor development and ability to assess and interpret motor performance levels accurately, and the goals the teacher is attempting to achieve in the physical education program. In this chapter the three levels of function that contribute to sport and functional skills, ways to facilitate development at each of those levels, adaptations that can be made to accommodate individuals with special needs, and techniques for programming instruction are addressed.

Levels of Function

The ultimate goal of physical education for children with disabilities is to equip them with motor skills that contribute to independent living. To plan these programs systematically, it is desirable to distinguish clearly the levels of function that contribute to acquisition of the many specific sport skills.

Each of three levels makes a unique contribution to independent functioning: (1) basic input functions, (2) general abilities, and (3) specific skills (Figure 4-1). The physical educator who understands the interrelatedness of these levels and can select intervention activities to facilitate functioning at any given level, depending on a student's needs, will realize success.

Basic input functions depend on the integrity and operation of the sensory input systems. These systems include **primitive** and **equilibrium reflex** reactions, the **vestibular** system, **refractive** and **orthoptic vision, audition,** and the **tactile** and **kinesthetic** systems. Before information can reach the central nervous system for processing, these systems must be intact and operational. The physical educator who automatically assumes these systems are functioning and that adequate stimulation is reaching the central nervous system disregards an important component of purposeful movement.[14]

The second level of functioning is made up of abilities. Like basic input functions, these prerequisites enhance the acquisition of skill. If the sensory input systems are functioning, abilities develop concurrently with movement experiences. Abilities prerequisite to skills include the perceptual-motor, physical, and motor fitness categories. They are not as readily forgotten and are maintained longer than are skills. Examples of

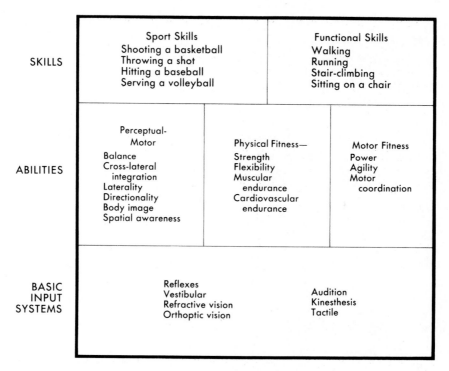

figure 4-1
Levels of motor learning.

perceptual-motor abilities are *balance, cross-lateral integration, laterality, directionality, body image,* and *spatial awareness*. **Physical fitness** prerequisites are *strength, flexibility, muscular endurance,* and *cardiovascular endurance*. **Motor fitness** requires *agility* and motor *coordination*. The uppermost level of functioning is skill. Skills are motor behaviors that are either specific to a sport or specific to functional living. Examples of skills are shooting a basketball, serving a tennis ball, climbing stairs, and sitting down in a chair. Proficiency at specific individual and team sport skills is usually developed through repetitious practice of the skill itself. However, nonspecific, general skills, such as walking or running, usually emerge as the central nervous system prerequisite components mature.

Incidental Versus Planned Learning

Most individuals learn from everyday interaction with the environment. This is particularly true if the environment is varied and the learner possesses all the prerequisites needed to convert environmental stimulation into

A creative teacher helps a child with no fingers enjoy arts and crafts. (Courtesy Dallas Independent School District.)

motor patterns. This is known as **incidental learning.** The more ready an individual is (i.e., the more developed cognitive and motor functions are), the more that can be gained from interaction with the environment. Conversely, the fewer the number of developed prerequisites, the less a person gains from environmental exchanges.

The individual with a disability is often denied opportunities to interact with varied environments. This is a hindrance, because for the central nervous system to develop normally, a wide variety of stimulation is necessary.[9] Thus attempts to protect these children from interaction with the environment often delay their development. Because of these delays, learners with disabilities do not always gain as much from incidental learning as do other learners.

Teachers of children with disabilities must be particularly sensitive to the needs of their students. Until a teacher determines the needs of students, appropriate intervention strategies cannot be planned. The adapted physical education teacher must ensure that each student's motor learning improves. The general approach of providing a wide variety of activities to all students gives no assurance that motor learning will result. It is true that the children may have fun and could possibly gain some physical fitness from their activities; however, the students will not make the same gains as would be possible if carefully planned intervention strategies were used.

Facilitating Skill Development

Children with disabilities frequently demonstrate **physical** and **motor development lags.** As a result, they often have difficulty learning chronologically age-appropriate skills. When developmental deficits become apparent, decisions about how to address the deficits have to be made. Questions that need to be answered include: Is it necessary to modify the teaching technique used or will modifications/adaptations best accommodate the student's needs? In the following sections three teaching techniques and several functional adaptations that are effective for accommodating the student with special needs are presented.

Teach Specific Skills: Top, Down

Teaching the skill directly is known as the **task-specific approach.** Advocates of this approach stress what skills

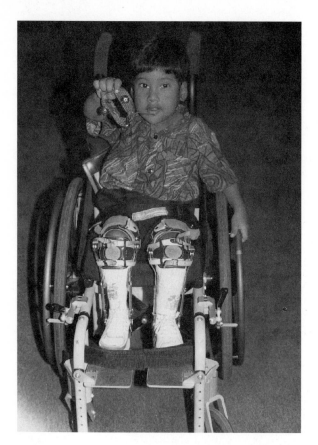

Every child can make music. (Courtesy Dallas Independent School District.)

Prerequisite Task Analysis
Stair climbing

Task Components	Contributing Prerequisites
Raise foot the height of the step (9 inches)	Balance, flexor strength in knee and hip
Place the foot on at least half the tread	Depth perception, kinesthetic perception, and spatial relations
Straighten the leg placed on the tread	Extensor strength in hip and knee
Raise the trailing leg so that advancing two steps is possible	Dynamic balance and bilateral coordination

an individual will need for productive independence as an adult in the community where he or she lives. In the case of the physical educator, the targeted behaviors focus on recreational sport skills that an individual would have an opportunity to participate in as an adult in the community. Prerequisites that are not the specific skill itself must relate to functional skills that can be used in the community for recreational purposes or provide a health benefit. The top, down approach places emphasis on the end of the skill sequence, the final motor countdown as an adult, rather than on what is to be taught next. When using the top, down approach, one needs to carefully monitor the progress of learners with disabilities as they move from elementary school to middle school to high school and then into adult life. To ensure that functional skills are being taught it is necessary to

gather information about the lesser restrictive environments the individual will function in as an adult. The focus of this approach emphasizes teaching skills and behaviors that are absolutely necessary for a person to function in a community environment.

To determine which skills an individual has in relation to skills that will be needed for ultimate functioning in the community requires the completion of an **ecological inventory** (community-based assessment). The ecological inventory provides critical information about current and future school and community environments (see Chapter 2). Selecting age-appropriate skills tends to maximize the normalization process during the life of a person with a disability. With the use of ecological assessment data, a major departure from traditional procedures is the need to take students into the community for part of the instruction. This enables the student to practice the skills in a natural setting.

When using a task analysis approach to assess students' repertoires, the educator can determine which motor skills are present and which are yet to be learned. Once the deficient skills are determined, they are prioritized and then analyzed to determine which portions have not yet been mastered; the specific missing components are then taught using a direct teaching method. If inefficient movements are not readily learned using the direct approach, the teacher probes the underlying ability components for deficits (see box above). If problems are found at the ability level, those prerequisites

table 4-1

Teaching Approaches and Their Relation to Growth and Development Principles

Principle	Implication	Bottom, Up Teaching Approach	Top, Down Teaching Approach
Each individual is unique.	Every child has a different motor profile.	Test for sensory input deficits and intervene to eliminate those before testing and programming for higher-level abilities and skills.	Test for specific functional motor skill deficits. If some are found, probe down into specific abilities that contribute to those skills. If deficits are found, probe down into sensory input areas.
	Every child learns at his or her own rate.	Select activities that appeal to the child and use those until the deficits are eliminated.	Program activities at the highest level of dysfunction. If the child does not learn quickly, probe down into contributing components for deficits.
Children advance from one stage of development to a higher, more complex stage of development.	Activities are selected appropriate to the level of development.	Select activities that are appropriate for the stage of development the child demonstrates.	Select activities specific to the skill deficits the child demonstrates. Begin an intervention program at the developmental level the child demonstrates.
	Progression to the next stage of development depends on physiological maturation and learning.	When a child appears to have mastered one stage of development, select activities appropriate for the next level of development.	When a child masters lower levels of a specific skill, select activities to promote learning of a more complex aspect of that skill.
Children learn when they are ready.	As neurological maturation takes place, we are capable of learning more.	Test from the bottom up and begin instruction with the lowest neurological deficit found.	Analyze a specific task from the top down until the present level of educational performance is found.
	There are critical periods of learning.	It is assumed the child will learn fastest if instruction is begun at the developmental stage at which the child is functioning.	The level of instruction determined by empirical testing verifies that the child is ready to learn.
Development proceeds from simple to complex.	Development begins with simple movements that eventually combine with other movements to form patterns.	Eliminate reflex and sensory input delays before teaching higher-level abilities and skills.	Functional skill deficits are identified. The pattern of the skill is analyzed to determine contributing components. Behavioral programs are constructed and implemented to develop pattern deficits.
	Development progresses from large to small movements (from gross to fine patterns).	Promote reflex and vestibular development to stabilize balance. Once balance becomes automatic, control of the limbs will follow.	Program to synthesize patterns that contribute to a specific skill.

can be directly taught or specific sensory input systems believed to contribute to the deficits at the ability level can be tested. When deficiencies are found, activities are selected to promote development at the lowest level probed.

The task-specific top, down approach may be the most realistic and expedient type to use with individuals with severe disabilities, but it may be inappropriate for higher-functioning children with disabilities. The essential question to ask when trying to decide whether to use this approach is "How much time is available?" Facilitating basic input systems and abilities before teaching specific skills takes time, perhaps years. Also, there is

evidence that children under the age of 12 years respond more readily than do older individuals. When the individual with a disability is older and severely involved and there is a limited amount of time available to develop functional skills needed to live in a natural environment, the task-specific approach may be the best intervention strategy.

Eliminate Deficiencies: Bottom, Up

Motor development is a progressive process. For each of us to learn to move efficiently, we must first be able to take environmental information into the central nervous system. Then this information must be processed

table 4-2

Teaching Approaches and Their Relation to the Generalization Process*

Principle	Implication	Bottom, Up Teaching Approach	Top, Down Teaching Approach
Generalization procedures	Activities to promote generalization are selected in particular ways.	Activity is selected to develop sensory input systems, reflexes, and abilities that are believed to be prerequisite to many skills that could be used in a variety of environments.	Functional age-appropriate activities are selected to promote appropriate skills in a variety of natural environments.
Generalization process	There is a degree to which the learning environment matches the natural environment.	At the basic levels (reflexes, sensory inputs, and abilities) the environment is controlled only to ensure that the basics are learned. No attention is paid to the type of environment the eventual skills will be used in.	Skills are practiced in environments that correspond closely to the environment in which the skill will be used (e.g., practice shooting baskets in the gym).
Retention	The more meaningful the skill, the longer it is remembered.	It is believed that once basic reflexes, sensory input systems, and abilities emerge, they remain stable (unless the child is traumatized in some way).	Activities are reviewed immediately after a lesson and then periodically to ensure retention.
Overlearning	Overlearning occurs when a skill or activity is practiced after it has been learned.	Overlearning occurs as the basic levels are interwoven into higher skill levels.	Ability levels prerequisite to skills should be substantially greater than minimum entry requirements needed to fulfill the needs of the task.

*A task is not considered learned until it can be demonstrated in a variety of environments.

or integrated so that it can be used to direct movement patterns and skills. Only after the information is received and processed can the brain direct the muscles to work. If anything goes wrong before the information reaches the muscles, movement is inefficient or nonexistent. Advocates of the developmental approach agree that the ultimate goal of education is to produce productive adults who can function independently in their communities. To achieve this goal, the developmentalist would intervene in a child's life as early as possible to determine whether age-appropriate basic input systems, abilities, and skills were functional. If any age-appropriate skills, abilities, and/or basic input systems were found to be deficient when the child was tested, then the developmentalist would select activities to promote development of the deficient areas. Thus if a child were found to have a severe orthoptic (eye alignment) problem that would interfere with eye-hand coordination development, the

child would be referred to a **visual behavioral specialist** for correction of the problem. If a child demonstrated failure to develop equilibrium reactions and/or adequate vestibular (inner ear) function, both of which are critical for balance development, activities to promote development in those areas would be prescribed.

The developmental approach can be considered a **bottom, up strategy** (see Figure 4-1). That is, the developmentalist first evaluates each of the sensory input systems and then tests the ability components to determine which deficits are in evidence. Once the deficits are identified, activities that promote functioning of each sensory input system found to be lacking are selected. The rationale is to progress to activities that facilitate development of the ability components. Only after each of these building blocks is in place will the developmentalist attempt to teach the specific sport or functional skills.

table 4-3			
The Relation of Teaching Approaches to Attention of the Learner			
Principle	Implication	Bottom, Up Teaching Approach	Top, Down Teaching Approach
Get the attention of the learner.	Help the child attend to relevant rather than irrelevant cues.	Permit the child to participate in a free activity of his or her choice each day if the child enters the room and immediately focuses on the beginning task.	Bats, balls, and other play equipment should be kept out of sight until time of use.
	Give a signal (sometimes called a "ready signal") that indicates a task is to begin.	Structure each day's lesson the same way so the child knows that when a given activity ends, the next activity will begin.	Teach the child precise signals that indicate a task should begin.
Provide the appropriate stimulation.	Stimulate the child to focus on the desired learning task.	Make the activities enjoyable so that the child will want to continue the task.	Use precise, detailed instruction that is designed around eliciting attention through the use of the following hierarchy: 1. Visual or verbal input only 2. Combine visual and verbal input 3. Combine visual, verbal, and kinesthetic instruction.

McLaughlin[12] documented the value of the approach when she followed up on children who were clumsy and who had received this type of evaluation and intervention at the University of Kansas Perceptual-Motor Clinic. Before intervention the children demonstrated varied sensory input and ability deficits. One to two years after the deficits had been eliminated and the children were released from the clinic program, every child was demonstrating age-appropriate motor skills.

It should be apparent that the developmental approach is not only time consuming, it also requires extensive knowledge of sensory input system function and ability level developmental trends. For individuals lacking the knowledge base, both testing and teaching techniques are discussed later in this chapter.

When attempting to determine whether to use a bottom, up approach in the adapted physical education program, the teacher must again ask: "How much time is available?" The younger the child and the more time available to the teacher, the more appropriate it is to use this strategy. Examples of how each of these two teaching methods is applied to achieve the same principles are given in Tables 4-1 through 4-7.

Note that when either the top, down task-specific or bottom, up developmental approach is used, considerable individual attention must be given to each child. Therefore, in order for these approaches to be effective, the teacher must structure the class so that it contains small groups of children with similar problems or so that stations with individual activities are available to address specific needs. When children who are in need of intensive intervention are identified, it is recommended that in addition to being served in an **inclusive environment,** they be given additional instruction in a small group or one-on-one setting (e.g., in an adapted physical education class).

table 4-4

Managing the Instructional Environment Through Teaching Approaches

Principle	Implication	Bottom, Up Teaching Approach	Top, Down Teaching Approach
Impose limits for use of equipment, facilities, and student conduct.	Children should learn to adhere to rules that are necessary in a social context.	Students are not permitted access to equipment and areas unless they have been given permission by the teacher.	The equipment and facilities a student has access to are specified in the behavioral program.
Control the social interaction among children.	Inappropriate social behavior among children may disrupt class instruction.	The teacher must consider the performance level and emotional stability of each child when grouping children for activities.	Tasks and environments are structured to reduce adverse interaction with peers.
Do not strive for control in all situations.	Children with disabilities must develop social skills that will promote social interaction in the natural environment. For this to occur, students must have an opportunity to adjust to situations independent from supervision or with minimum supervision.	Select activities that will meet the long-range goals of the students and promote social interaction. Pair children so that their interaction contributes to both students' objectives. Example: A child who needs kinesthetic stimulation might be given the task of pulling a child who needs to ride a scooter for tonic labyrinthine prone inhibition.	Permit the students to interact with others as long as progress toward short-term objectives is occurring.

Regardless of whether the teacher selects an indirect or direct teaching method, it is important to remember that all children must experience success when interacting with their peers. Successful interaction with others is necessary for the development of a healthy, positive self-concept. Frequently children with disabilities can participate in the regular physical education class if functional adaptations are made.

Functional Adaptations

Functional adaptations are modifications such as using an assistive device, changing the demands of the task, or changing the rules to permit students with disabilities to participate. Making functional adaptations in accordance with a child's needs may enable immediate participation in age-appropriate activities selected to enhance specific skills. The following are functional adaptations for children with physical, sensory, or motor deficits:

- Blind children can receive auditory or tactual clues to help them locate objects or position their bodies in the activity area.
- The blind read through touch and can be instructed in appropriate movement patterns through manual

---

table 4-5

Nature of Activity and Quality of Experience as They Relate to Two Teaching Approaches

Principle	Implication	Bottom, Up Teaching Approach	Top, Down Teaching Approach
Learning occurs best when goals and objectives are clear.	Clear goals provide incentives for children to learn.	The desired outcome is clear to the teacher (e.g., 5 seconds of post-rotatory nystagmus). The child may be advised of another goal (e.g., stay on the spinning scooter until it stops).	The goal and ongoing measurement of the attainment of the objectives that lead to the goal are shared by the teacher and the child.
The student should be actively involved in the learning process.	The greater the amount of learning time and the lesser the amount of dead time, the more learning that will occur.	The child stays active because activities that are enjoyable to the child are selected.	When and if the child learns to self-instruct and self-evaluate or do so with the help of peer tutors, the student will be active throughout the period. The well-managed class will have children work on nonspecific activities when not participating in behavioral programs.
Discourage stereotyped play activities that develop rigid behaviors.	Permitting children to participate in the same activity day after day deters learning.	The teacher must initiate new activities as soon as lack of progress is evidenced.	The ongoing collection of data makes lack of progress immediately apparent to the teacher and the child and serves notice that the activity should be changed.
Program more for success than failure.	Every satisfying experience decreases anxiety and increases confidence.	The teacher selects activities the child enjoys and from which the child gains a feeling of accomplishment.	The increment of the step sizes in the behavioral program is constantly modified to match the ability of the learner.

table 4-6

Training Regimens as They Relate to Teaching Approaches			
Principle	Implication	Bottom, Up Teaching Approach	Top, Down Teaching Approach
Rate of learning is affected by initial skill level and length of time practicing the skill.	Beginning students who are learning a new skill learn at a faster rate than intermediate and advanced learners; however, plateaus in learning do occur after initial learning.	At reflex and sensory input levels plateaus may not be seen, because learning is not cognitive. At ability levels (perceptual-motor, coordination, etc.) plateaus are apparent. Observe progress with care and change activities if plateaus are observed.	Plateaus will be identified immediately because of the precise data being collected. Provide rest between training trials and terminate activity before failure sets in.
The nature of the learner, the task, and the stage of the learner in learning the task must be considered.	Some research indicates that in the initial stages of motor learning distributed practice is more effective than mass practice.	Use specific time frames (e.g., 5 minutes) each day for each objective.	Highly organized lessons during which accurate data on progress are gathered provide immediate feedback about the effectiveness of the practice trials. When lack of progress becomes apparent, change the activity or the learning strategy.
	Short practices are better than long practices. Frequent practices are more effective than infrequent practices.	Divide the lesson plan into several activities. Provide activities for each objective daily or several times weekly.	
Stop instruction at or before the point of satiation on the task.	Plateauing occurs when a person is satiated with learning a task.	Selecting tasks that are novel may prevent satiation.	Monitor the increment of the step size carefully because as long as the learner can be reinforced with success on challenging tasks, the child may withstand satiation.
		Use a variety of activities to reach the same objective.	Use a variety of different types of programs for the child to move to so that satiation is countered.
Use the method of teaching that is best for the learner (whole, part, part-whole).	When the whole method is used, the entire task is taught at one time. The task is demonstrated (using visual and verbal cues); the child is challenged to learn the skill.	When working toward reflex normality or when stimulating sensory input systems, the entire task is presented.	Use this method when teaching complex tasks. If a child has difficulty with any part of the task, shape the response through programming.

table 4-6			
Training Regimens as They Relate to Teaching Approaches—cont'd			
Principle	Implication	Bottom, Up Teaching Approach	Top, Down Teaching Approach
	When the part method is used, break the task down into component parts and teach the parts using backward or forward chaining.	When teaching toward perceptual-motor abilities (e.g., size discrimination), teach the child to recognize differences between sizes.	Break the skill into parts and teach each specific part.
	The part-whole method involves teaching the component parts of the skill and then synthesizing the parts into the whole skill.	When teaching perceptual-motor abilities such as size discrimination, after teaching the learner to discriminate between two or three different sets of sizes, combine the sets gradually until the child can discriminate between a large set of different sizes.	Because it is difficult to establish behaviors in which one is built on the other, divide the skill into natural divisions, teach each section, and then combine them.

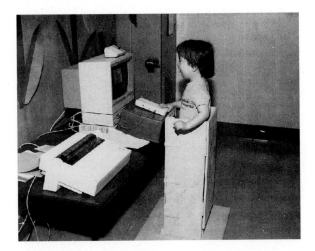

Assistive devices help a child use computer technology.
(Courtesy Dallas Independent School District.)

kinesthetic guidance (i.e., the instructor manually moves the student through the correct pattern) or verbal instructions.

- Deaf children can learn to read lips or learn signing so that they understand the instructions for an activity.
- Children with physical disabilities may have to use walkers, wheelchairs, or crutches during their physical education class.
- An asthmatic child may be permitted to play goalie in a soccer game, which requires smaller cardiovascular demands than the running positions.
- Rules may be changed to accommodate the variety of ability levels demonstrated by children in the class (see Chapter 5).
- A buddy, peer tutor, or paraprofessional may be assigned to help the student with special needs execute the required moves or stay on task.

In these examples functional adaptations are necessary for the student with a disability to participate in chronologically age-appropriate physical education activities. The approach is most beneficial when the only motor prerequisites lacking are those that are a result of the student's disabling condition or when the student is included to promote social interaction.

table 4-7

Relation of Teaching Approaches to Motivation Techniques

Principle	Implication	Bottom, Up Teaching Approach	Top, Down Teaching Approach
Children will learn better if the activity is pleasurable.	As a rule, children enjoy tasks at which they can be successful and dislike tasks where the failure risk is high.	Tasks that are enjoyable to children are selected to reach the specific objective.	Learning steps are sequenced close enough to ensure success.
Provide knowledge of results on task success.	Knowledge of results provides information to the learner as to the correctness of performance. Learners tend to persist at tasks they are successful with.	The students may or may not be advised about the specific objective the teacher is trying to reach; however, the child is advised about the objective to accomplish. Example: In trying to inhibit a positive support reflex, the teacher's objective may be to have the child demonstrate ability to flex the hips, knees, and ankles when there is pressure on the bottom of the feet. The child may be told that the objective is to stop bouncing on the trampoline 3 out of 5 times on command by doing a partial squat when the feet hit the bed of the trampoline.	Precise objectives should be built into the behavioral program to provide immediate feedback as to whether the task was mastered.
Apply a system of reinforcement for attainment of objectives.	Reinforcement strengthens the recurrence of behavior.	The teacher tells the child when he or she has done a good job.	Specific behaviors in a structured hierarchy are reinforced when the behavior occurs, because the learner then progresses to the next step in the hierarchy.
The social context of learning should be considered.	Learning is influenced by the presence or absence of others. Each student is influenced in some way by competition/cooperation with peers and the presence or absence of spectators or the teacher.	The child is made to feel as comfortable as possible so that the activity is enjoyable. It is believed that when the child feels successful, he or she will want to engage in play/competition with peers.	Social conditions will be directed toward the generalization of social behavior that exists in natural environments.

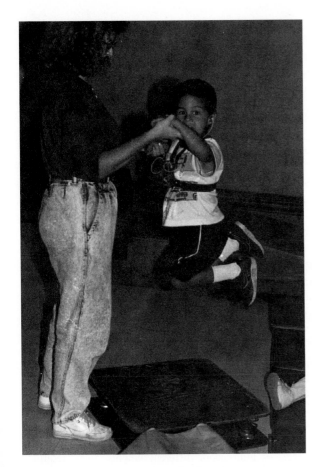

A child learns to jump on a bouncing board.

Programmed Instruction

Instructional strategies are the ways to arrange an educational environment so that maximum learning will take place. Factors that affect the type of instructional strategy selected include the levels of performance demonstrated by individual students in the class, the age of the learners, the comprehension levels of the students, the class size, and the number of people available to assist the teacher. An instructional strategy that meets the needs of a wide range of learners and can be delivered by a limited number of personnel is more valuable for ensuring that individual needs are met than is a strategy that presumes **homogeneous grouping.** For learners with disabilities who have heterogeneous needs, an instructional strategy that promotes individualized learning is not only desirable, but absolutely necessary.

Individualization of instruction can be realized through the use of programmed instruction. The major goals of programmed instruction are to promote students' abilities to direct their own learning and to develop a communication system between the student and the teacher that enables them to become independent of each other. The teacher's primary goals are to guide and manage instruction according to the student's individual needs and learning characteristics. The programmed instruction approach enables a teacher to cope with **heterogeneous groups** of children and to accommodate large numbers of children in the same class without sacrificing instructional efficiency.

To implement such a program, however, three major factors must be taken into consideration: (1) programming must be constructed on the basis of scientific principles[1]; (2) learners must be trained in specific behaviors[7]; and (3) learning principles must be applied through the use of programmed curricula.

The most expeditious way to manage an average-size class in a public school, using the individualized approach, is by means of instructional objectives that shift learning conditions to create task sequences. Prearranged instructional objectives take the form of self-instructional and self-evaluative programs appropriate for typical and atypical children. However, for the child who cannot self-instruct and self-evaluate, the teacher must assume the responsibility for directing instruction and monitoring progress. Task analysis and pattern analysis will facilitate development. A child functioning at a low level, like the child who strives to reach upper limits of development for competitive purposes, needs special types of programming and thus specific attention by instructors when the teacher-student ratio is low. Self-instructional and self-evaluative materials composed of prearranged objectives help students develop skills at their own rates.

Generalization to Community Environments

Time spent teaching skills in physical education training settings is wasted if the individual with disabilities cannot demonstrate competency in sport and recreation settings other than the schools and in the presence of persons other than the original teachers.[2] To ensure that generalization to community environments and activities does occur, simulated training conditions need to be developed. Although there are few studies in physical education that have examined generalization of motor skills and sport performance from instructional to community environments, Budoff[4] indicates positive results of softball training of mentally retarded persons in integrated community environments. On the other hand, the review of literature on simulated settings versus training in the applied settings on nonphysical education tasks is mixed. Browder, Snell, and Ambrogio[3] report successful generalization from simulated settings using vending machines, whereas Marchetti et al.[11] found that training an individual in pedestrian skills was significantly more effective when done in the community rather than in a **simulated training environment.** The more severe the disability, the more difficult it seems to be to generalize trained skills across environments.[16] It is critical that instruction not cease until the individual uses the new skills spontaneously and correctly in the community.

Principles of Programmed Instruction

The following principles of programmed instruction have been suggested by Lindvall and Bolvin[10]:

1. Objectives the students are expected to achieve must be clear and specific.
2. Objectives must be stated in behavioral terms.
3. Objectives must lead to behaviors that are carefully analyzed and sequenced in a **hierarchical order** so that each behavior builds on the objectives immediately preceding it and is prerequisite to those that follow.
4. Instructional content of a program must consist of a sequence of learning tasks through which a student can proceed with little outside help and must provide a series of small increments in learning that enable the student to proceed from a condition of lack of command of behavior to a condition of command of behavior.
5. A program must permit students to begin at the present ability level and move upward from that point.
6. A program must allow each student to proceed independently of other students and learn at the rate best suited to his or her own abilities and interests.
7. A program must require active involvement and response on the part of the student at each step along the learning sequence.
8. A program must provide immediate feedback to the student concerning the adequacy of his or her performance.
9. A program must be subjected to continuous study by those responsible for it and should be regularly modified in light of available evidence concerning the student's performance.
10. A program must accommodate the ability range of many students, thus enabling continuous progress.

These principles can be applied when a hierarchical behavioral program is designed for each child. When a hierarchical teaching sequence is used, a single task is broken down into small steps that are then arranged in order of difficulty. Pupils enter the sequence at their present level of performance and then advance at their own rate through the sequence. This sequencing of steps can be used for basic input systems, abilities, and skills. As children master one level of performance, they move on to the next. It is essential that the steps be arranged in a hierarchy to enable the students to progress from simple to more difficult levels of performance.

Progressively more difficult performance requirements are built into the program by shifting either the conditions under which the task must be performed or the criteria for success.[6] **Condition shifting** alters the conditions surrounding performance of the task, making it more or less difficult. To promote development of basic locomotor skills, the elementary school physical educator modifies time, space, force, and flow variables. Time variables are introduced when the learner is required to move faster, slower, to an even beat, or to an uneven beat. Space variables are manipulated by requiring the learner to move in different patterns (e.g., circle, figure eight, around a person or object) alone or with a partner. Force requirements can be changed by having the children jump lightly, jump while holding a heavy object, or jump from different heights. Flow requirements can be changed by hopping first on one foot, then on both, or doing the "Bunny Hop," or mirroring another student's moves. The same types of modifications can be made to increase the difficulty of a sport or recreation skill. For example, in bowling, conditions such as the performer's distance from the pins (space), the speed of the approach (time), the point at which the ball is released (flow), and the strength with which the ball is rolled or the size of the ball (force) can be changed to make the task more or less difficult.

Criterion shifting alters the level of acceptable performance by increasing the number of repetitions, the distance traveled, the speed, or the range of motion needed to accomplish the task. Examples of shifting criterion measures are building strength by increasing the number of repetitions or the amount of weight lifted, building cardiovascular endurance by increasing the distance run, and building flexibility by increasing the range of motion at a specific joint.

Once the teacher has decided whether to use a criterion- or condition-shifting program (or a combination of both), the teaching sequence should be decided on. There are several different strategies for developing standard teaching sequences. A standard procedure often used is as follows:

1. Select a behavior that needs to be developed (identify a long-range goal).
2. Identify a way to measure the behavior objectively.
3. Select the conditions or criteria that will be used to make the task more difficult.
4. Write your short-term objectives.
5. Arrange the short-term objectives in a hierarchy from simple to difficult.
6. Identify the materials or equipment that will be needed in the teaching sequence.

Examples of two teaching sequences—one using a shifting criterion and one using a shifting condition—are found in Figure 4-2. These examples focus on specific skills. The same type of teaching sequence can be developed for basic levels and for abilities. When programming to develop basic levels, such as vestibular function, the educator selects activities believed to facilitate that system and arranges them in a hierarchy. For example, the teacher may decide to use activities such as rolling, turning, or spinning to stimulate the vestibular system. A technique for determining whether the activities have been useful for activating the system would be to evaluate the duration of **nystagmus** immediately after the activity. A sequence of short-term objectives might be 3 seconds of nystagmus after 30 seconds of spinning, 3 seconds of nystagmus following 25 seconds of spinning, 3 seconds of nystagmus after 20 seconds of spinning, and so on, until the child demonstrates nystagmus for half the spinning time (e.g., 3 seconds of nystagmus after 6 seconds of spinning). The next step in the sequence would be to increase the time nystagmus is demonstrated (e.g., 5 seconds of nystagmus following 30 seconds of spinning). The sequence is continued until the child reaches the normally expected duration of nystagmus (10 seconds of nystagmus after 20 seconds of turning at a speed of 180 degrees per second).

When programming for abilities, the same format is used. If the need to develop cross-lateral integration has been identified, an objective measure of this ability would be decided on, such as the percentage of time the student uses the right hand to pick up objects on the left side of the body. A criterion- or condition-shifting sequence would be constructed, and activities to promote the behavior would be selected.

Whenever possible, the teaching strategy should be as self-directed as possible. If children are not able to read written instructions, pictures or figures that represent the action to be performed should be included.

Component Model of Functional Physical and Sport Activity Routines: An Assessment and Programming Strategy

Frequently persons with disabilities learn specific parts of sport skills (**splinter skills**) but do not possess the capability to put the parts together in a routine that enables them to participate in a recreational activity. Budoff[4] describes an integrated softball league in which many of the mentally retarded individuals had learned some of the softball skills; however, few had ever played the actual game. The players had to be taught how to use their skills in a game situation. Before participants can be taught to use their skills in a functional activity, a decision must be made about what must be learned to enable participation. One way to determine the skills necessary to perform in a functional activity in the community (i.e., what individuals with disabilities need to learn to enable them to participate in community physical activities) is to use the **component model of functional routines.**[15] This model breaks down a person's daily sport and other physical activity into a series of routines that are composed of several skills. Each routine is made up of a skill sequence that begins with natural cues needed in a playing environment and ends with the achievement of the specific sport behavior in a functional setting.[13] The focus of the physical play routines is the broad competencies needed to function in natural physical and sport environments in the community. Unlike the traditional ecological approach, the component model systematically divides sport and physical routines into structured subsets of physical skills and cues needed. Once these components are identified, they can be assessed and programmed.

Commercial Programs

Since 1980 several physical and motor programs have been made available commercially. The achievement-based curriculum development in physical education (I

STANDARD TEACHING SEQUENCE

The system requires only that the teacher note the child's progress using the following symbols: **X** = the steps (activities) in the standard teaching sequence that can be mastered by the student, in this case step nos. 1, 2, 3, and 4; / = immediate short-term instruction objective, in this case no. 5;* = goal, in this case no. 18. All behaviors between the present level (/) and the goal (*) are potential objectives (6 to 18).

Walks unsupported (step no.): ~~1~~ ~~2~~ ~~3~~ ~~4~~ 5 6 7 8 9 10 11 12 13 14 15 16 17 18* 19 20 21 22 23 24 25 26

Two-footed standing broad jump

Type of program: Shifting criterion
Conditions
    1. Both feet remain behind restraining line before takeoff.
    2. Takeoff from two feet.
    3. Land on two feet.
    4. Measure from the restraining line to the tip of the toe of the least advanced foot.
Measurement: Distance in inches.

Two-footed standing broad jump (inches)	60	62	64	~~66~~	~~68~~	~~70~~	~~72~~	74	76	78	80	82*	84
Date mastered				9/7	9/21	10/5							

The scoring procedure of the ongoing development of the person would be explained as follows. The program that the child is participating in is the two-footed standing broad jump. The child began the program at an initial performance level of 66 inches on September 7 and increased performance by 4 inches between September 7 and October 5. Thus the present level of educational performance is 70 inches (note the last number with an **X** over it). The child will attempt to jump a distance of 72 inches (immediate short-term objective) until he or she masters that distance. The child will continue to progress toward the goal, which is 82 inches (note the asterisk). It is a mistake in the applications of learning principles to ask the child to jump the 82 inches when it is known that the goal far exceeds the present level of educational performance. Unreasonable instructional demands from the learner by the teacher violate the principle of learning in small steps, which guarantees success for the child.

The same procedure could be used when teaching a child to throw a ball for accuracy. In the following example, a shifting condition program is used. For instance, two hierarchies that are known in throwing for accuracy are the size of the target and the distance between the thrower and the target. Thus a standard teaching sequence might be similar to the following sequence of potential objectives: demonstrate the ability to throw a 4-inch ball a distance of _____ feet and hit a target that is _____ feet square five out of five times.

Throwing for accuracy

Type of program: Shifting condition
Conditions
    1. Remain behind the restraining line at all times.
    2. Complete an overhand throw (ball released above the shoulder).
    3. If the ball hits any part of the target, it is a successful throw.

figure 4-2
Standard teaching sequence.

STANDARD TEACHING SEQUENCE—cont'd

The previous information would be contained in a curriculum book. However, the specific standard teaching sequence would be placed on a bulletin board at the performance area in the gymnasium. This would enable the performer to read his or her own instructional objective. The measurement of the performer's placement in the standard teaching sequence would be indicated on the prescription sheet.

Criterion for mastery: Three successful hits out of three.

DISTANCE OF THROW	SIZE OF TARGET	DISTANCE OF THROW	SIZE OF TARGET
Step 1. 6 feet	3 feet square	Step 10. 18 feet	2 feet square
Step 2. 9 feet	3 feet square	Step 11. 21 feet	2 feet square
Step 3. 12 feet	3 feet square	Step 12. 24 feet	2 feet square
Step 4. 15 feet	3 feet square	Step 13. 27 feet	2 feet square
Step 5. 18 feet	3 feet square	Step 14. 30 feet	2 feet square
Step 6. 21 feet	3 feet square	Step 15. 21 feet	1 foot square
Step 7. 24 feet	3 feet square	Step 16. 24 feet	1 foot square
Step 8. 27 feet	3 feet square	Step 17. 27 feet	1 foot square
Step 9. 30 feet	3 feet square	Step 18. 30 feet	1 foot square

The steps of the standard teaching sequence can be reduced and tasks can be added that are more or less complex as the situation requires.

STUDENT RECORDING SHEET

Throwing for accuracy (step no.)	1̶	2̶	3̶	4̶	5̶	6	7	8	9	10	11	12	13	14*	15	16	17	18
Date mastered																		

figure 4-2, cont'd
Standard teaching sequence.

CAN),[17] the Data-Based Gymnasium,[5] and Mobility Opportunities via Education (MOVE)[8] are excellent examples of commercial programs specifically developed to promote physical and motor capability.

Program Evaluation

To determine whether a physical education program is contributing positively to an individual's functional performance, the following questions must be answered[18]:

1. *Frequency:* Did the individual perform the activity during the last month?
2. *Independence:* Did the individual perform the physical activity independently?
3. *Social integration:* With whom did the individual do this activity during the last month?
4. *Physical integration:* Where has the individual done this activity during the last month?
5. *Limitations:* If the individual did not perform the activity, why not?
6. *Opportunity:* Has anyone else in the family done this activity during the last month?
7. *Preference:* How well does the individual like to perform the activity?
8. *Perceived importance:* Should the program work to improve the individual's performance in this activity?

Reporting the Results to Parents

Parents should always be informed of their children's educational performance levels and the goals and objectives of the school curricula. The Individuals with Disabilities Education Act (IDEA) requires that the parents be apprised of the educational status of their children and approve the individual education program (IEP) that has

Modified sports equipment opens the world to individuals with disabilities. (Courtesy RADVENTURES, Inc.)

been designed for them. When the procedures described in this chapter are followed by the teacher and the information is shared with the parents, there should be no question about the educational process. Parents may question whether appropriate goals have been selected for their children; usually, however, when evaluation results and the importance of their child's achieving as normal a performance level as possible are explained, parents agree with the professional educator's opinion.

It is important to point out to the parents their child's specific deficiencies and how those deficiencies interfere with the child's functional ability. Wherever possible, basic level and ability deficiencies should be linked to skill performance. That is, the educator should explain not only what deficits exist, but how those deficits relate to the child's present and future levels of performance ability. Once parents understand these relationships, they usually endorse the school's efforts on behalf of their children. In addition to pointing out a child's

deficiencies, it is important to tell the parent about areas of strength their child has demonstrated. Parents of children with disabilities need to hear positive reports as frequently as possible. Do not overlook that need.

SUMMARY

The goal of a physical education program for students with disabilities is development of motor behaviors that assist ultimate functional responses in community environments. Maximizing performance of the many specific skills of the physical education curriculum is the unique role of the adapted physical educator. Individuals with disabilities often possess limited motor skills. Thus the physical educator must determine which skills are needed and select appropriate intervention strategies to ensure that learning occurs. Teaching specific skills, fostering developmental sequences, and employing functional adaptations are three acceptable intervention strategies. The amount of time available, the age and readiness level of the learner, and the capabilities of the adapted physical education teacher dictate which intervention strategy to use. Programmed instruction facilitates development of a sequence of steps to follow to attain success with learning skills. Skill development sequences can be constructed by the teacher or purchased commercially.

Review Questions

1. What is the relationship between specific functional motor skills and general ability prerequisites to these skills?
2. What are some examples of making functional adaptations for age-appropriate motor skills, and what are arguments for and against such functional adaptations?
3. Identify three perceptual-motor abilities.
4. What are the differences between bottom, up (developmental) and top, down (task-specific) approaches?
5. Name two sensory input systems, two general abilities, and two specific skills.
6. What is meant by *incidental learning?* Why are some children with disabilities unable to learn as much through incidental learning as children without disabilities.

Student Activities

1. Talk with adapted physical education teachers about how they determine what objectives and activities to use with their students with disabilities. Try to determine whether

the teachers are using a top, down or bottom, up approach.
2. Observe a physical education class that includes students with and without disabilities. Make a list of the functional adaptations used during the class. Select the two adaptations you believe aided the children most and tell why those adaptations were so helpful.
3. List the ways in which a top, down testing and teaching approach would differ from a bottom, up testing and teaching approach.
4. Break the class into small discussion groups and have them share their bottom, up and top, down teaching approach suggestions for Billy Bogg's class with one another. Ask each group to agree on two suggestions for each teaching approach and share them with the rest of the class.
5. Develop a task analysis of a specific sport skill.

References

1. Bellamy T, Peterson L, Close D: Habilitation of the severely and profoundly retarded: illustrations of competence, *Educ Train Ment Retard* 10:174-186, 1975.
2. Billingsley F: Where are the generalized outcomes? An examination of instructional objectives, *J Assoc Persons Severe Handicaps* 9:186-192, 1984.
3. Browder D, Snell M, Ambrogio B: *Using time delay to transfer stimulus control within the behavioral chain of vending machine use with a comparison of training sites,* Unpublished manuscript, Bethlehelm, Pa, Lehigh University, Department of Special Education.
4. Budoff M: *The Massachusetts mixed softball league: a final report to Special Olympics International, Washington, DC,* Cambridge, Mass, 1987, Research Institute for Educational Problems.
5. Dunn JM, Frederick H: *Physical education for the severely handicapped: a systematic approach to a data based gymnasium,* Austin, Tex, 1985, PRO-ED.
6. Evans IM, Meyer L: *An educative approach to behavioral problems,* Baltimore, 1985, Paul H Brookes Publishing.
7. Gold M: *Task analysis: a statement and example using acquisition and production of a complex task by the retarded blind,* Champaign, 1975, Institute for Child Behavior and Development, University of Illinois at Urbana-Champaign.
8. Kern County Superintendent of Schools: *Mobility opportunities via education,* Bakersfield, CA, 1990, Author.
9. Kohen-Raz R: *Learning disabilities and postural control,* London, 1986, Freund Publishing.
10. Lindvall CM, Bolvin JD: *Programmed instruction in the schools: an application of programming principles in individually prescribed instruction,* Sixty-sixth Yearbook of the National Society of the Study of Education, Chicago, 1967, University of Chicago Press.
11. Marchetti AG et al: Pedestrian skill training for mentally retarded adults: a comparison of training in two settings, *Ment Retard* 21:107-110, 1983.
12. McLaughlin E: *Follow-up study on children remediated for perceptual-motor dysfunction at the University of Kansas perceptual motor clinic,* Unpublished master's thesis, Lawrence, 1980, University of Kansas.
13. Neel RS et al: *Teaching autistic children: a functional analysis approach,* Seattle, 1983, University of Washington, College of Education.
14. Quiros JB, Schrager OL: *Neuropsychological fundamentals in learning disabilities,* San Rafael, Calif, 1979, Academic Therapy Publications.
15. Snell M: *Systematic instruction of persons with severe handicaps,* Columbus, Ohio, 1987, Merrill Publishing.
16. Snell M, Browder D: Community referenced instruction: research and issues, *J Assoc Persons Severe Handicaps* 11:1-11, 1986.
17. Wessel JA, Kelly L: *Achievement-based curriculum development in physical education,* Philadelphia, 1986, Lea & Febiger.
18. Wilcox B, Bellamy GT: *Design of high school programs for severely handicapped students,* Baltimore, 1986, Paul H Brookes Publishing.

Suggested Readings

Falvey MA: *Community based curriculum: instructional strategies for students with severe handicaps,* Baltimore, 1986, Paul H Brookes Publishing.
Guess D, Noonan MJ: Curricula and instructional procedures for severely handicapped students, *Focus Except Child* 14:1-12, 1982.
Pyfer J: Teachers, don't let your students grow up to be clumsy adults, *J Phys Educ Rec Dance* 59:38-42, 1988.
Seaman JA, DePauw K: *The new adapted physical education,* Palo Alto, Calif, 1989, Mayfield Publishing.

chapter five

Delivering Services in the Most Inclusive Environment

Courtesy Dallas Independent School District.

Objectives

Explain the Regular Education Initiative (REI) and its implications for inclusion.

Define inclusion.

Suggest strategies for preparing the school and community for inclusion.

Describe the least restrictive environment continuum and each of its seven components.

Evaluate an existing physical education setting to determine its appropriateness for students with disabilities.

Evaluate appropriate physical education services, using the least restrictive environment design matrices.

Describe the role of the adapted physical educator in the transition process.

Describe techniques and strategies for the adapted physical education consultant.

Describe inclusive community-based leisure, recreation, and sports programs.

Task

As you read this chapter, think about the support services that Billy Bogg (see Chapter 2) will need to be successful in the regular physical education class.

Least Restrictive Environment and Inclusion—Federal Interpretation and Explanation

How best to meet the physical and motor needs of individuals with disabilities is a topic of continuing debate. It is clear that information gathered from a variety of assessment techniques, appropriate programming based on test results, intervention at least three times a week, and continual monitoring of student progress are critical factors that positively impact motor and physical development. However, there is continuing controversy over the most optimal setting for service delivery. The movement toward including all students with disabilities in the regular education program, which began in 1986 with the Regular Education Initiative (REI), continues to gain momentum in the closing years of this century. Despite pleas by authorities in the field[18,35,37] that it is to the benefit of students with disabilities to continue to provide a continuum of alternative educational placements, every state in this country is steadily moving toward total (full) inclusion for all students with disabilities. The New Mexico State Department of Education[43] defines **full inclusion** as follows:

> Full inclusion means that all children must be educated in supported, heterogeneous, age-appropriate, natural, child-focused classroom, school and community environments for full participation in our diverse and integrated society.

Part of this impetus is based on widespread notions regarding equity within the broader social context. According to Gallagher[13]:

> Clearly, there is concern for equity in education. Are children of poor families or families from culturally different backgrounds getting a fair chance at a quality education? Fairness and equity are the key concepts, and the educational reactions to such concerns have been to return to an educational setting where children of all levels of ability, achievement, motivation, and family backgrounds would be together, more or less, ensuring that no group has been siphoned off and placed in an inferior setting with less opportunity.

The National Association of State Boards of Education Special Education Study Group[43] recommended the following in order to create a new, inclusive system of education:

Recommendation 1: State boards of education must create a new belief system and vision for education in their states that includes *all* students. Once the vision is created, boards must provide leadership by clearly articulating goals for all students and then identifying the changes needed to meet those goals.

Recommendation 2: State boards should encourage and foster collaborative partnerships and joint training programs between general educators and special educators to encourage a greater capacity of both types of teachers to work with the diverse student population found in fully inclusive schools.

Recommendation 3: State boards, with state departments of education, should sever the link between funding, placement, and handicapping label. Funding requirements should not drive programming and placement decisions for students.

Assistant Secretary of Education Madeline Will wrote the position paper, "Educating Students with Learning Problems—A Shared Responsibility,"[41] that is generally considered the foundation for the regular education initiative that has fostered a widespread interest in inclusion. Will encouraged "special programs to form a partnership with regular education. The objective of this partnership for special education and the other special programs is to use their knowledge and expertise to support regular education in educating children with learning problems." The position paper encouraged more inclusive education for all students, particularly those with special needs. This was based on her belief that there are four fundamental problems in current special education practice:

1. Services meant to reach children are lost in a maze of distinct categories; children can fall through the cracks.
2. "Regular" and "special" education programs function separately. This reduces the accountability of the regular classroom educator. Children are "pulled out" of the regular classroom for special services, and this instruction is not coordinated with that received in the regular classroom.
3. Students in segregated programs are labeled and may be stigmatized; this may result in lowered self-esteem.
4. Eligibility requirements may create conflicts between parents and educators.

There are educators, however, who believe that there are serious flaws in the REI and the impetus toward inclusion. According to Kauffman and Hallahan[19]:

One of the primary hypotheses on which the REI is based is that students with disabilities would be best served by the improvement of education for all students, such that students of every description are fully integrated into regular classes, no student is given a special designation (label), costs are lowered by the elimination of special budget and administrative categories, the focus becomes excellence for all, and federal regulations are withdrawn in favor of local control. This hypothesis is parallel to Reagan-Bush economy theory, often known colloquially as a trickle-down theory, which is based on the presumption that the greatest benefits will be accrued indirectly by economically disadvantaged citizens under a policy designed to benefit more advantaged citizens directly.

The bottom line is that the trickle-down economic policy of the Reagan-Bush administration has caused the rich to become richer and the poor to become poorer. The vast gulf between the "haves" and the "have nots" has become an almost inseparable chasm. Many educators fear that the REI will cause the same type of class abuse—children in wealthy districts will receive better educational services than children from the inner city, and children without disabilities will receive a better education than children with disabilities. And Heaven help the children in the inner city with disabilities . . . they desperately need angels to see to their needs.

Federal Policy

The Education of the Handicapped Act mandates that a child with a disability should be educated in the least restrictive environment. This is true of the child's specially designed physical education program, as well. The regular education initiative, the national trend toward educating children with disabilities in the "regular" education program, has caused a flourish of interest in "inclusion."

Judith Heumann, assistant secretary of the Office of Special Education and Rehabilitation Services, and Thomas Hehir, director of the Office of Special Education Programs, have addressed issues related to the least restrictive environment (LRE) and inclusion in a memorandum to "Chief State School Officers." They note[16]:

> IDEA does not use the term "inclusion" . . . However, IDEA does require school districts to place students in the LRE. LRE means that, to the maximum extent appropriate, school districts must educate students with disabilities in the regular classroom with appropriate aids and supports, referred to as "supplementary aids and services," along with their nondisabled peers in the school they would attend if

not disabled, unless a student's IEP requires some other arrangement.

If the student's individual education program (IEP) goals and objectives cannot be met in the child's home school and in the regular education classroom, including the physical education classroom, even with supplementary aids and services, the least restrictive educational environment on the continuum must be selected. The intent is to provide each child with the opportunity to learn and demonstrate adequate progress in an educational environment that includes his or her typically developing peers.

Heumann and Hehir[16] describe some supplementary aids and services that have been used successfully in inclusion efforts. These include, but are not limited to:

- Modifications to the regular class curriculum
- Assistance of an itinerant teacher with special education training
- Special education training for the regular teacher
- Use of computer-assisted devices
- Provision of note takers
- Use of a resource room

According to Heumann and Hehir[16]:

> IDEA does not require that every student with a disability be placed in the regular classroom regardless of individual abilities and needs. This recognition that regular class placement may not be appropriate for every disabled student is reflected in the requirements that school districts make available a range of placement options, known as a continuum of alternative placements, to meet the unique educational needs of students with disabilities. This requirement for the continuum reinforces the importance of the individualized inquiry, not a "one size fits all" approach . . .

The Heumann/Hehir interpretation of the relationship between the LRE and inclusion outlines the following factors that must be considered in the determination of placement:

- The educational benefits to the student with a disability in the regular classroom (with support) in comparison with the educational benefits to the student in a special education classroom
- The "nonacademic," or social, benefits to the child with a disability derived from interaction with typically developing peers
- The extent of disruption of the education of other students

The legal, moral, and ethical bases of the LRE mandate make it imperative for physical educators to allow every child the opportunity to learn within the regular physical education class in the school closest to his or her home. Only when it has been determined that the child cannot make adequate educational progress in that environment or that the child is so disruptive that the education of other children is hindered should the members of the IEP committee consider an alternative placement. All too often, an alternative physical education placement is considered without exploring the regular physical education environment with supplemental aids and services.

According to Giangreco et al.[15]:

Inclusive education provides opportunities for teachers to model acceptance of human diversity in its many forms (e.g., culture, race, gender, disability). If we are to encourage the next generation to accept and value diversity, what better opportunity than welcoming students with disabilities into the classroom as full, participating members. The expanding diversity of the student population reflects the corresponding expansion of diversity in our communities, which highlights the need for students to learn how to live, work, and play harmoniously with people who have an ever-widening range of personal characteristics.

Inclusive education has been defined as education in which the following are true[15,33]:

- All students are welcomed into the regular education classes in their home/neighborhood school.
- Students are educated in groups that represent the greater society (i.e., approximately 10% of the students in any class/school have identified disabilities).
- A zero-rejection philosophy is in place, so no student, regardless of the nature or severity of the disability, is excluded.
- Students with varying abilities share a common educational experience, with specific modifications and accommodations to meet individual needs.
- Special education support is provided within the context of the general education program.

All Children Belong (ACB)[1] is a joint project of the National Parent Network on Disabilities and the Statewide Parent Advocacy Network of New Jersey and is supported by the DeWitt Wallace-Reader's Digest Fund. ACB's positions concerning inclusion are summarized in the box above.

Because of this growing trend toward a widespread, unilateral acceptance of inclusion, we have elected to include in this edition a variety of strategies for meeting

All Children Belong Position Statements

- Inclusion is a process, not a place, service, or setting.
- Children and youth with disabilities have the right to participate in the same neighborhood schools, classrooms, extracurricular activities, and community programs they would attend if they did not have a disability.
- Children and youth with disabilities should have all necessary supports to ensure successful experiences and achievement of potential.
- Children and youth with disabilities bring their inherent gifts to their schools and communities.
- Children and youth with disabilities must be afforded the dignity of risk.
- Communities should have the capacity to support participation of children and youth with disabilities in all aspects of community life.
- Children and youth with disabilities must be guaranteed their civil and educational rights as defined in Section 504 of the Rehabilitation Act of 1973, the Individuals with Disabilities Education Act of 1990, (IDEA) and the Americans with Disabilities Act of 1990 (ADA).
- The value system of the school and community should be based on the belief that all children belong.

Modified from All children belong, *Except Parent,* pp 43-46, July 1994.

the needs of students with disabilities in an inclusive setting. Our decision to provide this information is not intended to imply our belief that all students' needs can best be met in the regular physical education setting. Rather, we wish to promote active, meaningful participation in the most positive settings possible for all students with disabilities. General guidelines, including types of activities that will meet the needs of all students in various school levels, are included in this chapter, and more specific strategies are addressed in each of the chapters dealing with specific disabilities.

National Standards for Physical Education

The National Association for Sport and Physical Education (NASPE) has developed a text titled *Moving into the Future: National Physical Education Standards: A Guide to Content and Assessment.*[26] This standards-based document seeks to define "what a student should know and be able to do." It seeks to bring physical education into the third millenium by defining the student outcomes of a quality physical education program and by focusing on the need for authentic assessment protocols and practices that address the desired outcomes. The NASPE task force examined content and performance standards for children in kindergarten, second grade, fourth grade, sixth grade, eighth grade, tenth grade, and twelfth grade.

The NASPE task force determined the characteristics of a physically educated person and suggests[26]:

A physically educated person:
1. Demonstrates competency in many movement forms and proficiency in a few movement forms
2. Applies movement concepts and principles to the learning and development of motor skills
3. Exhibits a physically active lifestyle
4. Achieves and maintains a health-enhancing level of physical fitness
5. Demonstrates responsible personal and social behavior in physical activity settings
6. Demonstrates understanding and respect for differences among people in physical activity settings
7. Understands that physical activity provides opportunities for enjoyment, challenge, self-expression, and social interaction

These are the national standards for every physically educated individual. If inclusionary practices are to be effective and are to meet the needs of all learners, these standards must be maintained for every learner. Strategies for modifying educational practice to help all learners meet these standards are discussed in this chapter.

Preparing for Inclusion—A Proactive Approach

For inclusion to be effective within a given community and school, significant preparation must occur. Unfortunately, all too often inclusion "happens" without forethought, consensus building, values modification, or comprehensive in-service education. In this section suggestions are made for ensuring that inclusion is successful by preparing the community, administrators, parents, children, teachers, and paraprofessionals.

Preparing the Community

If members of the community are to embrace the notion and practice of inclusion, the most vital link is a school board committed to the education of all children. If the school board interprets federal and state education policy with all children in mind, the community is more likely to embrace the notion that children have a right to be educated within the least restrictive environment.

A broad-based public relations campaign needs to precede the initiation of inclusionary practice within the school district. An excellent example of this type of preparation is American Airlines' national training program to prepare its personnel to better accommodate travelers with disabilities. To kick off that training program, American Airlines invited the first deaf Miss America, Heather Whitestone, to give the opening address at their Dallas–Ft. Worth headquarters. The American Airlines "community" was prepared for the inclusion of travelers with disabilities via motivational and educational programs.

Within a given community, visible and effective individuals with disabilities need to be part of the public relations campaign to educate and motivate its citizens to embrace inclusionary practice in the schools.

Preparing Administrators

Administrative support for the inclusion of children with disabilities in regular education, including regular physical education, is vital if a nurturing educational environment is to be created. If the local campus administrator, principal, or dean of instruction supports the notion that children with disabilities should be integrated into the regular physical education program, then that administrator must be in a position to support the physical educator in a number of ways. The local campus administrator cannot expect that a physical educator can create a nurturing, supportive environment for a child with a disability—for any child, for that matter—if saddled with huge class sizes. It is not uncommon in some school districts for a physical educator to have a class size in excess of 80 students. It is impossible to address the needs of each child in a class of this size, and it is ridiculous to assume that even the best teacher could accommodate even one more child, particularly a child with a disability. The administrator committed to inclusion will do one of the following to ensure that quality physical education is received by all:

1. Decrease the class size by hiring additional professional personnel or arranging alternate scheduling patterns.

2. Decrease the student-teacher ratio by assigning trained paraprofessionals to assist the teacher.
3. Decrease the student-teacher ratio by assigning school volunteers to assist the physical educator in the gymnasium.
4. Use creative alternative scheduling patterns for service delivery. Perhaps it is more prudent to have students attend a quality physical education class three times a week if the class size is limited to 30 students than to have them attend a large, ineffective baby-sitting service daily if class size is in excess of 80 students.
5. Arrange for university/community college interns to provide vital extra hands.

In addition to limiting the student-teacher ratio in physical education, the campus administrator must also provide support for the physical educator by addressing other concerns:

1. The physical educator must be encouraged to attend classes and in-service presentations that address the education of children with disabilities in the regular physical education program.
2. The physical educator must be given release time to participate actively as part of the motor development team or the multidisciplinary team in the assessment/evaluation of the child's gross motor skills and in the creation and implementation of the child's **individual motor education plan (IMEP) or individual physical education plan (IPEP).**

Unfortunately, many school administrators believe special education and adapted physical education are simply peripheral responsibilities and focus their energies on test scores in the "regular" education program. Inclusion will never be really effective until principals are evaluated not only on the basis of test scores, but also on whether learners with disabilities meet their IEP goals and demonstrate those skills and abilities defined by NASPE as national standards.

Preparing Parents

Perhaps the most important phase of a successful inclusion program is the preparation of parents of children with and without disabilities. Certainly, a broad-based public relations campaign within the community is a good start, but carefully designed parent education programs are vital.

Parents of children with disabilities are often the primary advocates of inclusionary programs. On occasion, however, parents of children with disabilities are fearful of the regular education program. Particularly if their child has been educated in a self-contained special education program, they may like the safety and the security of that program. Parents fear that their child may be teased or hurt, laughed at, and ridiculed by typically developing children.

The best way to deal with these types of fears is to invite the parents to visit the regular physical education program before their child begins attending the class. If the parents have the opportunity to see a caring, nurturing teacher and a well-organized, child-centered physical education program, their fears will be reduced.

Preparing the parents of children without disabilities for inclusion may be the most difficult part of the development of an inclusionary education program. Most parents of children without disabilities are supportive of inclusionary efforts if, and only if, they believe their children's education will not be compromised. Parents of children without disabilities are concerned that:

- The teacher's time and energy will be exhausted dealing with a learner with disabilities.
- School resources and tax dollars will be allocated disproportionately for learners with disabilities.
- Their child's learning will be disrupted by a child with inappropriate learning behaviors—out of seat, acting out, and refusal behaviors, for example.
- Their child will begin to mimic inappropriate behaviors demonstrated by children with disabilities.
- Their child's safety will be compromised by a child with physically aggressive behavior.
- Their child's emotional well-being will be compromised by a child who is verbally aggressive or who uses foul language.
- Their child's health will be compromised by a child who vomits, drools, spits, is not toilet trained or who has a communicable disease (e.g., AIDS, syphilis).

The single most important strategy for preparing parents of children without disabilities for inclusionary practices, in addition to a broad-based public relations campaign, is gradual and thoughtful inclusion of children with mild disabilities, at first. If parents can see that their child's education is not compromised, they will be more likely to support inclusion.

Achilles Track Club sponsors a summer in Central Park for disabled children, which promotes family involvement. (Courtesy Achilles Track Club, New York, N.Y.)

Another significant strategy is to give parents of children with and without disabilities the opportunity to discuss their mutual and independent concerns in a carefully designed open forum. Often, if a parent becomes aware of the fears, needs, dreams, and hopes of another parent, an avenue of communication is opened that will transcend discriminatory practice.

Preparing Children

The single most effective strategy for preparing children with and without disabilities for inclusion is to begin inclusive education early. If infants, toddlers, and young children grow up learning together, as young adults there will be no question of "who belongs." In fact, if a school district was deeply committed to effective, inclusionary practice with a minimum of upheaval, the district would begin inclusionary practice in their birth to age 5 program and then gradually, as the children who grew up learning together moved into the primary grades, expand the program into the primary grades. Then, eventually, the program would be expanded into the middle and high schools. Although the total transformation would take up to 8 years, at the end of that time the school district would be a place in which all children could learn together.

In fact, if inclusion is well done, there are innumerable benefits for all children. According to Rogers[32]:

The presence of an included classmate should provide opportunities for growth for the entire class.
- Classmates can develop a sense of responsibility and the enhanced self-esteem which results from such responsibility.
- Classmates' understanding of the range of human experience can be enhanced.
- Classmates can benefit from their disabled classmates as role models in coping with disabilities. As a result of advancements in medical science, most of those presently nondisabled children will survive to become persons with disabilities themselves one day.
- Classmates are enriched by the opportunity to have had friends with disabilities who successfully managed their affairs and enjoyed full lives.

To ensure that this is a positive experience for all children, helping children without disabilities to understand what it is like to have a disability is an excellent first step. Children respond well to **empathy experiences** in which they have the opportunity to feel what it is like to have a disability. These empathy experiences help a child, in a concrete way, to learn and, hopefully, accept.

The child without a disability, or with a different disability, can be instructed to do one or more of the following:

1. Spend a day in a wheelchair.
2. Wear mittens when attempting to perform fine motor tasks.
3. Endeavor to trace an object reflected in a mirror.
4. Spend a day not speaking a word.
5. Spend a day with cotton wads, covered with vaseline, or a headset covering the ears.
6. Wear eye patches.
7. Use crutches for a day.
8. Spend a day with a yardstick splint on the dominant arm.
9. Listen to teacher instructions given in a different language.

In the physical education classroom, these empathy experiences might include instructions to:

1. Navigate an obstacle course in a wheelchair.
2. Wear mittens when trying to play catch with a friend.
3. Play in the gymnasium and on the playground using only gestures for communication.

4. Wearing a headset to cut out hearing, attempt to play in a game.
5. Wearing eye patches, allow a classmate to walk you around the playground and help you use each piece of equipment.
6. Kick a ball while supporting yourself on crutches.
7. With a yardstick splint on the dominant arm, catch, throw, and dribble with the nondominant hand and arm.
8. Participate in class when the teacher uses only sign language to communicate.

One of the most significant means of preparing an environment for a learner to be successfully included is to identify and encourage a "circle of friends" to be in place before the inclusion experience is attempted.[35] This helps provide a vital and humane transition into regular education services.

A child with a disability is given the opportunity to make friends in a controlled, reverse mainstream setting before attempting to move into the regular education/physical education setting. For example, if a 6-year-old girl with Down syndrome is hoping to participate in the regular education/physical education program, several 6-year-old girls would be asked to meet and play with the child in her classroom, preferably during a time in which interaction might occur (e.g., center time). Then, after the child had made friends, she would be included in the regular education/physical education program.

Preparing older students, middle and high school age, for inclusion needs to be approached altogether differently. These students are more likely to be accepting of an individual with a disability if they are able to understand the disability on an intellectual level. Honest communication of information regarding the nature of a disability will reduce fear. They are also more likely to interact with a classmate with a disability if given a leadership role (e.g., as a tutor, personal assistant, etc.). Only the truly mature adolescent is able to deal with peer pressure issues to only "hang with the in crowd." Selective assignment and recruitment of tutors and personal assistants must be used.

Preparing Professionals and Paraprofessionals, Including the Regular Physical Educator

For a child with even a mild disability to be educated in the regular education/physical education class, careful preparation must be made. There are three variables that must be considered before a decision is made to place a child in the regular education/physical education program:

1. The professional preparation of the educator to teach a child with disabilities
2. The attitude of the educator toward learners with disabilities
3. The nature of the educator's previous experience working with learners with disabilities

The first variable to be considered in the decision to include children with disabilities in regular education/physical education programs is the professional preparation of the teacher and the assistant. To serve children with disabilities in the regular education program, the teacher and the assistant must have the knowledge and skills outlined in the box below.

If the physical educator did not acquire this knowledge during undergraduate or graduate professional preparation, the educator must be provided access to this information through in-service preparation before a child with disabilities is included in the regular program. Subsequent, ongoing in-service training is vital in order to keep professional and paraprofessional staff on the cutting edge in the provision of services to learners with

---

Essentials for Regular Education Teachers and Assistants for Inclusion of Children with Disabilities

1. Knowledgeable of the physical, mental, and emotional characteristics of children with disabilities
2. Knowledgeable of the learning styles of children with disabilities
3. Able to use teaching techniques and methodologies appropriate for children with and without disabilities
4. Proficient in using behavior management strategies appropriate for children with and without disabilities
5. Able to modify play, games, and leisure, recreation, and sport activities to include children with disabilities
6. Capable of modifying curriculum objectives to meet the needs of children with disabilities
7. Able to modify evaluation and grading for children with disabilities

disabilities in a regular education/physical education setting.

The second variable that must be considered before placing a child with a disability in the regular classroom is the teacher's attitude toward teaching those with disabilities. If the teacher has a negative attitude about including a learner with a disability in the class, the learner will know it instantly and be devastated by it; the learner with a disability simply cannot be placed in a classroom or gymnasium in which he or she is not wanted.

Teachers may have negative attitudes toward a student with a disability for a variety of reasons, but attitudes are learned behaviors that, when necessary, can be changed. According to Clark, French, and Henderson[7]:

> It is important to find ways to teach physical educators the knowledge and skills necessary to work effectively with students with disabilities in the regular classroom and increase positive attitudes toward them. These are not mutually exclusive. Teachers may have negative attitudes toward students with disabilities because they do not know how to teach them.

Pre-professionals, those involved in preparation for careers as physical educators, express the intent to work with students with disabilities based on their role identity in society and their confidence in their ability to teach students with disabilities.[38]

Downs and Williams[10] studied 371 preservice physical education students in four European countries to determine their attitudes toward serving learners with disabilities in their future career. The researchers used the Physical Educators' Attitudes Toward Teaching the Handicapped (PEATH) developed by Rizzo.[31] They noted that learners with "some previous experience" with individuals with disabilities had a more negative attitude toward learners with disabilities than those who did not have this experience. It is important to consider the nature of the experience; clearly, a well-planned, structured experience improves the attitudes of individuals toward those with disabilities.

Downs and Williams[10] also noted that their European students expressed a more positive attitude toward teaching learners with physical disabilities than those with learning disabilities. They suggest:

> One could argue that people with physical disabilities are more suited to the physical activity setting since their "limitations" present only functional barriers whereas people with learning disabilities may be unable to grasp the fundamental, cognitive structures underlying the physical activity setting.

In addition, Downs and Williams[10] reported that women were more likely to express a positive attitude toward teaching individuals with disabilities than men. This is easily explained by societal expectations of women as nurturers and caregivers.

Clark, French, and Henderson[7] recommended preservice or in-service training that would include empathy experiences, values clarification, volunteerism, experiences with learners with disabilities, group discussions, and lectures as vehicles for attitude change. The following techniques are suggested for preservice or in-service presentations intended to alter the attitudes of physical educators toward the disabled.

Empathy experiences

The educator/physical educator would be provided experiences that simulate the experience of being disabled. For example, the individual would be asked to spend a day teaching in a wheelchair or to spend a night at home with his or her family while wearing a headset. Or the educator/physical educator would be asked to wear eye patches and a blindfold and allow a student to take him or her on a tour of the playground.

The same type of experience that might help a child understand the phenomenon associated with having a disability would help the professional or paraprofessional understand, as well. A truly remarkable account of an empathy experience is the true story of an entire football team, players and coaches, who shaved their heads to commiserate with a teammate who lost his hair as a side effect of chemotherapy for cancer.

"Humbling" experiences

The educator/physical educator would be exposed to information about the potential and the performance of individuals with disabilities. The physical educator might be asked, for example, to compare his or her running performance with the national marathon record of male and female wheelchair racers. Better still, the physical educator would be given the opportunity to compete against an elite disabled athlete. The teacher might have a chance to play tennis against a wheelchair-enabled tennis player, or the teacher might have the opportunity to bowl against a member of the American Wheelchair Bowling Association or to play golf against a low handicap player of the National Amputee Golf Association.

Observation experiences

The physical educator would be invited to attend a local or regional sports competition for individuals with disabilities. These would include events sponsored by, for example, the Special Olympics, the National Wheelchair Athletic Association, or the National Association of Sports for Cerebral Palsy. If this is not possible, the teacher would be given the opportunity to view tapes, for example, of the 1995 International Special Olympics Competition, the wheelchair athletes competing in the 1996 Boston Marathon, and the Paralympics in Atlanta during the summer of 1996.

Volunteer experiences

The educator/physical educator would be given the opportunity to volunteer, in a carefully supervised experience, to work with learners with disabilities. The mere act of volunteering does not cause a change in attitude. But a positive experience, one in which the educator perceives his or her work to be of value—one that allows for important and honest communication between the educator and the individual with a disability—can alter an attitude for a lifetime.

Values clarification

The educator/physical educator would be led by a trained psychologist or school counselor through the process of identifying and clarifying prejudices, attitudes, and notions about individuals with disabilities. These values might best be clarified in and through conversations with disabled adults or with parents of children with disabilities. This type of conversation should be led by a psychologist or counselor, at first, to ensure that the individuals have a quality human interaction. Clark, French, and Henderson[7] suggested that a "trigger story" may also help physical educators sort out feelings and attitudes toward teaching students with disabilities. For example, the physical educator would be asked to react to the following types of scenarios by identifying the emotions of the child, those of his or her classmates, and the fears or concerns the physical educator may have about the inclusion process:

Atlantis is a moderately mentally retarded, emotionally disturbed child who cries for an hour before being made to join the fifth grade physical education class. No one in the class has befriended her; indeed, her classmates taunt and jeer at her throughout.

or

Guadalupe is a 5-year-old child with mild spina bifida. He is ambulatory and loves to play. He is not being allowed to come to the gym with his classmates and is depressed because of the decision.

or

Johnny is a 14-year-old student-athlete with a cabinet full of medals and trophies for outstanding performance in wheelchair sports competitions. He has quadriplegic cerebral palsy but is an accomplished swimmer and archer. The "coach" has said, within Johnny's hearing, that Johnny should be in an institution.

This type of values clarification can also be encouraged by asking the physical educator to read books like *Breaking Through,* the Harry Cordellos story* or to watch movies, readily available on videotape, like *My Left Foot* or *Children of a Lesser God.*

Evaluating the Physical Education Environment for Inclusion

Facilities for physical education at the elementary, middle, and high school level vary extensively from district to district and from state to state. Most schools have an indoor gymnasium/play area and an outdoor playground area that is available for class use. Some inner-city schools, however, have no viable (safe, weapon-free, gang-free) playground area, and often the gymnasium is too small to allow appropriate activities.

Students with disabilities who receive physical education instruction within the regular physical education program share these facilities with children in their class. It is, of course, necessary to evaluate the facilities with regard to the safety of all the learners. In addition, it is vital that the physical educator critically appraise the facility with the unique needs of learners with disabilities in mind. The physical educator must ask the following questions regarding the learning environment:

1. Is the indoor gymnasium/play area accessible for a student who is wheelchair enabled, crutch enabled, or walker enabled?
2. Can the student with a physical or neurological

---

*Cordellos H: *Breaking through,* Mountain View, Calif, 1981, Anderson World.

disability make an easy transition from the indoor gymnasium/play area to the outdoor playground area?

3. If the gymnasium/play area is not easily accessible, what accommodations can be made to ensure that a student is not limited by a disability?

4. If the student is unable to make an easy transition from the indoor to the outdoor play area, because of stairs, for example, what accommodations can be made to ensure that the child is not limited program access by the disability?

5. Can the play areas be modified to provide a safe and secure nurturing learning environment for all learners?

6. Are there accessible washrooms close to the indoor gymnasium/play area and the outside playground area?

7. Can all learners, including those with disabilities, be safely evacuated from the indoor gymnasium/play area in the event of a fire?

It is important for the teacher to understand that Section 504 of the Rehabilitation Act of 1973 and subsequent legislation, specifically the Americans with Disabilities Act of 1990, mandate that all new public facilities must be built to ensure access for individuals with disabilities. In the event, however, that the teacher is serving in an old building, the law mandates that a "reasonable accommodation" must be made to ensure that the student has access to programs offered to others. For example, if the primary pathway from the gymnasium to the playground is down a set of stairs, a student in a wheelchair may be unable to get to the playground using that route. A reasonable accommodation is for the physical education teacher to have the entire class use an accessible route, one with a ramp, for example, so that the learner using the wheelchair feels part of the group.

The gymnasium and playground areas can be modified to make them more user-friendly for learners with disabilities. For example:

▪ A constant sound source could be placed in the gymnasium or on the playground to allow the visually impaired student to orient self in both settings.

▪ A "safety strip," made of a material different from that of the major play area, could surround the gym-

nasium or playground area to warn the visually impaired or blind student of walls or fences.

▪ The playground area must be completely surrounded by fences if a severely emotionally disturbed learner, a student with autism, or a "wanderer" or "runner" is to be allowed to play and/or recreate outside.

▪ The gymnasium should be well lighted to ensure best use by a student with a visual disability.

▪ The gymnasium should have good acoustics to ensure that a learner with a hearing impairment can hear the teacher's instructions.

▪ The teacher should have access to a microphone to speak at levels that can be heard by a student with a hearing impairment.

▪ Major equipment should always be stored in the same place in the gymnasium to provide consistency for the visually impaired and autistic learner.

Least Restrictive Environment Alternatives on a Continuum of Services

The least restrictive environment continuum provides a variety of alternatives to meet the unique needs of a student with a disability. In the past, the continuum commonly used in adapted physical education has only addressed issues related to placement and support personnel. The alternatives on a least restrictive environment continuum are much more complex than that and provide many more options for the IEP committee to consider.

Decker and Jansma[9] have cautioned that federal mandates to provide education in the least restrictive environment have been largely ignored and, indeed, that many school districts have as few as two "service delivery options." Their research in 452 schools throughout the United States indicated that "the most widely used continuum (50.7%) was not a continuum at all, but rather a single placement option: full-time regular class in a regular school." The frightening thing is that this study was conducted during the 1988 to 1989 school year, before the widespread national focus on inclusionary programs. It seems logical to concur that this widespread abuse of the "least restrictive environment" alternatives has escalated.

In a discussion regarding the provision of educational service in the least restrictive, most inclusive en-

figure 5-1

Least restrictive environment alternatives to provide a continuum of services. (Teaching style data from Mosston M, Ashworth S: *Teaching physical education*, New York, 1994, Macmillan.)

vironment, a number of factors must be considered. Specifically, these are:

- Curriculum
- Program participation
- Support personnel
- Teaching style
- Management of behavior
- Grading
- Equipment

Figure 5-1 illustrates the movement from the most restrictive educational environment, at the center of the circle, to the least restrictive educational environment, at the outside of the circle. In the most restrictive physical education environment, these factors exist:

- An adapted physical education curriculum is used.
- The student receives adapted physical education services in the home, hospital, or institution. (Note that with a preschool child the home may be considered the least restrictive environment.)
- The student's teacher is the adapted physical educator.
- The teacher uses a command teaching style.
- The student's behavior is managed by an individually designed behavior management plan.
- There is a reduction in expectations for the purpose of evaluation and grading.
- The student uses specially designed equipment in order to participate.

In the least restrictive physical education environment, these factors exist:

- The National Association for Sport and Physical Education (NASPE) National Standards for Physical Education are the basis of the school curriculum.
- The student is able to participate fully and independently in the regular physical education program.
- The student's teacher is the regular physical educator.
- The teacher develops individually designed programs for all learners in the program.
- The same behavior expectations exist.
- For the sake of grading, the teacher has the same expectations for the learner in all phases of evaluation.
- The learner uses the same equipment as all other learners.

When the IEP committee meets to determine the least restrictive environment for a learner with a disability, the committee members must first consider whether the learner can function in the regular physical education program with no alternatives or modifications. In some states, the law has been interpreted to mean that the learner must be given the opportunity to prove he or she can function in the regular physical education program before alternatives are even considered.

As alternatives are considered, every effort should be made to maximize participation in the regular physical education program. A student with mild to moderate dyslexia may participate under the following conditions:

- The physical education curriculum is based on the NASPE National Standards for Physical Education.
- The student is able to participate fully and independently in the regular physical education program.
- The student's teacher is the regular physical educator.
- The teacher develops individually designed programs for all learners in the program.
- The same behavior expectations exist for all students in the class.
- There are modifications of expectations in some phases of the evaluation process. Specifically, knowledge tests are administered orally.
- The learner uses the same equipment as all other learners.

The matrix allows a maximum of flexibility, designed to meet the unique needs of all learners. For example, a student with spina bifida who is wheelchair enabled may participate in the least restrictive physical education environment with these alternatives:

- The physical education curriculum is based on the NASPE National Standards for Physical Education.
- The student is able to participate fully and independently in some units (such as archery) but requires support in others (such as gymnastics) in the regular physical education program.
- The student's teacher is a regular physical educator who has consultative support from an adapted physical education specialist.
- The teacher develops individually designed programs for all learners in the program.
- The same behavior expectations exist for all students in the class.

- There are modifications of expectations in some phases of the evaluation process. For example, the student's cardiovascular fitness evaluation may be based on improvement in the number of minutes the student can wheel at a given rate without stopping.
- The learner uses the same equipment as all other learners and just happens to ambulate in a chair.

To consider the alternatives in the least restrictive environment continuum, each of the variables is considered separately. These are considered from the "least restrictive" to the "most restrictive."

Curriculum

The adoption of a given curriculum for use by all students within a given district, or for use by some students in a given district, is a key decision in the creation of an inclusive learning environment. Inclusionary practice mandates that every learner have access to the same curriculum.

- *NASPE National Standards for Physical Education as the basis of the school curriculum:* The National Association for Sport and Physical Education has determined the standards of performance in physical education. The least restrictive environment for all students is one in which these standards serve as the basis of the curriculum.
- *State education agency "essential elements" in physical education as the basis of the school curriculum:* Most states have developed their own standards or "essential elements" for all curricular areas, including physical education. These essential elements may not be as global as those outlined by NASPE and, subsequently, are more restrictive.
- *Local education agency physical education curriculum:* Many local districts have developed their own curriculum. Unfortunately, educators are known for "reinventing the wheel." Curricula developed at the local level tend to reflect only the interests and attitudes of local personnel and may, subsequently, not be as comprehensive.
- *Modified physical education curriculum:* According to Kelly[20]:

  Physical educators must examine how they, as professionals and their content area of physical education contribute to an inclusive school. This may involve issues such

as revising the physical education curriculum so that it reflects the needs and interests of all the students and the community at the expense of what the physical education staff has traditionally taught or valued in the past.

In some states, such as Wisconsin, the Department of Public Instruction (state education agency) actually spearheaded the development of a state-wide adapted physical education curriculum. It reflected a "separate but equal" philosophy. Before the major impetus toward inclusive education, many educators within local school districts developed their own adapted physical education curriculum. The goals, objectives, and standards are typically modified to meet the needs of many students with disabilities served by the local education agency.

Program Participation

In the determination of the least restrictive environment, there are many alternatives that may be considered by the IEP committee:

- *Full, independent participation in regular physical education:* In actuality, the regular physical educator has coped with the notion of inclusion for years. It has been relatively standard, albeit inappropriate, practice to give students the opportunity for "socialization" in art, music, and physical education to pacify parents interested in having their child educated with "typically developing peers."
- *Full, independent participation in regular physical education with younger students:* Occasionally it may be appropriate to integrate children with disabilities into physical education classes with younger children. This strategy, which is viable only at the elementary school level, may be appropriate with children with delayed social and play skills. Under no circumstances, however, should a child with a disability be integrated into a physical education class serving children more than 2 years younger. To place a mildly emotionally disturbed first grader in a physical education class with kindergartners may prove to be a humane and creative way of allowing the child to develop social and play skills that the child lacks. It would, however, be inhumane to place that same child in a kindergarten class when the child has reached fourth grade age. The child is not "included" in that environment; the

child is set apart for ridicule by the very nature of size differences.

▪ *Full, independent participation in some units, with support in others, in regular physical education:* On occasion, a decision about the least restrictive environment must be made on a unit basis. For example, a learner with a behavior disorder may be able to participate independently in individual activities, such as bowling, bocci, or in-line skating, but would be overwhelmed by a large-group game or sport activity. Support personnel would make it possible for the student to participate in large-group activities.

▪ *Full, independent participation in some phases of the daily lesson, with support in other phases, in regular physical education:* A mildly autistic learner, for example, may be able to participate in the structured warm-up/fitness phase of the physical education class but would be unable to handle a group game or sport without support.

▪ *Participation with support in some units, with separate physical education for other units:* A blind student, for example, may be able to participate in units such as bowling, wrestling, archery, bocci, billiards, and cross-country running with support from someone who gives verbal directions and/or serves as a "guide." That same student may receive instruction in a separate setting when the class is involved in a field hockey unit, for example.

▪ *Participation with support in some phases of the daily lesson, with separate physical education for other phases:* A student with muscular dystrophy, for example, may be able to participate in the "relaxation" phase of the daily lesson with a paraprofessional's help. However, when the rest of the class is involved in a group game or competitive sport activity, the student should receive instruction in seat- and bed-based leisure and recreation activities, such as Jarts, checkers, etc.

▪ *Separate, but equal, adapted physical education in the school building with typically developing peers:* In the event that a student requires a program participation limitation—separate, but equal, adapted physical education—a reverse mainstreaming model may be adopted. In that model, with parental permission, students without disabilities may be invited to participate in a physical education program specifically designed for students with disabilities. This is the basis of the Special Olympics Unified Sports concept. The intent of that instructional, recreation, and sports program is to allow individuals with mental retardation to be taught with, to recreate with, and to compete with individuals with disabilities.

▪ *Separate, but equal, adapted physical education in the school building with peers with disabilities:* Students with severe disabilities and/or delays may need to receive their physical education within a separate adapted physical education class. This may, in fact, be the least restrictive environment for a student with severe behavior disturbances, severe autism, Rett syndrome, or severe/profound mental retardation.

▪ *Adapted physical education in the home, hospital, or institutional setting:* Students with profound disabilities and/or chronic, terminal illness may need to receive physical education, as well as the rest of their educational services, in an institutional setting, the hospital, or their home. Students with an illness or injury that requires hospitalization or causes them to be homebound for more than 4 weeks (this time line may vary from state to state) require educational services, including physical education, in the hospital or home.

Support Personnel
No support required

The least restrictive environment in terms of support is that in which the regular physical education teacher requires no support in order to provide services.

Regular physical educator with adapted physical education consultant support

A slightly more restrictive environment is one in which the regular physical educator provides instruction and simply relies on an adapted physical education consultant for assessment/evaluation, IEP development, and sharing of ideas and equipment.

Same-age peer buddy

Often the only accommodation that must be made to allow a learner with a disability to function effectively within the regular physical education class is to ask a given learner in the same class, a learner the same age, to be a special "buddy." The buddy is asked to include the learner in play, games, or activities; often this is the only "ice breaker" necessary to allow the student to thrive in the regular program.

One's peers are powerful facilitators of learning. Once instruction becomes specific, it is not difficult for students to learn what it is they are to do and then communicate information to their peers. The peer instruction or modeling can be done by students with and without disabilities. Buddies must know what is to be done and have the ability to communicate with the learner.

The buddies should receive the same type of pre-service and in-service training as does the professional, although the learning needs to be adapted so that it is developmentally appropriate. Armstrong, Rosenbaum, and King[3] found that a controlled, direct-contact experience between children with and children without disabilities can significantly improve the attitudes of the nondisabled child toward the child with a disability.

Empathy experiences are particularly valuable in the training of peer buddies. Also, just like paraprofessionals, the buddy should have a specific job description. Working in close cooperation with the student's classroom teacher, this experience can be valuable for the peer buddy, as well as for the child with a disability.

While they are often very effective in elementary and high school programs (e.g., the Richardson, Texas, Independent School District Partners Program) peer buddy programs are often difficult to implement in middle school programs. Those students tend to be too concerned about their image to value association with an individual who is different.

Older peer buddy

A student who is unable to function within the regular physical education class with a same-age buddy may thrive if given the opportunity to work with an older buddy. This buddy should be carefully trained to help meet the special needs of the student without interfering with instruction and without setting the child apart from the others. This older, more mature student should receive training in the nature of the disability, in techniques for communicating effectively with the learner, and in methods of helping the learner (to move his or her wheelchair for example, or, if blind, to orient himself or herself in the gymnasium). Older students may serve as

excellent models and, if carefully chosen, may serve as a magnet to draw other students toward the student with a disability.

Older student as teacher's assistant

Teacher's assistants in physical education can be indispensable in individualized learning environments. They can assume several responsibilities that contribute to class management and record progress in physical education, such as setting up and storing equipment before and after class, collecting data on self and others, and assisting with the instruction of younger students. These students are often honor students who are released from school or are scheduled with younger and slower-learning children. These students need to be thoroughly familiar with the programming if their assistance is to be valuable.

The process of organizing a successful buddy/teacher's assistant program is complex. The steps are outlined as follows:

1. Discuss the peer buddy/teacher's assistant plan with the local campus administrator. Secure support and approval.
2. Discuss the peer buddy/teacher's assistant plan with the classroom teachers whose schedules will be affected. Secure support and approval (see Figure 5-6).
3. Schedule a preservice orientation meeting for all teachers and students. The preservice orientation should include a description of:
   a. The peer buddy/teacher's assistant program.
   b. The role and responsibilities of the peer buddies and teacher's assistants (see Figure 5-7).
   c. The characteristics of the children with disabilities who will be served. Care must be taken to protect, at all costs, the privacy rights of the children who will be served. Information may be shared, for example, about the nature of mental retardation, but specific information about "Deundrae" must not be shared.
4. Develop a schedule for each teacher and child involved in the program. Share copies with the principal.
5. Have ongoing in-service education with peer buddies and teacher's assistants during each lesson. Spend a few moments before each class reminding the students of their roles and responsibilities.

6. Evaluate the performance of the peer buddies and teacher's assistants during each lesson. Provide feedback (positive, whenever possible) with students after each lesson.

7. Arrange to honor the peer buddies and teacher's assistants at the end of the unit, semester, or year. Ask to be involved in the school's honor assembly and award certificates of participation or certificates of thanks during the award ceremony.

8. If possible, present a slide presentation that highlights the peer buddy/teacher's assistant program at a Parent-Teacher Association (PTA) meeting.

Strategies for Increasing Volunteer Support in the Gymnasium

1. Develop a poster recruiting campaign that features the fact that it is "fun" and a great "change of pace" to work with children with disabilities in a play, leisure, recreation, or sport setting.
2. Actively recruit volunteers on the basis of their athletic skills; it is easier to recruit someone who has the perception of being needed because of particular skills.
3. Form a "dad's club" that allows fathers to contribute to their child's education in a format in which they may be comfortable.
4. Indicate the potential for learning new skills, particularly those that might be marketable. This is particularly valuable in recruiting individuals who are unemployed or seeking alternative employment opportunities.
5. Share program goals and objectives with the volunteer. Share specific goals and objectives for specific children the volunteer serves.
6. Write a specific job description for the volunteer (see Figure 5-8). This is the key to successful volunteer recruitment and retention. The volunteer needs to understand his or her role within the program.
7. Ensure that the volunteer is recognized for his or her efforts. Help the children in the program express their thanks—this is perhaps the most valuable form of recognition for most volunteers. Develop a systematic strategy for recognizing the volunteer. This includes "volunteer highlights" in the adapted physical education newsletter, thank-you notes, plaques, and/or recognition dinners.

Adult volunteer as teacher's assistant

The adult volunteer must be carefully trained to meet the needs of the student with a disability in the regular physical education classroom. This may be a more effective learning environment (the least restrictive one) for a learner with behavior disorders that are difficult for another child to manage but that can be handled by an adult.

Recruitment and retention of volunteers. As funds become increasingly scarce, administrators and teachers have become more and more dependent on the use of volunteer resources to continue or improve programs. The effective recruitment and retention of volunteers is enhanced by effective communication (discussed later in this chapter). However, it is important for the regular physical education teacher or adapted physical education teacher to understand the nature of the volunteer to effectively use the volunteer to meet program goals.

Schools and school districts have begun the process of actively recruiting volunteers to work with children within the schools. Schools may be "adopted" by a corporation or a civic organization. Corporate employees or members of a civic group may each serve the school in a unique way as a part of the "adopt a school" program. The regular physical education teacher or adapted physical education teacher can increase the likelihood that a volunteer will choose to work in the gymnasium by following the suggestions in the box at left.

The use of volunteers in the schools can greatly enhance the opportunities that can be given to children with disabilities. The adapted physical educator can provide a chance for children to thrive and grow through the encouragement and help of program volunteers.

Physical education paraprofessional to provide support

The student's least restrictive physical education environment may be the regular physical education class with the support and assistance of a physical education paraprofessional. This paraprofessional literally serves as a second physical education teacher, who focuses interest and efforts on the children with special needs. In some instances the regular physical education teacher should insist that if one or more learners with disabilities are to be included in the physical education class, a paraprofessional must be available.

In many school districts paraprofessionals or teacher's aides are assigned to assist a teacher in a given program without regard to their training or background. As such, it is possible that the physical education teacher will need to ensure that the paraprofessional attend preservice and in-service programs regarding physical education and, if students with disabilities are to be served, regarding physical education for children with disabilities.

At the very least, the paraprofessional must have the opportunity to share the same types of learning experiences recommended for teachers. Clark, French, and Henderson[7] have recommended preservice or in-service training for physical education teachers that includes empathy experiences, values clarification, volunteerism, experiences with children with disabilities, group discussions, and lectures as vehicles for attitude change. This same type of preservice or in-service training must be included in the training regimen of the paraprofessional as well.

One of the most significant aspects of the supervision of a paraprofessional is the description of the paraprofessional's role and responsibilities. Most school districts have a job description for the paraprofessional. This description is, however, often vague regarding the specific role and responsibilities of the paraprofessional. In addition, the job description for the paraprofessional is usually prepared for the individual who will assist a classroom teacher. The duties and responsibilities of the paraprofessional working in the gymnasium are different from the duties and responsibilities of the paraprofessional in the classroom. As such, the regular physical education teacher or adapted physical education teacher must work closely with the building principal to design a specific job description, particularly if the paraprofessional is to help teach children with disabilities. An example of a description for one class period is listed in the box above.

A specific job description significantly alleviates potential problems. If respective roles and responsibilities are clear to both the physical education teacher and the paraprofessional, they can work together as a professional team, serving children in the best possible way. In addition, the wise physical educator should take every opportunity to reinforce the efforts of the paraprofessional. For example, the physical educator should write a letter to the principal praising the efforts of the paraprofessional. A copy should be shared with the para-

Example of Specific Responsibilities for a Physical Education Paraprofessional

Class 1, 8:00-8:45

7:55

Go to Room 103 to accompany Kaneisha to the gym. Insist she push her own chair.

8:00-8:15

Roam throughout the gymnasium while children are doing warm-up exercises, encouraging all the children to do well. If necessary, remind Kaneisha to do her modified warm-ups, which are posted on the wall.

8:15-8:40

Monitor Kaneisha's interactions with others in the class. Record and describe any inappropriate interactions on her behavior chart in the teacher's office. Refer to the description of appropriate and/or inappropriate behaviors on her chart.

8:40-8:45

Accompany Kaneisha to her room.

professional. Or, the physical educator should routinely orchestrate a class "thank-you" for the paraprofessional with cards, cake, and punch.

Special education paraprofessional to provide support

The presence of a special education paraprofessional in the gymnasium is more restrictive than if the student works with a physical education paraprofessional because of the stigma attached to having a "special ed" teacher accompany the learner to class. Every bit of information that applied to the physical education paraprofessional applies to the special education paraprofessional as well.

Adapted physical educator to provide student support

For a student to function within the regular physical education program, it may be necessary for a specialist trained in adapted physical education to intervene with the student in the gymnasium. Unfortunately, by necessity, this would reduce the amount of time the student would spend in the regular physical education program. In most districts the adapted physical education specialist has too large a caseload to spend individual time with each student each day. This type of arrangement may, however, demonstrate strategies to the regular physical educator that he or she may be able to use with this student and with other students with disabilities.

In some situations, if the adapted physical educator provides a model while supporting a student with a disability in the regular physical education setting, the regular physical educator and/or paraprofessional can then adopt that behavior to facilitate inclusion.

Adapted physical educator as teacher

Many school districts have not made a real commitment to quality adapted physical education programming. In some schools, for example, the caseload of the adapted physical educator may be 200+ students; there is no way that quality service can be delivered in that situation. A separate, but equal, service for students with disabilities has become a luxury, not a reality.

The adapted physical educator may provide direct service in some institutions or with a very specific type of student—those with traumatic brain injuries, for example—but, in general, staff priorities cause this form of direct service to students with disabilities and their parents to be rare.

Teaching Style

On occasion, there is a choice of placement of a learner with a disability. For example, there may be two physical educators in the same large high school. The IEP committee may need to evaluate the teaching style of both teachers to determine in which class the learner is likely to succeed. Certainly, a willingness to work with a student with a disability and a commitment to educating all are necessary and desirable traits in a teacher selected to work with a learner with a disability.

Learner's individually designed program

The essence of this teaching style is that the focus is on each individual student and his or her needs. A teacher who is already focusing on individual students can easily accommodate and serve a student who just happens to have a disability. The learner is empowered to design and develop a series of tasks and activities that meet his or her needs, and the teacher serves essentially as a consultant—the teacher helps the student by asking important questions, reinforcing appropriate tasks and activities, and redirecting the student's efforts if the tasks or activities are not developmentally appropriate.

Guided discovery

In this teaching style, the teacher asks questions, chooses and develops activities, and plans events to lead a student to a predetermined answer or solution.[25] The most common guided discovery teaching style in physical education is movement exploration. For example, a student who uses a wheelchair may be guided through the following activities at the same time as his other-ambulatory peers:

1. Can you move in a large circle on the floor?
2. Can you move in a large circle on the floor in a different way?
3. What can you do to make the circle smaller?
4. What can you do to make the circle even smaller?

This type of approach empowers all movers and respects the individual's unique responses to movement problems and challenges. This teaching style is one in which learners with disabilities can be easily included.

Self-check

In this teaching style, the teacher shares with the learner the skills needed to perform a task or activity individually.[25] The teacher has established criteria for successful accomplishment of a given task so that the individual learner can evaluate his or her own success. If the teacher is serving a student with a disability, the teacher can help the student establish challenging, yet attainable, standards for success. Once again, the emphasis on meeting the needs of individual students facilitates the inclusion of students with disabilities.

Reciprocal style

This teaching style is characterized by the establishment of learning partnerships.[25] While the teacher determines the activity or task and establishes the criteria for success, students work in partnership to provide each other feedback regarding performance. This teaching style easily accommodates learners with disabilities, even those who require the support of a same-age or older peer buddy to be successful. If every student has a

Innovative equipment designs enable individuals with disabilities to bike in tandem. (Courtesy Just 2 Bikes, Inc., White Bear Lakes, Minn.)

learning buddy, it is easy for the learner with a disability to have a buddy as well.

Command style

This teaching style has often been called the "traditional" teaching approach.[25] In this style, the teacher explains an activity, demonstrates the activity, and expects each learner to replicate the activity. The teacher-controlled atmosphere allows little individual variation in performance. This type of learning climate is not one in which a learner with a disability can expect to thrive, because the rigid expectations do not allow for individual differences.

Management of Behavior

Same behavioral expectations for all students

One of the critical issues in determining the appropriate, least restrictive environment is the ability of the learner with a disability to meet the behavioral expectations and standards set for every other learner. Too often, a learner with a disability is excluded from the physical education environment not because of a motor delay, but because of the learner's inability to follow class rules.

Slightly modified behavioral expectations

Regular physical educators are often willing to in-changes in behavioral expectations. For example, if a student with attention deficit disorder is unable to sit on a given spot while listening to directions, the teacher may accommodate the student by allowing the student to stay within a larger space (e.g., a free-throw circle).

Individually designed reinforcement system

As an example of this behavior management system, a deeply committed physical educator teaching a high school student with Down syndrome was willing to abide by the recommendations of the IEP committee and completed a behavior checklist each week to be sent home to the student's parents. When the student willingly participated in class activities more than 50% of the time, she earned a coupon that she could use to rent a video on the weekend.

Individual behavior management plan for the individual student

The most restrictive environment is one in which the student with a disability has an individual behavior management plan that is different from the plans of his or her classmates. It should be noted that an individual behavior management plan is almost impossible to implement in a physical education class without the support of an additional, trained adult in the gymnasium. Under no circumstances should a student, even an older student, be put in the position of implementing a behavior management plan for another student. The ethical and legal implications of a student being given the responsibility of managing the behavior of another student are frightening.

Grading

Same expectations in all phases of evaluation

The least restrictive environment in the physical education program is one in which learners with disabilities are able to meet the same expectations in all phases of the evaluation process. That includes the motor, physical fitness, knowledge, and behavioral components of grading.

Modifications of expectations in some phases of evaluation

Occasionally a learner with a disability may be successfully included in the regular physical education program with modifications in expectations for grading. For example, a learner with spastic cerebral palsy that affects the lower limbs might be evaluated in a physical fitness unit in terms of upper body strength or dexterity.

Equipment

Same equipment

Every learner within the class shares and uses the same equipment.

Similar, but different, equipment

It is possible to facilitate inclusion simply by changing the type of equipment available for student use. For example, a student with arthritis may not be able to participate in a volleyball game with a real volleyball but may be successful in a "volleyball" game that uses a beach ball instead. A child with a visual impairment may experience difficulty tracking a typical playground ball but would be able to participate in a game of catch if the ball were a bright, fluorescent color.

Specially designed equipment

It is possible to enhance opportunities for inclusion by providing the learner with a disability with specially designed equipment to meet his or her needs. For example, a student with cerebral palsy may be able to bowl by using an "automatic grip release" or a ramp. A student with a below-the-knee amputation may be able to participate in downhill skiing with an "outrigger" ski pole.

▪ ▪ ▪

Seven major variables may be considered in the process of developing a least restrictive learning environment for a student with a disability. The IEP committee can, and must, consider (1) the curriculum, (2) a program participation hierarchy, (3) the availability of support personnel, (4) the teaching style of the regular physical educator, (5) strategies for management of behavior, (6) grading, and (7) equipment when designing an individual, appropriate learning experience. These variables must be considered at each annual review, as the learner's skills, needs, and environmental demands change. For example, a learner with a severe emotional disturbance may receive his or her physical education services within a hospital designed for rehabilitation until the learner can receive outpatient services. As an outpatient, that learner may require physical education services in a school setting with a full-time instructional aide.

The point is that the nature of the least restrictive environment is an ever-changing process, certainly never a product carved in stone. As the individual student's needs change, the least restrictive environment alternatives must be reconsidered.

Determination of Appropriate Physical Education Placement

Least Restrictive Environment Spreadsheet

Art Reinhardt,[29] formerly an adapted physical education specialist in the Stevens Point (Wisconsin) Area Public Schools, developed a spreadsheet with which the physical educator can monitor the performance of children with disabilities within the regular physical education program. An adaptation of this spreadsheet is shown in Table 5-1.

This evaluation form allows the regular physical educator and the adapted physical educator to make significant decisions regarding intervention with a child functioning, at least temporarily, within the regular physical education environment. The process of quantifying behaviors required for successful participation in regular physical education is vital if thoughtful decisions are to be made regarding a child's ultimate placement; and the beauty of the spreadsheet is that repeated observations can be made and calculations performed instantly for review. In addition, quantifying behaviors allows the adapted physical educator to work closely with the regular physical educator to modify the program, if necessary, to allow the child to participate successfully in the program.

For example, the student described in Table 5-1 appears to have the skills and knowledge necessary to participate in the program but lacks the social skills necessary to function with partners or with groups, as indicated by average scores of 1 and 1.2 on "participation in groups" and "participation with partner," respectively. The professionals serving this child have several appar-

table 5-1

Class: K
Regular PE teacher: Mr. Shirly
Observer: Art Reinhardt
Date: 2/14/96

Observation	1st	2nd	3rd	4th	5th	Avg.
Psychomotor skills	2	2	2	2	2	2.0
Fitness	2	1	2	1	2	1.6
Knowledge/understanding	3	3	3	3	4	3.2
Attitude/behavior	1	2	2	1	1	1.4
Participation in groups	1	1	1	1	1	1.0
Participation with partner	1	1	1	2	1	1.2
Individual activities	3	3	3	2	3	2.8
TOTAL AVERAGE	1.8	1.8	2.0	1.7	1.8	

Activities and Comments

J.C. participated well in warm-up activities. Disrupted group parachute activity.
Rating scale: Give the point rating below for the student's performance on that given day.

1 point

If the student needs to be pulled from class and would require one-on-one assistance
If the regular PE program must be totally modified to meet the student's needs
If the student is unable to participate

2 points

If one-on-one assistance is required more than 50% of the time
If significant modifications must be made for more than 50% of the activities
If the student requires full assistance to participate

3 points

If partial assistance is required for 25% or less of the activities
If slight modifications to regular PE are necessary
If the student requires partial assistance to participate

4 points

No assistance is required
No modifications are necessary

Modified from Mainstream Physical Education Evaluation.

ent choices based on these data. The first option is to remove the child from the regular physical education class until the child acquires the social skills necessary to function with a partner or within a small group. The second option is to develop a behavior management system, implemented by a paraprofessional, to shape the child's social behavior while the child remains in the regular physical education class. The third, and least practical, option is to modify the regular physical education class so that the emphasis is on individual, self-testing activities that do not require a partner or group interaction.

Working Document for the IEP Committee: Least Restrictive Environment in Physical Education

The Irving (Texas) Independent School District designed a special education program design matrix for the IEP committee in their consideration of the least restrictive environment within the regular education program (Figure 5-2). The strength of this document is that it provides the members of the IEP committee with a working document that emphasizes a student's strengths and considers the realities of the regular education experience. The committee members then try to match the student's strengths with the educational opportunity that will be provided.

This type of proactive effort in determining the least restrictive environment for learners with disabilities may be modified for use in physical education as well. Examples of matrixes for a unit and a daily plan are presented in Figures 5-3 and 5-4, respectively. Figure 5-3 demonstrates how the student's strengths are matched by unit(s) in which the student is likely to experience success. Focusing on the student's strengths is of particular value in the IEP meeting; parents are often much more receptive to the ideas of the committee members if the emphasis is on what the student can do rather than what the student cannot do. In Figure 5-4, the student's strengths are matched with each phase of the daily lesson plan in the first grade physical education program.

If an IEP committee is truly focused on providing the best possible, least restrictive learning environment for a student, accommodations can be made to ensure success. Careful consideration of the student's abilities,

---

Program Design Matrix

To facilitate positive and constructive admission, review, and dismissal meetings (ARDs) for all students, this program design matrix was developed at Irving Independent School District. It was during a difficult ARD that this matrix was scratched out for all participants to see a "picture" of the student. Because it focused on the strengths of the student, the ARD was able to maintain a proactive focus that generated an individual education program (IEP) for the student's needs. The successful and positive ARD supported the need for this matrix.

The following is a guide to implement the matrix.

1. The matrix is given to the teacher before the ARD to fill in the schedule of a regular school day. Copies are to be made to hand to all those attending the ARD.
2. After review of student's testing, progress, etc., you could begin the use of the matrix, explaining that this will help develop the IEP and programming for the student.
3. Next, identify strengths of the student. Everyone should participate and feel comfortable with the identified strengths before doing a cross-check with the classroom schedule.
4. As you do a cross-check, mark an X in the appropriate box and column to signify the student's specific strength(s) that could allow the student to be able to be successful in the classroom. It does not mean that the child could not get support if needed.
5. Empty boxes could indicate areas of concern that the ARD committee needs to address or that a box is not applicable. Circling an activity identified as an area of need will alert the committee to be sure to develop strategies to meet the student's needs in that area. Through ARD discussion, areas that could provide support through modification, consultation, pullout, collaboration, etc., could be identified. It is not to be assumed that support services are to be provided at the specific time scheduled for an activity identified as an area of need. The time assigned will allow the ARD committee to see how much time during the day is needed to program for special education support. The bottom boxes allow times to be totaled, which will help transfer information onto the time sheet.
6. Support suggestions can include equipment, peer tutor, buddy classmate, modifications to the lesson or activity, support personnel, etc.

A

figure 5-2

Special education program design matrix to facilitate inclusion based on student's strengths.
A, Description of matrix.

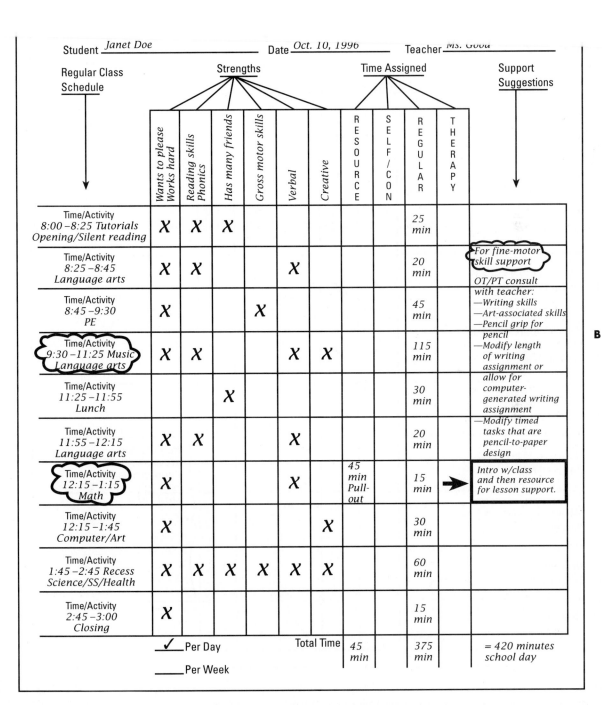

Student __Janet Doe__   Date __Oct. 10, 1996__   Teacher __Ms. Good__

Regular Class Schedule	Strengths						Time Assigned				Support Suggestions
	Wants to please / Works hard	Reading skills / Phonics	Has many friends	Gross motor skills	Verbal	Creative	RESOURCE	SELF/CON	REGULAR	THERAPY	
Time/Activity 8:00–8:25 Tutorials Opening/Silent reading	X	X	X						25 min		
Time/Activity 8:25–8:45 Language arts	X	X			X				20 min		For fine-motor skill support
Time/Activity 8:45–9:30 PE	X			X					45 min		OT/PT consult with teacher: —Writing skills —Art-associated skills —Pencil grip for pencil
Time/Activity 9:30–11:25 Music Language arts	X	X			X	X			115 min		—Modify length of writing assignment or allow for
Time/Activity 11:25–11:55 Lunch			X						30 min		computer-generated writing assignment
Time/Activity 11:55–12:15 Language arts	X	X			X				20 min		—Modify timed tasks that are pencil-to-paper design
Time/Activity 12:15–1:15 Math	X				X		45 min Pull-out		15 min	→	Intro w/class and then resource for lesson support.
Time/Activity 12:15–1:45 Computer/Art	X					X			30 min		
Time/Activity 1:45–2:45 Recess Science/SS/Health	X	X	X	X	X	X			60 min		
Time/Activity 2:45–3:00 Closing	X								15 min		
✓ Per Day ___ Per Week					Total Time		45 min		375 min		= 420 minutes school day

figure 5-2, cont'd

B, Example. (Courtesy Irving (Texas) Independent School District.)

Least Restrictive Environment Design Matrix (Unit)
High School Physical Education
First Semester

Student _Julia Hernandez_   Date _1/6/97_

Adapted Physical Education Teacher _Brett Favre_

Physical Education Teacher _Mr. Garcia_

Activity/ Unit	Good runner	Excellent flexibility	Works well independently	Responds well to music	Follows directions	Support Suggestions
September, Weeks 1 & 2 Fitness Evaluations	✔	✔			✔	
September, Weeks 3 & 4, October, Weeks 1 & 2 Individual Fitness	✔	✔			✔	
October, Weeks 3 & 4 Archery			✔		✔	
November, Weeks 1 & 2 Flag Football						_Remove for separate, but equal program with low pupil-staff ratio_
November, Weeks 3 & 4 Soccer						
December, Weeks 1 & 2 Volleyball						
December, Week 3 Creative Dance			✔	✔		

figure 5-3

Example of least restrictive environment design matrix (unit) to facilitate humane inclusion in high school physical education class.

Least Restrictive Environment Design Matrix
First Grade Physical Education
Daily Lesson Plan

Student ___*Dione Haley*___   Date___*9/7/96*___

Adapted Physical Education Teacher ___*Emmitt Smith*___

Physical Education Teacher ___*Cassandra Williams*___

Activity/ Unit	Student Strenghts				Support Suggestions
	Basic locomotor skills	*Balance*	*Rhythmic ability*	*Responds well to 1–1 instruction*	
9:40–9:45 Roll				✓	*Pair with a buddy for roll/ directions*
9:45–9:55 Warm-Ups to Music			✓		
9:55–10:10 Movement Exploration	✓				
10:10–10:20 Large-Group Activity				✓	*Pair with a buddy for parallel activity*
10:20–10:25 Relaxation				✓	*Pair with a buddy for relaxation activity*

figure 5-4
Example of least restrictive environment design matrix (daily lesson plan) to facilitate humane inclusion in first grade physical education class.

the schedule and plan of the regular physical educator, and the availability of support can all influence decisions involved in the construction of an appropriate learning environment.

Specific Strategies for Including Learners with Disabilities

Specific instructional strategies for including learners with disabilities in the regular physical education program are considered at the elementary, middle, and high school level. The reader is referred to the Suggested Readings at the end of this chapter for references that address inclusion techniques for specific types of disabilities.

Elementary Physical Education

According to Ratliffe, Ratliffe, and Bie[28]:

> Effective learning environments allow teachers to provide learning tasks, refine students' performance, and focus on students' skill and knowledge rather than on their behavior. Until such a learning environment has been established, most of the teacher's time is spent attending to students' behavior and trying to keep students on task.

Although the strategies outlined by these authors (see box at left) were designed for organizing instruction in the regular elementary physical education class, they are appropriate for any physical education setting. The teacher approaches classroom organization proactively and creates a situation that enhances learning and prevents inappropriate behavior.

Williams[42] addressed the fact that many activities typically used in elementary physical education programs are inappropriate not only for children with disabilities, but for any child. He identified the "Physical Education Hall of Shame" to help physical educators take a close look at decisions regarding games that are inappropriate for any learner. In 1992 the following activities were included:

- Dodgeball
- Duck, Duck, Goose
- Giants, Elves, and Wizards
- Kickball
- Musical Chairs
- Relay races
- Steal the Bacon

In 1994 the "Physical Education Hall of Shame" was expanded to include the following:

- Line Soccer
- Red Rover
- Simon Says
- SPUD
- Tag

The intent of the "Hall of Shame" is to encourage educators to focus on activities to avoid the following:

- Embarrassing a child in front of his or her peers
- Eliminating students from participation to allow only one "winner"

Strategies for Reinforcing Appropriate Behavior

1. Reward appropriate behavior (e.g., smiley faces, stars, "happy-grams," stickers, hugs, smiles, or free time).
2. Remove distractions from the area before starting a lesson.
3. Provide equipment of the same type and color for all children to help prevent fights.
4. Strategically place students who are likely to exhibit inappropriate behavior in designated spots within the gymnasium (e.g., close to the teacher or near children who will be good models).
5. Have students practice "stopping" an activity by placing equipment on the floor in front of their feet. Have students practice returning equipment to the original storage place.
6. Develop a strategy for transition from the classroom to the gymnasium that allows maximum control. For example, have the students practice walking in a line with hands behind the back.
7. Consider an immediate individual activity when students sit on their designated spot, waiting for further instruction. For example, have the children join in singing a song while waiting for the entire class to be seated.
8. Reward students who listen and cooperate by letting them choose equipment first and take turns first.
9. Stand near a disruptive student. Make your immediate presence known by placing your hand firmly on the student's shoulder.
10. Provide a designated time-out area separate from the group, but easily monitored.

Data from Ratliffe T, Ratliffe L, Bie B: *J Phys Educ Rec Dance* 62:24-27, 1991.

perceptual-motor integration processes are best served by using the bottom, up developmental model. Types of activities that have proved to be effective in resolving delays frequently demonstrated by young children whose development was compromised before, during, or after birth are discussed at length in Chapter 7. As often as possible, activities that address specific areas of development should be incorporated into the activity of children demonstrating those delays. When programs for these youngsters must be delivered in an inclusive setting, it is possible to address their specific needs and still benefit other students within the class. Games and activities that promote development in specific areas and are enjoyed by all children, regardless of ability level, are included in the supplement to this text, *Gross Motor Activities for Young Children with Special Needs.* Over 200 group activities to promote reflex and equilibrium development; tactile, proprioceptive, auditory, and visual sensory stimulation and discrimination; body image; locomotor patterns; cross-lateral integration; fitness; and relaxation are included in this booklet.

The Middle and High School Physical Education Program

Games analysis technique

One of the most successful techniques for designing physical education classes that appeal to and accommodate a wide range of ability levels is described in the book entitled *Changing Kids' Games* by Morris and Stiehl.[24] These authors suggest that an excellent way to pique students' interest and involvement in a physical education class is to engage them in a process that puts them in control of many aspects of the games included in the curriculum. They propose using a games' analysis technique in classes to enable students and teachers to identify and modify any aspect of a game or sport. Using a chalkboard or a flip chart, a teacher can lead the students through a process of systematically identifying the components that are included in the six categories that constitute a game.

The six categories included in every game are purposes, players, movements, objects, organization, and

1. *Purposes:* The purposes of a game include developing motor skills, enhancing self-worth, improving fitness, enjoyment, satisfaction, and/or developing cognitive skills. When deemed necessary, the components may be subdivided to identify specifics, such as which motor skills, what aspects of fitness, and which cognitive skills are included in the game.

2. *Players:* Analysis of the players category yields characteristics such as the number of players required, whether individual performance or group cooperation is needed, and the makeup of the groups. To create greater opportunities for students to be involved in a game, the number of team members could be increased, all teams could be made coeducational, efficient and inefficient movers could be placed on the same team, and students with disabilities and/or different cognitive levels could be included.

3. *Movements:* The components of the movement category include types (body awareness, locomotor versus nonlocomotor, reception versus propulsion, and physical attributes); locations, including personal space (levels, directions, and pathways) and general space; the quality of the movements (force, flow, and speed); relationships (objects, players, and group); quantity (number, unit of time, distance, and location), and sequences (task order within an episode). Students should be given the opportunity to alter the types of movement demands so that everyone has a chance to participate fully. Individual games could be changed to partner or small-group efforts, and a variety of different pathways from which players could choose could be built into the game. Players could be given the opportunity to play for a predetermined score rather than for time or vice versa.

4. *Objects:* The discussion of objects will center around the types and uses of the objects, the quantity needed, and where they are to be located. A game that requires everyone to use the same implements does not require much imagination. Why not give everyone the opportunity to use a

batting tee, or to swing at a slow pitch rather than a fast pitch, or to catch with the mitt of choice rather than the one the rules call for?

5. *Organization:* Organizational patterns include patterns in the game (lines, circles, or scattered), the number of players in the pattern, and locations of the players (close to one another or far apart, etc). Differences among students can become less discouraging if the students are given opportunities to change things so that they can be successful. Permitting the volleyball server to stand as close to the net as he or she chooses, designating specific players who have a difficult time keeping up to execute all of the throw-ins in soccer, working with peer partners who can help interpret written personal fitness program instructions, or allowing a hit after two bounces of the tennis ball can turn a dreaded class into a positive, uplifting experience.

6. *Limits:* Limits in games have to do with what is expected of players (the kind of participation and the movements that are necessary) and the environmental conditions (boundaries, time limits, scoring, and rules). Wider boundaries, modified rules, shoulder instead of forward rolls, spotting instead of executing a cartwheel, smaller goals to defend, and more than one chance to execute a correct serve can include students who might never have the opportunity to participate in a game with their classmates.

Students can be wonderfully creative when they are given an opportunity to analyze the components in a familiar game and are invited to invent ways to alter it by changing one or more components. In the beginning, the teacher may have to provide some examples, such as, if the game requires the use of one ball, what changes to the game would be necessary if two or more balls were used? How could the rules be changed if three rather than two teams were included in the game? What components would need to be modified to include the active participation of a student in a wheelchair? After the students catch on, they will have several ideas of their own to try. Once everyone agrees on the specific modifications, have them practice their newly designed game. An evaluation session should always follow. What did they like about their new game? What did they dislike? What other alterations would they like to try?

An example of one way to modify a game appears in Table 5-2. In the example, the game of ten pins has been changed to give the students an opportunity for more success, teamwork, and active participation. While the purposes of the game remain similar (knock down the most pins possible), the other components have been changed to better accommodate movement and skill differences. The number of pins has been reduced, the number of balls has been increased, and the dimensions of the lane have been widened and shortened. All players are given the opportunity to work with a partner and continue to roll the ball until all the pins have been knocked down. Players rotate among the stations so that everyone has a variety of opportunities to contribute to their team's accomplishments. A student with a disability who had movement limitations could easily participate at each of the three stations because how to perform the pin setting and ball-return tasks is not specified. Each team could decide how best to modify each of those roles to best accommodate the skill/capability level of each of their team members. A little thought and creativity on the students' parts can go a long way in increasing the sensitivity, enjoyment, and satisfaction of all of the team members. These are critical lessons that, once learned, will positively impact the quality of these students' and others' lives long after they have left the protective school environment.

This approach has been used successfully with middle and high school students. It is a major focus of the physical education curriculum in use in the seventh and eighth grades at Cal Young Middle School in Eugene, Oregon.[36] In an attempt to increase student participation and involvement in physical education, it was decided to try the games analysis approach. After gaining the support and approval of the administration and parents, the physical education teachers implemented the program to foster cooperation, creativity, and involvement of all the students. Students in the physical education classes were required to use a group approach to modify traditional games for the purposes of (1) maximizing the features of the game the students liked and minimizing those they did not like, (2) practicing the skills of the game, and (3) including students of all ability levels. For each of the traditional game units in the curriculum (i.e., softball, volleyball, soccer, etc.), teachers divided the class into equal teams, making a special effort to balance ability levels within each group. The

Name	Purposes	Players	Movements	Objects	Organization	Limits
Original Version						
Ten Pins	Compete	5 per team	Walk to line	10 pins	Teams	Lanes 8 ft wide
	Cooperate	3 players	Roll balls	1 ball per team	Line	Foul line 20 ft from
	Sportsmanship	1 player	Sets pins	Score sheet	One at a time	pins
	Reliability	1 player	Returns ball after	Pencil		Roll 2 balls each
	Team scoring most		player rolls 2			1 point per downed
	points in 20 rolls		balls or knocks 10			pin
	wins		pins down			Can't count ball if
						step on or over
						foul line
Changes						
Down Pins	Hit all pins	6 per team	Stand still	6 pins	Teams	Lanes 12 ft wide
	Cooperate	2 players	Roll 1 ball at a time	4 balls per team	2 at line	Foul line 15 ft from
					2 by pins	pins
					2 behind pins	
					One ball at a time	
	Help team down all	2 players	Set pins after all	Score sheet	Rotate to new posi-	Count only number
	pins		are downed		tion after 2	of times all pins
					downs	are down
	Compete	2 players	Return balls after 6	Pencil		Two players roll 1
	Attentive teamwork		pins are down			ball at a time un-
						til 6 pins are
						downed
	Team scoring most					Can't count pins hit
	strikes in 4 min-					if step on or over
	utes wins					foul line

groups, once formed, selected a team name that was positive and then proceeded to analyze the sport to determine the components of each of six categories.

After identifying the components of the game, the students listed things each of them liked and disliked about the game, and discussed and decided on ways to modify the game and the rules to better meet their needs and objectives. Modifications were expected to preserve the basic movements of the game (i.e., hitting, catching, throwing), yet accommodate the students' individual likes, dislikes, needs, and different levels of ability. Every aspect of the game could be altered, and all students, regardless of ability level, were given the option of using any modification the team members had agreed on.

Before beginning to play the game, each student selected his or her own objectives to achieve in the sport.

Afterward the students determined the extent to which those objectives were met (Figure 5-5). Student evaluations of their ability to meet their own objectives were not part of the class grading system.

During any given unit there could be as many as five different versions of the same sport being played in one class. When each team was satisfied with the game they had created, they presented it to the rest of the class.

Teachers reported that after the initial period of uncertainty and confusion, the vast majority of students embraced and enjoyed the process. Teachers also reported that they, personally, grew in their ability to admit to not always having the "right" answers and to trust the students' abilities to make good decisions and evaluate their own progress.

Self-Evaluation—Softball Unit

_____   _____
(First and last name)   (PE period)

Please rate yourself on the following questions. The rating scale is 1 (low) to 10 (high). Indicate which number best represents your contributions to your softball group. Your teachers hope that you will honestly evaluate yourself because this evaluation is not a part of your point total for the softball unit. The purposes are to have you see if you used your time constructively and in a positive manner for this 3-week instructional unit.

1. I gave some suggestions toward our team name. _____
2. I made a sincere effort to write down my own individual "likes and dislikes" about softball. _____
3. I contributed my ideas toward the game that we taught the class. _____
4. I understood most of the rules to the game that our group taught the class. _____
5. I thought I presented positive ideas and thoughts to my group. _____
6. I got along with the people in my group. _____
7. I became more acquainted with some people in my group that I did not know very well before we did the softball unit. _____
8. I tried to listen to other people's opinions in my group. _____
9. I was willing to try the new games that my classmates made up. _____
10. I became more aware of people's abilities and limitations. _____
11. I was willing to see adaptations made for people who needed some extra help when it came to practicing the skills of softball. _____
12. I learned to become more tolerant of my classmates' limitations. _____
13. I learned that if we can make modifications to the regular game of softball, we can have better participation by the entire class. _____
14. I have increased my awareness that everyone in my class has certain abilities and limitations when it comes to playing softball. _____
15. I would like to participate in another unit of instruction using some of the same ideas that were tried in the softball unit. _____

Please state the one thing you "liked the most" and "disliked the most" about the softball unit of instruction.

figure 5-5
Self-evaluation—softball unit. (Courtesy L. Temple and J.D. Kelly, Eugene, Ore.)

Individually selected modifications

One of the primary goals of education is to guide students toward taking the responsibility for making and following through on responsible decisions; physical education is an ideal setting for teaching students how to reach this goal. When students are provided with basic information about the value of an active lifestyle through well-designed courses and are given opportunities to make individual selections in the high school physical education program, there is a better chance that they will select activities they like and are motivated to succeed with. It is particularly important to include a va-

riety of opportunities to learn activities that are available in the community. When instruction is provided in activities students can engage in after leaving the school setting, they are more likely to make informed decisions and stay active throughout life.

An important step in ensuring that students develop the skills and knowledge needed to participate in community activities is teaching individual students how to analyze and adjust to the demands of specific game tasks. Physical education teachers should work with their students with disabilities to help them develop their ability to analyze the demands of activities that are included

advanced instruction, conditioning, and/or game modifications will be required to maximize their opportunity to participate successfully with their classmates. Game modifications appropriate for specific types of disabilities are addressed in those respective chapters.

Enhancing Instruction in Inclusive Settings Through Computer Technology

The single most significant advance in the science and art of teaching is the computer. Computer technology has made it possible for educators to open the world to learners.[27] In addition, computer technology has made possible computer-assisted instructional management and computer-assisted instruction. Computer-assisted instructional management is particularly important in the field of physical education, wherein teachers commonly have large caseloads. It is also particularly valuable to the adapted physical educator who is held accountable for the learner's progress toward specific goals and objectives.

There are a number of computer programs that have been developed to help physical educators generate IEPs. One of the best is the Observation, Analysis, and Recording System (OARS), developed by Luke Kelly and marketed by MAZE products.* This computer program assists the educator in the collection and maintenance of information regarding a student's performance. This is particularly valuable when the portfolio assessment process is used. An IEP generator, created by Barry Ankney and marketed by EBSCO Curriculum Materials,† allows the educator to create files of goals, objectives, and activities for students.

Word Processor

Word processors can be used to write and generate assessment reports, write weekly and/or daily lesson plans, maintain behavior records, maintain a record of skill acquisition, and generate communications with parents and other school personnel.[17]

The process of describing the results of assessments and evaluations, critical in effective adapted physical

effective format for recording and then reporting information.[30] The process of writing the evaluation report is made even simpler when phrases used often are saved for reuse in macro files. For example, the evaluator might save the phrase, "The Ohio State University SIGMA is a criterion-referenced instrument, validated by the wealth of research/literature on the process of normal and abnormal motor development." The evaluator can use a simple key stroke combination to write this statement instead of having to retype it each time it is used.

The word processor can also be used to manage the instructional process. For example, curriculum materials can and should be written and updated via computer programs. This provides an opportunity for constant and ongoing revision of curriculum, which prevents the curriculum from becoming stagnant.

Database

Database programs can be used to maintain student records, including demographic data, height and weight records, and physical fitness and motor performance scores, as well as to maintain a list of the child's medications. In addition, database programs can be used to organize information about equipment, music, or games (Table 5-3). These can be valuable as the physical educator makes decisions, for example, about the type of games that would be appropriate for a particular child, with a particular objective. Information stored in the database can be retrieved for easy use by the physical educator.

The American Alliance for Health, Physical Education, Recreation and Dance markets a database management program named "Physical Best," which stores individual information regarding physical fitness. A similar product, "Physical Education FIT-N-DEX" by Cramer Software Group,* also allows physical educators to enter students' fitness scores and print profiles and summaries regarding performance.

Many database programs are integrated with statistics and/or graphics packages that can convert data from

---

*8 Randolph Court, Charlottesville, VA 22901.
†P.O. Box 1943, Birmingham, AL 35201.

*P.O. Box 1001, Gardner, KS 66030.

Sample "Window" of Database of Music for Young Children

Song	Album	Author	Area	Level
All part of you	Activities and	Stallman	Body Ident	1
Walk don't run	Activities and	Stallman	Locomotor	1
Your body	Activities and	Stallman	Body Ident	1
Jello	Aerobic dances	Glass	Imitation	2
Kangaroo	Aerobic dances	Glass	Body awareness	2
Bouncing back	Aerobics for	Stewart	General	1

an already-existing file into, for example, bar, line, or pie graphs. Or, data can be analyzed statistically by merging scores maintained within the database with "canned" statistical packages that can do things as simple as compute means and standard deviations or complete more sophisticated analyses of variance.

Spreadsheet

Spreadsheet programs can be used to monitor grades, keep significant records of use of instructional time, or maintain an operating budget. For example, a spreadsheet can be used effectively to give the instructor an accurate report of curriculum areas addressed, activities selected for remediation, the number of minutes spent on a given area (e.g., equilibrium or body image), and the total percentage of time devoted to the areas emphasized.

Special Programs

The Apple "Newton" MessagePad can be used as part of an ongoing portfolio assessment process. With this hand-held computer the teacher can readily add data to behavioral checklists and to formal assessment instruments, and can rapidly store data (translated in the teacher's own writing) for later assimilation into an individual student's portfolio.

Computer technology can be used to translate any document you send home to parents into several different languages. A software package titled, "Language Assistant" translates Spanish, in particular, for Windows, Macintosh, and DOS. There are also interactive programs that allow teachers to learn to speak Spanish, for example.

Software such as "Printshop" can create banners, posters, and notes that can be used to motivate, generate interest, and inform students, parents, and members of the greater school community regarding the adapted physical education program. This type of software usually includes a wide selection of graphics that can be generated on the computer. This same type of program can be used to create overhead transparencies for classroom lecture.

Software such as "Certificate Maker" allows the teacher to create sophisticated certificates to thank students, parents, other school personnel, and community personnel for their support. Printing these certificates on paper that looks like parchment allows a framed copy to be a handsome gift or token. This is particularly important in the development of a strong inclusion network—thanking people for their help goes a long way toward strengthening their commitment.

Software exists that makes it possible for students and teachers to create excellent school newspapers. The software helps the user create columns, headings, and banner headlines like a real newspaper. An adapted physical education—or inclusion—newsletter that highlights student success is an excellent way to communicate program development. As always, names cannot be shared without parent/student permission.

CD-ROM computer technology allows teachers to save, on a CD, videos of children moving, playing, and dancing. It allows teachers to save pictures of children involved in play activities. It allows teachers to save audiotapes of children reporting their movement successes. See Chapter 10 for more information about the portfolio assessment process.

These computer games—golf, tennis, football, baseball, etc.—allow even a child with limited movement potential to play with a peer. Programs such as "Maniac Sports" allow a student who is confined to bed the opportunity to experience hang gliding, mountain climbing, and downhill skiing vicariously. For example, a learner in the last stages of Duchenne muscular dystrophy may have only limited control of one hand. With that hand the learner can manipulate the joystick. This type of software also exists for high school students studying the human body and the way it works.

State-of-the-art technology allows physical educators instant access to other professionals through systems such as Quick Net, America Online, and the Internet. Communication capability is constantly expanding, and the physical educator who will participate in the professional world of the third millennium must be familiar with such technology.

Grading (Marking) Children with Disabilities in an Inclusive Setting

A grade in any subject should promote educational goals and should reflect educational aims and objectives. For programs to be most effective, established objectives must indicate the desired goals of instruction so that they become the criteria on which grades are based. If the criteria are valid, successful measurement will result in valid evaluation. The grade, if one desires to translate behavioral performance, could reflect how well these criteria have been met.

The complexity of grading physical education classes is magnified when an attempt is made to evaluate the performance of students with disabilities. The one common denominator among all students is the mastery of individual performance objectives. If students are graded on the basis of how well they meet their IEP objectives, a student with poor posture, a student with a cardiac disorder, an obese student, and a student who has just had surgery can all be properly evaluated for their grades in the class.

The following criteria might be applied to students to determine how well they have met objectives in the adapted physical education class:

1. *Performance:* The standard of performance in ref-

tensity of work for cardiac and postoperative students

2. *Persistence:* Accomplishment of individual performance objectives determined in the IPEP

Suggestions for recording and computing the grade are as follows:

1. Since the grade may involve some subjective judgments on the part of the instructor, the student should be observed and graded many times throughout the semester (daily or weekly).
2. Numerical ratings (recorded on the exercise card and in the roll book or on a class spreadsheet) can be given to the student; in this way the student and the instructor are always aware of the student's progress toward stated behavioral objectives.
3. These numerical grades can be averaged and then should be considered, along with other factors that may influence the final grade (knowledge examinations and health factors, if they are considered), to determine the final mark for the semester.
4. Objective measurements should be used to test skill and knowledge.

Collaboration and Inclusion

The collaborative process, one in which two or more professionals share responsibilities, and subsequently thoughts and ideas, is often a difficult one for educators. It is particularly distressing to some professionals when the necessity for collaboration is thrust on them by programs, such as "inclusion," or by administrators. Always, the most successful collaborations are those that spring from grassroot, teacher-based efforts and that emerge naturally as professionals learn to trust each other and themselves.

According to Giangreco, Baumgart, and Doyle[14]:

> The inclusion of students with disabilities in general education classrooms can serve as a catalyst to open classroom doors and change staffing patterns so that teachers can build collaborative alliances with other teachers and support personnel in order to have ongoing opportunities to engage in professional dialogue, problem solving, and various forms of co-teaching.

The adapted physical educator and the special educator, those with special training in pedagogy designed to meet the unique needs of learners with disabilities, may contribute their unique skills to the collaborative process. The roles of the adapted physical educator and special educator are listed in the box below.

The adapted physical educator must work in close cooperation with regular physical education personnel who are providing services to children with disabilities in the regular physical education class. The physical educator may assume several roles in the capacity of delivering services to children with disabilities. Whatever the role, it is clear that an organizational system needs to be developed that coordinates the efforts of aides, volunteers, and special and regular classroom teachers who deliver services, as well as itinerant and resource room teachers if they are involved in the program.

Specific job descriptions, such as those provided in this chapter, are vital to the collaborative process. Shared responsibility necessitates significant communication and specific delineation of responsibilities. Regular, ongoing team meetings are necessary if this type of communication is to work. In addition, there must be a way for team members involved in the collaboration to communicate with others regularly. Many teachers have found shared lunch periods and/or common planning periods to be good times to discuss common problems and to create solutions.

Maguire[22] noted that there are four types of skills necessary for collaboration between educators in the school setting:

1. Exchanging information and skills
2. Group problem solving
3. Reaching decisions by consensus
4. Resolving conflicts

Exchanging Information and Skills

All professionals involved in collaboration must be able to share information and skills in a nonthreatening, nurturing way. As is true of all collaborative efforts, a teacher who is confident of his or her ability is delighted to share and receive information and skills from others. While this type of information sharing can be accomplished in formal, in-service training experiences, often the most effective information sharing occurs in small doses as professionals work together on an ongoing basis. This type of mutual learning occurs when teachers learn from watching another's behavior (modeling), observe another teacher's portfolio assessment, and share assessment/evaluation data.

Group Problem Solving

Historically, teachers have had their own, autonomous classroom or gymnasium. Decisions made within their room have been made independently. Collaborative teaching necessitates that teachers learn to make group decisions and solve problems together. The skills required for group problem solving include:

- Identifying the problem
- Stating the problem
- Listing solutions
- Comparing solutions
- Deciding on the solution to the particular problem

Reaching Decisions by Consensus

Although it is a more time-consuming process than making decisions by a vote, the collaborative process necessitates that all team members feel comfortable with group decisions. To reach consensus requires open and

Special Roles of the Adapted Physical Educator and Special Educator

1. Assess/evaluate learners with disabilities.
2. Provide diagnostic/testing information for other educators.
3. Develop an individually designed educational program to meet each student's unique needs.
4. Modify activities to meet each student's unique needs.
5. Develop specific behavior management plans.
6. Coordinate instruction in regular education and special education settings.[39]
7. Provide input regarding grading and retention or promotion.[39]
8. Plan for transfer of skills from the special education environment to the general education setting.[39]
9. Direct small-group or individual instruction in general education classes.
10. Team teach in regular education classes.
11. Direct preteaching and postteaching experiences to prepare for and review material.
12. Communicate with parents of students with disabilities.

tion and needed to determine how best to use the money to serve its students, the teachers (and in the best educational environment, the students, too) would meet together to discuss and prioritize needs. Together, all involved would come to a decision that all could accept.

Resolving Conflicts

As is true of any human community, conflicts may arise among members of that community. Teachers involved in a collaborative effort may find that there are times when disagreements occur and conflicts arise. One of the most important aspects of a collaborative effort is the willingness of those involved to address disagreements and conflicts openly and honestly. Left to fester, or left unaddressed, disagreements and conflicts will grow out of proportion. This type of open discussion requires professionals who are secure in their own skills and competencies. In the event that professionals cannot solve a dispute by themselves, a negotiator may be required to help find resolution.

The Consultancy and Inclusion

Impetus toward inclusionary practices in adapted physical education has drastically and dramatically changed the nature of adapted physical education in the schools and, at the same time, the nature of services provided by the adapted physical educator. Many adapted physical educators have been thrust into the role of consultant. Once placed in that role, concerns these individuals express include:

- The unique and specific needs of students with disabilities cannot be met in the regular physical education program, particularly in large classes, regardless of the nature of support provided.
- I have spent thousands of hours preparing to teach learners with disabilities and now I have to depend on others (who are usually not nearly as committed or well trained) to provide services.
- I am responsible for assessment and implementation of an IEP, and if I'm lucky I see the student and am able to monitor progress once a month.
- I fear that when I am not in the building, the program I designed is not being implemented and my student has been relegated, once again, to watch-

that I need to help my students don't care about them and don't want them in their classes.
- Because I am not an active presence in the lives of my students, I can't possibly make a difference in the quality of their lives.

For many physical educators specially trained to provide services to children and adults with disabilities, the process of changing roles from direct service provider to that of consultant has been difficult. Thrust into the often unwanted role, the adapted physical education consultant must create an educational environment that can be maintained without daily supervision. The responsibilities of the adapted physical education consultant, in an "inclusive" through an "intensive" educational environment, are included in Table 5-4. The regular physical educator can indeed provide an excellent program for students with disabilities if their adapted physical education consultant provides the following services:

- Assessment and evaluation of motor performance
- Evaluation of the learning environment
- IEP development
- Grading modifications
- Curriculum modifications
- Activity modifications
- Behavior management strategies
- Communication skills
- Provision of specialized equipment

With this type of comprehensive support, a student with disabilities may be able to learn and thrive in the regular physical education setting, and the regular physical educator will be willing to serve children with special needs.

In the event that the student is unable to participate successfully without additional personnel support, the adapted physical education consultant may play a crucial role in the creation of a successful inclusion program. The adapted physical education consultant can:

1. Create a personnel support program.
2. Identify student needs.
3. Determine the least intrusive personnel continuum that will meet the student's needs (e.g., a peer buddy is much less intrusive than a full-time paraprofessional).
4. Develop a training program.

table 5-4			
Levels of Service Delivery—Adapted Physical Education Consultancy			
Levels of Intervention	Purpose of Intervention	Relationship to Educational Environment	Implementors
Level 1: Inclusive	Evaluate motor performance and placement options. Provide consultation: IEP development Grading modifications Curriculum modifications Activity modifications Behavior management techniques Communication skills Provision of specialized equipment	Student will receive physical education in a regular program.	Physical educator
Level 2: Inclusive with support	Evaluate motor performance and placement options. Assist or provide training for support personnel. Provide consultation: IEP development Grading modifications Curriculum modifications Activity modifications Behavior management techniques Communication skills Provision of specialized equipment	Student will receive physical education with support in a regular program.	Physical educator with support from: Peer buddy Teacher's assistant (student) Volunteer Paraprofessional Related service personnel Adapted physical education specialist
Level 3: Intensive	Evaluate motor performance and placement options. Assist or provide training for support personnel. Team teach or provide one-on-one instruction.	Student will receive physical education in a staff-intensive (low student-teacher ratio) program.	Adapted physical education specialist with support from: Paraprofessional Related service personnel Classroom teacher

5. Write specific job descriptions for support personnel.

It is vital that important communication be established with the principal, teachers, and parents of students with and without disabilities if a successful student support program is to be implemented. Specific strategies to follow when initiating student support programs in physical education are presented in the box on p. 145. In addition, communications with building personnel are a vital part of this process. Ongoing communication (Figure 5-6) helps a teacher feel like part of an important effort.

Creating concise job descriptions may be the single most important part of the consultancy process. Specifically, a job description allows the adapted physical education consultant to ensure some quality control; it helps maintain accountability. The job description should include specific task requirements, dates/time involved, the extent of responsibility, the hierarchy of authority, and allowance for "storms." Sample job descriptions used in a large, urban school district adapted physical education consultancy are presented in Figures 5-7, 5-8, and 5-9. Each job description is written in very different terms, using different language depending on whom

gram be used as a reinforcer for good work in the classroom. For example, those students who had turned in homework assignments each day of a given week would be given the opportunity to serve as "peer buddies" or "student assistants" in the following week.

3. Secure permission of parents of students without disabilities in order for them to participate in the program. Outline potential benefits of participation in the program for students involved:
   a. Opportunity to learn responsibility
   b. Opportunity to assume a leadership role
   c. Chance to interact with children with different needs and abilities
4. Schedule a preservice orientation meeting for all teachers, students, and their parents. Include:
   a. A description of the program
   b. Roles/responsibilities of all involved
   c. Characteristics of children with disabilities (use empathy experiences)
5. Provide in-service training for all teachers and students involved in the program. Invite parents to attend as well.
6. Develop a specific schedule for each classroom teacher whose children will be involved in the program.
7. Plan ongoing in-service education during each class period. Spend a few moments before each class reminding the student support personnel of their roles and responsibilities.
8. Informally evaluate the performance of the student support personnel; provide positive feedback whenever possible.
9. Honor the student support personnel at the end of the year in the student award assembly. NOTE: The greater the student perception of program importance, the greater the participation.

MEMO

To: Mary Nelson, Aurora King, and Kim Le
From: Jean Pyfer, Adapted Physical Education Consultant
Re: Older Student Assistant Program
Date: August 30, 1996

I would very much like to continue the Adapted Physical Education Student Assistant Program that was so successful last year at Albert Sydney Johnston Elementary School. I appreciate your cooperation in the program and hope that it will continue to flourish and grow.

During this year, I would like to involve your fifth graders as student assistants in the adapted physical education program. There are, still, a number of students who need their IEP goals/objectives to be met in a class with a small student-teacher ratio. In addition, a number of students can participate in ™regularʃ physical education with minimal support from an older student. Your students help provide a vital ™extra pair of handsʃ and, in the process, learn some valuable skills.

Please find below a schedule for the semester and the number of students who would be of help.

Developmental Center Class Play room	MWF	9-9:40	2 students
Support for 1 student with spina bifida Gymnasium	TThF	1-1:40	1 student

The criterion for selecting the student(s) that participate on any given day will always be yours. I would ask, however, that you create an environment in your class so that participation in this project is considered to be a reward for good behavior and completion of class work.

I look forward to working with you again. I'll be in touch soon.

figure 5-6
Memo sent to classroom teachers by an adapted physical education specialist serving as a consultant in a large, urban district. As in all illustrations, the names and dates have been changed to protect confidentiality.

Job Description: Peer Buddy

Peer buddy: Molly Pyfer
Student: Cole
Physical education teacher: Dave Auxter
Physical education: Monday, Wednesday, and Friday,
8:00 to 8:45 AM

Every time your class goes to PE:
1. Walk behind Cole in line. Take his hand if he starts to get out of line. Ask him, "Cole, walk with me, please." If he says, "No," drop his hand.
2. Sit next to Cole in the gymnasium.
3. Follow Mr. Auxter's directions so Cole can watch you and learn from you.
4. If Cole is not doing what the class is doing, tell Cole, "Watch me."
5. During free play, ask Cole, "Will you play with me?" If he says, "No," leave and go play with other friends.
6. If Cole does play with you, tell him, "I like playing with you, Cole."
7. If Cole hits, spits, or tries to wrestle with you, leave him and tell Mr. Auxter.

figure 5-7
Job description for a peer buddy for a second grader with Down syndrome.

Job Description: Physical Education Volunteer

Volunteer: Beth Ann Huettig
Students: Alex, Talitha, Lashundra, and Jesus
Physical education teacher: Jean Pyfer
Physical education: Tuesday and Thursday, 10:10 to 10:50 AM
- Provide instructional support for Alex, Talitha, Lashundra, and Jesus.
- Please use the following strategies for encouraging appropriate behavior:
  1. Praise the child if "on task."
  2. Praise another child, in close proximity, who is "on task."
  3. Remind the child verbally regarding the task. For example, "Alex, we are all doing warm-ups now"; *or* "Alex, I'd like you to join the other children and do your sit-ups."
  4. Physically assist the child with the task. For example, sit down next to Talitha and help her hold onto the parachute handle.
- If the child demonstrates "off-task" or disruptive behaviors after using the four steps, request the teacher's assistance.
- Beth, remember you are responsible solely to me. If one of the children is abusive or aggressive, please let me intervene.

figure 5-8
Job description for an adult volunteer in an elementary physical education program.

---

it is written for. It is vital that the information in the job description be shared verbally, as well, for the support person who is unable to read. A translator may be required to communicate the components of the job description to a student, volunteer, or paraprofessional who uses a language not used by the consultant.

The job description can be used informally, as a simple method of communicating with support personnel. If it is determined that the job is not being done well—that is, the student with disabilities is not being served well, several options exist, including:

1. Evaluate job performance in relation to the job description and provide supervisory support. Revise the job description if necessary.
2. Find another peer buddy, older student assistant, or volunteer.
3. Use the job description as a type of contract and

ask school personnel to sign the contract in front of the building principal.

The essence of the adapted physical education consultancy is communication. An example of a letter written to motivate, as well as inform, a regular physical education teacher who is serving students with disabilities in the regular class is presented in Figure 5-10. This type of letter is extremely effective for building cooperative teams with school personnel because it is personal and it compliments the physical education teacher. This is particularly important in school settings in which the teachers feel unempowered. A consultant who is willing to take the time to thank and honor a teacher for his or her service to students with disabilities will have created

Contained Classroom, Carthage Middle School
From: Jean Pyfer, Adapted Physical Education Consultant
Responsibilities for: Alejandro Moreno
Physical education: 11:00 to 11:50 AM every day

- Allow Alejandro to wheel himself to the gymnasium every day. Please leave 5 minutes before passing time so that Alejandro will not be late.
- Please watch quietly as Alejandro does his modified warm-ups with the class. Please note that his exercises are posted in the coach's office on the back of his door. He knows his exercises, but he may "pretend" he doesn't to avoid them.
- As the class begins their group activity, please use another student (one who hasn't dressed for activity) to work on skills with Alejandro. For example, if the class is playing basketball, demonstrate to the student how to bounce pass to Alejandro. Carefully monitor the activity to ensure that his peer is not too rough.
- When the class begins laps at the end of class (outside or inside), Alejandro should start his as well. At the beginning of the year, he was able to roll 2 times around the gymnasium in 10 minutes. Build, please, throughout the year by adding 1 lap per month. I would like him to be able to roll 6 times around the gymnasium in 10 minutes. Reward good effort with the football cards I gave you.
- You are responsible for Alejandro's safety and well-being in the gymnasium. If you have difficulty with his behavior, call me and we will develop a specific behavior management plan. If he has a "bad" day (swearing, refusing, etc.) report it to his classroom teacher.

figure 5-9
Job description for a paraprofessional for middle school physical education.

a strong program supporter. The letter also provides a summary and review of communication that is important documentation of one's program and efforts. Copying the letter to the physical educator's principal and any other administrative "higher-ups" is reinforcing to the teacher. In addition, it provides the principal and the

remembering to take the time to thank school personnel who serve students well. A simple handwritten or computer-generated thank-you note is a marvelous tool for reinforcing good efforts and developing a team of individuals willing to serve students with disabilities. Perhaps most effective is a note, voice tape, or work of art created by the student (with the help of the classroom teacher or art teacher) to thank his or her peer buddy, older student assistant, volunteer, or paraprofessional. This type of thank you is also very important for the regular physical educator. Samples of notes sent to paraprofessionals who really served children well are presented in Figures 5-11 and 5-12. Sending a copy to building principals and area special education coordinators enhances their impact.

One of the most difficult aspects of the adapted physical education consultancy is being accountable for one's actions and for the supervision one has provided to school personnel. Job descriptions, letters that outline responsibilities and summarize conversations, correspondence regarding support personnel programs, and copies of thank-you notes help document efforts. As important, the adapted physical education consultant must:

1. Keep a copy of original assessment data, as well as the written report shared with the IEP committee.
2. Attend as many IEP meetings as possible. There is simply no substitute for face-to-face communication with parents, regular educators, building personnel, and related service personnel.
3. Keep a copy of the IEP and carefully document visits to campus sites to monitor achievement of goals/objectives.
4. Maintain careful logs that document:
   a. Direct student contact, including the date, length of time spent with the student, and the purpose on that date (e.g., assessment, team teaching, or modeling teaching behavior)
   b. Time spent in consultancy, including the date, length of time spent in collaboration, the personnel with whom you consulted, and the purpose on that date (e.g., modifying grading,

Dave Auxter
Physical Education Teacher
Lincoln Elementary School

September 1, 1996

Dear Dave,

Thank you for the *wonderful* work you do with our special children. I consult with hundreds of physical education teachers in the district, and I believe you to be among the very best. Your classroom management, organization, and commitment to *really teaching* movement skills is exemplary.

I so appreciate the special place your have in your heart, and the special place you have made in your classes so that our atypically developing children can be included with their peers. You provide a safe, nurturing, and consistent environment in which they can learn and enjoy movement and play. You have embraced the notion that all our children have a right to be educated . . . and you do it so well.

Dave, I wanted to provide a written review of our collaboration regarding some of the special children attending Lincoln Elementary School and what, if any, modifications are needed for them to continue to thrive in your physical education program.

Juan Garcia

Please continue to allow Juan to use the modified warm-up exercises he used last year. His weight gain over the summer prevents us from increasing the number of repetitions/resistance in his exercises. Juan knows you and knows what you expect, and I believe he will have another good year with you. His behavior seems much improved—in the gym and the classroom. As always, any encouragement is vital. [Note for readers: Juan has spina bifida and uses a wheelchair for ambulation.]

Chuck Nelson

As we discussed, Chuck has Duchenne muscular dystrophy, a disability associated with ever-increasing loss of muscle tone and strength. At present, Chuck has particular difficulty getting up from a sit and moving into a stand. In addition, he has problems with stop/start activities and those that require a rapid change in direction.

In addition, Chuck is beginning to have difficulty maintaining an erect sitting posture, and this may adversely affect his ability to assume the cross-legged/cross-armed sitting position you ask of your students during your introduction and between warm-up exercises. As you begin your "heart healthy" runs and other physical fitness components of your program, please be aware that Chuck will fatigue easily. He tries very hard to do what his peers do . . . and does not like to be singled out because of his disability.

Lucy Anderson

Lucy's classroom teacher, Ms. Joslyn, has very wisely chosen to gradually introduce Lucy into the physical education program. Actually, movement is one of her particular strengths—she does not have a gross motor delay at this point, typical of children with Down syndrome. She was successful in her kindergarten physical education program at Washington Elementary School and should experience more success here because of the gradual introduction to your program, smaller class size, and your wonderfully structured program.

The one time she is likely to experience difficulty is during free play . . . I'd be grateful for an extra eye on her.

Jason Washington

It's hard to believe Jason is really in the fifth grade. He should continue to participate in regular physical education during warm-up activities, skill-learning sessions, and free play. If, however, your class is going to engage in activities like dodgeball, team basketball, or team soccer, Jason must return to his class. Ms. Joslyn is aware of this and will welcome him back. [Note for readers: Jason is a learner whose movements are characterized as "awkward" and "clumsy". He has a severe learning disability. His mother overfeeds to "reward" him and, subsequently, he also struggles with obesity.]

Dave, if I could clone you, I could retire. If only I had teachers like you all over the district to serve our children.

Please know I have nominated you as the Elementary Physical Education Teacher of the Year in the Texas Association of Physical Education, Recreation and Dance. If you are selected . . . and I expect that . . . I trust we will celebrate.

Yours,

Emily Unger
Adapted Physical Education Consultant
XXX Public Schools

cc: *Catherine Smith,* Principal, Lincoln Elementary School

figure 5-10
Letter written to motivate and inform a regular physical education teacher serving students with disabilities.

Thank you, Thank you, Thank you.

We
would not have been able to
participate in the
community-based swimming program
without your help!

Much love,

Ernesto,
Juan,
Sharonda,
&
Glenn

Dr. Carol says "you are an angel!"

cc. Mr. Garcia, Principal, Caillet Elementary School

figure 5-11
"Thank-you" note sent to a paraprofessional who accompanied four wheelchair-enabled children to a community-based swimming program and assisted in the locker room. The children signed the thank-you.

with the student's physician and/or related service personnel

5. Be visible on the local school campus on the day you are delivering service. In addition to signing in at the office, make a point of speaking to the building principal, office secretary, the child's regular and/or special educator, and the physical educator.

6. If the student has made progress or accomplishes a goal/objective, be certain to send a note home to the student's parent, and leave copies with the child's regular and/or special educator and the physical educator.

7. Keep transportation logs to verify campus visits.

One of the unique difficulties associated with the consultancy is demonstrating, in a systematic way, the efficacy of your program and the effect it has on the lives of students with disabilities. As more and more school districts and school systems demand accountability of their staff members, the responsibilities of the consultant become more clear—the consultant must keep and maintain a "paper trail" to document service delivery.

Transition

The activities and skills learned in the physical education class should be applicable to community leisure and

MEMO

To: Sharon Black
From: Carol Huettig, Adapted Physical Education Consultant
Subject: Deundrae Bowie, Dunbar Learning Center
Date: December 1, 1996

I can't thank you enough for your efforts on Deundrae's behalf. He is so lucky to have you as a mentor and friend. Your willingness to provide him with special help has truly enhanced the quality of his life. His dribbling skills have really improved, as has his ability to maneuver his wheelchair.

I thank you, once again, for your professionalism, dedication, and concern for your students.

cc: Mr. Moore, Principal, Dunbar Elementary School
      Dr. Pittman, Area Coordinator

figure 5-12
"Thank-you" memo sent to a paraprofessional.

recreation activity. The intent of the physical education program from kindergarten through the senior year of high school must be to prepare all students, particularly those with disabilities, for a life enhanced and enriched by quality leisure and recreation experiences.

According to Dattilo and Jekubovich-Fenton[8]:

> The trend toward inclusive leisure services focuses attention on participants' strengths as opposed to weaknesses, thus providing all participants—including people with mental retardation—with choices of age-appropriate recreation activities in which they can participate with their peers.

Active participation in leisure and recreation activities after leaving the school-based setting is only effective if the student has had the opportunity to learn, while in school, the skills needed to function with success in the community.

Because few school districts hire therapeutic recreators to help in the transition process, the role of the adapted physical educator and regular physical educator becomes ever more important. Krebs and Block[21] outlined the eight responsibilities of the adapted physical educator in the transition process, which are summarized in the box at right.

A model inclusive leisure, recreation, and sports program, Promoting Accessible Recreation Through Networking, Education, Resources and Service (PARTNERS), has demonstrated success in providing transition from rehabilitation services to a community-based leisure, recreation, and sports program. The multidimensional program includes the following components:

- *AIM for Independence—activity instructional program:* The quality instructional program is designed to give individuals with disabilities and their families and friends an opportunity to explore a variety of activities, including skiing, scuba diving, canoeing, kayaking, waterskiing, stunt kite flying, sledge hockey, and weight training.
- *Equipment rental program:* The specially designed equipment necessary for an individual with a disability to participate in some leisure and recreation activities is often prohibitive financially. PARTNERS makes equipment such as sit-skis, bi-skis, and mono-skis available for rental.
- *Sports development program:* While providing a youth sports development program, PARTNERS is designed particularly to be sensitive to groups of individuals with an interest in a particular activity.

Transition Responsibilities of the Adapted Physical Educator

1. Identify accessible community-based resources and programs in which an individual with a disability would be made welcome.
2. Provide instructional and technical support to personnel within local leisure and recreation facilities.
3. Analyze the environments in which learners could participate in leisure and recreation programs and identify specific skills required for participation. These include gaining access to the facility, making choices regarding participation, skills required to prepare for the activity (changing into swimwear, for example, and using a locker), equipment necessary for participation, and motor skills and fitness levels required to participate.
4. Determine levels of support required (see Figure 5-1 for least restrictive environment continuum alternatives).
5. Identify personnel who may be available to provide support.
6. Participate actively in the individual transition plan (ITP) meeting.
7. Implement the program.
8. Conduct ongoing program evaluation.

Data from Krebs P, Block M: *Adapt Phys Act Q* 9:305-315, 1992.

For example, if a number of individuals wish to explore winter camping, the staff mobilizes to provide needed instruction and to help find accessible facilities and necessary equipment.

- *Education and advocacy:* PARTNERS provides education and advocacy to enhance the likelihood that an individual with a disability who chooses to participate in a leisure, recreation, and sports program will be extended the hospitality and welcome that any individual has a right to expect.

The Denver Parks and Recreation Program provides a program titled Transition to Recreation Activities in the Community (TRAC) in which a certified therapeutic recreator provides direct services and support to individuals making a transition from a hospital or rehabilitation program into the community.

It is only through a comprehensive school-based

a successful transition into the community as an active participant, making independent choices regarding activities that meet his or her needs.

Inclusion in Leisure, Recreation, and Sports

The Americans with Disabilities Act of 1990, P.L. 101-336, has expanded the federally mandated accessibility requirements of Section 504 of the Rehabilitation Act of 1973. The findings of Congress included the following[2]:

- Some 43,000,000 Americans have one or more physical or mental disabilities, and this number is increasing as the population as a whole is growing older.
- Historically, society has tended to isolate and segregate individuals with disabilities, and despite some improvements, such forms of discrimination against individuals with disabilities continue to be a serious and pervasive social problem.
- Discrimination against individuals with disabilities persists in such critical areas as employment, housing, public accommodations, education, transportation, communication, recreation, institutionalization, health services, voting, and access to public services.
- Individuals with disabilities continually encounter various forms of discrimination, including outright intentional exclusion; the discriminatory effects of architectural, transportation, and communication barriers; overprotective rules and policies; failures to make modifications to existing facilities and practices; exclusionary qualification standards and criteria; and segregation and relegation to lesser services, programs, activities, benefits, jobs, or other opportunities.

In essence, the Americans with Disabilities Act of 1990 expands the mandates of Section 504 of the Rehabilitation Act of 1973. That law indicated that no individual can, solely on the basis of a disability, be denied access to publicly supported facilities and programs. The Americans with Disabilities Act of 1990 expands that to include privately owned public facilities. The law states that:

owns, leases (or leases to), or operates a place of public accommodation.[2]

In addition, the law mandates that individuals with disabilities should be able to participate in the programs and activities of the public facility in the most integrated setting appropriate to the needs of the individual. A reasonable accommodation must be made to ensure access. A reasonable accommodation may include modifications of rules and policies, provision of assistive devices, or provision of support personnel.

However, despite federal and state mandates regarding access to community leisure, recreation, and sports programs, many adults with disabilities do not participate in recreation activities. Sands and Kozleski[34] asked 131 adults without disabilities and 86 adults with disabilities to complete a survey that addressed their perceived quality of life. Their findings regarding participation in recreation activities were frightening:

- Thirty-five percent of adults with disabilities had not attended a movie in the past year (compared with 5% of adults without disabilities).
- Eighty-three percent of adults with disabilities had not participated in a community group in the past year.
- Eighty percent of adults with disabilities had not gone to an athletic club in the past year.
- Sixty-four percent of adults with disabilities had not attended a live theatre performance in the past year.
- Sixty-four percent of adults with disabilities had not attended a music performance within the community in the past year.
- Fifty-eight percent of adults with disabilities had not attended a sporting event within the community in the last year.

Four hundred and thirty-four athletes participating in Wheelchair Sports USA, U.S. Association for Blind Athletes, and U.S. Cerebral Palsy Athletic Association national competitions completed a survey addressing disability-related problems that made it difficult for individuals with disabilities to participate in sports.[12] The athletes identified the following non–medically oriented problems: lack of transportation, lack of equipment or equipment failure, lack of support personnel (guides), and difficulty with orthotics or prostheses. They identified the following medically oriented problems: general medical problems, pressure sores or skin breakdown, difficulties with medication, and seizures.

While these data point dramatically to the obstacles to participation, widespread changes have occurred in leisure, recreation, and sports programs to increase the participation of individuals with disabilities. One of the most dramatic results of the emphasis on inclusion of individuals with disabilities in all public programs and facilities can be seen in the efforts of the National Park Service and the U.S. Forest Service to provide opportunities for individuals with disabilities to use and enjoy the programs and opportunities offered in the national parks.[11] The national parks listed in the box below are accessible to individuals with disabilities.

Brasile[5] addressed the development of leisure and recreation skills of adventitiously injured individuals, within a social context. He suggested that an individual with a new physical disability moves through a series of developmental stages toward total social reintegration and participation in integrated leisure, recreation, and sport activities. He suggests that the individual participates before the injury in "typical life course participation." Immediately following the injury, the individual may participate in leisure, recreation, and sport activities for the primary purpose of postinjury rehabilitation. Then, the individual may participate in parallel activities, such as wheelchair basketball, amputee golf, or Paralympic track and field. In the last stages of recovery, the individual may be involved in total social reintegration that includes participation in integrated or "inclusive" leisure, recreation, and sport activities.

The Amateur Sports Act of 1978 (P.L. 95-606) encourages the integration of persons with and without disabilities in sports competition. The U.S. Olympic Committee provides assistance to amateur athletic programs for inclusion of individuals with disabilities in training and competition programs with individuals without disabilities. This theme is also expressed in the Rehabilitation Act of 1973 (P.L. 93-112) and the Education for All Handicapped Children Act of 1975.

In some cases integration requires creative strategies. Special Olympics International has developed several creative programs designed specifically to enhance integration of individuals with and without disabilities into sports programs. The Partner's Club Program is designed to encourage high school–age students to seek coaching certification and to be actively involved as coaches of athletes who are mentally retarded. The Unified Sports Program is designed to foster the integration of individuals with and without disabilities into training and competition programs by matching participants on the basis of age and ability. Then, children with and without disabilities can train and compete together, being mutually dependent on each other for the outcome of the

National Parks Accessible to Individuals with Disabilities

Denali National Park and Preserve
Grand Canyon National Park
Death Valley National Monument
Sequoia National Park
Mesa Verde National Park
Rocky Mountain National Park
Everglades National Park
Gulf Islands National Seashore
Mammoth Cave National Park
Blue Ridge Parkway
Prince William Forest Park

Data from Ellis W: *Sports n' Spokes* 17:47-51, 1992.

Canoeing in the wilderness can be enjoyed by individuals with all levels of physical abilities. (Courtesy American Canoe Association, Springfield, Va.)

pate in integrated play with their peers in public school physical education programs.

Part of the growth of leisure, recreation, and sports programs is due to an increased desire of individuals with disabilities to participate in leisure and recreation activities and to their willingness to serve as self-advocates in finding resources and programs that will address their needs.

One of the major developments in leisure and recreation programs nationally is the trend toward participation by individuals with and without disabilities in programs with an emphasis on outdoor, environmental experiences. The Breckenridge Outdoor Recreation Center in Breckenridge, Colorado, is known for exceptional wilderness programming for challenged individuals. It is based on the philosophy that:

> There is therapeutic value in wilderness programming. Wilderness adventures can be strong tools for attitude changes and psychological growth . . . providing experiences that bring out the best of the human spirit . . . the real mission has to do with empowerment; instilling in participants the sense that who they are and who they can be is a product of their own hand, heart, and vision. Climbing, backcountry travel, and survival training are not ends in themselves. Rather, such activities are methods to attain other goals.[23]

The innovative program includes the following winter activities: downhill and cross-country skiing, sit-skiing, mono-skiing, helicopter skiing, ice sledding, winter camping, backpacking, solo trips, and ropes courses.

More and more community-based leisure and recreation programs are being made available to individuals with disabilities. The most promising of these are programs that encourage individuals with disabilities to participate with individuals without disabilities. Wilderness Inquiry II of Minneapolis, Minnesota, has a model program that includes wilderness canoeing, backpacking and hiking, cross-country skiing, and dog sledding. Wachtel,[40] a participant in Wilderness Inquiry II, described his experience as follows:

> This type of trip is really at the cutting edge of recreational experiences. Most trips that include disabled people are trips that do for people; decisions are made for disabled people, and disabled people are cared for and allowed to have an experience. This trip, as an integrated trip, was not a care-for trip, it was a do-with trip. It was a trip with disabled people.

foot, jumping, and trick skiing. Adventures, Inc., has developed a balloon basket customized and certified to fly passengers with disabilities. The Vinland Center has developed a comprehensive program for children and adults with disabilities. Vinland's programs are whole person in nature and focus on wellness, positive lifestyles, fitness, and productivity.

The Wisconsin Lion's Camp focuses on the development of individual competency through the use of a challenging "in the trees" ropes course, rock climbing, and aquatic activities. Other camping-based programs focus on the unique needs of the chronically ill child. Camp John Marc Myers, for example, in Bosque County, Texas, has been designed to give children with special health needs the chance to learn new skills, form peer relationships, and develop greater independence and self-esteem. Camp John Marc Myers is based on the following philosophy[6]:

> Chronic disease and physical disability can rob children of the chance to just be kids, leaving them to spend the precious years of their youth watching from the sidelines. In lives that are filled with doctors, hospitals, and the painful awareness that they are not like other children, the chance to be a 'normal' kid is rare. Going away to camp gives children with special health needs that chance. The feeling of freedom experienced through camping provides an invaluable opportunity for these children to overcome preoccupation with illness and feelings of isolation.

Other programs offer children with disabilities the opportunity to learn more community-based leisure and recreation skills. Kathy Corbin's "Never Say Never" program is a nonprofit organization that teaches golf to physically challenged individuals. The National Amputee Golf Association provides clinics in local schools or community centers to teach golf skills and golf-teaching skills to those with amputations. The U.S. Tennis Association has a series of clinics that they offer in the public schools to teach beginning tennis to children with and without disabilities. The American Wheelchair Bowling Association works in close cooperation with the American Bowling Association to develop integrated bowling leagues.

Some colleges and universities offer sports camps for children with physical disabilities. Ball State University in Muncie, Indiana, the University of Texas at Arlington, and the University of Wisconsin–Whitewater are known for their children's sports training camps.

SUMMARY

The whole process of providing adapted physical education services has changed dramatically since the advent of the Regular Education Initiative (REI) and the move toward provision of services in the regular physical education program. Many adapted physical educators fear that the widespread inclusion of students with disabilities in the "regular" physical education program will seriously compromise the education of students with disabilities. There are, however, strategies and procedures that can be used to ensure that appropriate services are provided.

Physical educators deeply committed to providing quality adapted physical education services have to cope, adjust, and create new collaborative and consultative procedures for providing services in inclusive settings. Careful preparation, communication, and documentation are needed for the process to work.

Review Questions

1. What is the regular education initiative? How does it impact the placement of students with disabilities in educational settings?
2. What are the seven components of the least restrictive environment continuum included in this chapter? How could they be used to determine the placement of a student with disabilities in physical education?
3. How can the least restrictive environment design matrices included in this chapter be used to evaluate appropriate physical education services for a student with disabilities?
4. What techniques and strategies does an adapted physical education consultant need to facilitate the inclusion process?
5. What does the term *inclusion* mean?
6. What are the characteristics of an inclusive, community-based leisure, recreation, and sports program?
7. What factors can be considered when grading a person with a disability who is being served in an inclusive physical education setting?

Student Activities

1. Describe where Billy Bogg would fit on the least restrictive environment alternatives continuum. Provide a rationale for your selection.

2. Write a job description for a peer buddy assigned to work with Billy in an inclusive physical education class.
3. Interview a parent who is adamant about "full inclusion" and a parent who prefers his or her student to be educated in a safe and secure "special education" program. Compare.
4. Evaluate a physical education setting to determine if it is appropriate for a student with disabilities to be included in the regular physical education program.
5. Write a job description for an older student (fourth grade) who will be assisting a first grader who uses a wheelchair for ambulation in the regular physical education program.
6. Develop a list of empathy experiences that a professional might experience in preparation for including a student with a disability in the regular physical education program.

References

1. All children belong, *Except Parent,* pp 43-46, July 1994.
2. Americans with Disabilities Act of 1990, PL 101-336, Alexandria, Va, 1991, National Mental Health Association.
3. Armstrong RW, Rosenbaum PL, King SM: A randomized controlled trial of a 'buddy' programme to improve children's attitudes toward the disabled, *Dev Med Child Neurol* 29:327-336, 1987.
4. Belka DE: Let's manage to have some order, *J Phys Educ Rec Dance* 62:21-23, 1991.
5. Brasile F: Inclusion: a developmental perspective. A rejoinder to "Examining the concept of reverse integration," *Adapt Phys Act Q* 9:293-304, 1992.
6. Camp John Marc Myers, Special Camps for Special Kids, Dallas, Tex.
7. Clark G, French R, Henderson H: Attitude development of physical educators working with the disabled, *Palaestra* 1:26-28, 1986.
8. Dattilo J, Jekubovich-Fenton Q: Trends: leisure services for people with mental retardation, *Parks and Recreation,* pp 46-52, May 1995.
9. Decker J, Jansma P: Physical education least restrictive environment continua used in the United States, *Adapt Phys Act Q* 12:124-138, 1995.
10. Downs P, Williams T: Student attitudes toward integration of people with disabilities in activity settings: a European comparison, *Adapt Phys Act Q* 11:32-43, 1994.
11. Ellis W: Accessible camping in the national parks, *Sports n' Spokes* 17:47-51, 1992.
12. Ferrara M et al: A cross-disability analysis of programming needs for athletes with disabilities, *Palaestra,* pp 32-42, Fall 1994.
13. Gallagher J: The pull of societal forces on special education, *J Spec Educ* 27:521-530, 1994.

..... *learning: a practical guide to empowering students and teachers,* Baltimore, 1994, Paul H Brookes Publishing.

16. Heumann J, Hehir T: *Questions and answers on the least restrictive environment requirements of the Individuals with Disabilities Education Act,* US Department of Education, Office of Special Education and Rehabilitative Services, Nov 23, 1994.

17. Huettig C, Reinhardt A: A joint university and public school commitment to adapted physical education, *Palaestra* 2:23-26, 1986.

18. Kauffman J: The regular education initiative as Reagan-Bush education policy: a trickle-down theory of education of the hard-to-teach, *J Spec Educ* 23:256-278, 1989.

19. Kauffman JM, Hallahan DP, editors: *The illusion of full inclusion,* Austin, Tex, 1995, PRO-ED.

20. Kelly L: Preplanning for successful inclusive schooling, *J Phys Educ Rec Dance,* pp 37-39, Jan 1994.

21. Krebs P, Block M: Transition of students with disabilities into community recreation: the role of the adapted physical educator, *Adapt Phys Act Q* 9:305-315, 1992.

22. Maguire P: Developing successful collaborative relationships, *J Phys Educ Rec Dance,* pp 32-36, Jan 1994.

23. Mobley M, Marlow P: Outdoor adventure: a powerful therapy, *Palaestra* 3:16-19, 1987.

24. Morris GS, Stiehl J: *Changing kids' games,* Champaign, Ill, 1989, Human Kinetics

25. Mosston M, Ashworth S: *Teaching physical education,* New York, 1994, Macmillan.

26. National Association for Sport and Physical Education: *Moving into the future: national physical education standards: a guide to content and assessment,* St Louis, 1995, Mosby.

27. Rademaker B, Shirer W, Stocco D: *Project communicate: computer aided instruction for handicapped students,* Mosinee, Wis, 1990, Mosinee School District.

28. Ratliffe T, Ratliffe L, Bie B: Creating a learning environment: class management strategies for elementary physical education teachers, *J Phys Educ Rec Dance* 62:24-27, 1991.

29. Reinhardt A: *Computer assisted instruction and management in adapted physical education,* A working draft of the Wisconsin Department of Public Instruction Adapted Physical Education Curriculum, 1992.

30. Reinhardt A: Personal communication, 1994, adapted physical education specialist, Stevens Point (Wis) Area Public Schools.

33. Sailor W: Special education in the restructured school, *Teacher Remed Spec Educ* 12(6):8-22, 1991.

34. Sands D, Kozleski E: Quality of life differences between adults with and without disabilities, *Educ Train Ment Retard Dev Disabil* 29:90-101, 1994.

35. Shanker A: Inclusion and ideology, *Except Parent,* pp 43-46, Sept 1994.

36. Temple L, Kelly JD: *Break the rules: everyone plays.* Presentation at the American Alliance of Health, Physical Education, Recreation and Dance convention, Portland, Ore, 1995.

37. Stein J: Total inclusion or least restrictive environment? *J Phys Educ Rec Dance* 65(12):21-25, 1994.

38. Theodorakis Y, Bagiatis K, Goudas M: Attitudes toward teaching individuals with disabilities: application of planned behavior theory, *Adapt Phys Educ Q* 12:151-160, 1995.

39. Voltz D et al: Collaborative teacher roles: special and general educators, *J Learning Disabil* 27:527-535, 1994.

40. Wachtel L: Thoughts on a wilderness canoe trip, *Palaestra* 3:33-40, 1987.

41. Will M: *Educating students with learning problems—a shared responsibility,* Report to the secretary, Washington, DC, 1986, US Department of Education.

42. Williams N: The physical education hall of shame, part 2, *J Phys Educ Rec Dance,* pp 17-20, Feb 1994.

43. *Winners all: a call for inclusive schools,* Report of the National Association of State Boards of Education, Study Group on Special Education, Alexandria, Va, Oct 1992.

Suggested Readings

The Canadian National Education Steering Committee of the Moving to Inclusion Initiative has developed a series of booklets that address inclusion techniques for use with students with the following disabilities: amputation, cerebral palsy, hearing impairment, intellectual disability, multiple disabilities, physical awkwardness, visual impairment, and wheelchair use. These booklets, which were published in 1994, are available through the Canadian Association of Health, Physical Education, and Recreation, 1600 Promenade James Naismith Drive, Gloucester, Ontario K1B 5N4.

Facilitating Learning

Objectives

Differentiate between behavior management techniques for reducing disruptive behaviors in a group setting versus with individuals.

Describe the techniques that can be used to identify behaviors that need to be learned or changed.

Describe three intervention strategies that can be used to facilitate learning a new skill.

Explain a contingency management program.

Give three examples of techniques to facilitate generalization.

Identify two ways to determine the effectiveness of generalization.

Task

As you read this chapter, think about the off-task behaviors that Billy Bogg demonstrated during his testing session (see Chapter 2). Try to anticipate ways Billy's behavior might disrupt a regular physical education class if he were included, as well as specific strategies a teacher could use to lessen or eliminate those behaviors.

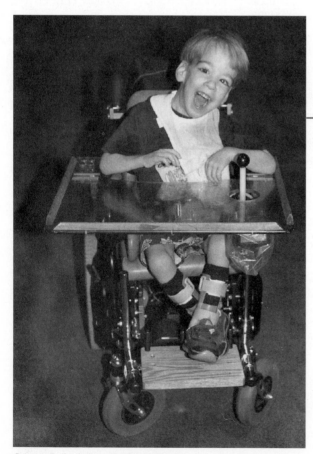

Courtesy Dallas Independent School District.

The benefit of physical education programs can be maximized if acceptable principles of learning and development are applied to instruction. Teachers of children with disabilities bear the responsibility for ensuring that learning takes place. In the past, teachers often were assigned to children with disabilities on the basis of tolerance or because they enjoyed working with these children. The physical education programs that

teachers not only must enjoy their work, but also must be masterful at designing educational environments that promote maximum learning. Maximizing learning involves the ability to generalize skills from the instructional settings to functional use in natural, integrated community environments.

Teachers of learners with disabilities must be able to test children, interpret test results, write appropriate long-range goals and short-term objectives that lead to those goals, and apply principles of learning, development, and behavioral strategies that contribute to classroom learning. In addition to these skills, the teacher provides patterns of behavior for the child to copy. From their teachers, immature children learn how the environment works and how persons cope with changing environments.

Teachers must be emotionally stable, flexible, and empathetic toward atypical behavior while encouraging learning. To best understand what the child with a disability is experiencing, teachers must be sensitive enough to perceive the importance of even the slightest change in the child's behavior. This degree of understanding provides a medium through which a child may better understand his or her own behavior and then modify it. This is no easy task. Being in contact with anxiety-provoking persons often stretches the teacher's emotional capacities. Some of the behaviors that teachers often tolerate are implied rejection from the child and conflicting demands, which range from demanding that immediate needs be met to severe withdrawal, aggressive tactics, and immature behavior.

Teachers who work solely with normally developing children may be unaccustomed to the many behaviors demonstrated by students with disabilities. If inclusion is going to succeed, teachers must understand and accept the behavior patterns of atypical children while designing and implementing programs that ensure learning progress. The best defense a teacher has is knowledge of what is occurring coupled with teaching and behavioral strategies to move the child beyond present levels of educational performance.

The research on the effectiveness of behavior management techniques in improving learning is impressive; however, its use in applied settings is not as widespread as it could be. There is a significant need to incorporate what is known about behavior management systematically in American schools.

Behavioral management technology provides the teacher with information about how to structure the environment to produce changes in pupil behavior, thus allowing maximum learning to take place. The technology can be used either to teach and maintain physical and motor skills or to lessen or eliminate disruptive behaviors. The general process is the same in both instances; however, certain techniques are beneficial in facilitating step-by-step learning of motor skills, whereas others are effective for managing disruptive behavior.

The physical education teacher should establish learning environments that permit students to be productive. The environment must be arranged to facilitate skill learning and discourage disruptive behavior because disruptive behavior by one student interferes with that student's learning, as well as with the learning of the others in the class. There are several strategies physical education teachers can use to teach skills and manage classroom behavior; however, the most effective intervention programs are based on actual student performance data. Whether one is attempting to identify behaviors or skills that need to be learned or behaviors that need to be changed, the procedure is the same:

1. Identify the behavior that needs to be learned or changed.
2. Select an intervention strategy.
3. Determine an appropriate reinforcer.
4. Consistently reinforce the student's efforts to comply.
5. Reevaluate to ensure that learning or change has occurred.

Identifying Behaviors That Need to Be Learned or Changed

Student performance data can be gathered by using a formal instrument to assess motor, physical, or behavioral performance, or by observing the students as they per-

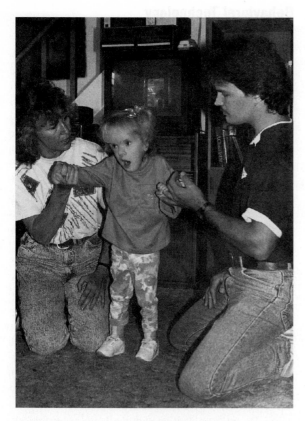

Parents are the child's most important teachers.

form in educational settings. Formal physical and motor assessment instruments are presented in Chapter 2 of this text; formal observational instruments that can be used to identify teacher and student behaviors in educational settings are included in the Suggested Readings at the end of this chapter. Regardless of whether the behavior to be studied involves performance or learning of tasks, or disruptive actions, the data collected must be accurate. If a formal instrument is not used, a measuring system must be developed that clearly identifies the behavior to be observed and enables the observer to systematically gather baseline data about the behavior.

When collecting baseline behavioral data, it is necessary first to select a measurement system and then decide who will observe and how often. Measuring systems available for collecting and recording behavior include the following components:

- **Permanent product recording:** A system that involves counting actual behaviors that are demonstrated
- **Event recording:** The number of times a specifically defined behavior occurs within a time interval (e.g., counting the number of times a student steps away from a line within one class period)
- **Duration recording:** The length of time a behavior occurs (e.g., how long a student can stay on a specific task)
- **Interval recording:** The occurrence or nonoccurrence of a behavior within a specific time interval (e.g., the teacher may observe that Jim was active during only two of the five 1-minute observation periods)

The method selected depends on the type of behavior, the kind of data to be gathered, and the ease of implementation by the observer. The most common behavior measurement systems used in physical education are event, duration, and interval recordings.

Event recording produces frequency data that can be converted into percentages. Percentages and frequencies are appropriate measures for skill behaviors done in blocks of tasks (see box on p. 159). Percentages can be computed by counting the number of baskets made out of 10 shots, or the number of successful kicks out of 5 at a goal in soccer. Frequency data are simply the number of occurrences of the behavior. To compare frequencies, the observation periods should be equal in length, and the student should have the same opportunity to demonstrate the behavior during each observation period. Frequency data can be converted into rate information. Rate is simply the number of times a behavior occurs within a certain time limit, such as the number of times a student is able to set up a volleyball in 20 seconds.

Duration recordings are useful if the length of time a student engages in a behavior is of interest. For example, observers may note the amount of time a student requires to move from one activity to the next or how long a student is active or inactive. Duration can be recorded in actual time limits (e.g., Jack was on task for 5 minutes) or in percentages (e.g., Ralph was active for 40% of the time) (see box on p. 160).

Interval recordings are particularly useful for the regular class teacher because they do not require that stu-

Behavior observed: Objectives completed by Sue on recording sheet
Data reported: Frequency and percentage of short-term objectives completed each day
Time of observation: Individualized skill development and prerequisites; period of the class for 5 periods

Day	Number of Expected Objectives Achieved	Number Completed	Percentage Completed
1	4	(3)	75%
2	4	(2)	50%
3	5	(5)	100%
4	5	(4)	80%
5	5	(3)	60%

Example 2: Simple Frequency

Student ___Jim___   Observer ___Mr. Jones___

Behavior observed: Talk-outs by Jim during instruction by teacher; talk-outs are verbalizations loud enough to be heard by the instructor

Data reported: Frequency of talk-outs and rate of talk-outs per 5 minutes of instruction time

Time of observation: Entire time teacher instructs

Day	Number of Minutes	Number of Talk-Outs	Frequency
1	5	3	3
2	5	2	2
3	5	1	1
4	5	0	0
5	5	0	0

dents be observed continuously. McLoughlin and Lewis[18] have described advantages of this system and several of the different recording systems:

This technique does not require counting or timing behaviors. Instead, the observer simply notes whether or not a behavior is present or absent during a specified time interval. For example, if a teacher is interested in observing staying on task, smiling, or swearing, the classroom day may be broken into short time periods, such as 15- or 5- or 3-minute intervals. One of several variations of interval recording can be used:

1. **Whole-interval time sampling:** The observer notes whether the target behavior occurs continuously during the entire interval. That is, if 5-minute intervals are being used, the observer notes for each interval whether the behavior occurred *throughout the interval.*

2. **Partial-interval time sampling:** The partial-interval method requires only that the observer determines whether the behavior occurs at least once during the interval. That is, if the observation period has been broken down into 20-minute intervals, the observer notes for each interval whether the behavior has occurred at all during that time.

3. **Momentary time sampling:** Observation occurs only at the end of each time interval (see Example 2 in the box on p. 160). That is, if the observation period is broken down into 3-minute intervals, the teacher checks the student only at the end of each interval and notes if the target behavior is occurring at that moment.

Observers must be trained to evaluate and record data accurately and consistently. Peer teachers and aides also can be trained to assist in and monitor the data collec-

Duration Recording

Example: Duration and Percent Data

Student Sue   Observer Jim

Behavior observed: Time working on self-directing task

Data reported: Amount of time (duration) on task; observer starts timing when child moves to learning stations

Time of observation: Five-minute intervals for observational periods during a class session

Day	Time	Number of Minutes	Percentage of Time
1	9:00-9:05	1:00	20%
2	9:10-9:15	1:30	30%
3	9:00-9:05	1:15	25%
4	9:25-9:30	2:00	40%
5	9:20-9:25	3:00	60%

tion. Someone other than the performer (teacher, aide, tutor) observes for only a short period each day; however, it is long enough to obtain an accurate picture of the student's behavior (Table 6-1). The most effective data collection system requires that the students be able to evaluate themselves as to whether they did or did not demonstrate that behavior.

The collected data must be studied by the teacher to determine whether the behavior is effectively contributing to the learning process or deterring learning. If the behavior being observed relates to performance of a skill or learning task, the greater the number of successful occurrences, the better. If the behavior being monitored is disruptive (undesirable), the fewer the number of occurrences, the better (see Example 2 in the box on p. 159).

Selecting an Intervention Strategy to Facilitate Learning

The central purpose of the physical education program is to develop positive physical and motor behaviors that result in improved health and recreational activity. Intervention programs can be used to teach, maintain, or strengthen a new behavior or to weaken or eliminate undesirable behaviors.

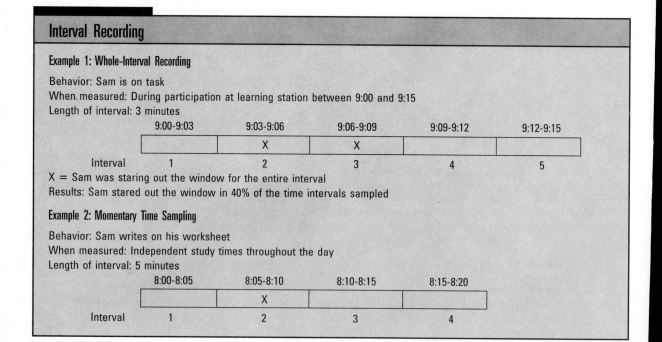

Interval Recording

Example 1: Whole-Interval Recording

Behavior: Sam is on task

When measured: During participation at learning station between 9:00 and 9:15

Length of interval: 3 minutes

	9:00-9:03	9:03-9:06	9:06-9:09	9:09-9:12	9:12-9:15
		X	X		
Interval	1	2	3	4	5

X = Sam was staring out the window for the entire interval

Results: Sam stared out the window in 40% of the time intervals sampled

Example 2: Momentary Time Sampling

Behavior: Sam writes on his worksheet

When measured: Independent study times throughout the day

Length of interval: 5 minutes

	8:00-8:05	8:05-8:10	8:10-8:15	8:15-8:20
		X		
Interval	1	2	3	4

table 6-1			
Measures of Behavior			
Measure	Derivation	Example	Application
Percentage	Number of correct trials out of a block of trials	Seven basketball goals are made out of a block of 10 trials $\frac{7}{10} \times 100 = 70\%$ accuracy	A measure of accuracy without regard for time or proficiency
Frequency	$\frac{\text{Count of behavior}}{\text{Observation time}}$	Pupil tutor feeds back three times in 3 minutes $= \frac{3}{3}$	How often a distinct behavior occurs within a period of time
Duration	Direct measures of length of time	A child is off task for 45 seconds	The total length of time a continuous behavior occurs
Intervals	Number of fixed time units in which behavior did or did not occur	Children are observed for 20 seconds; then the observer records whether the behavior occurred during the interval; observers then repeat the process (usually data are expressed in terms of percentage of intervals during which the behavior occurred) $\frac{4 \text{ intervals}}{10 \text{ intervals total}} \times 100 = 40\%$ of intervals	When behavior occurs over a time frame

The amount of productive behavior being demonstrated is the primary criterion for determining whether an intervention program is needed. To make this decision, the teacher must refer to the student's educational objectives and compare the behavior being demonstrated with those objectives. If a behavior to be learned or maintained is not being demonstrated consistently, an intervention program is needed. If time off task and/or disruptive behavior is occurring to the extent that meaningful learning is not occurring, an intervention program is needed.

When a skill or behavior is being taught, maintained, or strengthened, several techniques can be selected to facilitate the performance. These include modeling, shaping, prompting and fading, chaining, and repetition. Each of these is described here.

Modeling

Modeling refers to demonstration of a task by the teacher or reinforcement of another student who performs a desirable behavior in the presence of the target student. When a teacher actually performs the desirable behavior, he or she is teaching the target student how the task is to be performed. When another student is used as the model and performs a task correctly, the teacher praises the behavior in the presence of the target student. For example, if a teacher wants all the children to maintain a curled back while doing sit-ups, those children who keep their backs curled are pointed out by the teacher and praised while they do their sit-ups. All other children who then perform the task correctly are also reinforced. Modeling can lead to a fairly close approximation of the desired response. Refinement of the response could be done at another time. The model, particularly in motor tasks that are continuous and cannot be broken into component parts, is a very efficient way of promoting learning. Still pictures, movies, or videotapes also may be used. The intent of the model is for the student to imitate the behavior that is demonstrated.

Shaping

Shaping involves the reinforcing of small, progressive steps that lead toward a desired behavior. It is the development of a new behavior through the use of an ap-

Procedures for Shaping a Behavior.

Procedure	Example
1. Define the behavior.	Balancing on one foot with eyes open for 10 seconds
2. Define a reinforcer.	Knowledge of task success
3. Determine the present level.	2 seconds on the task
4. Outline a series of small steps that lead to the desired behavior.	16 increments of ½ second each
5. Advance the learner on a predetermined criterion.	Each step three times in a row
6. Define the success level.	90%

Equine therapy is a creative, nurturing way to facilitate learning and help in the development of psychosocial skills. (Courtesy Texas Special Olympics.)

propriate reinforcer. The technique of shaping is used to teach new behaviors and is particularly valuable in the performance phase of acquiring a skill. When shaping a new motor response, the physical education teacher has the choice of waiting for the learner to demonstrate the next small step toward the goal or helping the learner attain the objective through the use of a physical prompt. In either case, the specifically defined task (step) must be reinforced. The procedures for shaping a behavior are listed in Table 6-2.

Prompting and Fading

Prompting techniques can be included in any behavior management system. Prompting and **fading** involve providing just enough assistance so that the student realizes some success at the task and then gradually withdrawing the help. Usually prompting will enable a successful response or a close enough approximation so that shaping can be used to improve the performance level. Types of prompts include physical, auditory, and visual.

  Physical priming,[1] or prompting, involves physically holding and moving the body parts of the learner through the activity. An auditory prompt may involve clapping the hands or blowing a whistle to gain attention or terminate activity. Visual prompts would involve hand signals that could be used to gain attention and terminate activity, footprints that indicate where one should stand or position the body for a skill, or visual targets.

  Prompting should be used with the idea of elimi-

nating the primers as quickly as possible so that the learner can begin to function independently. A general rule for prompts is to provide no more assistance than is necessary to elicit a successful outcome. Prompts should be reduced (faded) as soon as possible to eliminate the learner's dependence on them. Students should be taught to reduce their dependence on the teacher and increase their ability to function independently. A way of structuring the environment from the most to the least assistance might involve (1) providing a great amount of physical help combined with verbal instruction, (2) providing a lesser amount of physical help combined with verbal instruction, (3) providing demonstration with verbal instruction, (4) providing verbal instruction only, (5) providing visual cues only, and finally (6) having the learner seek the auditory and/or visual cues needed to understand the task and be successful.[30]

  Prompts can be combined with other behavioral management techniques to facilitate the learning of physical skills. One other technique that can be used in combination with prompting is **positive reinforcement.**[10] Combining positive reinforcement with auditory, visual, and/or physical prompts tends to reduce avoidance behaviors.[7]

  Prompts are valuable if the tasks can be quickly learned. If the learner is not able to perform the task in

Examples of Skills Taught by Backward Chaining

Behavior	Task Sequence
Pass receiving in football	(1) Catch pass; (2) run and catch pass; (3) make cut, run, and catch pass; (4) release from line, run, cut, and catch pass.
Tackling in football	(1) Tackle ball carrier; (2) run pattern to intersect and tackle ball carrier; (3) release blocker, run pattern to ball carrier, and tackle ball carrier; (4) administer technique to neutralize blocker, release blocker, run pattern to ball carrier, tackle ball carrier.
Shooting a soccer goal	(1) Shoot soccer goal; (2) dribble and shoot soccer goal; (3) receive a pass, dribble, and shoot soccer goal.
Passing a soccer ball	(1) Pass soccer ball; (2) bring ball under control and pass soccer ball; (3) dribble, bring ball under control, and pass soccer ball.
Leg takedown in wrestling	(1) Take opponent to the mat; (2) secure legs and take opponent to the mat; (3) shoot move for legs, secure legs, and take opponent to the mat; (4) set up move, shoot move for legs, secure legs, and take opponent to the mat.
Fielding a ball and throwing a player out at first base in softball	(1) Throw to first base; (2) field the ball and throw to first base.

a relatively short period of time, the teacher probes through prerequisite components to determine which ones are missing and need to be learned before the skill can be performed.

Chaining

Chaining is a process of leading a person through a series of teachable components of a motor task. Each teachable component represents a discrete portion (link) in a task. When these portions or links are tied together, the process is known as chaining. Some skills can be broken into components and taught by the chaining process more easily than others. Self-help skills are easily broken into parts. Clearly, grasping a spoon is an essential link in the process of eating; however, it is a behavior distinctly different from scooping the food with the spoon or placing the food in one's mouth. Each of these components is a necessary link that must be tied together (chained) to accomplish the skill of self-feeding. Continuous physical skills do not break into discrete teachable components and are difficult to chain. Other physical skills, such as the lay-up shot in basketball, can be broken into discrete components that lend themselves to chaining.

When **forward chaining** is being used, the first step is taught first, the second step is taught second, and so

on, until the entire task is learned. Most teachers use forward chaining when teaching motor and physical tasks.

When the last of the series of steps is taught first, the process is known as **backward chaining.** Teaching a basketball lay-up by means of backward chaining requires that the student (1) stand close to the basket, reach high with the arm, and shoot the basketball; (2) jump from the inside foot, reach high with the arm, and shoot the basketball; (3) run-jump from the inside foot, reach high with the arm, and shoot the basketball; and (4) dribble a ball while running, jump from the inside foot, reach high with the arm, and shoot the basketball. The value of backward chaining is that the individual is reinforced during each step by completing the task successfully.

Self-help tasks, such as tying a shoe and dressing, are easily and effectively taught by backward chaining, as are skills used in team play. Examples of the analysis of these tasks are given in Table 6-3.

Repetition

Repetition is the act of practicing the same physical movement over and over again. Repetition can be varied into massed or distributed schedules. Massed practice occurs all at once, whereas distributed practice sessions are spaced out over a period of several days or months. In general, distributed practice is considered the best technique for promoting learning and ensuring retention of a skill. Repetition can result in overlearning of a target skill, which, in turn, enhances the possibility of generalizing motor and physical skills from a class setting to a community recreational setting.

Intervention strategies for weakening or eliminating disruptive behaviors include techniques that are more effective in group settings and those that focus on specific behaviors demonstrated by an individual. Because reinforcement is intrinsically tied to controlling disruptive behaviors, a discussion about the process is introduced here. Ways to apply reinforcement to weaken or eliminate disruptive behavior follow.

Reinforcement

Reinforcement is a strategy that follows and strengthens a behavior. The discussion that follows focuses on positive reinforcers because they yield the most lasting results. Positive reinforcers include teacher or peer praise, material rewards, activities a student enjoys doing, and success on a task. Positive reinforcement is constructive because it helps individuals feel good about themselves.

Selecting Reinforcers

Reinforcers may be intrinsic (internal) or extrinsic (external). Intrinsic reinforcement comes from within the learner. Often knowledge of success on a task or the satisfaction of participating is sufficient reinforcement. Extrinsic reinforcement comes from outside the learner. Examples of extrinsic reinforcement are praise and other rewards from a person who acknowledges the learner's achievement. One objective of a reinforcement program is to move the learner from dependence on extrinsic reinforcers to seeking intrinsic reinforcers. Once learners no longer have to rely on teachers for feedback, they can direct their own learning. It is important that both the learner and the teachers agree on what the reinforcer will be and how the system of reinforcement will work.

Reinforcement Procedures

Contingency management is a way of controlling the use of reinforcers. A **contingency agreement** is an agreement between the student and the teacher that indicates what the student must do to earn a specific reward. A **token economy** is a form of contingency management in which tokens (external reinforcers) are earned for de-

sirable behavior. This type of system can be used with a single student, selected groups of students, or classes of students. Lewis and Doorlag[15] suggest the following procedure for setting up a token economy:

1. Specify the behaviors that earn tokens.
2. Use tokens that are appropriate for the student.
3. Pose a menu (a list) of the types of available reinforcers.
4. Allow students to suggest reinforcers for the list.
5. Revise the menu regularly.
6. Use a clear record system (of distributing the tokens) that is accurate.
7. Give students frequent opportunities to cash in their earned tokens.
8. The cash-in system should take a minimal amount of time.
9. Provide clear rules to staff and peer tutors for distribution of tokens.
10. Gradually reduce the value of the tokens to increase reliance on more natural reinforcers.

Token economy systems that have proved successful in the physical education program include those that allow students to "cash-in" their tokens to buy the following:

▪ A given number of minutes of supervised free play

Learning to persist in life is more important than winning. (Courtesy Adapted Physical Education Department, Jefferson Parish Public School System, New Orleans, La.)

- The privilege of being the "assistant" teacher for a given class
- The privilege of 5 to 10 minutes of uninterrupted one-on-one play time with the physical education teacher
- The right to eat lunch with the physical education teacher
- A poster of a sports star
- Recreation and sport equipment

Relatively inexpensive recreation and sport equipment can be purchased to support the token economy system. Children love having the privilege to earn jump ropes, balls, juggling scarves, or hackey-sacs. Parent-Teacher Associations often are willing to help with fundraising to help provide the physical education teacher with this type of equipment. There are corporations that have fund-raiser/promotional campaigns (e.g., Campbell Soup Company) that may help the physical education teacher secure this type of equipment without buying it out of an already small budget or an equally small personal salary.

Several examples of different types of reinforcers appropriate for use in school settings are presented in Table 6-4. Social and activity reinforcers have special appeal, since they are usually available at no cost to the teacher.

fully controlled so that the student continues to strive toward desirable goals. The frequency that reinforcers are given is called the **reinforcement schedule** (Table 6-5). Schedules of reinforcement should move from **continuous** (a reinforcer every time the desirable behavior occurs) to a **fixed-interval ratio** (e.g., one reinforcer for every three instances of desirable behavior). The schedule should be changed eventually to a **variable-interval ratio** (e.g., one reinforcer for every three instances of desirable behavior followed by one reinforcer for every five instances of desirable behavior, or one reinforcer every minute followed by one reinforcer every 3 minutes). The variable-interval ratio is the most effective because when students are unable to predict when they will be reinforced, they tend to persist at a task.

Intervention Strategies to Control Disruptive Behaviors

Much of the previous discussion concerns the uses of reinforcement to increase efforts toward learning tasks. Very often, reinforcement procedures are used to decrease undesirable behaviors. The undesirable behaviors must be eliminated or substantially reduced so that the student can focus attention and effort on positive learning habits.

Because of self-concept and attention deficits, children with disabilities may disrupt classrooms and make

table 6-4		
Classroom Reinforcers for Use in a School Setting		
Social-Verbal	Manipulative	Token
Elementary Students		
Hug Positive comments ("Good job"; "That was a nice play") Pat on the back	Helping teacher Being team leader Time in the game center Choosing a game Extra minutes of recess Extra minutes of free-time activity	Paper certificate Stars Positive note sent to parents Medal
Adolescents		
Gesture of approval Handshake Positive comments ("Great job"; "You did it"; "Great effort")	Choosing class activity	Sports equipment Posters Positive note sent to parents T-shirt

table 6-5

Intermittent Schedules of Reinforcement

		Effects on Behavior	
Name of Schedule	Definition of Schedule	Schedule in Effect	Schedule Terminated (Extinction)*
Fixed ratio (FR)	Reinforcer is given after each X responses	High response rate	Irregular burst of responding; more responses than in continuous reinforcement, less than in variable ratio
Fixed interval (FI)	Reinforcer is given for first response to occur after each X minutes	Stops working after reinforcement; works hard just prior to time for next reinforcement	Slow gradual decrease in responding
Variable ratio (VR)	Reinforcer is given after X responses on the average	Very high response rates; the higher the ratio, the higher the rate	Very resistant to extinction; maximum number of responses before extinction
Variable interval (VI)	Reinforcer is given for first response after each X minutes on the average	Steady rate of responding	Very resistant to extinction; maximum time to extinction

From Walker HM: *The acting-out child: coping with classroom disruption,* New York, 1979, Allyn & Bacon.
*See pp. 169-170 for discussion on decreasing inappropriate behavior.

it difficult for themselves and others to learn meaningful motor skills. When behavioral technology is applied to classroom management, it must be systematic, consistent, and concerned with both preventing disruptive behavior and promoting positive behavior. There are two levels of classroom management: one for the group and another for individuals within the group.

Controlling Group Behavior

There are some techniques for managing behavior that are particularly effective for groups. These include positive teacher attitudes, prevention, establishing and enforcing class rules, teacher intervention, flexibility in planning, appealing the values, controlling the environment, and giving students leadership opportunities. Each of these techniques is discussed here.

Positive teacher attitudes have a powerful impact on learning of social behavior and physical skills. Some behaviors a teacher can demonstrate that will motivate a class to perform to their maximum include[25]:

1. Be positive. Students work harder to gain rewards than they do to avoid punishment.
2. Teach enthusiastically. Use a comfortable verbal

pace, varied inflection, and an encouraging tone of voice.
   a. Set realistic expectations. Students will strive toward goals they believe they can accomplish.
   b. Inform students about their progress. Students need to know they are on track and improving.
   c. Reinforce every legitimate effort. Students are more motivated to persist when their efforts are noticed and reinforced.

The single most effective method for controlling behavior is prevention. The most significant technique for controlling behavior is to *"Catch 'em being good!"* This proactive teaching response, in which the teacher consistently and enthusiastically embraces "good" behavior, allows the teacher and the students to focus on "good" behavior. It must be noted that it is crucial that when addressing the behavior of a child or children, the focus is on behavior. When praising a child for good behavior, it is necessary that other children understand that it is the behavior that is being praised, so that those not being praised do not get the unintentioned message that they are somehow "bad." Examples of appropriate responses include the following:

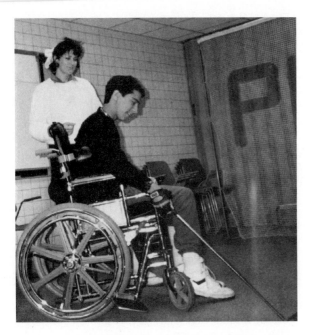

Verbal correction promotes learning. (Courtesy "Never Say Never," Kathy Corbin's Golf for the Physically Challenged.)

- "Juan, thank you for being such a good listener."
- "I really like the way that Thelma is following directions."
- "Carlos, I'm really proud of you for putting your ball away."
- "Way to be, Jason! I like the fact that you shared your toy with Julianna."

This basic good teaching technique of "catch 'em being good" is one of the basic elements of preventive planning, which consists of establishing class rules and enforcing them in the least intrusive ways possible. Rules for class conduct should communicate to students the behavior expected by the teacher. Effective class rules should be (1) few in number, (2) a statement of behavior desired from the student, (3) simple and clearly stated in a positive way, and (4) guidelines that the teacher can enforce. For example, a well-stated rule is: "When lined up at the door waiting to pass to the next class, keep your hands to yourself."

Clearly stated expectations lead to appropriate classroom behavior. They provide learners with rules of conduct and identify behavior that will be rewarded. It is suggested that a list of rules be placed where students can observe it each day. The consequences for breaking rules should also be made clear to the students. These must be posted in the native languages of the children served. For example, if a school serves a large number of Hispanic students, rules and consequences should be posted in both English and Spanish.

When serving young children or nonreaders, rules and consequences must be reviewed before each class period; in some situations, rules and consequences may need to be repeated periodically throughout the class.

Rules cannot take care of every situation; often there is disruptive behavior not covered by the rules. The difficult decision each teacher must make is whether to intervene and stop the disruptive behavior. Teachers have a responsibility to interfere with behaviors that:

- Present a real physical danger to self or others
- Are psychologically harmful to the child and others
- Lead to excessive excitement, loss of control, or chaos
- Prohibit continuation of the program
- Lead to destruction of property
- Encourage the spread of negativism in the group
- Lead to conflict with others outside the group
- Compromise the teacher's mental health and ability to function[28]

If the teacher does decide it is necessary to intervene to control disruptive behavior, several techniques are effective in controlling disturbances. Some specific techniques that have been identified by Redl[23] to manage disruptive students in a physical education setting are as follows:

- **Planned ignoring:** Much of children's behavior is designed to antagonize the teacher. If this behavior is not contagious, it may be wise to ignore it and not gratify the child.
- **Signal interference:** The teacher can use nonverbal controls, such as hand clapping, eye contact, frowns, and body posture, to indicate to the child disapproval and control.
- **Proximity control:** The teacher can stand next to a child who is having difficulty. This is to let the child know of the teacher's concern regarding the behavior.

- **Interest boosting:** If a child's interest is waning, involve the child actively in class activities of the moment and let him or her demonstrate the skill that is being performed or discussed.
- **Reduction of tension through humor:** Humor is often able to penetrate a tense situation, with the result that everyone becomes more comfortable.
- **Hurdle lesson:** Sometimes a child is frustrated by the immediate task. Instead of asking for help, the child may involve his or her peers in disruptive activity. In this event, select and structure a task in which the child can be successful.
- **Restructure of classroom program:** If the teacher finds the class irritable, bored, or excited, a change in program might be needed.
- **Support from routine:** Some children need more structure than others. Without these guideposts they feel insecure. Structure programs for those who need it by clearly defining the rules, boundaries, and acceptable limits of behavior, as well as adhering to the same general routine each day.
- **Direct appeal to value areas:** Appeal to certain values that children have internalized, such as a relationship between the teacher and the child, behavioral consequences, awareness of peer reaction, or appeal to the teacher's power of authority.
- **Removal of seductive objects:** It is difficult for the teacher to compete against balls, bats, objects that can be manipulated, or equipment that may be in the vicinity of instruction. Either the objects have to be removed or the teacher has to accept the disorganized state of the group.

In addition, whenever possible, students should be given opportunities to provide leadership within the class,[22] be given opportunities to select activities,[25] and engage in planning sessions on ways to modify games to include a wide range of student abilities (see Chapter 5).

Handling the Disruptive Student

The behavior problems of special students frequently contribute to their placement in special physical education programs. When special students are placed in the physical education class, teachers are often concerned that their problem behaviors will interfere with the operation of the classroom.

Behaviors that interfere with classroom instruction,

One athlete reinforces another athlete's performance. (Courtesy Achilles Track Club, New York.)

impede social interaction with the teacher and peers, or endanger others are considered **classroom conduct problems.** Examples of inappropriate classroom behaviors are talking out, fighting, arguing, being out of line, swearing, inappropriate use of equipment or facilities, noncompliance, and avoiding interactions with others. Breaking the rules of the game, poor sportsmanship, and immature and withdrawn behaviors also fall under this category. Behaviors that interfere with the special student's motor skill development are considered **skill problems.** Typical skill problems result from poor attending behavior and failure to attempt tasks with a best effort.

Problem behaviors are exhibited in one of three ways: (1) there is a low rate of appropriate behaviors, (2) there is a high rate of inappropriate behaviors, or (3) the appropriate behavior is not part of the student's repertoire. Knowing the characteristics of the behavior is important, since different management strategies are linked to each.

Low rate of appropriate behaviors

Students with **low rates of appropriate behaviors** do exhibit appropriate behaviors, but not as frequently as expected or required. For example, a student may be able to stay on task only 50% of the time. Also, students may behave appropriately in one setting but not another. For instance, the special student may work well on individual tasks but may find it difficult to function in group games. To alleviate these problems, the teacher sets up a systematic program to generalize on-task behaviors from one situation to another. An example of facilitating the generalization of on-task behavior toward functioning in a group setting is to gradually move a student from an individual task to a task that is paralleled by another student, to a task where two students assist each other in being successful (such as taking turns spotting one another during free weight lifting).

High rate of inappropriate behaviors

Inappropriate behaviors that occur frequently or for long periods are troublesome to teachers. Examples are students who do not conform to class rules 30 to 40 times a week, those who talk during 50% to 60% of class instruction, those who use profanity 5 to 10 times in one class period, and those who are off task 70% to 75% of the class period. To overcome these **high rates of inappropriate behavior,** the physical education teacher attempts to decrease the frequency or duration of the undesired behavior by increasing appropriate behaviors that are incompatible. For instance, to decrease the incidence of hitting a peer while in class, the teacher can increase the rate of performing tasks or decrease the time between tasks.

Appropriate behavior not part of the student's repertoire

Students may not yet have learned appropriate behaviors for social interaction or classroom functioning. For instance, they may not know sportsmanship conduct in class games. Teachers must provide instruction to help students acquire new behaviors. Behavior problems do not occur in isolation. Events or actions of others can initiate or reinforce inappropriate behaviors. To understand and manage classroom problems, the teacher should examine the student in relation to the target behavior. For example, classmates who laugh at clowning or wisecracks tend to reinforce that type of disruptive behavior; as a result, the disruptive student continues to exhibit the undesirable behavior.

Students show inappropriate behavior when they have not learned correct responses or have found that acting inappropriately is more rewarding than acting appropriately. These behavior problems do respond to instruction.

Methods for decreasing a student's inappropriate behavior

Several methods for decreasing inappropriate behavior are available. Walker and Shea[28] have proposed the following continuum of behavior modification interventions:

1. **Reinforcement of behavior other than the target behavior:** A reinforcer is given at the end of a specified period of time, provided that a prespecified misbehavior has not occurred during the specified time interval.
2. **Reinforcement of an appropriate target behavior:** A reinforcer is given following the performance of a prespecified appropriate target behavior.
3. **Reinforcement of incompatible behaviors:** A reinforcer is given following the performance of a prespecified behavior that is physically and functionally incompatible with the target behavior.
4. **Extinction:** The reinforcer that has been sustaining or increasing an undesirable behavior is withheld.
5. **Stimulus change:** The existing environmental conditions are drastically altered to ensure that the target behavior is temporarily suppressed.
6. **Nonexclusionary time-out:**
   a. Head down on a desk or table in the work area in which the target behavior occurred.
   b. Restriction to a chair in a separate area of the classroom but able to observe classroom activities.
   c. Removal of materials (work, play).
   d. Reduction or elimination of room illumination.
7. **Physical restraint:** It may be necessary to restrain a child physically if he or she loses control and becomes violent.
8. **Negative practice or satiation:** The target behavior is eliminated by continued and increased reinforcement of that behavior.
9. **Overcorrection:** The repeated practice of an appropriate behavior in response to the exhibition of an inappropriate target behavior.

10. **Exclusionary time-out:**
    a. Temporary distraction: When a student's behavior has reached the point at which he or she will not respond to verbal controls, the student may have to be asked to leave the room (to get a drink, wash up, or deliver a message—not as punishment, but to distract the student).
    b. Quiet room: Some schools provide quiet spaces for students to use when it becomes necessary to remove oneself from a group setting.
    c. In-school suspension.

Consistent Management Techniques

There is consensus that successful schools use systems of firm, consistent management. Research confirms that

Attempting a new skill may require encouragement from a friend. (Courtesy Wisconsin Lions Camp, Rosholt, Wis.)

clearly structured, secure environments permit students to master the objectives of the program. Haring[6] indicates that "teaching . . . necessitates finding a method of instruction which allows the child to learn."

The preconditions for the application of learning principles are that there must be a precisely defined short-term instructional objective, and there must be incentives for the learner to master the objective. If either of these preconditions is not satisfied, the effect of the program is minimized. Effective learning is the result of mutual understanding between the student and the teacher. The student must understand what is expected and the consequences of not performing to expectations. Homme[8] provides nine rules to follow when using behavior management techniques:

1. Praise the correct objective.
2. Praise the correct objective immediately after it occurs.
3. Praise the correct objective after it occurs and not before.
4. Objectives should be in small steps so that there can be frequent praise.
5. Praise improvement.
6. Be fair in setting up consequences for achieving objectives.
7. Be honest and provide the agreed-on consequences.
8. Be positive so that the child may achieve success.
9. Be systematic.

Praise the Correct Objective

To implement this principle effectively, persons involved with instruction (teachers, school administrators, parents, and related service personnel) must know precisely the objective or behavior that the learner is to carry out. That behavior must be praised only if it is achieved. The application of this principle must be consistent among all persons who work with the child.

There are two ways that this learning principle can be violated by a teacher, parent, or school administrator. First, he or she may provide praise even though the objective has not been achieved; second, he or she may neglect to provide praise even though the objective has been achieved. In the first case, the learner is being reinforced for doing less than his or her best and consequently will have a lessened desire to put forth maximum effort on subsequent trials. In the second case, if the teacher does not deliver the agreed-on consequence (explicit or implicit), the student's desire to perform the instructional task again will be reduced.

Praise Immediately After Completion of the Task

Learners need to receive feedback immediately after task performance. Homme[8] indicates that reinforcing feedback should be provided 0.05 second after the task for maximum effectiveness. Immediacy of feedback on task performance is particularly important with children functioning on a lower level. If there is a delay between task performance and feedback, the child may be confused as to what the praise is for. For example, if a child walks a balance beam correctly but confirmation of task mastery is provided late (for instance, as the child steps off the beam), the behavior of stepping off the beam may be strengthened to a greater degree than the desired objective of walking the beam. Thus the timing of the feedback (immediately after the task has been completed) is important.

Praise at the Appropriate Time

If a child is praised for performing an objective before it is completed, there is a good chance that he or she will expend less effort to meet the objective.

Make Sure Objectives Are in Small Steps

If the step size is small, there will be a greater rate of success. As has been indicated, disruptive behavior may be triggered by lack of success. This principle may therefore be applied in attempts to control disruptive behavior in the classroom. Thus if a child often exhibits many different types of disruptive behavior, objectives can be postulated to reduce the occurrence of these disruptive behaviors in small steps. For children with disabilities, learning by small steps permits much-needed success.

Praise Improvement

The acquisition of skill toward an objective should be praised. Providing appropriate consequences for improvement may in some instances violate the principle of praising the correct objective. However, on tasks that cannot be broken into small steps, it is necessary to praise improvement. To do so, the instructor must know precisely the student's present level of educational performance. When the performance reflects an improvement on that level, the student must be reinforced with praise. Improvement means that the learner is functioning on a higher level than before. Therefore it is unwise to praise or provide positive consequences to students

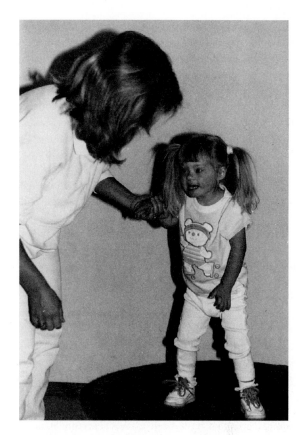

A well-designed home-based motor program greatly enhances motor development.

who perform at less than their best effort, since to do so may encourage them to contradict their potential.

Be Fair in Setting Up Consequences

When there are specific objectives to be achieved to develop skill or appropriate classroom behavior, specific consequences can be arranged to support the development of these objectives. However, if such arrangements are to be made between the learner and the teacher, there must be equity between the task and the incentives. If the learner does not have sufficient incentive to perform the tasks or to behave appropriately, he or she is unlikely to do so. This learning principle operates at very early ages.

In our clinical experience, we set up a target objective for an 18-month-old boy with Down syndrome to learn to walk. The task involved walking from one chair to another, which was placed 8 feet away. If the child walked the full distance, he was allowed to play for 15 seconds with the toys that were placed on top of the chairs. When this period elapsed, he would return to the task of walking a prescribed distance of 8 feet 1 inch, a short distance farther than the previous time. After a time, the child refused to participate in the activity. The child's mother suggested that he be permitted to play with the toys for 30 seconds rather than 15 seconds. This procedure was employed, and the child again engaged in the instructional task. It was inferred that the child would participate in tasks if the opportunity to play was commensurate with the effort put forth to master the objective. In our opinion, this is an example of equity between incentive and performance.

Be Honest

Agreements between teachers and learners must be honored by both. If there is an implicit or explicit arrangement between the teacher and the learner and the teacher does not follow through with the arrangement when the learner has upheld his or her end of the bargain, then the learning conditions will be seriously weakened. It is not uncommon for teachers to inadvertently forget the arrangements that have been made. Therefore it is important for teachers to have records of arrangements between themselves and the learner. Forgetting the preconditions between learner and teacher may have a negative impact on the pupil's learning at a subsequent time.

If the teacher requests that a learner perform a specific task, the teacher must not provide the desirable consequences unless the learner achieves the proper objective. Honest delivery of the agreed-on consequences is similar to praise for the correct behavior. However, praise for the correct behavior usually connotes a specific short-term task, whereas an agreed-on consequence may involve a contractual arrangement between two parties. Principals and teachers who set policies may achieve positive results with the application of this principle.

Be Positive

The objective should be phrased positively so that the learner can achieve the stated objective (e.g., "Walk to the end of the balance beam"). An example of a negative statement is "Don't fall off of the balance beam."

In the negative instance, the child is avoiding failure, and there can be little value in mastering the desired behavior.

Be Systematic

To make the greatest positive impact on children with disabilities, it is necessary to apply all the learning principles all the time. Inconsistency confuses the learner with regard to the material to be learned and the type of behavior to maintain during class. The consistent use of modern behavioral technology enhances a child's ability to learn desirable behaviors. This learning principle is the most difficult one for teachers of emotionally disturbed children to master.

Techniques to Ensure Persistence of Learning or Change

Maintenance is perpetuation of a trained behavior after all formal intervention has ceased. To determine whether a trained behavior is being maintained, it can be formally assessed, observational data can be gathered, and/or individuals who interact with the student can be interviewed. The most powerful indication that behavior has really been impacted and is being maintained is the extent to which the behavior has been generalized to other settings.

Generalization

Generalization is the ability to use a learned skill or way of behaving in places other than the instructional setting. The success of instruction can be measured by the extent to which a learned way of behaving can be used in a variety of practical settings. Such generalization assists with independence and adds to the quality of life for persons with disabilities.

In the past, generalization was an expected, yet unplanned, outcome of instructional programs[26]; however, during the past 20 years generalization has been more systematically planned and evaluated. Studies have documented that generalization of motor skills can be successfully taught. More recently, studies are being conducted to determine the process and variables that control generalization of all types of behaviors to applied settings. LeBlanc and Matson[14] have developed a social training program that helps preschool children with disabilities to generalize behaviors to other social settings. The program uses protocols for modeling, feedback, and time-out from reinforcement. Other instructional packages directed at self-management, self-modeling, self-assessment, discrimination training, and cooperative efforts can be used for physical skill development.[2,17]

Although a number of considerations are a part of the development and application of generalization techniques, two are of paramount importance: (1) the techniques should support the generalization of functional motor skills to nontraining settings, such as recreational environments in the community and the home; and (2) the techniques should be reasonably efficient. *Efficiency* refers to the use of a skill in an applied setting with a minimum amount of training or assistance to produce the desired results. To ensure transfer of learning to applied settings, it is critical that specific generalization goals be incorporated into the severely disabled student's educational program.[24]

Morris[19] describes three types of generalizations: (1) response maintenance, (2) situation or setting, and (3) response generalization:

1. **Response maintenance generalization** includes changes that are maintained even after the behavior modification has stopped.
2. **Situation or setting generalization** includes changes that occur from one environment to another, and/or from one person to another.
3. **Response generalization** refers to changes in behavior that was not targeted for intervention.

Generalization variables

There are two basic forms of generalization in the curriculum content of physical education: (1) generalization of the acquired motor skills and (2) generalization of the cognitive and social dimensions that enable participation with others. Clearly, if the skills of a physical sport (e.g., basketball, soccer, or softball) are acquired but the social skill is inappropriate for participation in culturally acceptable environments in the community, then the person with a disability will not have the opportunity to express the attained skills.[29]

When using generalization procedures, the adapted physical educator should consider the cognitive and social ability levels of the student, the acquired level of proficiency of the target skill, and the features of the natural environment. The cognitive and motivational levels of the individual with disabilities and his or her attitude toward the skill are other dimensions of generali-

zation. Also, it is important to understand the student's attitude toward competition. Some individuals do not enjoy participating in activities where there are winners and losers. If these individuals participate in competitive sports, they may be motivated by focusing on the importance of their contributions to the team effort rather than on bettering their opponents.[4,16]

Considerations for generalization

There are at least two different types of environments associated with the process of generalization. One is the **instructional environment,** and the other is the natural environment. Instructional environments are settings where the education of students with disabilities is of explicit concern. **Natural environments** are those settings where the motor skills that are learned in school are actually used (e.g., community environments). Natu-

When the appropriate intervention strategy is used, every individual can perform to a higher standard. (Courtesy Canadian Association of Athletes with a Mental Handicap.)

ral environments are those in which individuals without disabilities function and in which individuals with disabilities should be taught to function.

To facilitate generalization from educational to community environments, it is recommended that the teacher (1) develop a management system to assess the generalized effect of the motor skill training program in nontraining environments, (2) determine the effects of training on the motor function of persons with disabilities, (3) analyze the ecological variables (i.e., community situations in which the motor skills will be used), and (4) manipulate environmental variables to facilitate the generalization of the use of the motor skills.[29]

Generalization is an important issue for students with severe disabilities because they typically do not learn motor skills sufficiently to enable participation in natural environments. Some persons with disabilities have difficulty generalizing newly learned motor behaviors to other settings, persons, and stimuli because of their limited motor capabilities. It is desirable to establish a comprehensive repertoire of motor behaviors that will permit not only sufficient immediate opportunities for participation in the community, but also motor skills that can be recombined to permit other opportunities to participate in an expanding number of recreational activities in the natural community. Fostering the ability to generalize across similar events in dissimilar settings is essential. A person can be aided in generalizing to new environments if he or she is taught the cues and correction procedures used in natural settings.

Cues and correction procedures

Cues and correction procedures are used to increase the probability that a skill learned in one setting will generalize to a second setting. The procedures range from those that provide maximum assistance to those that offer minimum guidance, and from those that occur exclusively in instructional environments to those that occur exclusively in natural environments.[5] There are three important considerations in the utilization of cues and correction procedures for generalization:

1. Know the cues and correction procedures that non-disabled persons typically use when performing a specific motor skill in the natural environment.
2. Know the specific motor response required to perform the particular skill.

3. Know how to use the environmental cues and correction procedures that shape and develop motor responses.

All three component parts of the instructional process must be fully comprehended, and detailed attention must be given to these three essential aspects of instruction.

Self-Management

Self-management of behavior should be taught to persons with disabilities.[21] The technique requires that the control over behavior be shifted from the teacher or parent to the student. Self-management has been used to teach individuals with disabilities play and social skills, and to lessen disruptive behavior.[12,13] The effectiveness of a variety of self-management procedures has been demonstrated in classroom settings. It has been shown that students can regulate their behavior by selecting appropriate goals; self-instructing; and monitoring, reinforcing, and evaluating responses.[3,9,20] Self-management procedures consist of one or more of the following strategies:

- *Goal setting:* Teaching students to select numerical targets to achieve leads to higher performance than not selecting goals or selecting vague goals.[11,27]
- *Self-instruction:* Teaching individuals to direct their own task performance is critical for independent functioning.
- *Self-evaluation:* Teaching individuals to observe, record, evaluate their performance according to a standard, and reward their own successes promotes ongoing growth and independence.[20]

Learning by Self-Correction

A mode of behaving that contributes to successful independent functioning in the community is learning to **self-correct.** Adults must learn to think about the effectiveness of their behaviors in order to identify aspects in need of change. Obviously, it is necessary that the individual have the cognitive ability needed to reflect on his or her performance and determine where or how errors occurred. The ability to learn by correction varies according to the learner's cognitive capabilities and the complexity of the task being attempted.

SUMMARY

Learning is facilitated and changes in behavior occur when a systematic process is used. New skills and behaviors can be learned and inappropriate behaviors can be diminished when appropriate procedures are followed. First, the behavior to be learned or changed must be identified. Second, intervention strategies and appropriate reinforcers must be selected. Finally, reinforcement must be consistently applied, and change in behavior validated. The maintenance of a learned skill or behavior can be verified through reevaluation in the educational or community setting. The true measure of learning is the extent to which the skill or behavior generalizes across several environments and contributes to independent functioning. The ability to use cues and correction and self-management procedures, and to learn by correction facilitates the process of generalization.

Review Questions

1. What techniques can be applied to maximize student achievement in motor skill development?
2. What are some positive teacher techniques that can be used to adapt instruction to the needs of the learner?
3. Describe some techniques for recording data that extend present levels of performance.
4. Describe the different ways in which performance can be measured.
5. Name and describe some behavioral techniques for facilitating the development of positive behavior.
6. Indicate some principles for establishing class rules.
7. What are some techniques that can be used to manage disruptive classroom behavior?
8. List different types of reinforcers.
9. What are some of the characteristics of a teacher that can maximize the development of motor and social skills for individuals with disabilities?
10. What is generalization, and how does it apply to independent recreational sport and physical activity in the community?
11. What are some principles that may guide the physical educator to generalize the physical education activities learned in a class setting to activity outside of class?
12. How does the appropriate utilization of cues and correction procedures help a person with disabilities to generalize meaningful motor skills learned in physical education instruction?

Student Activities

1. Identify one acting-out behavior Billy Bogg demonstrated (see Chapter 2) that might create problems in a regular physical education class setting and present this behavior to the rest of your class.
2. For each behavior presented in the preceding activity, suggest behavior modification techniques that could be used by the teacher to reduce the potential for Billy's behavior to disrupt the class.
3. Make a list of class rules other than those suggested in this chapter that would minimize disruptive behavior in a physical education class.
4. Set up a contingency management system for a class. Indicate procedures for the administration of the system.
5. Conduct an ecological assessment of the community to determine what activities should be included in physical education programs for individuals with disabilities in your community.
6. Working in small groups, identify possible differences in cues and correction procedures of tasks in the instructional setting and in a natural environment setting.
7. Develop a behavior management checklist and use it while observing a child with a disability participate in a physical education class. Discuss your observations with the rest of your class.

References

1. Bellamy GT, Horner RH, Inman DP: *Habilitation of the severely and profoundly retarded,* Specialized Training Program Monograph No 2, Eugene, 1977, Center on Human Development, University of Oregon.
2. Berg WK et al: A demonstration of generalization of performance across settings, materials, and motor responses with profound mental retardation, *Behav Modif* 19:119-143, 1995.
3. Ellis DN, Cress PJ, Spellman CR: Training students with mental retardation to self-pace while exercising, *Adapt Phys Educ Q* 10:104-124, 1993.
4. Ellis ES: The role of motivation and pedagogy on the generalization of cognitive training by the mildly handicapped, *J Learning Disabil* 19:66-70, 1986.
5. Falvey MA: *Community-based curriculum: instructional strategies for students with severe handicaps,* Baltimore, 1986, Paul H Brookes Publishing.
6. Haring N, editor: *Developing effective individualized programs for severely handicapped children and youth,* Washington, DC, 1977, US Office of Education, Bureau of Education for the Handicapped.
7. Hoch TA et al: Contingency contracting, *Behav Modif* 18:106-128, 1994.

8. Homme L: *How to use contingency contracting in the classroom,* Champaign, Ill, 1970, Research Press.

9. Hughes CA, Korinck L, Gorman J: Self-management for students with mental retardation in public school settings: a research review, *Educ Train Ment Retard* 26:271-291, 1991.

10. Jayne D et al: Reducing disruptive behaviors by training students to request assistance, *Behav Modif* 18:320-338, 1994.

11. Kahle AL, Kelley JL: Children's homework problems: a comparison of goal setting and parent training, *Behav Ther* 25:275-290, 1994.

12. Kohler FW et al: Promoting positive supportive interactions between preschoolers: an analysis of group oriented contingencies, *J Early Intervention* 14:327-341, 1990.

13. Kohler FW et al: Using group-oriented contingency to increase social interactions between children with autism and their peers, *Behav Modif* 19:10-32, 1995.

14. Leblanc LA, Matson JL: A social skills training program for preschoolers with developmental delays, *Behav Modif* 19:234-246, 1995.

15. Lewis RB, Doorlag DH: *Teaching special students in the mainstream,* Columbus, Ohio, 1983, Charles E Merrill Publishing.

16. Licht BC, Kistner JA: Motivational problems of learning-disabled children: individual differences and their implications for treatment. In Torgesen JK, Wong BYL, editors: *Psychological and educational perspectives on learning disabilities,* New York, 1986, Academic Press.

17. Lonnecker C et al: Video self monitoring and cooperative classroom behavior in children with learning and behavior problems: training and generalization effects, *Behav Disord* 20:24-34, 1994.

18. McLoughlin JA, Lewis RB: *Assessing special students,* Columbus, Ohio, 1981, Charles E Merrill Publishing.

19. Morris RJ: *Behavior modification with exceptional children,* Glenview, Ill, 1985, Scott, Foresman.

20. Nelson RJ, Smith DJ, Colvin G: The effects of a peer-mediated self-evaluation procedure on the recess behavior of students with behavior problems, *Remed Spec Educ* 16:117-126, 1995.

21. Nelson RJ et al: A review of self-management outcome research conducted with students who exhibit behavioral disorders, *Behav Disord* 16:169-179, 1991.

22. Pierangelo RA: *A survival kit for the special education teacher,* West Nyack, NY, 1994, Center for Applied Research in Education.

23. Redl F: Managing surface behavior of children in school. In Long HJ, editor: *Conflict in the classroom,* Belmont, Calif, 1965, Wadsworth.

24. Sailor W, Guess D: *Severely handicapped students: an instructional design,* Boston, 1983, Houghton Mifflin.

25. Spodek B, Saracho ON: *Dealing with individual differences in the early childhood classroom,* New York, 1994, Longman.

26. Stokes TF, Baer DM: An implicit technology of generalization, *J Appl Behav Anal* 10:349-367, 1977.

27. Swain A, Jones G: Effects of goal-setting interventions on selected basketball skills: a single subject design, *Res Q Exerc Sport* 66:51-63, 1995.

28. Walker J, Shea T: *Behavior management,* Columbus, Ohio, 1988, Charles E Merrill Publishing.

29. Warren SF et al: Assessment and facilitation of language generalization. In Sailor W, Wilcox B, Brown L: *Methods of instruction for severely handicapped students,* Baltimore, 1985, Paul H Brookes Publishing.

30. Zhang J, Horvat M, Gast DL: Using the constant delay procedure to teach task-analyzed gross motor skills to individuals with severe intellectual disabilities, *Adapt Phys Educ Q* 11:347-358, 1994.

Suggested Readings

Darst PW, Zakrajsek DB, Mancini VH, editors: *Analyzing physical education and sport instruction,* Champaign, Ill, 1989, Human Kinetics Books.

Gardner R et al: *A behavioral analysis in education,* Pacific Grove, Calif, 1994, Brooks/Cole Publishing.

French RW, Henderson HL, Horvat M: *Creative approaches to managing student behavior in physical education,* Park City, Utah, 1992, Family Development Resources.

Jansma P, French R: *Special physical education, physical activity, sports, and recreation,* Columbus, Ohio, 1994, Charles E Merrill Publishing.

Metzler MW: *Instructional supervision for physical education,* Champaign, Ill, 1990, Human Kinetics Books.

part three

Generic Educational Needs

The types of educational needs that can effectively be addressed in physical education settings include motor, physical fitness, and psychosocial developmental delays. In this section conditions that contribute to developmental delays are identified, ways to determine levels of function are presented, and intervention strategies to overcome delays are discussed.

chapter s e v e n

Motor Development Delays

Objectives

Explain the importance of motor development.

Provide examples of how sensory input delays affect movement.

Explain the differences between sensory input systems and abilities.

Discriminate between functional and sport skills.

Describe an example of a content analysis.

Task

Before you read this chapter, review Billy Bogg's motor test results in Chapter 2 and note any motor development delays he demonstrated. As you read this chapter, select three activities for each of Billy's delays that you could include in his physical education program to improve his motor development.

Courtesy Dallas Independent School District.

There is no question about the importance of motor development. In addition to it being a critical component of movement efficiency, it is also widely believed to underlie **perceptual, cognitive,** and **affective function.**[3] How infants' bodies grow and change has been widely studied in this country since 1920. From that time through the 1940s, Shirley, McGraw, and Gesell carefully observed and documented hundreds of **motor milestones** normally developing children demonstrate during their first few years of life. Those observations became the basis for the majority of motor development screening instruments available to us today (see Chapters 2 and 10 for specific screening instruments). Such instruments are frequently used to determine whether an infant is progressing neurologically at the expected rate, because motor milestones are among the first visible indicators of central nervous system maturation. However, even though motor development screening instruments can be used to identify *where* a child is performing in comparison to normal expectations, such instruments do not provide information indicating *what* is interfering with the slowly developing child's progress. That information must be *predicted* from formal sensory input, sensory integration or psychological tests developed specifically for those purposes, or informal clues provided by the child. More direct, absolute measures are, however, under development.

In the closing decade of this century, developmental psychologists, movement scientists, neuroscientists, and others are joining forces to try to build on the work of the early developmentalists to better understand the processes by which infants and children gain mastery over their bodies. Careful studies are being conducted to determine what aspects of nature and nurture are critical for maximal motor development. Advanced technology is being used to identify and monitor factors that impact favorably on a child's motor competence.[3] However, until those intricacies are sorted out, the educator responsible for facilitating motor and physical development must use existing formal or informal techniques to identify and remediate motor development delays that impact movement efficiency.

There is no one test that has been developed to identify all the underlying **neurological components** that contribute to motor competency. Tests are available that have been developed for the express purpose of measuring reflex development, vestibular efficiency, kinesthetic awareness, sensory integration, and perceptual-motor efficiency; however, in every case actual **neurological validity** must be assumed because the technology to verify the truthfulness of the instrument has not been developed or is too invasive to use with humans. If an educator has access to professionals trained in administering and interpreting the formal tests that are available, the assistance of these professionals should be sought. However, in the absence of formal, predictive information, the educator can use informal observational techniques that have been validated clinically by individuals with extensive experience with children who have movement difficulties. Educators can have confidence in these techniques because recently, studies from around the world are verifying what practitioners have been reporting for the past 25 years. That is, individuals with movement problems do indeed process neurological information

differently from the more capable mover. (See the *Adapted Physical Activity Quarterly* cited in the Suggested Readings at the end of this chapter.) To enable a child with motor development delays to move more efficiently, it is imperative that the underlying cause of the problem be identified and remediated.

In this chapter, the types of motor development delays most frequently demonstrated by school-age children with or without diagnosed disabilities are described. (Motor development problems experienced by younger, at-risk children are addressed in Chapter 10.) The material has been organized according to the motor development model presented in Chapter 4. Sensory input system and ability components that underlie sport and functional skills are identified. Clues indicating developmental delay of the components are outlined, and activities to facilitate development in those areas are suggested. A technique for analyzing developmental lags at the skill level is explained. In addition, a sensory input systems screening test that can be used to probe for underlying developmental delays is presented.

Facilitating Motor Development

Physical educators have traditionally included exercises, individual stunts and tumbling, games, sports, rhythmic activities, and gymnastics in their curricula. Often these activities are selected according to teacher bias. More recently, teachers have been sensitized to the need to provide appropriate learning environments for students who demonstrate a wide range of abilities. These teachers are exercising greater care in selecting meaningful activities to include in their programs. Rather than following a set, unchanging curriculum, they are selecting activities based on their learners' demonstrated needs.

Once the evaluation of the learner's needs has been carefully completed and the behavioral objectives clearly stated, the physical educator is ready to select activities that will enable the student to progress. The three most important factors to keep in mind when selecting activities are (1) appropriateness for reaching the specific objectives, (2) adequate practice time to ensure that learning will occur, and (3) modification of the activity to make it increasingly more challenging.

The physical education activities selected depend on whether the teacher is using a bottom, up or top, down instructional strategy. When the bottom, up approach is used, initial attention is focused on the basic input systems followed by domains of abilities. In the following section each of the basic input systems is described, clues that indicate the system is not fully developed are given, and individual activities that will promote development are suggested. Group activities to use to facilitate development of these systems are included in the handbook *Gross Motor Activities for Young Children with Special Needs,* which accompanies this text.

Basic Input Systems

The vestibular, visual, kinesthetic, tactile, reflex, and auditory systems are considered basic input systems because sensations arising from these systems' receptors provide the basic "stuff" from which perceptual-motor abilities and motor skills are built. These systems normally develop during the first 5 years of life. After they are functioning, perceptual-motor and motor skill development occurs. Should any one or a combination of these systems fail to fully develop, all motor development is delayed and/or interfered with in some way.[1,2] For this reason, it is imperative to identify and remediate basic input system delays as early in life as possible. The point at which it becomes too late to attempt to facilitate development of any of these systems is not really known; however, some writers suggest that if such delays are still present at age 12 years, the educator's time might be better spent teaching the child to accommodate to the delay.

Reflexes

Reflexes are innate responses that all normal children develop (Table 7-1). Reflexes that affect movement are of interest to the physical educator because students whose reflex maturation is delayed have inefficient movement patterns. In general, there is a series of reflexes that should appear and disappear during the first year of life. These early (primitive) reflexes are layered over by (integrated into) voluntary movement patterns. As a child begins to move voluntarily, a different set of reflexes appears. These later automatic patterns are equilibrium reflexes. They help maintain upright posture and should remain with us throughout life.

A child would be considered developmentally delayed in reflex development if any of the following conditions existed:

1. The primitive reflexes do not appear during the first year of life.

2. The primitive reflexes appear at the normal time but do not disappear by the end of the first year of life.
3. The equilibrium reflexes do not appear by the end of the first year of life.
4. Equilibrium reflexes do not persist throughout life.

Primitive reflexes. **Tonic labyrinthine reflexes** (supine and prone) help maintain trunk extension when the child is supine and help maintain trunk flexion when the child is prone. If either of these reflexes does not become integrated, the following movement problems will be exhibited:

1. Supine
   a. Difficulty doing sit-ups
   b. A tendency to extend the trunk during the backward roll
   c. Rolling over on the side when trying to rise from a back-lying position
2. Prone
   a. Difficulty doing a full push-up
   b. Inability to extend the body fully when lying belly down on a scooter

These two reflexes are under the control of the **labyrinthine portion of the inner ear.** To facilitate integration of these reflexes, the physical educator should have the child perform activities that require lifting the head against the pull of gravity.

To promote integration of the tonic labyrinthine supine reflex, the child should do activities such as the following, which require flexing the head and body from a back-lying position:

1. Hold knees to chest and rock back and forth several times.
2. Do egg rolls.
3. Do V-sits.
4. Do partial sit-ups.

To promote integration of the tonic labyrinthine prone reflex, the physical educator should have the child do activities such as the following, which require extension of the head and body, starting in a front-lying position:

1. Do wing lifts.
2. While lying prone on a scooter, roll down a ramp and toss a beanbag at a target hung overhead.
3. Seal walk while looking at the ceiling.
4. Rock back and forth on the tummy while holding ankles with hands.

table 7-1			
Primitive and Equilibrium Reflex Development			
Reflex	Age	Age Inhibited	Effect on Movement Patterns
Primitive Reflexes			
Flexor withdrawal	Birth	2 months	Uncontrolled flexion of leg when pressure is applied to sole of foot
Extensor thrust	Birth	2 months	Uncontrolled extension of leg when pressure is applied to sole of foot
Crossed extension 1	Birth	2 months	Uncontrolled extension of flexed leg when opposite leg is suddenly flexed
Crossed extension 2	Birth	2 months	Leg adducts and internally rotates, and foot plantar flexes when opposite leg is tapped medially at level of knee (scissor gait)
Asymmetrical tonic neck	Birth	4-6 months	Extension of arm and leg on face side or increase in extension tone; flexion of arm and leg on skull side or increase in flexor tone when head is turned
Symmetrical tonic neck 1	Birth	4-6 months	Arms flex or flexor tone dominates; legs extend or extensor tone dominates when head is ventroflexed while child is in quadruped position
Symmetrical tonic neck 2	Birth	4-6 months	Arms extend or extensor tone dominates; legs flex or flexor tone dominates when head is dorsiflexed while child is in quadruped position
Tonic labyrinthine, supine position	Birth	4 months	Extensor tone dominates when child is in supine position
Tonic labyrinthine, prone position	Birth	4 months	Flexor tone dominates in arms, hips, and legs when child is in prone position
Positive supporting reaction	Birth	4 months	Increase in extensor tone in legs when sudden pressure is applied to both feet simultaneously
Negative supporting reaction	Birth	4 months	Marked increase in flexor tone in legs when sudden pressure is applied to both feet simultaneously
Neck righting	Birth	6 months	Body rotated as a whole in same direction head is turned
Landau reflex	6 months	3 years	Spine, arms, and legs extend when head is dorsiflexed while child is held in supine position; spine, arms, and legs flex when head is ventroflexed while child is held in supine position
Equilibrium Reflexes			
Body righting	6 months	Throughout life	When child is in supine position and initiates full body roll, there is segmented rotation of the body (i.e., head turns, then shoulders, then pelvis)
Labyrinthine righting 1	2 months	Throughout life	When child is blindfolded and held in prone position, head raises to a point where child's face is vertical
Labyrinthine righting 2	6 months	Throughout life	When child is blindfolded and held in supine position, head raises to a point where face is vertical
Labyrinthine righting 3	6-8 months	Throughout life	When child is blindfolded and held in an upright position and is suddenly tilted right, head does not right itself to an upright position.
Labyrinthine righting 4	6-8 months	Throughout life	Same as labyrinthine righting 3, but child is tilted to left

Data from Fiorentino MR: *Reflex testing methods for evaluating CNS development,* Springfield, Ill, 1970, Charles C Thomas.

table 7-1

Primitive and Equilibrium Reflex Development—cont'd

Reflex	Age	Age Inhibited	Effect on Movement Patterns
Optical righting 1	2 months	Throughout life	Same as labyrinthine righting 1, but child is not blindfolded
Optical righting 2	6 months	Throughout life	Same as labyrinthine righting 2, but child is not blindfolded
Optical righting 3	6-9 months	Throughout life	Same as labyrinthine righting 3, but child is not blindfolded
Optical righting 4	6-8 months	Throughout life	Same as labyrinthine righting 4, but child is not blindfolded
Amphibian reaction	6 months	Throughout life	While child is in prone position with legs extended and arms extended overhead, flexion of arm, hip, and knee on same side can be elicited when pelvis on that side is lifted
Protective extensor	6 months	Throughout life	While child is held by pelvis and is extended in air, arms extend when child's head is moved suddenly toward floor
Equilibrium-supine position	6 months	Throughout life	While child is supine on a tiltboard with arms and legs suspended, if board is suddenly tilted to one side, there is righting of head and thorax and abduction and extension of arm and leg on raised side
Equilibrium-prone position	6 months	Throughout life	Same as equilibrium-supine, except child is prone on tiltboard
Equilibrium-quadruped position	8 months	Throughout life	While child balances on all fours, if suddenly tilted to one side, righting of head and thorax and abduction-extension of arm and leg occur on raised side
Equilibrium-sitting position	10-12 months	Throughout life	While child is seated on chair, if pulled or tilted to one side, righting of head and thorax and abduction-extension of arm and leg occur on raised side (side opposite pull)
Equilibrium-kneeling position	15 months	Throughout life	While child kneels on both knees, if suddenly pulled to one side, righting of head and thorax and abduction-extension of arm and leg occur on raised side
Hopping 1	15-18 months	Throughout life	While child is standing upright, if moved to the left or right, head and thorax move right and child hops sideways to maintain balance
Hopping 2	15-18 months	Throughout life	While child is standing upright, if moved forward, head and thorax move right and child hops forward to maintain balance
Hopping 3	15-18 months	Throughout life	While child is standing upright, if moved backward, head and thorax move right and child hops backward to maintain balance
Dorsiflexion	15-18 months	Throughout life	While child is standing upright, if tilted backward, head and thorax move right and feet dorsiflex
See-saw	15 months	Throughout life	While child stands on one foot, another person holds arm and free foot on same side; when arm is pulled forward and laterally, head and thorax move right and held leg abducts and extends
Simian position	15-18 months	Throughout life	While child squats down, if tilted to one side, head and thorax move right and arm and leg on raised side abduct and extend

The **positive support reflex** causes the legs to extend and the feet to plantar flex when the child is standing. Clues to its presence are apparent if there is an inability to bend the knees when attempting to jump or there is no "give" at the knees and hips on landing.

When the **negative support reflex** is present, there is flexion of the knees, hips, and ankles when pressure is removed from the feet. Inability to inhibit the expression of the reflex causes the following problems:

1. Loss of explosive power during vertical jumps because the legs bend as soon as the weight is taken off the feet
2. Inability to maintain extension of the legs while bouncing on a trampoline

Both of these reflexes are caused from pressure to the soles of the feet. A child may have either the positive or the negative support reflex, but not both at the same time. To facilitate integration of these reflexes, the physical educator should use activities that increase pressure on the soles of the feet while the child controls the position of the legs.

To eliminate the positive support reaction, the child should flex the lower limbs while applying pressure to the soles of the feet. The following activities are suggested:

1. Bounce on an air mat and suddenly stop by bending the knees.
2. Play stoop tag.
3. Bunny hop.
4. Bounce on inner tubes and/or small trampolines (with the child's hands being held to reduce the chance of falling).

To eliminate the negative support reaction, the child should extend the lower limbs while applying pressure to the soles of the feet. The following activities are suggested:

1. While lying prone on a gym scooter, use the feet to push off from the wall; keep legs extended as long as the scooter is moving across the floor.
2. Bounce while sitting on a "hippity-hop" ball.
3. Practice jumping up vertically and putting a mark on the wall.
4. Bounce on an air mat and try to keep legs straight.

Presence of the **asymmetrical tonic neck reflex** enables extension of the arm on the face side and flexion of the arm on the skull side when the head is turned. Positioning the arms in this fashion when the head is turned is often referred to as the *classic fencer's position.* Early in life this reflex serves to direct the child's visual attention toward the extended hand. If it persists beyond the tenth month of life, it interferes with bringing the hands to the midline when the head is turned and thus prevents turning the head while creeping and throwing and catching a ball.

Activities that facilitate integration of this reflex include movements that require the child to turn the head toward his or her flexed limbs, such as:

1. Practice touching the chin to various parts of the body (e.g., shoulder, wrist, knee).
2. Balance on hands and knees while holding a beanbag between the chin and one shoulder. Then place the hand on the face side of the body on the hip.
3. Hold a beanbag between the chin and one shoulder. Crawl down the mat while keeping the object between the chin and the shoulder.
4. Do a no-hands ball relay where the students have to hold a tennis ball between their chin and chest, and pass it to one another without using their hands or feet.

When the **symmetrical tonic neck** reflex is present, the upper limbs tend to flex and the lower limbs extend during **ventroflexion of the head.** If the head is **dorsiflexed,** the upper limbs extend and the lower limbs flex. If this reflex does not become fully integrated within the first year of life, the child will demonstrate the following:

1. Instead of using a **cross-pattern creep,** the child will bunny hop on both knees up to the hands.
2. If, while creeping, the child lowers the head, the arms will tend to collapse.
3. If, while creeping, the child lifts the head to look around, movement of the limbs will cease.

Activities that require the child to keep the arms extended while the head is flexed, and the arms flexed while the head is extended will promote integration of this reflex. Examples of such activities include the following:

1. While balancing on hands and knees, look down between the legs, then look up at the ceiling. Keep the arms extended and the legs flexed.
2. With extended arms, push against a cage ball while looking down at the floor.
3. Practice doing standing push-ups against a wall while looking at the ceiling.

4. Do pull-ups (look up when pulling up, and look down when letting one's self down).

Equilibrium reflexes. The **protective extensor thrust reflex** causes immediate extension of the arms when the head and upper body are tipped suddenly forward. The purpose of the reflex is to protect the head and body during a fall. The reflex is used during handsprings and vaulting. If the reflex does not emerge, the child will tend to hit the head when falling.

To develop this reflex, the child needs to practice extending the arms and taking the weight on the hands when the head and upper body are tipped toward the floor. The following activities represent ways to accomplish this:

1. While the child is lying prone on a cage ball, roll the ball slowly so that the head, shoulders, and arms are lowered toward the floor. Roll the ball far enough so that the child's weight gradually comes to rest on his or her hands.
2. Practice handstands while someone holds the child's feet in the air.
3. Practice mule kicks.
4. Wheelbarrow with a partner holding the child's knees.

Presence of the **body righting reflex** enables segmental rotation of the trunk and hips when the head is turned. As a result of this segmental turning, children can maintain good postural alignment and maintenance of body positions. Without it, for example, when doing a log roll, the child will tend to turn the knees, then the hips, and then the shoulders.

To promote development of the body righting reflex, the child should practice turning the head first, then the shoulders, followed by the hips. The child should start slowly and then increase the speed from both a standing position and a back-lying position.

Labyrinthine and **optical righting reactions** cause the head to move to an upright position when the body is suddenly tipped. Once the head rights itself, the body follows. Thus these reflexes help us maintain an upright posture during a quick change of position. Without these reflexes the child will fall down often during running and dodging games and even tend to avoid vigorous running games.

The labyrinthine reflexes are under control of the inner ear, whereas the optical righting reactions are primarily controlled by the eyes. Labyrinthine reflexes are facilitated when the head is moved in opposition to gravity. Any activity requiring the child to move the head in opposition to the pull of gravity will promote development of this reflex (see tonic labyrinthine prone and supine activities). Clinical observation indicates that poorly developed optical righting reactions most frequently accompany orthoptic visual problems (poor depth perception). Once the depth perception problem is corrected, the optical righting reactions begin to appear.

Like the labyrinthine and righting reactions, the other equilibrium reactions help us maintain an upright position when the center of gravity is suddenly moved beyond the base of support. If the equilibrium reactions are not fully developed, children fall down often, fall off chairs, and avoid vigorous running games.

Almost all of these types of equilibrium reactions are the result of stimulation of muscle spindles and/or the Golgi tendon apparatus. Both muscle spindle and Golgi tendon apparatus reactions result from sudden stretch (or contraction) of the muscles and tendons. To promote these equilibrium reactions, the child should participate in activities such as the following, which place sudden stretch (or contracture) on the muscles and tendons:

1. Bouncing on an air mat while lying down, balancing on all fours, or balancing on the knees
2. Tug of war
3. Crack the whip
4. Wrestling
5. Scooter activities with a partner pulling or pushing the child, who is seated on the scooter

Vestibular system

The vestibular receiving mechanism is located in the inner ear. As the body moves, sensory impulses from the vestibular system are sent to the cerebellum and to the brainstem. From these two areas, information about the position of the head is sent to the **extraocular muscles of the eye,** to the **somatosensory strip in the cerebral cortex**, to the stomach, to the cerebellum, and down the spinal cord. Accurate information from this mechanism is needed to help position the eyes and to maintain static and dynamic balance. When maturation of the system is delayed, students may demonstrate the following problems:

1. Inability to balance on one foot (particularly with the eyes closed)

Sensory Input Systems Screening Test

	Pass	Fail

Reflex Test Items—Check Pass or Fail

1. Tonic labyrinthine supine—(TLS)
   While lying on back, can bend knees to chest, wrap arms around knees, and touch head to knees. Child should be able to hold position for 10 seconds.
2. Tonic labyrinthine prone—(TLP)
   While lying face down on mat with arms at side, child can lift head and upper body and hold off mat for 5 seconds.
3. Positive support reaction—(PSR)
   Child is able to jump into air and, on landing, flex ankles, knees, and hips while maintaining balance for 5 seconds.
4. Equilibrium reactions
   When placed on a tilt board, child will move hands out to side and maintain balance for 3 seconds when the board is suddenly tipped 15 degrees to one side and then to other side (check each side independently).
   Check child in each of these positions:
   a. Seated, start with hands in lap—move right
   b. Seated, start with hands in lap—move left
   c. On two knees, start with hands on hips—move right
   d. On two knees, start with hands on hips—move left
   Place child on all fours on tilt board and tip board 15 degrees to one side and then to the other. Child can maintain "all fours" position while holding head in a neutral position.
   e. When tipped to right
   f. When tipped to left

Vestibular Test Items—Check Pass or Fail

1. Seat child in a desk chair that can be rotated 360 degrees. Have child rest hands in lap or on arms of chair. Child should tip head down slightly (30 degrees). Turn chair 10 complete turns in 20 seconds (1 complete rotation every 2 seconds). Stop chair and watch child's eyes. Child's eye should flick back and forth for 7 to 13 seconds. After a 2-minute rest, repeat turning procedure in opposite direction. Check eye movement again.
   a. Turn to right
   b. Turn to left

Fixation (Ocular Control)—Check Pass or Fail

1. Child should sit in a chair facing a seated evaluator. Child can fixate with both eyes on an object held 18 inches in front of the nose at eye level for 10 seconds.
2. Child should sit in a chair facing a seated evaluator. Cover child's left eye with your hand or a card. Child can fixate with right eye on an object held 18 inches in front of the nose at eye level for 10 seconds.
3. Child should sit in a chair facing a seated evaluator. Cover child's right eye with your hand or a card. Child can fixate with left eye on an object held 18 inches in front of the nose at eye level for 10 seconds.
   NOTE: Any tendency to turn the head to one side, to blink excessively, or for the eyes to water could be an indication that the child needs to be referred to a visual development specialist for a refractive and orthoptic visual exam.

Courtesy Jean L. Pyfer, Texas Woman's University, Denton, Tex., and Robert Strauss, Trinity University, San Antonio, Tex.

	Pass	Fail

Ocular Alignment (Depth Perception)—Check Pass or Fail

NOTE: On all of the following items start with the child looking at the object with both eyes. Then cover one eye and begin your observation.

1. Child is seated in a chair facing a seated evaluator. Child can fixate on an object held 18 inches in front of the nose at eye level without moving right eye as left eye is covered for 3 seconds. (Note whether the right eye moves and in what direction.)
2. Child is seated in a chair facing a seated evaluator. Child can fixate on an object held 18 inches in front of the nose at eye level without moving left eye as right eye is covered for 3 seconds. (Note whether the left eye moves and in what direction.)

Convergence-Divergence Ocular Control—Check Pass or Fail

1. Child is seated in a chair facing a seated evaluator. Child can visually follow with both eyes an object moved slowly from 18 inches directly in front of the nose (eye level), to 4 inches from the eyes (midpoint), and back to 18 inches. (Note whether the eyes move equally without jerking.)

Visual Tracking—Check Pass or Fail

1. Child is seated in a chair facing a seated evaluator. Child can visually pursue with both eyes without moving the head an object held 18 inches from the eyes as the object is moved in the following patterns:
   a. A square (12-inch sides)
   b. A circle (8- to 10-inch diameter)
   c. An X (10-inch lines)
   d. A horizontal line (12 inches)
2. Child is seated in a chair with left eye covered facing a seated evaluator. Child can visually pursue with the right eye without moving the head an object held 18 inches from the eyes as the object is moved in the following patterns:
   a. A square (12-inch sides)
   b. A circle (8- to 10-inch diameter)
   c. An X (10-inch lines)
   d. A horizontal line (12 inches)
3. Child is seated in a chair with right eye covered facing a seated evaluator. Child can visually pursue with the left eye without moving the head an object held 18 inches from the eyes as the object is moved in the following patterns:
   a. A square (12-inch sides)
   b. A circle (8- to 10-inch diameter)
   c. An X (10-inch lines)
   d. A horizontal line (12 inches)

   NOTE: During all tracking tasks, note any tendency for the eyes to (1) jump when the object moves across the midline of the body, (2) jump ahead of the object, (3) jerk while pursuing the object, (4) water, or (5) blink excessively. The watering and/or excessive blinking could be an indicator of visual stress, and such cases should be referred to a visual development specialist for a refractive and orthoptic visual exam.

Kinesthesis—Check Pass or Fail

1. Can touch finger to nose three times in alternating succession with index fingers while eyes are closed. (Failure if the child misses the tip of the nose by more than 1 inch.)

2. Inability to walk a balance beam without watching the feet
3. Inability to walk heel to toe
4. Inefficient walking and running patterns
5. Delays in ability to hop and to skip

Children who demonstrate the clues listed above and who fail to demonstrate nystagmus after spinning are believed to have vestibular development delays and are in need of activities to facilitate development. *Concentrated activities to remediate balance problems that result from poor vestibular function should be administered by someone trained in observing the responses of such a child.* However, some activities can be done in fun, nonthreatening ways in a physical education class or on a playground with the supervision of parents or teachers.

CAUTION: Anyone who uses vestibular stimulation activities with children should observe closely for signs of sweating, paleness, flushing of the face, nausea, and loss of consciousness. These are all indications that the activities should be stopped immediately. Also, spinning activities should not be used with seizure-prone children. Avoid rapid spinning activities.

The following vestibular stimulation activities should be nonthreatening to most children:

1. Logroll on a mat.
2. Spin self while prone on a gym scooter by crossing hand-over-hand; stop and change direction.
3. Lie on a blanket and roll self up and then unroll.
4. Let the child spin himself or herself on a scooter, play on spinning playground equipment, go down a ramp prone on a gym scooter, or do other such nonthreatening activities that give the child an opportunity to respond to changes of his or her position in space (movement or spinning should not be so fast as to be disorienting or disorganizing).

Visual system

Both **refractive** and **orthoptic vision** are important for efficient motor performance. Refractive vision is the process by which the light rays are bent as they enter the eyes. When light rays are bent precisely, vision is sharpest and clearest. Individuals who have poor refractive vision are said to be nearsighted (myopic) or farsighted (hyperopic) or have astigmatism. The following problems are demonstrated by children with refractive visual problems:

1. Tendency to squint
2. Tendency to rub the eyes frequently
3. Redness of the eyes

Orthoptic vision refers to the ability to use the extraocular muscles of the eyes in unison. When the extraocular muscles are balanced, images entering each eye strike each retina at precisely the same point, so that the images transmitted to the visual center of the brain match. The closer the match of the images from the eye, the better the depth perception. The greater the discrepancy between the two images that reach the visual center, the poorer the depth perception. Clues to orthoptic problems (poor depth perception) are as follows:

1. Turning the head when catching a ball
2. Inability to catch a ball or a tendency to scoop the ball into the arms
3. Tendency to kick a ball off center or miss it entirely
4. Persistence in ascending and descending stairs one at a time
5. Avoidance of climbing apparatus

The physical educator is not trained to test for or correct refractive and orthoptic visual problems. However, a simple screening test that can be used to determine whether the possibility of a serious orthoptic **(depth perception)** problem exists is described in the screening test for developmental delays (see box on pp. 186-187). Individuals who fail the ocular alignment portion of the screening test should be professionally evaluated by a visual behavioral specialist (optometrist or ophthalmologist who has specialized training in **orthoptics**). Students suspected of having refractive vision problems should be evaluated by either an optometrist or an ophthalmologist.

Kinesthetic system

The kinesthetic receptors are specialized **proprioceptors** located in the joints, muscles, and tendons throughout the body. Information from the kinesthetic receptors informs the central nervous system about the position of the limbs in space. As these joint receptors fire, sensory impulses are sent to the brain and are recorded as spatial maps. As the kinesthetic system becomes more developed, judgment about the rate, amount, and amplitude of motion needed to perform a task improves. Refined movement is not possible without kinesthetic awareness. Possible signs of developmental delays of the kinesthetic system are:

1. Inability to move a body part on command without assistance
2. No awareness of the position of body parts in space
3. Messy handwriting
4. Poor skill in sports that require "touch," such as putting a golf ball, basketball shooting, and bowling

Activities to promote kinesthetic function include any activity that increases tension on the joints, muscles, and tendons. Selected activities that have proved useful in promoting kinesthetic function are:

1. Games involving pushing (or kicking) a large cage ball
2. Lying prone on a scooter, holding onto a rope, and being pulled by a partner
3. Using the hands and feet to propel one's self while seated on a gym scooter
4. Doing any type of activity while wearing wrist and/or ankle weights

Tactile system

The tactile receptors are located throughout the body and respond to stimulation of body surfaces. Some of the receptors lie close to the surface of the body; others are located more deeply. A well-functioning **tactile system** is needed for an individual to know where the body ends and space begins, and to be able to tactually discriminate between pressure, texture, and size. Children who are **tactile defensive** are believed to have difficulty processing sensory input from tactile receptors. Behaviors demonstrated by the tactile-defensive child include:

1. Low tolerance for touch (unless the person doing the touching is in the visual field of the student)
2. Avoidance of activities requiring prolonged touch, such as wrestling or hugging
3. Avoidance of toweling down after a shower or bath unless it is done in a vigorous fashion
4. Tendency to curl fingers and toes when creeping

Activities believed to stimulate the tactile system and promote sensory input processing should begin with coarse textures and progress (over time) toward finer-texture stimulation. A sequence of such activities follows:

1. Present the child with a variety of different-textured articles (nets, pot scrubbers, bath brushes). Have the child select an article and rub it on his or her face, arms, and legs. (Tactile-defensive children will usually select the coarsest textures to use for this activity.)
2. Using an old badminton net, play "capture me" while crawling around on a mat. The teacher should toss the net over the child as the child tries to crawl from one end of the mat to the other. When the child has been captured, rub the net over exposed parts of the body as the child struggles to escape. Repeat the activity with the child chasing and capturing the teacher.
3. Construct an obstacle course with several stations where the child must go through hanging textures (strips of inner tube, sections of rope) and/or squeeze through tight places.
4. Using a movement exploration teaching approach, have the students find various textures in the gym to rub a point or patch against (e.g., rough, smooth, wavy).

Motor Ability Level

Abilities emerge after sensory input systems begin to stabilize, usually during the fifth through the seventh years of life. Development of these abilities requires not only intact information from the sensory input systems, but also the capacity to integrate those signals in the brain. When all sensory input systems are functioning and cortical reception and association areas are intact, domains of abilities and motor skills emerge and generalize with practice. Weakened, distorted, or absent signals from the sensory input systems will detract from the development of abilities, as well as from all other motor performance. This is not to say that specific abilities and motor performance cannot be taught in the absence of intact sensory information. Specific functions can be taught, but only as splinter skills. A **splinter skill** is a particular perceptual or motor act that is performed in isolation and does not generalize to other areas of performance. If hard neurological damage or the age of the learner prevents development of the sensory input systems, it becomes necessary to teach splinter skills. In such cases the top, down approach (task analysis) is recommended. If, however, it is believed that sensory input systems are fully functioning and cortical integration is possible, practice in the following activities should promote development of a wide variety of perceptual-motor abilities from which motor skills can emerge.

Balance

Balance is the ability to maintain equilibrium in a held position (static) or in moving positions (dynamic). Balance ability is critical to almost every motor function. Some literature suggests that until balance becomes an automatic, involuntary act, the central nervous system must focus on maintaining balance to the detriment of all other motor and cognitive functions.[1,2] Balance development is dependent on vestibular, visual, reflex, and kinesthetic development. When these systems are fully functioning, high levels of balance development are possible. Clues to poor balance development include:

1. Inability to maintain held balance positions (e.g., stand on one foot, stand heel to toe) with eyes open
2. Inability to walk heel to toe on a line or on a balance beam
3. Tripping or falling easily
4. Wide gait while walking or running

Activities that can be used to promote static balance include:

1. Freeze tag—the children play tag; the child who is caught is "frozen" until a classmate "unfreezes" the child by tagging him or her. "It" tries to freeze everyone.
2. Statue—the child spins around and then tries to make himself or herself into a "statue" without falling first.
3. Tripod—the child balances by placing forehead and both hands on the floor; knees balance on elbows to form tripod balance.
4. The child balances beanbags on different parts of the body while performing balancing positions.

Activities that can be used to promote dynamic balance include:

1. Hopscotch
2. Various types of locomotor movements following patterns on the floor
3. Races using different types of locomotor movements
4. Walk forward heel to toe between double lines, on a single line, and then on a balance beam; make this more demanding by having the child balance a beanbag on different body parts (e.g., head,

shoulder, elbow, wrist) while walking the balance beam

Laterality

Laterality is an awareness of the difference between the two sides of the body. Children who have not developed laterality often demonstrate balance problems on one or both sides. Delays in the development of laterality may be indicated by the following types of behavior:

1. Avoiding use of one side of the body
2. Walking sideways in one direction better than in the other
3. Using one extremity more often than the other
4. Lacking a fully established hand preference

Laterality is believed to develop from intact kinesthetic and vestibular sensory inputs. If these two input systems are believed to be functioning adequately, then a child will benefit from activities that require differentiation between the two sides of the body. Examples include the following:

1. Wear ankle and/or wrist weights on the weak (unused) side of the body while climbing on apparatus, moving through obstacle courses, and kicking, bouncing, throwing, or catching a ball.
2. Walk a balance beam while carrying objects that weigh different amounts in each hand (i.e., carry a small bucket in each hand, with different numbers of beanbags in each bucket).
3. Push a cage ball with one hand only.
4. Use only one hand in tug of war.

Spatial relations

Spatial relations concern the ability to perceive the position of objects in space, particularly as they relate to the position of the body (Figure 7-1). Development of spatial relations is believed to depend on vestibular, kinesthetic, and visual development. Problems may be indicated by:

1. Inability to move under objects without hitting them or ducking way below the object
2. Consistently swinging a bat too high or low when attempting to hit a pitched ball
3. Inability to maintain an appropriate body position in relation to moving objects
4. Inability to position the hands accurately to catch a ball

figure 7-1
A child must have spatial relationship abilities to fit the body through the circular tunnel.

If it has been determined that none of the prerequisite input systems is delayed, spatial relations can be facilitated by practice in the following activities:

1. Set up an obstacle course with stations that require the child to crawl over, under, and through various obstacles.
2. Place a 10-foot taped line on the floor. Give the child a beanbag and ask him or her to place the beanbag halfway down the line. If the child makes an error, ask him or her to walk from one end of the line to the other, counting the number of steps. Then have the child divide the number of steps in half, walk that far, and place the beanbag down at that point. The child should then stand to the side of the line and look from one end of the line to the beanbag. Continue practicing until the child is successful at estimating where, on several different lengths of line, the midpoint is.
3. Repeat activity 2 with the child wearing ankle weights.
4. Place several chairs around the room with varying distances between them. Ask the child to point to the two chairs that are closest together, furthest apart, or a given distance from one another (i.e., 3 feet, 10 feet, 6 feet). If the child makes an error on any task, have him or her walk the distance between the chairs and/or measure the distance with a measuring tape.

Ocular-motor control

Ocular-motor control includes the ability to fixate on and visually track moving objects, as well as the abil-

figure 7-2
Activities that contribute to the development of visual systems.

ity to match visual input with appropriate motor response (Figure 7-2). Observed deficiencies might include:

1. Failure to visually locate an object in space
2. Failure to visually track a softball when attempting to hit it
3. Failure to visually track a fly ball or ground ball
4. Failure to keep a place when reading
5. Difficulty using scissors or tying shoelaces
6. Poor foot-eye coordination
7. Messy handwriting

Ocular control can be improved with practice if a child does not have serious orthoptic (depth perception) problems. If an individual does have depth perception problems, participation in ocular control activities can worsen their visual difficulties. Once it is ascertained that no depth perception problems exist, the following

figure 7-2, cont'd
Activities that contribute to the development of visual systems.

activities can be used to promote ocular control of the eyes.

Fixation

1. The child sits and rocks back and forth while keeping his or her eyes on a tape on the wall directly in front of him or her.
2. The child lies on his or her back with eyes fixated on a point on the ceiling. The child then stands up (or does a series of stunts) while continuing to fixate on the spot.
3. The child is in a standing position while fixating on a designated point on the wall. The child then jumps and turns 180 degrees and fixates on a designated point on the opposite wall.
4. The child is in a standing position, fixating on a designated point on the wall. The child then jumps and turns completely around (360 degrees) and again fixates on the original point.

Convergence/divergence

1. Draw two X's on the chalkboard (at the child's shoulder height) approximately 36 inches apart. Have the child stand centered about 2 inches in front of the board and move his or her eyes back and forth between the two X's.
2. Have the child sit at a table and look from an object on the table to an object on the wall directly ahead; continue back and forth 10 times. The table should be about 15 inches from the wall.
3. The child sits with arms extended and thumbs up, looking back and forth from one thumb to the other.
4. The child sits with one arm extended and the other flexed so that the hand is about 6 inches from the nose with thumbs up. Have the child look back and forth from one thumb to the other 10 times.

Visual tracking

1. The child lies on his or her back. Have the child visually track lines, pipes, or lights on the ceiling, without moving the head.
2. The child lies on his or her back. Attach a small ball to a string and swing the ball horizontally above the child's head. The child should track the swinging ball with his or her eyes and then point to it as it swings. (The ball should be suspended approximately 16 inches above the child's head.)
3. The child throws a ball up in the air and follows the path of the ball with his or her eyes until it hits the floor. Repeat several times, and encourage the child not to move his or her head while tracking the ball.
4. The child either sits or lies on his or her back. Have the child hit a suspended ball with the hand and visually track the movement of the ball.

Cross-lateral integration

Cross-lateral integration is the ability to coordinate use of both sides of the body. It normally follows the development of balance and laterality. A child who has not developed cross-lateral integration by age 8 years is said to have a **midline problem** because there is difficulty using the hands efficiently at and across the center of the body. Teachers will note the following problems demonstrated by a child with a midline problem:

1. Difficulty using both hands to catch a ball
2. Tendency of eyes to jump when trying to visually track an object that is moving from one side of the body to the other
3. Inability to master a front crawl stroke with breathing while trying to swim
4. Inability to hop rhythmically from one foot to the other
5. Tendency to move the paper to one side of the body when doing paper and pencil tasks

Activities that will promote cross-lateral integration are as follows:

1. The child crawls down a rope or line on the floor, crossing hands back and forth over the line (rope) going forward, then crossing feet back and forth while crawling backward.
2. The child picks up objects (from the right side of the body) with the right hand and places them in a container on the left side of the body. This should be repeated using the left hand. The child picks up one object at a time.
3. The child plays "pat-a-cake."
4. The child practices swimming the front crawl with breathing.

Body awareness

Body awareness is a broad term that includes how people picture their body, their attitude toward their body, and their knowledge of personal bodily capabilities and limitations. Body awareness develops from all sensory input system information, as well as from personal experiences with the body. Indications of a poorly developed body awareness are:

1. Lack of knowledge of where body parts are located
2. Distorted drawings of self
3. Lack of knowledge about what specific body parts are for
4. Poor motor planning

Activities that can be used to facilitate a child's body awareness include:

1. Give verbal commands to the child (e.g., touch your knees, touch your ankles, touch your ears, touch your shoulders, etc.).
2. Have the child stand with eyes closed. The teacher touches various body parts, and the child identifies them. Then have the child touch the same part that the teacher touches and name the part.
3. Trace an outline of the child's body on a large piece of paper or with chalk on the floor. Then have the child get up and fill in the details (e.g., facial features, clothes, shoes). Perhaps make an "own self" body puzzle. After the child is finished drawing, laminate the body shape; cut it into pieces for the child to reassemble.
   a. Have the child name all the body parts.
   b. Leave out a part and see if the child notices it.
   c. Have the child trace around the teacher and name all the body parts.
   d. Have the child trace certain body parts on the drawing with different colors (e.g., yellow for feet, blue for arms, etc.).
4. Draw an incomplete picture of a person on the chalkboard and have the child fill in the missing parts.

Skill Level

Skills are motor acts that are necessary to perform a specific activity. Skills are categorized as functional or sport specific. **Functional skills** include locomotor patterns, such as crawling, creeping, walking, running, jumping, hopping, sliding, and skipping. **Sport-specific skills** include kicking a soccer ball or a football, shooting a basketball, serving a volleyball, and ice skating. As explained in Chapter 2, content, prerequisite, and/or ana-

tomical task assessment analyses are conducted to determine which parts of a skill are lacking. Once the missing components are determined, skills are developed by directly teaching these components and by practicing the actual movement under a variety of conditions.

Examples of task analyses are presented in Chapter 4. An example of using a content analysis of discrete tasks to determine missing components of a lay-up basketball shot is as follows: After watching the student attempt the lay-up shot, the physical educator determines which components are contributing to the student's inability to perform the task successfully. If, for example, the student is performing all parts of the task correctly except timing the jump to occur just before the body reaches the area under the basket and directing the ball to the correct point on the backboard, those are the two components that require attention.

To correct the jump-timing problem, it may be necessary to mark an area on the floor where the jump should be executed for a right-hand lay-up. The student practices approaching the mark and landing on it consistently with the left foot. When that movement becomes habitual, the student practices the approach and adds a jump off the left foot when reaching the mark on the floor. Then to direct the student's attention to the correct place to rebound the ball, an area can be marked on the backboard. The student then practices the correct approach, jump, and striking the outlined area on the backboard with the ball in one continuous motion. Minor adjustments may need to be added to modify the amount of force the student uses when releasing the ball.

Once a skill is learned, it should be practiced under a variety of conditions to ensure the learner's ability to use the skill in a variety of situations and environments. Conditions that can be modified include time (fast/slow, even/uneven), space (straight/circular/zigzag, high/low, alone/with others, inside/outside), force (light/heavy, soft/hard), and flow (synchronized/unsynchronized, run/walk/hop, twist/turn). (See Chapter 4 and *Gross Motor Activities for Young Children with Special Needs,* which accompanies this text, for additional examples.)

Additional examples of teaching skill components are routinely included in regular physical education, motor-learning, kinesiology, and techniques texts and curricula. The reader is referred to those sources for specific examples.

SUMMARY

Motor development is a critical component of movement efficiency, as well as perceptual, cognitive, and affective function. It is essential that a child's motor development progress be monitored to ensure growing competence. Some predictive tests have been developed to measure basic input and ability level function; however, the technology to probe actual neurological function is still being developed. In the absence of formal assessment, it is possible to observe children's movement patterns to determine whether they demonstrate developmental delays at the sensory input, ability, and/or skill levels. When delays are identified, every effort should be made to select activities that will promote development. The earlier in life a delay is identified and intervention is begun, the better the opportunity to remediate the delay. For children beyond the age of 12 years, deficient skills should probably be taught directly.

Review Questions

1. Why is it important to monitor children's motor development as they grow?
2. Give three examples of how primitive refexes differ from equilibrium reflexes.
3. Provide three examples of movement behaviors a child would demonstrate if he or she lacked depth perception.
4. How does vestibular development impact balance ability?
5. Identify two behaviors a child might demonstrate if bilateral coordination has not yet developed.
6. Describe two behaviors a child who is tactile defensive might demonstrate.
7. When should functional and motor skills be directly taught?

Student Activities

1. Working in small groups, share your list of Billy Bogg's motor development delays and the activties you selected to alleviate those delays with other class members. Share your group's information with the rest of the class.
2. Observe an occupational therapist administering a sensory integration evaluation. Report on the types of test items used.
3. Interview a visual behavior specialist to determine the types of techniques used to remediate depth perception problems.
4. Observe the movements of a person who has cerebral palsy. Identify which primitive reflexes the person exhibits.
5. Conduct a content analysis of one functional skill and one sport skill. Identify each component required to successfully perform each of the skills.

References

1. Kohen-Raz R: *Learning disabilities and postural control,* London, 1986, Freund Publishing.
2. Quiros JB, Schrager OL: *Neuropsychological fundamentals in learning disabilities,* San Rafael, Calif, 1979, Academic Therapy Publications.
3. Thelen E: Motor development: a new synthesis, *Am Psychologist* 50:79-95, 1995.

Suggested Readings

Adapt Phys Act Q 11:111-235, 1994.
Pyfer J: Teachers, don't let your students grow up to be clumsy adults, *J Phys Educ Rec Dance* 59:38-42, 1988.
Seaman JA, DePauw K: *The new adapted physical education: a developmental approach,* Palo Alto, Calif, 1989, Mayfield Publishing.

Physical Fitness Deficiencies

Courtesy Canadian Association of Athletes with a Mental Handicap.

Objectives

Cite the causes of poor physical fitness and the purposes of physical fitness programming.

Determine a unique physical fitness need.

Describe the different types of physical fitness tests and their implications for programming.

List the basic principles for conducting a physical fitness program for individuals with disabilities.

State the physical fitness characteristics and problems associated with specific disabilities.

Construct a circuit training program.

Explain the problems associated with overweight, underweight, and obesity.

Task

Review Billy Bogg's test results (see Chapter 2) to determine whether he demonstrated any physical fitness deficiencies. As you read this chapter, identify potential activities that could be used to improve Billy's physical fitness.

One of the objectives of physical educators is to assist students in developing their **physical fitness** levels. Individuals who are physically fit are healthier, able to perform motor skills competently, and able to perform daily living activities without undue fatigue.

Physical fitness is considered a prerequisite to healthful and recreational living, not an end in itself. Physical fitness can be health related inasmuch as it preserves healthful function of the body over extended periods into adult life. Physical conditioning can keep the

197

cardiovascular and muscular systems from deteriorating and can assist in maintaining good mechanical posture. Good alignment of the body is particularly important to persons with disabilities because it enhances appearance, which aids in social development. Physical fitness programs for individuals with disabilities should contribute in every way possible to independent life patterns.

The lack of physical development and **low vitality** of persons with disabilities constitute a major concern of physical education. Chronically ill persons with **debilitating conditions** are particularly prone to poor physical vitality and development. Persons with cardiorespiratory conditions such as chronic bronchitis and various heart defects also show a tendency toward poor physical fitness. Increasing numbers of **medically fragile** children who are now being educated in the public schools represent a serious challenge for the physical educator. Children with disabilities and children without disabilities often lack the physical and motor abilities that are prerequisite to successful participation in sports and the activities of daily living. This chapter includes a discussion of physical fitness and special problems demonstrated by persons who are undernourished, obese, visually impaired, and/or mentally and physically impaired.

Definition of Physical Fitness

The American Alliance for Health, Physical Education, Recreation and Dance (AAHPERD) describes physical fitness "as a physical state of well-being that allows people to perform daily activities with vigor, reduce their risk of health problems related to lack of exercise, and establish a fitness base for participation in a variety of activities."[24]

Developing and maintaining an appropriate level of physical fitness is critical for persons with disabilities because, frequently, the disabling condition itself interferes with the ability to move efficiently. The problem is compounded when physical fitness levels are not adequate, because appropriate levels of muscular strength, joint flexibility, muscular endurance, and cardiovascular endurance are requisite for movement efficiency. A sedentary lifestyle that results from inadequate levels of physical fitness and lack of movement efficiency can contribute to a number of health problems, including obesity, spinal disk deterioration, osteoporosis, and coronary heart disease.

The benefits of exercise that promotes physical fitness include:

- Increases and maintains muscular function[23]
- Reduces depression[6]
- Increases longevity as a result of improved cardiovascular function[22]
- Improves sleep patterns[4]
- Lessens back aches and diminishes fluid retention in varicose veins[4]
- Facilitates weight reduction and enhances insulin production in persons who have diabetes[4]
- Contributes to independent living and mobility[10]
- Enhances postural stability[17]
- Prevents or delays the onset of osteoporosis[4]
- Enables a person with severe disabilities to lift the head, roll over, and maintain a sitting position
- Enables a person with moderate to mild disabilities to engage in leisure time activities in the community

Thus, participating in activities to improve physical fitness enhances a person's attitude about life, enhances his or her ability to perform activities of daily living, enhances sport and leisure skills, and improves and maintains health.

Once minimum levels of physical fitness are achieved, development and use of motor fitness can contribute to additional physical fitness development. That is, once an individual begins to use agility, balance, and coordination in daily living activities, as well as in games and sports, physical fitness levels continue to rise, and health continues to improve.

Physical Fitness in the United States

Although the United States appears to be involved in a fitness boom, there is evidence that the general population is not as active as one would believe. According to Payne and Hahn,[21] only 12% of the adult population engages in vigorous physical activity 3 or more days a week for 20 or more minutes. They also report that only slightly more than 20% of the adult population is mildly to moderately active for at least 30 minutes 5 or more times per week. Major cardiovascular diseases account for almost 40% of the leading causes of death in this country.[21] Because conditions that contribute to cardiovascular disease have their beginning in childhood, there is renewed concern about the status of childhood fitness. This concern is justified because (1) the nation's school-

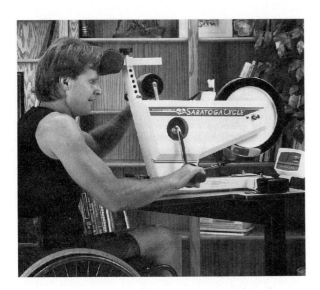

Saratoga Cycle. (Courtesy Saratoga Access and Fitness.)

children have become fatter and less fit during the past decade; (2) if this trend continues, it is predicted that these children will be at greater risk for illness when they become adults; and (3) less than one half (46%) of physical education teachers have as their major goal improvement of physical fitness of students.[12] It is apparent that children in the United States are not as physically fit as experts believe they should be, and it is evident that youth with disabilities are less fit than their peers without disabilities.

All physical fitness test results that have been normed using children and youth with disabilities have shown lower physical fitness levels than results normed using children who lack disabilities.[7,24,28] Individuals with moderate mental retardation do poorer on cardiorespiratory function tests than those with mild retardation.[7] Males and females between the ages of 6 and 18 years who are mentally retarded are heavier than individuals the same age who are not retarded.[7] Individuals between the ages of 10 and 17 years who have visual impairments and those with spinal neuromuscular conditions have higher percentages of body fat than those the same age with no disabilities.[28] Males and females between the ages of 10 and 17 who have visual impairments,[28] moderate mental retardation, or Down syndrome[7] have less flexibility (sit-and-reach test) than youth without those

disabilities. It is evident that physical educators who serve children and youth with disabilities must address the physical fitness deficiencies these youngsters demonstrate.

Causes of Poor Physical Fitness

Several factors contribute to poor physical fitness, including health status, developmental delays, lack of opportunity, and/or lack of confidence by the child or the caregiver. Examples of health status problems include obesity; asthma and other chronic respiratory problems; susceptibility to infectious diseases, including the common cold; poor nutrition; inadequate sleep; motor limitations such as paralysis, muscle dystrophy, or cerebral palsy[3]; and cardiopulmonary or metabolic limitations, including advanced cyanotic heart disease, cystic fibrosis, scoliosis, and undernutrition.[3]

Developmental delays that can impact physical fitness levels include abnormal reflex development, delayed vestibular function, poor vision, delayed crosslateral integration, inadequate spatial awareness, poor body image, and any other factor that limits the ability to move efficiently.

Lack of opportunities to participate in physical fitness activities results from environmental barriers, such as limited access to community, group, or private exercise facilities[6]; insufficient programs as a result of inadequate testing procedures; lack of instructor knowledge; or limited curriculum offerings in the school system.[30]

Caregivers, including parents, medical personnel, and educators, sometimes encourage children to "take it easy" because they fear the children will overdo or hurt themselves during activity participation.[3] Also, some individuals with disabilities may be exceptionally self-conscious, and they may lack self-confidence. Their fear of failure may result in avoidance of both instructional and extracurricular physical activity.[20] It is important to determine why a person's fitness is low (i.e., why they are avoiding physical activity) so that the physical fitness program that is developed will focus on cause, as well as effect.

The physical educator is the ideal person to address the deterrents to exercise; however, before a program can be implemented, the student's present level of performance must be ascertained. With those results in hand, a physical fitness program can be established to benefit the student.

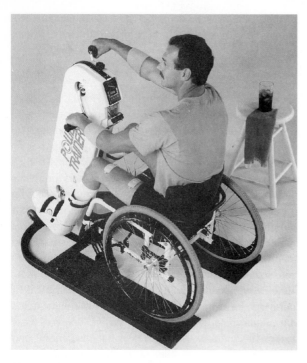

Muscle-Stim Power Trainer offers muscle stimulation for inactive leg muscles. (Courtesy Sinties Scientific, Inc.)

Evaluating Physical Fitness

The full evaluation of the physical fitness of a child with a disability requires comprehensive assessment of ability areas identified through research (see Chapter 2). One does not just measure strength as a single entity. Rather, one measures the strength of specific muscle groups, such as the knee extensors, elbow flexors, or abdominal muscles. In the same manner, when flexibility is evaluated, it is necessary to determine range of motion at specific joints in the body. A severe loss of strength in any muscle group or limited range of motion in any joint could seriously affect the attainment of specific daily living or sport skills. Thus a full evaluation of physical education needs would involve assessing the strength of major muscle groups, range of motion of many joints, and factors that affect cardiovascular efficiency.

It should be obvious that there is seldom enough time or personnel in a school system to assess every child comprehensively. Therefore the physical educator usually only samples some physical and motor fitness

components. Which components are measured is usually determined in one of two ways. Either a specific test (e.g., Physical Best and Individuals with Disabilities) is administered, or test items that measure specific aspects of a given daily living skill or motor skill are selected and administered.

The ultimate purpose of preevaluation in the areas of physical fitness is to determine which activities will meet the unique needs of the child with disabilities. The procedures to be employed for determining the needs in the areas of physical fitness are as follows:

1. Identify motor skills to be taught in the physical education program that contribute to physical fitness and can be expressed as recreational skills and activities of daily living for independence in the community.
2. Select physical fitness areas associated with the skills needed for independent living in the community.
3. Identify levels of physical fitness necessary for independent recreation and activities of daily living in the community.
4. Test for present levels of educational performance in the physical fitness domain.
5. Compare the child's performance with normative community standards to determine whether there is sufficient discrepancy to indicate an educational need.
6. If it is determined that there are physical fitness needs, establish long-range goals and short-term objectives that lead to those goals.

Types of Physical Fitness Tests

There are at least three different orientations to physical fitness testing. One type is **"health-related fitness,"** which refers to those components of physiological functioning that are believed to offer protection against such degenerative diseases as obesity, disk degeneration, and coronary heart disease.[14] A second type includes tests designed to develop aspects of physical fitness such as optimal strength, endurance, and flexibility to be used in sport activities. A third orientation, which is preferred by Evans and Meyer[8] for individuals with disabilities, is a function-specific type of physical fitness that relates to independent functioning in the community.

Health-related tests include measures of **cardiovascular/cardiorespiratory endurance, abdominal**

strength, percentage of body fat, and flexibility. The performance of children and youth with disabilities has been measured using items included in the Health-Related Physical Fitness Test and the Prudential FIT-NESSGRAM. These types of tests are meaningful when individuals with mild or moderate cognitive and physical disabilities are being evaluated. AAHPERD has incorporated those test items in their newly developed Physical Best and Individuals with Disabilities evaluation (see Chapter 2). At this writing, Winnick and Short[29] are in the process of converting Project UNIQUE into a criterion-referenced health-related test. Nonambulatory severely and profoundly involved students would benefit from the test items and curriculum presented in Mobility Opportunities Via Education (MOVE) (see Chapter 2).

Individuals with severe disabilities who are ambulatory require functional physical fitness tests that relate specifically to what an individual needs to meet the daily demands of the environment. Examples of such test items would be walking to develop endurance to walk to and from one's home from designated areas in the neighborhood, developing sufficient balance to remedy a wide shuffling gait, and specific practice to lengthen tight heel cords so that the entire foot will strike the ground when walking. The type of fitness test selected depends on the goals and objectives of the physical education program.

Programming for Physical Fitness

Physical fitness encompasses muscular strength and endurance, flexibility, **body composition,** and cardiovascular endurance. Each of these factors must be addressed in the training program.

Muscular Strength

Muscular strength is the ability to contract a muscle against resistance. Types of contraction include:

- **Concentric:** Muscle tension is greater than the amount of applied resistance, so that the muscle shortens and movement occurs.
- **Isometric (static):** Muscle tension equals the amount of applied resistance, so that no movement occurs.
- **Eccentric:** Resistance is greater than the muscle tension, so that the muscle lengthens without relaxing.

Muscular strength can be improved by using the overload principle. The **overload principle** is applied by gradually increasing the resistance (load or weight) used over time (days or months). **Isotonic exercises** use progressive resistance with free weights or the Nautilus or Universal weight machines. When isotonic exercises are being performed, the greatest resistance is during the start or finish of the movement. **Isokinetic exercises** provide resistance throughout the entire range of motion. Isokinetic exercise machines include the Cybex and Orthotron. When isometric exercises are being performed, the resistance is so great that the contracting muscles do not move.[21]

Muscular Endurance

Muscular endurance is the ability to continue to contract a muscle against resistance. Muscular endurance is developed by gradually increasing the number of repetitions completed during an exercise period.

Flexibility

Flexibility is the range of motion possible at any given joint. Flexibility can be improved through the use of static stretching, which is accomplished by slowly lengthening a muscle group that surrounds a joint and then holding the extended position for 30 to 60 seconds.

Body Composition

Body composition refers to the muscle, bone, fat, and other elements in the body.[21] Usually in a discussion of physical fitness, the term is used to express the percentage of body fat in comparison with lean tissue. Overweight and obese individuals have high percentages of body fat. There is controversy as to what percentage of body fat is most desirable; however, most fitness experts would agree that levels less than that 30% are healthiest.

Cardiovascular Endurance

Cardiovascular endurance refers to the ability of the heart and vessels to process and transport oxygen from the lungs to muscle cells for use. The greater the cardiovascular endurance, the longer the period of time that a person is able to continue exercising. Cardiovascular endurance can be improved by persisting at activities that increase the heart rate to between 60% and 90% of maximum.

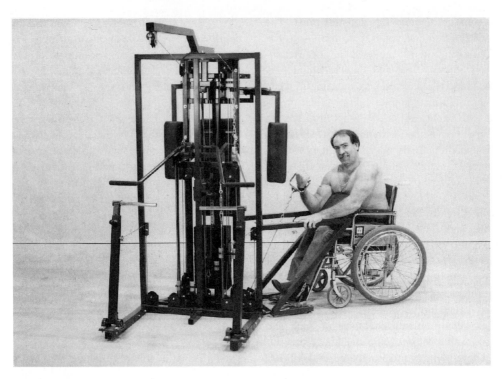

Equalizer 5000 Home and Office Gym. (Courtesy Equalizer Exercise Machines.)

Principles of Training

In 1990 the American College of Sports Medicine (ACSM) made recommendations in the following five areas for achieving and maintaining physical fitness:

1. *Mode of activity:* It is recommended that any continuous physical activity that uses large-muscle groups and that can be rhythmic and aerobic be used.[21] Activities such as walking, running, in-line skating, hiking, rowing, stair climbing, swimming, dancing, and cycling are suggested.

2. *Frequency of training:* Frequency of training refers to the number of times per week a person should exercise. Rest periods are interspersed between training sessions to permit the body to recover.[9] For aerobic conditioning programs, the ACSM recommends at least three, but not more than five, sessions per week.[25] For resistance training, the classical frequency is three times per week.[18] However, some advanced programs of re-

sistance training may be as frequent as six times per week.[27]

3. *Intensity of training:* Intensity refers to the magnitude (percentage of one's capacity) of exercise during one exercise session. Usually the higher the intensity, the greater the benefit from the activity. In aerobic activity the faster the pace, the greater the intensity. In resistance training, the heavier the weight, the greater the intensity.[15] With individuals with disabilities, low to moderate intensity will provide these advantages: (1) less chance of cardiovascular problems, (2) possibly fewer injuries, and (3) a greater probability that the students will continue their exercise programs after formal instruction.

4. *Duration of training:* Duration refers to the length of time a person exercises at a given time. Duration of exercise applies primarily to cardiorespiratory endurance development. The ACSM recom-

mends 20 to 60 minutes of sustained activity. High-intensity activities (80% to 90% of maximum heart rate) require shorter periods of time; activities that generate a lower level of intensity (less than 70% of maximum heart rate) require longer periods of time. The duration time should include at least a 10-minute warm-up period and a 5- to 10-minute cooldown period. When one is working with students who have disabilities, it is better to begin with a shorter duration of less intense activity and gradually work toward lengthening the time and intensity of the activity.

5. *Resistance training:* The goal of resistance training is to improve overall muscular strength and endurance. To develop and maintain a healthy body composition, the ACSM recommends moderate intensity strength training at least twice weekly. The workout should consist of one set of 8 to 10 repetitions of 8 to 10 exercises.[21] Isotonic or isokinetic exercises of major muscle groups should be included. To develop strength, it is recommended that 60% of the maximum resistance a person can move be used. The number of times the weight is moved depends on the repetition continuum selected. The training effect is increased in proportion to the number of times an exercise is repeated, up to a point.[2] It is recommended that exercises be repeated three to six times in a row (one set) to increase strength.[9] Once a student can repeat the exercise six times in a row with ease, the number of sets should be increased by one. As the amount of resistance is increased, the number of repetitions is decreased and then gradually increased.

Maximum voluntary contraction is the ability to use (recruit) as many muscle fibers as possible to develop force. As a muscle begins to tire, more muscle fibers are recruited to move the force. The maximum voluntary contraction is the last repetition of an exercise when maximum force can be generated before the muscle fatigues. Successful training programs include at least one maximum voluntary contraction.[27] For the sedentary person the maximum voluntary contraction will occur after very few repetitions have been completed. Students with disabilities who are just beginning exercise programs should be closely monitored to prevent injuries that may occur because of muscle fatigue.

A child experiences success with a 3-foot-high basketball hoop. (Courtesy Dallas Independent School District.)

Developing Training Programs

The American Academy of Pediatrics[1] and the National Strength and Conditioning Association[19] agree that strength training is permissible for children under the age of puberty only when expert supervision is provided.

Fitness instruction for students with disabilities should be conducted in conformance with the individual education program (IEP). This means that there should be measurable, observable objectives and that present levels of educational performance should be determined for each student when the activity program is begun. To accommodate the changing demands of the ability level of each learner, the following principles are suggested:

1. *Individual differences:* Every student's IEP should be based on specific assessment data that indicate the unique needs for alleviating deficits in prerequisites for self-sufficient living.
2. *Overload/shaping principle:* Increases in strength and endurance result from small increments of workload greater than the present ability. Overload can be achieved in the following ways:
   a. Increase the number of repetitions or sets.
   b. Increase the distance covered.
   c. Increase the speed with which the exercise is executed.

d. Increase the number of minutes of continuous effort.

e. Decrease the rest interval between active sessions.

f. Any combination of the above.

3. *Maintenance or development of physical fitness:* Training sessions can be used to maintain or develop physical fitness. The data on the frequency of the training will indicate whether the training results maintain or develop physical fitness levels.

4. *Physical fitness for a purpose:* Values gained from exercises should be relevant to development of functional skills and/or health components. Exercises are highly specific; they need to be done at intensity levels commensurate with the ability of the student.

5. *Active/voluntary movement:* Benefits are greatest when the exercise is active (done by the student) rather than passive (done by the therapist or teacher). When the student performs the activity, it is possible to provide behavioral measurement and apply learning principles from research and demonstration.

6. *Recovery/cooldown:* Students should not lie or sit down immediately after high-intensity exercise. This tends to subvert return of blood to the heart and cause dizziness. Cooldown should entail continued slow walking or mild activity.

7. *Warm-up:* At least 10 minutes of warm-up exercises using movements specific to training should precede high-intensity exercise sessions or competitive games. The warm-up is particularly important for persons with chronic respiratory problems or cardiovascular conditions. Warm-ups should emphasize stretching exercises that facilitate range of motion (flexibility) rather than ballistic (bouncing) exercises.

Examples of ways to write behavioral physical fitness goals are provided in the box on p. 205.

Contraindications

Physical educators should know what exercises or activities are contraindicated for each individual. Lasko-McCarthey and Knopf[16] recommend avoiding the following movements during exercises:

▪ Head circles that involve circumduction/hyperextension of the cervical spine

▪ Trunk circling that involves flexing the spine from a standing position with the legs straight

▪ Shoulder stands

▪ Hyperextension of the spine from a prone (face-down) position

▪ Standing toe touches with straight legs

▪ Bilateral straight-leg raises

▪ Sit-ups with feet held and hands behind head

▪ Sit-ups with straight legs

▪ Trunk twists from a standing position

▪ Deep knee bends (squats)

▪ Bench press performed with the feet on the floor

▪ Hip flexor stretches from a prone (face-down) or kneeling position

▪ Hurdle stretches

▪ Prone flies from a standing position

▪ Military presses with head extended (dorsiflexed)

▪ Isometric exercises for individuals over age 40 or those with a history of cardiovascular disease

▪ Immediate rest after intense exercise

In addition, the medical records of individuals with disabilities should always be reviewed to determine whether specific exercises or activities have been identified as contraindicated by medical personnel.

Static Stretching Exercises

Adapted physical education requires that tasks be adapted to the ability level of each learner. When this occurs, each student with a disability can be accommodated. Usually individuals with disabilities have tight muscles and connective tissue, which limits joint range of motion. Stretching is an important activity for increasing movement of desired joints. Lasko-McCarthey and Knopf[16] recommend the following practices for achieving a permanent increase in flexibility: (1) engage in a 5- to 10-minute warm-up before stretching; (2) do not apply too much force to the stretch; (3) hold the stretch for a duration of 30 to 60 seconds; (4) do not perform stretching if pain, infection, or edema is present; and (5) incorporate stretches at the end of the cooldown to prevent adaptive shortening and promote relaxation of muscles.

Walk-Run Program for Cardiovascular Endurance

A walk-run program has at least two variables that can be manipulated to make it more or less difficult: (1) the

Behavioral Statements for Development of Physical Fitness

Many physical fitness tasks are measurable. Usually, if measure can be incorporated into a task, performance difficulty can be prescribed for the individual learner. Below are statements that involve physical and motor tasks requiring specifications of measurement to be ascribed to the tasks. Many children with disabilities will be able to participate in these tasks at their ability level if objectives are sequenced.

1. Walk a specified distance at a heart rate of 120 beats per minute.
2. Jog and walk alternately 50 steps for a specified distance.
3. Run in place lifting the foot a specified distance from the floor a specified number of times for a specified period of time.
4. Run in place 100 steps in a specified amount of time.
5. Run a specified distance in a specified period of time.
6. Perform a modified push-up a specified number of times.
7. Perform a modified chin-up a specified number of times.
8. Climb a rope a specified distance in a specified amount of time.
9. Perform toe raises with a specified amount of weight a specified number of repetitions.
10. Perform a sit-up (modified if necessary) a specified number of repetitions; sit-up difficulty can be modified by performance on an incline, where gravity assists with the sit-up.
11. Perform a specified number of dips on the parallel bars (lower and raise the body by straightening and bending the arms) with a specified amount of weight attached to a belt. If one dip cannot be done, reduce the range of motion of the dip.
12. Perform arm curls with a specified weight and a specified number of repetitions.
13. Curl the toes and pick up a specified number of pencils or sticks of the same size; move them a specified distance to a target of a specified size over a specified time frame.
14. Perform a wrist roll in which a rope of specified length has a weight of specified pounds attached to it a specified number of repetitions over a specified time frame.
15. Perform toe curls with a towel with the heels flat on the floor; bunch up the towel under the feet, and put a weight of a specified number of pounds on the towel a specified distance from the toes.
16. Perform a wrist curl in which the wrist is over the edge of a table or a chair; then bend and straighten the wrist, holding a weight of a specified amount a specified number of repetitions.
17. Jump and reach a specified height.
18. Throw a medicine ball of specified weight from a sitting position a specified distance.
19. Run a specified distance over a specified period of time.
20. Run around a hoop 4 feet in diameter a specified number of times over a specified time frame.
21. Leap over a rope placed at a specified height.
22. Leap over two lines on the floor that are a specified distance apart.
23. Step up and then down on a bench of a specified height a specified number of repetitions over a specified time frame.
24. Run in a figure-eight fashion around a specified number of cones set a specified distance apart a specified number of times during a specified time frame.
25. Perform a shuttle run in which the parallel lines are a specified distance apart a specified number of trips in a specified amount of time.

distance that the individual should run and (2) the length of time permitted to travel the prescribed distance. Suggested distance intervals are 1 mile, 1¼ miles, 1½ miles, 1¾ miles, and 2 miles. Suggested target criterion times for each distance could be 15 minutes for 1 mile, 17 minutes for 1¼ miles, 20 minutes for 1½ miles, 24 minutes for 1¾ miles, and 28 minutes for 2 miles. The learner should be reinforced for improving performance on each subsequent day.

Jumping Rope for Cardiovascular Endurance

When a cardiovascular fitness program is being conducted for individuals with disabilities, each individualized program should have specific objectives tailored to the present level of ability of the student. A continuum of exercise activities can be used to accommodate individual differences. A procedure for constructing an individualized physical fitness program of rope jumping may be as follows:

1. Make a 4-minute musical tape recording that uses a cadence of 70 jumps per minute.
2. Test the students to determine how long they can jump without a rest interval.
3. Prescribe each individual to continue for 2 seconds longer each day.
4. When an individual can continuously jump for 4 minutes, substitute another tape that uses a cadence of 80 jumps per minute.

Under these conditions there would be two stations of different frequencies, but each person at each of those stations would be performing for specific lengths of time commensurate with their present levels of ability. Increasing cadences could be added to the program as individuals increase in cardiovascular endurance. Another factor that could be introduced into the program to make it more or less difficult would be to vary the length of the rest intervals between repeated bouts of exercise.

Modification of the Physical Fitness Training System

Training systems can be modified to accommodate persons with disabilities. All students need to participate in activities that are commensurate with their needs with respect to workloads. However, specific types of disabilities require special adaptations to adequately meet unique physical activity needs. General disabilities that need special accommodation are those of sensory impairment, physical impairment, and intellectual impairment.

Accommodation of Individual Differences

Physical fitness activities for students with disabilities must be individually tailored to abilities and the severity of the condition. The goals of the exercise program among persons with disabilities will vary depending on the type of impairment and will differ from those of individuals with no disabilities.[23]

There are at least four ways that exercises can be modified to accommodate the ability level of each student with a disability:

1. The number of repetitions can be modified to make the task easier or more difficult. The fewer the number of repetitions, the less difficult the activity.
2. The position of the body in relation to gravity during the activity can be modified. Strength exercises done using gravity for assistance are the least demanding (e.g., executing a sit-up on a slant board with the head higher than the feet). Strength exercises done in a side-lying position will eliminate the effect of gravity (e.g., going from a full body extension to a crunch position while in a side-lying position). Exercises done against gravity are the third most demanding (e.g., executing a sit-up from a supine position or on a slant board with the head lower than the feet). The most demanding strength exercises are those done with resistance and against gravity (e.g., individual leg extensions from a sitting position while wearing ankle weights).
3. The time that it takes to complete a set of repetitions can be shortened or lengthened. The shorter the time interval for completing the work, the more difficult the exercise task.
4. The number of sets of repetitions can be modified. Greater numbers of sets are associated with more intense and difficult training regimens. The number of sets can be decreased to accommodate the individual's present level of ability. Applying these principles to interval training for persons with disabilities will permit participation in and benefit from these exercise routines.

Circuit Training

Accommodation for individual differences for most students with disabilities can be easily accomplished if a circuit training program is used. Circuit training involves using a different type of exercise at each of a series of stations. Individual differences can be accommodated by altering the intensity and workload required of each student (Figure 8-1). To meet the individual physical needs of each student in circuit training, the following modifications can be made:

1. Develop a wide variety of activity levels, the lower of which can accommodate most individuals with disabilities.
2. Assign students with disabilities to only those stations in the circuit that meet their assessed needs.
3. Modify the nature of the activity at each station so that each student can participate at the appropriate ability level.
4. Provide peer assistance, if available, and special instructions for use of specific apparatus or equipment.

Name of exercise	Developmental levels*				
	I	II	III	IV	V
	Wt.	Wt.	Wt.	Wt.	Wt.
Two arm curl	40	50	55	60	65
Military press	50	60	65	70	75
Deep knee bends	70	80	85	90	95
Dead lift (straight leg)	70	80	85	90	95
French curl (or dip) with dumbbell	10	15	20	25	30
Situps (time)	--	--	--	--	--
Bench step-ups (time)	--	--	--	--	--
Bench press	55	60	65	75	85
Lateral raises (dumbbell)	5	10	15	20	25
Pushups (time)	--	--	--	--	--

*When 10 repetitions are reached, advance to the next developmental level.

figure 8-1
A suggested circuit training program.

Accommodating for Specific Types of Disabilities

Students with varying types of disabilities may need specific accommodation in circuit training exercises. Visually impaired and deaf students need assistance with communication systems that provide them with instructional information, whereas students with physical disabilities need accommodation for impaired motor functioning. Students who are mentally retarded or who have a specific learning disability, on the other hand, may need assistance in comprehending the task. The following are suggestions for accommodating visually and physically disabled students.

Visual Disabilities

Students with visual impairments need confidence to cope with training programs. They may need for the exercise environment to be modified, or they may need help from others to participate in training activities. Some environmental aids and supplemental assistance that may enable the student with a visual disability to benefit from circuit training can be found in the box at right.

Circuit Training: Environmental Aids and Supplemental Assistance for Students with Visual Disabilities

1. Provide boundaries that define the general exercise area to facilitate mobility of the student within the exercise area.
2. Use boundaries to define the location of each specific exercise station.
3. Use sighted peers, if available, to help the student with visual disabilities move from station to station and to comprehend each task.
4. Provide a complete explanation of the way to use specific apparatus or equipment.
5. Arrange the exercise area the same way every time so that the student with visual disabilities will be able to move through a familiar environment.
6. Arrange for enlarged type or braille descriptions of the activity at each session.
7. Physically move the student through the exercise several times.
8. Plan the circuit so that movement to different areas for exercise is minimized.
9. Provide initial reference points that indicate where the student starts in the circuit.
10. Use brightly colored objects as boundaries to assist students with residual vision.

Physical Disabilities

Students with physical disabilities may need accommodations to physically move through the environment and to manipulate exercise equipment. Some accommodations to enable these individuals to participate in circuit training follow:

1. Select activities that involve functional body parts (e.g., if the legs are impaired, prescribe activities for the arms).
2. If an individual has limited function of the wrists and fingers, place pads on the forearms and select activities that will enable the individual to move the weights with the padded forearms.
3. If necessary, attach weights to the body or attach a body part to a piece of equipment with Velcro straps (e.g., if the student has difficulty keeping the feet in bicycle stirrups, attach the feet to the pedals with Velcro straps) (Figure 8-2).
4. Establish an exercise environment that is accessible for students in wheelchairs.

Selected Fitness Problems

As mentioned earlier in this chapter, the problems of underdevelopment and low physical vitality are closely associated with a great number of organic, mental, physiological, and emotional problems discussed throughout this book. However, two major problem areas transcend the others: malnutrition and overweight.

Malnutrition

The term **malnutrition** means poor nutrition, whether there is an excess or a lack of nutrients to the body. In either instance, the malnourished individual has relatively poor physical fitness and other serious disadvantages.

It is important that the cause of physical underdevelopment be identified. One cause of physical underdevelopment may be a lack of physical activity, which, consequently, does not provide an opportunity for the body to develop its potential. However, some children are physically underdeveloped partially because of **undernutrition.** When a person's body weight is more than 10% below the ideal weight indicated by standard age and weight tables, undernutrition may be a cause. Tension, anxiety, depression, and other emotional factors may restrict a person's appetite, causing insufficient caloric intake and weight loss. The most severe emotional

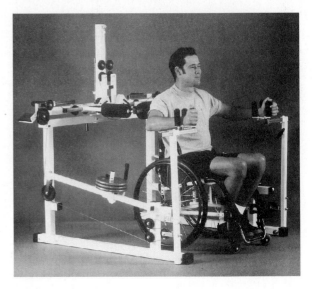

figure 8-2

The Uppertone system enables individuals without hand grip strength to develop and maintain upper body strength. (Courtesy GPK, Inc.)

disturbances causing insufficient caloric intake and weight loss are **anorexia nervosa** and/or **bulimia.** Impairment in physical development may also ensue. In culturally deprived areas, common in the urban inner city, children may lack proper nutrition as a result of insufficient food resulting from poverty or the use of money for other priorities (e.g., drugs), idiosyncrasy, or loss of appetite caused by some organic problem. Proper nutrition and exercise go hand in hand in growing children. One without the other may cause lack of optimum physical development. The role of the physical educator in dealing with the underweight person is to help establish sound living habits with particular emphasis paid to proper diet, rest, and relaxation.

Students from affluent families should be encouraged to keep a 3-day food intake diary, after which, with the help of the teacher, a daily average of calories consumed is computed. After determining the average number of calories taken in, the student is encouraged to increase the daily intake by eating extra meals that are both nutritious and high in calories.

The physical educator must be sensitive to the unique problems of the homeless child, the child living

A high ropes course provides a physical challenge and an opportunity for physical development. (Courtesy Wisconsin Lions Camp, Rosholt, Wis.)

in poverty, and the nutritionally abused child. A change in caloric intake is not a simple matter of the child understanding the relationship between caloric intake and health. Often the child is a victim, unable to control the powerful forces around him or her. The physical educator may take the lead in arranging for the child to have a federally or state-subsidized free breakfast or free lunch. This may be the only meal the child eats during the day. In addition, the physical educator may use fresh fruit as a reward, always seeking an opportunity to allow the hungry child to earn the reward.

Overweight

Many persons in the United States are **overweight. Obesity,** particularly in adults, is considered one of the great current medical problems because of its relationship to cardiovascular problems and other diseases. The frequency of overweight among patients with angina pectoris, coronary insufficiency, hypertension, and coronary occlusions is considerable.

Overweight may be defined as any excess of 10% or more above the ideal weight for a person, and obesity is any excess of 20% or more above the ideal weight. Obesity constitutes pathological overweight that requires correction. Several factors must be considered in determining whether a person is overweight. Among these are gender, weight, height, age, general body build, bone size, muscular development, and accumulations of subcutaneous fat.

In the past, sufficient attention has not been given to the diagnosis of overweight among many children in our society. The incidence of overweight among children in our schools has been estimated at 10% or more—a rate of such significance that attention to prevention and remediation should be provided by public school doctors, nurses, and health and physical educators.

Overweight persons have a greater tendency to contract diseases of the heart, circulatory system, kidneys, and pancreas. They also have a predisposition to structural foot and joint conditions because of their excess weight and lack of motor skill to accommodate the weight.

The basic reason for overweight is that the body's food and caloric consumption is greater than the physical activity or energy expended to utilize the calories. Consequently, the excess energy food is stored in the body as fat, leading to overweight. In many instances overeating is a matter of habit. Thus the body is continually in the process of acquiring more calories than are needed to maintain a normal weight.

Overweight and obesity have many causes. Among them are (1) caloric imbalance from eating incorrectly in relationship to energy expended in the form of activity; (2) dysfunction of the endocrine glands, particularly the pituitary and the thyroid, which regulate fat distribution in the body; and (3) emotional disturbance.

There is impressive evidence that obesity in adults has its origin in childhood habits. There seems to be a substantial number of overweight adults whose difficulty in controlling their appetite stems from childhood. The social environment may have some influence on obesity. In the preschool years, thinness rather than obesity is the general developmental characteristic of children. However, during the early school years and up to early adolescence, children seem susceptible to excess fat deposition.

A belief prevalent among some authorities is that a

high percentage of obesity is caused by emotional problems. They theorize that children at the age of 7 years are particularly susceptible to obesity from overeating in order to compensate for being unhappy and lonely. Evidently, eating may give comfort to children. This particular period is significant because it is when children are transferring close emotional ties from the family to peer relationships. If children do not successfully establish close friendships with other children, they feel alone. A compensatory mechanism of adjustment is eating, which gives comfort. Eating also may be used as a comfort when children have trouble at home or at school.

Adverse effects of obesity

Obese children, in many instances, exhibit immature social and emotional characteristics. It is not uncommon for obese children to dislike the games played by their peers, since obesity handicaps them in being adept at the games in which their peers are adequate. These children are often clumsy and slow, objects of many stereotyped jokes, and incapable of holding a secure social position among other children. Consequently, they may become oversensitive and unable to defend themselves and thus may withdraw from healthy play and exercise. This withdrawal from activity decreases the energy expenditure needed to maintain the balance that combats obesity. Therefore in many instances obesity leads to sedentary habits. It is often difficult to encourage these children to participate in forms of exercise that permit great expenditures of energy.

Obesity may be an important factor as children form ideas about themselves as persons and about how they think they appear to others. The ideas that they have about themselves will be influenced by their own discoveries, by what others say about them, and by the attitudes shown toward them. If the children find that their appearance elicits hostility, disrespect, or negative attention from parents and peers, these feelings may affect their self-concept. Traits described by their parents and peers may affect their inner feelings and may be manifested in their behavior, since children often assess their worth in terms of their relationships with peers, parents, and other authority figures.

When children pass from the child-centered atmosphere of the home into the competitive activities of the early school years, social stresses are encountered. They must demonstrate physical abilities, courage, manipula-

A student develops age-appropriate sport skills. (Courtesy Adapted Physical Education Department, Jefferson Parish Public School System, New Orleans, La.)

tive skill, and social adeptness in direct comparison with other children of their age. The penalties for failure are humiliation, ridicule, and rejection from the group. Obesity places a tremendous social and emotional handicap on children. Therefore educators should give these children all possible assistance and guidance in alleviating or adjusting to obesity.

Programming for the obese child

Since overweight children often cannot perform the activities of the physical education program efficiently, it is not uncommon for them to dislike many of these activities. As a result of their inability to participate in the program, they are often the objects of practical jokes and disparaging remarks made by other children. In such an environment, obese and overweight boys and girls become unhappy and ashamed and often withdraw from the activity to circumvent emotional involvement with the group. The physical educator should attempt to create an environment that will enable the obese child to have successful experiences in the class, thus minimizing situations that could threaten the child's position as a person of worth. The physical educator is also chal-

table 8-1	
Behavior Management Techniques to Control When Conducting a Weight Control Program	
Program Punishers	Program Reinforcers
Poor program advice	Adequate program advice
Inappropriate schedule for activity	Convenient and regular routine
Musculoskeletal injury	Care of self and free from injury
Lack of progress in program	Measureable progress
Peer disapproval	Social approval

Guidelines for a Safe and Effective Weight Control Program

1. Know your desirable weight.
2. Count calories.
3. Try to calculate the energy expenditure through controlled workouts.
4. Do not cut out the food you like; cut down on the amounts you eat.
5. Seek medical treatment in the case of a glandular dysfunction.
6. Seek counseling when emotional causes are at the root of the problem.
7. Seek counseling on the consequences of obesity to the total personality.
8. Disrupt sedentary ways of living.

lenged in regard to developing the attitudes of the nondisabled majority. Consequently, proposing to the class the acceptance of children who are different is an important and worthwhile goal of the physical educator.

Conducting a weight control program

The conduction of a weight control program should follow the basic procedures according to the instructional process of the Education of the Handicapped Act. First, there must be a goal—a desirable body weight that the individual is to achieve. Next, the present level should portray the weight of the person at the present. Third, short-term instructional objectives that lead from the present weight to the eventual goal must be developed. For instance, if the present body weight is 100 pounds and the desirable body weight is 90 pounds, then the series of short-term objectives could be in 1- or 2-pound increments. The weight loss goal will be reached most quickly if diet control is practiced while the exercise program is conducted. Appropriate goal setting will contribute not only to immediate weight loss, but also to changes in lifelong diet and exercise habits.

The use of behavioral management techniques contributes to success in weight control programs by controlling the positive influences and minimizing the negative variables of the program. Some of the positive aspects of behavior management that will strengthen weight control behaviors are (1) encouragement by the instructor, (2) a safe environment that keeps the student free from injury, (3) a variety of activities to reduce boredom, (4) a regularly scheduled routine, (5) a compatible, supportive social group, (6) feedback about progress toward short-term objectives that have been set, and (7)

social reinforcement when weight losses occur. Punishing features that should be minimized are (1) poor program advice, (2) inconvenient time and place, (3) muscle soreness and/or injury, (4) lack of progress, and (5) disapproval of participation in the program by peers and family. Table 8-1 portrays these variables.

There can be no one program for the remediation of children who are overweight. It is necessary that the true cause of the problem be found. When the cause of overweight or obesity is known, several avenues are available for treatment. Some rules to be applied for successful weight control are provided in the box above.

Obese or overweight students should be guided into activities that can be safely performed and successfully achieved. This will tend to encourage them to participate in more vigorous activities. Some of the activities that can be used to combat obesity are general conditioning exercises, jogging, dancing, rhythmical activities, swimming, and sports and games. Much can be done for these children through individual guidance, encouragement, and selection of the proper developmental experiences.

Weekly weigh-ins in which a certain number of pounds is scheduled to be lost in a given week provide program incentives. Sustained reduction may afford opportunities for establishing permanent patterns for exercise and eating. The value of the weigh-in is that it projects a precise goal for the student to achieve each

A world-class athlete with paraplegia works out regularly to maintain upper body strength. (Courtesy Abu Yilla, Dallas, Tex.)

week. Furthermore, the exercise program in which the student engages should be progressive. Exercises based on calculated energy expenditures are initiated with slight progression ensured in the program with each successive day of attendance. Suggested activities are walking, jogging, bicycle riding, rope jumping, swimming, stair and hill climbing, and stepping up on, and down from, a bench.

Spot reducing

Loss of weight results in a decrease in the amount of stored adipose tissue; however, which stores of adipose tissue will decrease cannot be predicted. Therefore it really is impossible to spot reduce.

Educational versus medical diets

If a physician indicates that there is a pathological condition that is associated with the weight condition, then a medically prescribed diet and exercise program should be provided by the physician. When no medical

pathological condition exists and the obesity can be treated by a change in caloric intake and by raising the energy expenditure, then an educationally prepared prescription can be conducted. The educational prescription involves changing behaviors that enable the individual to conform to lifestyle patterns that may be maintained over a long period. According to Steiner,[26] only 10% of persons who sustain rapid and large weight losses achieve lifetime weight control. Fad diets should be discouraged because of their potential threat to nutritional balance and their short-lived results.

Family Involvement in Active Lifestyles

Lifestyles of physical activity are shaped in part within the school setting and in part within the home. The family unit provides the primary social learning environment for the child. Parents serve as role models for children's attitudes and practices, and the extent to which the parents participate in physical activity does impact their child's attitude and behavior.[13] When family members support and cooperate with teachers, participation in physical activity is reinforced. For this reason, teachers should routinely reach out to the home to communicate their program goals and seek support.[5]

Effective collaboration of schools and families to facilitate physically active leisure lifestyles for persons with disabilities involves a blend of convenience, acceptability of information sent to the home, home-based curricula, and family learning opportunities. When these factors are controlled, the vast majority of families participate with the school to enhance their child's well-being.[11] Some successful components of a parent training program follow:

- Home packets that list the values of exercise, suggest types of activities, identify community resources, and highlight upcoming special physical activity events can be distributed to students on a regular basis by the physical education teacher.
- *Family fun nights* can be used to generate interest in the physical program, raise awareness of the value of exercise, and inform all members of the family about the joy and benefits of regular participation in physical activity. The evening should be a mini-health fair aimed at improving health habits. Events can be structured that demonstrate games and activities that individuals and families should participate in to enhance their health.

▪ Family scorecards should be distributed to families to allow them to record the amount and frequency of physical activity in which the child with a disability and the family participate. The scorecard should include specific activities for which points can be earned, the activities and points earned by the student, and the activities and points earned by the family as a whole.[13]

Implications for Physical Education

Physical education has emerged with new importance as awareness of the deleterious effect of inactivity on the sedentary adult population has increased. Through the efforts of many disciplines, the public is beginning to realize that proper exercise can be a deterrent to many characteristics of premature physiological aging, as well as to their concomitant diseases.

Research and studies have resulted in new concepts about the type of physical fitness activities best suited for adults. Acquisition of motor skills in physical education could encourage participation in ongoing physical activity, which in itself assists in maintaining physical fitness and controlling weight. Continuity of well-planned activities can serve as a preventive conditioner.

A multidisciplinary approach has resulted from medicine's concern for premature cardiovascular disease and the positive effects of proper exercise. The physician, physical educator, exercise physiologist, sports nutritionist, and many other professionals are lending their skills to help solve the problem of lack of physical fitness among adults. With the implementation of many medically oriented adult physical education programs, there is an increased need for trained teachers of adapted physical education who understand the problems and needs of the adult population. Establishing individual physical education programs for adults is one of the greatest challenges of our time.

SUMMARY

There are three purposes of physical fitness: (1) to promote and maintain health, (2) to develop prerequisites for maximum performance of daily living skills, and (3) to develop prerequisites for leisure and sport skills. Each person possesses a unique composition of physical and motor abilities and therefore should be assessed and pro- *vided with an individual program that will contribute to his or her development. Activity programs should be constructed so that the physical and motor fitness tasks can be adapted to the ability level of each learner. Circuit training can be used to develop a wide range of performance levels. Fitness training should include both resistance training and aerobic activities. Programs of activity should include mode of activity, frequency of training, intensity of training, duration of training, and resistance training. Physical and motor fitness is important for all persons. Although collectively persons with the same disability may be similar, each student with a disability needs an individualized physical fitness program.*

Physical and motor fitness programs are beneficial as deterrents to obesity. Weight control is a product of energy expenditure and balanced caloric intake. Therefore the amount of exercise is an important factor in the control of obesity. Behavior management techniques may assist in weight control.

Family interest and involvement in physical activity enhances the probability that a child will have a positive attitude toward and participate in an active lifestyle. Teachers should reach out to the home to encourage understanding of and participation in healthful activities.

Review Questions

1. Describe the components of physical fitness.
2. What are the causes of low physical fitness?
3. How would one determine a unique physical fitness need for an individual for functional skill?
4. What are the principles for conducting a physical fitness program?
5. What are some behavioral management principles that can be applied to conduction of a weight control program?

Student Activities

1. Select five group activities that could be used in a regular kindergarten class that would be fun for the class and also address Billy Bogg's physical fitness deficiency (see Chapter 2).
2. Working in small groups, with each group assigned a particular muscle group (e.g., abdominals, quadriceps, biceps), develop four levels of strengthening exercises (with, without, and against gravity, and against gravity with resistance) for your assigned muscle group.
3. Construct a circuit training program that includes three levels of activities to promote shoulder girdle strength,

abdominal strength, quadricep endurance, and cardiovascular endurance.

4. Design and implement a weight reduction program of exercise and diet that incorporates behavior management principles.
5. Evaluate and design a program for persons who are overweight.

References

1. American Academy of Pediatrics: Weight training and weight lifting: information for the pediatrician, *Physician Sportsmed* 11:157-161, 1983.
2. Bar-Or O: Trainability of physical fitness measures, *Physician Sportsmed* 17:70-82, 1989.
3. Bar-Or O: Importance of differences between children and adults for exercise testing and exercise prescription. In Skinner JS, editor: *Exercise testing and exercise prescription for special cases,* Philadelphia, 1993, Lea & Febiger.
4. Carlucci D et al: Exercise: not just for the healthy, *Physician Sportsmed* 19(7):47-54, 1991.
5. Cooper P: *Update on comprehensive school health programs in West Felciana Parish.* Paper presented at the Louisiana Association for Health, Physical Education, Recreation, and Dance, New Orleans, La, 1992.
6. Coyle CP, Sanatiago MC: Anaerobic exercise training and depressive symptomatology in adults with physical disabilities, *Arch Phys Med Rehabil* 76:647-652, 1995.
7. Eichstaedt C et al: *Physical fitness and motor skill levels of individuals with mental retardation,* Normal, Ill, 1991, Illinois State University Printing Service.
8. Evans IM, Meyer L: *An educative approach to behavior problems,* Baltimore, 1985, Paul H Brookes Publishing.
9. Fleck SJ, Kraemer WJ: Resistance training: basic principles, *Physician Sportsmed* 16:160-171, 1988.
10. Hamdorf PA et al: Physical training effects on the fitness and habitual activity patterns of elderly women, *Arch Phys Med Rehabil* 73:603-607, 1992.
11. Hearn MD et al: Involving families in cardiovascular health promotion: the CATCH feasibility study, *J Sch Health* 23:22-31, 1992.
12. Humphrey JH: *An overview of childhood fitness,* Springfield, Ill, 1991, Charles C Thomas.
13. Johnson CC et al: CATCH: family process evaluation in a multicenter trial, *Health Educ Q* 2:S91-S106, 1994.
14. Katch FI, McArdle WS: *Nutrition, weight control and exercise,* ed 2, Philadelphia, 1983, Lea & Febiger.
15. Kraemer WJ, Fleck SJ: Resistance training: exercise prescription, *Physician Sportsmed* 16:69-81, 1988.
16. Lasko-McCarthey P, Knopf KG: *Adapted physical education for adults with disabilities,* ed 3, Dubuque, Iowa, 1992, Eddie Bower publishing.
17. Lord SR, Caplan GA, Ward JA: Balance, reaction time, and muscle strength in exercising and nonexercising older women: a pilot study, *Arch Phys Med Rehabil* 74:837-839, 1993.
18. McDonagh MJ, Davies CT: Adaptive response of mammalian skeletal muscles to exercise with high loads, *Eur Appl Physio* 52:139-155, 1984.
19. National Strength and Conditioning Association: Position statement on prepubescent strength training, *Natl Strength Condit* 7:27-31, 1985.
20. Pagenoff SA: The use of aquatics with cerebral palsied adolescents, *Am J Occup Ther* 38:469-473, 1984.
21. Payne WA, Hahn DB: *Understanding your health,* ed 4, St Louis, 1995, Mosby.
22. Pommering TL et al: Effects of an aerobic program on community-based adults with mental retardation, *Ment Retard* 32:218-226, 1994.
23. Poser CM, Ronthal M: Exercise and Alzheimer's disease, Parkinson's disease and multiple sclerosis, *Physician Sportsmed* 19(12):85-92, 1991.
24. Seaman JA, editor: *Physical best and individuals with disabilities: a handbook for inclusion in fitness programs,* Reston, Va, 1995, American Association for Active Lifestyles and Fitness.
25. Sparling PB, Tinklepaugh MP: *A fitness primer: a guide to exercise and diet for enhanced health,* Dubuque, Iowa, 1991, Kendall/Hunt Publishing.
26. Steiner MM: *Clinical approach to endocrine problems in childhood,* St Louis, 1970, Mosby.
27. Tesch PA, Colliander EB, Kaiser P: Metabolism during intensity heavy-resistance exercise, *Eur Appl Physio* 55:362-366, 1986.
28. Winnick J, Short F: *Physical fitness testing for the disabled: project UNIQUE,* Champaign, Ill, 1985, Human Kinetics.
29. Winnick J, Short FX: *A health-related criterion-referenced test for adolescents with spinal cord injuries.* Paper presented at the annual meeting of the National Consortium of Physical Education and Recreation for Individuals with Disabilities, Alexandria, Va, 1995.
30. Wiseman DC: *Physical education for exceptional students: theory to practice,* Albany, NY, 1994, Delmar Publishers.

Suggested Readings

American College of Sports Medicine: *American College of Sports Medicine fitness,* Champaign, Ill, 1993, Human Kinetics.

Corbin CB, Lindsey R: *Concepts of fitness and wellness with laboratories, ed. 8,* Dubuque, Iowa, 1994, Brown/Benchmark.

chapter **n i n e**

Psychosocial Delays

Courtesy Texas Special Olympics.

Objectives

Describe the nature of infant mortality in the United States.

Explain the impact of prenatal exposure to drugs on children with and without disabilities.

Describe the nature of abuse and neglect on children with and without disabilities.

Explain the relationship of poverty and homelessness to inadequate psychosocial development in children.

Describe some of the causes of violence in our society and explain the impact of that violence on children and the schools.

List some of the signs/symptoms that a child or adolescent may be a gang member or a "wannabe."

Explain the development of play behaviors.

Describe the nature of the physical education setting in which children with psychosocial delays may learn and thrive. Address the eight things children need in order to detoxify the learning environment.

Task

Review Billy Bogg's assessment information in Chapter 2 and individual education program (IEP) in Chapter 3. As you read this chapter, think about the play behaviors Billy needs to develop and describe teaching strategies you would use to accomplish his psychosocial long-term goals and short-term objectives.

ducators must respond to the increased psychosocial needs of the infants, children, and adolescents they serve. Children with and without disabilities are entering the public school system unprepared, understimulated, abused, abandoned, homeless, unloved, frightened, distrustful, tired, hungry, and unkempt. Because any of these factors may have a serious detrimental impact on the **psychosocial development** of any child and may cause the child to be at risk for failure in school and in the society in general, they are considered in this chapter.

Children with disabilities may also demonstrate delayed psychosocial development. Factors specific to these children that contribute to this delay are also discussed. In addition, strategies for enhancing psychosocial development in or through participation in developmentally appropriate play, games, leisure and recreation, and sports in a well-designed physical education program are considered.

Marian Wright Edelman, president and co-founder of the Children's Defense Fund, released data indicating that one of three children will live in poverty, drop out of school, or be abused or neglected before reaching adulthood[6]:

> These shameful numbers have small, individual faces and feelings and suffering . . . At a time when nearly 16 million children are poor, almost 3 million are abused and neglected, and 400,000 drop out of school, Congress should be strengthening rather than permanently shredding federal child protections and recklessly slashing child investments.

Our children should be proclaimed an endangered species. Our most precious natural resource is being squandered; millions of children are growing up feeling unempowered and disenfranchised. During this critical time, state and federal legislators continue to allocate more and more money for prisons and less and less money for child care, child welfare, child protective services, and education programs. Karen Thomas[60] wrote:

> On playgrounds, in school hallways, on street corners, and in their homes, children in New York City and Washington, D.C. [and Dallas, Los Angeles, St. Louis, Houston—addition, ours], are fantasizing about the day that their lives will abruptly end. They are picking colors for the satin of their coffins, instructing their parents what they would like to be buried in and describing details to make their funerals different from the others they have already witnessed. *Kids are playing funeral* [emphasis ours].

The physical educator, standing before a gymnasium full of 60 children, can assume that at least 20 of those children are at significant risk for school failure because of overwhelming poverty, homelessness, abuse, and/or inappropriate or nonexistent parenting. These numbers are even higher in large, urban school districts. This is an overwhelming, humbling experience. It is even more overwhelming and more humbling when the physical educator really knows and loves the children reflected in those statistics.

At-Risk Infants, Children, and Adolescents

A growing number of infants, children, and adolescents in this society are **at risk.** The societal forces acting on these children are overwhelming. They include poverty, homelessness, prenatal maternal neglect or abuse, child abuse, violence, classism, and racism. According to Geoffrey Cowley[8]:

> Children have never had it easy. A fair proportion have always been beaten, starved, raped or abandoned, and until quite recently even the loved ones faced daunting obstacles . . . Nearly one in four is born into poverty, a formidable predictor of lifelong ill health, and a growing number lack such basic advantages as a home, two parents, and regular access to a doctor. Every year thousands die violently from abuse or preventable accidents. Millions go unvaccinated against common childhood diseases . . . *American children remain the most neglected in the developed world* [emphasis ours].

Infant Mortality

The most obvious indication of the neglect that Cowley[8] describes is the fact that the United States ranks behind 19 developed nations in its infant mortality rate. The National Center for Health Statistics[28] released information recently that indicated that the U.S. infant mortality rate reached a record low of 7.9 infant deaths for every 1000 births in 1994, down from 8.3 in 1993. However, there has not been a reduction in the infant mortality rate for black infants; rather, there has been a significant increase. In fact, the black infant mortality rate was 16.5 per 1000 births in 1994, making them almost 2½ times more likely than white infants to die before their first birthday.

Almost as frightening as the infant mortality rate is the number of infants born in the United States with low birth weight and **shortened gestation.** According to the National Commission to Prevent Infant Mortality, there has been an escalation in the number of low birth weight and very low birth weight infants born in the United States. This is true, in part, because of the increasingly sophisticated technology that allows for intensive prenatal and perinatal intervention. In fact, in neonatal centers characterized by aggressive neonatal and perinatal management, death rates as low as 21% have been seen in very premature or very low birth weight infants.[40]

Still, at issue is the fact that low birth weight infants are more likely to die than infants of normal weight, often because of lack of access to high-technology neonatal centers. Infants with low birth weight (less than 5½ pounds) are 40 times more likely to die within their first month and 20 times more likely to die within their first year than are infants weighing more than 5½ pounds at birth.[8]

Of equal importance is the fact that the immature and incomplete in utero development of these children causes them to be at serious risk for developmental disabilities throughout their lives. These low birth weight infants who survive have high risks of deafness, blindness, mental retardation, and other disabilities.[18] In addition, these infants will be at a serious disadvantage in every skill required for adequate, much less successful, performance in school.[55]

Alcohol and Other Drug Abuse

According to Greer[20]:

> We are facing the emerging of what some are now calling a **"bio-underclass";** a frightening proportion of the next generation of school children will have impairments which, in the words of Dr. Harold Nickens of the American Society of Addiction Medicine, may require the medical community "to define an entirely new, organic brain syndrome" based on the physical and chemical damage done to fetal brains by drug-abusing mothers.

The escalation of the use and abuse of alcohol and other drugs has had a profound impact on the quality of life of millions of infants, children, and adolescents with and without disabilities. Over 1 million women in the United States who use and abuse alcohol, nicotine, marijuana, cocaine, or other drugs may give birth to babies with developmental delays. Fetal alcohol exposure is the nation's leading known cause of mental retardation, surpassing Down syndrome and spina bifida. The figures are staggering. Between 5000 and 10,000 children are born with severe fetal alcohol syndrome each year.[8] According to Dr. Ira Chasnoff, president of the National As-

sociation for Perinatal Addiction Research and Education, about 11% of all newborns, or 375,000 infants, were exposed to drugs in utero.[9]

Characteristics of infants exposed to drugs in utero

Wiliams, Howard, and McLaughlin[69] found that infants with fetal alcohol syndrome (FAS) are affected by central nervous system dysfunction, craniofacial defects, and growth retardation. Neonates with FAS exhibit poor sucking behaviors, disrupted sleep behaviors, tremors, abnormal reflexes, hypertonia, and inability to ignore extraneous stimuli in the environment.[65] In later infancy, these researchers noted continued disruption in sleep behaviors, delays in motor development, poor visual recognition memory, spoken language delays, and difficulty with verbal comprehension.

In their early school years, victims of fetal alcohol abuse often exhibit poor **impulse control,** difficulty with skills related to socialization, excessive demands for body contact, and continued delays in fine and gross motor behavior.[12,65] Streissguth et al.[54] noted that the problems associated with FAS persist well into adolescence. Adolescents exhibit difficulty with cause-effect relationships; difficulty with social interactions and friendships, including social withdrawal; poor attention; dependency; and difficulty with conduct in group situations (e.g., school and work settings).

Greer[20] reported that children exposed to cocaine in utero—those born addicted to cocaine—face overwhelming odds. The results of early research suggest that the cocaine-addicted infant may suffer from poor **body-state regulation,** tremors, chronic irritability, and poor visual orientation. Crack-abusing women are giving birth to babies with small heads, missing bowels, and malformed genitals who suffer strokes and seizures as infants.

Those infants exposed to drugs in utero who survive the tenuous first year demonstrate the characteristics of any postdrug impairment syndrome, including difficult withdrawal experiences.[18] Rotholz et al.[47] found a greater likelihood of passive behaviors, even in the learning environment, among young children who had been exposed to crack/cocaine. Because a child engaged in early learning needs to be an active learner, the child exposed to crack/cocaine is at early risk for school failure.

Waller[64] noted that crack-exposed children between

the ages of 5 and 17 years continued to exhibit behaviors that interfered with learning or work, including:

- Violent tendencies
- Inappropriate social behavior
- Hyperactivity
- Learning difficulties
- Apparent lack of conscience; lying and stealing
- Tendency to isolate self from others
- Lack of impulse control
- Little or no understanding of cause and effect

It is almost impossible to imagine the impact of this prenatal child abuse—women literally abusing their babies with alcohol, crack, heroin, PCP, and **poly drugs** when the infants are in utero. The child protective service agencies, child welfare agencies, and the foster care system are being bombarded. Not only have these infants been "abandoned" during the prenatal experience, but often these infants are subsequently abandoned on the streets and in the hospitals. The women who give birth to these infants commonly continue to be drug abusers and often are unable to care for themselves, much less an infant.

Abandoned infants and children, without extended family willing to assume responsibility, generally are placed in protective custody of the state. The first placement is generally in a foster care home. A study of the foster care system in New York demonstrated an escalated need and increased demand on the child protective service system in recent years. In 1980, 19% of the children placed in foster homes were under the age of 5; in 1990, over 50% of children placed in foster homes were under the age of 5. This dramatic increase is directly attributable to crack abuse.[42]

U.S. schools are facing the same overwhelming need. The Los Angeles Unified School District has developed a pilot preschool program designed to serve children exposed prenatally to crack. According to Wehling[67]:

> The pilot preschool program in the Los Angeles Unified School District is one of the first in the nation to tackle a problem that many educators fear is about to explode nationally: a surge in the number of drug-damaged children entering public schools. These children present a variety of developmental, neurological, and behavioral challenges—including unusually short attention spans, hyperactivity, sudden temper flare-ups, speech and language delays, poor task organization, and an exaggerated need for structured routine.

A child engages in solitary play. (Courtesy Callier Center for Communications Disorders, Dallas, Tex.)

The National Association for Perinatal Addiction Research and Education has led the nation in its efforts to examine the impact of in utero exposure to drugs. The research is scarce, however, for a number of reasons. The women, infants, and children involved tend to be transient, and this makes it difficult to do research on the long-term effects of the in utero drug exposure on children as they grow. Research also is difficult because it is impossible to isolate the variables that may cause the child to have developmental delays—poverty, malnutrition, lack of medical intervention, and environmental deprivation from drug-related delays. It also is difficult to complete such research because each child appears to be affected differently, depending on the mother's drug(s) of choice. It is difficult, for example, to examine the effects of perinatal cocaine addiction on a newborn infant because most cocaine addicts tend to use other drugs (poly drugs, heroin, PCP, marijuana, and alcohol) as well. The National Association for Perinatal Addiction Research and Education, acknowledging difficulty with control of all variables, studied the long-term consequences of perinatal addiction in 263 children. The following findings were reported[67]:

- Children of drug-using mothers were more likely to be born prematurely and generally weighed less, were shorter, and had smaller head circumferences. As infants, they were unusually irritable and had a low threshold for overstimulation.
- By 3 months, the mean weight of drug-affected children had caught up with that of infants in a drug-free control group; by 12 months, the two groups were not significantly different in body length.
- Through age 2, head circumference measurements remained smaller in drug-affected children.
- Drug-exposed children scored within the normal range for cognitive development and are not considered to be brain-damaged. However, they require a structured learning environment and patient, one-on-one attention from teachers and caregivers.

Tarr[57] completed a meta-analysis of 56 studies that examined the physical and psychomotor development of neonates/infants prenatally exposed to drugs. Her findings regarding these neonates/infants include:

- Lower birth weight
- Decreased length (height) at birth
- Smaller head circumference
- Significant decrease in Apgar scores at 1 and 5 minutes (NOTE: **Apgar scores** are numerical indicators of an infant's status immediately after birth; they reflect behavioral indices, including breathing, color, heart rate, and muscle tone.)
- Significantly lower score on the Bayley Psychomotor Development Index (which evaluates body control, gross motor behavior, and fine motor skills) at 6, 12, 18, and 24 months

Poverty and Homelessness

Dr. Lillian Parks, superintendent of the East St. Louis schools, said, "Gifted children are everywhere in East St. Louis, but their gifts are lost to poverty and turmoil and the damage done by knowing they are written off by their society."[34] A privately funded report by the National Center for Children in Poverty[56] has just released data indicating that the number of American children under the age of 6 years living in poverty has reached a record high of 6 million, or 26% of that age group.

Nearly 42% of American children grow up in low-income families,[19] and roughly one in four children is poor, versus one in eight adults, and the consequences are manifold. Poor children are more likely to suffer from low birth weight, more likely to die within the first year of life, more likely to suffer hunger or abuse while growing up, and less likely to benefit from immunizations or adequate medical care.

A 3-year study by the Washington-based children's advocacy group, Food Research and Action Center, conducted face-to-face interviews with individuals in more than 5000 low-income households.[29] Their findings are startling:

- Four million children under the age of 12, one of every 12 children in the United States, experienced hunger.
- Of the four million children identified as experiencing hunger, the average child was hungry five days in the previous month and five months in the previous year.
- Another 9.6 million low-income children are at risk of hunger.

Victor Sidel, a physician involved in the research, noted, "Hunger, even if there are no direct signs of malnutrition, can affect children's health, can affect their ability to learn."[29] Clearly, a child whose basic needs, including adequate and nutritious food, are not being met cannot be free to learn, to grow, and to move toward self-actualization. The primary concern of a child who is hungry is food and this predominates thought. In addition, hungry children are more likely to get colds, suffer from headaches, have difficulty concentrating, and be irritable than children who have been fed.

Mayor Ray Flynn, chairman of the Conference of Mayors Task Force on Hunger and Homelessness, suggested that increases in hunger, homelessness, and poverty are "one of the most dramatic changes that swept across our country."[46] Poverty is particularly threatening to families headed by single women.

These single-parent families, headed by women, represent 34% of the homeless population.[3] The New York City Department of Health reported that in 1987, 40% of homeless women studied had had no prenatal care at all. As a result, these women are dangerously at risk for low birth weight babies and difficulties with pregnancy.

The picture of adults that comes to mind when the

term *homeless* is mentioned must be erased. Recent data released by the U.S. Conference of Mayors indicate that 43% of homeless people are children. It is frightening to note that in the last edition of this text (1993) we reported that one in four homeless people is a child.[46] In just 3 years, that figure has almost doubled. It is reasonable to expect that between 100,000 and 150,000 homeless *children* sleep in emergency shelters, welfare hotels, abandoned cars, or abandoned buildings every night.

Characteristics of homeless children

The U.S. Department of Education estimates that there are more than 220,000 homeless school-age children in America. Those who make it to school are frightened, exhausted, hungry, and disenfranchised. The children feel unempowered and overwhelmed by the uncertainty of their lives. Homeless children are among those most at risk for delays in psychosocial development because they are denied the most basic of human rights—to be warm and protected and safe. According to Bassuk[3]:

> During critical, formative years, homeless children lack the basic resources needed for normal development. They undergo experiences resulting in medical, emotional, behavioral, and educational problems that may plague them forever.

Homeless shelter workers report that homeless children often suffer from depression and rage, and their aspirations and expectations are low.[45] Homeless teenagers are particularly susceptible to the ravages of the streets—drug and alcohol abuse, violence, gangs, pregnancy, and juvenile crime. It is startling to note that the response of homeless children and adolescents to their situation has been compared to that of **posttraumatic stress syndrome,** which is most typically associated with the effects of war.

Homeless children experience more acute and chronic medical problems than do poor children who have homes. Health care workers find high incidences of diarrhea and malnourishment, as well as asthma and elevated blood levels of lead, in shelter children.

The Children's Defense Fund, an active child advocate agency, has reported that homeless children are three times more likely to have missed immunizations than are poor children with homes. As a result, there has been an overwhelming resurgence of once-rare childhood diseases.

Homeless children are at high risk for health and behavior problems. Lack of consistent health care, adequate nutrition, and adequate rest causes significant health risks for the homeless child. In combination with a disordered, chaotic life led at the mercy of child welfare, child protective services, and homeless shelters, these homeless children usually find it impossible to develop psychosocial competence. In addition to a chaotic family life, if a family exists, homeless children frequently also experience loss of friends, loss of familiar neighborhood surroundings, school disruptions, exposure to many strangers, and threatening situations on the streets and in the shelters.

Wood et al.[70] concluded that homeless children have a significant risk of present and future developmental delays, behavior disorders, academic problems, and nutritional deprivation. Homeless children experience a great risk of present and future health problems that affect the quality of life.

A federal law, the Stewart B. McKinney Homeless Assistance Act, enacted by Congress in July 1987, together with its amendments of 1990, mandates that *all* children, including homeless children, have a right to access a free, appropriate public education and that school residency laws may not be used to prevent homeless children from attending school.[53] In the past, homeless children were often denied access to school because of a lack of address as a "legal and permanent resident" of a district and/or because parents were unable to locate or provide health records. In addition, parents of homeless children fail to register their child for school because of the seemingly impossible obstacles of providing transportation to and from shelters/abandoned cars/empty buildings, of sending the child to school clean and in clean clothes, and of securing needed school supplies. In addition, the parents may be fearful that their child will be taken away from them by social service agencies, they may be concerned that the child will be teased, and/or the child may be afraid to attend school.

Yon[71] reminds us that:

> It is important not to lose sight of the realities in the political economy that contribute to the plight of homeless children in the first place. The dramatic changes in family composition, the restructuring of the postindustrial economy, and the reduction in social welfare during the past 12 years have increased homelessness on an unprecedented scale.

Interaction with a gentle animal may lead to interaction with gentle human beings. (Courtesy Adapted Physical Education Department, Jefferson Parish Public School System, New Orleans, La.)

Parental Instability

One of the major issues in the psychosocial development of infants, young children, and adolescents, with and without disabilities, is the presence of a stable, caring, and nurturing, primary adult (parent) in their lives. Without the security of a stable, caring, and nurturing adult, children are not free to explore the world around them and, subsequently, are at significant risk for developmental delays.

The U.S. Census Bureau reported that 56% of Anglo children, 38% of Latin-American children, and 26% of African-American children live in a "nuclear family," with biological parents and siblings.[61] While a slight majority of children still live in nuclear families, a rising number live with single parents, other relatives, in foster homes, in institutions, in homeless shelters, or on the streets.

One in every four children in this country lives in a single-parent household, and most of these single parents are women living in poverty. While single parents can be very effective parents, when the parenting process is complicated by lack of money and support, parenting becomes a very difficult skill.

Often in hopes that they will now "have someone who loves me," children are having children. These children, who are often incapable of caring for themselves, certainly lack the parenting skills necessary to raise a child, particularly if that process is made more difficult because of poverty, insufficient education to seek and keep a good job, lack of support from the father, and lack of access to appropriate child care.

Sixty of 1000 young women between the ages of 15 and 19 years gave birth in 1992.[59] While this is down from 62/1000 in 1991, these infants are often at risk because of inappropriate and/or nonexistent prenatal care and subsequently are more likely to give birth to low birth weight babies. Then, often, a teen parent is faced with the difficult role of parenting a child with special needs.

An estimated 3.4 million children live in a household headed by a grandparent.[2] In almost one third of these households, the parent, who may be involved in significant drug use/abuse and/or may be incapable of parenting, is not involved in child rearing at all.

Large numbers of children have been neglected or abandoned by parents addicted to drugs and alcohol. David Liederman, executive director of the Child Welfare League of America, has noted that as many as

500,000 children in this country are in foster care.[15] The number of children under the age of 3 in foster care doubled in a 5-year period. The General Accounting Office indicated that 58% of the youngest children in foster care have serious health-related problems, including (1) fetal alcohol syndrome, (2) low birth weight, (3) cardiac defects, (4) HIV infection or AIDS, and (5) developmental delays.[15] Many move into the foster care system and may live in as many as seven homes before they reach the sixth grade.

Violence

The schools are simply a microcosm of the greater society, which is characterized by escalating violence and by the real and noxious presence of gangs. Increasingly the schools are becoming places in which violence is common and in which gangs meet, conduct their "business," and recruit new members.

Children and adolescents are faced with violence on a daily basis. A bulletin board, made by a prekindergarten class in an inner-city elementary school in central Dallas, celebrated Martin Luther King's birthday. Each 4-year-old child in the class was asked to complete the statement, "I have a dream. . ." Eighteen of the 22 children in the class responded with such statements as: "I have a dream . . . the shooting will stop"; "I have a dream . . . my momma won't get dead"; or "I have a dream . . . the guns will stop so I can sleep."

These 4-year-old children, and other victims like them, experience symptoms similar to those of posttraumatic stress disorder, including anxiety; a heightened sense of hearing, smell, and sight; and hypervigilance or "tuning out" the environment.[66] While these symptoms prepare the child for "fight or flight" reactions in stressful situations in the streets or in their homes, they interfere significantly with learning in school. Unable to tune out the background, or tuning it out completely, makes it difficult for these children to attend to the important tasks of learning.

A recent KidsPeace survey found that, as a group, children ages 10 to 13 think they are more likely to die or be abused than they are to start smoking or drinking.[41] That type of hopelessness breeds desperation. Capers wrote[5]:

> If society places little value on your life or your feelings, you respond in one of two ways. Either you believe what you see and hear about yourself and give in to it, or you do

anything to save whatever fragment of self-esteem or ego you have. Either way, violence may seem a logical response.

Speaking to the Association of Black Foundation Executives in Dallas, Marian Wright Edelman described the significant toll that violence has on our children[38]:

- Every day, 135,000 American children bring a gun to school.
- Every 2 hours a child is fatally shot.
- Over half of all violent crimes committed against young people ages 12 to 19 occur on or near school property.
- The Harlem Hospital in New York reports that the majority of children admitted with gunshot wounds have already lost a family member to a fatal gun-related injury.
- A study in the *New England Journal of Medicine* found that young men in Harlem are less likely to live to age 40 than their counterparts in Bangladesh.
- Homicide is the leading cause of death among black youth ages 18 to 24.

Thomas[60] offers more data that support the notion that violence has reached an untenable level in this society and that it is devastating to our children. She notes that a recent study of fourth and fifth grade students in New Orleans found that more than 50% of the fifth graders had already been a victim of a violent act, 90% of the children reported having witnessed some type of violence, 70% had seen weapons being used in confrontations, and 40% had seen dead bodies.

As Edelman noted, violence often occurs on or near the school grounds. The Center for Disease Control and Prevention released data from a 1993 survey that indicated that violence within the school setting is a major health problem for teenagers.[49] The findings indicated that 11.8% of teenagers surveyed brought weapons to school in the previous month; 24% had an illegal drug offered, given, or sold to them in the previous year; 16.2% said they had been in a fight in the previous year; and 7.3% were threatened or injured with a weapon while at school.

The *Metropolitan Life Survey of the American Teacher, 1993: Violence in America's Public Schools* polled a national sample of 1000 third to twelfth grade teachers, 1180 third to twelfth grade students, and 100 police department officials. The most frightening finding was that "23% of students (6.8 million children and adolescents) and 11% of teachers (273,000) have been victims of violence in and around their schools."[58]

Gang Culture

Many children and adolescents in this society do not feel secure, loved, wanted, needed, or respected. The gang, as a sociological phenomenon, has always been present in cultures in which individual members of that culture feel unempowered and disenfranchised. In many real ways, the gang replaces the family as the primary source of security. In addition, participation in a gang may provide the gang member with a sense of power and recognition missing in other relationships.

Gang has been defined as[25]:

. . . a formal or informal association of three or more persons who have a common name or identifying signs, color or symbols, who individually or collectively engage in a pattern of criminal activity involving felony crimes and violent misdemeanor offenses.

The gang culture has a profound influence within the schools. In many school districts, high school–age gang members recruit students from middle schools in their area, and middle school gang members recruit from elementary schools. It is not unusual for children in the first and second grades to be members of gangs.

Teachers and parents need to be aware of the early signs of gang activity and gang membership:

- The child decreases the amount of communication with family members.[25]
- The child's personality changes abruptly.[25]
- The child has a new circle of friends and "hangs" with them; he or she does not bring these friends home.
- The child no longer communicates with old friends.
- The child begins wearing a particular color or style of clothing, excluding other clothes he or she used to wear.
- The child uses a walking gait that he or she did not use before (e.g., the child struts).
- The child begins to use a language that includes slang the parent or teacher does not understand.
- The child's schoolwork begins to suffer, and grades fall.
- The child is truant more often.
- The child's clothing, posters, notebooks, diaries, etc., have graffiti-like symbols on them.[25]

- The child becomes confrontational with teachers and parents and may exhibit violent behavior.[25]
- The child ignores hobbies or other activities that used to be important in order to "hang" with friends.
- The child has a tattoo or other distinctive mark on the skin, including self-inflicted scars from knives or rubbing erasers on the skin until it bleeds, picking the scab, and repeating the process until a scar exists.
- The child begins to carry weapons, such as pocket knives, sharpened screwdrivers, switchblades, or guns.

The very nature of the gang culture leads gang members into direct confrontation with law enforcement personnel. Graffiti is used to claim territory and to mark an area as that of the gang. Violence is typical. Gang members feel that any disrespect (being "dissed") is just cause for retaliation. Intimidation techniques include, but are not limited to, extorting lunch money, forcing others to pay "protection" money, beatings, rapes, drive-by shootings, and murder.

While gangs have long been thought to be a vestige of the inner city, nothing could be further from the truth. In fact, gangs are now a common phenomenon in small, rural communities. Part of the reason for this phenomenon is that gang members from large cities literally recruit members in smaller, rural areas in order to expand membership.[16]

In addition, there is a growing number of gang "wannabes." These children and adolescents who want to be part of a gang may actually be more dangerous than gang members themselves; the "wannabe" may be willing to participate in a violent ritual in order to prove worthy of gang membership. The bottom line is that many children and adolescents in small, rural areas also do not feel secure, loved, wanted, needed, or respected. A gang becomes a natural and viable place, in their minds, to find what they need.

Child Abuse and Neglect

According to James Barbarino, outgoing president of the Erikson Institute, a child development research center in Chicago[36]:

If you take almost any major social problem in America and treat it like those nested Russian dolls, what you will get to is that child abuse would be the last doll—because it is such a profound wound in developing children.

The U.S. Advisory Board on Child Abuse and Neglect, completing a nationwide research project, found that fatal abuse or neglect is much more widespread than previously believed; at least 2000 children are killed each year, and over 140,000 children are seriously injured because of neglect or abuse.[42] Although frightening, these data reflect the fact that most child abuse is an abuse of power. The most helpless, the youngest children, those least likely to be able to defend themselves, are the victims. Data indicated that 53% of the children killed as a result of abuse are under the age of 1 year.[11]

The cycle of violence for children who grow up in violent homes escalates. The Texas Council on Family Violence[14] has indicated that children who grow up in violent homes, as opposed to children who grow up in homes where violent behavior is not tolerated, are 6 times more likely to commit suicide, 24 times more likely to commit sexual assault, 50 times more likely to abuse alcohol or drugs, 74 times more likely to commit crimes against other people, 53% more likely to be arrested as a juvenile, and 38% more likely to be arrested as an adult. Violence does, indeed, breed violence. The student who is exposed to violence in the home cannot leave that at home. The student who threatens or verbally or physically abuses other children and/or the teacher is one who has learned these behaviors. Thus, often the student who is most difficult to teach is the very student who most needs the constancy of support, love, and nurturing in the classroom.

The American Association for the Protection of Children (AAPC) reported the following distribution of cases reported to child protective service agencies: 27% physical abuse, 15% sexual abuse, 46% neglect, 9% emotional maltreatment, and 4% other.[11]

Rampant poverty, economic instability, unemployment, sanctioned societal violence ("spare the rod, spoil the child"), a family history of abuse, and substance abuse are among the primary factors in the continued growth in child abuse reports and fatalities.[32] In addition, the persistent, ridiculous notion that children are somehow the "property" of parents creates situations where abuse is perpetuated. An animal removed from the custody of an abusive owner is not returned to that owner. A child, however, is often returned by the courts to an abusive parent, even after several referrals to the child welfare system.

Children with disabilities are even more at risk for abuse than other children.[26] In fact, the very nature of children with some disabilities puts them in jeopardy. For example, Elizabeth Rahdert, a research psychologist in the division of clinical research at the National Institute on Drug Abuse suggested[10]:

> When you have infants and children fetally exposed to crack, they may be easily excitable, hyperarousable and do more crying. So if the child is impaired and the mother or care giver is impaired, the situation is even more explosive and dangerous.

The research literature provides growing evidence that children who are abused or neglected are at greater risk of becoming emotionally disturbed, language impaired, mentally retarded, and/or physically disabled, whereas children with disabilities may be at greater risk of abuse or neglect.[13,30,37,68]

Children with disabilities and their susceptibility to abuse

Children with disabilities may have one or more of the following characteristics, which make them more susceptible to child abuse and neglect than children without disabilities:

- Need for expensive medical intervention or therapy and the pressure that puts on the caregiver
- Inability to follow expected developmental patterns in motor, speech, social, and play skills
- Dependency on others to take care of basic daily living needs
- Dependency on others to take care of social or friendship needs
- Inability to take control of own life, which causes long-term need for caregiver
- Inability to effectively communicate needs and wants[26]
- Inability to participate in reciprocal relationships[26]
- Lack of knowledge about sex and misunderstanding of sexual advances
- Inability to differentiate between acceptable and nonacceptable touch
- Inability to defend self[26,68]

Parents of children with developmental disabilities may be more prone to abuse because of the following:

- Their obligation to provide constant care with concomitant financial and time restraints
- Their guilt, denial, and frustration[62]
- Their lack of understanding regarding the developmental sequence of the learner with a developmental delay
- The tendency to compare the development of the child with that of nondelayed children
- Failure to develop appropriate expectations regarding the child's behavior
- Frustration because of intervention, and perceived intrusion, by care providers (e.g., teachers, therapists, social workers, etc.)
- Frustration because the child is incapable of a reciprocal relationship
- Frustration due to the child's inability to express needs and wants and subsequent feelings of helplessness
- Disputes between couples regarding care of the child with a disability
- Alcohol and drug abuse[62]
- The parents' own developmental delay (Verdugo, Bermejo, and Fuertes[62] noted that 25% of parents with mental retardation were involved in the maltreatment of their developmentally delayed child.)

Verdugo, Bermejo, and Fuertes[62] examined the families of 445 children and adolescents between birth and 19 years of age in one of the largest regions in Spain. They found parental maltreatment of children and adolescents with disabilities in 11.5% of the families and found evidence of the following:

Physical neglect	92%
Emotional neglect	82%
Emotional abuse	65%
Physical abuse	31%
Exploitation of labor	4%
Sexual abuse	2%

The researchers found that the less functionally impaired child was more likely to be abused than the more functionally involved child. The one interesting exception was the child with severe speech defects. The percentage of maltreated children with severe speech defects was 75%; 37% of these children did not speak. This points again to the significant parental need for reciprocity and communication.

Psychosocial Deficits of Children and Youth with Disabilities

At-Risk Children and Youth with Disabilities

It is important to note that the students receiving special education services in the United States are disproportionately at-risk minority children. The Public Education Association of New York reported:

> Classes for the emotionally handicapped, neurologically impaired, learning disabled and educable mentally retarded are disproportionately black. . . . Classes for the speech, language, and hearing impaired are disproportionately Hispanic.[27]

Kozol[34] wrote:

> Nationwide, black children are three times as likely as white children to be placed in classes for the mentally retarded but only half as likely to be placed in classes for the gifted: a well-known statistic that should long since have aroused a sense of utter shame in our society.

Children with disabilities face even more problems than children without disabilities; this is particularly true of at-risk children, poor or homeless children, or abused children who happen to have disabilities. Their lives are more complex and more frightening because of an even more overwhelming sense of lack of power than that experienced by children facing only the disabilities.

Children and Youth with Disabilities

Children with disabilities may find it difficult to experience typical psychosocial development for a number of reasons. They may face rejection, overt or covert, by their parents, siblings, teachers, or peers. These rejections are generally borne of fear, guilt, pity, or the process of equating disability with illness. In ancient Greece and Rome, for example, infants with disabilities were perceived to be disgusting to the gods and were abandoned to die. In the Middle Ages, individuals with disabilities were believed to be possessed by "evil spirits." Unfortunately, some of this type of mentality persists. One has only to read about the treatment of children with acquired immunodeficiency syndrome (AIDS), for example, to understand the nature of prejudice toward children with disabilities.

The psychosocial development of children with disabilities may be seriously affected by the prejudice of others. In fact, the prejudice of others may predispose the child to have low self-esteem. Children with disabilities may be overprotected and, subsequently, prevented from developing age-appropriate play and interaction skills. Well-meaning parents and teachers may keep children with disabilities from participating in activities with their siblings and peers.

Individuals with disabilities generally experience more problems in individual and social development and adjustment than do their peers without disabilities.[17] Some of the problems with psychosocial development are a function of the prejudice and expectations of others. Some of the problems may be a function of the behaviors of children with disabilities. Some disabilities cause, by their very nature, serious difficulties in social interaction skills. The autistic child or the child with childhood schizophrenia, for example, is deemed to be disabled primarily because of the difficulties the child experiences in interacting with other people.

Some of the ways in which children with disabilities may differ socially from others are as follows:

- They may have difficulty with basic communication skills and, as such, lack ability to relate to others and respond appropriately.
- They may lack impulse control.
- They may have significant difficulty following, or be unable to follow, directions and rules.
- They may have difficulty in age-appropriate social interactions with peers and teachers, particularly in a structured school environment.
- They may be verbally or physically aggressive toward self, peers, and teachers.
- They may be totally passive in the social environment, avoiding interaction with others and exhibiting completely subservient behavior in any interaction with another.
- They may demonstrate no interest in play or the play environment.
- They may have difficulty taking turns and sharing equipment, particularly toys, balls, etc.
- They may have difficulty understanding social cues and, subsequently, respond inappropriately to others.
- They may exhibit difficulty processing and understanding gestures, facial expressions, and vocal inflections that are crucial to understanding the context of an interaction with another.
- They may exhibit "out-of-control" behaviors or

temper tantrums, particularly in response to overstimulation or a change in routine.
- They may exhibit developmental delays in play behaviors basic to the social development of children.

Psychosocial Assessment

A comprehensive psychosocial assessment may be requested for a child experiencing significant psychosocial delays. This assessment is usually completed by a psychologist or educational diagnostician. The physical educator may, at the request of the child's parents, participate in some phases of the evaluation. In addition, the results of a psychosocial assessment may be shared in an individual education program (IEP) meeting for a child with a psychosocial delay.

There are several psychosocial assessment techniques, including: (1) naturalistic observations, (2) sociometric measures, (3) teacher ratings, (4) norm-referenced social assessments, and (5) content-referenced social assessments. A brief description of each of the methods follows.

Naturalistic Observations

The single most effective technique for evaluating a child's psychosocial behavior is observation of the child

Two children engaged in solitary play. (Courtesy Dallas Independent School District.)

in settings/activities in which the child is completely comfortable. The child may be observed interacting with others, children and adults, in a variety of natural social settings, which in the school setting may include playground time, recess, and lunch, for example. To assess a child's psychosocial development, however, the observations must also include the child interacting and playing with siblings, peers, and adults in his or her home, within the neighborhood, on playgrounds, and within familiar groups, such as church groups. The frequency of specific behaviors is observed and recorded. Observations must be collected across a variety of environments to provide a fairly complete picture of the child's psychosocial behavior. Technology, including the use of videotaping, makes the process of collecting psychosocial data much more efficient.

Sociometric Measures

An effective technique for determining the social behaviors of children includes a process in which children are asked to specify which classmates they would prefer to interact with in a given situation (e.g., "Name two classmates with whom you like to play best"). This process provides crucial information to the physical educator about a child's friendships, if the child has any friends, and may help the physical educator to identify a "popular" student who might be an effective peer buddy for a child lacking social skills.

Teacher Ratings

Teacher rating scales have been used for many years to gather social data. One instrument, the Social Behavior Assessment tool,[52] analyzes 136 social skills necessary to perform a variety of environmental, interpersonal, self-related, and task-related behaviors. The essential question that is answered by the teacher is whether each behavior is important for success in the class. This type of information can help identify which social skills a child must have to benefit fully from a specific classroom experience.

Normative-Referenced Social Assessment

Selected normative-referenced social assessment instruments are the Brigance, Pyramid Scales,[7] the Vineland Adaptive Behavior Scales,[51] the Scales of Independent Behavior,[4] and the Gesell Developmental Schedules. Most of these tests have subtests that represent domains

of social behavior, including: (1) personal independence, (2) socialization, (3) self-direction, (4) expressive and receptive language, (5) play skills, (6) self-help skills, and (7) **locus of control.**

Normative-referenced test results can provide the physical educator with information about a student's general social behavior and the psychosocial developmental age at which the child is functioning. Parent reports can also provide clues about where a child is functioning. For example, you will recall that Billy Bogg's mother (see Chapter 2) reported that she was concerned because he demonstrated the social and play skills of a much younger child. In fact, Billy preferred solitary play to other types of play and made no attempt to initiate communication or play with other children. The sensi-

The development of trust is often difficult for children. (Courtesy Wisconsin Lions Camp, Rosholt, Wis.)

tive physical educator can help Billy by gradually preparing him to function as a member of a larger group.

Content-Referenced Social Assessment

Content-referenced social assessment requires the acquisition of information about what an individual can and cannot do within the context of the play, games, and leisure, recreation, and sport activities that are critical components of the specific physical education curriculum of a given school district. The information received from such an assessment may be used to make relevant instructional decisions to enhance social behavior. The prerequisites for such an assessment of individual social abilities within the context of play, games, and leisure, recreation, and sport activities are as follows:

1. Operationally defined social abilities to be developed
2. A sequence of play, games, and leisure, recreation, and sport activities that progress from lower to higher demands for social skills of participants
3. Entry procedures to determine the present level of play, games, and leisure, recreation, and sport ability of the learner and the specific psychosocial delays demonstrated within a specific social context

Psychosocial Delays and Their Implications for Physical Education for At-Risk Children and Youth, Including Those with Disabilities

James Garbarino, director of the Family Life Development Center at Cornell University, has noted that our children are growing up in a world so "socially toxic" that all are at risk simply by being in the environment. According to Garbarino[48]:

> In a physical toxic environment, you see the effects first and worst among the most vulnerable. In a socially toxic environment, it's the same. We see the effects first among children with disabilities, poor children.

The **social toxins** that affect our children—violence, poverty, hunger, homelessness, inadequate parenting, abuse and neglect, drug abuse, racism, and classism—seriously compromise the quality of life of our children. These multivaried "pollutants" precipitate a delay in the psychosocial development of our children. They are particularly devastating to those infants and children in the critical early years of development.

Indeed, the very foundation of all psychosocial development lies in the early years between birth and 3 years. In the first year of life, infants who are raised in a caring, nurturing environment in which their needs are met will learn to be trusting, loving, and caring children, adolescents, and adults. In contrast, infants who are raised in an environment characterized by chaos, violence, abandonment, poverty, and inconsistency learn to be fearful, mistrustful, wary, anxious, impulsive, and stressed.

Grazyna Kochanska, a research psychologist at the University of Iowa, has found that social conscience emerges in young children between the ages of 18 months and 3 years.[35] A conscience, an internal sense of right and wrong, emerges when the child develops secure maternal attachments (based in large part on the mother's ability to meet the child's needs), lives with consistent discipline, and has a history of shared good times with his or her parents.

According to Lorraine Wallach,[63] one of the founders of the Erikson Institute:

> Development in the first five or six years should prepare children for successful school experiences. When they enter elementary school, they are expected to have the social and cognitive skills that will make them good group members who are reasonably cooperative with adults. However, many children have not been prepared for this step. They do not come to school eager to learn and to put aside their immediate wants in order to be part of the group and win the teacher's approval. Rather, they arrive at school with all the internal stress and external fears that result from living with violence. Managing this stress takes all their energies, which are then not available for tasks such as learning to read and write or learning mathematics, history, or science [or learning to play and move efficiently—addition ours].

Garbarino identified eight things that children need in order to overcome the social toxicity in their environment: (1) stability, (2) security, (3) affirmation of worth, (4) time with parents, (5) belief in ideology, (6) access to basic resources, (7) community, and (8) justice.[48] Children have these same basic needs within the school environment. These needs are consistent within the physical education setting, as well, and each is discussed with specific strategies for meeting the child's psychosocial needs in the physical education environment.

Stability

1. *The single most important variable in maintaining stability in the physical education environment is a professional educator able to exhibit consistent, calm, and nurturing behavior; there is no room for volatility when teaching children whose lives are in chaos.*
2. Class rules need to be posted in clear view and must remain consistent. They should be posted in the primary languages of the children whenever possible.
3. Rules need to be written in specific, behavioral terms. For example, "Be good!" has little or no meaning to young children who have been raised in chaos.
4. Class rules need to be written in positive, rather than negative, terms. For example, "Keep your hands and feet to yourself," conveys a much more positive message than "No hitting or kicking."
5. There should be rewards for following the rules, as well as consequences for breaking the rules.
6. Consequences for breaking the rules need to be provided as choices to help the children learn cause-effect and *must be the same for every child, every time.* According to Sparks[50]:

All students, but especially at-risk students, must accept responsibility for the decisions they make. This is a learned process. At-risk students often refuse to acknowledge this responsibility by accepting very little ownership in a decision. They often look for excuses, blame someone else, or even society in general for a situation they do not like or cannot control.

Security

1. *The single most important variable in maintaining security in the physical education environment is a professional educator able to exhibit consistent, calm, and nurturing behavior; there is no room for volatility when teaching children whose lives are in chaos.*
2. The routine should be consistent from class to class, with the same schedule followed every day.
3. If there must be a break from routine (e.g., the teacher knows he or she is taking a personal day or there is to be a special event that will affect the schedule) the children need to be warned so that they can prepare.
4. It must be infinitely clear to all children that verbal and physical abuse of others will not be tolerated.
5. Verbal or physical abuse of children is *never* a consequence of misbehavior. Even in districts or states in which corporal punishment is allowed, the physical educator must *never* allow that to be part of the program. By its very nature, it perpetuates the violence and chaos that have caused the children to be at risk in the first place.

Affirmation of Worth

1. *The physical educator must know and use each child's name.*
2. Expect excellence from all your students. O'Neil[44] has suggested that having high standards for at-risk students is vital if they are to be successful and is crucial to their self-esteem.
3. Always "catch 'em being good" and acknowledge that behavior.
4. Praise often and well.
5. The emphasis in the physical education setting must be on cooperative, not competitive, experiences. At-risk children have difficulty experiencing success in cooperative experiences. Competition, by its very nature, causes some children to lose; these children simply do not need to lose any more than they already have.

Time with Teacher

1. While it may be difficult to find time every day for each child (particularly if there are 60+ children in each class), warm-up time, station time, and relaxation time offer excellent opportunities for interpersonal communication—a compliment, a question, or a pat on the back (ask for permission to touch a child until you know the child will be receptive to your touch).
2. Use time with you as a reward for good behavior. A student or a small group of students can be rewarded if you do something as simple as have lunch with them in the cafeteria, buy them a soft drink and talk for 5 minutes after school, or shoot baskets with them for 5 minutes during your lunch break.

Belief in Ideology

1. The student must be given the opportunity to feel that his or her life matters and that there is some sense in the "big picture." This is desperately hard for many of our children who have come to believe that their only options are prison or death. The physical educa-

tor can help with this process in a small but significant way.

2. Give students specific responsibilities as part of the class experience. For example, most young children would almost kill, literally, to be line leader. Develop a system so that all children have the opportunity to assume responsibility and be rewarded for performing the given task.

3. Load your gymnasium with pictures or posters that represent ethnic, cultural, gender, and ability diversity.

4. Invite role models, such as area athletes and/or professional or college/university athletes, including those with disabilities, to participate in your program as a guest speaker or mentor.

Access to Basic Resources

1. Playground areas are often disregarded in school planning, particularly in urban, poor school districts. Organize a community/parent campaign to design and build a playground area.

2. Use inexpensive and homemade equipment so that, when appropriate, each child has access to his or her own piece of equipment. (NOTE: You would be amazed at the number of children who have never had a balloon with which to play.)

Community

1. The focus in play, games, and leisure, recreation, and sport activities must be on the adoption of the philosophy espoused in the "New Games" movement.[39,43] In this philosophy, individuals have an opportunity to learn to move while learning cooperative, rather than competitive, behaviors. There is no winner and, subsequently, no loser in the "New Games" movement. For example, instead of trying to score a "kill" in a competitive volleyball game with only six people per side, a "New Games" volleyball game would include as many people as want to play, who work together to see how long they can keep the volleyball from hitting the ground.

2. Develop a parent physical education newsletter that the children write (a wonderful strategy for cooperative learning with the regular educator or language arts teacher).

3. Invite parents to help as volunteers in the physical education program. (See Chapter 19 for more information about programs involving parent participation.)

4. Use ethnic and culturally diverse music for warm-ups and rhythm/dance activities.

5. Expand the curriculum to include ethnic and culturally diverse play, games, and leisure, recreation, and sport activities.

Justice

1. Every child must be treated the same way as every other child, all the time, if children are to believe the physical educator to be just.

Model Physical Education and Recreation Programs for At-Risk Children and Youth

The physical educator is in a unique position to address some of the issues that plague at-risk children. In fact, in and through play, games, and leisure, recreation, and sport activities, the physical educator can help children who have psychosocial delays by providing the opportunity to develop social skills necessary to function within play, games, and leisure, recreation, and sport activities. Many of the skills necessary to participate successfully in the physical education program are those necessary to participate successfully within the schools and within society at large.

Hellison[22] and his associates at the University of Illinois–Chicago Circle have developed an innovative, model physical education and sports program for at-risk children and youth that is based on the notion that the physical education class, or a team within a class, is a microcosm of the greater society and that children can learn to develop values and behaviors necessary to participate in play, games, and leisure, recreation, and sport activities; those social skills are at the very foundation of an individual's ability to function within the society at large.[24]

The intent of the program is to develop the child's self-responsibility and social responsibility. According to Hellison[22]:

. . . self-responsibility is conceptualized as empowering at-risk youth to take more control of their own lives, to learn how to engage in self-development in the face of a variety of external forces, including socialization patterns, peer pressure, self-doubt, lack of concepts and skills, and limited vision of their own options. Social responsibility is conceptualized as the development of sensitivity to the rights, feelings, and needs of others. Indicators include movement beyond egocentrism and ethnocentrism, recognition of the rights and feelings of others, caring and compassion, service to others, and concern for the entire group's welfare.

Their programs have been based on the notion that children, even those who are most seriously at risk, can learn the social and emotional skills necessary to function in play, games, and leisure, recreation, and sport activities, and perhaps more important, can generalize those skills to participation in the larger society.

Hellison has suggested a four-level model of behavior or value development for the physical education program, which is outlined in the box below.

At-risk children and youth are given the opportunity to develop fundamental skills necessary for human interaction. Indeed, many of these children and youth simply have not been taught basic skills necessary for communicating basic needs, for negotiating, and for expressing emotions that are socially appropriate. They have learned, and their models have used, verbal and physical aggression to communicate; young people simply reflect what they have learned and what they have seen. Specific strategies for modifying games to better meet students' needs are presented in Chapter 5.

These children are given specific program responsibilities and are taught how to follow through and complete a task. As they learn, they are gradually weaned from adult control to increased student independence. Hellison and his associates have incorporated the use of student logs and/or diaries in which the student explains behavior and indicates his or her progress on skills at each of the four levels of social development.[21,23]

The culmination of the acquisition of socially de-sirable behaviors includes the student's efforts to provide help, care, and support for others. Hellison and his colleagues provide the opportunity for children to learn the skills that are expected of them within the larger society, in a structured environment that allows them to self-test and grow.

PROJECT YES: A Break from Tradition is an exciting and innovative, community-based, recreation program for at-risk children and youth and targets low-income, high-crime sectors of towns and cities; the project is usually implemented in or near public housing projects.[31] The program has a multidisciplinary design with an emphasis on multiculturalism and includes physical and health education, including drug awareness, nutrition, health, safety, and self-empowerment.

Psychosocial Skills Necessary for Successful Participation in Play, Games, and Leisure, Recreation, and Sport Activities

Socialization is the process of learning how to behave appropriately in social settings—that is, how to interact with others. At-risk children and children with disabilities often have difficulty interacting with others in a socially appropriate way. Instruction to teach developmentally appropriate social behaviors follows the same procedures as those for teaching motor skills. In the process, the learner interacts within a social environment (the play, game, or leisure, recreation, or sport activity), adapts to the characteristics of the environment, and thus changes actions so that he or she is better able to engage in the social process. Fostering, nurturing, guiding, influencing, and controlling social behavior is possible in a designed environment with practical objectives structured by the physical educator. If the teacher is successful, at-risk children with and without disabilities move to higher levels of social skills.

Fundamental to the acquisition of social skills in children is the development of play behavior. These play behaviors are developmental in nature. That is, most children begin to develop play behavior with onlooker behavior before they engage in parallel play. In addition, each stage of play requires more sophisticated social skills. The complexity of the movement experience increases throughout the stages. The stages and teaching strategies to encourage the development of psychosocial behavior necessary for play behavior include:

Hellison's Four-Level Model of Behavior/Value Development

Level 1: Sufficient self-control to respect the rights and feelings of others
Level 2: Participation and effort in program activities
Level 3: Self-direction with emphasis on independence and goal-setting
Level 4: Caring about and helping others

Data from Hellison D: *J Phys Educ Rec Dance* 61:38-39, 1990.

1. *Nonpurposeful solitary activity:* The child wanders about the play area, not engaged in any obviously purposeful activity, or sits and plays with fingers or toes, pats head, or spins in circles, for example.

   The physical educator wants to encourage purposeful activity, so perhaps the best strategy is to redirect the child's behavior. For example, if the child is patting his or her head, put a tambourine or drum in front of the child to encourage the child to make music.

2. *Onlooker:* The child follows the movement/activity of other children or adults in the learning area. This, the first of the stages of development of play behavior, is basic to the process of learning to play. The child learns to play by watching others.

   The physical educator can encourage onlooker behavior in children without play skills (e.g., children with autism) by drawing attention to the play behavior of others. For example, the teacher can sit next to the child and say, "Look at Juan, he is keeping the balloon in the air all by himself!" Onlooker behavior can also be encouraged by using bright, colorful toys and equipment and by using music.

3. *Purposeful solitary play:* The child participates in purposeful play. For example, the child may use a shovel to fill a bucket, or climb a ladder to slide down a slide.

   The physical educator can encourage purposeful solitary play by reinforcing the child's efforts to engage in that play. It is difficult, however, not to limit the child's creativity in that process. Unfortunately, adults often have stereotypical notions of child's play and reinforce those stereotypes.

4. *Elaborate solitary play:* The child develops sophisticated play behaviors, which allows the child to develop a repertoire of skills to prepare him or her for play with others. The child makes a castle in the sand, for example.

   The teacher can enhance this play by providing ever-increasing opportunities for elaborating on a play theme. For example, if the child is building in the sand, the teacher can help by providing a bucket of water.

5. *Parallel play:* The child participates in individual play in the same space as another child participating in individual play. Two children play with shovels and pails in the sandbox.

   The physical educator can encourage this type of behavior by providing two children with the same type of equipment to use in a designated space. This works best if both children have identical equipment (e.g., they both have red plastic buckets and blue shovels).

6. *Parallel play with interaction:* The child participates in individual play in the same space as another child participating in individual play and demonstrates an interest in the activity of the other child. The child may ask for help or make suggestions to the other.

   The physical educator can encourage this type of interaction by pointing out commonalities in the play behavior of two or more children. For example, the teacher might say, "Look, boys and girls, Taleisha and Bubba can both dribble that soccer ball through the cones." In addition, the teacher can encourage this interaction if children are given different tools or toys.

Children participating in parallel play. (Courtesy Dallas Independent School District.)

Children participating in cooperative play. (Courtesy Dallas Independent School District.)

7. *Participatory play:* The child engages in play, sharing a space and toys with another child. Two children share a station, taking turns tossing a beanbag into a clown's mouth.

   The physical educator can encourage participation in play by ensuring that the activity is developmentally appropriate, interesting, and allows for success.

8. *Cooperative play:* The child cooperates with others in play to accomplish a common goal. The two children tossing the beanbags into the clown's mouth begin to count how many they can throw into the clown's mouth without missing.

   The physical educator can encourage cooperative play behavior by choosing activities that require cooperation. In addition, the teacher can compliment cooperative behavior. For example, "Lashundra, great pass! You really set Tim up for the score."

9. *Competitive activity:* The child participates in an activity in which the intent is winning. The two children playing with the clown face decide to see who can toss the most into the clown face and compare performance.

The physical educator can teach competitive behavior, but it is very difficult for at-risk children, particularly at-risk children with disabilities, and may in fact result in psychosocial behaviors that are contrary to the intent of social development. One has only to watch the **socially aberrent behaviors** of our country's professional athletes to understand that competition does not, in and of itself, encourage socially appropriate, sports (wo)manlike behavior.

Hierarchy of Incentives for Demonstrating Socially Appropriate Behavior

There may be a hierarchy of incentives for demonstrating developmentally appropriate behavior in social situations. Children learn appropriate behavior, as their social conscience evolves, from models who are capable of demonstrating appropriate behavior in social situations. Children and adults without a strong social conscience, and without a perception of right and wrong, exhibit behavior in social situations based on incentives that may not be related to an inherent, gut-level sense of what behavior is appropriate. Kohlberg[33] suggests the following sequence of psychosocial development. Social behavior in the child or adult without a well-defined morality may be based solely on avoidance of punishment; the more evolved child or adult may exhibit developmentally appropriate social behavior simply to maintain self-respect and self-esteem. Kohlberg's hierarchy is detailed in the box on p. 234.

An understanding of Kohlberg's hierarchy is crucial for the physical educator. A child who is unloved, unwanted, uncared for, and in other ways neglected may not respond to the threat of punishment or may be unable to care about a potential reward. If the child comes from a situation in which cause and effect has not been addressed fairly, specifically if the child is treated differently for exhibiting the same behaviors on two different occasions (e.g., if Mom is sober, I can say "hello"; if Mom is drunk and I say "hello," she'll hit me), the child comes to school either unwilling to act or acting out.

If the child is socially immature and exhibits appropriate social behavior only to avoid punishment, the physical educator committed to the notion that corporal punishment is unethical, immoral, and counterproductive may be hard pressed to develop a plan that provides a

Kohlberg's Hierarchy of Psychosocial Development

1. Obey rules to avoid punishment.
   If there is no punishment, the rules will not be obeyed.
2. Conform to obtain rewards.
   If there are no rewards, there may be inappropriate social behavior.
3. Conform to obtain approval from others.
   If there is little recognition from the group, there is little incentive to maximize participation.
4. Conform to avoid censure by authority figures.
   If there is no authority censure, there is insufficient incentive to participate.
5. Conform to maintain the respect of the social community.
   If the social community cannot express respect, there is insufficient incentive to participate.
6. Conform to maintain self-respect and integrity.
   If there is little desire to be a person of integrity, there is less incentive to participate.

Data from Kohlberg L: The cognitive-development approach to moral education. In *Values, concepts, and techniques,* Washington, DC, 1971, National Education Association.

Freedom to explore a beautiful natural environment may enhance the development of a sense of self-worth. (Courtesy Wisconsin Lions Camp, Rosholt, Wis.)

punishment that will be fair, consistent, and still a deterrent.

If the child demonstrates socially appropriate behavior only when that behavior is rewarded, the physical educator must give serious consideration to the nature of the reward. For example, if the child is hungry, earning a "smiley face" sticker may have little or no meaning; earning an apple may reward behavior and meet the child's basic need—hunger. If the child with spina bifida, for example, is "bribed" at home with money, the chances that a teacher can effect behavioral change at school without that reinforcement are remote. A significant parent-teacher conference is vital at this point to determine the value structure reinforced in the home and that which is appropriate in the school setting.

The child who exhibits certain social behaviors to obtain approval from others can provide a real challenge for the physical educator. Specifically, the child or adolescent may be much more interested in demonstrating

social behaviors endorsed and supported by his or her gang—defiance, violence, and aggression—than in demonstrating social behaviors that have been deemed appropriate by the larger society. This also causes problems for children whose life on the streets demands certain social behaviors for survival that are not acceptable in most other social situations, including school.

The child who conforms to avoid censure by authority figures is atypical among at-risk children and youth. One of the major problems in school settings today is that many of our children have little or no regard for authority figures—particularly if the authority figures represent a different culture or are perceived by the children to be part of the system that is abusive to them. The physical educator must earn respect and, subsequently, authority from his or her students by consistently attempting to create a learning environment that is caring and nurturing and meets the needs of the students.

Obviously, it is hoped that children and adolescents will demonstrate appropriate social behavior in order to maintain the respect of the social community and to maintain self-respect and integrity. This is a difficult and long-term process that requires careful planning and thought.

A child who spends his day in a wheelchair can play on a scooter in the gym. (Courtesy Dallas Independent School District.)

Psychosocial Goals and Objectives of the IEP

Psychosocial goals and objectives are a crucial part of the IEP. The very nature of a carefully developed physical education program, which includes developmentally appropriate play, games, and leisure, recreation, and sport activities, gives the physical educator the opportunity to focus on the attainment of psychosocial goals and objectives.

An annual goal or short-term objective that involves psychosocial behavior possesses all of the characteristics of other well-written goals and objectives and includes the following characteristics:

▪ It should contain a psychosocial ability that can be generalized from the microsociety of play, games, and leisure, recreation, and sport activities to the larger society.

▪ It should be observable in the play, games, and lei-

sure, recreation, and sport activities in the physical education class and in the community-based environment.

▪ It should be measurable to determine the effectiveness of the proposed strategies for intervention.

▪ It must have the capability of being developed through classroom intervention.

▪ It must represent a social ability concept, conscience, or moral imperative, as well as a specific behavior in the class.

For example, one of Billy Bogg's long-range goals (see Chapter 3) was:

By May 15, Billy will participate with the whole class in a low-organized game.

The short-term objectives leading to that goal were:

Short-term objective 1: By November 15, Billy will complete individual activities at three stations without being reminded to stay on task.
Short-term objective 2: By January 15, Billy will participate in parallel activity with a classmate for a minimum of 3 minutes.
Short-term objective 3: By March 15, Billy will participate in a small-group activity for a minimum of 3 minutes.

Billy's long-term and short-term objectives met all the criteria for the development of appropriate psychosocial goals and objectives.

SUMMARY

Children with and without disabilities in this society are at serious risk. Children are among the most neglected of our people. Children with and without disabilities are entering the public school system unprepared, understimulated, abused, homeless, unloved, fearful, tired, hungry, and unkempt. Any and all of these factors have an impact on the psychosocial development of these children. In combination, the effect is devastating.

At-risk individuals and individuals with disabilities sometimes demonstrate delayed psychosocial development. Factors that contribute to this delay include differences in appearance and behavior, overprotective environments, lack of opportunity to interact with others in play, and rejection by others.

Psychosocial development can be promoted through participation in developmentally appropriate play, games, and leisure, recreation, and sport activities in a

*well-designed physical education program. That pro-
gram must carefully address the student's needs, play
skills, and motivations for social interaction and create
a nontoxic learning environment.*

Review Questions

1. Explain the relationship between maternal prenatal neglect and low birth weight infants.
2. List some of the reasons why children with disabilities
are more at risk for child abuse and neglect than other
children.
3. Describe the impact of poverty and homelessness on infants and children.
4. Describe the turbulent nature of the schools in contemporary society.
5. Describe the hierarchy of development of play behavior.
6. Describe Hellison's model physical education program
for at-risk children and youth.
7. Describe the nature of a "New Game."
8. Describe the eight fundamental needs of children in a
nontoxic physical education environment. Name some
specific strategies that can be used to manufacture this
environment.

Student Activities

1. Interview a physical education teacher working in the inner city and a physical education teacher working in an
affluent suburb. Compare and contrast their experiences.
Ask specific questions regarding the "out-of-school"
lives of their children.
2. Volunteer at a shelter for the homeless or at a shelter for
abused women and children.
3. Observe a child with a disability at play with other children. Determine the nature of the child's play.
4. Describe specific teaching strategies you would use to
encourage Billy Bogg to move from purposeful solitary
play into cooperative play.

References

1. Anderson J: What will happen when crack babies grow up?
The Dallas Morning News, March 24, 1990.
2. Barker L: Grandparents raising kids aren't alone, *The Dallas Morning News,* Nov 8, 1994.
3. Bassuk EL: Homeless families, *Sci Am* 265:66-72, 1991.
4. Bruininks RH et al: *Scales of independent behavior,* Allen,
Tex, 1984, DLM Teaching Resources.
5. Capers C: You must listen to understand, *The Dallas Morning News,* April 30, 1995.
6. Children's group blasts poverty, abuse, *The Dallas Morning News,* March 29, 1995.
7. Cone JD: *The pyramid scales,* Austin, Tex, 1984, PRO-ED.
8. Cowley G: Children in peril, *Newsweek* (special issue),
summer 1991.
9. Crack children, *Newsweek,* pp 62-63, Feb 12, 1990.
10. Crack hurts parental instinct, *The Dallas Morning News,*
March 17, 1990.
11. Daro D, McCurdy K: *Current trends in child abuse reporting and fatalities: the results of the 1990 annual fifty state
survey,* The National Center on Child Abuse Prevention
Research, a working paper, 1991.
12. D'Entremont D: *Intervention strategies for school age children,* Rep No CG023529, University of Southern Maine
(ERIC Document Reproduction Service No ED 334514).
13. Diamond LJ, Jaudes PK: Child abuse in a cerebral-palsied
population, *Dev Med Child Neurol* 1:12-18, 1987.
14. Easley J: We are failing to protect our children, *The Dallas Morning News,* March 16, 1995.
15. Foster-care hike, parents' addiction linked, *The Dallas
Morning News,* April 28, 1994.
16. Gangs/recruiters find fertile turf beyond big city, *Milwaukee Journal Sentinel,* June 18, 1995.
17. Gaylord-Ross RJ, Holvoet J: *Strategies for educating students with severe handicaps,* Boston, 1985, Little, Brown.
18. Green C: Infant mortality rate may rise: poverty, drug use,
AIDS among factors cited in panel's report, *The Dallas
Morning News,* Feb 27, 1990.
19. Green C: Something is robbing our children of their future, *Parade Magazine,* March 5, 1995.
20. Greer JV: The drug babies, *Except Child,* pp 382-384, Feb
1990.
21. Hellison D: Making a difference—reflections on teaching
urban at-risk youth, *J Phys Educ Rec Dance* 61:33-45,
1990.
22. Hellison D: Physical education for disadvantaged youth, *J
Phys Educ Rec Dance* 61:37, 1990.
23. Hellison D: Teaching PE to at-risk youth in Chicago—a
model, *J Phys Educ Rec Dance* 61:38-39, 1990.
24. Hellison D, Templin T: *A reflective approach to teaching
physical education,* Champaign, Ill, 1991, Human Kinetics.
25. *Hillsborough County Street Gang Awareness,* Hillsborough
County, Fla, Hillsborough County Anti-Drug Alliance
Multi Agency Gang Related Committee.
26. Huettig C, DiBrezzo R: *Factors in abuse and neglect of
handicapped children.* Paper presented at American Alliance of Health, Physical Education, Recreation and Dance
National Convention, Las Vegas, April, 1987.
27. *I hated the school, barriers to excellence,* Boston, 1985,
National Coalition of Advocates for Children.
28. Infant mortality declines, but not among blacks, *Milwaukee Journal Sentinel,* July 10, 1995.
29. Jasperse P: Four million U.S. kids "hungry," *Milwaukee
Journal Sentinel,* July 20, 1995.

30. Jaudes PK, Diamond LJ: The handicapped child and child abuse, *Child Abuse Negl* 9:341-347, 1985.
31. Jones D, Winn G, Dooley E: PROJECT YES: a break from tradition, *J Phys Educ Rec Dance* 66(2):41-47, 1995.
32. Kenyon R: The deceptive peace of the countryside, *Wisconsin: The Milwaukee Journal Magazine,* Aug 12, 1990.
33. Kohlberg L: The cognitive-development approach to moral education. In *Values, concepts, and techniques,* Washington, DC, 1971, National Education Association.
34. Kozol J: *Savage inequalities: children in America's schools,* New York, 1991, Crown.
35. Leroux C, Schreuder C: Crucial beginnings: a child's first few months can determine its future, *The Dallas Morning News,* Nov 29, 1994.
36. Lev A, Brandon K: Rescuing the children: a new tactic against abuse: intervention, *The Dallas Morning News,* Sept 6, 1994.
37. Lifka BJ: Hiding beneath the stairwell—a dropout prevention program for Hispanic youth, *J Phys Educ Rec Dance* 61:40-41, 1990.
38. Miller R: Children's advocate tallies toll of violence, *The Dallas Morning News,* May 8, 1995.
39. *More new games . . . and playful ideas from the New Games Foundation,* Garden City, NY, 1981, A Headlands Press Book.
40. Msall M et al: Multivariate risks among extremely premature infants, *J Perinatol* 14(1):41-47, 1994.
41. Myers L: Poll finds that children are afraid of the future, *The Dallas Morning News,* May 17, 1995.
42. *A nation's shame: fatal child abuse and neglect in the United States,* Washington, DC, 1995, US Advisory Board on Child Abuse and Neglect.
43. *New games,* Garden City, NY, 1976, A Headlands Press Book.
44. O'Neil J: Transforming the curriculum for students "at-risk," *Curriculum Update,* pp 1-3, 6, 1991.
45. Rafferty C: No home address: the increasing number of children growing up homeless may face long-term emotional dangers, *The Dallas Morning News,* Feb 8, 1994.
46. Rise in urban needy reported, *The Dallas Morning News,* Dec 21, 1989.
47. Rotholz D et al: A behavioral comparison of preschool children at high and low risk from prenatal cocaine exposure, *Educ Treatment Child* 18(1):1-18, 1995.
48. Rummler G: Children's world may be "socially toxic," *The Dallas Morning News,* Aug 15, 1994.
49. Schoolyard violence a threat to students, *The Dallas Morning News,* March 31, 1995.
50. Sparks W: Promoting self-responsibility and decision making with at-risk students, *J Health Phys Educ Rec Dance* 64(2):74-78, 1993.
51. Sparrow SS, Balla DA, Cicchetti DV: *Vineland adaptive behavior scales,* Circle Pines, Minn, 1984, American Guidance Service.
52. Stephens TM: *Social skills in the classroom,* Columbus, Ohio, 1978, Cedars Press.
53. Stewart B: McKinney Homeless Assistance Amendment Act, PL 100-645, 1990 US Code, *Cong Admin News* (104 Stat) 4673, 1990.
54. Streissguth A et al: Fetal alcohol syndrome in adolescents and adults, *JAMA* 265:1961-1967, 1991.
55. Study charts disabilities of premature babies, *The Dallas Morning News,* Sept 22, 1994.
56. Study says 26% of kids under 6 are living in poverty, *The Dallas Morning News,* Jan 30, 1995.
57. Tarr S: *Physical and psychomotor development of neonates/infants prenatally exposed to drugs: a meta-analysis,* Dissertation, Denton, Dec 1994, Texas Woman's University.
58. Teachers and students victims of violence at school, *Natl Assoc Sport Phys Educ News,* winter 1994.
59. Teen birth rate falls for 1st time in years, *The Dallas Morning News,* Oct 26, 1994.
60. Thomas K: This is sick: kids planning their funerals, *The Dallas Morning News,* March 23, 1995.
61. Traditional families on wane, study finds, *The Dallas Morning News,* Aug 30, 1994.
62. Verdugo M, Bermejo B, Fuertes J: The maltreatment of intellectually handicapped children and adolescents, *Child Abuse Negl* 19(2):205-215, 1995.
63. Wallach L: Children coping with violence: the role of the school, *Contemp Educ* 65(4):182-184, 1994.
64. Waller M: Crack babies grow up: what happens when drug-exposed children get older, *Am School Board J,* pp 30-31, June 1994.
65. Warren K, Bast R: Alcohol-related birth defects: an update, *Public Health Rep* 103:638-642, 1988.
66. Wasserman J: Surviving the mean streets, *The Dallas Morning News,* Jan 12, 1995.
67. Wehling D: The crack kids are coming, *Principal,* pp 12-13, May 1991.
68. Westcott H: The abuse of disabled children: a review of the literature, *Child Care Health Dev* 17:243-258, 1991.
69. Williams B, Howard V, McLaughlin T: Fetal alcohol syndrome: developmental characteristics and directions for future research, *Educ Treatment Child* 17(1):86-97, 1994.
70. Wood DL et al: Health of homeless children and housed, poor children, *Pediatrics* 86:858-866, 1990.
71. Yon M: Education of homeless children in the United States, *Equity Excellence Educ* 28(1):58-62, 1994.

Suggested Reading

Fluegelman A, editor: *New games book,* Garden City, NY, 1976, A Headlands Press Book.

Needs of Specific Populations

In this section, specific types of disabilities are described. Each condition is defined, characteristics are given, means of testing are suggested, and specific programming and teaching techniques are detailed. Because of the growing number of services required for children 5 years old and younger, we have added a chapter on assessing and programming for infants, toddlers, and preschoolers with disabilities.

Infants, Toddlers, and Preschoolers

Courtesy Dallas Independent School District.

As we approach the closing years of the twentieth century, it is becoming increasingly clear that traditional educational practices that have served our society well in the past must be modified. Technology that enables us to access information at a moment's notice, a growing appreciation of the values and contributions of different cultures, and the continuing increase in numbers of individuals who function in very different ways on a variety of levels challenge us to explore new ways of "educating" people to function fully in our society. We are beginning to realize that if our society is going to survive and grow, all students, regardless of gender, ethnicity, and functional capacity, must be adequately prepared to participate successfully in a multicultural society that is increasingly dependent on advanced technology. A curriculum that provides students with information, skills, and problem-solving capabilities that will serve them in their career and community must be embraced. Intervention strategies that address the developmental needs of the individual and evaluation techniques to assess the success of those interventions must be developed and implemented. The sooner in life individual needs are addressed, the better the child's chance of growing into a productive adult.

We have chosen to address the needs of infants, toddlers, and young children in a separate chapter in this edition because of the unique, diverse, and comprehensive needs of children in the earliest stages of development. Early and developmentally appropriate intervention during the crucial years in which central nervous system development is marked and pronounced has a profound impact on cognitive, language, social-emotional, and motor performance. Attention to these factors is important for all children; however, it is critical for children who are born at risk for failure to thrive and failure to develop along expected lines.

In this chapter we introduce the most recent theories of intellectual development, as well as the gross motor, cognitive, receptive and expressive language, symbolic play, drawing, fine motor, constructive play, self-help, and emotional characteristics of the typically developing child from birth through 5 years. Techniques for identifying the developmental level of young children and intervention strategies to facilitate their developmental processes are explained. In addition, federal mandates that address required services for at-risk infants, toddlers, and young children are discussed. The central role of the parents in this process is emphasized. The characteristics and importance of developmentally appropriate learning environments designed to facilitate the primary learning tool of the young child—play—are highlighted.

The Eight Types of Intelligence—The Philosophical Foundation of Early Intervention

Howard Gardner,[15] in the *Frames of Mind: The Theory of Multiple Intelligences,* suggests that if educators are to conceptualize cognition, it must be considered in a far broader realm than that typically used to identify or quantify an individual's ability to think and learn. Specifically, Gardner suggests that those instruments used typically to assess and evaluate intelligence tend to ignore many types of human intelligence in lieu of measuring those that are easier to measure, namely linguistic and mathematical abilities.

Gardner's theory of multiple intelligence has been widely embraced by enlightened educational communities. His theory continues to be ignored by those satisfied with the status quo. Gardner defines "intelligence" as the ability to solve problems or create products valued within one or more cultural settings. His emphasis on multicultural settings is of particular value in consideration of the philosophy. His work has gained particular reknown as educators seek to explore and define strategies to evaluate the intelligence of children representing a wide variety of cultures and as they seek educational intervention strategies that meet their diverse needs.

Widely used norm-referenced linguistic and mathematically based "intelligence tests" have widespread cultural, racial, socioeconomic, and gender biases. Historically, these very tests have been used to include and exclude children from particular learning environments and experiences. The tracking of black and poor children, which provided the impetus for *Brown v. Board of Education* (Kansas), 1954, is a practice that, unfortunately, still exists. If Gardner's theory of multiple intelligences was widely embraced and practiced, educational assessment would more appropriately and equitably evaluate the performance and potential performance of all children. And, as important, educational intervention would be more appropriate and equitable.

Of particular interest to the preschool adapted physical education specialist, or movement/play specialist, is the fact that the movement/play behaviors that are the focus of the preschool movement/play program would be embraced as a vital and integral part of the total education process. Movement/play would be recognized for its significant potential in the lives of young children.

Each of Gardner's theorized intelligences is considered here with examples of the behaviors of infants, toddlers, and young children that reflect these intelligences.

Linguistic Intelligence

Linguistic intelligence is expressed in and through the use of oral language (receptive and expressive) and the use of written language (reading and writing). It represents a sensitivity to and interest in the use of words, the sound and rhythm of words, and the functions of language—to express wants and needs, to convince, to share, and to explain.

The young child demonstrates this intelligence by:
- Cooing and babbling
- Scribbling and drawing
- Asking questions
- Repeating nonsense rhymes
- Telling stories
- Identifying simple words or signs
- Rote counting

Logical-Mathematical Intelligence

Logical-mathematical intelligence reflects an individual's ability to group and sequence objects, to order and reorder them, to describe their quality and quantity, and to see and understand patterns.

The young child demonstrates this intelligence by:
- Separating dinosaurs from zoo animals
- Stacking rings, diminishing in size, on a base
- Collecting sticks and separating the long ones from the short ones
- Sequencing blocks in patterns, such as 3 blue, 2 red, 3 blue
- Arranging balls from the largest to the smallest

Musical Intelligence

Musical intelligence reflects an individual's ability to recognize sounds and distinguish one from another, identify and see patterns in music, be sensitive to rhythm and time variables, know and appreciate timbre and tone, and express feelings and emotions through music.

The young child demonstrates this intelligence by:
- Seeking one particular "favorite" musical instrument

- Turning off the tape recorder if he or she does not like the music
- Asking to sing a favorite song, over and over
- Clapping or toe tapping to a particular rhythm or beat
- Singing or humming
- "Rapping" a favorite saying

Spatial Intelligence

Spatial intelligence includes the ability to identify shapes and differentiate between objects in terms of size, to see commonalities in shape or size, to perceive the visual world accurately, to perform simple transformations of visual images, and to recreate a graphic image of a visual representation, such as maps or graphs.

The young child demonstrates this intelligence by:
- Putting puzzles together
- Drawing self
- Sorting objects by shape and size
- Copying a given figure
- Drawing a particular shape in a variety of positions[13]
- Identifying a child who is larger or smaller than self
- Identifying a child who is taller or shorter than self

Bodily-Kinesthetic Intelligence

Bodily-kinesthetic intelligence is characterized by ability to use the body in highly differentiated and skilled ways, for expressive and goal-directed purposes.

The young child demonstrates this intelligence by:
- Crawling, creeping, and walking in, around, and between objects
- Using gestures to express needs/wants
- Using facial expressions to convey emotions
- Reaching to get a favorite toy
- Hurling a ball
- Jumping over a set of blocks, arranged in an ever-taller sequence
- Kicking a ball

Interpersonal Intelligence

The interpersonal intelligence is one in which an individual can identify and empathize with the feelings and emotions of others.

The young child demonstrates this intelligence by:
- Crying if another child cries

- Telling a parent or other caregiver if a friend is hurt or sad
- Comforting a friend who is upset
- Noticing that the parent or caregiver is having a "bad day"
- Making independent choices about play

Intrapersonal Intelligence

The intrapersonal intelligence is one in which the individual is able to identify his or her own feelings, emotions, and motives and is basically inner directed (i.e., internally driven).

The young child demonstrates this intelligence by:
- Seeking solitary play experiences
- Expressing emotion in sociodramatic play experiences
- Preferring an independent plan-do-review process to a group process

In later works, Gardner identified yet another form of intelligence. At first, he suggested that it might be a "spiritual" intelligence; in recent works he has called it "naturalist" intelligence. In fact, it appears that the eighth intelligence is probably a combination of "spirituality" and a profound sense of "nature." Gardner[20] suggested that:

> The intelligence of the naturalist involves the ability to recognize important distinctions in the natural world (among flora, fauna). It can also be applied to man-made objects in our consumer society (cars, sneakers, etc.). Obviously, this skill is crucial in hunting or farming cultures, and it is at a premium among biologists and others who work with nature in our own society.

The young child demonstrates this intelligence by:
- Identifying flowers with similar petals
- Collecting leaves and sorting them
- Preferring to be outside to being inside
- Wanting to take care of the class pet

Perhaps only when educators, lawmakers and voters, and school board members acknowledge that there are *at least* eight different types of intelligence . . . and that in order to thrive and grow, our society needs individuals with each of these types of intelligence . . . and that the educational system must nurture each child representing every culture, race, socioeconomic status, and gender . . . will the educational system truly meet the needs of its constituents—all its constituents.

Developmentally Appropriate Assessment of Infants, Toddlers, and Preschoolers

While the move toward assessment that acknowledges multiple forms of intelligence has been embraced by some educators, there is a desperate need for assessment that is sensitive to the unique needs of infants, toddlers, and young children (i.e., developmentally appropriate practice). This is crucial because assessment drives eligibility, placement, and programming decisions.

In this section, we address **developmentally appropriate movement/play assessment** for infants, toddlers, and young children with an emphasis on play-based, transdisciplinary assessment practices and the development of a movement/play portfolio assessment process to follow the child from infancy through adulthood.

Shepard[41] has suggested three basic principles to guide assessment of young children:

1. Only testing that can be shown to lead to beneficial results should take place.
2. Assessment methods, particularly the language used, must be appropriate to the development and experiences of the children being tested.
3. Assessment features, including content, form, evidence of validity, and standards for interpretation, must be tailored to the specific purpose of the assessment.

Before passage of P.L. 99-457, The Education of the Handicapped Amendments of 1986, assessment and intervention efforts directed toward children under 5 years of age focused on those children with obvious disabilities, such as Down syndrome, cerebral palsy, or visual impairment. P.L. 99-457 represents a major step toward meeting the needs of individuals with disabilities because, in addition to serving children with recognized disabilities, infants and toddlers with less well defined problems, who are highly likely to experience developmental delays, now qualify for services. This inclusion has far-reaching implications for screening, assessment, and intervention activities.

Tasks and opportunities relevant to screening and assessment outlined in P.L. 99-457 include:

1. Use of a multidisciplinary approach to screen and assess children from birth through 5 years of age
2. Identifying infants and young children with known disabilities and developmental delays; and at states' discretion, identifying children from birth

through 2 years of age who are at risk for developmental delays (including physical delays)

3. Planning comprehensive services for young children with special needs, including a model of periodic rescreening and reassessment

4. Involving the family in all levels of assessment, identification, and intervention

Levels of services included in the law are:

1. Child Find activities

2. Developmental and health screening, including administration of screening instruments, questioning of parents, and administration of medical, vision, and hearing examinations

3. Diagnostic testing, including formal testing, parent interviews, and home observation

4. Individual program planning[31]

Traditionally, many adapted physical educators serving young children with disabilities have been involved with **Child Find** searches and developmental screening. However, the expansion of services mandated by P.L. 99-457 has enabled the physical educator to become more fully involved in identifying and remediating delays evidenced by a wider range of young children. This is a distinct opportunity to have a positive impact on the lives of growing numbers of at-risk children in those critical early periods of life before school age.

Guidelines for Screening and Assessment of Infants, Toddlers, and Preschoolers

The following guidelines for screening and assessing young children are recommended by Meisels and Provence[32]:

1. Screening and assessment are services—as part of the intervention process—and not only as means of identification and measurement.

2. Processes, procedures, and instruments intended for screening and assessment should be used only for their specified purposes.

3. Multiple sources of information should be included in screening and assessment.

4. Developmental screening should take place on a recurrent or periodic basis. It is inappropriate to screen young children only once during their early years. Reassessment should continue after services have been initiated.

5. Developmental screening should be viewed as

only one path to more in-depth assessment. Failure to qualify for services based on a single source of screening information should not become a barrier to further evaluation for intervention services if other risk factors (e.g., environmental, medical, familial) are present.

6. Screening and assessment procedures should be reliable and valid.

7. Family members should be an integral part of the screening and assessment process. Information provided by family members is critically important for determining whether to initiate more in-depth assessment and for designing appropriate intervention strategies. Parents must give complete, informed consent at all stages of the screening process.

8. During screening or assessment of developmental strengths and problems, the more relevant and familiar the tasks and setting are to the child and the child's family, the more likely it is that the results will be valid.

9. All tests, procedures, and processes intended for screening and assessment must be culturally sensitive.

10. Extensive and comprehensive training is needed by those who screen and assess very young children.

Selected motor assessment instruments that are appropriate for use with preschool children are included in Table 10-1.

Transdisciplinary, Play-Based Assessment

The Individual with Disabilities Education Act (IDEA) mandates, in both Part H (birth to 3 years) and Part B (3 to 5 years), a comprehensive assessment of children to determine eligibility and to serve as the basis for placement and educational programming decisions. The standard within the profession is **transdisciplinary, play-based assessment (TPBA),** described by Linder[28] as follows:

> Transdisciplinary play-based assessment involves the child in structured and unstructured play situations with, at varying times, a facilitating adult, the parent(s), and another child or children. Designed for children functioning between infancy and 6 years of age, TPBA provides an opportunity for developmental observations of cognitive,

table 10-1				
Selected Motor Assessment Instruments for Infants, Toddlers, and Preschoolers				
Test/Description	Source	Age	Components	Reference
Alberta Infant Motor Scale (AIMS) (1994) A tool for assessing the early postures of the developing infant	Piper & Darrar: Motor Assessment of the Developing Infant W.B. Saunders Company 6277 Sea Harbor Drive Orlando, FL 32821	0-19 mo	Prone, supine, sit, stand postures	Content-referenced
Bayley Scales of Infant Development II (1992) This new, revised scale is sensitive to differences between children who are at risk for developmental delay and those who are not	The Psychological Corp. 555 Academic Court San Antonio, TX 78204	1-42 mo	Posture, locomotor, fine motor	Norm-referenced
Brigance Diagnostic Inventory—Revised (1991) A widely used, teacher-friendly scale that also includes speech and language, general knowledge and comprehension, social and emotional development, reading readiness, basic reading skills, manuscript writing, and basic math assessment techniques	Curriculum Assoc., Inc. 5 Esquire Road North Billerica, MA 10862	Birth-7 yr	Preambulatory, motor skills, fine motor, gross motor, self-help skills	Content-referenced
Callier-Azusa Scale (1978) A developmental scale designed to aid in the assessment of deaf-blind and profoundly disabled children. It also includes daily living skills, cognition, communication, and language, and social-developmental milestones	The University of Texas at Dallas The Callier Center for Communication Disorders 1966 Inwood Road Dallas, TX 75235	Birth-7 yr	Postural control, locomotion, fine motor, visual-motor, and visual, auditory, and tactile development	Content-referenced
DeGangi-Berk Test of Sensory Integration (1983) An excellent instrument for use by individuals familiar with sensory integration theory and development	Western Psychological 12031 Wilshire Blvd. Los Angeles, CA 90025	3-5 yr	Postural control, bilateral motor integration, reflex integration	Content- and norm-referenced

table 10-1				
Selected Motor Assessment Instruments for Infants, Toddlers, and Preschoolers—cont'd				
Test/Description	Source	Age	Components	Reference
Denver Development Scale II (1988) This easy-to-use screening tool also includes screening for language and personal-social skills (self-help)	Ladoca Publishing Found. 5100 Lincoln Street Denver, CO 80216	Birth-6 yr	Gross motor skills, fine motor–adaptive skills	Content-referenced
Hawaii Early Learning Profile (HELP) (1988) A curriculum-imbedded developmental checklist that also includes cognitive, language, social, and self-help skills	VORT Corp. P.O. Box 601321 Palo Alto, CA 94306	0-36 mo	Gross motor, fine motor, self-help	Content-referenced
Miller Assessment for Pre-schoolers (1988 Rev.) An instrument that also includes evaluation of a child's speech and language and cognitive abilities, and provides guidance in determining whether a child's behavior during testing ranges from severely dysfunctional to normal	The Psychological Corp. 555 Academic Court San Antonio, TX 78204-2498	2.9-5.9 yr	Sense of position and movement, touch, basic movement patterns, gross motor, fine motor	Content-referenced
Movement Assessment of Infants (1980) An instrument that enables the evaluator to determine whether a child is developing normally during the first year of life	Movement Assessment of Infants P.O. Box 4631 Rolling Bay, WA 98061	Birth-12 mo	Muscle tone, primitive reflexes, equilibrium reflexes, volitional movement	Content-referenced
Peabody Developmental Motor Scales (1983) A curriculum-imbedded assessment tool that is widely used by preschool teachers	DLM Teaching Resources One DLM Park Allen, TX 75002	Birth-83 mo	Fine motor, gross motor	Norm-referenced
Test of Sensory Functions in Infants (1989)	Western Psychological 12031 Wilshire Blvd. Los Angeles, CA 90025	4-18 mo	Reaction to tactile deep pressure adaptive motor functions, visual-tactile, integration, ocular-motor	Content-referenced

social-emotional, communication and language, and sensorimotor domains.

The assessment process must be **transdisciplinary;** that is, it should be done by a team of individuals with a commitment to infants, toddlers, and young children representing various disciplines. The child's parent(s) is the most important member of the team—the parent is the best source of information about the child. Professionals with unique abilities and skills in one or more of the domains are a vital part of the team as well. These professionals may include, but are not limited to (1) an educational psychologist, (2) a speech and language therapist, (3) an occupational therapist, (4) a physical therapist, (5) a movement/play specialist, and (6) a play therapist. A transdisciplinary approach to assessment with infants, toddlers, and young children allows the team members to gain vital information regarding the child's development and to share that information with other professionals.

It is vital that the professionals and parents understand their feelings during the evaluation process. Simeonsson[42] found a significant disparity between the feelings that parents acknowledged they felt during the evaluation process and those that the professionals attributed to them:

	Parental Feelings During Transdisciplinary Evaluation (%)	Feelings Professionals Attribute to Parents (%)
Afraid	17	70
Angry	8	24
Confused	13	61
Worried	42	89

In order for the parents and professionals to function as part of the transdisciplinary team effectively, honest and open communication between them is vital so that this type of misperception does not persist.

The preschool movement/play specialist may add a unique perspective to the transdisciplinary team because of specific competencies. Cowden and Torrey[5] suggest the "adapted motor developmentalist" should have the following competencies:

- Knowledge of normal and abnormal motor development
- Curriculum- and judgment-based assessment techniques
- Appropriate response-contingent toys/materials for

sensory stimulation and physical and motor development
- Strategies for relaxation, socialization, and play

The assessment process is sensitive to the unique needs of the child and allows flexibility in order to see the child's very best. In and through play—the most natural phenomenon of early childhood—the assessment team has the opportunity for developmentally appropriate observations within the cognitive, social-emotional, communication and language, and sensorimotor domains.

The more traditional assessment/evaluation model is inappropriate for infants, toddlers, and preschoolers for a number of reasons:

- Infants, toddlers, and preschoolers are not comfortable with strangers. It is frightening to meet a stranger, much less be asked to leave a parent to go with a stranger into a room to "play."
- Young children are uncomfortable outside of their natural setting—their home, their neighborhood, their child care setting. Little children will not behave "naturally" when asked to perform outside of their "natural setting."
- Young children may be asked to "play" with an evaluator, but the child does not control the situation—the unfamiliar adult does. The child is asked to "play" without his or her favorite toys, and to facilitate evaluation, the child may find a toy he or she enjoys playing with and then be asked to return the toy to move on to another task.
- Assessment protocols often discriminate against a child with a disability. For example, most "intelligence tests" rely heavily on language; the performance of a child may be significantly affected by a dialect unfamiliar to the examiner.
- Many developmental assessment scales assume that there is a "typical" developmental sequence; many children with disabilities simply do not acquire developmental milestones in a "typical" way.
- Many of the tasks that infants, toddlers, and young children are asked to perform have little or no meaning for the child or the child's parent(s). This has, unfortunately, been part of the clinical "mystique," which has presumed that the professionals have the answers and the parent(s) are dependent on the professionals for information.

The TPBA process can and must be used in the motor assessment process as well. The motor assessment instrument presented in the box on pp. 250-251 was designed to evaluate motor development delays in preschoolers 3 years of age and older. Data are collected through observation of play in structured and unstructured situations. It provides wonderful information for the parent and preschool adapted physical education specialist developing the individual education program (IEP) and the individual family service plan (IFSP).

Comprehensive Motor Assessment

The assessment of movement and play behaviors in infants, toddlers, and young children requires a special sensitivity to the fact that major developmental changes occur during the crucial years from birth to 5 years. (See Chapter 7 for a discussion regarding the evaluation of primitive and equilibrium reflex development and strategies for promoting and extinguishing given reflexes.)

Federal mandates require a child's assessment to include results of standardized and validated tests, particularly when decisions are being made about eligibility (see Table 10-1). These instruments are developmental scales that allow the preschool adapted physical education specialist to evaluate the progress of the infant, toddler, and young child in relation to "typical" child development. Typical child development is considered later in this chapter under Ages and Stages—Understanding Typical and Atypical Development.

While federal mandates require that a child's assessment include results of standardized and validated tests, information can be gathered for a comprehensive and formal assessment using the TPBA approach and while honoring the unique needs of the child. Formal assessment and the TPBA process are compatible. For example, the preschool adapted physical education specialist may observe most of the motor and play components of the Brigance Diagnostic Inventory of Early Development–Revised while simply observing the infant, toddler, or child engaged in play in the home, child care center, or preschool classroom. To maintain an emphasis on child-appropriate assessment, strategies sensitive to the needs of the child can be used to gain information regarding the skills the child does not demonstrate during natural or structured play. For example, to see the child perform particular skills, the assessment specialist

can administer a certain component to a child, or a small group of children, while telling the children a story with puppets. The evaluator may use hand puppets and tell a story about animals who "do" the skills that the evaluator needs to see. A pony puppet may be used to tell a brief story in which the pony gallops, for example. Or a puppy puppet may be used to tell a story in which the puppy catches a bounced ball.

Ecological Assessment

Whenever possible, the assessment and evaluation of an infant, toddler, or young child should be completed in the child's most natural environment—the home, child care setting, or neighborhood play area. In addition to being sensitive to the child's natural environment, the assessment must be culturally and socioeconomically, as well as gender, sensitive.

The Portfolio Assessment Process

Sensitivity to the fact that assessment is not, and should never be, a "6-month" or "annual" or "3-year comprehensive" event but rather a day-to-day, ongoing process has led educators to the portfolio assessment. Just as caring parents have historically saved documentation of their child's progress—pictures, drawings, height/weight information, "new" words, etc., caring educators must begin to save, carefully, documentation of the progress of the children they teach.

The **portfolio assessment process** allows educators to address each of the eight types of intelligence to carefully document and monitor the progress of the infants, toddlers, and preschoolers they serve.[22] If the parent and teacher are sensitive to the fact that their role should not be intrusive, but rather supportive, not as the director of learning but as the facilitator, the portfolio is a natural and obvious conclusion. If the educator is actively watching and learning from the children, the teacher will become adept at documenting each child's progress.

The preschool movement/play specialist has a great deal to contribute to the child's total portfolio. In fact, this specialist may contribute information and data for the portfolio in all eight types of intelligence. Contributing this type of data to the preschool educator helps validate the active play and learning process and encourages teachers and parents to perceive the adapted physical educator as a professional who can make a signifi-

Motor Development Delay Indicators: 3 Years and Older*

I. Muscle tone status (check all that apply):
   a. Low tone (proprioceptive problems):
     Difficulty holding up head _____
     Slumped posture _____
     Tendency to put legs in a W position when sitting _____
   b. High tone (overflow/tension):
     Stiff body movements _____
     Fisting of one or both hands _____
     Grimacing of mouth or face when concentrating _____

II. Strength and endurance—demonstrates any of the following:
     Tires during play before other children _____
     Gets out of breath before other children _____
     Has breathing difficulties sometimes _____

III. Equilibrium/extensor muscle control (check all that apply):
   a. Does not raise and control head when:
     Lying face down _____
     Balancing on hands and knees _____
     Sitting _____
   b. Does not roll from front to back _____
   c. Does not prop on forearms _____
   d. Does not reach for a toy when:
     Lying face down _____
     Balancing on hands and knees _____
     Sitting _____
   e. Cannot remain standing without support _____

IV. Equilibrium/flexor muscle control (check all that apply):
   a. Has difficulty with the following moves from a back-lying position:
     Rolling from back to front _____
     Sitting up _____
     Standing up _____
     Reaching for toy _____

V. Equilibrium when moving (check all that apply):
     Does not use sequential movement when rolling (head, shoulders, hips, followed by legs) _____
     Standing/walking/running on balls of feet _____
     Uses a wide base of support during walk/run _____
     Loses balance when suddenly changing directions _____
     Does not put arms and hands out to break fall _____
     Avoids walking on narrow supports (balance beam, curb) _____

VI. Visual status (indicators of depth perception problems)—demonstrates any of the following:
     Both feet are not off ground momentarily when running _____
     Does not jump down from bottom step _____
     Watches feet when moving on different surfaces _____
     Marks time when ascending and descending stairs _____
     Avoids climbing apparatus _____
     Turns head when catching ball _____
     Cannot bounce and catch playground ball with both hands _____
     Misses ball when kicking _____

*Activities that can be used in preschool and elementary grades to promote motor development can be located in the handbook *Gross Motor Activities for Young Children with Special Needs,* which accompanies this text.

Motor Development Delay Indicators: 3 Years and Older—cont'd

(NOTE: Children demonstrating three or more of the preceding eight behaviors should be referred to a visual development specialist for an orthoptic visual examination.)

VII. Coordination (check all that apply):

    a. Does not bring the hands together at midline when:

        Lying down   _____

        Sitting up   _____

    b. Does not demonstrate the following:

        Uses arms in opposition to legs when crawling   _____

        Uses arms in opposition to legs when walking   _____

        Uses arms in opposition to legs when running   _____

        Arms are bent at waist height when running   _____

        Use of both arms to assist during jump   _____

        Slides leading with one side of body   _____

        Gallops   _____

    c. Does not demonstrate the following when kicking:

        Swings kicking leg behind body when preparing to kick   _____

        Follows through with kicking leg after contact   _____

VIII. Additional information:

    a. What are the primary means of moving during play?_____

    _____

    b. What motor skills does the child avoid?_____

    _____

    c. Can the child imitate a movement pattern that is demonstrated?_____

    d. Can the child demonstrate a sequence of movements when requested to do so?

    _____

    e. Check the stages of play the child demonstrates:

        Solitary (onlooker, or ignores others)   _____

        Parallel (plays alongside or with similar toys)   _____

        Associative (follow the leader)   _____

        Cooperative (social interaction)   _____

IX. Comments/observations/concerns_____

_____

_____

---

cant contribution. Examples of movement and play data that might be collected to reflect each of the eight types of intelligence are included here.

Linguistic intelligence

- A child tells a story about a favorite movement, and the story is recorded on an audio tape.
- A toddler says "ball" when he or she wants the teacher to roll the ball to the child; the teacher records the utterance on the child's daily log.

- The child sings a simple "rap" song while jumping; the teacher videotapes the child.

Logical-mathematical intelligence

- A child builds a tower with giant soft blocks and the teacher takes a picture of the structure.
- A group of children line up to form a "train," and the teacher videotapes the group performing to the song, "Chug-a-Long Choo Choo."

Musical intelligence

- Several children dance to Hap Palmer's "What a Miracle"; the teacher videotapes the child being assessed.
- A child walks to the beat of a drum; the teacher notes the progress.
- An infant looks about to find the source of a sound; the teacher notes the milestone.

Spatial intelligence

- A toddler can trap a 13-, 10-, 8-, or 6-inch ball rolled to the child sitting in a V-sit position; the parent notes the ability and shares that information with the motor specialist.
- An infant crawls toward and reaches a toy; the preschool movement/play specialist records that on the ongoing motor development assessment instrument.

Bodily-kinesthetic intelligence

- A 9-month-old child creeps on all fours. The teacher takes a picture of the child moving in this position.
- A 2-year-old toddler hurls a ball; the teacher records the progress on the child's portfolio.
- A 5-year-old with Down syndrome climbs up and down a set of five stairs, holding the railing; the teacher records the milestone.
- A child slides down a playground slide for the first time; the teacher catches the "first" on film.

Interpersonal intelligence

- A child engages in parallel play in a sandbox. The teacher videotapes the play.
- A child identifies the children he or she likes to play with and those he or she does not like to play with; the teacher records this on a sociogram.

Intrapersonal intelligence

- A child describes the way he or she feels when playing a simple game with a friend. The teacher catches this on audiotape.

Naturalistic intelligence

- A child names a flower on a nature walk; the teacher notes it.

- A child describes how he or she feels while playing in the sunshine; it is recorded on audiotape.

▪ ▪ ▪

Contemporary communication, technology, and computer capabilities now make it possible for parents and teachers to save vast amounts of information about the development of young children. Baby boomers have sepia photographs of their parents as children and their grandparents as adults. The children of the 1990s, and most certainly those of the third millennium, have audio and visual memories stored on CD-ROM. The technology exists to begin a portfolio for every infant that can follow the child throughout his or her development. The beauty lies in the capability to save and store information that could, potentially, increase the likelihood that infants, toddlers, and young children can grow and learn in the best possible way. When the infant makes the transition into a toddler program, when the toddler makes the transition into a preschool program, and when the preschooler makes the transition into first grade, his or her teachers will have a comprehensive and complete record of the child's progress.

The most significant questions related to the assessment process with infants, toddlers, and preschoolers are:

1. Does the assessment process yield important information that relates to eligibility, placement, and programming?
2. Does it do no harm? That is, can the infant, toddler, or preschooler be hurt in any way by the process; if so, it should not be done under any circumstance.
3. Does the assessment discriminate against children on the basis of culture, socioeconomic base, or gender? It must not.
4. Does the process provide information that the parents and other practitioners can use?

Assessment can be intrusive. A transdisciplinary, play-based approach to assessment completed in the child's natural ecosystem reduces the potential that the assessment may be frightening to the child or parent.

Assessment can also be discriminatory. Recognizing eight different types of intelligence and monitoring progress using a portfolio assessment minimizes that possibility as well. Most important, the unique sensitivities of an infant, toddler, or young child must be respected and acknowledged.

Ages and Stages—Understanding Typical and Atypical Development

It is vitally important that the preschool movement/play specialist be aware of the development of the whole child. It is also necessary for the educator to embrace the notion that there is no such thing as a "typical" child. Each child is a unique being who develops in a unique way.

The description of the approximate ages at which a child usually acquires a new skill is charted for ease of understanding (Table 10-2). Certainly, the educator must know what is typical in order to deal with a child with delays or disabilities. But it must be understood that each child develops uniquely. For example, it is not uncommon for an abused or neglected child to demonstrate typical gross and fine motor development but demonstrate marked delays in social-emotional, cognitive, receptive, and expressive language development.

Not only does the preschool movement/play specialist need to understand and identify delays, but the knowledge of "typical" development makes it possible for the educator to sensitively teach the whole child. For example, let's consider Billy Bogg, whose comprehensive motor assessment was presented in Chapter 2.

A complete psychoeducational assessment of Billy Bogg at age 40 months may have found him functioning at the following developmental levels:

Cognition	50 months
Receptive language	48 months
Expressive language	48 months
Gross motor	20 months
Social-emotional	18 months

Given that assessment information, the preschool movement/play specialist would know Billy would *probably* be able to:

- Follow along in a book being read.
- Try to read a book from memory.
- Classify food or people by function.
- Understand approximately 2500 words.
- Understand words associated with direction (e.g., "forward"/"backward," "above"/"below," "top"/"bottom").

- Retell a story.
- Describe differences and similarities in objects.
- Use five- to six-word sentences.
- Walk down stairs, marked time, one hand held.
- Walk backward.
- Hurl a tennis ball while standing.
- Begin to comply with simple requests.
- Resist change.

With that information, the educator can better plan and design an appropriate learning environment for the whole child. An understanding of "typical" development allows the educator to better meet the needs of the child in early childhood intervention and preschool programs for children with disabilities.

Early Childhood Intervention Programs—Birth to Age 3 Years
Infants, Toddlers, Young Children, and Their Families

Federal mandates to provide educational services to infants, toddlers (IDEA, Part H), and preschoolers (IDEA, Part B) have opened a window of opportunity for adapted physical education professionals. However, the strategies for intervention with infants, toddlers, and preschoolers are significantly different from those used in traditional educational programs. The most recent legislation has emphasized the importance of the family unit in providing early services to infants and children. Steps were taken to ensure that the family takes a central role in providing for their children, particularly, those children with high probability for lagging in their developmental process.

The Families of Children with Disabilities Support Act of 1994 was reauthorized and enacted as P.L. 103-382, and included as Part I in the IDEA. This legislation provides financial assistance to states to support system changes that put an emphasis on the family unit in the provision of services. The mandates support the following initiatives:

- To develop and implement, or expand and enhance, a statewide system of family support for families of children with disabilities
- To ensure the full participation, choice, and control by families of children with disabilities
- To enhance the ability of the federal government

Text continued on p. 258.

table 10-2

Ages and Stages of Typical Child Development

Months	Typical Gross Motor Development	Typical Play Development	Typical Fine Motor/Constructive Play	Typical Cognitive Development
0-3	Optical righting (2 mo)—child uses vision to align head when body is tilted; labyrinthine righting prone (2 mo)—when body is tilted, head orients to normal position	Gets excited when a toy is presented; shakes rattle if placed in hand	Puts fist in mouth; brings hands to chest and plays with hands and fingers; refines movements that satisfy needs (e.g., thumb sucking)	Follows object with eyes; continues actions to produce interesting reactions (e.g., kicks, coos, babbles)
3-6	Labyrinthine righting supine (6 mo)—when body is tilted, head orients to normal position; body righting (6 mo)—when body is tilted, body orients to normal position	Smiles, laughs in response to parent's speech, smile, or touch; enjoys simple songs, tickling, vocal games	Early grasping patterns emerge; plays with hands and feet; rubs, strikes, and shakes things to make noise; reaching patterns develop; uses both hands together; reaches and grasps objects	Uncovers partially hidden object; imitates simple familiar actions
6-12	Supine and prone equilibrium reactions (6 mo); hands and knees equilibrium reactions (8 mo); sitting equilibrium reaction (10-12 mo); cruises holding onto furniture	Likes to bang things together; begins to imitate social games; prefers play with a parent to play with a toy; bites/chews toys; explores environment with adult help	Imitates simple actions (e.g., clapping, lying down; thumb begins to help with grasp; loves to shake and bang toys; begins to move intentionally; real pincer emerges at 12 months; begins to release objects)	Uncovers hidden object; imitates somewhat different actions; puts familiar actions together in new combinations; moves to get toy
12-18	Standing equilibrium (15 mo); walks up stairs, marking time; stands alone; walks alone with wide base of support; starts and stops walking; pushes a playground ball back and forth with a partner; makes a whole-body response to music; pulls or pushes a toy while walking	Enjoys piling objects and knocking them down; engages in solitary play; swings on a swing; plays alone contentedly if near an adult; likes action toys but plays with a variety of toys; uses realistic toys on self (e.g., pretends to brush hair with brush)	Stacks hand-sized blocks; combines objects; puts on/takes off pan and jar lids; takes objects out of a container; begins to scribble; holds crayon in hand with thumb up	Modifies familiar actions to solve new problems; imitates completely new actions; activates toy after adult demonstration

Typical Social-Emotional Development	Typical Development of Receptive Language	Typical Development of Expressive Language	Typical Development of Self-Help
Begins to find ways to calm and soothe self (e.g., sucking); draws attention to self when distressed; learns adults will answer (if, indeed, an adult answers); likes face-to-face contact; responds to voices	Notices faces of others; coos in response to pleasant voice; may stop crying when someone enters room	Cries and makes vowellike sounds; uses "different" kinds of cries; makes pleasure sounds	Depends on parent for everything
Cries differently in response to adults; shows excitement when adult approaches to lift, feed, or play; regards adult momentarily in response to speech or movement; smiles when parent smiles; laughs and giggles; smiles at mirror image	Turns eyes and head toward sound; responds to sound of own name	Varies tone to express feelings; new sounds emerge; stops making sounds when adult talks; begins vocal play; squeals; babbles; coos; "talks" to toy or pet	Depends on parent for everything
Asserts self; demonstrates curiosity; infant tests relationship with caregiver; exhibits anxiousness over separation; shows awareness of difference between parent and "stranger"; gives hugs and kisses; likes to play simple adult-child games; exhibits sensitivity to other children (e.g., cries if another child cries); demonstrates emotions—joy, fear, anger	Shows interest in sounds of objects; understands and recognizes own name; understands "no" and "stop"; imitates simple sounds; gives objects on request	Makes same sounds over and over; uses gestures; imitates adults' sounds; enjoys simple games such as "peek-a-boo"; appears to sing along with familiar music; asks for toys/food by pointing and making sounds; says "da-da" and "ma-ma"	Pulls off own socks; feeds self finger foods; holds bottle independently to drink
Demonstrates initiative; imitates; "me do it" attitude; explores (if feels safe); exploration inhibited if child feels insecure; begins to comply with simple requests; resists change; demonstrates affection with parent; follows simple one-step directions; initiates interactions with other children	Recognizes names of people and some objects; points to some objects; responds to a simple command; points to 1-3 body parts when asked; acknowledges others' speech by eye contact, speech, or repetition of word said	Jabbers; understands simple turn-taking rules in simple play; tries to communicate with "real words"; uses 1-3 spoken words; calls at least 1 person by name	Spoon-feeds and drinks from cup with many spills; sits on toilet supervised for 1 minute

Continued.

table 10-2

Ages and Stages of Typical Child Development—cont'd

Months	Typical Gross Motor Development	Typical Play Development	Typical Fine Motor/Constructive Play	Typical Cognitive Development
18-24	Walks down stairs, marked time, 1 hand held; walks backward; hurls a tennis ball while standing	Engages in parallel play; likes play that mimics parent's behavior; adds sounds to action (e.g., talks to a teddy bear); play themes reflect very familiar things (e.g., sleeping, eating); engages in play beyond self (e.g., child holds doll and rocks it)	Builds tower of 4 blocks; turns a key or crank to make a toy work; fits simple shapes into form boards; pours/dumps objects out of a container; scribbles vigorously; begins to place scribbles in specific place on paper	Points to pictures of animals or objects; chooses pictures to look at; points to mouth, eyes, nose; looks for familiar person who has left room; uses stick to get out-of-reach toy
24-30	Runs; jumps over a small object; stands on tiptoes momentarily	Likes rough and tumble play; pretends with similar objects (e.g., a stick becomes a sword); uses a doll to act out a scene; imitates adult activity in play (e.g., pretends to cook or iron)	Stacks 5-6 objects by size; nests cups by size; puts together simple puzzles; dresses/undresses dolls; strings objects; turns doorknob; scribbles begin to take on forms and become shapes; imitates circular, vertical, and horizontal strokes; rolls, pounds, and squeezes clay	Points to and names pictures; likes "read-to-me" books; loves stories that include him or her; points to arms, legs, hands, fingers; matches primary colors
30-36	Walks to and kicks a stationary playground ball; climbs on/off child-sized play equipment	Shares toys with encouragement; plays with other children for up to 30 minutes; pretend play reflects child's experience; pretends with dissimilar objects (e.g., a block becomes a car)	Draws a face; makes pancakes with clay; moves fingers independently; snips on line using scissors	Understands "front"/"back" and "in"/"out"; matches objects that have the same function (e.g., comb, brush)
36-48	Stands on 1 foot for 5 seconds; walks up stairs, alternating feet; runs contralaterally; hops on "best" foot 3 times; catches a bounced playground ball; throws a ball homolaterally; does a simple forward roll	Plays with an imaginary friend; prefers playing with other children to playing alone; pretends without any prop (e.g., pretends to comb hair with nothing in the hand); pretends after seeing, but not experiencing, an event; assumes "roles" in play and engages others in theme; acts out simple stories	Builds 3-D enclosures (e.g., zoos); makes specific marks (e.g., circles, crosses); draws a simple face; drawings represent child's perceptions (adult should not try to name/label); makes balls and snakes out of clay; cuts circles with scissors	Fills in words and phrases in favorite books when an adult reads; corrects adult if adult makes an error in reading (or tries to skip part of the story); points to thumbs, knees, chin; matches brown, black, gray, white; names red and blue when pointed to; matches simple shapes; understands "over"/"under"; classifies animals, toys, and modes of transportation

Typical Social-Emotional Development	Typical Development of Receptive Language	Typical Development of Expressive Language	Typical Development of Self-Help
Expresses emotions by acting them out; likes cuddling; follows simple rules most of the time; begins to balance dependence and independence; "no" becomes a favorite word; remains unable to share	Recognizes common objects and pictures; follows many simple directions; responds to "yes" or "no" questions related to needs/wants; listens as pictures are named; points to 5 body parts when asked; understands approximately 300 words	Uses simple 2-word phrases (e.g., "Bye-bye, Daddy" or "Cookie, more"); uses simple words to request toys, reject foods, or answer simple questions; "favorite word" may be "no"; names familiar objects; has an expressive vocabulary of at least 25 words; refers to self by name	Chews food; begins using fork
Separates easily from mother in familiar situations; exhibits shyness with strangers; tantrums when frustrated; imitates others' actions; may be bossy and possessive; identifies self with children of same age and sex	Understands simple questions; understands pronouns ("I," "me," "mine"); follows a related 2-part direction; answers "what" questions; understands approximately 500 words	Begins to put together 3- and 4-word phrases; says first and last name; uses "I" and "me"; asks simple questions; uses "my" and "me" to indicate possession	Uses spoon, spills little; takes off coat; puts on coat with help; washes and dries hands with help; gets drink from fountain; helps when being dressed; tells adult regarding need to use toilet in time to get to toilet
Comforts others; relates best to one familiar adult at a time; begins to play with others with adult supervision; is conscious of and curious about sex differences	Listens to simple stories; follows a 2-part direction; responds to simple "yes" or "no" questions related to visual information; points to pictures of common objects by use (e.g., "Show me what you eat with"); understands approximately 900 words	Begins to tell stories; plays with words/sounds; has 300-word vocabulary; asks "why" and "where" questions; adds "ing" to words	Stabs food with fork and brings to mouth; puts on socks and shirt
Begins to say "please" and "thank you"; shows affection for younger siblings; enjoys accomplishments and seeks affirmation; begins to form friendships	Answers "who," "why," and "where" questions; responds to 2 unrelated commands; understands approximately 1500 words	Begins to use tenses, helping verbs; uses simple adjectives—"big," "little"; uses language imaginatively when playing; uses 3-4 word sentence; repeats simple songs; asks lots of questions; uses speech to get/keep attention of others; has 900- to 1000-word vocabulary; repeats simple rhymes	Eats independently, with little help; brushes hair; spreads with knife; buttons/unbuttons large buttons; washes hands independently; uses tissue, with verbal reminder; uses toilet independently, with assistance to clean and dress self; puts on/takes off shoes and socks (Velcro closures); hangs up coat (child-sized cubbies)

Continued.

table 10-2				

Ages and Stages of Typical Child Development—cont'd

Months	Typical Gross Motor Development	Typical Play Development	Typical Fine Motor/Constructive Play	Typical Cognitive Development
48-60	Walks down stairs, alternating feet; walks to an even beat in music; jumps forward 10 times consecutively; hops on nonpreferred foot; catches using hands only; gallops with one foot leading; slides in one direction; throws contralaterally; swings on a swing and self-propels	Plays a table game with supervision; acts out more complex stories; creates stories that reflect that which child has not experienced; plays cooperatively with 2 or 3 children for 15 minutes	Prints first name; repeats patterns in structure (e.g., 3 red blocks, 3 blue, 3 red); draws self with primary and secondary parts; creases paper with fingers; begins to distribute shapes/objects evenly on paper; begins to draw bodies with faces; completes 8-piece puzzle; threads small beads on string	Follows along in a book being read; tries to read book from memory; names green, yellow, orange, purple; names circle and square when pointed to; understands "forward"/"backward," "above"/"below"; classifies food/people
60-72	Gallops with either foot leading; may skip; bounces and catches tennis ball	Plays several table games; engages in complex sociodramatic play	Combines drawings of things he knows (e.g., people, houses, trees); draws pictures that tell stories; folds paper diagonally and creases it; colors within the lines; pastes and glues appropriately	Retells story from a picture book; reads some words by sight; names triangle, diamond, rectangle when pointed to; understands "right"/"left"; classifies fruits and vegetables; matches letters

to identify those programs that help or hinder family support in families of children with disabilities
▪ To provide technical assistance and information, and evaluate programs

The shift toward embracing the family in the early intervention process represents an entire philosophical and pedagogical shift from past practices. The growing societal awareness of the importance of early intervention for positively impacting the quality of children's lives and the current national emphasis on parental involvement in programs for at-risk children have the potential for dramatically modifying educational experiences of all children.

Central to early childhood intervention is a respect for the family unit—in whatever form that takes. The child must be seen as part of that dynamic unit with the parent (or parent substitute) as the infant's primary and most significant teacher. Dawkins et al[8] acknowledged that there has been a wonderful transformation in the provision of services to infants, toddlers, and young children:

> The "family-centered approach" has become the foundation of early intervention. Families are seen as having enormous strengths and making the critical difference that enables a child to reach his or her potential. In the family-centered approach, families are allowed to choose their role at each stage and professionals are there not to direct, but to support the family and provide services.

To consider movement/play intervention with an infant or young child, it is vital that the movement/play specialist be sensitive to the unique needs of the child within the family unit and to the needs of the parent(s) in response to the child. The interactions of the child and parent may be seriously compromised if the infant has a disability or if the parent is ill prepared for the role.

Stern has described a representational model that helps explain the complexities of the infant-parent interaction.[9] It is vital that the educator who hopes to inter-

Typical Social-Emotional Development	Typical Development of Receptive Language	Typical Development of Expressive Language	Typical Development of Self-Help
Begins to describe feelings about self; acknowledges needs of others and may offer assistance; starts to initiate sharing; tends to exaggerate; shows good imagination	Understands approximately 2500 words; knows words associated with direction (e.g., "above," "bottom")	Uses adjectives; uses past tense; can retell a story; defines simple words; can describe differences in objects; can describe similarities in objects; uses 5-6 word sentence	Cuts easy food with knife; does laces; buttons smaller buttons; uses toilet independently; uses zipper
Asks for help from adults; cares for younger children; waits for turn for adult attention; has "best friend"; seeks autonomy	Participates in conversation without dominating it; understands words related to time and sequence; understands approximately 10,000 words; understands opposites	Participates in give-take conversation; uses words related to sequence; uses "tomorrow" and "yesterday"	Dresses self completely; makes simple sandwiches; brushes teeth alone; likes to make simple purchases; can assist in setting table, making beds; complete independence in bathing

vene successfully understand the nature of the interaction. This is particularly important when planning intervention with a family unit unlike that of the movement/play specialist. Every attempt must be made to see every parent as an individual of value—as one who wants the best for the child (Figure 10-1).

The interaction between the infant and the parent is complex because the actions of the infant and the parent may represent hopes, fears, and dreams that the parent finds difficult, if not impossible, to articulate and may be a result of learned behavior. Subsequently, the infant's and parent's actions may be grounded in representations that are often difficult to understand. The relationship between the infant and parent, and their unique representations are considered here.

The initial actions of the infant are reflex behaviors (rooting, for example) and responses to basic physiological needs (crying when hungry, for example). Subsequent actions are a result, at least in part, of the primary caregiver's responses to the initial actions. The infant's life is driven by the need to create a "global pattern perception" in which there is constancy and a predictable routine. Indeed, if the parent is able to make a natural response to the baby's natural needs, the baby will have a regular, schedule-based and predictable routine, which, as with older children, is the critical basis for the infant's development.

Stern described the "motherhood constellation,"[9] a complex of hopes, fears, dreams, and needs that have an impact on the mother and the way the mother acts and reacts to her child:

- *Survival and growth:* The mother believes her primary responsibility is to keep the baby alive and growing. The mother's major fear is that something may happen to the baby. This shared, common instinct is one of the reasons why members of this society react so violently to mothers who abandon their infants in trash bins or kill their children.

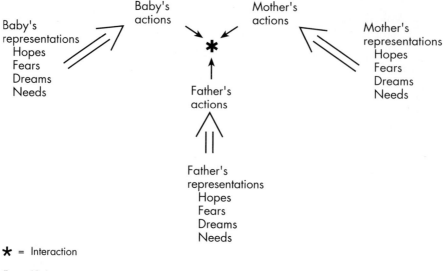

★ = Interaction

figure 10-1
Stern's model for infant-parent interaction analysis before caregiving.

- *Fear re competence:* The mother fears that she will be unable to fill her role as a mother, that she lacks the basic skills required for meeting the needs of the infant. Unfortunately, all too often this fear is well grounded. We are aware of one child who was born naturally, full term, and healthy. The very young mother took the child home but did not understand she needed to feed her child, who was hospitalized with severe malnutrition and dehydration 4 days after being released into the mother's care. The child now has profound mental retardation and severe quadriplegic spastic cerebral palsy as a result of the profound deprivation. And, as one would expect, the mother is guilt ridden.

- *Primary relatedness:* The mother fears she will be unable to love the baby or that the baby will be unable to love her. The mother knows that society expects that the infant and mother will have a natural bond and that the mother will be the primary and most important person in the infant's life. The significant bond between the infant and the mother is relatively set by 12 to 18 months. These bonds tend to take one of three forms: (1) secure attachment pattern; (2) insecure attachment pattern; or (3) disorganized attachment pattern. Insecure and/or dis-

organized attachment patterns are typical in very young mothers and in mothers who are abusing drugs. Insecure and/or disorganized attachment patterns are also typical in the mothers of children with infantile autism or those born addicted to drugs. The infant may be unable to make the responses expected by the mother. Thus begins a vicious cycle in which the infant-mother connection evolves into one that is confusing and frightening for both.

- *Validation as caregiver:* The mother, particularly if the child is her first, is in desperate need of validation. That is, the mother needs to have other women perceive her to be a good mother. The new mother is, in particular, in need of validation from her own mother. If her relationship with her own mother has been secure, she is more likely to be able to form a secure attachment with her new baby. If her relationship with her own mother has been insecure or disorganized, she is more likely to form an insecure or disorganized attachment pattern with her new baby.[9]

- *Identity reorganization:* The process of becoming a mother causes a vast reorganization of a woman's identity. The woman goes from being her mother's daughter to being her child's mother and, usually at the same time, moves from being a wife to being a parent. This causes significant adjustments in her perception of self. The same type of identity reorganization occurs in professional women who have a first child; the woman may have been validated as a professional in the workplace and now seeks validation in the role of parent. This process may be complicated by the fact that job requirements are often relatively basic—do this, and you will be perceived to be a good employee. Being a parent is simply not that easily defined, and this may result in confusion.

The mother's perception of the baby is complex and is formed, at least in part, by seeing the baby in diverse roles: (1) baby as individual being; (2) baby as my son/daughter; (3) baby as my husband's son/daughter; (4) baby as a grandchild; (5) baby as a sibling; and/or (6) baby as a niece/nephew. The mother's perception of the baby begins while the fetus is still in utero, and these perceptions are heightened by seeing a sonogram and/or feeling the baby move and kick.

The mother's expectations of the infant are heightened, as well, when the infant achieves basic milestones related to growth and development. For example, when the child first sits up independently and manipulates an object (at approximately 7 to 8 months), the mother's expectations may change and the child may be envisioned as a pianist or author. When the child first walks independently (at 11 to 13 months), the mother's expectations may change and the child may be envisioned as an architect or firefighter.

Not as much research has been done on the role of the father in this process. But the father, if involved, shares many of the same questions and fears regarding validation as a parent and, most certainly, shares expectations regarding the child and the child's future. And there is a great deal of evidence that the father suffers from a significant period of confusion when the infant replaces the father as the predominant interest in the wife's existence. The father may experience the following:

- Concern regarding ability to care for and support the infant and mother—financial and emotional concerns
- Fear regarding ability to assume the role of father
- Concern with loss of primary importance in his wife's (girlfriend's) life
- Expectations regarding his child's future

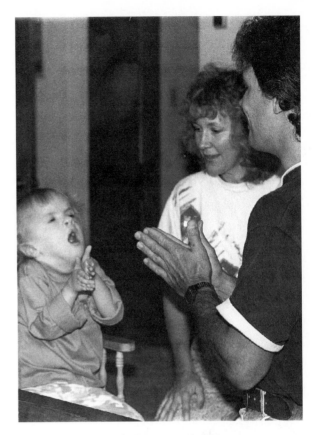

Parents stimulate learning in a home-based program.

Infant-Parent Relationships in Infants with Disabilities

The myriad of actions and representations of the infant, mother, and father, especially when complicated by actions and representations of members of the extended family, is difficult enough in the growth and development of an infant/child who develops typically. The process is much more complex when the infant/child has a developmental delay or disability.

There are early indicators that an infant may be at risk for delay and/or disability. Typically, these infants present one of two profiles: the "model" baby or the "irritable" baby. The "model" baby is lethargic, prefers to be left alone, and places few demands on parents. These behaviors, which cause these babies to be perceived to be "good" babies, may be due to neurological or neuromuscular pathology. A typically developing infant seeks contact with the parents, particularly the mother, engages in social interaction (at 7 weeks the infant seeks to make eye contact), and makes his or her needs known.

The "irritable" baby cries excessively, sleeps fitfully, is difficult to console (does not respond to rocking, caress), and has difficulty nursing/eating. Mothers of infants later diagnosed as having attention deficit disorder or attention deficit–hyperactivity disorder have suggested that the fetus is "irritable" within the uterus and that the kicking and other movements of the fetus are not like those of other children. Again, these behaviors may have a neurological or neuromuscular basis.

Other behaviors associated with atypical infant development (potential indicators of developmental delay or disability) include the following:

- Lack of response to sound (parent's cooing or singing)
- Lack of response to smile
- Limited imitation of parent expressions, gesture, or vocalizations
- Difficulty with gaze behavior (avoiding eye contact or staring)
- Limited response to parent play attempts
- Unnatural attachment to objects

Comprehensive and early medical evaluation of infants makes it possible for a child with a potential for developmental delay or disability to be identified early in many cases. In fact, many potential delays or disabilities may be identified when the fetus is in utero.

Early identification of an at-risk fetus or infant provides the parents with early warning and may give them the opportunity to begin the grief process. However, this grief process is as complex and multidimensional as the actions and representations of the infant, parents, and members of the extended family. Typically, the grief process is similar to that described by Kubler-Ross in her classic works regarding death and dying. The grief of parents and others when confronting the delay or disability of an infant is often much more profound than that of an individual dealing with the death of an individual who has lived a long and purposeful life.

The contrast between the expectations and dreams for the infant and the reality is often vast. The parent who dreams of his or her child being the first woman president of the United States grieves unbelievably when the parent learns that that is most probably not an option for the daughter with Down syndrome.

The stages of grief that a parent may experience in response to an infant with a delay or disability are detailed in Table 10-3. Also presented is a range of appropriate responses from the professional educator.

The parent moves through these phases of grief in a fluctuating way—simple events may cause the parent to experience all these feelings all over again. For example, if the infant is still unable to walk at age 3 years, the parent may begin the grieving process all over again. If the child requires placement in a preschool program for children with disabilities at age 3, the parent may need to envision the dream all over again. The professional working with the parent must consistently focus on honest, open communication and redirect the parent to focus on the child's abilities rather than disabilities.

Early Childhood Intervention in Natural Settings

Best practices in **early childhood intervention (ECI)** acknowledge that infants and toddlers between birth and 3 years of age must be educated in their most natural environments. In fact, an amazing number of infants and toddlers spend time outside the home in regulated and unregulated child care centers.[26] This is directly related to drastic changes in society and its demands on parents (see Chapter 9). Specifically, increasing numbers of children receive care outside the home because of the following:

- Increased numbers of parents/families unable to provide care within the home
- Increased numbers of parents/families unwilling to provide care within the home
- Increased numbers of parents/families living in poverty and the subsequent need for both parents (if there are two parents) to work
- Increased numbers of single parents, particularly young women, trying to support their child(ren)
- Increased numbers of children with significant developmental delays and disabilities with special needs because of improved medical technology that allows infants to survive who would have died in the natural selection process in earlier civilizations

The **ECI natural settings initiative** is in direct response to programs that in the past served typically developing infants and toddlers, and infants and toddlers

table 10-3

Stages of Parental Grief and the Role of the Educator in Response to Infants with Developmental Delays or Disabilities

Stage	Parent's Behavior	Role of the Educational Professional
Denial	The parent does not acknowledge that the infant has a delay or may have a disability. In the initial stages of grief, this is a self-protective mechanism that keeps the parent from being totally destroyed by this information.	During this time, the professional working with the parent may help in the following ways: Share information about the infant and the infant's progress; far too often, the parent is exposed only to what the infant cannot do rather than what the infant can do. Deal with the present rather than projecting the future. Express a willingness to listen. Use open-ended questions to allow the parent to discuss feelings and thoughts. Share information in writing (simple, direct writing) so the parent can review the information in private and on the parent's terms.
Negotiation	During this stage parents may try to negotiate or "make a deal" with their God or a force in the universe. The parents may promise to "do good works" in order to have their infant cured.	The professional working with the infant and the parent should continue to work with the parent as if in denial.
Guilt/grief	During this stage the parent may experience tremendous guilt and grief. This is particularly true if the cause of the delay or disability is genetic or a result of parental alcohol/other drug abuse. This is often a time in which parents may blame each other for the child's disability. This is difficult if there is no blame to be had; it is devastating if one of the parent's behavior did, indeed, have a cause-effect relationship in the disability.	The professional working with the infant and the parents should: Encourage parents to express guilt and "get it in the open" Encourage parents to examine their belief system Help parents meet other parents who have experienced the same thing—contact existing support groups or help parents make contact with parents of other infants Share realistic expectations regarding their infant's development Reinforce any parent attempt to play/interact with infant
Depression	The parent may become overwhelmed with the contrast between the expectation and the reality. Stern described a mother's reaction to having a severely disabled infant as a narcissistic wound.[9] The depression, ultimately, allows parents to abandon their dream and may help the parent move to self-acceptance.	The professional dealing with the parent who is depressed must do so with great care, since the parent is very fragile at this time. The professional must keep an open line of communication that is nonjudgmental and caring.
Anger	Though this may be the most difficult stage for the professional to deal with, when the parent finally gets angry, the parent is on the way to healing (a process that may take a lifetime).	During this time, the professional must: Acknowledge that anger directed toward him or her may be displaced (or the parent may simply be angry with the motor specialist) Encourage the parent to express anger Encourage the parent's effort to play with the child and help the parent develop skills to avoid directing the anger toward the child

with developmental delays or disabilities, in training/ school centers or provided programs in hospital-based or university-based clinical settings. Advocacy groups such as Advocacy Incorporated and the Association for Retarded Citizens have lobbied actively for service provision in the most inclusive and natural setting. According to Crais[6]:

> The suggested changes involve moving from client-centered to family-centered services, from professionally-driven to family-driven decision making, and from focusing on problems to identifying and developing family and child strengths.

Specifically, the focus is on a family-centered approach, in which the family and its culture are honored. Winston[47] and Crais[6] have suggested that the following underlying principles must be the crux of the family-centered, natural setting initiative:

1. Families are the constants in their children's lives, whereas service systems and professionals may only be sporadic.
2. Services should be ecologically based and therefore focus on the mutual influence of the contexts surrounding the child and family.
3. Families should be equal partners in the assessment and intervention process.
4. Services should foster families' decision-making skills and their existing and developing skills while protecting their rights and wishes.
5. Professionals need to recognize the individuality of children and their families and to modify their own services to meet those needs.
6. Services must be delivered using a coordinated, "normalized" approach.

This has resulted in ECI mandates, at the federal and state level (most states), that expect the family-centered **individual family service plan** (IFSP) process, including assessment, IFSP development, and service delivery (see Chapter 3), to relate to the family's ability to choose services that reflect and support the child in the family's natural settings. Basic to this process is the fact that a natural environment is a setting that is natural or "normal" for the child's age peer who has no disabilities and includes home and community settings in which children without disabilities participate. These natural settings include:

▪ Home

▪ Family and for-profit/not-for-profit agency child care settings
▪ Church and synagogue programs and activities
▪ Community playground
▪ Park and recreation department programs and activities
▪ Library "reading times"
▪ Restaurants
▪ Grocery stores

The assessment and the IFSP must provide information regarding the infant or child's eligibility and the level of functioning in the areas of (1) cognitive development; (2) physical development, including vision and hearing, gross and fine motor skills, and nutrition status; (3) communication development; (4) social-emotional development; and (5) adaptive development or self-help skills.[35] In addition, the assessment must include the child's unique strengths and needs "in relation to the child's ability to function in settings that are natural or normal for the child's peers who do not have disabilities, including home and community settings in which children without disabilities participate."[35]

Recent mandates also require parent input regarding their child's functional abilities and the extent of their participation in settings that are natural or normal for their child's age peers without disabilities. The focus is on the family's perception of their needs if they are to provide quality parenting in natural environments.

Mandates exist that ensure that each child and family has a plan of services that meets the unique needs of the child and family and reflects and supports the collaborative partnership between parents and professionals. The program must provide service coordination and an IFSP for all eligible children (Table 10-4).

The IFSP must[35]:

▪ Be written within 45 days of referral.
▪ Be jointly developed through a face-to-face meeting of a team of professionals that includes the parents.
▪ Be based on information from a comprehensive evaluation and assessment performed by an interdisciplinary team.
▪ Be developed to include the services to be provided, the child's ability to function in natural environments, and the family's ability to meet the child's needs.

table 10-4

Comparison of the Individual Education Plan and the Individual Family Service Plan

	Individual Family Service Plan	Individual Education Plan
Focus	Family centered and needs based	Child centered
Children served	Children from birth to age 3 years with developmental delays	Children from age 3-22 years with disabilities
Emphasis	Education in natural environment	Education in least restrictive environment
Eligibility	Based on developmental delay, atypical development, or medical diagnosis	Based on educational need
Response to referral	Requires development of an IFSP with 45 days of referral	Requires development of an IEP within 90 days of referral
Provision of services	Services continually provided 12 months of year	Services provided during 9-month school year, unless identified concern re regression necessitates extended year services
Progress review	6-month and annual reviews (arranged by ECI service coordinator)	Annual reviews and 3-year comprehensive evaluations
Team participants	Parent(s) of child	Parent(s) of child
	Other family members or child care persons, as requested by parent	Other family members, as requested by parent
	Advocate(s) or person(s) outside family, as requested by parent	Advocate(s) or person(s) outside family, as requested by parent
	A minimum of 2 professionals from different disciplines	Child's special educator
		Representative from regular education
		Related service personnel
		Building principal (or representative)
	Service coordinator	Case manager
	Person directly involved in evaluation/assessment	Professional able to interpret assessment data
Contents	Summary of child's health/medical history	Statement of present level of educational performance
	Statement describing present level of:	
	Cognitive development	
	Physical development, including vision and hearing, gross/fine motor skills, and nutrition skills	
	Communication development	
	Social-emotional development	
	Adaptive development or self-help skills	
	Description of child's unique strengths and needs in relation to ability to function in natural settings: home, child care, neighborhood, community playground, church, restaurants, grocery stores, etc.	
	Review of need for assistive technology: assessment, services, and devices	
	Statement of major outcomes and strategies for achieving outcomes	Annual goals and short-term objectives
	FILM (frequency, intensity, location, and method of delivering services)	Statement of specific educational services to be provided
	Summary of opportunities for inclusion in family and community life, and with peers	Statement re extent to which student will participate in regular education program
	Starting dates and expected length of services	Projected dates for initiation/duration of services

Continued.

table 10-4

Comparison of the Individual Education Plan and the Individual Family Service Plan—cont'd

	Individual Family Service Plan	Individual Education Plan
	Transition plan for child leaving program (beginning at 2 years)	Transition plan for student leaving program (beginning at 14 years)
	Medical and other services required and method of payment	Appropriate objective criteria and evaluation procedures
Procedural safeguards	Families are protected by procedural safeguards outlined in Part H of IDEA	Families are protected by procedural safeguards outlined in Part B of IDEA
Additional features	With agreement of family, the IFSP may include: Integrated summary of procedures for identifying family's concerns, priorities, and resources Statement regarding family's ability to enhance their child's development, as identified by family Description of intervention required to meet needs of family and payment plans	

- Coordinate services with all other providers, including child care providers.
- Address the need for assistive technology assessment, services, and devices.
- Include a statement that describes the child's health and medical history.
- Include a statement that describes the present level of development.
- Contain major outcomes and strategies for achieving outcomes.
- Include FILM (frequency, intensity, location, and method of delivering services).
- Contain a summary of opportunities for inclusion in family and community life, and with peers.
- Address starting dates and expected length of services.
- Include medical and other services required and the method of payment.
- Include a transition plan, beginning at 2 years, into preschool programs.

With the permission of the family, the IFSP may also include a summary of procedures for identifying the family's concerns, priorities, and resources. In addition, it will include information regarding the family's ability to enhance their child's development. If required, it may stipulate plans for intervention required to meet the needs of the family.

The Movement Program and the ECI Natural Settings Initiative

The ECI natural settings initiative has a broad and comprehensive impact on the preschool adapted physical education specialist and movement/play specialist. It is no longer appropriate for the movement/play specialist to pull children out of their natural settings to provide intervention, including intervention with parents, in a clinic based in a service agency, on a public school campus, or on a university campus. Far too often in the past, an infant or toddler was removed from the familiar home and neighborhood environment and brought into an enhanced learning environment (i.e., a clinical setting with all the materials and equipment [toys, for example] necessary). While the opportunity for learning and development was great during the time the child was receiving services within the clinic, there was little or no opportunity for transfer of the learning experience into the home or neighborhood. Also, parents were often overwhelmed by the clinical setting and became observers rather than active participants in the learning process.

The preschool movement specialist must be prepared to provide services in settings described as "natural" for children from birth to age 3 years. Settings in which it is appropriate for the preschool movement/play specialist to provide services include:

- Home
- Child care
- Neighborhood
- Community playground

Intervention within a child's natural setting provides many advantages for the preschool movement/play specialist. The first, and most important, is that an infant or toddler will be most at ease in the familiar environment. The specialist will have the opportunity to see the child moving in his or her most natural play environment and will be able to develop a movement/play program designed to work within that context.

The second advantage is that the specialist will have an opportunity, in the home, child care setting, or neighborhood, and on the community playground to provide meaningful intervention with the parent in a context familiar to the parent or other caregiver. Strategies can be developed to help the parent develop skills for facilitating the child's development in the environment most familiar to both the parent and the child. The likelihood that the parent will become an active participant in the child's learning is enhanced.

There are, however, some disadvantages and problems associated with provision of services in the natural setting. These disadvantages and problems, which are increased in inner-city and other poverty-stricken areas, including Native American reservations and camps for transient migrant workers, include:

- The very safety of the professional may be compromised within a given community, particularly in the late afternoon and evenings. Unfortunately, there are simply some homes and some neighborhoods in which the lives of professionals (even when traveling in pairs) are in jeopardy.
- The health of the professional may be compromised in homes in which basic health care standards are not met (cleanliness, lack of appropriate immunizations).
- The provision of services in a clinical setting provided professionals the opportunity, if only for a brief time, to meet an infant/toddler's basic health and safety needs. For example, infants and toddlers were often bathed and fed nutritious meals while attending the clinic. That type of opportunity is not readily available in some homes and neighborhoods.
- The professional feels as if he or she has no base—and limited connection with other preschool professionals.

Movement and Play in The Individual Family Service Plan

The trend toward intervention within the natural context can be effective only if the goals and objectives (and the specific strategy for accomplishing these objectives) are functional, can be generalized, can be integrated within the natural setting, are measurable, and reflect a hierarchical relationship between long-range goals and short-term objectives. Notari-Syverson and Shuster[36] believe it is necessary to put real-life skills into the IFSP. This is true of movement and play, as well. Examples of goals and objectives are considered here:

- *Functionality:* Will the movement or play skill increase the child's ability to interact with people and objects in the environment? For example, facilitating the development of sitting equilibrium increases the likelihood that a child will be able to sit and play with a toy. An appropriate annual goal may be: "The child is able to retain sitting equilibrium while being bounced on a mattress with hands held."
- *Generality:* Can the movement or play skill be used in several different settings? For example, if a child is able to grasp and release small objects, the child can:

  At home—help pick up toys and put them in a bucket.

  At child care—build with large Duplo blocks.

  On the playground—collect and stack twigs.

  An appropriate annual goal may be: "The child is able to grasp and release a variety of small objects."
- *Integrated in natural setting:* Can the movement or play skill be used within the child's daily environment? For example, if a child is able to participate in parallel play, he or she can:

  At home—sit and look at a book while the parent looks at a newspaper.

At child care—share a water table with another child.

On the playground—share a sandbox and engage in filling and pouring like another child.

An appropriate annual goal may be: "The child is able to engage in parallel play with adults and peers."

- *Measurable:* Can the movement or play skill be measured? A goal or objective is of absolutely no use if the educator or parent cannot determine if the objective has been met. For example, "The child will be able to run better" is not an appropriate goal or objective. An appropriate annual goal may be: "The child will be able to run, using arms in opposition to the legs."

- *Annual goals and objectives:* Can the movement/ play goals and objectives be expressed in hierarchical fashion? The only appropriate annual goals and objectives are those in which the objectives can build on one another, leading to an annual goal.

Role of the Preschool Movement/Play Specialist with Infants and Toddlers in Natural Settings

The role of the preschool movement/play specialist is the same in each of the natural settings—home, child care setting, neighborhood, and community playground. The first responsibility is the completion of a comprehensive, developmentally appropriate, ecological assessment and the initiation of the portfolio assessment process.

After the completion of the initial assessment and the initiation of the ongoing portfolio assessment process, the preschool movement specialist working with infants and toddlers is responsible for working closely with the parents or caregivers to help them understand the importance of play to the infant and toddler and to help them acquire the skills necessary to facilitate play. It is clear that infants and toddlers are more responsive to parents who are playful than to those that are not and that infants and toddlers develop stronger bonds with parents who play with them.[25]

There are several techniques for introducing parents to the play process. These include[25]:

1. Informal discussions regarding developmental milestones in typically and atypically developing children

2. Films and videotapes that illustrate child development

3. Films and videotapes that demonstrate parent-child interaction

The most effective strategies, however, are those in which the preschool movement/play specialist actually demonstrates the techniques for the parent with the infant or toddler and then allows the parent to practice under a watchful eye. These strategies and techniques are described in the following sections.

Modeling strategies and techniques for enhancing sensory stimulation
VESTIBULAR STIMULATION

1. Hold and rock the infant or toddler in your arms or rock in a rocking chair.
2. Bounce the infant or toddler on your lap with the child lying on his or her stomach, sitting, and standing.
3. Gently pat the bed or couch cushion next to the infant or toddler while the child lies prone.
4. Dance, holding the infant or toddler in your arms.
5. Carry the child in a baby backpack.

TACTILE/PROPRIOCEPTIVE STIMULATION

1. Do infant massage. Hold (or lie down next to) the infant or toddler and gently stroke the child with the fingertips and fingers. Apply slightly more pressure as the massaging hand moves down the long bones in the arms and legs, and down the spine.
2. Play with the child's fingers and toes.
3. Introduce Koosh balls and squishy animals for the child to hold and feel.
4. Grasp the child's feet and gently pump up and down while chanting or singing a simple song: "Molly is kicking, kicking, kicking, Molly is kicking all day long." (sung to "London Bridge")
5. Lift and move the child's arms and legs, stretch and bend.
6. Use different types of materials to gently rub on the child's body—flannel, silk, cotton, fake fur, terry cloth, feathers, sponge, etc.
7. Wiggle the child's fingers and toes in water, sand, cereal, whipped cream, etc.
8. Help the child do finger play in a scoop of pudding on the child's high chair tray.
9. Plan simple games such as "This Little Piggy" while touching and pulling gently on the baby's toes and fingers.
10. Let the child pound on chunks of refrigerated cookie dough.
11. Put pillows on the floor for the child to crawl and creep on or over.
12. Let the toddler push and pull objects such as laundry baskets.

AUDITORY STIMULATION

1. Talk, coo, and sing to the baby.
2. Read, read, read. (If the parent cannot read, help the parent select auditory tapes of simple books or, better still, urge the parent to participate in a parent/child literacy program.)
3. Tell the child simple stories that include the child. Use the child's name often in the story.
4. Expose the infant or toddler to different types of music—classical, jazz, rock, and country-western.
5. Allow the infant or toddler to stimulate his or her own auditory system using rattles.
6. Attach a large jingle bell to the child's arm or foot using a ponytail holder; help the child kick the foot.

VISUAL STIMULATION

1. Expose the newborn to black/white contrasts.
2. As the infant matures, expose the baby to vibrant, primary colors.
3. Imitate the baby's gestures and expressions.
4. Encourage the child to look at self in a mirror.
5. Jiggle a brightly colored toy or noisemaker in front of the child's face. When the child's eyes locate the object, jiggle it again.

OLFACTORY STIMULATION

1. Hold the child very close to the body, allowing the child to pick up the body's unique odor.
2. Expose the child to the varying odors of perfumes and spices.

Modeling strategies and techniques for enhancing the development of equilibrium behaviors

SUPINE EQUILIBRIUM

1. With the infant or toddler supine, jiggle a bright toy or noisemaker above the child's face (no closer than 12 inches).
2. With the child supine on your lap, with the head supported by a hand under the head, gently bounce the infant or toddler on your lap.
3. Put a brightly decorated sock on the baby's foot to encourage the child to reach for his or her toes.
4. Lie on your back with the child supine on your chest. Supporting the child's head and body, roll from side to side.

PRONE EQUILIBRIUM

1. With the infant or toddler in the prone position, place a bright toy or noisemaker in front of the child's head to encourage the child to lift the head.
2. With the infant or toddler in the prone position, walk your fingertips up the child's back, with fingers on either side of the spine.
3. Use textures to stimulate the muscles in the baby's back and neck, including a paintbrush, washcloth, and sponge.

4. Lie on your back with the child prone on your chest. Supporting the child's head and body, roll from side to side.
5. Put a rolled-up towel under the child's shoulders, allowing the hands and arms to move freely in front of child. Blow bubbles for the child to track or use a music box or rhythm instrument to encourage the child to hold the prone position, bearing weight on the forearms.

SITTING EQUILIBRIUM

1. Hold the child on your lap, supporting the child's head on your chest, and gently rock from side to side.
2. Hold the child on your lap, supporting the child's head on your chest, and gently bounce the child up and down.
3. Prop the child up in a sitting position using pillows. Put toys or musical wind-ups above eye level to encourage the child to hold the head up.
4. Place the baby in a high chair, infant seat, or walker. Hold a toy in front of the child and encourage the child to reach for it.
5. Prop the baby in the corner in a sitting position with pillows for support. Encourage the child to reach for a toy and play with it while sitting.
6. When the child can sit independently, place a number of toys within the child's reach and a number just beyond easy reach so that the child has to adjust equilibrium to get the toys.
7. Play games such as "Pat-a-Cake."
8. With the child seated on a mattress or pillow, gently pull or push the child to force the child to regain equilibrium.
9. Let the older child sit on a rocking-horse, etc.
10. With the child in a sitting position, put a bucket in front of the child and objects to be placed in the bucket at the sides and near the back of the child.
11. Put a wheeled toy in front of the child and let the child roll it back and forth, causing the child to need to readjust equilibrium.

STANDING EQUILIBRIUM

1. With the child supine, put the palms of your hands against the bottom of the child's feet and push gently.
2. After child has head righting capabilities, hold the child in a standing position with the child's feet on your lap. Bounce the child and gently move the child from side to side, keeping the feet in contact with the lap.
3. Play "Soooooo Big"—lift the child above your head while keeping the child in a vertical position.
4. While supporting the child in standing position, "dance" back and forth, and forward and back, keeping the child's feet in contact with the floor.
5. Let the child stand on your shoes as you dance about the room.

Modeling strategies and techniques for developing simple locomotor competency

ROLLING

1. Gently lift the infant's right hip from the supine toward the side-lying position; alternate and lift the left hip from the supine toward the side-lying position. Let the return happen naturally.
2. If the infant is supine, place a favorite toy on either side of the child's head to encourage the child to roll the head to look for the toy.
3. Place the child on a blanket or towel on the stomach or back. Gently raise one side of the blanket to assist the child in rolling to the side. (NOTE: Do not use this activity if the infant arches his or her back during the roll.)
4. Jiggle a favorite toy or noisemaker in front of the child's eyes (never closer than 12 inches) while the child lies supine; when the child focuses on the toy, slowly move it to a position at the side of the child's head on the crib mattress.
5. Place the child on a small incline so that the child has a small hill to roll down.
6. With the child supine, gently bend one leg and bring the leg across the midline of the body. Go slowly so that the child's body follows the movement.

PULL TO SITTING

Sit with your back against a support and with your knees bent to make an incline for the child to lie on. The baby lies with the head near the knees and the hips cradled by your chest, so that the child faces you. Carefully, and with head support, round the baby's shoulders toward you and lift the baby into a sitting position. As the baby develops strength and sitting equilibrium, gradually reduce the amount of support.

CRAWLING

1. Sitting on the floor with your legs stretched out, place the child over your leg and shift the child so that the child's hands are in contact with the floor, and gently roll the child toward his or her hands so that the child gradually takes more weight on the hands.
2. Repeat the above, but this time, shift the weight so that the child gradually takes more weight on his or her knees.
3. Place the child on a carpet or mat and remove shoes and socks. Place a favorite toy in front of the child to encourage the child to move toward the toy. If needed, help the child move by placing a palm against the child's foot so that the child has something to push off from.

CREEPING

1. Place a bolster or rolled-up towel in front of the child and encourage the child to creep over it to get to a favorite toy.
2. Make a simple obstacle course with sofa cushions, pillows, rolled-up towels, and rolled-up newspapers, and encourage the child to move through the obstacle course toward a favorite toy.

PULL TO STANDING

1. Place a favorite toy on the edge of the seat of a sturdy, cushioned chair or sofa; when the child expresses interest in the toy, move it back just a little from the edge.
2. When child is in a sitting or kneeling position, periodically throughout the day grasp hands and pull gently to standing.

CRUISE

1. Put a small, child-sized chair with metal feet on a tile or wooden floor. Help the child pull to stand near the chair and "cruise," holding weight on the chair.
2. Put several well-cushioned chairs close together and increase interest in cruising by placing toys on the chair seats.

Modeling strategies and techniques for facilitating/scaffolding symbolic play behavior

1. Imitate the infant or toddler's facial expressions and gestures.
2. Demonstrate simple strategies for the child to communicate the following and model parent response[38]:
   a. Behavioral regulation
      (1) Requesting objects
      (2) Requesting actions
      (3) Protesting
   b. Social interaction
      (1) Greeting
      (2) Calling
      (3) Requesting social routine
      (4) Requesting permission
      (5) Show off
   c. Joint attention
      (1) Commenting
      (2) Requesting information
      (3) Providing information.

Strategies and techniques for scaffolding learning

The preschool movement/play specialist may help the parent develop the **scaffolding** skills necessary to gently nudge the child toward more sophisticated symbolic play as he or she moves through the sequence of development of symbolic play skills.[2,16,38,46]

PRE-PRETENSE OR ACCIDENTAL PRETENSE

The child puts a comb in his or her hair or a telephone to his or her ear. The adult can help scaffold learning by responding, "Emily, you're combing your hair," or the adult can pretend to put a telephone to his or her own ear and say, "Hello, Hannah. This is . . ."

SELF-PRETEND

The child actually pretends to do *familiar* things. The most typical are eating and sleeping. The adult can help scaffold learning by saying, "Is it good? Can I have some, too?" or the adult can cover the child and say out loud, "Ssshhhh, Molly is sleeping."

OTHER-PRETEND

The child pretends to do things that he or she has seen significant others do. For example, the child may pretend to feed a baby or drive a car. The adult can help scaffold learning by saying, "Lashundra, what a good mommy you are being, feeding your baby." Or the adult may sit down next to the child and make "vvvvvvrooooom" sounds. The adult may facilitate other-pretend play by providing appropriate "props" after a trip, for example, to the grocery store: garbage bags, boxes of food, an old wallet, for example.

IMAGINARY OBJECTS AND BEINGS

The child not only uses a variety of real or child-sized replicas of real objects in play, but also uses imaginary objects to engage in pretend behavior. For example, the child might ride an imaginary horse or pretend a block is an ice cream cone. The adult may provide support for play by joining in—riding an imaginary horse while twirling a rope or giving the child another "scoop" of ice cream. This type of play is best facilitated when the child has access to props that can be "anything"—blocks, for example.

ANIMATED PLAY

The child uses toy people and toy animals, for example, and assigns them words or actions. The toy horse may gallop across the range while "neeeeiiiiighing." The adult can facilitate play by galloping and then jumping over "fences."

SEQUENTIAL PLAY (30 MONTHS+)

The child is moving into sophisticated play scenarios, and the play represents a sequence of events. For example, the child may "go to the store, buy groceries, bring them home, and fix dinner." The adult can scaffold learning by asking simple questions about the sequence, but should not intrude on or change the child's plan.

Modeling strategies and techniques for facilitating constructive play behavior

1. Put four blocks or small animals on the floor. Pick one up and put it into a small box. Pick up a second block and put it into the box. Pick up a third block and put it into the box. Wait for the toddler to pick up the last block and put it into the box.
2. Sit near the child and stack two blocks. Stack three, etc.
3. Sit near the child and roll play dough in your hands. Offer some to the child.

Demonstrating how simple materials found in the home or other settings can be used to facilitate play and the development of gross motor and fine motor skills

1. Use mattresses as "trampolines."
2. Provide pillows as "mountains" for climbing over and rolling down.
3. Provide wooden spoons, strainers, funnels, and old pans to make music or pretend to "cook."
4. With the child lying on a quilt, pick up an edge of the quilt to help the child roll from the stomach to the back.
5. Put a favorite toy just "out of reach" of the child to encourage crawling, creeping, cruising, or walking to the toy.

Demonstrating how simple toys can be made out of inexpensive materials found in the home or easily obtained through donations

1. Attach objects securely to a dowel and tie it across the crib (large hair curlers, clean jar lids, plastic rings).
2. Put dry oatmeal, cereal, or macaroni in film canisters.
3. Make building blocks out of 2 × 4s (saw and sand the blocks).
4. Recycle empty cereal boxes as building blocks.
5. Use cardboard rolls from paper towels and toilet paper for building and rolling.
6. Make available things to crumple and crinkle—waxed paper, aluminum foil, tissue, used wrapping paper, newspaper, etc.
7. Clean a 1-liter soda bottle and fill it with water. To enhance the effect, add food coloring. Close the lid tightly and seal with duct tape. To help the child with discrimination of weight, etc., put varying amounts of water in a number of bottles.

Helping the parent select toys that facilitate communication between the parent (or other caregiver) and the child

1. Toys that draw attention to the parent's actions
   a. Push toys that make noise
   b. Musical instruments
   c. Rattles
2. Toys that draw attention to the parent's face
   a. Bubbles
   b. Balloons
   c. Pinwheels
   d. Scarves
3. Toys that facilitate reciprocal interaction
   a. Puppets
   b. Push toys (cars, trains, trucks)
   c. Balls

Helping the parent select toys that empower the child

1. Toys that allow the child to see cause and effect (I bang pan with spoon and make noise.)
2. Toys the child can push and pull
3. Toys where the child can follow the action (Ball is dropped into the top and rolls down the series of chutes.)

▪ ▪ ▪

A comprehensive, parent-focused, early childhood intervention program based in natural settings has the potential to prepare a 3-year-old child for participation in "regular day care" or for continued home/community involvement. If a child deemed at risk for developmental delays exhibits a disability at age 3 years, the child will usually make the transition into a preschool program for children with disabilities within a community agency or public school program. The role of the movement/play specialist in the 3- to 5-year-old program is discussed in the following section.

The Preschool Program for Children Ages 3 to 5 Years

A natural and logical extension of a quality early childhood intervention program is a quality preschool program for children ages 3 to 5 years to help prepare the children for school. Washington, Johnson, and Mc-Cracken[44] wrote:

When former President George Bush and the nation's governors hammered out their six most important national education goals in 1989, this goal emerged as the first—**Goal One: "By the year 2000, all children will start school ready to learn."**

Three objectives were specified to achieve Goal One:

- All children with disabilities and from less-advantaged families would have access to good quality, appropriate preschool experiences.
- Every parent would devote time every day to help their preschoolers learn, and they would have access to training and support needed to do that.
- Children would receive the nutrition and health care needed to arrive at school healthy.

The critical components necessary for children to achieve their potential are:

- Health
- Nutrition
- Family and community stability

- Cultural competence
- Self-esteem
- Quality of early learning experience

Improvements in even one component increase children's opportunities to succeed in school and life.

Given blatant poverty, the abuse and neglect of young children, homelessness, and cultural deprivation, the quality of the early learning experience becomes even more important. The importance of a quality preschool learning experience has been well documented in the research literature. The most noteworthy of the studies is the Perry Preschool Project,[4] which is a comprehensive, longitudinal study of 123 black children from families with low incomes—children who were believed to be at risk for school failure. The study examined the long-term effects of participation versus nonparticipation in a high-quality early education program.

Children ages 3 and 4 years were selected at random from a single school attendance area and were randomly assigned to an experimental group that received high-quality preschool education or to a control group that did not. Information was collected annually on these children from ages 3 to 11 years, and then at ages 14, 15, and 19. The following variables were considered: family demographics; child abilities, attitudes, and scholastic performance; involvement in delinquent and criminal behavior; use of welfare assistance; and employment.

The results were astonishing and demonstrated lasting benefits of quality preschool education. When compared with the control group, the individuals in the experimental group demonstrated the following:

- Improved cognitive performance during early childhood
- Improved scholastic performance during school years
- Decreased delinquency and crime
- Decreased use of welfare assistance
- Decreased incidence of teenage pregnancy
- Increased graduation rates
- Increased frequency of enrollment in postsecondary education and vocational training programs
- Increased employment

Not only is this evidence impressive from a human success standpoint, but it is also incredible because the return on the dollar is so significant. "Over the lifetimes of the participants, preschool is estimated to yield economic benefits with an estimated present value that is over seven times the cost of one year of the program."[4] Unfortunately, current legislative thrusts ignore the simple findings. If society spends 1 dollar to educate a 3-year-old child, it will save $7.00 later on costs associated with special education, social services, unemployment, and prisons.

Perhaps a quality preschool experience is so effective because it drastically affects the perceptions of the children, the parents, and the teachers. Expectations are high—and children rise to meet those expectations. "Preschool, then, enables children to better carry out their first scholastic tasks. This better performance is visible to everyone involved—the child, the teacher, the parents, and other children. Children realize they have this capacity for better scholastic performance and believe and act accordingly, developing a stronger commitment to schooling. Teachers recognize better scholastic performance and react to it with higher expectations and eventually with scholastic placements that reflect these higher expectations."[4]

A quality preschool learning environment is one in which expectations for children's performance are high and the learning environment encourages active exploration. A quality learning environment for 3- to 5-year-old children is play based.[29] A child's natural drive to play is encouraged, fostered, and respected. Play is a vehicle through which a child's motor, language, social-emotional, and cognitive skills are scaffolded in and through interaction with another child or a gentle, caring adult.

Play by any name—symbolic play, fantasy play, make-believe, pretend play, dramatic play, imaginative play—is the very foundation or focus of the development of cognition, social-emotional skills, and language.[2] According to Gowen[16]:

> It is during this second developmental period (preoperational) that children begin to develop their symbolic function, or representational competence. This is the function that allows children to go beyond the limitations of immediate experience by using symbols to represent (re-present) past experiences and to imagine future possibilities.

Rubin, Fein, and Vandenberg,[40] in their significant review of the research regarding symbolic play, indicate that it is at the very core of the development of a diverse set of abilities, including creativity, sequential memory, group cooperation, receptive vocabulary, conceptions of kinship relationships, impulse control, spatial perspective-taking skills, affective perspective-taking skills, and cognitive perceptive-taking skills.

Vygotsky[43] emphasized the role of representational play, or fantasy play, as a leading factor in child development:

> Play creates a zone of proximal development in the child. In play, the child always behaves beyond his average age, above his daily behavior; in play it is as though he were a head taller than himself. As in the focus of a magnifying glass, play contains all developmental tendencies in a condensed form and is itself a major source of development.

One of the major features of all symbolic play is that the children playing make rules regarding the play. Although it may not appear to be rule-governed behavior, even the most basic pretend play has rules that the child takes very seriously. A sensitive adult will hear the protests of a child to another child or to the adult (e.g., "Not that way"; "That isn't a horse"; "You can't cook with that"; or "That goes in the blocks center."

In and through rules over which the child has some control, the child learns to function in a rule-governed society. According to Berk and Winsler[3]:

> Adults and peers scaffold young children's play, nurturing the transition to make-believe and its elaboration throughout the preschool years. Representational play serves as a unique, broadly influential zone of proximal development within which children advance themselves to ever higher levels of psychological functioning.

In most child care and preschool settings, this play-based, quality educational environment is one that is centers based. That is, there are unique, separate, and distinct areas within the classroom that are specifically designed and equipped for active exploration.

Dodge and Colker[12] recommend the following centers for the preschool classroom:

- Blocks
- House corner
- Table toys
- Art
- Sand and water
- Library
- Music and movement
- Cooking
- Computers
- Outdoors

Other preschool educators recommend different center configurations:

- Discovery (science)
- Sociodramatic play
- Creative arts
- Language and literacy
- Active play
- Blocks and manipulatives (mathematics)

A center provides children the opportunity to explore and interact with a wide variety of materials that engage a whole spectrum of senses, encourages sensory integration, and allows the children to be involved in an extended process of "pretend" and real play. For example, a sociodramatic play center may include the following:

- Child-sized furniture, including a stove, refrigerator, sink, comfortable chair, sofa, kitchen table and chairs, doll bed, ironing board/iron, stroller
- Play props, including pots and pans, cooking and eating utensils, coffee pot, glasses and cups, broom, mop, etc.
- Baby dolls reflecting diversity—cultures, genders, and ability
- Doll clothes
- Dress-up clothes
- Full-length mirror
- A puppet theatre and puppets reflecting a variety of people, animals, etc.
- An area that can be used to simulate a post office, grocery store, restaurant, etc., and the necessary props to stimulate play

Given this type of play support, the young child who is just developing sociodramatic play skills will be "nudged" toward more sophisticated play. Eventually, the child will not need actual objects to stimulate play but will be able to substitute any object for another in play.

Quality Movement/Play Experiences in Preschool Programs
NASPE Position Statement

The process of preparing every child for a successful school experience includes providing quality movement/play experiences. A position statement of the The National Association for Sport and Physical Education (NASPE), developed by the Council on Physical Education for Children (COPEC), describes appropriate and inappropriate practice in movement programs for young

children in a 21-page pamphlet titled *Developmentally Appropriate Practice in Movement Programs for Young Children Ages 3-5*.[11] The major premises outlined by NASPE and COPEC are presented here.

Three-, four-, and five-year-old children are different from elementary school-age children[11]

Widespread condemnation of the American public school system in the 1980s and early 1990s caused an academic "trickle down" that has had a devastating impact on the education of young children. Specifically, a knee-jerk response to the criticism caused academicians and administrators to allow curricula to "trickle down" to younger grades. For example, material that was once considered appropriate for the sixth grade is now being introduced in the fourth and fifth grades. What was once considered appropriate for first graders is now being introduced in prekindergarten and kindergarten classes. According to Shepard[41]:

> Because what once were first grade expectations were shoved down to kindergarten, these shifts in practice were referred to as the "escalation of curriculum" or "academic trickle-down." The result of these changes was an aversive learning environment inconsistent with the learning needs of children. Developmentally inappropriate instructional practices, characterized by long periods of seatwork, high levels of stress, and a plethora of fill-in-the-blank worksheets, placed many children at risk by setting standards for attention span, social maturity, and academic productivity that could not be met by many normal 5-year-olds [much less children with disabilities and developmental delays—comment ours].

This has been true not only in "academic" content areas but in movement/physical education programs as well. This "trickle down" effect has seriously compromised the movement/play experience of young children as children have been expected to:

- Sit and wait "forever" for a turn.
- Sit and listen "forever" to directions given by an adult.
- Participate in an activity predetermined by an adult and given no choice regarding participation.
- Participate in large-group activities when the child is not yet able to play with another one-to-one.
- Share equipment.
- Use modified equipment—mini-basketballs, shortened baskets, large plastic bats—with a stereotypical expectation regarding the use of the equipment.

- Use equipment in a stereotypical, adult-determined way.
- Perform skills for which they are not ready, because the teacher or parent does not understand developmental sequence (e.g., a 5-year-old trying to bat an arched, pitched ball).
- Play cooperatively, or heaven forbid, compete with other children when the child is developmentally at onlooker, solitary play, or parallel play stages.

Preschoolers are ready for movement and play activities that prepare them for school. But they are, by nature and design, not prepared for activities that would be part of the school curricula for 6-year-olds. There is a vast difference in capability and interests of 3-year-olds and 6-year-olds.

Young children learn through interaction with their environment[11]

Preschoolers learn only through active play and active involvement with their environment. They do not learn by watching someone else perform or by listening to directions—they learn by doing and experimenting and experiencing.[17] Active, experiential play is the very foundation for the active learning center and the outdoor play center.

Teachers of young children are guides or facilitators[11]

Vygotsky has theorized that all children learn best when their learning is scaffolded or supported by an adult or another child.[3] Traditional practice in education, including physical education, embraces the teacher as the "giver of wisdom" and the child as the "learner." Vygotsky[43] and other early childhood educators have reminded us that that, simply, is not the way young children learn.

The preschool physical educator or preschool adapted physical education specialist must, by necessity, rethink and reevaluate traditional teaching models and strategies and embrace a model in which the teacher is simply (but very importantly) an unobtrusive facilitator of children's learning. Preschool children hate whistles, unless they happen to be blowing them; lines, unless they happen to be drawing them; and speeches, unless they happen to be giving them.

The preschool physical educator best serves preschoolers by becoming a facilitator of learning. The role of the facilitator includes the following:

1. Observing children in play.
2. Observing children moving—their locomotor and nonlocomotor patterns, their receipt-propulsion skills, and the way they use equipment and materials.
3. Recreating the learning environment by including materials that encourage further exploration of the environment or enhance self-testing. For example, if the child is successfully running and jumping off an incline ramp that is 6 inches at the tallest point into a large landing mat, ask the child if he or she would like to try running and jumping off an incline ramp that has been raised so that it is 12 inches at the tallest point.
4. Redirecting the child's learning and activity, with permission. For example, if the child is bobbling a balloon in the air with ease, ask the child if he or she would like to try bobbling two balloons at the same time.
5. Honoring and respecting the play of children. Powell[37] notes that a teacher honors the play of children by asking questions about the play and by joining the play, but only if invited by the child.
   a. *Ask* to join their play and respect their decision if they choose to play without you.
   b. Engage in parallel play so that a child can observe you without being told what it is he or she should do. For example, if a child is having difficulty pushing a wheelbarrow because the load is not distributed equally, position yourself near the child and redistribute materials in your wheelbarrow as a model.
   c. Support the child's play by providing adequate time and appropriate equipment and materials to challenge the child.

Young children learn and develop in an integrated fashion[11]

Physical education must not be a separate, 30-minute period of time. Movement must be, inherently, an integral part of all learning, in all centers, and an important part of every special activity. For example, in the blocks and manipulatives center, children will engage in gross motor activity when given the opportunity to build using large foam or wooden blocks. In the music center, children will engage in gross motor activity when given the opportunity to perform locomotor and nonlocomotor actions to music. In the language and literacy center, children will have the opportunity to use their large muscles and engage in gross motor activity when given the opportunity to "be" the turtle or snake or rabbit in the story.

Planned movement experiences enhance play experiences[11]

The preschool adapted physical education specialist may plan movement experiences for children—but *under no circumstances should children be required to participate in those experiences.* Young children have such widely diverse motor capabilities, play skills, and needs that it is developmentally inappropriate to force a child into any activity. A **developmentally appropriate movement experience** allows individual, solitary activity and a choice to participate in small- and/or large-group activities. For example, the adapted physical education specialist may have a plan to involve children in a "snowball fight" with rolled-up socks or white yarn balls. If a child is ready—physically, motorically, neurologically, and socially—he or she will choose to participate. If the child is not ready, the preschool adapted physical education specialist must have some other option—independent play on a scooter, play with balloons, play with large playground balls—readily accessible. The movement program for young children with disabilities—indeed, for any young children—must be designed to meet their needs and be responsive to their interests.

▪ ▪ ▪

The focus of this chapter continues to be the need for movement/play programs for young children with and without disabilities to focus on the needs and interests of the children, not the needs and interests of the adults. The activity suggestions that follow must be used within the broader framework of developmentally appropriate practice. Specifically, when one is working with young children, the movement activities must always be presented as a choice—not an expectation. If the movement activities are appropriate, most children will be drawn to them and will want to participate. If the movement activities are inappropriate, children will choose not to participate, will act out if made to participate, or will lose interest quickly.

The intent of a quality movement/play program for

preschoolers with and without disabilities is to provide young children access to neurodevelopmentally appropriate activities that enhance the development of:

- Equilibrium
- Sensory discrimination
- Body image
- Basic locomotor and nonlocomotor competency
- Cross-lateral integration
- Receipt and propulsion skills
- Fitness.

Examples of activities that enhance the development of each of the above follow. Additional activity suggestions can be found in the handbook *Gross Motor Activities for Young Children with Special Needs,* which accompanies this text.

Equilibrium

A young child develops equilibrium in static positions and movements, at first, in which the center of gravity is very close to a large base of support (i.e., in the supine and then the prone position). As the child develops, he or she begins to "be in balance" in static and dynamic situations in which the center of gravity is farther away from a smaller base of support (e.g., walking on tiptoes on a balance beam). The intent of these activities is to develop tone and strength in the muscle groups that provide shoulder and hip stability and to enhance postural adjustments.

Supine equilibrium
BUBBLE OUT

Ask the child to lie on his or her back and try to break bubbles with a finger as you blow them over his or her face and chest.

Prone equilibrium
TRAMPOLINE FUN

Ask the child to lie on his or her stomach on a mini-trampoline. Sit next to the child and push the mini-trampoline at various spots near the child's body. Vary the pressure and the area of focus. NOTE: A nap mat or 1-inch-thick play mat placed over an inner tube makes a great, inexpensive mini-trampoline.

Sitting equilibrium
LITTLE RED WAGON

Ask the child, or a group of children, to sit on a crash-type mat or clean mattress. To the song, "Little Red Wagon," the children can act out the experience of "joltin' up and down in the little red wagon." The song can be found on the cassette *Hello Everybody* by Rachel Buchman.

Hands and knees equilibrium
PET PARADE
Ask a number of children to get into a hands/knees position on a long scooterboard and "parade by" by moving their scooterboard with their hands. To make it a great deal of fun, the pets can wear special costumes for the parade.

Kneeling equilibrium
RODEO RIDER
Ask the child to straddle a bolster, with the knees on a mat on both sides. Let the child pretend to be a "rodeo rider" and lift either end of the bolster and try to roll it back and forth while the child sits on it. This is even more fun if the children sing "Rodeo Rider" from the cassette *What I Want to Be* from Kids Songs.

Standing equilibrium
BODY BOOGIE
Ask the children to stand and join you in the dance, "Swing, Shake, Twist and Stretch," on the record/cassette *Walter the Waltzing Worm* by Hap Palmer.

Sensory Discrimination

Movement/play programs for 3- to 5-year-old children with and without disabilities focus on the development of sensory discrimination, although profoundly delayed children may require ongoing sensory stimulation. The intent is to provide children with the opportunity to integrate sensory stimuli so that they can make an appropriate motor output. Examples of activities to stimulate the development of sensory discrimination follow.

Tactile discrimination
LINE-EM-UP
Ask the child to sit in a long V-sit position with his or her eyes closed. Roll a variety of balls to the child (yarn, whiffle golf, tennis, 6-inch playground ball, volleyball, 20-inch beach ball, etc.) and ask the child to arrange the balls from "smallest" to "biggest." NOTE: If the child peeks, the child needs to peek.

OBSTACLE COURSE
On a mat, establish an obstacle course with mats, rolled-up towels, bolsters, incline mats, beanbag chairs, etc. Ask the children, one at a time, to move through the obstacle course with his or her eyes closed. NOTE: If the child peeks, the child needs to peek.

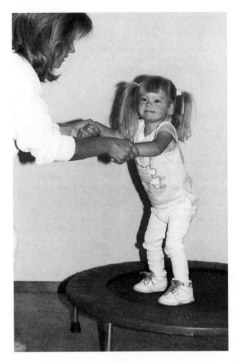

Equipment for the home provides play opportunity for child and parent.

Vestibular discrimination
SPIN-A-WAY
Ask the child to sit on a scooter board, holding the handles. The teacher spins the child 180, 360, or 720 degrees and then stops the child. Ask the child to spin self the same number of times.

Proprioceptive discrimination
PULL-A-THON
Ask the child to close his or her eyes. Tie jump ropes to a variety of objects that can be pulled (scooters with other kids sitting on them, a tire, a wagon with a mat in it, etc.). Let the child pull one "object" and replace it. Then let the child pull all "objects" until the child finds the one he or she pulled first.

Auditory discrimination
YOU CAN'T FIND ME
Ask two or more (depending on the auditory discrimination capability of the child) children to hide, each using one rhythm instrument. Ask a child to close his or her eyes and try to locate the child shaking the tambourine, for example, as opposed to the child beating on the drum.

YOU CAN'T CATCH ME, I'M THE GINGERBREAD MAN

Ask the children to crawl or creep while trying to catch the child who is reciting, "Run, run, as fast as you can . . . You can't catch me, I'm the gingerbread man." This is even more fun if the class has already heard the story, "The Gingerbread Man."

Visual discrimination

TEXAS ROUND-UP

Blow up several dozen balloons (several different colors) and put them on a parachute in the corner of a room. The children play "cowgirl" or "cowboy" and try to "round up" the balloons after they have escaped. (The teacher and several children lift the parachute up into the air to send the balloons flying.) Particular children are asked to "round up the little doggies" by collecting balloons of one color.

Body Image

Having a good body image indicates that a child has an internal understanding of how the body works, how the parts of the body relate to one another, how much space the body occupies, and what the body looks like. The development of body image can be enhanced by activities as simple as participating in the dance, "What a Miracle" on Hap Palmer's *Walter the Waltzing Worm* record/cassette. Or the activities can be more complex, as in the following example.

MY OWN SPECIAL MOVEMENT

A group of children sit in a circle. Each child is asked to show a "special" movement. The teacher can help prompt. For example, if the child is asked to show a special movement and the child simply shrugs the shoulders, the teacher can thank the child for sharing the "shoulder shrug." Then the activity starts. The group chants the child's name while doing *the child's* shoulder shrug 3 times. For example, the group chants "Tommy, Tommy, Tommy" while shrugging the shoulders 3 times, once for each time the name is repeated.

　　If the next child, Maria, chooses a hand clap as her movement, the group practices saying, "Maria, Maria, Maria" while clapping 3 times. Once the group has practiced, the activity starts over. The group chants, "Tommy, Tommy, Tommy" while shrugging and then "Maria, Maria, Maria" while clapping.

　　The number of children in the circle is determined by the children's interest and attention span. This is an empowering activity—having your own movement and having others chant your name—so most tend to stay involved. This is a particularly wonderful activity if a child in the group has limited movement potential. For example, if Roshard's athetoid cerebral palsy limits his volitional move-

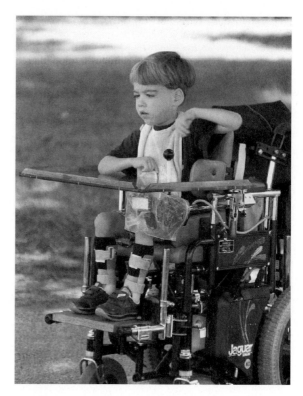

A motorized chair gives a child the opportunity to control his destiny.

ment to a head roll, the group can chant, "Roshard, Roshard, Roshard" while rolling their heads.

Basic Locomotor and Nonlocomotor Competency

Locomotor and nonlocomotor skills can be enhanced as young children are given every opportunity to explore movements and their variables: time, space, force, and flow. Examples of how basic movements can be modified by manipulating those four variables follow.

TIME

The child swings his or her arms to:
1. A 4-4 beat
2. The song "Freeze" on the cassette *We All Live Together II* by Greg and Steve
3. The beat of a drum
4. Follow the arm-swinging motion of a partner

SPACE

The child creeps:
1. Forward and backward
2. Up and down an incline mat
3. In, around, and between a series of obstacles
4. Through a tunnel
5. On a "crazy sidewalk"

   A series of mats is placed on varying surfaces, such as beanbag chairs, so that the surface "gives" when the student moves, causing postural adjustments.

FORCE

The child runs:
1. While pushing a wheelbarrow
2. While pulling a partner sitting on a scooter, each holding one end of the rope
3. While pumping arms and legs vigorously
4. While trying to get as high off the ground as possible

FLOW

The child pushes his or her wheelchair:
1. 3 times and then stops
2. Forward 3 times, stops; backward 3 times, stops
3. In an alternating pattern, right hand, left hand, right hand, left hand
4. "Wheelies" (wheels on ground) right 3 times, and "wheelies" left 3 times

Cross-Lateral Integration

Cross-lateral integration is the ability to coordinate the use of both sides of the body, particularly in activities that require movement about the midline of the body. Examples of activities that may facilitate the development of cross-lateral integration follow.

RIBBON ACTIVITIES

The child holds a wand with a ribbon of Mylar or crepe paper and makes the following movements, alternating hands:
1. Figure eight, which crosses the midline of the body
2. Huge X's, which cross the midline of the body

BALL ACTIVITIES

1. The child, while sitting, rolls a ball all the way around the body.
2. The child performs alternate-hand dribbling in front of the body.

Receipt and Propulsion Skills

Receipt and propulsion skills are simply those that involve the process of "taking in" an object and then "sending it out." Examples of activities that facili-

tate the development of receipt and propulsion skills follow.

RECEIPT

1. Ask the child to sit in a long V-sit, and roll a series of balls to the child, asking the child to roll them back. The intensity (quickness) should be adjusted so that the child is successful.
2. Ask the child to lie supine and "bobble" a balloon above the body using knees and feet.
3. Ask the child to sit and "trap" as many balloons as possible with the arms and legs.

PROPULSION

1. Ask the child to wad newspaper into balls as quickly as possible and then throw them as far as possible.
2. Scatter balls and beanbags of as many different sizes, weights, and textures as possible in a given space. Ask the child to throw them all to another space, over a net, for example.
3. Scatter balls and beanbags of as many different sizes, weights, and textures as possible in a given space. Ask the child to kick them all to another space, over a net, for example.

Fitness

Fitness activities for young children, ages 3 to 5, should be redundant. If a young child is involved in a quality, developmentally appropriate movement program, the child will develop and maintain fitness. The natural inclination of a young child to move—to play—if honored, should provide the child ample opportunity to develop strength, flexibility, and cardiovascular endurance. Any attempt to structure that fitness experience may encourage fitness in the preschooler but will ultimately serve to discourage the child from a lifetime of fitness commitment.

Activities designed particularly for the young child who is wheelchair enabled or who has limited movement potential can be found in the handbook that accompanies this book, *Gross Motor Activities for Young Children with Special Needs*. However, a more structured movement activity program may be necessary.

The Indoor Active Learning Center

The active learning center for preschoolers with and without disabilities, like other centers designed in the developmentally appropriate learning environment, should provide children with the opportunity to move, self-test, explore, interact, and play. Ideally, the preschool movement/play specialist should create the active learning center with the children. And, most certainly, the specialist should be sensitive to the needs of the children and create and recreate the environment on the basis of the materials and equipment to which the children are drawn. The following materials and equipment enhance the learning environment and encourage active exploration and active experiences in movement and play:

- Mats of different types and densities, including "crash-type" mats
- Large foam-filled forms of different shape (pyramids, cubes, donut holes, etc.) for kids to roll on, jump on, climb in, around, over and through (e.g., Lakeshore Tumble Forms and Giant Climb and Play Blocks)
- Large empty boxes for children to climb in, around, over, and through
- Giant tumble balls (17-, 23-, and 30-inch)
- Hippity hops
- Large balls for catching (10- to 13-inch)
- A wide variety of small balls and beanbags to throw
- Tricycles and child-sized safety helmets
- Scooters and child-sized safety helmets
- Wagons and wheelbarrows
- A variety of scooterboards, with and without handles
- Sheets and blankets to make "forts" and tunnels
- Steps for climbing and a slide for sliding
- An incline ramp
- Nets and ropes for climbing
- Big trucks, cars, etc.
- Hula hoops
- Balloons
- Parachutes (6-, 12-, and 20-foot)
- Tug-of-war rope and shorter ropes for pulling and jumping over
- Cones
- Paper and markers to identify a play area (e.g., "Pooh's house")

This indoor active learning center provides a wealth of opportunity for children to explore and move. It provides a myriad of experiences that enhance learning in other centers as well. For example, the active learning center is a vital part of a centers-based, developmentally appropriate program. The children should have the opportunity to participate in independent, adult-supported play experiences. In addition, the active learning center

can provide a wonderful opportunity for enhancement of a given theme or unit. For example, if the preschoolers are learning about "winter," activities in each of the centers may enhance this learning and make it more real. The following are examples of the types of activities that may occur in each center.

SCIENCE OR DISCOVERY CENTER

To examine ice and its properties, the teacher can freeze water on cookie sheets and let the children feel how slippery and cold the ice really is. Then they can watch it melt and, if possible, refreeze.

SOCIODRAMATIC PLAY CENTER

The children may pretend to make hot chocolate or warm cider on the stove. The children may get all dressed up to go out in the "cold weather."

CREATIVE ART CENTER

The children can use cottonballs ("snowballs") in their art. The children can cut or tear white paper and make snowflakes.

RHYTHM AND MUSIC CENTER

The children can sing and dance to "Frosty the Snowman."

LANGUAGE CENTER

The children can read the story of "Frosty the Snowman" and then act out the story. The children can make up stories re "Hannah [the child's name] the Snowman."

COOKING CENTER

The children can make "snowball" cookies by cutting prepackaged rolls of refrigerated sugar cookie dough into small quarters, sprinkling the cookies with shaved coconut, and baking the cookies (of course, with the teacher's help).

BLOCKS AND MANIPULATIVES CENTER

The children can use blocks and Duplos/Legos to build snowpeople and snow forts.

ACTIVE PLAY CENTER

1. The children may pretend to be people cutting and stacking firewood and shoveling snow.
2. The children may pretend to be ice skaters, skating on pieces of waxed paper on the wood or tile floor.
3. The children can use large building blocks to make snow forts and have a "snowball" fight using yarn balls or rolled-up white socks.
4. The children can ride tricycles and pretend to be snowmobilers.
5. The teacher can fold a large rope between panels of a mat. Several children can ride on the "sleigh" while the teacher and other children are the horses. To make it even more fun, the children can jingle "sleigh bells" and sing "Jingle Bells."

6. The teacher can push children lying prone on scooterboards, and the children can pretend to be sledding.

Movement is an end in itself. Children need to move, and they must be given every opportunity to do so. It may be easier for the preschool movement/play specialist to convince other preschool educators to involve children in gross motor activity if they believe the activity will reinforce learning that occurs in other centers. The opportunities for learning that are inherent in the active learning center are endless and meet the needs of young children to use their bodies and to participate in play, all the while reinforcing other learning.

As mentioned earlier, the equipment, materials and other props simply help the preschool adapted physical educator establish the learning environment. The learning opportunities are endless. They are endless, however, only if each child has adequate play opportunities. There is nothing so sad as seeing a group of young children in a huge open play space with only two or three balls to share.

Careful preparation of the play environment will maximize learning opportunities and minimize the potential for arguments. The key to the preparation of any learning environment for young children is the creation of at least 2.5 play units per child. Sharing is one of the things that preschoolers really struggle with—to force them to do something for which they are developmentally unprepared is to create conflict between children. Fewer play units (play materials, equipment, and spaces) increase the likelihood that children will argue about materials, equipment, and space.

Wetherby[45] describes the different types of play units:

> Simple Play Unit—a play area that occupies one child and is not conducive to cooperative interaction.
> Complex Play Unit—a play area that occupies up to four children, such as a sand table with pouring utensils for each child or a puppet stage with puppets for each child.
> Super Play Unit—a play area that occupies up to eight children, such as a dramatic play area with eight costumes or a block area with at least 25 interlocking or 50 unit blocks per child.

We would like to suggest another play unit category that has not been considered before in the literature. With young children, the leap from independent, solitary play in a simple play unit to play in a complex play unit may be overwhelming. A "partner" play unit is developmentally appropriate as children learn first to deal with one

Active Learning Center, Indoors: Play Unit Analysis

Following is a sample evaluation of an indoor active learning center that a preschool adapted physical education specialist would complete before involving young children in its use. Required: 2.5 play units per child.

Materials, Equipment, Spaces	Number of Play Units
Simple play units (1 point each)	
5 tricycles	5
3 wheelbarrows	3
2 small slides (height = 6 feet)	2
2 small balance beams (6 inches wide, 6 inches long)	2
6 scooter boards (2 feet × 3 feet)	6
3 wooden trucks	3
3 plastic fire trucks	3
2 "jumpin jiminy"	2/26 play units
Partner play units (2 points each)	
3 small pull wagons (1 child pulls, 1 rides)	6
2 two-seat rockers	4
6 huge (refrigerator/stove) empty boxes	12/38 play units
Complex play units (4 points each)	
1 cassette player with songs for dancing	4/42 play units
Super units (8 points each)	
1 large parachute with handles for 16	16/58
	68 play units

Play area is adequate to support quality play of 27 children!

other child and then with small groups of children. Teachers must create opportunities for play with only one other child as well. Play unit analyses for indoor and outdoor active play centers are presented in the box above and in the box on p. 282.

The Outdoor Active Learning Center

The outdoor play experience for young children with developmental delays or disabilities should be an exten-

Active Play Center, Outdoors: Play Unit Analysis

Following is a sample evaluation of an outdoor play area that a preschool adapted physical education specialist would complete before involving young children in its use. Required: 2.5 play units per child.

Materials, Equipment, Spaces	Number of Play Units
Simple play units (1 point each)	
5 tricycles	5
3 wheelbarrows	3
2 small slides (height = 6 feet)	2
2 small balance beams (6 inches wide, 6 inches long)	2
6 scooter boards (2 feet × 3 feet)	6
3 wooden trucks	3
3 plastic fire trucks	3
2 "jumpin jiminy"	2/26 play units
Partner play units (2 points each)	
3 small pull wagons (1 child pulls, 1 rides)	6
2 two-seat rockers	4/10 play units
Complex play units (4 points each)	
1 water table (with a spoonful of dishwashing detergent)	4/4 play units
2 buckets	
2 measuring cups	
2 watering cans	
4 bubble makers	
Super units (8 points each)	
1 large sandbox	8
5 buckets	
5 shovels	
4 rakes	
4 pancake turners	
2 sieves	
1 small parachute with handles for 8	8
1 large play structure	8/24 play units
	64 play units

Play area is adequate to support quality play of 25 children!

sion of learning that occurs within the home, day care center, recreation center, and active learning center. As in every other setting, the outdoor play of young children needs to be respected and valued, and may serve as a scaffold for the development of:

- More complex and sophisticated play
- Gross and fine motor skills
- Interpersonal skills
- Communication and language

The opportunity to play and learn outdoors is as vital to a child as the air he or she breathes. Children, as resilient animals, will find a way to play—in almost any outdoor setting. Being able to use "outdoor voices" and to do the things that come naturally to many children—running, jumping, climbing, swinging, hanging—creates the opportunity for a joyful learning experience. However, as Rivkin[39] reminds us:

> Although no person or government planned it, habitats for children, especially in industrialized countries, have been greatly altered—often destroyed—in this century, especially in recent decades . . . Children's access to outdoor play has evaporated like water in sunshine.

Unfortunately, this alteration and destruction of play environments for children—the ruination of their "habitats"—has compromised the quality of young children's lives. In many urban environments, children simply do not "go out to play," even in their own yards, for fear of drive-by shootings or kidnapping, contact with drug paraphernalia, or contact with toxic substances. In fact, many children have the opportunity to play outdoors only under the supervision of teachers and assistants in the day care or preschool program. A vital and integral part of a total early childhood education program, the outdoor play experience should be a part of the daily schedule.[33] Children must have the opportunity to play outside every day. The only exception, of course, would be during inclement or dangerous weather, including weather "warnings," storms with lightning, severe heat or severe cold, and, particularly for children with asthma and other respiratory problems, ozone and other pollution alerts.

Most preschool educators would agree that the ideal outdoor play setting is one in which the child has the opportunity to interact with and learn from nature. It is vital not only for their physical and social development, but may inherently be vital for the development of their

figure 10-2
Natural outdoor play area.

souls. The ideal preschool outdoor play area would be nature based (Figure 10-2) and would include the following:

- Flowers, bushes, and trees native to the area
- Natural play surfaces: grass (short and tall grasses), dirt, sand, hills and valleys
- Apparatus for climbing, swinging, and hanging: trees, rocks, vines
- Apparatus for balancing, self-testing: tree stumps, fallen logs
- Play areas for digging and pouring: dirt/mud, sand, stream/pond
- Play materials for building and stacking: rocks, twigs
- Play materials for sorting and classifying: flowers and weeds, leaves, seeds (acorns)

In the event that the outdoor play area is not in a natural setting, there are still ways for the creative preschool physical educator to help design an outdoor play area that meets the fundamental needs of young children (Figure 10-3). The *"asphalt" play area* could include the following:

- Flowers, bushes, and trees native to the area (flower boxes, potted trees, potted bushes)
- Natural play surfaces: wood chips, grass (short and tall grasses), sand, dirt, pea gravel, "hills and valleys" (incline ramps)
- Apparatus for climbing, swinging, hanging, and sliding: "trees," "large rocks," "vines," (net climbers, tire climbers, swings, slides, steps/ladders, horizontal poles, vertical poles)
- Apparatus for balancing, self-testing: railroad ties,

figure 10-3
"Asphalt" outdoor play area.

"tree stumps" (4 × 4s), "fallen logs" (balance boards)

▪ Play areas for digging and pouring: sandbox, dirt/mud, sand table, sand, water table, "stream/pond" (plastic swimming pool), sprinkler, garden plots

▪ Play materials for building and stacking: plastic blocks, rocks, wooden blocks, twigs

In some inner-city areas it is virtually impossible to maintain a developmentally appropriate outdoor play area because of theft and vandalism. Large play structures that can be cemented into the ground may be the only option to provide any play spaces for children. And, amazingly, educators have to be concerned that parts of those play structures will be disconnected to be sold to gain recycling dollars. There are, thankfully, some cre-ative play structures that provide access for all children that are difficult to disassemble and difficult to hurt.

Basic Standards for the Preschool Outdoor Play Area

The preschool physical educator or the preschool adapted physical education specialist must determine the safety and developmental appropriateness of the outdoor play area. The following must be considered:

1. Is the outdoor play area large enough to allow children to move freely (75 to 100 square feet per child)? If the play area is not that large, can scheduling patterns be devised to limit the number of children using the outdoor play area at any given time?

A tricycle provides an opportunity for development of motor competency. (Courtesy Dallas Independent School District.)

2. Can the teachers and assistants see all children in the outdoor play area without obstruction?
3. Is the area accessible to all children?
4. Is the area adjacent to bathrooms and water fountains? Are those accessible to all children?
5. Is there a phone available in the event of an emergency?
6. Does the outdoor play area provide areas that are sunny and areas that are shaded?[12]
7. Is the area fenced in to provide protection? Is there an area that serves as a buffer between the street and the play area?
8. Are there child-sized places to rest and relax (e.g., child-sized picnic tables or benches)?
9. Is the area free of debris, litter, and broken glass?[12]
10. Are playground structures no taller than twice the height of the tallest preschooler using the play area?

11. Does any of the equipment have rust, cracks, or splinters?[12]
12. Are there any hazards, such as sharp edges or places where a child can be pinched?

Careful attention should be paid to the safety of the outdoor play area. Careful review of safety standards, on a daily basis, is a vital part of the role of the preschool physical educator.

Extending Learning Center Activities Outdoors

Far too often, outdoor play time is considered a "recess" time or a time for teachers to regroup. The outdoor play time is one of the most vital and significant parts of the day and can, if carefully planned, not only prove crucial in the development of more complex and sophisticated play skills, gross and fine motor skills, interpersonal skills, and communication/language skills, but may also enhance learning opportunities initiated in indoor learning centers. The following are examples of how activities that are part of the "centers experience" can be expanded and enhanced in learning activities out-of-doors.

SOCIODRAMATIC PLAY

Children wearing dress-up hats and "pretending to be" wear the hats outside and:
1. Put out the fire in the house (playground structure).
2. Use the wagons as ambulances when playing doctor.
3. Climb on buildings (climbers) as construction workers.
4. Chase robbers in squad cars (tricycles).

CREATIVE ART

1. Children use large brushes and water, and "paint" the outside of the building.
2. Children make sand sculptures in the sandbox.
3. Children make texture rubbings on trees, with leaves and flowers.
4. Children make shadow drawings.

DISCOVER (SCIENCE)

1. Children fly kites to experiment with the wind.
2. Children slide down slides to experience gravity.
3. Children collect acorns, seeds, leaves, weeds, flowers, etc., for a collage.

BLOCKS AND MANIPULATIVES (MATHEMATICS)

1. Children collect and arrange rocks in sequence from large to small.
2. Children see how many "laps" they can drive on their tricycle in a given amount of time.
3. Children take large foam and large wooden blocks outside to create structures that augment those that already exist.

LANGUAGE AND LITERACY

Children act out stories learned in the classroom. They become large muscle/gross motor activities when "acted out" outside. Examples:

1. "Billy Goat Gruff" (incline ramps/play structure as bridge)
2. Pocahontas (outdoor play area is the wilderness)

MUSIC

Children move to music while climbing, hanging, swinging, bending, stretching, and twisting on apparatus, trees, rocks, etc.

▪ ▪ ▪

This approach allows the "inside" and "outside" learning experiences to augment and enhance each other. Outdoor play does not require any justification and certainly is not designed to supplement anything. It is, inherently, a vital and integral part of the child's total educational experience.

Preschool Inclusion Programs

If this society is, indeed, committed to the notion that *all* individuals should have the opportunity to learn together—a commitment not based on administrative feasibility or perception of cost reduction—the best possible place to begin inclusionary practices is with infants, toddlers, and young children. Yet, Lamorey and Bricker[27] estimated that less than one third of young children eligible for early intervention services are receiving those service in integrated or inclusive settings.

Young children are, inherently, very accepting of other children. Their curiosity is natural and, if their questions are answered honestly, they accept their playmates naturally and without hesitation. A true, child-sensitive inclusion program would begin with inclusive infant, toddler, and preschool programs. As children who have played together enter school together, they are able to learn together and, eventually, be citizens together in peace.[30] Millspaugh and Segelman[34] suggested that preschoolers are so willing to accept other children with disabilities because each preschooler is virtually disabled in the so-called adult-designed world. According to them, "Society systematically handicaps all small children by making drinking fountains too high to manage, stairs too deep to climb, and toilet paper dispensers too far (away) to reach."[34] A checklist that can be used to evaluate the extent to which a child with a severe disability is actually included in a preschool activity program is presented in the box on p. 287.

A publication written for the W.K. Kellogg Readiness Initiatives, supported by the W.K. Kellogg Foundation in cooperation with the National Association for the Education of Young Children, *Grassroots Success: Preparing Schools and Families for Each Other,*[44] suggested that schools that are ready for children:

Physical educators must appraise play facilities with the needs of students with disabilities in mind. (Courtesy Collier Center for Communicative Disorders, Dallas, Tex.)

Preschool Movement/Play Inclusion Checklist for Children with Severe Disabilities

Student:_____ Age:_____ Date:_____ **Y/N**

1. Is the child in a position to participate in all phases of the movement/play activity? If the child uses a wheelchair or crutches, is the activity taking place on a surface that is accessible? _____

2. Does the child participate in the same movement/play activities as the other children? If not, are the modifications kept to a minimum? _____

3. Does the child engage in movement/play activities at the same time as the other children? _____

4. Is the child actively involved, or does the child spend a great deal of time watching others move/play? _____

5. Does the child receive physical assistance from an adult only when absolutely necessary? _____

6. Is the adult careful not to interrupt the play of the child? _____

7. Does the child receive only the most unobtrusive prompts from adults to help the child participate in the activity? _____

8. Do other children seek out the child for play (e.g., ask the child to play)? _____

9. Does the child seek out other children for play? _____

10. Does the child have gestures, signs, or pictures to help him or her communicate if the child is unable to communicate verbally? _____

11. Do teachers interact with the child the same way as they do with the other children—the same type of praise, stickers, hugs, etc.? _____

12. Does the child have the same opportunities as other children for responsible roles in the active learning center (e.g., selecting music, distributing equipment)? _____

- Welcome all children and families in the community.
- Design curriculum content and daily routines that promote children's self-motivated learning: social, emotional, cognitive, and physical.
- Offer challenging, hands-on, relevant learning activities that build on what children already know and prepare them to contribute to a democratic society.
- Ensure that staff are well prepared to work with the ages and abilities of the children.
- Use appropriate methods to assess children's progress and evaluate possible special needs.
- Prepare environments that enable children to construct knowledge and understanding through inquiry, play, social interaction, and skill development.

As is true of school-based inclusive adapted physical education programs (see Chapter 5), a great deal of preparation must occur to address attitudes and empathies, abilities and skills, and, most important when addressing inclusive learning with preschoolers, the developmental appropriateness of the learning environment. Children with diverse abilities and disabilities can learn and thrive together in developmentally appropriate learning environments with few, if any, modifications in curriculum or pedagogy.[23]

Educators within the Dallas Public Schools, like many other school districts in the nation, have developed programs to meet the unique needs of preschoolers within their community, sensitive to the unique needs and backgrounds of their children. On two of the district's campuses, Macon Elementary School and Walnut Hill Elementary School, principals, educators, parents, and the instructional specialists in preschool programs for children with disabilities have developed inclusive, developmentally appropriate, centers-based programs to meet the needs of all preschoolers.

The Macon Project

Under the remarkable leadership of Dick Knox, Principal of Macon Elementary School for over 10 years, educators have created a unique, totally inclusive preschool program that serves *all* children between the ages of 3 and 5 years. This includes children whose primary educational placement is:

- A preschool developmental center, a learning environment designed for children with severe and profound delays and, often, who are medically fragile
- A preschool program for children with disabilities classroom, a learning environment designed for children with identified disabilities
- A preschool speech program, a special program for children with delays in expressive or receptive speech and/or articulation problems
- Prekindergarten, a program for children at risk for school difficulty because of low socioeconomic status or a nonenriched home environment
- Kindergarten, a voluntary program designed to prepare young children for a successful school experience

Research by Huettig, Tomlinson, and Hudson[24] has shown that preschoolers with and without disabilities learn more effectively in a developmentally appropriate, centers-based program than in a more traditional education program. The preschoolers in the Macon Project share nine distinct learning centers in mixed-age, mixed-ability groupings approximately 10 hours per week. The learning centers include:

- Language and literacy
- Science/discovery
- Mathematics
- Blocks and manipulatives
- Creative art
- Music and rhythms
- Active play
- Cooking

All preschoolers are given the maximum opportunity to learn the way young children learn best—through hands-on, active learning.

The Walnut Hill Project

The Walnut Hill Project is also designed to promote an inclusive, developmentally appropriate learning environment, but it serves a different group of children. Walnut Hill's visionary principal, Joanne Hughes, believes that all preschoolers can and should receive their educational services together and should learn in a dynamic, active, hands-on program. The Walnut Hill Project includes children whose educational placement is:

- A preschool program for children with disabilities classroom, a learning environment designed for children with identified disabilities
- A preschool speech program, a special program for children with delays in expressive or receptive speech and/or articulation problems
- A preschool total communication program, a program designed for children with the diagnosis of autism
- Kindergarten, a voluntary program designed to prepare young children for a successful school experience

These preschoolers share the following learning centers: sociodramatic play, blocks and manipulatives, science, and mathematics. In the early stages of the project, sociograms were developed by charting the responses of all the children to the questions, "Who do you like to play with?" and "Is there anybody you do not like to play with? The children's responses were charted as they pointed to pictures of their classmates on a tagboard. Each child was asked to answer the same questions 6 days later. The preschoolers had a remarkable "test-retest" correlation coefficient of 0.84 in response to the question, "Who do you like to play with?"[21] All children with disabilities were chosen by their kindergarten peers as someone they wanted to play with.

Cooperative Preschool

Another major preschool inclusion initiative in the Dallas Public Schools is the Cooperative Preschool Program at three branches of the YWCA of Metropolitan Dallas. With the cooperation of Dr. Phyllis Neuman, Executive Director, the Dallas Public Schools has three PPCD (preschool program for children with disabilities) classrooms, with a special educator and a teacher assistant, in three YWCA child care centers. In that setting, the children with special needs from the Dallas Public Schools share the child care environment with their typically developing peers in a natural setting. The special educator is responsible for implementation of the IEP within that setting.

Role of the Preschool Adapted Physical Educator in Inclusion Programs

The preschool adapted physical educator plays a unique role when serving children with disabilities in inclusion programs. It is crucial that the adapted physical educator provide services to all the preschoolers being served by the program. The last thing that should occur is pulling the children with disabilities out for segregated, separate programs. For example, when providing services to the 8 children with disabilities served at one of the YWCA cooperative preschool programs, the adapted physical educator developed a movement program for all of the 3-, 4-, and 5-year-old children being served (approximately 35 children).

The responsibilities of the preschool adapted physical educator include the following:

1. Address the gross motor and play goals/objectives on the IEPs of each of the children with disabilities.
2. Collect data for each child's portfolio assessment, those children with and without disabilities.
3. Create a learning environment in which all the children, those with and without disabilities, have the opportunity to work on gross motor and play skills. The key to a successful, developmentally appropriate motor/play learning environment is the work done before the children are present to prepare the learning environment.
4. Coordinate and plan the learning experience to support the theme or focus of the child care or preschool program.
5. Model appropriate motor and play behavior for all students.
6. Encourage age-appropriate interaction between all students.
7. Provide support for the children with disabilities who are having difficulty with a gross motor or play skill, not by separating the children for individual instruction, but by encouraging a small group of children to work together.
8. Model and provide consultative support for the child care teachers and assistants and other pre-

---

PARENT NOTE

It is very important that you know…

You can be very proud of _____ . Your child did some great things this week:

      Played in a small group

      Caught a bounced 6-inch playground ball

You could help at home by:

      Complimenting play at home that doesn't include fighting

      Playing catch with your child

Thank you for sharing your great kid with me.

      Emily Unger, Preschool Motor Specialist

figure 10-4
Parent note.

PPCD Newsletter
September 2, 1996

Dear Parents,

We are learning a great deal together…and want you to know how well we are doing!

We Are Learning to:	Things to Do at Home
Walk on a 6-inch balance beam.	Hold your child's hand while the child practices walking on a curb.
Throw a small ball, overhand, at a target.	As you finish looking at the paper, wad up each piece of paper and ask the child to throw it as hard as possible.
Jump	Rake leaves with your child and jump into them.
Act out stories.	Tell your child a story and act it out together.
Identify body parts.	Ask your child to draw a picture of you and ask the child to explain it to you.
	Go on a nature walk and collect leaves, seeds, etc.

figure 10-5
PPCD newsletter.

school regular and special educators and their paraprofessionals.

9. Communicate with parents through notes and newsletters (Figures 10-4 and 10-5).

An example of including all children in a learning center that reflects a child care or preschool theme is provided in Figure 10-6. In this example, the theme for the week was "transportation," and the preschool adapted physical educator created an active learning center to support that theme. The active learning center, indoor or outdoor, for preschoolers with and without disabilities, designed to support a transportation theme would include the following:

- A marked roadway for automobiles, busses, and trucks with tricycles, scooter boards, and wagons, including stop signs, etc.

- An incline ramp with crash mat to simulate an airplane take-off
- Different-sized boxes for the children to decorate as race cars, police cars, firetrucks, etc.
- A "crazy" roadway created with a series of mats to provide a variable surface for the cars to move on
- An obstacle course for the automobiles, buses, and trucks to move on, over, between, and through
- A cassette player with a tape including the following songs: "The Freeze" (*We All Live Together,* Volume 2); "Yellow Submarine" *(Mod Marches);* "Chug A Long Choo Choo" (*Preschool Aerobic Fun,* Georgiana Stewart)

Once the active learning center is designed to expand on the theme, the role of the preschool adapted physical educator is one of facilitator. Following are ex-

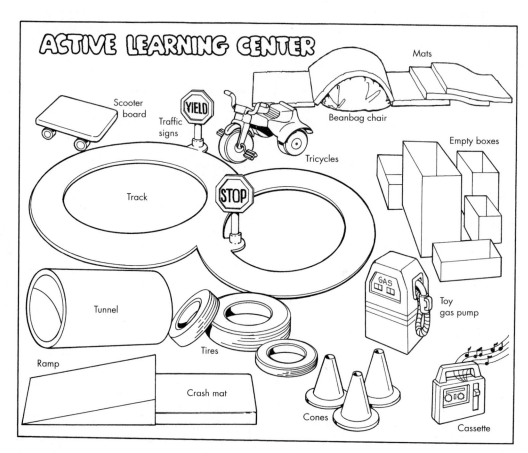

figure 10-6
Active learning center to support a transportation theme.

amples of techniques that can be used to address IEP goals/objectives and still serve all the children in the program:

- If a 4-year-old with Down syndrome is having difficulty with jumping skills, the teacher may position himself or herself near the "airplane take-off area" and offer to spot for all the children as they run and jump into the crash pad. All children gravitate to a teacher who is actively supporting and encouraging children.
- If a 3-year-old child with low muscle tone is having difficulty lifting his head and shoulders when in a prone position, the teacher may sit on the floor and play "race car" by letting children get on scooterboards on their stomachs and then push them so they race until they run out of gas.
- If a 5-year-old with spina bifida is using a wheelchair to ambulate, the teacher can help her decorate her wheelchair as a police car and then work with all the children on starting/stopping activities in the figure-eight raceway.
- If a 4-year-old child with ADHD (who has difficulty playing with other children) has an annual goal that reads, "Jeremiah will be able to participate in a small-group cooperative play activity," the teacher may invite three or four children to play "Freeze," a parallel play activity.

If preschoolers with disabilities are receiving services from a preschool adapted physical education teacher, it is usually as a consultant rather than as a direct service provider. Thus the major task of the teacher is to help local campus staff follow through and continue the activity and actions throughout the week when the teacher is not present. Refer to Chapter 5 to learn strategies regarding the consultancy.

Atypical Play Behavior

Curry and Arnaud[7] wrote:

> For young children, play is the most natural and spontaneous of activities, on a part with eating, sleeping, talking, moving, and elimination. Accordingly . . .
> 1. Play is a lawful, predictable phenomenon that shows clear developmental regularities, although the degree to which these regularities are expressed is much influenced by the child's environment.
> 2. Play serves to integrate complex cognitive, emotional, and social elements in the child's thinking and behavior.
> 3. Disturbances in play often reflect disturbances in the child's personality and social functioning.

The preschool movement/play specialist, as an acute observer of children's behavior, may note disturbances in a child's play that should alert the specialist to a potential problem.[7] The play behavior of young children with disabilities may reflect their developmental delays. Bergen[1] stated:

> Most at-risk young children engage in the first stage of play development (sensorimotor/practice play) although the quantity and quality of the play is influenced by the nature and severity of their handicaps, biological risk, or environmental risk conditions. For example, visually impaired, autistic, and motorically-impaired children have narrower ranges of sensorimotor play behaviors, severely multiply-handicapped [sic] children initiate less sensorimotor play, and abused/neglected children may be hypervigilant and less exploratory. Down syndrome and hearing impaired children, however, seem to show sensorimotor play behaviors that are very similar to those of children who are not at risk.

The preschool movement/play specialist, always a careful observer of young children at play, must be sensitive to the following types of idiosyncrasies in play:

1. Significant preoccupation with a single play theme (NOTE: Most young children seek repetition as a means of gaining and keeping control of their environment. Any parent who has been urged to read it "one more time" or any teacher who has grown weary of a particular song or dance understands this phenomenon.)
2. Unchanging repetition of a play theme:
   a. May indicate an emotional disturbance or a cognitive delay
   b. May indicate a need for control of part of the child's life, as is typical of children living with abuse and neglect or parental drug abuse
3. Unusual or morbid play themes (drive-by shooting, funeral): may indicate a child has had the experience and is trying to put it into perspective
4. Imitation of sexual acts and practices: May indicate the child is being or has been sexually abused or molested
5. Lack of awareness of other children:
   a. May indicate a developmental delay (in children age 3+)
   b. May indicate an emotional disturbance

6. Fragmentary play—an inability to sustain play:
   a. Typical of children younger than 3 years; in older children it may indicate a developmental delay or attention deficit disorder
   b. May indicate that a child is unable to cope with a significant, acute, or chronic trauma
7. Difficulty separating self from a play role (e.g., the child is a Power Ranger, not Sally playing "Power Ranger"): typical of a child who has been treated aggressively
8. Difficulty joining groups at play without disrupting: typical of a child with a developmental delay
9. Tendency to lash out and spoil play (knock down the block structure) of other children: may indicate the child has a disability that makes it difficult to participate, so the child acts out in frustration

Management of Behavior in the Preschool Learning Environment

The beauty of the developmentally appropriate, play-based, learning environment is that behavior problems are minimized. The following environmental variables encourage appropriate behavior and minimize behavior problems:

- A small student-teacher ratio (Young children demand and require the attention and care of adults. A ratio of no more than 8 : 1 is vital.)
- Age-appropriate, child-driven activity
- A routine that the child can count on during the day
- Child choices regarding activity
- A daily schedule sensitive to a child's basic needs—nutritious snack and lunch time, quiet or nap time
- A daily schedule that provides an opportunity for solitary, partner, small-group, and large-group activities
- A daily schedule that allows for a mix of indoor and outdoor play
- A quiet place where a child can "retreat" at any time during the day
- An adequate number of play units (There must be a sufficient number of materials so children are not expected to share.)

If these basic variables are controlled, most children's behavior will be controlled as well. To encourage

consistency, just as in any other setting, rules must be clear and concise—brief and understandable.

The most basic strategy for establishing a positive learning environment in which a preschooler will be successful is to be proactive and to "catch 'em being good" whenever possible. There are some important constraints, here, however, for the preschool movement/play specialist to consider.

The preschool adapted physical educator is aware that there are effective and ineffective ways to acknowledge the play (work) of the young child. Programs such as High Scope acknowledge that if an adult praises a young child, the child gets two messages. First, the child learns that the adult can praise or withhold the praise; inherent here is a power that is frightening to the child. If an adult says, "Good boy" or "Good girl," the child may be concerned or frightened that if he "messes up" he may no longer be "good." If an adult says, "I'm proud of you," the child may be concerned that the adult will not be "proud" if she doesn't do it "right" next time.

Professionals need to consider the difference between using encouragement and praise.[18] Encouragement acknowledges the adult's interest in the play/work of the child and reinforces that play/work. The use of praise inherently causes a value judgement—"good" and "bad"; "appropriate" and "inappropriate"; "right" and "wrong." The young child, still inherently so dependent on the adult, quickly understands that "if my actions can be 'good,' they can also be 'bad'; if my behavior is 'appropriate,' it can also be 'inappropriate'; and if my work can be 'right,' it can also be 'wrong.'" This is very frightening to a young child.

Encouragement, however, acknowledges interest in and respect for a child's efforts and is specific enough that there is no sweeping judgment of "goodness," "badness," "rightness," or "wrongness." Examples of encouragement are:

You jumped 2 feet!
You threw that ball and hit the target!
You bobbled the balloon 8 times before it hit the floor!
You hopped on your other foot! All right!
You wheeled your chair up the ramp! Way to be!
Show me how you run fast. Whew . . . that was fast!
You climbed over that huge cube mat!

Teachers who care about children and their feelings struggle with a way to communicate caring and love without communicating "power." Adults who use the following type of language need to leave the field:

No—not like that!
No way.
You can't be serious.
Your brother was such a great kid, what happened to you?
Why can't you be like . . .

Young children (and older children and adults, for that matter) do not need to be treated with that type of disrespect. There is nothing to be gained, and young souls to be lost.

Cultural Diversity in the Active Learning Centers

The preschool motor/play specialist needs to be particularly sensitive to the diverse cultures, socioeconomic backgrounds, genders, and abilities/disabilities of the children served. Even very young children begin to develop stereotypical notions regarding performance and potential. The wisest response from educators is to openly address issues related to culture, socioeconomic forces, gender, age, and ability/disability, and, specifically, be willing to address the many questions that young children will raise.

According to Derman Sparks and the A.B.C. Task Force[10]:

Research data reveal that:
- Children begin to notice differences and construct classificatory and evaluative categories very early.
- There are overlapping but distinguishable developmental tasks and steps in the construction of identity and attitudes.
- Societal stereotyping and bias influence children's self-concept and attitudes toward others.

Even the young child is engaged in the process of sorting and categorizing. By age 3 many children have begun to notice gender, racial, and cultural differences and may have begun to notice children with physical disabilities, in particular. This process begins earlier. According to Derman-Sparks and the A.B.C. Task Force[10]:

By 2 years of age, children are learning the appropriate use of gender labels (girl, boy) and learning color names, which they begin to apply to skin color. By 3 years of age (and sometimes even earlier), children show signs of being influenced by societal norms and biases and may exhibit "pre-prejudice" toward others on the basis of gender or race or being differently abled. Between 3 and 5 years of age, chil-

dren try to figure out what are the essential attributes of their selfhood, what aspects of self remain constant. By 4 or 5 years of age, children not only engage in gender-appropriate behavior defined by socially prevailing norms, they also reinforce it among themselves without adult intervention. They use racial reasons for refusing to interact with children different from themselves and exhibit discomfort and rejection of differently abled people. The degree to which 4-year-olds have already internalized stereotypic gender roles, racial bias, and fear of the differently abled forcefully points out the need for antibias education with young children.

Antibias education is particularly crucial if young children with disabilities are to be included in preschool programs.[30] Froschl and Sprung[14] observed 158 preschoolers between the ages of 2½ and 5 years. They noted that girls and children with disabilities were likely to be overhelped and overpraised. They wrote:

If a 3-year-old boy and girl are getting ready to go out to play and are attempting to put on jackets, the girl is more likely to receive help. If both receive help, the girl will probably have her jacket put on for her, the boy will be shown a technique for putting it on himself. If the same situation arises and one child is disabled, it is the disabled child who will have the jacket put on, whether a girl or a boy. This is the beginning of the syndrome of "learned helplessness."

The preschool movement/play specialist must be part of the cadre of professionals who are willing to create a learning environment in which each child is embraced and nurtured. There are vast opportunities to explore cultural, socioeconomic, gender, age, and ability/disability issues within the learning environment. Henninger[19] wrote:

To insure that multicultural play experiences happen, learning centers must be arranged in such a way that diversity issues encountered elsewhere and those inherent in the materials themselves can be understood as children select materials and engage in playful interactions with them and their peers. Rather than "visiting" these multicultural experiences for brief, disconnected learning opportunities children can more naturally experience diverse cultures when multicultural materials and activities are integrated into the art, manipulative, housekeeping, dramatic play, and outdoor learning centers.

To create an antibias learning environment within the active learning center, the preschool adapted physical educator must do the following:

1. Display posters and photographs of people that re-

flect a broad variety of cultures, socioeconomic status, gender, age, and ability/disability.

  a. Posters and photographs should empower all children.

  b. Posters and photographs should correctly reflect daily life with an emphasis on movement, sport, recreation, and leisure activities.

2. Use records/cassettes of various types of music common to the cultures of children in the program.

  a. Ask parents to share records/cassettes of music that reflects their culture.

  b. Use a broad assortment of records/cassettes that feature males and females as lead performer.

  c. Choose a broad assortment of records/cassettes that feature young and old performers.

  d. Use records/cassettes that reflect diversity.

    (1) "You Are Super the Way You Are" *(Joining Hands with Other Lands)*

    (2) "Mi Casa, My House" *(Joining Hands with Other Lands)*

    (3) "Somos El Barco" *(Head First and Belly Down)*

    (4) "Sister Rosa" (The Neville Brothers)

    (5) "Native American names" *(Joining Hands with Other Lands)*

    (6) "La Bamba" *(Dancin' Magic)*

    (7) "Shake It to the One You Love the Best" *(Shake It to the One You Love the Best,* Cheryl Mattox)

  e. Use records/cassettes that honor young children as they are.

    (1) "Ugly Duckling" *(We All Live Together,* Volume IV, Greg and Steve)

    (2) "What a Miracle" *(Walter the Waltzing Worm,* Hap Palmer)

    (3) "Free to Be You and Me" *(Free to Be You and Me,* Marlo Thomas)

    (4) "Self Esteem" (B.E.S.T. Friends)

3. Use records/cassettes that include culturally distinctive instruments.

4. Provide a variety of cultural musical instruments:

  a. Kenyan double stick drum

  b. Zulu marimba

  c. Indian sarangi

  d. Mexican guiro

  e. West African balaphon

  f. Japanese den den

  g. Native American dance bells

  h. Chilean rainstick

5. Teach dances that reflect a variety of cultures and experiences.

  a. Ask parents and grandparents of the children to teach the songs and dances of their childhood.

  b. Provide materials of color that have cultural connotations to enhance celebrations and studies of different cultures (e.g., red and gold to celebrate Chinese festivals, and red, white and green to represent the Mexican flag for Cinco de Mayo celebrations).

6. Introduce simple games that reflect a variety of cultures and experiences. Ask parents and grandparents of the children to teach simple games.

7. Use language that is gender-free when referring to the activities and play of children. If the child, for example, is zooming about the room "pretending to be," be certain the words you use reflect no bias. The child is a "firefighter," a "member of the police force," a "postal worker," etc.

8. Read and act out stories of children involved in diverse play, sport, leisure, and recreation experiences.

The creation of an antibias active learning center provides young children with yet one more learning experience that honors young children. The preschool adapted physical education specialist can also help embrace diversity by encouraging the preschool educators to provide dolls, puppets, and puzzles for the classroom that reflect children with disabilities.

SUMMARY

New federal and state initiatives have had a dramatic impact on early childhood intervention and preschool education programs. A heightened respect for the integrity of the family unit, in whatever form, and a sense that infants, toddlers, and young children should be educated in the most natural, least restrictive environment has placed a new emphasis on providing services to infants and toddlers within the home and the child's community and on providing educational services to preschoolers in private and public child care and other natural settings.

The preschool movement/play specialist or the preschool adapted physical education specialist has a unique role to play in the child development process. The specialist's role, like that of other adapted physical educators, has changed drastically, and the professional must now be a consultant, or a teacher of teachers—including the parent.

A developmentally appropriate learning environment for infants, toddlers, and young children is one in which adults are sensitive to the unique needs of the children and are responsive to those needs. The learning environment allows active exploration with others and with materials. A developmentally appropriate learning environment for movement reflects the same needs.

Review Questions

1. Compare and contrast the behavior of a typically developing infant, toddler, or preschooler with that of an infant, toddler, or preschooler who has a delay or disability.
2. Explain the differences between IDEA, Part H, and IDEA, Part B, mandates.
3. List and describe each of Gardner's eight forms of intelligence.
4. Explain how you could assess a young child to determine his or her level of each of Gardner's eight forms of intelligence.
5. Describe modeling techniques that parents or teachers could use to improve an infant's or toddler's motor and play skills.
6. Describe developmentally appropriate assessment practices for preschool-age children.
7. Describe developmentally appropriate intervention programs for preschool-age children.
8. Describe a developmentally appropriate preschool learning environment.
9. Describe essential elements of an antibias active learning center.

Student Activities

1. Visit a child care center and evaluate the play units in their outdoor play area. Write a paper describing what you saw and your evaluation of the adequacy of the play units.
2. Using the motor development delay indicators tool presented in this chapter (see box on pp. 250-251), evaluate the movement of a preschooler.
3. In small groups, discuss the types of preschool movement programs that might have prevented or diminished Billy Bogg's perceptual-motor deficits. Share your group's observations with the rest of the class.
4. Working in small groups, design an active learning center for indoor play and one for outdoor play. Present your group's center to the rest of the class and explain the purpose of each component and why it was included in the plan.

References

1. Bergen D: *Play as the vehicle for early intervention with at-risk infants and toddlers.* Paper presented at the annual conference of the American Educational Research Association, Chicago, April 1991.
2. Berk L: Vygotsky's theory: the importance of make-believe play, *Young Child,* Nov 30-39, 1994.
3. Berk L, Winsler A: *Scaffolding children's learning: Vygotsky and early childhood education,* Washington, DC, 1995, National Association for the Education of Young Children.
4. Berrueta-Clement J et al: Changed lives: the effects of the Perry Preschool Program on youths through age 19, *Monographs of the High/Scope Educational Research Foundation,* No 8, Ypsilanti, Mich, 1985, High/Scope Press.
5. Cowden J, Torrey C: A ROADMAP for assessing infants, toddlers, and preschoolers: the role of the adapted motor developmentlist, *Adapt Phys Act Q* 12:1-11, 1995.
6. Crais E: *"Best practices" with preschoolers: assessing within the context of a family-centered approach,* Chapel Hill, NC, 1991, Carolina Institute for Research on Infant Personnel Preparation, Frank Porter Grahman Child Development Center.
7. Curry N, Arnaud S: Personality difficulties in preschool children as revealed through play themes and styles, *Young Child,* May 4-9, 1995.
8. Dawkins C et al: Perspectives on early intervention, *Except Parent,* Feb 23-27, 1994.
9. *A Day with Daniel N. Stern, M.D.* Presentation sponsored by the Texas Association for Infant Mental Health, Feb 20, 1995.
10. Derman-Sparks C, ABC Task Force: *Anti-bias curriculum: tools for empowering young children,* Washington, DC, 1989, National Association for the Education of Young Children.
11. *Developmentally appropriate practice in movement programs for young children ages 3-5,* Reston, Va, 1994, National Association for Sport and Physical Education.
12. Dodge D, Colker L: *The creative curriculum for early childhood,* Washington, DC, 1992, Teaching Strategies.
13. Eddowes EA: Drawing in early childhood: predictable stages, *Dimens Early Child,* pp 16-18, fall 1995.
14. Froschl M, Sprung B: Providing an anti-handicappist early childhood environment, *Interracial Books Child Bull* 14:7-8, 1983.

15. Gardner H: *Frames of mind: the theory of multiple intelligences,* New York, 1983, Basic Books.
16. Gowen J: The early development of symbolic play, *Young Child,* pp 75-84, March 1995.
17. Hayes T, Shaffer K, Wiens A: *Promising practices: active learning lab.* Presentation at the Texas Education Agency "Promising Practices" conference, Austin, Tex, fall 1994.
18. Hendrickson-Pfeill S: Encouragement, *Communication Skill Builders,* 1990.
19. Henninger M: Supporting multicultural awareness at learning centers, *Dimens Early Child,* pp 20-23, summer 1995.
20. Howard Gardner on the eighth intelligence: seeing the natural world—an interview, *Dimens Early Child,* pp 5-6, summer 1995.
21. Huettig C, Powell C, Hughes, J: *The Walnut Hill Project: preschoolers and their choice of playmates,* Research in progress, Dallas, Texas, Independent School District.
22. Huettig C, Pyfer J: *The motor portfolio assessment process with young at-risk children.* Presentation at the First Annual National Conference on At-Risk Children and Youth, Denton, Tex, June 1995.
23. Huettig C, Tomlinson D: *The Macon project: a developmentally appropriate school-based inclusion project for at-risk children.* Presentation at the First Annual National Conference on At-Risk Children and Youth, Denton, Tex, June, 1995.
24. Huettig C, Tomlinson D, Hudson C: *The Macon Project: a developmentally appropriate preschool inclusion project* (in press).
25. Hughes F, Elicker J, Veen L: A program of play for infants and their caregivers, *Young Child,* pp 52-88, Jan 1995.
26. Lally J: The impact on child care policies and practices on infant/toddler identity formation, *Young Child,* pp 34-36, Nov 1995.
27. Lamorey S, Bricker D: Integrated programs: effects on young children and their parents. In Peck C, Odom S, Bricker D, editors: *Integrating young children with disabilities into community programs,* Baltimore, 1993, Paul H Brookes Publishing.
28. Linder T: *Transdisciplinary play-based assessment: a functional approach to working with young children,* Baltimore, 1993, Paul H Brookes Publishing.
29. Linder T: *Transdisciplinary play-based intervention: guidelines for developing a meaningful curriculum for young children,* Baltimore, 1993, Paul H Brookes Publishing.
30. Lubeck S: The politics of developmentally appropriate practice: exploring issues of culture, class, and curriculum. In Mallory B, New R, editors: *Diversity and developmentally appropriate practices: challenges for early childhood education,* New York, 1994, Teachers College Press.
31. Meisels SJ: Developmental screening in early childhood: the interaction of research and social policy. In Breslow

L, Fielding JE, Love LB, editors: *Annual review of public health,* vol 9, Palo Alto, Calif, 1988, Annual Reviews.
32. Meisels S, Provence S: *Screening and assessment: guidelines for identifying young disabled and developmentally vulnerable children and their families,* Washington, DC, 1989, National Center for Clinical Infant Programs.
33. Miller K: *The outside play and learning book: activities for young children,* Mt Ranier, Md, 1989, Gryphon House.
34. Millspaugh, F, Segelman M: Neither fear nor pity: public-service announcements about differences. In Harmonay M, editor: *Promise and performance: children with special needs,* Cambridge, Mass, 1977, Ballinger Publishing.
35. *"Natural Environment" draft policy recommendations,* Texas Interagency Council on Early Childhood Intervention, March 31, 1995.
36. Notari-Syverson A, Shuster S: Putting real-life skills into IEP/IFSP's for infants and young children, *Teach Except Child,* pp 29-32, winter 1995.
37. Powell C: Personal communication, 1995, Instructional Specialist, Preschool Program for Children with Disabilities/Speech and Language Pathologist, Dallas, Texas, Independent School District.
38. Prizant B, Meyer E: Socioemotional aspects of communication disorders in young children and their families, *Am J Speech-Lang Pathol* 2:56-71, 1993.
39. Rivkin M: *The great outdoors: restoring children's right to play outside,* Washington, DC, 1995, National Association for the Education of Young Children.
40. Rubin K, Fein G, Vandenberg B: Play. In Hetherington E, editor: *Handbook of child psychology, vol 4, Socialization, personality, and social development,* New York, 1983, John Wiley & Sons.
41. Shepard L: The challenges of assessing young children appropriately, *Phi Delta Kappan,* pp 206-212, Nov 1994.
42. Simeonsson R: Family involvement in multidisciplinary team evaluation: professional and parent perspectives, *Child Care Health Dev* 21:109-215, 1995.
43. Vygotsky L: The role of play in development. In Cole R et al, editors: *Mind in society,* Cambridge, Mass, 1978, Harvard University Press.
44. Washington V, Johnson V, McCracken J: *Grassroots success preparing schools and families for each other,* WK Kellogg Readiness Initiatives, Washington, DC, 1995, National Association for the Education of Young Children.
45. Wetherby A: *Communication and language intervention for preschool children,* Buffalo, NY, 1992, Educom.
46. Wetherby A: *Best practices for enhancing communication and education for children with autism or pervasive developmental disorder.* Presentation at the Region X Education Service Center, Richardson, Tex, Aug 20, 1994.
47. Winston P: *Working with families in early intervention: interdisciplinary perspectives,* Chapel Hill, NC, 1990, Carolina Institute for Research on Infant Personnel Preparation.

Suggested Readings

Bredekamp S: *Developmentally appropriate practice in early childhood programs serving children from birth through age 8,* Washington, DC, 1992, National Association for the Education of Young Children.

Dodge D, Colker L: *The creative curriculum for early childhood,* Washington DC, 1992, Teaching Strategies.

Nelsen J, Erwin C, Duffy R: *Positive discipline for preschoolers,* Rocklin, Calif, 1995, Prima Publishing.

Piper MC, Darrah J: *Motor assessment of the developing infant,* Orlando, Fla, 1994, WB Saunders.

Mental Retardation

Objectives

Define mental retardation.

Explain the variability of characteristics among individuals who are mentally retarded.

Recognize the need for differential programming for individuals who are severely mentally retarded.

Select appropriate activities depending on the age and level of functioning of each person.

Explain procedures for appropriate placement and programming of individuals in the least restrictive environment.

Scenario

Kaneisha is a 16-year-old girl who attends an urban high school that serves children with severe/profound mental retardation. In her most recent 3-year comprehensive assessment, it was determined that she has an IQ of 35. Kaneisha has been living with her grandmother and her two younger brothers since the age of 13 years. At that time, she saw her mother murdered on her front porch in an ill-fated drug deal. Since that time, she has experienced serious depression and cries often and easily.

Kaneisha is a truly gifted natural athlete. A streetball basketball player, she averaged 18 points per game in Special Olympics basketball competition in 1994 and 1995. Her bowling average is 118. She can put the shot a distance of 6.5 meters. She runs the 100-yard dash in 17 seconds.

Task

As you read this chapter, think about how Kaneisha could use her athletic skill after she finishes school. Make a list of the types of activities she might want to learn so that she can stay active after her school years. Also think about the type of support systems and other skills and knowledge (transportation, money handling, social interaction) she will need to participate successfully in activities in a large urban area.

I t is now recognized that mental retardation is not a fixed, unalterable condition that condemns an individual to a static, deprived lifetime of failure to achieve. Rather, today we understand that cognitive, psychomotor, and affective behaviors are dynamic processes that, if properly stimulated, can be developed further than ever before imagined. Early concepts of mental retardation viewed the condition as an inherited disorder that was essentially incurable. This notion resulted in hopelessness on the part of professionals and social and physical separation of persons who were mentally retarded. After years of research and innovative programming, it is now recognized that intelligence and other functions depend on the readiness and experience of the child, the degree and quality of environmental stimulation, and many other variables.

In the late 1960s and early 1970s institutions that served persons with mental retardation began designing and implementing educational programs intended to develop independent living skills to enable these persons to function in community settings. As institutionalized individuals rose to the challenge of these educational programs, a movement began to promote their placement in communities. During the 1970s thousands of persons with mental retardation were removed from institutions and allowed to take their rightful place as contributing members of communities.

As institutions began to develop viable educational programs, public schools took up their responsibility toward young children with mental retardation who lived in the communities. Professionals trained in appropriate teaching techniques were hired by the school systems to provide educational opportunities for these children. As a result of efforts by both institutions for persons with mental retardation and public school systems, all except those individuals who are the most severely mentally retarded are living, going to school, and working in the community. Today, these individuals have more opportunities for optimum social interaction than ever before.

However, the social awareness and commitment required to maximize the physical and social community opportunities for individuals with mental retardation are still in their infancy.

Definition

The labels assigned to different groups of individuals with mental retardation vary depending on who is doing the labeling.[38] Traditionally, levels of retardation were determined by IQ scores. The 1994 edition of the *Diagnostic and Statistical Manual of Mental Disorders,*[2] while recognizing the importance of adaptive functioning, bases severity of intellectual impairment on the following IQ scores: (a) mild = 50 or 55 to approximately 70; moderate = 35 or 40 to 50 or 55; severe = 20 or 25 to 35 or 40; and profound = below 20 or 25. The definition of mental retardation that was adapted by the American Association on Mental Retardation (AAMR) in May 1992 reads as follows[1]:

> **Mental retardation** refers to substantial limitations in certain personal capabilities. It is manifested as significantly subaverage intellectual functioning, existing concurrently with related disabilities in two or more of the following applicable **adaptive skill areas:** communication, self-care, home living, social skills, community use, self-direction, health and safety, functional academics, leisure, and work. Mental retardation begins before age 18.

The AAMR 1992 definition differs from past definitions in three ways:

1. Mental retardation refers to substantial limitations in certain, but not all, personal capabilities. The personal capabilities identified include cognitive, functional, and social abilities.
2. Mental retardation is manifested as significantly subaverage intellectual functioning plus related disabilities in two or more specific adaptive skill areas. The inclusion of at least two specific adaptive skill areas ensures the inclusion of individuals who are limited in fully accessing independent functioning in our society.
3. The fact that mental retardation must be evident before age 18 is clearly stated; however, the condition may not always be of lifelong duration. The recognition that mental retardation is not necessarily permanent speaks directly to a point many of us have argued for years. That is, with appropriate and timely intervention services, individuals

who are born mentally retarded can be taught to perform to acceptable (normal) personal and social standards. Clearly, we must increase our efforts to use the most up-to-date information and technology to help individuals who are mentally retarded advance to the point where they can become fully functioning, independent citizens in society.

The AAMR classification system includes only two levels: mild and severe retardation. The diagnostic system is divided into six parts: (1) intellectual functioning and adaptive skills, (2) psychological and emotional considerations, (3) health and physical considerations, (4) etiological considerations; (5) environmental considerations, and (6) appropriate supports. Use of this diagnostic system yields an overall profile of each mentally retarded individual that should greatly facilitate programming for these students.

In applying the definition, the following four assumptions are essential:

1. Specific adaptive disabilities often coexist with strengths in other adaptive skills or other personal capabilities.
2. The existence of disabilities in adaptive skills occurs within the context of community environments typical of the individual's age peers and is indexed to the person's individualized needs for support.
3. With appropriate supports over a sustained period, the life functioning of the person with mental retardation will generally improve.
4. Valid assessment considers cultural and language diversity.

According to the AAMR definition, mental retardation is environmentally determined; therefore an IQ score is not used to determine the severity of retardation. Instead, individuals are assessed in 10 adaptive skill areas: communication, home living, community use, health and safety, leisure, self-care, social skills, self-direction, functional academics, and work.

The level of retardation (mild or severe) is based on functioning in the adaptive skill areas and on the amount of support the individual needs. The four levels of support are:

1. *No support needed:* The person is either self-sufficient or can procure needed supports on his or her own.

2. *Minimal support:* The person needs intermittent help or support in areas such as case management, transportation, home living, physical health, employment, and self-advocacy.
3. *Substantial/extensive support:* The person needs regular, ongoing support, which includes instruction, assistance (such as attendant care), and/or supervision within a designated adaptive skill area.
4. *Pervasive/consistent support:* The person needs constant care on a 24-hour basis, which may include the maintenance of life-support systems.

The public schools have not adopted the AAMR definition. Rather, they are adhering to the definition that appears in the Rules for Implementing the Individuals with Disabilities Education Act (IDEA). That definition reads[57]:

> Mental retardation means significantly subaverage general intellectual functioning existing concurrently with deficits in adaptive behavior and manifested during the developmental period that adversely affects a child's educational performance.

Most schools consider an IQ score lower than 70 as significant subaverage general intellectual functioning. Thus IQ scores lower than 70 accompanied by deficits in adaptive behavior qualify a student for the mental retardation classification and services. If the public schools in this country were to adopt AAMR's two sug-

table 11-1

Characteristics of Mild and Severe Levels of Mental Retardation	
Mild Retardation	**Severe Retardation**
IQ of 70 to 35	IQ of 35 or below
Insufficient school progress in regular class	Needs training focusing on self-help skills
Minimum educability in reading, writing, spelling, math	Likely to be dependent on others for care
Capacity for school adjustment to a point	Noticeable motor deficits
	Physical and motor problems
Needs special adaptation for appropriate education	Restricted movement
Can manage independently in the community	Skeletal deformities
Can make productive adjustments at an unskilled or semiskilled level	Sensory disorders
	Seizure disorders

gested levels of mental retardation, IQ scores and adaptive behaviors that might be used to assist in identifying types of needed services at each of the two levels of retardation could be defined in a manner similar to that presented in Table 11-1.

Incidence

Because the newer definitions of mental retardation depend on adaptive behaviors, as well as a lowered IQ score, the number of citizens classified as retarded is far lower than that reported in past years. For example, the number of children and youth reportedly served by Part B of P.L. 94-142 and Chapter 1 of the Elementary and Secondary Education Act during 1987 to 1988 was 539,717. During the 1992 to 1993 school year, the number of children and youth reported to be served under federal requirements was 484,871.[72]

Before 1988 many children with an IQ score of less than 85 (1 standard deviation below the mean score of 100) who were having difficulty adapting to school requirements would have been placed in special education programs. However, since that time the cutoff score for the classification of mental retardation was reduced to 70 (2 standard deviations below the mean score of 100). Thus, just by changing the definition, the incidence of mental retardation in this country was reduced from 16% to 3% of the population.[36]

Causes

The causes of mental retardation include, but are not limited to:

- Chromosomal abnormalities, such as Down syndrome and fragile X syndrome
- Genetic metabolic disorders such as phenylketonuria (PKU) and Tay-Sachs disease
- Infections such as rubella and meningitis
- Poisoning from lead or drugs
- Traumatic head and brain injury
- Socioeconomic and environmental factors, including poverty[9]

Characteristics

Although research tends to generalize the characteristics of mental retardation, these individuals are diverse in cognitive, social, and physical functions. The performance of athletes with mental retardation in the 1995 Special Olympics International games, where performance exceeded expectations, is testimony for their competence. On the other hand, some persons with mental retardation are unable to participate in regular sport events and need modification of the activities to be successful in their efforts to play. Other persons with severe mental retardation may not be ambulatory or have the physical capability needed to participate in play of any sort.

Because of the diversity within the group, it is difficult to generalize a set of characteristics to the total population. However, there are general characteristics that are representative of the group. The cognitive and physical characteristics of this population provide basic guidelines and alert the physical educator to the potential nature of the physical education programs they need.

Cognitive Characteristics Related to Skill

The cognitive capabilities of persons who are mentally retarded may vary greatly. In addition to the considerable variability in intelligence as measured by standardized tests, individuals will demonstrate variance in processing information, comprehension, and memory. However, some may have aspects of intelligence that are superior to many with so-called "normal" intelligence. For instance, some persons with mental retardation have phenomenal memories.

As a group, persons who are mentally retarded are not as adept in perceptual attributes that relate to motor skills as are comparable nonretarded individuals. They may be clumsy and awkward and lack balance, which would affect their ability to perform motor tasks efficiently. A review of the literature reveals that there are many perceptual and cognitive characteristics that may inhibit the learning of motor skills. Examples are less preparation and slower actual movement times.[70] Also, when compared with other persons, they are less able to spontaneously predict changing conditions of a motor task. They are slower than others to estimate the amount of time needed to plan activities,[33] and to intercept moving objects.[19] Yabe et al.[78] reported that as subjects with IQs of 40 and above increased in chronological age, their reaction times and individual variability decreased. Thus it is reasonable to expect individuals who are mentally retarded to continually grow and develop. Well-designed physical education programs can promote this growth.

Persons with severe mental retardation most likely have adverse performance in social, cognitive, language, and motor development. Many students who are severely mentally retarded have difficulty interacting with others. This may stem from abnormal behavior, which may include self-abusive acts, as well as behavior that is injurious to others. Furthermore, stereotypical behaviors and bizarre acts such as rocking back and forth, waving the hands in front of the eyes, and making strange noises may also adversely affect social interaction with others. In addition, those individuals who are severely mentally retarded may have problems with self-help skills, such as dressing, feeding, and basic motor functioning.

Attention, Memory, and Decision Making

Two important aspects to learning motor skills are the attention that one gives to the instructional task and the ability to remember and respond to movement cues. De-Pauw and Ferrari[25] indicate that individuals who are not mentally retarded have a more difficult time performing tasks when some interference occurs than do persons with mental retardation. Thus once individuals who are mentally retarded are on task, they are not distracted by extraneous cues and information. Furthermore, Newell[52] found no difference between subjects who were mentally retarded and those who were not on adopting memory strategies for the recall of movement cues on a motor task. Thus it would seem that persons with mental retardation can make improvements in their movement accuracy if they are helped to understand and remember essential movement information.

Decision-making capability varies widely among persons with mental retardation. Some persons with mental retardation may be able to make decisions that enable independent functioning in the community, whereas others may be totally dependent on others for cognitive decisions. One unique study that focused on the impact of exercise on problem-solving skills reported that moderate-intensity exercise (55% to 60% $Vo_{2\ max}$) for 20 minutes resulted in an increase in speed of problem solving in teenagers with average IQ scores of 60.[20] It has also been shown that persons with mental retardation can be made aware of **exertion levels** during physical exercise[6] and can successfully engage in **self-management practices.**[29]

Persons who are severely mentally retarded frequently have impaired cognitive and language development. Many are unable to respond to simple commands.

An adolescent with mental retardation experiences the challenge of an "in-the-trees" ropes course. (Courtesy Wisconsin Lions Camp, Rosholt, Wis.)

Thus it is difficult for them to grasp instruction. Furthermore, they may lack the ability to generalize skills learned in one setting to another setting. They often have problems with language. This further makes communication during instruction difficult.

Motor Development Delays

Motor delays are very common among persons who are severely mentally retarded. Delays in developing postural reflexes[55] impact the ability to perform such basic tasks as grasping objects, holding the head up, sitting, standing, and walking. In addition, these delays, to varying degrees, negatively impact their motor and physical capabilities. They may be less capable in areas of strength, flexibility, agility, coordination, and balance.

Postural Development

Many individuals who are mentally retarded have postural abnormalities that include malalignment of the trunk or the legs. One of the most obvious postural deficiencies is that of the protruding abdomen, which may be associated with obesity[61] and/or lack of abdominal strength. In addition, because of depth perception problems and/or delayed vestibular and equilibrium reflex development, there may be a tendency to hold the head flexed, externally rotate the legs, and use a wide base of support when walking and running. Delays in reflex development always result in delays in the appearance of motor milestones.[35]

Physical Fitness Development

The cardiovascular system is less well developed in many individuals who are mentally retarded; however, it is usually very low in individuals who are profoundly retarded.[17,45] In many individuals, regardless of retardation level, poor respiration and susceptibility to respiratory infections may accompany the underdeveloped cardiovascular system. There is, however, strong evidence that physical fitness, including cardiovascular endurance, can be developed through training regimens.

Canadian Special Olympic athletes who were given the opportunity to participate in the Manitoba Special Olympics Medallion Program demonstrated outstanding improvement in physical fitness and performance levels. The Medallion Program is a 6-month-long intensive, three-times-a-week training program for selected Special Olympic athletes in Manitoba. The program combines both fitness and skill-specific training similar to generic sport training, as well as nutritional counseling.[5] The Canadian program verifies what many of us who have worked closely with these individuals through the years believe: when individuals with mental retardation are given appropriate practice opportunities and guidance, they will demonstrate high levels of fitness and motor performance.

Individuals with mental retardation who have not been given opportunities to exercise and build work capacity demonstrate low levels of function.[18] When provided instruction in physical fitness and given opportunities to practice, they will demonstrate improvement, but at a slower rate than their peers who are not retarded.[17,56] Investigations using subjects who are mentally retarded indicate that it is possible to strengthen all muscle groups when using appropriate training regimens.[5,62,79]

Social Development

The social characteristics of individuals who are mentally retarded also vary greatly. Some persons with mental retardation are dependable, cooperative, and can delay their gratification, whereas others are self-centered and impulsive.[64]

Competition

Competition is an important motivator to bring out the best efforts of athletes. While evidence exists that persons who are mentally retarded can benefit through competition such as Special Olympics, some youngsters who are retarded may not understand the concept of competition. The athlete who is severely mentally retarded may not comprehend "run as fast as you can," "jump as high as you can," and "score more points than your opponent." Also, studies show that besting an opponent is not important to some persons with mental retardation,[80] and as a result, their competitive performance is not adversely affected by anxiety.[58] Because individuals with mental retardation frequently demonstrate lower levels of self-determination than others in the same situations,[75] their workouts must be supervised by individuals willing to motivate them to persist.

Testing to Determine Functioning Levels

Development of the individual education program (IEP) requires that present functioning levels be determined. Several formal tests that can be used with students with mental retardation are listed in Table 2-1. Preference should be given to measuring physical fitness, locomotor skills, object-handling skills, and balance. Reliable strength measures can be obtained from individuals who are mentally retarded.[69] When strength is being measured, it is suggested that the mean of three trials be used to best represent the individual's capability.[40,41] For those individuals who appear to demonstrate poor posture, postural alignment should be assessed and followed by specific programming to correct any abnormalities. Other acceptable ways to evaluate the functioning levels of this population are task analysis and observation of the students as they perform a hierarchical sequence of activities. These techniques are described in Chapters 4 and 6.

One of the most difficult problems of testing individuals with mental retardation is determining whether poor comprehension or poor motor development is the reason for their inability to perform a specific task. Because it is difficult to determine whether a student who is mentally retarded understands directions given during test situations, the following suggestions may help the evaluator elicit the best performance possible:

1. If, after the student has been told what to do, the response is incorrect, demonstrate the position or movement.
2. If demonstration does not elicit the correct performance, manually place the student in or through the desired position or pattern.
3. Use positive reinforcement (praise, tokens, free play) to encourage the student.

When students who are severely mentally retarded are tested, it may be necessary to use an anatomical task analysis (see Chapter 2) to determine their level of capability.

Because persons with mental retardation who participate in competitive sports such as Special Olympics are more likely than most athletes to experience sport-specific injuries,[71] it is strongly recommended that physical examinations that are tailored to each athlete be administered before participation. Athletes with Down syndrome should always be assessed for **atlanto-axial instability** before participation.

Special Considerations

The three most common causes of mental retardation are fetal alcohol syndrome (FAS), Down syndrome, and fragile X syndrome. Because of their prevalence in this country, each of these causative factors is discussed here.

Fetal Alcohol Syndrome

Fetal alcohol syndrome is the leading known cause of mental retardation (2.2 in 1000 live births).[9] It is caused by maternal alcohol abuse during pregnancy and results in severe mental retardation because of impaired brain development. More than 80% of children with FAS have prenatal and postnatal growth deficiencies, microcephaly, and characteristic facial features (saddle-shaped nose and gap between the front teeth). Poor motor coordination, hypotonia, and attention deficit–hyperactivity disorders are characteristic of half of the children.[13] The severest form of FAS results from the mother's heavy

drinking during pregnancy; lesser degrees of alcohol abuse result in milder forms of FAS.[9]

Down Syndrome

Down syndrome is the most common chromosomal disorder leading to mental retardation. The incidence rates are about 1 in 1000, of whom 80% score between 25 to 50 on IQ tests.[8] Some physical characteristics of individuals with Down syndrome are:

- Small skull
- Slanting, almond-shaped eyes
- Ears slightly smaller than average
- Flat-bridged nose
- Protruding tongue
- Palmar crease
- Short stature
- Short fingers
- Short limbs
- Short neck
- Overweight
- Substantial delays in reflex integration
- Varied levels of mental retardation
- Looseness of joints
- Lack of muscle tone during infancy

There has been considerable interest by researchers concerning the specific physical and motor characteristics of individuals with Down syndrome. There is evidence that when compared with the general population, this population differs in the following ways:

- May demonstrate less power and strength[63]
- May function lower than average on cardiovascular measures[45]
- May have deficient leg strength associated with lower cardiovascular measures[45]
- May begin the aging process earlier than expected[51]
- May have less capability for decision making that relates to motor control[47]
- May have difficulty in planning goal-directed movements[39]
- May evidence a greater incidence of obesity
- May have atlantoaxial instability

It is believed that effective programs of physical activity may significantly impact physical and psychomotor deficiencies. Clinical intervention programs that begin early in life can promote reflex integration, vestibular function, and kinesthetic impulses that impact muscle tonicity. Development of these input systems is critical to gaining locomotor and object control patterns and skills. Other intervention programs have also been shown to be effective. Ulrich et al.[72] demonstrated facilitation of stable walking patterns through the use of treadmill programming. Once locomotor and object skills are developed, the child with Down syndrome will be more likely to participate actively with peers and perhaps reduce the chance of developing obesity.

Atlantoaxial instability

The atlantoaxial segments of the cervical spine of children with Down syndrome may have a tendency for development of localized anomalies that are in danger of atlantoaxial dislocation. As a result of this potential danger, in 1983 a group of physicians, including experts in sports medicine and the surgeon general of the United States, met at the Joseph P. Kennedy, Jr., Foundation to discuss the perceived dangers of atlantoaxial instability among individuals with Down syndrome. Of particular concern were the thousands of athletes in Special Olympics with Down syndrome.

The incidence of atlantoaxial instability is in question. The range of incidence is reported to be from 10% to 30% of the population with Down syndrome. However, the public health department reports a 10% incidence.[4]

Atlantoaxial instability is a greater than normal mobility of the two upper cervical vertebrae—C1 and C2—at the top of the neck. The condition exposes the victims to possible serious injury if they forcibly flex the neck, because the vertebrae may shift and thereby squeeze or sever the spinal cord. A dislocation involves an actual displacement of the bone from the normal position in the joint. Awareness of the significance of the atlantoaxial instability can aid in the prevention of injuries at the upper cervical spine level. The instability is due to (1) the laxity of the transverse ligament that holds the odontoid process of the axis (C2) in place against the inner aspect of the inner arch of the atlas (C1) and (2) abnormalities of the odontoid. These conditions allow some leeway between the odontoid and the atlas, especially during flexion and extension of the neck. This results in an unstable joint. The atlantoaxial instability can be gradual and progressive.

The two types of symptoms of atlantoaxial dislocation are observable physical symptoms and neurological signs. Some of the behavior symptoms are:

- Deterioration in ambulatory skills
- Changes in bowel or bladder function
- Changes in neck posturing, neck pain, or limitations of neck movement
- Weakness of any of the extremities
- Progressive clumsiness and loss of coordination[14]

Some of the neurological signs associated with atlantoaxial dislocation are:

- Hypersensitivity
- Hyperreflexiveness
- Cloneness (there are certain abnormalities that are present in neurological examinations)
- Extensor plantar responses (i.e., abnormalities detected in the neurological examination)[14]

Precautionary measures to use with atlantoaxial instability. Special Olympics has taken the lead in the formulation of policies for the participation of athletes with Down syndrome who may have atlantoaxial instability. Tens of thousands of individuals with Down syndrome have participated in Special Olympics over the past 20 years. Although officials of Special Olympics International believe that none have suffered injury related to atlantoaxial instability while participating in Special Olympics training or competition, as a precaution, Special Olympics has developed a policy concerning participation in Special Olympics by individuals with Down syndrome.

Professionals in physical education need to be aware of the potential injury-inducing activities and situations for persons with atlantoaxial instability. The adapted physical educator should be aware of the student's medical status, including the condition of the atlantoaxial joint. Hopefully, results of medical examinations will be kept in the student's permanent health file at the school. The following guidelines from Special Olympics policy and the Committee on Sports Medicine[12] should be followed:

1. Check the medical files to determine which individuals have the atlantoaxial instability condition.
2. Restrict participation in gymnastics, diving, the butterfly stroke in swimming, the diving start in swimming competition, the high jump, soccer, and any warm-up exercises that place pressure on the muscles of the neck.
3. Discuss the medical options and the situation with the parents or guardians of the student.
4. Have the parents sign a consent form allowing the

child to participate in the physical education program.

5. Design a physical education program with activities that are not contraindicated for those with atlantoaxial instability.
6. Watch for the development of symptoms indicating a possible dislocation.
7. Adhere to the physician's recommendations.
8. Contact the parents and explain the importance of screening.

Further considerations. Davidson[24] has studied the recommendations for implementation of sports programs for students with Down syndrome at risk for atlantoaxial instability. His analysis of scientific information of the risk factor of permanent injury as a result of atlantoaxial instability requires consideration. He notes that the published papers on the issue indicate that there are no data with which to determine the incidence of atlantoaxial dislocation in contrast to instability among individuals with Down syndrome, and that there is little or no evidence that indicates that instability constitutes a predisposition for dislocation. He also notes that there is no evidence that the current roentgenogram criteria of atlantoaxial instability are predictive of a tendency toward dislocation. Furthermore, inasmuch as the evidence provided by Special Olympics indicates no knowledge of accidents in a 17-year history, he questions policies that would potentially exclude tens of thousands of individuals with Down syndrome every year from many sports on the basis of the evidence published to date.

Fragile X Syndrome

Fragile X syndrome is the most common inherited cause of mental retardation, and it is recognized as being second only to Down syndrome as a specific chromosomal cause of developmental disability.[8] Prevalence rates are estimated to be 1 in 1250 in males and 1 in 2250 in females.[54]

Cause

The condition is a result of an abnormally long X chromosome that appears to have "fragile" ends, hence its name.[68] The fragile site on the X chromosome results in a folic acid deficiency.[26] The fragile X syndrome usually expresses itself less fully in females because they have two X chromosomes, with one being normal and the other abnormal. Because males have only one X

chromosome, the condition manifests itself more fully. In addition, two distinct categories of variation at the fragile X locus have been identified. A mosaic premutation results in milder deleterious features than the fuller, nonmosaic, mutation.[8] The fuller mutation is the one associated with the developmental delays that impact development.[8]

Characteristics

Approximately 95% of the males with the full mutation are mentally retarded (moderate to severe range), whereas only about 50% of the females with the full mutation are mentally retarded; however, those who are not retarded usually demonstrate learning disabilities.

There are several differences in the physical features between the genders, with males being more affected than females. When full expression of the condition prevails, there are several distinct physical features in the newborn male. The baby may be large and have a high forehead, heavy lower jaw, large, low-set ears, and a large head, nose, hands, and feet. These features become more prominent with age with the face narrowing and lengthening.[54] Other distinguishing characteristics in males are large testicles (70% of the time), strabismus (56%), mitral valve prolapse (50%), hypotonia, and joint laxity (50%).[34] Behaviors demonstrated by males include autistic-like behaviors such as hand flapping, perseveration, hand biting, and poor eye contact. Frequently these children are hyperactive, have attention deficits, and engage in aggressive outbursts.[76]

Females have an increased prominence of ears, but few of the other physical characteristics that the males demonstrate.[76] They tend to be shy, depressed, anxious, hypersensitive, somewhat hyperactive as children, and socially impaired as adults.[8]

Whereas most young boys with fragile X syndrome demonstrate moderate mental retardation, some (estimates vary between 25% and 75%) tend to deteriorate cognitively with age. The greatest change in cognitive ability is seen between the ages of 8 and 13 years.[77] By adulthood the majority of males test in the moderate to severe range of mental retardation.[8] Interestingly, these males frequently have good verbal expressive skills and long-term memory; however, they have definite deficits in processing sequential information, receptive language skills, visual-spatial abilities, visual-motor coordination, and short-term memory.[8]

Approximately 50% of the females are mildly mentally retarded; those who are not retarded usually have learning disabilities, particularly in the area of mathematics.[65] Most of the females with fragile X syndrome, regardless of degree of affect, demonstrate deficits in short-term memory for nonverbal information, deficits in mental flexibility, and visual-motor performance deficits.[8]

Both genders frequently have sensory motor integration deficits that result in delayed balance (probably related to recurring middle ear infections), poor coordination, motor planning deficits, and tactile defensiveness.[34]

Intervention strategies

The physical limitations of the males require careful motor programming. Hypotonia and joint laxity could predispose students to a tendency to hyperextend joints during contact sports; strabismus could create depth perception difficulties that would limit success in games and sports requiring object control; and prolapsed mitral valve might limit cardiovascular endurance. Activities such as weight training could contribute muscle tone and greater joint stability, as well as enhanced self-esteem.

Both genders should receive sensory integration activities, particularly vestibular, kinesthetic, and tactile stimulation, as early in life as possible. Later in life, when motor skills are being learned, short-term memory lapse and difficulty mastering sequential information will require that attempts be made to teach the whole task in the context where it will be used.[48] The greater the teacher's success at presenting the "whole picture," the easier it will be for the student to learn.

Teaching Strategies

Persons with mental retardation constitute a very heterogeneous group. Many techniques of instruction are necessary to elicit a desired response. Therefore it is difficult to make generalizations that may be helpful in the instruction of physical education activities for persons with mental retardation. However, as a guide, some teaching principles are given in the box on p. 308.

Every student, regardless of disability, can learn.[27] The teaching methodology selected for use with individuals who are severely retarded depends on their age. All children who are mentally retarded should engage in a bottom, up developmental program in the early ages

Adult Special Olympians participate in a "new games" clinic. (Courtesy Wisconsin Special Olympics.)

of life because they need to develop their sensory motor and perceptual motor systems, as well as learn the basic elements of fundamental movement skills. A bottom, up approach is critical for persons who are severely or profoundly involved because of the extent to which they are motorically delayed. The Special Olympics Motor Activities Training Program (MATP) is designed for this population.

Older individuals who are severely retarded learn specific skills best when a defined instructional procedure that employs a top, down teaching approach is used. That procedure includes (1) assessing the present level of the student in defined target skills, (2) arranging the skills in an appropriate sequence so that objectives can be identified, (3) providing clear cues during the instructional process, (4) providing precise feedback immediately after the task is completed, (5) including strategies to promote generalization of skills to meaningful community environments, and (6) measuring and evaluating the performance gains to enable appropriate subsequent instructional decisions.

Behavior modification coupled with task analysis is usually recommended when teaching students who are mentally retarded.[7] This system involves selecting a signal or a request to cause the desired behavior. After selecting the skill to be taught, divide it into its component parts. Teach the parts using backward or forward

Strategies for Teaching Physical Education to Persons with Mental Retardation

1. Employ Methods That Are Compatible with Individualized Instruction

Use strong visual, tactile, and auditory stimuli for the children who are more severely involved, because these often bring the best results.

Have many activities available, because the attention span is short.

Use a systematic style of instruction where the behaviors are defined, measured, modeled, and monitored for acquisition.

Keep verbal directions to a minimum. They are often ineffective when teaching children who are more severely retarded.

Use demonstration as an effective instructional tool. It is particularly effective to use a peer demonstrator.

Use **manual guidance** as a method of instruction. The proprioceptors are great teachers of movement. The less ability the child has to communicate verbally, the more manual guidance should be considered as a tool for instruction.

Help students to develop sound self-management procedures so that they can learn to plan and complete tasks independently, evaluate their own performance, compare their performance with a standard, and make adjustments.[50]

Provide opportunities for choice of activities to foster self-motivation and decision making[11]; these practices decrease social avoidance and reduce problem behavior[31] and noncompliance.[15]

2. Involve Students Actively in Activities They Can Do Successfully

Structure the environment in which the activity takes place so that it challenges the students yet frees them from the fear of physical harm and gives them some degree of success.

Analyze tasks involved in activities to be sure you are clear about all the components of the skill you are about to teach.

Work for active participation on the part of all the students. Active involvement contributes more to neurological development than does passive movement.

Modify the activity so that each child can participate up to his or her ability level.

3. Facilitate Participation in Group Activities

Use markers to indicate where students are to participate.

Have students hold hands as they organize for instruction (e.g., in a circle).

Use peer partners during group exercises.[46]

Use a token or point system to reward compliant behavior.[18]

4. Interact Appropriately with Students

Be patient with smaller and slower gains of students who are more severely involved. Often gains that seem small when compared with their peers are tremendous for students who are retarded.

Do not underestimate the ability of students who are mentally retarded to perform skilled movements. There is a tendency to set goals too low for these children.

Convey to all students that they are persons of worth by reinforcing their strengths and minimizing their weaknesses.

5. Teach for Generalization to Community Environments

Remember that children with lower levels of cognition must be taught to play. This means that physical education programs are responsible for creating the play environment, developing basic motor skills that are the tools of play, identifying at what play level (self-directed, onlooker, solitary, parallel, associative, or cooperative) the child is functioning, and promoting development from that point.

Use effective maintenance and generalization programs to ensure that the skills attained in physical education are used in community settings.[22] If possible, teach the skills within the community-based setting that will be used for leisure, recreation, or sports participation.

Create a safe play environment, but do not necessarily provide security to the extent that the students are unduly dependent on you for physical safety.

chaining. If the task is a continuous one (such as running or jumping), shaping, rather than task analysis, is more appropriate. Once the physical skill has been performed, reinforce the student (see Chapter 6).

The Physical Education Program

Knowledge of the characteristics of persons who are mentally retarded provides information about the types of programs that need to be implemented to serve them. However, designing whole physical education programs around these characteristics for the purpose of teaching groups of these persons may not meet the needs of individuals within the group. Clearly, the assessed needs of each individual must be taken into consideration when the individual physical education program is being designed.

It is true that individuals who are mentally retarded have developmental lags in intellectual quotients and usually have parallel lags in motor and social development. Table 11-2 shows the mental and chronological ages of individuals who are mentally retarded, with a conversion of motor behaviors one would expect from individuals with delayed mental ages. Children with a chronological age of 2 to 5 years who are mildly retarded would be expected to attempt locomotor patterns. Those between 6 and 9 years would be attempting to learn to jump and balance on one foot briefly, as well as learning to throw. This information provides a good basis for constructing curricula for group activity because it is simple and straightforward. However, full assessments of the physical education needs of persons who are mentally retarded will reveal deviations from behaviors indicated in Table 11-2.

Every effort must be made to provide each student who is mentally retarded with an appropriate physical education program that will promote the motor growth and development of that child. Children under the age of 9 years will benefit from a physical education program that focuses on promoting sensory input and perceptual-motor integration. Older students should be taught to perform culturally relevant community-based recreational skills that can be used throughout their lives to promote and maintain a healthy lifestyle in social settings.

table 11-2

Conversion of Behavior in Physical Education Activity Adjusted for Mental Age of Persons with Moderate Mental Retardation

Chronological Age	Activities for Normal Children by Chronological Age	Activities for Those with Mild Mental Retardation Adjusted for Mental Age	Mental Age
4 to 8 years	Generalization of running, jumping as subroutines into play activity; low organized games (i.e., Follow the Leader, Tag).	Learning to run; balance on one foot; manipulate objects; engage in activity that requires simple directions.	2 to 4 years
8 to 12 years	Can play lead-up games to sport skills that involve throwing and catching. Can play games of competition where there is team organization. Can learn rules and play by them.	May be able to generalize running and locomotor skills into play activity. May be able to play games of low organization and follow simple direction. May socially interact in play; may play by self, or may play in parallel.	4 to 6 years
12 to 17 years	Can play games of high organization. Can further develop skills that involve racquet sports and balls and require high levels of skill. Can participate in team games and employ strategies in competitive activity.	Can participate in modified sport activity. Is better in individual sports (e.g., swimming, bowling, and track), where there is a minimum of social responsibility. Can throw and catch balls, but it is difficult to participate in meaningful competitive activity.	6 to 8 years
Over 17 years	Can participate independently in recreational activities in their chosen community.	Can participate in community recreational sport and physical activity in special programs and with assistance from others.	Over 10 years

Numerous studies have demonstrated that individuals who are mentally retarded benefit from physical fitness training coupled with reinforcement.[21,62,74,79] Treadmill exercise regimens that are individualized have been proved to be safe and beneficial for improving and maintaining cardiovascular fitness.[3] In addition, training in a modified form of judo was a valuable therapeutic, educational, and recreational tool for some persons with mental retardation. A biweekly, 6-month program resulted in gains in physical fitness, as well as developmental skills, such as walking, stair climbing, running, jumping, and hopping.[32] Appropriate motivation, high teacher expectations, and carefully designed learning sequences appear to be the keys to promoting learning among individuals who are mentally retarded.

Physical education programs should be based on the nature and needs of the learner. As mentioned previously, there is great variability among the populations of individuals who are mentally retarded. This is attributable to inherent differences between mild and more severe retardation, causes, and the many other disorders that accompany the condition.

Disorders associated with mental retardation may be sensory impairments such as blindness, being hard of hearing, or deafness; emotional disturbances; and neurological disorders such as cerebral palsy, muscular dystrophy, and problems in perception. It becomes apparent that physical education programs for persons who are mentally retarded must meet a multitude of needs at all age levels and all levels of intellectual and physical development.

Programming Principles

Both the broad curriculum and the everyday activities of the physical education program should meet the needs of students with varying levels of development. The principles in the box at right may be used to guide the program.

Whenever possible, students who are mentally retarded should be integrated with their peers in regular physical education classes. If they cannot participate successfully in regular classes, they should be given special developmental physical education commensurate with their capacity and needs. It is recognized that the regular physical education class may not provide adequate placement for all students who are mentally retarded. These children have social and motor deficits that

---

Programming Principles for the Physical Education Program for Persons with Mental Retardation

1. Select Activities That Meet the Needs of the Students in the Class

Select activities to meet the students' interest levels. However, precaution should be taken against participation in one particular activity to the exclusion of others. Be aware of students' tendency to favor the single activity with which they are most familiar.

Consider individual differences when selecting the activities. There are many games that allow for differences in abilities among class members.

Select activities according to the needs of the students who are mentally retarded.

2. Include Appropriate Physical and Social Opportunities

Select sensory-perceptual-motor activities to promote specific and general development of the young child who is retarded and to develop recreational skills of older students to make it possible for these individuals to integrate socially with peers and members of their families now and in later life in community activity.

Select activities primarily on the basis of the development of motor skills; however, chronological ages should bias your selection of activities. Whenever possible, the activities should be age appropriate as well.

Provide a broad spectrum of activities that have recreational and social significance for later life.

Teach specific social skills that are meaningful within a specific social environment so that the behavioral change results in functional social performance.[49]

Work for progression toward skill development. For young children, use sensorimotor activities that contribute to sensory input system development; for older children, use task analysis with sequential progression methodology.

---

make it difficult for them to participate equally with members of the regular class. Consequently, they often are found on the periphery of activity and do not involve themselves in the games and activities of the physical education class. An effort must be made to integrate persons who are mentally retarded into regular class activities; however, if this is not possible, special physical education programs should be adapted to the particular needs of the children.

Modifications, Adaptations, and Inclusion Techniques

Regardless of the level of retardation, all students should be provided with an appropriate physical education program. The physical educator is cautioned against generalizing about the motor functioning level and learning capability of the student who is mentally retarded. As in all cases of students with disabilities, the children and youth should be thoroughly tested for motor skill functioning level and physical fitness before decisions are made as to what type of physical education program is needed. If testing shows a student to be deficient in areas of motor behavior performance, a thorough task analysis should be completed before the student's program is determined. Program adjustments may be required to ensure maximum benefit for students with mental retardation. In this section ways to meet the needs of students with mild to severe mental retardation in a segregated or inclusive setting are addressed.

Adaptations for Students Who Are Mildly Retarded

The most apparent difficulty for persons with the mildest forms of mental retardation is comprehension of complex playing rules and strategies. Often the student who is mildly retarded who is included in the regular physical education class is inappropriately accused of trying to cheat, when in reality, he or she honestly does not understand what the rule or proper move is. Such accusations by peers or teachers often lead to momentary or prolonged rejection of the student who is retarded. Rejection leads to feelings of low self-esteem, which contribute directly to withdrawal or retaliation on the part of the student. Acting out then becomes an everyday occurrence, and before long these students are perceived by peers or teachers as being troublemakers. The vicious cycle can be avoided if the teacher anticipates comprehension difficulties and acts to counter them before they occur. Some suggestions for dealing with lack of understanding of rules or playing strategies are as follows:

1. Place the student in a less demanding position.

2. Overteach and constantly reinforce cognitive aspects of each game.

3. Help the other students in the class develop an understanding and sensitivity toward the student's learning difficulties.

If the student who is retarded has a propensity toward excessive body fat, this problem will be detected when the AAHPERD Health Related Fitness Test or a similar assessment is given early in the school year to all students. Every student identified as having excessive body fat should be provided with appropriate aerobic activities and, possibly, nutritional counseling to reduce body fat stores. There is a need for routine health-related testing of all students in all schools, at every level. The sooner children learn the importance of controlling body fat levels through diet control and exercise, the better the chance that these good habits will carry over to adulthood.

To enhance the probability that children with mental retardation will interact with their families and peers in healthful leisure time pursuits, care must be taken to teach the student to play games and sports that are typically pursued in community settings. The child who finds success and enjoyment in vigorous activity at a young age will continue participation as an adult.

Students with more significant levels of mental retardation exhibit performance ranges from very poor motor skill and physical fitness levels to quite acceptable performance ability. Traditional studies done by Hayden,[37] Cratty,[16] and Rarick, McQuillan, and Beuter[60] showed the motor development of children with IQs between 36 and 52 to lag 2 to 4 years behind that of children with normal intelligence. However, the performance level of these mentally retarded persons may reflect the type of motor development programs afforded them.

Modifications for Students Who Are Severely Retarded

With the development of new instructional technology in the late 1970s, it was possible to demonstrate the competence of individuals with severe mental retardation. Project MOVE and the Data-Based Gymnasium are examples of programs that use instructional technology for improving the movement capability of persons who are severely involved.[28,44] The Association for Persons with Severe Handicaps is a professional and parent group that has developed instructional procedures based on research and demonstration, and provided opportunities for persons with severe mental retardation.[55] Through implementation of the available information from research and demonstration (i.e., best practice), it has been demonstrated that it is possible to maximize the potential of this group of individuals for meaningful participation in society. Physical education, which develops the motor capabilities of this group, is an integral and important part of their education.

It is true that these children who are severely mentally retarded often demonstrate delayed motor development milestones early in life and learn slower than children who are not retarded. However, the early childhood intervention programs that are gaining in popularity may help offset the marked motor delays more involved children demonstrate when they reach school age.

When designing the adapted physical education program, the physical educator should work closely with both the physical and occupational therapists, who often test students who are severely involved to determine range of motion and level of reflex development. Consultation with the therapists and creative modification of traditional physical education activities will benefit students who are severely delayed. Some common activities used by physical and occupational therapists with this population follow:

1. To stretch hip and knee flexors, remove the student who is nonambulatory and severely mentally retarded from a sitting position and allow him or her to stretch out on a mat.
2. To improve range of motion, encourage the individual to reach for an object held just a few degrees beyond the range of capability. To hold interest, permit the person to reach the object occasionally.
3. Place the student face down on the mat and place a pillow or bolster under the upper chest. Encourage the student to look up (lift head) from this position as often as possible.
4. Place the student who is severely mentally retarded face down on a long scooter. Pull the scooter and encourage the individual to try using the hands and feet to propel himself or herself.
5. Place the student in a supine position on an air mat or trampoline. Gently bounce the surface around the student.

6. Praise every attempt the student makes to initiate movement.
7. Hook a lightweight Theraband strip or an elastic loop around each of the student's limbs (one at a time) and encourage him or her to pull against the loop.

Special Olympics International has developed training materials for use with individuals who are severely mentally retarded.[66] Activities in the Special Olympics Training Program (MATP) are broken down into the following components: dexterity, reaching, grasping, releasing, posture, head control in prone and supine positions, sitting in a chair, rolling, crawling, use of an electric wheelchair, sensory awareness, visual-motor, auditory-motor, and tactile awareness. Each of these activities is sequenced to maximize the potential for learning. The motor development curriculum promotes improvement in coordination and control of the body when performing a variety of motor activities. It is designed to develop age-appropriate sport and recreation skills, as well as physical fitness, sensory awareness, and the sense of being part of a group. Included in the curriculum is a motor activities assessment instrument that should be used to evaluate mobility, dexterity, striking, kicking, and aquatic activity, as well as manual and electric wheelchair mobility skills. Also included are Special Olympics activities specifically adapted for severely mentally retarded athletes. These include aquatics, track and field, basketball, bowling, gymnastics, softball, volleyball, and weight lifting. Each sport is task analyzed for inclusion of the motor activities in the guide. Criteria and standards are identified to inform the teacher as to when the skill or the task has been mastered. Furthermore, data sheets on which to record types of instruction used (physical assistance, physical prompts, demonstration, verbal cues, and visual cues) are included. Spaces are also provided for recording the type of reinforcement used (i.e., edible, social, token, etc.), as well as the schedule of reinforcement (continuous, fixed, or intermittent).

Integration

The ultimate goal of sports and physical activity for persons who are mentally retarded is participation in integrated physical activity in natural community environments. For the most part, integration models for acquiring physical skills for persons with mental retardation in the public schools offer a choice of participation in regular or special physical education programs. It is becoming increasingly apparent that routinely exposing persons with mental retardation to students without mental retardation in regular physical education class (mainstreaming) may have a detrimental effect on the student with mental retardation.[7,60] Without systematic attention to the needs of the individual during the integration process in physical activity, self-esteem and social interaction may suffer.

Individuals with disabilities have a basic right to be provided opportunities that will lead to their full integration into community recreational settings. (Special Olympics has initiated several such integration programs, which are detailed later in this chapter.) To achieve this integration, the process should include the following opportunities:

1. There should be a continuum of lesser restrictive environments in both instructional settings in the schools and in community recreational environments, and they should be coordinated for the benefit of each individual.
2. Persons with mental retardation should be placed in the most appropriate environment that is commensurate with the individual's social and physical abilities.
3. Persons with mental retardation should be provided with a support system commensurate with

their needs to adapt to present restrictive environments and advance to lesser restrictive environments.

When this procedure to achieve integration is used, individuals with disabilities will have a much greater opportunity to interact successfully in community recreation settings than they now have. Just placing students who are mentally retarded in a regular physical education class and hoping they gain all that is needed has not been successful. The current mainstreaming practice of chance placement must be replaced by a carefully planned integration process.

Continuum of Lesser Restrictive Environments

To enable individuals with disabilities to progress toward integration into community recreation programs, a continuum of lesser restrictive environments is needed. Three major environments that would promote participation of individuals with disabilities in a sport activity are (1) a training environment restricted to individuals with disabilities, (2) a mixed or integrated athletic competition, and (3) a normal community environment (Figure 11-1). A persons-with-disabilities-only training/playing environment, where athletes receive special training from teachers and trained peer tutors, is a critical starting place for many individuals who are mentally retarded. They need opportunities to learn basic fundamental movement skills before being placed with persons

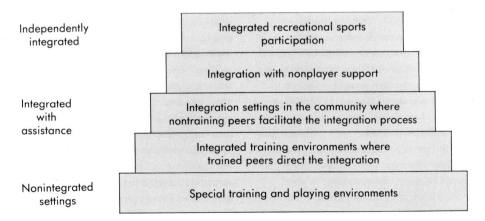

figure 11-1
Continuum of lesser restrictive environments that enable progression toward independent recreational participation in a specific sport activity.

who do not have a disability. The next most appropriate environment is mixed or integrated athletic competition, where the composition of the team is at least 50% athletes without disabilities. This step is important because to facilitate functioning in natural settings, athletes who are mentally retarded need exposure to peers who are not retarded and who have specific training in principles of integration. The next step would be participation in integrated settings with nontrained peers without disabilities who are willing to assist with the integration process. In the fourth step, individuals who are mentally retarded would participate in integrated leisure, recreation, and sport activities with the assistance of nonparticipants. The ultimate goal is to participate without assistance in natural community, school, and recreation environments, such as churches, YMCAs, and community recreation programs. Modifications of the major integration environments may be made to serve the unique needs of each athlete. It is most important that the thrust of integration be a process to move the students through the continuum of restrictive environments in specific sports to lesser restrictive environments to independent recreational functioning in sport activities that occur in communities.

Physical skill is one variable to consider for placement of persons with mental retardation in integrated settings with persons who are not mentally retarded. The ability to adapt to others when participating in activity is critical for successful integration of individuals into leisure, recreation, and sport activity. The ability to cooperate and work harmoniously with others, compete, display sportsmanship, respond to coaching and instruction, and control one's emotions is necessary social behavior if a person is to participate successfully in an integrated leisure, recreation, or sport activity. In addition to considering the physical and social abilities of individuals who are mentally retarded, the social complexity and the entry level of skill required to participate need to be considered. Individual sports, such as track and field, bowling, or swimming, require less social ability than team sports with complex rules, such as basketball or soccer.

Specific examples of integration techniques follow.

Marathon running integration

A project was designed to integrate Special Olympics athletes into 5- and 10-kilometer marathons. This project was conducted by a committed volunteer who was a marathon runner and coach of Special Olympics track athletes. The athletes participated in a series of training and competitive environments. The first environment was made up of all Special Olympics athletes who were trained for distance running. However, to advance to a lesser restrictive environment, it was necessary for the athletes to acquire greater skill. To achieve this, Special Olympics runners were given additional training with marathon runners who were also mentally retarded. After additional skill and higher performance levels were achieved, the prime athletes were integrated in training with adult marathon runners who were not retarded. The final step of the integration process was competition with runners in a regular marathon. Thus athletes progressed through three training environments—Special Olympics training, extended Special Olympics training conducted by a parent, and integrated training with competitors who were not mentally retarded in 5- and 10-kilometer races.

Softball integration

There is a concept in the integration process that is known as **reverse mainstreaming.** In this procedure, persons who are not mentally retarded are integrated into activities designed for persons who are retarded. Modification of this technique was initiated in the development of the Massachusetts Special Olympics softball integration project.[10] Special Olympics International subsequently funded the Research Center for Education Achievement to study the effects of Special Olympics softball integration on coaches and players who were mentally retarded and those who were not retarded. (The integrated softball game is composed of teams wherein at least 50% of the players are not mentally retarded.) Reverse mainstreaming can be used with individuals with any type of disability.

Integrated softball is a lesser restrictive environment than traditional Special Olympics, where a different social support system is provided to produce positive results. Through construction of social networks of lesser restrictive environments in which individuals who are retarded and those who are not participate on the same team, impressive social and physical gains can be made.

Budoff[10] has conducted research on integrated (Special Olympics) softball. In this activity, the individuals who are not retarded participate on the same team as an

Stable paddle boats allow freedom and independence for adolescents with severe mental retardation.

equal number of players who are retarded. Budoff, in comparing the play of the players who are retarded in integrated softball with other softball games made up entirely of players who are retarded, makes the following comments: "The contrast between the mixed (integrated) and all-mentally retarded [sic] teams is so stark as to make the same slow-pitch softball game look like a dramatically different game." As a result of a 3-month season of integrated softball, the athletes who were mentally retarded demonstrated lateral movement and intelligent positioning for the ball as it was coming toward them. There were few "dead spots" where players were immobile and did not move when a ball was directed to them. The team members worked well together. To explain this phenomenon, Budoff comments that "it seems that playing alongside of non-handicapped players helped to steady their [mentally retarded players] game, even when there were no overt signs of instruction."

An integrated team promotes the playing and understanding of the players who are mentally retarded because (1) the coach and the non–mentally retarded players are commited to teaching and supporting the players who are retarded and (2) the players who are not retarded serve as models on the field. According to Budoff[10]: "There seems to be no doubt of the individual develop-

ment observed in the play and sense of the game among handicapped players during this past season on the integrated (mixed) teams." Thus there are strong indications that an integrated environment in sport activity is a critical factor that benefits individuals who are mentally retarded.

Integrated basketball with adolescents who are severely mentally retarded

The previous descriptions of integrated activity with participants who were not retarded were based on modeling procedures and intuitive coaching techniques. Many of the athletes in both the marathon running and integrated softball projects had the potential for integrated activity without a highly technical support system. However, there are persons with mental retardation who may always need support systems for integrated play in sports.

Pilot research has been done on integrated basketball play with individuals who were severely retarded.[7] In this activity an equal number of college students preparing for professional roles in human service served as player-coaches. The rules of the basketball game were modified so that the athletes who were mentally retarded were required to perform the basic skill aspects of the game. The modified rules were (1) a player who was mentally retarded could travel and double dribble; (2) players who were not retarded could not dribble, shoot the ball, or pass to a teammate who was not retarded; and (3) only players who were mentally retarded could shoot. To increase scoring, another modification to the game was to award 1 point when the ball hit the rim. This modification provided more reinforcement to the conditions of play.

Each player who was not retarded was paired with a specific athlete with mental retardation. This athlete-coach then provided direct instruction as to when and to whom the ball was to be passed, when to dribble, and when to pass. These specific behaviors were reinforced. Thus play and technical instruction were combined. It is to be emphasized that when this procedure is being used, the stimulus cues and reinforcing properties by peer player-coaches are withdrawn as the athlete who is mentally retarded improves social and physical skills and can perform tasks without the cues. The limitations to this type of integrated play are that the desirable ratio of player-coach volunteers is 1 to 1. Furthermore, prerequisite training is needed for direct instruction by player-coaches.

Role of Player-Coaches

The roles assumed by the player-coaches in the complex social interactive game (e.g., basketball and softball), which may require direct coaching of social and cognitive strategies, appeared to be critical to the integration process. The complexities of the social and cognitive judgment of the athletes in marathon running were not as great as in basketball and softball. Therefore the demand on the coaches was not as great. Nevertheless, attention by the coach was necessary to adapt integrated environments and training regimens to be commensurate with the ability of the athletes who were mentally retarded.

In all three integration environments there was commitment by those who conducted the coaching. The attitudes of the coaches involved in all three projects support the notion that in an educational setting with teachers who favor integrating individuals with disabilities, mainstreaming has a reasonable chance of success. On the other hand, the evidence also suggests that where teachers oppose integration, the prognosis for success is not good. Thus because Special Olympics is a volunteer

activity for coaches, it is logical to assume that volunteers bring with them good attitudes toward the integration process.

Competition and Integration

The evidence from these integration programs is that they were beneficial to the performance of athletes with mental retardation. Inasmuch as there is some debate on the value of competition (as compared with play) for persons who are mentally retarded, the preliminary findings from these studies would indicate support for the findings of Karper, Martinek, and Wilkerson.[43] Their study investigated the effects of competitive and noncompetitive learning environments on motor performance in mainstreamed physical education classes. They found that the performance of the students who were mentally retarded dropped during noncompetitive learning following a competitive event. Although there is no way of knowing whether competition was the cause for behavioral changes, the effects of competition on the performance of athletes who are mentally retarded may be a significant and fruitful avenue for future research.

Community-Based Opportunities

Opportunities to learn motor skills and participate in leisure and recreation using learned skills should be available to all persons beyond the normal years of public-sponsored education. After leaving school, individuals must be able to find recreation using the skills and activities taught during the formal years of schooling. Opportunities for such recreation should be available to persons of all ages and capability levels. Those who have not had opportunities to participate and to learn motor skills should be provided with instruction in skills and ways of using leisure time for physical activity.

Children who are mentally retarded need to be taught to play regardless of their level of retardation. Fine, Welch-Burke, and Fondario[30] propose a three-dimensional model designed to enhance leisure functioning of individuals with mental retardation. Levels of social play are autistic, solitary, parallel, cooperative, and competitive. Levels of cognitive play are functional, constructive, dramatic, and games with rules. Areas of skill development range from acquisition of prerequisite fine and gross motor skills and functional play to toy play, art, simplified table games, exposure to the community, self-initiated play, and leisure education. Following is their five-step model designed to promote achievement of higher levels of play:

1. Assess current levels of skill and play.
2. Set goals consistent with individual needs.
3. Teach goal behaviors.
4. Generalize newly learned skills to higher levels of skill and to other environments.
5. Teach individuals to apply skills in natural environments.

Recreational opportunities for children who are mentally retarded should be provided after the school day terminates, during school vacations, and after formal educational training. There should be adequate provision in the recreation program for vigorous activity, such as sports, dancing, active games, swimming, and hiking. Intramural and community sports leagues should be provided to reinforce skills developed in the instructional program. In addition, winter snow games should be made available. Camping and outdoor education programs are other ways of affording expression of skills and interests.

Recreation

Recreational activities for persons with mental retardation should take place in a community-based integrated setting whenever possible. Recreational activities should be designed to stimulate interaction between individuals who are mentally retarded and those who are not.[23] Adults who are mentally retarded are more apt to integrate socially when they are given the opportunity to select leisure activities of interest to them.[11]

In conjunction with the recreation program, special events scheduled throughout the school year serve to stimulate interests, motivate the children, and inform the community about the progress of the physical education program and about the abilities of youngsters who are mentally retarded. Examples of such events are demonstrations for PTA meetings, track and field meets, swimming meets, play days, sports days, "hoop-it-up" and "pass-punt-kick" contests, hikes, and bicycle races.

Overcoming Barriers to Full Recreation Inclusion

Some of the barriers to full inclusion in recreation programs that adults with mental retardation face are[42]:

- Restrictive attitudes of parents and family
- Opposition from some members of the community

- Lack of widely available guidelines for pla... and implementation of integrated programs
- Lack of skill

Part of the solution to overcoming these barriers is fostering and improving social relationships.[53] What is needed is a community commitment to provide programs for all the citizens. Some ways a community can meet the needs of its citizens with mental retardation are as follows:

1. Develop guidelines for planning and implementing integrated recreation programs.
2. Provide opportunities for individuals who are retarded to socialize with persons who are not retarded.
3. Use existing materials to train personnel to work with individuals who are mentally retarded.
4. Change attitudes toward persons with mental retardation by "showcasing" their capabilities during local fairs and festivities.

Volunteer Assistants

Individuals who are severely mentally retarded often require individual attention. Volunteers trained in specific duties can be of assistance to the instructional program, as well as to after-school and vacation recreation programs. Parents of children who are retarded, members of high school and college service clubs, and scouting groups are becoming increasingly active as volunteers. Instructors can seek out these people and ask them to become involved with the programs for individuals who are mentally retarded. A 1- or 2-hour training session can be planned to teach these volunteers what needs to be done, how to do it, what to expect from individuals who are retarded, and how to deal with behavior problems.

The Home Program

The amount of time that the physical educator is involved personally with students who are mentally retarded is relatively small. If maximum benefits are to be derived from programs, it is necessary to have a follow-up of activities taught in the form of a home program. An educational program for parents describing the children's program and its purpose should be provided for implementation in the home. Parents should receive direction and assistance in methods for involving their children in physical activity taking place in the neighborhood and the home.

Special Olympics

Probably no single program has done as much to foster the participation of individuals who are retarded in physical activities as has the Special Olympics program. This program, which is now international in scope, was begun in 1968 by the Joseph P. Kennedy, Jr., Foundation. The program includes training in physical fitness and sports and provides competition for children and adults who are retarded at the local, district, state, national, and international levels. Special Olympics also has been instrumental in developing integration programs for athletes who are mentally retarded.

The Special Olympics philosophy is expressed by its motto: "Let me win, but if I cannot win, let me be brave in the attempt." The stated mission of Special Olympics is[67]:

> . . . to provide year-round sports training and athletic competition in a variety of Olympic-type sports for all children and adults with mental retardation, giving them continuing opportunities to develop physical fitness, demonstrate courage, experience joy, and participate in a sharing of gifts, skills, and friendship with their families, other Special Olympic athletes, and the community.

The philosophy and mission are supported by four basic programs:

1. *Special Olympic Sports Skill Program:* Based on illustrated guides for each sport, which include the rules under which the athletes must compete, task-analyzed skills, goals and objectives, and pretraining and posttraining assessments.
2. *Unified Sports Program:* Uses an equal number of players with and without mental retardation to participate in the sponsored events. Principles that guide this program are age and ability groups. Usually, unified teams compete with other unified teams.
3. *Special Olympics Motor Activities Training Program (MATP):* Serves persons with severe mental retardation.[66] The program provides a wide range of activities and stresses the following points:
   a. Training should be fun.
   b. Ultimately athletes should be able to choose their own activities.
   c. Activities should be age appropriate.
   d. Participants should demonstrate their newly developed skills to significant others.
   e. The participants' functioning level guides activity selection.
   f. Even partial participation has value.
   g. Creativity should be used when providing community-based sports and recreational activities.
4. *Demonstration Sports Program:* Explores and researches the appropriateness of incorporating new sports into the Special Olympics program.

Twenty-two official sports are offered in the Special Olympics national and international programs—alpine and Nordic skiing, basketball, bowling, diving, Frisbee throwing, floor hockey, gymnastics, figure skating, field hockey, physical fitness and weight training, rhythmic movements, softball, speed skating, walking, poly hockey, soccer, swimming, track and field events, volleyball, and wheelchair events.

Some of the rules of the Special Olympics sports program are as follows:

1. Athletes can participate beginning at age 8 years.
2. Competition is conducted according to age and ability.
3. Competition must be preceded by at least 8 weeks of training.
4. Records of performance levels during practice must be submitted before competition to establish competition divisions.
5. Head coaches must be formally trained.
6. Event managers must complete formal training.

SUMMARY

Mental retardation refers to substantial limitations in certain personal capabilities. It is manifested as significantly subaverage intellectual functioning, existing concurrently with related disabilities in two or more of the following adaptive skill areas: communication, self-care, home living, social skills, community use, self-direction, health and safety, leisure, functional academics, and work. Mental retardation begins before age 18 but may not always be of lifelong duration. The prevalence of mental retardation in the population is approximately 3%. Two levels are recognized: mild retardation and severe retardation. Persons with mental retardation can be expected to learn and develop.

Physical educators can expect to have students with mental retardation in the classes they teach. Although their motor skills and physical fitness levels may be lower than the students who are not mentally retarded, these students can be taught and can improve. Carefully selected teaching strategies and program adaptations will yield positive motor development results. Students should be tested to determine their specific motor strengths and weaknesses, as is true for most performance-based abilities. Physical education programs should be designed around these test results.

Physical education programs in the public schools should provide assistance for transition of the recreational skills acquired in physical education classes to independent, integrated recreational activity in the community. Participation in recreation, home programs, and Special Olympics should be encouraged. Special Olympics has taken the lead in developing programs to include individuals who are mentally retarded in integrated sports activity.

Review Questions

1. What is the history of the social perception of persons with mental retardation as contributing members of the community?
2. What are the essential concepts for determination of who is mentally retarded?
3. What are the intellectual and adaptive response levels of mental retardation classifications?
4. What is reverse mainstreaming?
5. What are five specific teaching strategies that can be used with persons who are mentally retarded?
6. How are adaptations for physical activity different for persons with mild retardation and persons with severe retardation?
7. What is the need or lack of need for supplemental programs outside of school and beyond formal education for individuals who are mentally retarded?
8. What Special Olympics programs are available for persons with mental retardation?
9. What is necessary to conduct a successful process of integration of persons with and without retardation in community sports activities?

Student Activities

1. Develop an individual transition plan for Kaneisha that will enable her to stay physically active after leaving the public school setting.

2. Diagram a personal futures plan that can be used with Kaneisha for the next 5 years that will provide her the support/knowledge/skills she needs in order to stay active after leaving school.
3. Locate one of the journals that deals with mental retardation. (Some of these journals are *Adapted Physical Activity Quarterly; Palaestra: The Forum of Sport, Physical Education and Recreation for the Disabled; Exceptional Children; Retardation; Education and Training of the Mentally Retarded;* and *American Journal of Mental Deficiency.*) Look through recent issues for articles that present teaching techniques that might be applied to conducting physical education programs for students who are mentally retarded.
4. Visit classes in which youngsters with mental retardation are included. Compare the performance of these students with that of the other students in the class. List the ways their performance and/or behavior differs.
5. Talk with a physical education teacher who has worked with students who are mentally retarded and ask which teaching strategies have proved to be successful with specific types of learners on specific tasks.
6. Observe a Special Olympics meet. Describe how the meet was conducted to accommodate the different abilities of the participants so all could engage in meaningful competition.

References

1. American Association on Mental Retardation: *Classification in mental retardation,* Washington, DC, 1992, The Association.
2. American Psychiatric Association: *Diagnostic and statistical manual of mental disorders,* vol 4, Washington, DC, 1994, The Association.
3. Anchuthengil JD et al: Effects of an individualized treadmill exercise training program on cardiovascular fitness of adults with mental retardation, *J Ortho Sports Phys Ther* 16:229-237, 1992.
4. Antony RM: Atlantoaxial instability: why the sudden concern, *Adapt Phys Act Q* 3:320-328, 1986.
5. ARA Consulting Group: *The Winter Medallion Program of Manitoba Special Olympics: an evaluation,* Winnipeg, Canada, 1994, The Group.
6. Arnold R, Ng N, Pechar G: Relationship of rated perceived exertion to heart rate and workload in mentally retarded young adults, *Adapt Phys Act Q* 9:47-53, 1992.
7. Auxter DM et al: *Prediction of playing basketball and basketball skills among persons with severe mental retardation,* Unpublished paper, Washington, DC, 1987, Special Olympics International.
8. Baumgardner TL, Green KE, Reiss AL: A behavioral neu-

rogenetics approach to developmental disabilities: gene-brain-behavior associations, *Curr Opin Neurol* 7:172-178, 1994.

9. Berkow R, Fletch AJ, editors: *The Merck manual of diagnosis and therapy,* Rahway, NJ, 1992, Merck Research Laboratory.

10. Budoff M: *The evaluation of the mixed teams softball in Massachusetts Special Olympics—coaches' views,* Cambridge, Mass, 1987, Research Institute for Educational Problems.

11. Bullock CC, Mahon MJ: Decision making in leisure: empowerment for people with mental retardation, *JOPERD* 63:36-39, 1992.

12. Committee on Sports Medicine: Atlantoaxial instability in Down syndrome, *Pediatrics* 74:152-154, 1984.

13. Committee on Substance Abuse, Committee on Children with Disabilities: Fetal alcohol syndrome and fetal alcohol effects, *Pediatrics* 91:1004-1006, 1993.

14. Cooke RE: Atlantoaxial instability in individuals with Down's syndrome, *Adapt Phys Act Q* 1:194-196, 1984.

15. Cooper LJ et al: Analysis of the effects of task preferences, task demands, and adult attention on child behavior in outpatient and classroom settings, *J Appl Behav Anal* 25:823-840, 1992.

16. Cratty BJ: *Motor activity and the education of retardates,* ed 2, Philadelphia, 1974, Lea & Febiger.

17. Croce R: Effects of exercise and diet on body composition and cardiovascular fitness, *Educ Train Ment Retard* 25:176-187, 1990.

18. Croce R, Horvat M: Effects of reinforcement-based exercise on fitness and work productivity in adults with mental retardation, *Adapt Phys Act Q* 9:148-178, 1992.

19. Croce R, Horvat M: Coincident timing by nondisabled mentally retarded, and traumatic brain-injured individuals under varying target-exposure conditions, *Percept Motor Skills* 80:487-496, 1995.

20. Croce R, Horvat H, Roswal G: A preliminary investigation into the effects of exercise duration and fitness level on problem solving ability in individuals with mild mental retardation, *Clin Kines* 48(3):48-54, 1994.

21. Curtis CK: Are education students being prepared for mainstreaming? *Educ Canada,* summer 1985.

22. Danforth DS, Drabman RS: Community living skills. In Matson JL, editor: *Handbook of behavior modification with the mentally retarded,* New York, 1990, Plenum Press.

23. Dattilo J, Schlein SJ: Understanding leisure services for individuals with mental retardation, *Ment Retard* 32:53-59, 1994.

24. Davidson RG: Atlantoaxial instability in individuals with Down syndrome: a fresh look at the evidence, *Pediatrics* 81:857-865, 1988.

25. DePauw K, Ferrari N: The effect of interference on the performance on a card sorting task of mentally retarded adolescents, *Phys Educator* 43:32-38, 1986.

26. De Vries LB et al: The fragile X syndrome: a growing gene causing familial intellectual disability, *J Intellect Disabil* 38:1-8, 1994.

27. Dunn JM, Fait H: *Special physical education: adapted, individualized, developmental,* Dubuque, Iowa, 1989, Wm C Brown.

28. Dunn JM, Morehouse JW, Fredericks HD: *Physical education for the severely handicapped: a systematic approach to a data based gymnasium,* Austin, Tex, 1986, PRO-ED.

29. Ellis DN, Cress PJ, Spellman CR: Using self management to promote independent exercise in adolescents with moderate mental retardation in a school setting, *Educ Train Ment Retard* 27:51-59, 1992.

30. Fine A, Welch-Burke C, Fondario L: A developmental model for the integration of leisure programming in the education of individuals with mental retardation, *Ment Retard* 23:289-296, 1985.

31. Foster-Johnson L, Ferro J, Dunlap G: Preferred curricular activities and reduced problem behaviors in students with intellectual disabilities, *J Appl Behav Anal* 27:493-504, 1994.

32. Gleser JM et al: Physical and psychological benefits of modified judo practice for blind mentally retarded children: a pilot study, *Percept Motor Skills* 74:915-925, 1992.

33. Grskovic JA, Zentail SS, Stormont-Spurgin M: Time estimation and planning abilities: students with and without mild disabilities, *Behav Disord* 20:197-203, 1995.

34. Hagerman R: Behaviour and treatment of the fragile X syndrome. In Davies KE, editor: *The fragile X syndrome,* Oxford, 1989, Oxford University Press.

35. Haley S: Postural reactions in infants with Down syndrome: relationship to motor milestone development and age, *J Am Phys Ther* 66:17-22, 1986.

36. Hardman ML, Drew CPJ, Egan MW: *Human exceptionality: society, school, and family,* Boston, 1987, Allyn & Bacon.

37. Hayden F: *The nature of physical performance in the trainable retardate.* Paper presented at the Joseph P Kennedy, Jr, Foundation Third International Scientific Symposium on Mental Retardation, Boston, 1966.

38. Hickson L, Blackman LS, Reis EM: *Mental retardation: foundations of educational programming,* Boston, 1995, Allyn & Bacon.

39. Hodges NJ et al: Visual feedback processing and goal directed movement in adults with Down syndrome, *Adapt Phys Act Q* 12:52-59, 1995.

40. Horvat M, Croce R, Roswell G: Magnitude and reliability for measurements of muscle strength across trials for individuals with mental retardation, *Percept Motor Skills* 77:643-649, 1993.

41. Horvat M et al: Single trial versus maximal or mean values for evaluating strengths in individuals with mental retardation, *Adapt Phys Act Q* 12:176-186, 1995.
42. Ittenbach RF et al: Community adjustment of young adults with mental retardation: overcoming barriers to inclusion, *Palaestra* 11(2):32-42, 1994.
43. Karper WB, Martinek TJ, Wilkerson JD: Effects of competitive/non-competitive learning on motor performance of children in mainstream physical education, *Am Correct Ther J* 39:10-15, 1985.
44. Kern County Superintendent of Schools: *Mobility opportunities via education (MOVE)*, Bakersfield, Calif, 1990, The Superintendent.
45. Kim S, Kwang HK: Cardiorespiratory function of educable mentally retarded boys, In Yabe K, Kusano K, Nakata H, editors: *Adapted physical activity: health and fitness*, New York, 1994, Springer-Verlag.
46. King D, Mace FC: Acquisition and maintenance of exercise skills under normalized conditions by adults with moderate and severe mental retardation, *Educ Train Ment Retard* 28:311-317, 1990.
47. Latash ML, Almeida GL, Corcos DM: Preprogrammed reactions in individuals with Down syndrome: the effects of instruction and predictability of the person, *Arch Phys Med Rehabil* 74:391-398, 1993.
48. Maes et al: Cognitive functioning and information processing of adult mentally retarded men with fragile-X syndrome, *Am J Med Genet* 50:190-200, 1994.
49. Martin JE et al: Consumer-centered transition and supported employment. In Matson JL, editor: *Handbook of behavior modification with the mentally retarded*, New York, 1990, Plenum Publishing.
50. Monroe H, Howe C: The effects of integration and social class on the acceptance of retarded adolescents, *Educ Train Ment Retard* 6:21-24, 1971.
51. Nakaya T, Kusano K, Yare K: Decreasing motor ability in adults with Down's syndrome. In Yabe K, Kusano K, Nakata H, editors: *Adapted physical activity: health and fitness*, New York, 1994, Springer-Verlag.
52. Newell R: Motor skill orientation in mental retardation: overview of traditional and current orientation. In Clark JH, Humphrey J, editors: *Motor development: current selected research*, vol 1, Princeton, NJ, 1985, Princeton Book.
53. Newton SJ et al: A conceptual model for improving the social life of individuals with mental retardation, *Ment Retard* 32:393-402, 1994.
54. Patel BD: The fragile X syndrome. *Br J Clin Pract* 48(1):42-44, 1994.
55. Patton J, Payne J, Smith M: *Mental retardation*, Columbus, Ohio, 1986, Charles E Merrill Publishing.
56. Pitetti KH, Rimmer JH, Fernhall B: Physical fitness and adults with mental retardation: an overview of current research and future directions, *Sports Med* 16:23-56, 1993.
57. PL 101-476 Rules, *Federal Register,* Sept 29, 1992.
58. Porretta DL, Moore W, Sappenfield C: Situational anxiety in Special Olympics athletes, *Palaestra* 9(3):48-50, 1993.
59. Rarick GL: *The factor structure of the motor domain of trainable mentally retarded children and adolescents,* Unpublished study, Berkeley, 1977, University of California.
60. Rarick GL, McQuillan J, Beuter A: *The motor, cognitive and psychosocial effects of the implementation of P.L. 94-142 on handicapped children in the school physical education programs,* Grant No G007901413, Berkeley, 1981, University of California.
61. Rimmer JH, Braddock D, Fujiura G: Prevalence of obesity in adults with mental retardation: implications for health promotion and disease prevention, *Ment Retard* 31:105-110, 1993.
62. Rimmer J, Kelly L: Effects of a resistance training program on adults with mental retardation, *Adapt Phys Act Q* 8:146-153, 1991.
63. Schantz OJ: Adaptation in students with Down's syndrome: an experimental study on the trainability of strength and power. In Yabe K, Kusano K, Nakata H, editors: *Adapted physical activity: health and fitness,* New York, 1994, Springer-Verlag.
64. Schroeder SR et al: Self-injurious behavior, In Matson JL, editor: *Handbook of behavior modification with the mentally retarded,* New York, 1990, Plenum Publishing.
65. Smith S: Cognitive deficits associated with fragile X syndrome, *Ment Retard* 31(5):279-283, 1993.
66. Special Olympics International: *Special Olympics motor activities training guide,* Washington, DC, 1989, Special Olympics International.
67. Special Olympics International: Adapted physical education sports skill assessment resource manual, *Special Olympics Bull,* Washington, DC, 1991, Special Olympics International.
68. Steinbach P et al: Molecular analysis of mutations in the gene FMR-1 segregating in fragile X families, *Hum Genet* 1993, 92:491-498.
69. Suomi R, Surburh PR, Lecius P: Reliability of isokinetic and isometric measurement of leg strength on men with mental retardation, *Arch Phys Med Rehabil* 74:848-853, 1993.
70. Surburg PR: The influence of task incompletion of motor skill performance of mildly retarded adolescents, *Am Correct Ther J* 40:39-42, 1986.
71. Tanji JL: The preparticipation exam, *Physician Sportsmed* 19:61-69, 1994.
72. Ulrich BD et al: Developmental shifts in the ability of infants with Down syndrome to produce treadmill steps, *Phys Ther* 75:17-23, 1995.

73. US Department of Education: Sixteenth Annual Report to Congress on the Implementation of the Individuals with Disability Education act, 1994.
74. Weber R, French R: Downs syndrome adolescents and strength training, *Clin Kines* 42:13-21, 1988.
75. Wehmeyer ML, Metzler CA: How self-determined are people with mental retardation? The national consumer survey, *Mental Retard* 33:111-119, 1995.
76. Wiebe E, Wiebe A: Fragile X syndrome, *Can Fam Physician* 40:290-295, 1994.
77. Wiegers AM, Curfs LMG, Fryns JP: A longitudinal study of intelligence in Dutch fragile X boys, *Birth Defects: Original Article Series* 28(1):93-97, 1992.
78. Yabe K et al: Developmental trends of jumping reaction time by means of EMG in mentally retarded children, *J Ment Defic Res* 29:137-145, 1985.
79. Zetts RA, Horvat MA, Langone J: Effects of a community-based progressive resistance training program on the work productivity of adolescents with moderate to severe intellectual disabilities, *Educ Train Ment Retard Dev Disabil,* pp 166-178, June 1995.
80. Zoerink DA, Wilson J: The competitive disposition: views of athletes with mental retardation, *Adapt Phys Act Q* 12:34-42, 1995.

Suggested Readings

Eichstaedt C, Lavay B: *Physical activity for individuals with mental retardation: infant to adult,* Champaign, Ill, 1992, Human Kinetics.
Luckasson R et al: *Mental retardation: definition, classification, and systems of support,* ed 9, Washington, DC, 1992, American Association on Mental Retardation.
Rimmer JH: *Fitness and rehabilitation programs for special populations,* Dubuque, Iowa, 1994, Wm C Brown.

chapter twelve

Autism

Courtesy Dallas Independent School District.

Scenario

Phillip is a third grader who was diagnosed with autism at age 4 years. He received his educational services, until age 7, in a highly structured, self-contained classroom with other children who had also been diagnosed as autistic. He had begun to make progress and had exhibited the following skills: bowling, using a two-handed push from a squat position; swimming a human stroke (dog paddle) a distance of 10 feet independently; running a distance of 100 yards without stopping; walking the length of a low, 4-inch balance beam while holding the teacher's hand; and riding a stationary bicycle for 15 minutes. In addition, he was able to follow simple two- and three-word instructions, would demonstrate interest in several simple tasks, and had bonded strongly with the paraprofessional.

When he began third grade, however, his parents insisted that he be included totally in the regular third grade program, including physical education. Repeated lawsuit threats caused school personnel to attempt to include him in the regular third grade, even though professionals with significant experience in the education of individuals with autism did not believe this was a good idea.

Even when accompanied by a paraprofessional assigned full time to provide instructional support for him, Phillip demonstrated the following behaviors in the regular third grade classroom: head banging and other self-injurious behavior; projectile vomiting, as often as 20 times a day; and physical attacks on the classroom teacher, paraprofessional, and other children.

In the gymnasium, as part of the third grade physical education class that included three classes (80+ students), Phillip fought to stand in front of the large circulating floor fan and would watch the fan for the entire class period. Any attempt to remove him from the fan caused violent acting-out behavior that included biting, pinching, kicking, and striking.

Task

As you read this chapter, think about other physical education placement experiences that would better meet Phillip's needs.

Definition

Three different forms of autism are described in the literature: classic autism, Asperger's syndrome, and Rett syndrome. **Classic autism,** originally known as Kanner's syndrome, was first described by Dr. Leo Kanner in 1943.[21] The principal characteristics of classic autism are significant developmental delays, global and comprehensive language disorders, abnormal and stereotypical behavior patterns, social isolation, and usually, but not always, mental retardation.

In 1944 Hans Asperger introduced an autistic disorder that is now widely known as **Asperger's syndrome.**[37] This condition, known as "high-level autism" shares many of the same symptoms as classic autism; however, distinguishing characteristics include motor clumsiness and a family history of Asperger traits.

Rett syndrome is a neurological disorder first described in 1966 in Germany by A. Rett.[33] The condition

is characterized by normal development during the first 6 to 18 months of life, followed by loss of acquired gross and fine motor skills, impaired language skills, gait apraxia, and stereotypical hand movements.[34]

Incidence

School personnel have reported increasing numbers of students with autistic behaviors. National awareness of the growing prevalence of autism was evidenced when the condition was first listed as a disability in P.L. 101-476, the Individuals with Disabilities Education Act (IDEA), which became effective October 1, 1990.

Reports of the incidence of classic autism range from 4 in 10,000 to 21 in 10,000 births,[4] and males evidence the condition 3 to 5 times more frequently than females.[15] Estimates of the incidence of Asperger syndrome range from 2.6 to 3 in 10,000 births, with males being affected 10 times more frequently than females.[15] The prevalence of Rett syndrome is estimated at 1 in 10,000 to 1 in 15,000 female births.[17]

Causes

Causes of classic autism have been widely studied. Classic autism is now recognized as a neurological impairment with a wide variety of underlying pathological conditions, including epilepsy, fragile X chromosome abnormality, hydrocephalus, lactic acidosis, immune system abnormalities,[31] and neurotransmitter dysfunction.[9] However, the most consistent pathological finding that has been identified is a brainstem abnormality characterized by an enlarged fourth ventricle, prolonged brainstem transmission time, and damaged brainstem nerve nuclei.[14]

Reports of an association between autism (or Asperger's syndrome) and affective disorder have only recently appeared in the literature. Delong and Nohria[10] conducted ongoing, repeated interviews to study the family, including the extended family, and the history of 420 relatives of 40 children and adolescents with autistic spectrum disorders. Neuropsychiatric diagnoses were recorded according to the Family History Research Diagnostic Criteria. In addition, notations were made that included a history of psychiatric hospitalization, specific psychiatric diagnoses, use of psychotropic drugs (particularly lithium), suicide or attempted suicide, and postpartum depression. Of the 20 children and adolescents with autistic spectrum disorder associated with neurological disorders, 18 had a *negative* family history of major affective disorder, including major depression and bipolar disorder. That is, there was no family history of major affective disorder in the families of those individuals. In contrast, of the 20 children and adolescents with autistic spectrum disorder but without neurological disorder, 14 had a *positive* family history of major affective disorder.[10] It appears there may be a relationship between affective disorder and autism in some children.[9]

The cause of Rett syndrome is unknown; however, because only females are affected, it is assumed that it is a result of a dominant mutation of an X-linked gene, which would be lethal in a male fetus.[23] Because individuals with Rett syndrome demonstrate many autistic-like behaviors, inaccurate diagnosis is common.[23] It is possible that cellular immune system abnormalities are associated with the neurological regression characteristic in Rett syndrome.[6,31] Cortical atrophy, especially in the frontal lobes, hypoplasia of the corpus callosum, and brainstem narrowing have been identified.[30] Abnormal neurotransmitter function has been suggested as a causal agent.[14] One distinguishing characteristic that has been reported is lack of nystagmus after spinning.[13] Lack of nystagmus strongly suggests a brainstem-vestibular abnormality; however, the technology to validate this hypothesis has not yet been developed.

Cognitive, Motor, Physical, Behavioral, and Psychosocial Characteristics

Classic Autism

The two primary formal classification systems used to identify autism are the DSM-IV-R system developed by the American Psychiatric Association (1994)[1] and the ICD-10 system developed by the World Heath Organization (1987).[42] For a formal diagnosis of autism, the DSM-IV-R system requires that at least eight of the following behaviors be demonstrated:

1. Qualitative impairment in reciprocal social interaction as manifested by at least two of the following:
   a. Marked lack of awareness of the existence of feelings of others
   b. No or abnormal seeking of comfort at times of distress
   c. No or impaired imitation
   d. No or abnormal social play
   e. Gross impairment in ability to make peer friendships
2. Qualitative impairment in verbal and nonverbal communication and in imaginative activity, as manifested by at least one of the following:
   a. No mode of communication, such as communicative babbling, facial expression, gesture, mime, or spoken language
   b. Markedly abnormal nonverbal communication, as in the use of eye-to-eye gaze, facial expression, body posture, or gestures to initiate or modulate social interaction
   c. Absence of imaginative activity, such as play acting of adult roles, fantasy characters or animals, lack of interest in stories about imaginary events
   d. Marked abnormalities in the production of speech, including volume, pitch, stress, rate, rhythm, and intonation; and stereotyped and repetitive use of speech
3. Markedly restricted repertoire of activities and interests, as manifested by at least one of the following:
   a. Stereotyped body movements (e.g., hand flicking or twisting, spinning, head banging, complex whole-body movements)
   b. Persistent preoccupation with parts of objects
   c. Marked distress over changes in trivial aspects of environments (e.g., insisting that exactly the same route always be followed when shopping)
   d. Markedly restricted range of interests and a preoccupation with one narrow interest (e.g., interested only in lining up objects, in amassing facts about meteorology, or in pretending to be a fantasy character)
4. Onset during infancy or childhood

The World Health Organization (1987) criteria for autism are less descriptive and impose a time limitation on the onset of the condition. Specific criteria are:

- Qualitative impairments in reciprocal social interaction
- Qualitative impairments in communication
- Restricted, repetitive, and stereotyped patterns of behavior, interests, and activities

Developmental abnormalities must have been present in the first 3 years for the diagnosis to be made.

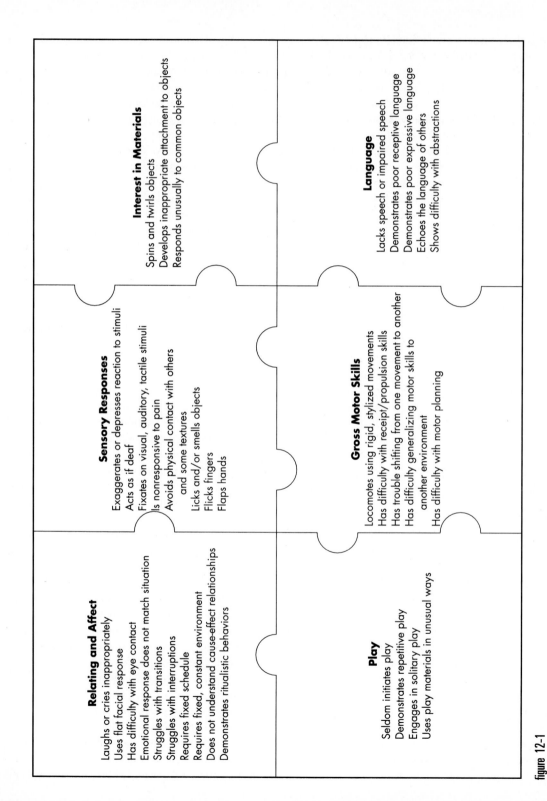

Relating and Affect

Laughs or cries inappropriately
Uses flat facial response
Has difficulty with eye contact
Emotional response does not match situation
Struggles with transitions
Struggles with interruptions
Requires fixed schedule
Requires fixed, constant environment
Does not understand cause-effect relationships
Demonstrates ritualistic behaviors

Sensory Responses

Exaggerates or depresses reaction to stimuli
Acts as if deaf
Fixates on visual, auditory, tactile stimuli
Is nonresponsive to pain
Avoids physical contact with others
  and some textures
Licks and/or smells objects
Flicks fingers
Flaps hands

Interest in Materials

Spins and twirls objects
Develops inappropriate attachment to objects
Responds unusually to common objects

Play

Seldom initiates play
Demonstrates repetitive play
Engages in solitary play
Uses play materials in unusual ways

Gross Motor Skills

Locomotes using rigid, stylized movements
Has difficulty with receipt/propulsion skills
Has trouble shifting from one movement to another
Has difficulty generalizing motor skills to
  another environment
Has difficulty with motor planning

Language

Lacks speech or impaired speech
Demonstrates poor receptive language
Demonstrates poor expressive language
Echoes the language of others
Shows difficulty with abstractions

figure 12-1
The autism puzzle. (Developed by Virginia Nelson, Autism Specialist, Dallas Independent School District, together with Carol Huettig and Jean Pyfer.)

Current research has identified other delays as well. Klin and Volkmar[25] found that precursors of social interaction such as joint attention, pointing for showing, and participation in early imitative experiences (e.g., "peek-a-boo") were lacking. Manjiviona and Prior[29] found that 66.7% of high-functioning children with autism had definite motor problems, as measured on the Test of Motor Impairment-Henderson revised, and performed at a level significantly lower than that of their same-age peers.

Temple Grandin, a high-functioning individual with autism who has earned a Ph.D. in animal science, described her particular difficulty with social skills. She and other individuals with autism tend to identify with Star Trek heroes Data and Mr. Spock. She believes most human beings have some innate and implicit knowledge of social conventions and codes; she also believes she and other individuals with autism lack that knowledge.[16] She said: "I couldn't figure out what I was doing wrong. I had an odd lack of awareness that I was different. I thought the other kids were different. I could never figure out why I didn't fit in."[35]

Howard Gardner,[12] in his classic work, *Frames of Mind,* suggested that individuals with autism demonstrated a variety of intelligences, including logical-mathematical and musical intelligence, but had particular difficulty with intelligences associated with social-emotional skills—the interpersonal and intrapersonal types of intelligence (Figure 12-1).

Asperger's Syndrome

Diagnostic criteria for Asperger's syndrome, similar to those described in classic autism, include the following characteristics:

- Severe impairment in reciprocal social interaction
- All-absorbing, circumscribed interest
- Imposition of routine or interest
- Speech and language problems in spite of superficially excellent expressive language skills
- Limited understanding of nonverbal expressive language skills

Motor clumsiness[15]

Manjiviona and Prior[29] found that 50% of children with Asperger's syndrome had definite motor problems, as measured on the Test of Motor Impairment–Henderson revised, and performed at a level significantly lower

than that of their same-age peers. They noted, however, that because of similar results with high-functioning children with autism, motor clumsiness may not be a valid diagnostic criterion for Asperger's syndrome.

Perhaps the major difference between an individual with classic autism and one with Asperger's syndrome is this: persons with Asperger's syndrome can tell us of their experiences, their inner feelings and states, whereas those with classic autism cannot. With Asperger's syndrome there is self-consciousness and at least some ability to introspect and report.[35] The individual with Asperger's syndrome is typically bright, with average or above-average intelligence. The individual with Asperger's syndrome is often highly verbal, but verbalizations may be unusual in content and may reflect bizarre interests and fascinations.[40]

Rett Syndrome

Diagnostic criteria for Rett syndrome are as follows:

1. Necessary criteria:
   a. Apparently normal prenatal and perinatal periods
   b. Apparently normal psychomotor development through the first 6 months
   c. Normal head circumference at birth
   d. Deceleration of head growth between ages 5 months and 4 years
   e. Loss of acquired purposeful hand skills between ages 6 and 30 months, temporally associated with communication dysfunction and social withdrawal
   f. Development of severely impaired expressive and receptive language, and presence of apparent severe psychomotor retardation
   g. Stereotypical hand movements such as hand wringing/squeezing, clapping/tapping, mouthing, and "washing"/rubbing automatisms appearing after purposeful hand skills are lost
   h. Appearance of gait apraxia and truncal apraxia/ataxia between ages 1 and 4 years
   i. Diagnosis tentative until 2 to 5 years of age
2. Supportive criteria:
   a. Breathing dysfunction
      (i) Periodic apnea during wakefulness
      (ii) Intermittent hyperventilation
      (iii) Breath-holding skills
      (iv) Forced expulsion of air or salivation

  b. Electroencephalography (EEG) abnormalities
    (i) Slow waking background and intermittent rhythmical slowing (3 to 5 Hz)
    (ii) Epileptiform discharges, with or without clinical seizures
  c. Seizures
  d. Spasticity, often with associated development of muscle wasting and dystonia
  e. Peripheral vasomotor disturbances
  f. Scoliosis
  g. Growth retardation
  h. Hypotropic small feet
3. Exclusive criteria:
  a. Evidence of intrauterine growth
  b. Organomegaly or other signs of storage disease
  c. Retinopathy or optic atrophy
  d. Microcephaly at birth
  e. Evidence of perinatally acquired brain damage
  f. Existence of identifiable metabolic or other progressive neurological disorder
  g. Acquired neurological disorder resulting from severe infections or head trauma[42]

Rett syndrome is devastating for the family and child. A girl with Rett syndrome appears to be perfectly normal during the first 6 to 18 months of life and exhibits typical social, emotional, language, cognitive, and motor development. At some point between her first and second birthday, a relentless regression begins. Iyama[19] describes the process as follows:

> She stops playing with toys. She stops responding to the spoken word and stops using the few single words she has learned. She becomes withdrawn and loses interest in social interaction. She may stop walking. Purposeful hand use is replaced by stereotypic hand movements. The lost developmental skills are never recovered, and she moves through childhood at a level of profound mental retardation.

In the girl's early preschool years motor performance is severely compromised by ataxia and difficulty with motor planning; this causes the girl to fix her joints into positions of stability, reducing her ability to change positions.[5] The regression appears to reach a plateau during the early school years. While no further loss occurs (there is little left to lose), few functional skills are acquired after this time. In adolescence and early adulthood motor deterioration is pronounced, and typically the young woman experiences muscle wasting, spasticity, and scoliosis and becomes dependent on a wheel-chair for ambulation. In addition, calcium deficiencies may cause low bone density and leave her more susceptible to breaks.[5]

Testing

Sacks[35] wrote, ". . . if we hope to understand the autistic individual, nothing less than a total biography will do." Without intending to, he makes a strong case for the use of portfolio assessment strategies for the learner with autism. (See Chapter 10 for a more comprehensive explanation of the portfolio assessment process.) A comprehensive ecobehavioral assessment is crucial if the educational progress of the learner with autism is to be measured and if the student's individual education plan program (IEP) is to be appropriate and maximize progress. This is particularly vital for the learner with autism because more traditional assessment strategies are difficult; the very nature of autism makes performance-on-request assessment impossible.

Ongoing observational data regarding the learner in a variety of settings are vital to the entire process. The child's learning behavior must be evaluated: in the home; in natural settings such as the grocery store; in a variety of school settings, including the classroom, playground, lunchroom, and library; in small- and large-group activities; in structured and free play; in academic/prevocational work experiences; and during leisure and recreation time. Motor competency must also be evaluated in each of the settings listed above.

Information regarding the motor performance of the learner with autism may include (1) videotapes of the learner moving in a variety of settings (e.g., navigating stairs in the home, pushing a grocery cart in the grocery store, using a piece of playground equipment, using a broom in a work setting, swimming, or engaging in a simple dance with peers); (2) photographs that represent the learner's play behavior (e.g., block structures); (3) narratives describing the learner's social interaction/play behaviors; and (4) teacher and parent anecdotal records. This information may be supplemented by medical data, behavior frequency counts, behavioral checklists, developmental rating scales, and formal assessment/evaluation instruments.

Formal assessment/evaluation is a critical part of a comprehensive portfolio assessment process. The Childhood Autism Rating Scale (CARS) allows the educational diagnostician or specially trained assessor to

Dallas Society for Autistic Children

1. Difficulty in mixing with other children.

2. Acts as deaf.

3. Resists learning.

4. No fear of real dangers.

5. Resists change in routine.

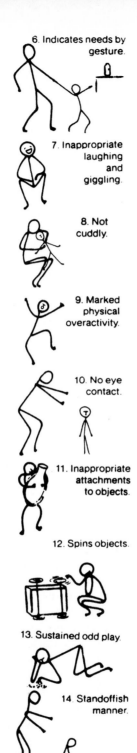

6. Indicates needs by gesture.

7. Inappropriate laughing and giggling.

8. Not cuddly.

9. Marked physical overactivity.

10. No eye contact.

11. Inappropriate attachments to objects.

12. Spins objects.

13. Sustained odd play.

14. Standoffish manner.

Author:
Prof. J. Rendle-Short
M.D., M.R.C.P., M.R.A.C.P.
University of Queensland
Brisbane Children's Hospital
Australia

Designed By Nena Williams

evaluate the child's abilities in the following areas: (1) relating to people; (2) imitation; (3) emotional response; (4) body use; (5) object use; (6) adaptation to change; (7) visual response; (8) listening response; (9) taste, smell, and touch response and use; (10) fear or nervousness, (11) verbal communication; (12) nonverbal communication; (13) activity level; (14) level and consistency of intellectual response; and (15) general impressions. The evaluator is able to share with parents and teachers a total score indicating that the child is in the nonautistic, mildly to moderately autistic, or severely autistic range.[38]

In addition, there are several instruments that teachers find useful for identifying autistic behaviors and referring students for diagnostic testing. These instruments vary in length and sophistication. For example, the Autism Behavior Checklist (ABC)[26] is a 57-item questionnaire that requires yes/no answers. The Behavioral Summarized Evaluation (BSE) is a 20-item paper/pencil scale developed for use by professionals and paraprofessionals. It appears to be most effective in the identification of severely affected children with autism and mental retardation.[3] A simpler instrument is presented in Figure 12-2. This instrument, the Autism Prescreening Checklist, which was developed by the Dallas Independent School District Autism Task Force, includes 14 behavioral signs and symptoms of autism.[8] Preschool and elementary teachers are taught to use this instrument so that children with autistic-like behaviors can be identified early and more extensive testing can be initiated.

One of the best instruments for evaluating the learning of the adolescent, young adult, or adult with autism has been developed by the North Carolina TEACCH (Treatment and Education of Autistic and related Communication–Handicapped Children) program. This instrument identifies and evaluates functional skills: (1) vocational skills, (2) independent functioning, (3) leisure skills, (4) vocational behavior, (5) functional communication, (6) interpersonal behavioral, and (7) community integration. Specific job requirements are evaluated, and the individual with autism is evaluated on the basis of (1) independence level, (2) productivity output, (3) qual-

figure 12-2
Behavioral signs and symptoms of autism. (Courtesy Dallas Independent School District.)

ity of work, (4) speed/rate of work, (5) attendance/punctuality, (6) ability to follow instructions, (7) willingness to accept criticism, (8) flexibility, (9) grooming/appearance, and (10) social behavior.[27]

Special Considerations: Facilitated Communication

The devastating impact of autism on the child and the child's family creates a situation in which the parents, in particular, are often extremely vulnerable to quick fixes or "cures" for a condition for which there is, at least at present, no cure. One of the most controversial practices in the education of individuals with autism is facilitated communication. This practice involves using a helper to support the hand, wrist, or shoulder of a learner while the learner makes selections on a communication device such as a keyboard. Claims were made that with this simple assistance, the learner with autism could be freed to express thoughts, feelings, and emotions. Travis Thompson wrote[41]:

> Facilitated communication appears to be a classic example of the self-fulfilling prophesy. The facilitator wants to believe that the person with a severe cognitive and language disability is actually of normal to superior intellectual ability. A technique is created which makes the false belief come true (Facilitated Communication) and the specious validity of the belief is perpetuated.

Essentially, wide and vast claims were made initially to support the practice of facilitated communication. Claims that children "locked" in autism were being freed to express their true intellect were made as parents flocked to yet another quick fix. Comprehensive study of the technique by researchers of the John F. Kennedy Center for Research on Human Development and other educators has indicated, however, that well-intentioned facilitators lead the learner to an answer. Indeed, the American Psychological Association, the Academy of Child and Adolescent Psychiatry, the American Association of Mental Retardation, and the American Academy of Pediatrics have denounced the practice.[2]

Teaching Strategies

Selecting the proper teaching strategy depends on the severity of symptoms demonstrated by the learner with autism. One-on-one instruction has been found to be effective when provided by a variety of individuals, in-

cluding the classroom teacher, paraprofessional, and peer tutors. Small-group instruction, with three to four students, has also been found to be effective.[20]

Classroom and physical education instruction for the higher-functioning children with autism requires, as with all learners with autism, a set routine and careful transition from one part of the instructional day to another. The children may, for example, prepare for the arrival of the adapted physical education teacher by selecting an appropriate "task" card from their "daily task chart." The task card may simply say, "PE," or it may be a photograph of the adapted physical education teacher. The children may prepare for a supervised walk or jog by selecting a laminated picture of a person walking or jogging. A speech and language therapist with training in augmentative communication may be particularly helpful in establishing the classroom routine.

Most physical education instruction for children with autism occurs in a self-contained setting. This setting, like the child's classroom setting, must be very structured and include transitions between activities. Each child should have a designated exercise spot to begin the class, to perform stationary exercises, and to serve as a "home base." There should be a definite, predictable routine during each class session. Each class session should start with the same set routine. This may simply be saying "good morning" to each child individually and then waiting for or prompting a greeting in return. If warm-ups are to be done to music, the physical education teacher should use the same songs over and over; a new song may be introduced after others have been mastered. If laps are to be run, the children should always run on the same path and in the same direction. If a given motor skill is to be practiced, the same class organization and equipment should be used. If the class is working on catching, for example, the teacher should use the same size and color ball. Exchanging a red playground ball for a yellow Nerf ball could be a terrible distraction. When using terms to describe a given activity or motion, the teacher should use the same terms. For example, if each child is assigned a plastic dot to serve as his or her home base, the teacher should refer to the plastic dot by calling it a "dot" and not use interchangeable terms such as "circle" or "spot." This type of consistency is crucial if the teacher is to maximize learning and avoid acting-out behaviors.

The physical educator working with a learner with

autism must, if possible, adopt the behavior management system used by the child's classroom teacher and, hopefully, the child's parents.[18] This consistency is vital if the child is to make the transition from the classroom to the gymnasium or playground. One of the most successful strategies for the management of behavior of learners with autism is to redirect inappropriate behavior. Since the learner with autism does not understand cause-effect relationships, it is ineffective to scold the child for misbehavior or to say "no." It is much more effective to redirect existing behavior. For example, if the child is kicking furniture, replace the furniture with a ball. If the child is biting his or her fingers, replace the fingers with a cracker. If the child is spinning about the room, place the child on a scooter board and encourage the child to spin in an appropriate play activity.

Another technique for managing behavior is to simplify the task if the child is misbehaving while attempting a task. Often, a learner with autism "acts out" as a result of frustration. Simplifying the task at hand may allow the child to succeed at the task while reducing inappropriate behaviors.

If the child is acting out or is "out of control," moving the child to a less stimulating area may allow the child to regain control of his or her behavior. For example, the child may be asked to return to a seat in the classroom or may be separated from the rest of the children to reduce noise levels, confusion, and distractions, which overstimulate the child with autism.

Perhaps most important, whenever possible the learner with autism should be encouraged to communicate instead of "act out." For example, if the child does not wish to participate in a given activity, the teacher should be delighted if the child says "no," or shakes his head instead of striking out or biting or pinching or having a tantrum. The child should be rewarded, then, by being allowed to not participate in the activity.

No studies involving teaching strategies for Rett syndrome have been reported to date in the literature. However, because of the similarities between Rett syndrome and autism, it is assumed that the female with Rett syndrome would benefit from the same structured physical education program suggested for other learners with autism. A top, down task-specific teaching approach that includes physical, visual, and verbal prompts using peer tutors should be attempted. Gait apraxia and breathing dysfunction may prohibit the inclusion of cardiovascu-

lar endurance training. Also, the possible presence of brainstem-vestibular abnormality would negate the use of vestibular stimulation activities. Music therapy has been reported to be successful with girls with Rett syndrome; perhaps a music-oriented, dance-based physical education program may be successful for the individual with Rett syndrome.

No studies suggesting teaching strategies specific to Asperger's syndrome are reported in the literature. However, because Asperger's syndrome is believed to be a form of autism, the same type of physical education program, with an emphasis on the use of language skills, may be effective.

Parents as Teachers

The parents of a child with autism struggle with the various stages of grief typical of any parent of a child with a significant developmental delay or disability. However, their struggle is unusual. Sacks wrote:

> And yet the parents of an autistic child, who find their infant receding from them, becoming remote, inaccessible, unresponsive, may still be tempted to blame themselves. They may find themselves struggling to relate to and love a child who, seemingly, no longer loves them back. They may make superhuman efforts to get through, to hold on to a child who inhabits some unimaginable, alien world; and yet all their efforts may seem to be in vain.[35]

It is vital to engage the parents in the physical education process, as in every facet of their child's education, in order to prevent, whenever possible, a downward "transactional spiral." This downward spiral may result as parents attempt to intervene, are met with no response or an inappropriate response, and then avoid the child and the intervention. Or, parents may attempt to demonstrate love and affection and as a result of rebuff choose not to continue to try to demonstrate love and affection. In essence, the education process should be devoted to maximizing the benefits for the child and the family, minimizing maladaptive behaviors of the child and members of the family, and maximizing learning and mutual satisfaction.[24]

Sport, leisure, and recreation skills may provide the parents with a format for engagement—there may be some commonality and shared love of the activity—that may help the parent and child with autism transcend communication barriers.

Empowering the parents of children with autism is

Parents must become involved with their child's play early in their child's life.

ting. Parent stress may skew perceptions regarding behavior. However, both parent and teacher perspectives give more information about the learner that is vital in the design and implementation of the learner's IEP.

Parents have been used as part of the evaluation process. In some creative and innovative programs, parents are actually part of the instructional team. A remarkable program, the North Carolina TEACCH has trained and used parents as co-teachers. This unique program is based on three crucial principles that acknowledge the dynamics of family interaction and the impact of that interaction on the professional attempting to intervene. Schopler et al.[37] describe those three concepts:

> First, it serves as a reminder that professional-family relations are defined not only by the expertise communicated from the professional to the parent but also by the parent's resources, aspirations and questions directed at the professional. . . . Second, and equally important, is the recognition that handicapped children and even infants have an impact on their parents every bit as real as the effect parents have on their children. Third, the interaction concept is probably most important for the TEACCH model in evaluating the outcome of educational and other intervention efforts. That is, the outcome is the product of two kinds of change. Either the child acquires better skills or reduces dysfunctional behavior, on the one hand, or the environment (home, school, community) develops greater acceptance of the child's deficits, on the other hand.

Acknowledging the vital interactive process and empowering the parents as teachers may have a vast impact on the physical education of the learner with autism. A home-based program to supplement the school-based program may have exciting results. Armed with information about facilitating play, supporting movement attempts, and interacting in and through movement activities, the parent may become more effective.

The Physical Education Program

The types of activities included in the physical education program for the learner with autism depend on the age of the child and the severity of his or her disability. The older the student, the more important it is to develop functional, prevocational, work-related, and leisure and recreation skills. The younger the student, the greater the focus on more basic motor components.

Vigorous, aerobic exercise two or three times daily is critical because it effectively reduces self-stimulatory and off-task behaviors and increases time spent on aca-

vital. They have unique and valued insight and information about the child that may enhance the education process. The role of the parent in the assessment/evaluation process has been examined. In a comparison of teacher and parent perceptions regarding the severity of autism as measured on the Autism Behavior Checklist and the Vineland Adaptive Behavior Skills, there was a significant disparity between parent and teacher perceptions. This was particularly dramatic in the perception of motor competency.[39] This disparity is not, in itself, a bad thing. The learner with autism may function very differently in the home than he or she does in the school set-

demic and vocational tasks.[11,22,28,32] However, physical education programs for individuals with autism of all ages should include exercise that promotes the development of cardiovascular endurance.

Kindergarten Through Third Grade

The physical education program for young children with autism, kindergarten through third grade, should emphasize cardiovascular-respiratory endurance activities, whole-body movement, dance and rhythm activities, activities to foster primary body part identification, and the development of onlooker and parallel play skills. Cardiovascular-respiratory endurance activities should be the basis of the program. The child should be engaged in vigorous, cardiovascular-respiratory activities with the heart rate in the target heart rate zone for at least 20 minutes per day. A general approximation of the target heart rate zone is 60% to 75% of the maximum heart rate. The maximum heart rate is calculated by subtracting the child's age from 220. For example, a 5-year-old child would have a maximum heart rate of 215 beats per minute. This child's training heart rate zone would be 129 to 161 beats per minute (0.60 × 215 = 129; 0.75 × 215 = 161). Cardiovascular-respiratory endurance activities for young children with autism may include aerobic walking, stationary cycling, and structured aerobic dance that emphasizes use of large muscle groups.

The development of equilibrium responses is a fundamental component of the physical education program of young children with autism. These equilibrium activities include the following.

SCOOTER BOARD ACTIVITIES

Depending on the child's level of development, the child should assume a supine, prone, sitting, or kneeling position on a scooter board. Initially, the activity will be teacher initiated and teacher controlled. Gradually, the teacher should fade out involvement so that the scooter-spinning activity is child initiated and child controlled.

CRAZY SIDEWALK

Place a mat, or series of mats, over the top of other, pliable objects. Then, depending on the child's developmental level, ask the child to crawl, creep, walk, or run over the top of the ever-shifting surface.

MAGIC CARPET RIDE

Have the child assume a supine, prone, sitting, all-fours, or kneeling position on a mat or blanket. Hold the edge of the mat or blanket and pull the child about the room.

Whole-body movement is also a curricular priority for the young child with autism. This includes "wrap-em-ups" (roll the child in a sheet or blanket, grasp the edge and lift, roll the child out of the sheet or blanket), log rolls, egg rolls, shoulder rolls, and forward/backward rolls.

In addition, simple songs and dances may be used to encourage the development of primary body part identification skills and rhythmic responses, as well as to provide an ideal opportunity for the child to be engaged in parallel play with peers. At the least, the child is sharing the same music with classmates. Songs and dances for young children with autism should have the following characteristics: (1) simple, clear, and often repeated directions; (2) repetitive phrasing; (3) even beat; (4) dominant rhythm instrument; and (5) nonintrusive "background" accompaniment. Hap Palmer and Greg and Steve songs and dances are particularly effective.

A crucial focus of the physical education program for young children with autism is the development of age-appropriate playground skills. Sacks[35] wrote:

> At one such school, as I approached, I had seen some children in the playground, swinging and playing ball. How normal, I thought—but when I got closer I saw one child swinging obsessively in terrifying semi-circles, as high as the swing would go; another throwing a small ball monotonously from hand to hand; another spinning on a roundabout, around and around; another not building with bricks but lining them up endlessly, in neat, monotonous rows.

The adapted physical educator, working with the classroom educator and the child's parent, needs to develop a systematic plan for developing skills necessary for successful participation in playground activities. A child with autism who is able to "pump" a swing and swing independently has a wonderful opportunity to participate in parallel play with other children also swinging.

Technology now exists to provide wonderful interactive toy experiences for young girls with Rett syndrome. Specifically, there are toys that combine bright colors and sounds, and allow the girl to experience cause-effect relationships as she uses adaptive switches on computers.[5] In addition, music therapy has been seen to have a positive impact on the lives of girls with Rett syndrome.[5] Indeed, the physical educator may enhance the child's life by including music and dance as part of the physical education curriculum.

Fourth Through Sixth Grade

The physical education curriculum for children with autism in the fourth through sixth grades continues to emphasize cardiovascular-respiratory endurance activities. These activities may include aerobic walking, stationary cycling, aerobic dance, jogging/running, and stationary rowing.

The development of "functional" locomotor skills is a vital part of the physical education curriculum for children in these grades. The child should be given the opportunity to develop walking, running, and jumping skills in the following situations:

1. Ask the child to move over different surfaces:
   a. Sidewalk–grass–sidewalk
   b. Grass–sand–grass
   c. Dry sidewalk–icy sidewalk–dry sidewalk
   d. Dry linoleum–wet linoleum–dry linoleum
2. Ask the child to move over, around, and through objects/obstacles:
   a. Step in and out of holes.
   b. Walk around puddles.
   c. Jump over puddles.
   d. Step over an object or series of objects.
   e. Walk up and down inclines.
   f. Walk up and down stairs.
   g. Vary number of stairs.
   h. Vary height of stairs.
   i. Vary surface of stairs (carpeting, linoleum, wood).
   j. Walk through a revolving door.
3. Ask the child to move carrying an object(s):
   a. Walk carrying a bag of groceries.
   b. Walk carrying an umbrella.
   c. Walk with a backpack.
   d. Run with a ball tucked under the arm.
4. Ask the child to push or pull an object:
   a. Walk, pulling a wagon.
   b. Walk, pushing a wheelchair.
5. Ask the child to lift objects of varying size and weight from different levels—off the floor, from a cupboard, etc.

More sophisticated equilibrium activities are also an important part of this program. These include self-testing balance activities. The child moves, for example, on a tapered balance beam. Or the child steps from one stone to another as the stones get smaller. Bouncing activities are also emphasized. using a mini-trampoline, an air

The child who is autistic requires cardiovascular activities. (Courtesy Dallas Independent School District).

mattress, or a gym mat placed on top of a tire, help the child "bounce" while sitting, kneeling, or standing.

Rhythm activities and low-organization games are important to children in this age range. Rhythms and games may be used particularly well to develop body image. In addition, these activities may be used to teach skills such as taking turns and sharing equipment.

More sophisticated use of playground equipment, including receipt and propulsion activities with balls, must be a part of this curriculum if the young child with autism is to have the opportunity to share recess and playground time. The young individual with autism may experience good success in playground activities such as shooting baskets.

Middle School Through High School

In the middle school and high school the primary curricular emphasis continues to be cardiovascular-respiratory endurance. In addition, there is an emphasis on the development of leisure and recreation skills. These include bowling, fishing, horseshoes, bocci, horseback riding, roller skating, skateboarding, and one-on-one basketball.

In addition, the adapted physical educator must work closely with the learner's vocational education co-ordinator to ensure that the learner has the necessary mo-tor skills to do a job. Specific job tasks need to be iden-tified, and then a task analysis needs to be done to de-termine which motor skills need to be taught. For ex-ample, if the learner is preparing for work at a nursery or as a gardener, then the prerequisite skills involving gross motor behavior would include (1) raking leaves, (2) digging with a shovel, (3) moving a wheelbarrow, (4) picking up and hauling large bags of peat moss, (5) using a trowel, etc.

Decisions regarding the activities that are taught should be based on the child's need to function within the community and on the accessibility of leisure and recreation facilities to the child. For example, it is un-fair to foster a love of horseback riding in a child from a poor family if the child's only access to a horse in-volves expensive rental. It would seem much more hu-mane to help the child develop the skills needed to par-ticipate in activities with other children in the neighbor-hood, such as one-on-one basketball. IDEA mandates that every child over the age of 14 must have a transi-tion plan included as part of the IEP. It is important that the adapted physical education IEP include plans to help the child use leisure and recreation skills within the com-munity.

Modifications, Adaptations, and Inclusion Techniques

Only the most highly functioning child with autism is capable of successful placement within the regular physical education setting. For most children with au-tism, the physical education setting is extremely restric-tive; that is, the very nature of the physical education experience often includes large numbers of children, making a great deal of noise, in an unstructured setting. A large number of variables need to be considered be-fore a decision is made to place a child with autism into the regular physical education setting. The box above de-scribes the *only* type of setting that may be appropriate for a child with mild autistic tendencies.

Characteristics of a Regular Physical Education Setting Appropriate for Children Who Are Mildly Autistic

Class Dynamics

The teacher-student ratio must be less than 1:20.
The class must be highly structured.
The class routine must be consistent.

Instructional Staff

The physical education teacher must be willing to cre-ate an environment that will facilitate learning for the autistic and the nonautistic child.
A physical education aide or special education aide must be present.
The physical education staff must be willing to work closely with special education personnel to learn strategies for managing the instructional environ-ment.

Instructional Program

The focus of the instructional program must be indi-vidual skills rather than group games and team sports.

Gymnasium and/or Playground

The gymnasium must be relatively free of distractions—fans, standing equipment, etc.
The playground must be surrounded by a fence.

More severely involved youngsters respond favor-ably to a top, down task analytical instructional model that includes physical, visual, and verbal prompts to guide learning.[7] These students must receive physical education instruction within a small-group, self-contained setting. Once again, the class must be very structured. This structure may include limiting opportu-nity for "out-of-seat" activity for all but the one child taking a turn. For example, all the children in the class may be physically and verbally prompted to remain in their respective "cubbies" (chairs) while one child is "spotted" in the performance of a forward roll.

A successful inclusion strategy for the learner with autism may be reverse mainstreaming. To give the learner with autism the opportunity to interact with typi-cally developing peers, other children may be included in the small-group physical education experience. These children need, however, to be aware of the nature and needs of the learner with autism.

The use of peer tutors to assist the child with autism in attending to specific tasks may be very beneficial[36]; however, although it gives the learner with autism an opportunity to interact with typically developing peers, the "peer tutor" designation separates the learners by the very designation of special status to the "peer tutor." The use of peer tutors must be part of a carefully designed instructional program. Peer tutors must be well trained for their role. They must be given specific instruction about the nature of autism and the behaviors they should expect from their peers with autism. The peer tutors must be very mature children who can accept the atypical interaction skills, the inability to play, and the inability to form meaningful peer relationships, characteristic of learners with autism. The peer tutor may function best in the role of "demonstrator."

Community-Based Opportunities

One of the major issues in the preparation of children and adults with autism for community-based experiences of any kind, including sport, athletic, leisure, recreation, and fitness activities, is that the individual with autism has difficulty generalizing skills taught in one setting into another. The physical education program for children and adults with autism must, by its very nature, include education in the settings in which the individual is likely to participate. Vital in this process is a family, neighborhood, and cultural evaluation of sport, athletic, leisure, recreation, and fitness patterns. The learner with autism may be able to acquire all the skills necessary to bowl. However, if no one in his or her family and no friends in the neighborhood enjoy bowling, it is unlikely that the skills will be used. This evaluation must be part of the process of developing the learner's IEP early in the child's life. It is much too late to determine appropriate familial, neighborhood, and cultural skills in the development of the transition plan.

Sports and Athletics

An individual with autism, because of vast communication and social-emotional ramifications, may never function well in a traditional community-based sports/athletics program. Most of these programs tend to emphasize competition, and most individuals with autism have difficulty competing; in fact, they may struggle to participate in cooperative, play-based activities.

Leisure, Recreation, and Fitness

Enlightened parks and recreation programs, as well as other community-based programs, that emphasize individual and/or cooperative experiences rather than competition may provide an avenue of success for the individual with autism. The individual with autism may experience particular success in leisure and recreation activities such as swimming, gymnastics, bowling, aerobic dance, horseshoes, fishing, bocci, horseback riding, roller skating, skateboarding, shooting baskets, cross-country skiing, tandem bicycling as the rear partner, and canoeing with an experienced partner. They may experience success in fitness activities such as walking or jogging on a treadmill, stationary cycling, or tethered/lap swimming.

SUMMARY

Because of the increasing numbers of children with autism, the condition is now included as a disorder that qualifies affected students for special education services. Forms of autism are classic autism, Asperger's syndrome, and Rett syndrome. Characteristics common to all forms of autism are communication difficulties, abnormal behaviors, and poor social skills. Physical education programs require set routines and careful transition between each part of the instructional day. Students with classic autism or Asperger's syndrome should participate in daily vigorous physical exercise. Students with Rett syndrome will benefit from a structured top, down, task-specific teaching approach that relies heavily on music and dance. Behavior modification techniques and use of peer tutors may be beneficial in helping the student focus on each physical education task.

Review Questions

1. Name some characteristics of a regular physical education setting appropriate for children with mild autism.
2. Name and briefly explain the three types of autism.
3. What types of activities should be included in physical education classes that serve young children with autism or Asperger's syndrome?
4. Give some examples of equilibrium activities that could be included in a physical education program for children with autism.

5. Give some examples of behaviors children with autism might demonstrate. Explain redirection and give examples.
6. Describe three strategies a teacher could use to manage the behavior of children with mild autism in a physical education class.
7. Explain how Asperger's syndrome and Rett syndrome differ.

Student Activities

1. Outline alternatives to the "regular" physical education program for Phillip that you can share with his parents at the multidisciplinary team meeting.
2. Prepare suggestions for Phillip's parents for a home-based physical education program.
3. Develop a rationale for the principal of Phillip's school to explain what his individual physical education program should be.
4. If the parents continue to insist on Phillip's being educated in the regular physical education program, what will your response be at the multidisciplinary team meeting?
5. Read *Emergence Labeled Autistic* (1986, Arena Press), the remarkable autobiography of Temple Grandin, a woman with autism who earned a Ph.D. and has a successful consulting business devoted to the humane treatment of farm animals. Develop an individual physical education program for a young "Temple" and for Phillip that would prepare them for adult community-based leisure and recreation activities.

References

1. American Psychiatric Association: *DSM-IV-R Diagnostic and statistical manual of mental disorders (revised)*, Washington, DC, 1994.
2. APA denounces facilitated communication for autistic students, *Spec Educ Rep*, Sept 7, 1994.
3. Barthelemy C et al: The behavioral summarized evaluation: validity and reliability of a scale for the assessment of autistic behaviors, *J Autism Dev Disord* 20:189-203, 1990.
4. Batshaw M, Perret Y: *Children with handicaps: a medical primer*, Baltimore, 1986, Paul H Brookes Publishing.
5. Braddock S et al: Rett syndrome: an update and review for the primary pediatrician, *Clin Pediatr*, pp 613-626, Oct 1993.
6. Budden S et al: Cerebrospinal fluid studies in the Rett syndrome: biogenic amines and beta endorphins, *Brain Dev* 12:81-84, 1990.
7. Collier D, Reid G: A comparison of two models designed to teach autistic children a motor task, *Adapt Phys Act Q* 4:226-236, 1987.
8. Dallas Independent School District Autism Task Force: *Autism prescreening checklist*, 1988, Adapted with permission of Randal-Short, University of Queensland, Brisbane Children's Hospital, Australia.
9. Delong R: Children with autistic spectrum disorder and a family history of affective disorder, *Dev Med Child Neurol* 36:674-688, 1994.
10. DeLong R, Nohria C: Psychiatric family history and neurologic disease in autistic spectrum disorders, *Dev Med Child Neurol* 36:441-448, 1994.
11. Elliott R et al: Vigorous, aerobic exercise versus general motor training activities: effects on maladaptive and stereotypic behaviors of adults with both autism and mental retardation, *J Autism Dev Disord* 24:565-575, 1994.
12. Gardner H: *Frames of mind: the theory of multiple intelligences*, New York, 1983, Basic Books.
13. Gillberg C: The borderland of autism and Rett syndrome: five case histories to highlight diagnostic difficulties, *J Autism Dev Disord* 19:545-559, 1989.
14. Gillberg C: Autism and pervasive developmental disorders, *J Child Psychol Psychiatry* 31:99-119, 1990.
15. Gillberg I, Gillberg C: Asperger syndrome—some epidemiological considerations: a research note, *J Child Psychol Psychiatry* 30:631-638, 1989.
16. Grandin T: An inside view of autism. In Schopler E, Mesibov G, editors: *High-functioning individuals with autism*, New York, 1992, Plenum Press.
17. Hagberg B: Rett's syndrome: prevalence and impact on progressive severe mental retardation in girls, *Acta Paediatr Scand* 74:405-408, 1985.
18. Howlin P, Rutter M: *Treatment of autistic children*, New York, 1987, John Wiley & Sons.
19. Iyama C: Rett syndrome. In Barness LA et al, editors: *Advances in pediatrics*, vol 40, St Louis, 1993, Mosby.
20. Kamps D et al: A comparison of instructional arrangements for children with autism served in a public school setting, *Educ Treat Child* 3:197-215, 1990.
21. Kanner L: Autistic disturbances of affective contact, *Nervous Child* 2:217-250, 1943.
22. Kern L et al: The effects of physical exercise on self-stimulation and appropriate responding in autistic children, *J Autism Dev Disord* 12:399-419, 1982.
23. Killian W: On the genetics of Rett syndrome: analysis of family and pedigree data, *Am J Med Genet* 24:369-376, 1986.
24. Klin A, Cohen D: Theoretical perspectives on autism, *The Signal: Newsletter of the World Association for Infant Mental Health* 2:7-11, April-June 1994.
25. Klin A, Volkmar F: Autism and the pervasive developmental disorders. In Nospitz JD, editor: *Basic handbook of child psychiatry*, New York, 1993, Basic Books.

26. Krug D, Arick J, Almond P: Autism behavior check-list for identifying severely handicapped individuals with high levels of autistic behavior, *J Child Psychol Psychiatry* 21:221-229, 1980.

27. Landrus R, Mesibov G: *Preparing autistic students for community living: a functional and sequential approach to training,* Chapel Hill, 1985, Division TEACCH, Department of Psychiatry, University of North Carolina.

28. Levinson L, Reid G: The effects of exercise intensity on the stereotypic behaviors of individuals with autism, *Adapt Phys Act Q* 10:255-268, 1993.

29. Manjiviona J, Prior M: Comparison of Asperger syndrome and high-functioning autistic children on a test of motor impairment, *J Autism Dev Disord* 25:23-39, 1995.

30. Nihei K, Naitoh H: Cranial computed topographic and magnetic resonance imaging studies on the Rett syndrome, *Brain Dev* 12:101-105, 1990.

31. Plioplys A: Lymphocyte function in autism and Rett syndrome, *Neuropsychobiology* 29:12-16, 1994.

32. Quill K, Gurry S, Larkin A: Daily life therapy: a Japanese model for educating children with autism, *J Autism Dev Disord* 19:625-635, 1989.

33. Rett A: Uber ein eigenartiges hirnatrophisches syndrom bei hyperammonamie im kindersalter, *Weiner Med Wochenschrift* 116:723-726, 1966.

34. The Rett Syndrome Diagnostic Criteria Work Group: Diagnostic criteria for Rett syndrome, *Ann Neurol* 23:425-428, 1988.

35. Sacks O: A neurologist's notebook: an anthropologist on Mars, *The New Yorker,* pp 106-125, Jan 3, 1994.

36. Schleien S, Heyne L, Berken S: Integrating physical education to teach appropriate play skills to learners with autism: a pilot study, *Adapt Phys Act Q* 5:182-192, 1988.

37. Schopler E: Convergence of learning disability, higher level autism, and Asperger's syndrome, *J Autism Dev Disord* 15:359, 1985 (editorial).

38. Schopler E et al: *The Childhood Autism Rating Scale (CARS),* Los Angeles, 1988, Western Psychological Services.

39. Szatmaria P et al: Parent and teacher agreement in the assessment of pervasive developmental disorders, *J Autism Dev Disord* 24:703-717, 1994.

40. Thompson R et al: *Pervasive developmental disorder: new subtests, new criteria.* Presentation at Texas Speech-Language-Hearing Association, Houston, April 22, 1995.

41. Thompson T: *A reign of error: facilitated communication.* Presentation at The John F Kennedy Center for Research on Human Development, Nashville, Tenn, Jan 1993.

42. World Health Organization: *Mental disorders,* Glossary and guide to their classification in accordance with the tenth revision (draft) of the International Classification of Diseases, 1989.

chapter thirteen

Specific Learning Disabilities

Objectives

Define the term *specific learning disability.*

Explain the controversy about the importance of motor development to the cognitive functioning of individuals with specific learning disabilities.

Cite at least three motor development delays demonstrated by individuals identified as having specific learning disabilities.

List at least five teaching strategies to use when working with students who have specific learning disabilities.

Identify five examples of off-task behaviors students with attention deficit disorder might demonstrate in a physical education class.

Identify three techniques that might be effective in keeping a student with attention deficit disorder on task during a physical education class.

Courtesy Dallas Independent School District.

Scenario

Miguel is a second grader. In his classroom and particularly in the gymnasium, he is a study in nonstop human motion. He finds it impossible to sit still when directions are being given or attendance is being taken; he fidgets and giggles, and pokes and prods classmates near him. He is unable to follow directions. More specifically, he is unable to listen long enough to get directions.

In game situations he becomes easily frustrated if he is not the center of attention. For example, in a game of Duck Duck Goose, he cries if he is not the chosen child. During station activities he runs from station to station, never completing the assigned activity, disrupting children on task, and occasionally taking play equipment from the station.

In parachute activities he constantly tries to climb

under the parachute to stick his head through the center hole. In fact, the physical education teacher has simply given up on the idea of including parachute activities in the curriculum.

In tag games he runs around the gymnasium, tagging people randomly and often too hard. When the class is involved in dance activities, he runs to the tape recorder and pushes the buttons randomly.

Task

As you read this chapter, think about Miguel's behaviors. Try to determine why he is frequently off task, and what could be done to reduce his acting-out behaviors.

Probably no disability has proved to be more controversial or has undergone more name changes than what we now call **specific learning disability.** Confusion about the condition is reflected in the number of terms associated with disability. Over the past 30 years, individuals with these disabilities have been classified as perceptually handicapped, brain injured, brain damaged, minimal brain dysfunctionate, dyslexic, and/or developmentally aphasic. In every case, the term was selected in an attempt to convey the fact that persons with a specific learning disability have normal intelligence but fail to demonstrate the same academic competencies as do the majority of individuals whose IQs fall within the normal range.

Definition

Specific learning disability was defined in the Individuals with Disabilities Education Act (IDEA) of 1990. It is a disorder in one or more of the basic psychological processes involved in understanding or using language, spoken or written, which may manifest itself in the imperfect ability to listen, think, speak, write, spell, or perform mathematical calculations. Such disorders include such conditions as perceptual disabilities, brain injury, minimal brain dysfunction, dyslexia, and developmental aphasia. The term does not include children who have learning problems that are primarily the result of visual, hearing, or motor disabilities; mental retardation; emo-

tional disturbance; or environmental, cultural, or economic disadvantage.[18]

Incidence

Estimates of the prevalence of the condition range from 2% to 10% of the population,[3] depending on the number of characteristics included in the definition. Regardless of which characteristics are included, it is widely accepted that 70% to 90% of the children identified as having a specific learning disability are male; however, there is growing speculation that both genders are equally affected but males are identified more frequently because they tend to act out more and be more disruptive than females.[3] In 1977 there were approximately 800,000 individuals with learning disabilities. By 1990, the incidence of learning disability had more than doubled (i.e., more than 2 million). As would be expected, research on this disability has greatly increased in recent years. At this writing, specific learning disability is the most prevalent disabling condition of individuals in the United States.

Causes

What is known is that children who were once believed to be daydreamers, inattentive, mischievous, or just plain "dumb" in school do indeed have an organic basis for their behaviors.[29] Technologically sophisticated equipment has been used to document neurological differences in the brains of persons with specific learning disabilities as compared with normal individuals.[16,22,25,32] Yet, neither the specific impact of neurological differences, the subcategories of the disability, nor the causes have been identified. The best we can do at this point in time is to describe the behaviors demonstrated by this varied group of learners and share whatever has been found to work successfully with them.

For more than 30 years theorists have postulated that sensory-perceptual-motor functioning delays underlie specific learning disabilities. To date, no definitive empirical evidence exists to support this theory; however, it is important that the physical educator be aware of the historical perspectives surrounding the controversy. The reason why many special educators took such a firm stand against the position that motor impairments may affect cognitive processing dates back to the 1960s. During that decade the perceptual-motor theories of Kephart[27] and Frostig and Maslow[21] were emerging.

The development of functional independent leisure skills can enhance the quality of life. (Courtesy Wisconsin Lions Camp, Rosholt, Wis.)

These pioneers proposed that the basic "stuff" from which cognitive information was constructed included perceptual and motor components. The thinking was that if educators could identify that perceptual-motor delays existed and intervene with a program to overcome the delays, cognitive function would be facilitated. Special educators with little or no background in motor development seized on these theories as the possible answer to resolving the academic learning problems manifested by learning-disabled populations. In an attempt to "cure" individuals with learning disabilities, Kephart's and Frostig and Maslow's programs of activities were tried on groups of students who were learning disabled. Almost without exception, the wholesale application of these theories proved disappointing. In most cases the student improved in motor function but demonstrated no immediate change in reading or mathematical ability. As a result, many special educators abandoned the notion that there could be a causative relationship between motor and cognitive functioning.

As the perceptual-motor theories faded in popularity, other neuropsychological theories emerged that advanced the belief that cognitive function could be facilitated by controlling types and qualities of sensory and motor experiences. These theories differed from earlier ones in that they advanced the notion that before there can be efficient perceptual-motor and cognitive functioning, sensory input stimuli must be organized so that it can be utilized by the central nervous system.

Prominent advocates of a definitive relationship between the sensory, motor, and cognitive domains were Ayres,[5,6] deQuiros and Schrager,[15] and Dennison and Hargrove.[14] Ayres, a well-known researcher in the area of sensory integration therapy, advocated that "learning and behavior are the visible aspects of sensory integration"[6] and that sensory integration results from sensory stimulation and motor activity. Schrager and deQuiros believed that primary learning disabilities had their bases in vestibular, perceptual modality, and cerebral dysfunctions. They advocated the use of sensory-perceptual-motor activities to assuage vestibular and perceptual problems. Dennison built on Sperry and Ornstein's model of brain function and developmental optometry's theories and developed a program of specific movements to use to enable individuals to access different parts of the brain. He called his approach educational kinesiology.

Research studies have validated that both sensory integration and educational kinesiology have a positive impact on perceptual-motor function; however, their value for enhancing cognitive functioning has been less apparent.[11,24] Studies that have reported academic gains from sensory integration therapy programs suffer from sampling, group assignment, treatment, and analysis inadequacies.[24] The one study located that studied the efficacy of educational kinesiology concluded that the treatment was not effective in improving academic skills as measured by the Comprehensive Test of Basic Skills for Language, Arithmetic, and Reading.[11]

Obviously, the controversy will not be easily settled. Carefully designed research studies that delineate specific types of motor components and their possible effect on cognitive functions will need to be completed and replicated. Longitudinal studies that follow individuals who have been exposed to contemporary sensory-perceptual-motor intervention programs will need to be carried out. Dialogue among educators, neurologists, visual and hearing specialists, and researchers will need to be initiated and fostered. The questions to be answered must be approached with open minds, honest and critical analysis, and persistence.

Characteristics

All children differ in their psychomotor, cognitive, and behavioral characteristics. Likewise, children with learning disabilities differ from one another, and there is considerable overlap in abilities between the child with learning disabilities and other children. However, there are some similar group characteristics that differentiate individuals with specific learning disabilities from non-disabled individuals.

Children can differ in motor performance for many reasons, including (1) neurophysiological differences, (2) language differences, (3) sensory input processing differences, (4) problems processing information, and (5) memory.

Neurophysiological Differences

Most of the research and theory on learning disability has been done by cognitive theorists. However, in the last 15 years there has been increased emphasis on neurophysiological functioning of the brain as it relates to learning disability. Studies of the brains of individuals with specific learning disabilities have been done using electroencephalography (EEG), auditory brainstem-evoked response (ABER), regional cerebral blood flow (rCBF), and magnetic resonance imaging (MRI). The purpose of this research is to determine whether any significant differences exist between the brain structure and function of normal individuals and those with learning disabilities. Some **neurophysiological differences** have been reported.

Using EEG, Johns[25] demonstrated that the evoked potentials of groups of students with learning disabilities were significantly different from those of students with no learning problems. Other investigators have reported significant differences in regions of blood flow,[32] brainstem-evoked responses during speech-processing tasks,[22] and the width of the structure connecting the two hemispheres of the brain.[16] Neurophysiological tools such as these show great promise for early identification of children with specific learning disabilities. Once unique brain structure and function profiles are identified and correlated directly with specific learning difficulties, it will be possible to develop educational intervention strategies specific to each child's individual needs.

Language Differences

The physical education teacher should recognize individual language usage differences among students with learning disabilities.[17] Such knowledge can be used to modify teaching strategies that involve communication through language. There are at least three language categories: (1) receptive language, (2) expressive language, and (3) inner language.

Receptive language involves the ability to comprehend the meaning associated with language. Deficits in receptive language may be either visual or auditory. Visual deficits are reflected by the inability to organize and interpret visual information appropriately. For example, a child may be unable to interpret facial gestures appropriately. Auditory receptive language deficits may be reflected in failure to follow directions or inability to discriminate among sounds.

Expressive language involves the ability to communicate feelings, emotions, needs, and thoughts through speaking and gesturing (facial or manual). Auditory deficits are expressed through impaired speech, whereas visual expressive language deficits refer to problems in writing. Problems in visual expressive language are inability to reproduce simple geometric forms, persistent reversal of letters, rotation or inversion of letters, or reversed sequence of letters.

Inner language processes refer to the ability to transform experience into symbols. This, of course, is dependent on experiences. Inasmuch as young children gain much of their experience with the world through play and motor activity, environmental exploration with the body is an important aspect of the development of inner language.

Sensory Input–Processing Differences

An analysis of perceptual attributes important to skilled motor performances indicates that exteroceptors (e.g., eyes, ears, and tactile receptors) and proprioceptors (e.g., vestibular and kinesthetic receptors) are important avenues for receiving information from the environment. Deficits in information from these senses may result in deficits in performance of physical activities.

There is evidence that persons with learning disabilities may be impaired in their ability to balance. Good balance depends on accurate information from the vestibular system, as well as normal reflex and depth perception development. When vestibular information is not received or processed efficiently, impaired balance results. Persisting primitive reflexes and/or a delay in development of postural (equilibrium) reflexes also inhibit a person's ability to achieve and maintain balance. Depth perception deficiencies interfere with an individual's ability to use visual cues in the environment to assist in balancing. Impaired balance interferes with postural and locomotor efficiency, as well as foot-eye and hand-eye coordination.

Children with learning disabilities also may possess deficits in kinesthetic perception. These deficits limit knowledge of precise position and rate of movement of body parts in space. Kinesthesis is an essential prerequisite for sophisticated, refined sport skills that require precise movements, such as putting a golf ball, shooting a basketball, setting a volleyball, and any other movements that require qualitative forces for success. Most physical education activities require an awareness and control of body parts in space (i.e., kinesthetic perception). Thus kinesthesis is considered an important prerequisite for movement control, which generalizes to many other physical and sport activities.

Szklut, Cermak, and Henderson[41] estimate that 60% to 95% of these children have poor static and dynamic balance, coordination problems, low muscle tone, poor spatial orientation, and delayed acquisition of equilib-

Aquatic experiences can open a new world. (Courtesy Wisconsin Lions Camp, Rosholt, Wis.)

rium reactions. Morrison, Hinshaw, and Corte[33] also report that this population demonstrates significantly more primitive reflexes and vestibular and equilibrium delays than children without disabilities.

Many children who have learning disabilities are uncoordinated and lack control of motor responses. Individuals with poorly developed balance and kinesthetic systems tend to have problems in changing directions or body positions. As a result, these individuals commonly have difficulty learning to perform efficient specific sport and motor skills.

Problems Processing Information

There is evidence that many persons with learning disabilities may differ from their unaffected peers as a result of their inability to process information efficiently.[10] Information processing relates to how one retains and manipulates information. It refers to how information is acquired, stored, selected, and then recalled. Although there appears to be agreement that as a group the population with learning disabilities has problems in information processing, the specific locus of the problem is disputed. Cermak[12] indicates that processing deficits appear in the speed of rehearsal strategies. On the other hand, Karr and Hughes[26] indicate that the problem may not be a processing deficit. They demonstrated that this population is able to handle information associated with increased task difficulty in the same manner as nondisabled persons; however, a problem may exist in the very early input stages of the processing mechanism (i.e., getting information into the processing system). Individuals with learning disabilities often demonstrate motor performance behaviors that provide clues about inappropriate receipt or use of information received through the visual and auditory mechanisms.

For instance, the six extraocular motor muscles of the eye must be controlled in such a way that objects of attention are fixated at the same points on each retina. If one or more sets of the extraocular muscles of the eye are weakened, one or both eyes will misalign and depth perception will be impaired. Individuals with impaired depth perception will misjudge where objects are in space. As a result, they will be unable to catch and kick balls, will descend stairs one at a time, and will avoid climbing apparatus. Figure-ground perception involves the ability to distinguish an object from its background. It requires selecting and attending to the appropriate visual cue among a number of other cues that are irrelevant to that task at a particular moment. If the visual object to which the individual is to respond is not well defined, then chances are that the motor task will be less proficient than desired. Individuals with poor depth perception almost always demonstrate deficits in visual figure-ground perception.

Another visual characteristic that may be impaired in this population is ocular saccadical abilities, which permit the learner to refix the eye on differing targets accurately and quickly. The ocular saccadical ability is required in those sports in which an individual must concentrate on a moving ball, as well as a moving target (e.g., in football, when a quarterback throws a ball to a second receiver after seeing that the first potential receiver is covered; in basketball, when focusing on a rebounding ball and then refocusing vision to find an outlet player to pass to). Any visual deficiency that interferes with visual discrimination needed for proficient performance of a given sport will impair the performance of that sport.

The auditory mechanism may not be as critical as the eye in performance of sport activity; however, impaired ability of the individual to utilize auditory information may result in performance that is below normative expectations. Some of the sport activities requiring auditory discrimination and perception are dancing and floor routines in gymnastics. Auditory figure-ground discrimination is important to skill proficiency. Any time there are extraneous auditory sounds, auditory figure-ground perception is needed (e.g., when players participating in a noisy gym must attend closely to hear the coaches' instructions and officials' calls).

Ayres[6] suggests that individuals who are learning disabled may have deficits in motor planning. Eichstaedt and Kalakian[19] describe motor planning as the ability to execute behaviors in the proper sequential order. Sport skill tasks require the integration of discrete component parts in sequence for task success. When one is learning a motor task, each component part of the skill must be planned and carried out in sequence before the skill can be executed correctly. With practice, the skill becomes a subroutine that is stored in long-term memory, and motor-planning requirements are lessened. However, when one is learning new skills that are composed of component parts that must be sequenced, each component part must be present for the skill to be learned. Individuals with learning disabilities who demonstrate difficulty with motor planning may not have the necessary components (e.g., vestibular, kinesthetic, or visual information) available to them.

Memory

Many individuals with learning disabilities also have deficits in long-term and short-term memory. Four steps are necessary for learning to occur: (1) a stimulus must be registered in the brain, (2) that stimulus must be maintained while its relevance is determined, (3) the stimulus must be processed in light of material present in long-term storage, and (4) the stimulus must be placed in long-term storage. Thus deficits in either short-term or long-term memory limit the benefits of prior experiences and practice.

Memory is also a prerequisite for closure, which is the ability to recognize a visual or auditory experience when only part is presented. The partial image is compared with complete images that are stored in the memory for identification. An example of visual closure occurs when a baseball player is batting. The batter must make inferences as to where the ball will be when it crosses the plate. If a batter is not able to estimate where the ball will cross the plate, it is impossible to determine where the bat should be swung. More experienced batters have more comparative images stored in their memory bank; thus they are better able to estimate the flight of an incoming ball than is the less experienced batter.

Individuals with learning disabilities also may be deficient in cue selection, which is the ability to attend to relevant cues and block out irrelevant stimuli. Individuals with memory, visual, or auditory deficits will not make efficient cue selections.

■ ■ ■

Any one or all of these factors will affect the success level of a child in physical education. Children with cognitive processing problems may not understand or remember instructions. Perceptual difficulties lead to spatial awareness or body image problems. Hyperactivity interferes with a student's ability to attend to instructions about, or persistence at, a task. Clumsy motor performance caused by delayed reflex and/or vestibular development or depth-perception problems directly influences a student's ability to master basic movement tasks and to combine those tasks into complicated patterns necessary to succeed in sport or leisure activities.

It is, however, difficult to group all children with specific learning disabilities together when trying to determine precisely what movement difficulties they will demonstrate. In an attempt to determine whether a clear-cut motor profile is demonstrated by this population, Pyfer[36] administered a wide variety of tests over an 11-year period to approximately 400 children with learning disabilities. Analysis of those data revealed that approximately 12% demonstrated no motor delays, 75% scored average on some tests but below average on other tests, and the remaining 13% were severely delayed in all areas tested. The youngsters who demonstrated motor delays were deficient in balance, spatial awareness, body image, visual-motor control, and/or fine motor development. These findings agree with those of the studies cited earlier in this chapter. That is, no one performance profile characterizes all individuals with learning disabilities. These children constitute a heterogeneous group, and as such they need to be treated as individuals. Haubenstricker[23] proposes that before appropriate prescriptive activities are selected, efforts must be made to determine particular movement characteristics of the students with specific learning disabilities. He proposes that

the earlier the problem is identified and the longer the remediation is carried out, the better the chances are for eliminating the problems.

Testing to Determine Motor-Functioning Levels

Appropriate tests to use with this population include any instruments that will provide information about the functioning of sensory input systems (vestibular, kinesthetic, visual efficiency, and reflex development), balance, fine motor control, and visual-motor control. An instrument that can provide several clues about the motor-functioning level of this population is the Bruininks-Oseretsky Test of Motor Proficiency. Helpful subtests for pinpointing possible vestibular, kinesthetic, visual efficiency, bilateral coordination, and physical fitness delays are the gross motor and upper limb coordination subtests and the visual-motor control section of the fine motor subtest. Rather than using the subtest scores to determine whether delays exist, it is recommended that the evaluator examine performance of specific components of the subtests. Specific clues to developmental delays are as follows:

- A marked difference (5 or 6 seconds) between ability to balance with the eyes open and ability to balance with the eyes closed, and inability to walk heel to toe on the floor suggest vestibular delay.
- If the student watches his or her feet while walking the balance beam and has trouble with static balance tasks with the eyes open and closed, the problem is probably visual (e.g., depth perception or visual acuity).
- Ability to execute activities requiring coordination of the limbs on one side of the body but not on opposite sides of the body suggests that bilateral integration has not yet occurred.
- Difficulty executing sit-ups and/or push-ups suggests deficient abdominal and shoulder girdle strength. To determine whether a reflex delay or weak abdominal muscles are causing difficulty in executing sit-ups, ask the student to get into a tucked position while lying on his or her back (e.g., the student puts his or her arms around bent legs and holds the forehead to the knees). If the student is unable to get into the tucked position or to hold it for at least 5 seconds, a persisting tonic labyrinthine supine primitive reflex may be the cause.

- A depressed running speed and agility score could be an indication of agility or visual deficiency.
- Difficulty catching a bounced or thrown ball indicates either poor depth perception or poor visual tracking skills.
- Any tendency to hold the head cocked and close to the paper during pencil-and-paper tasks and/or to go outside of the lines when tracing mazes and cutting around a circle suggests eye alignment problems.

If vestibular, kinesthetic, or bilateral integration delays are suspected, the student should be referred to occupational therapy for sensory integration testing. Possible visual problems may be referred to the school nurse for additional screening; however, frequently medical personnel do not have experience in evaluating visual misalignment and depth perception problems. These problems can best be evaluated by a **visual development specialist** with specific training in orthoptic vision. In some areas of the country, optometrists have specialized in this aspect of vision; in other areas ophthalmologists have the specialized training. Before making such a referral, one should contact the school principal for permission to do so, because, technically, referrals made by the school system must be paid for by the school system. School districts are usually very reluctant to assume responsibility for this type of follow-up, and the teacher is instructed not to advise the parent about the suspected problem. Commands of this sort place conscientious teachers in very difficult positions. Should the teacher put the child first and advise the parent about his or her suspicion, or should the teacher honor the superior's decision and let the student continue to experience failure?

Special Considerations
Attention Deficit Disorders

Over the years many terms have been used to describe inattentive and impulsive behaviors demonstrated by some children. Although originally identified in the 1930s,[40] research did not focus on this continuum of behaviors until the 1960s,[39] when the term *hyperkinetic impulse disorder* surfaced.[31] This was replaced by the term *hyperactive child syndrome* in the 1970s, and by *attention deficit disorder* (ADD) in the 1980s.[38]

Individuals with ADD have difficulty attending in school, work, and social situations. They are easily distracted and frequently make careless mistakes because they tend to rush through tasks without thinking. They have difficulty organizing their schoolwork and other responsibilities. They often appear to be daydreaming and/or not listening. When they do attempt tasks, their work is usually very messy and only partially completed. These individuals typically make every effort to avoid activities that demand sustained self-application, mental effort, and/or close concentration. They also have difficulty "reading" social situations and, as a result, make comments out of turn, initiate conversations at inappropriate times, and intrude on others. They are often judged by others as lazy, uncaring, and unreliable, when in reality they simply cannot focus their attention for any length of time.

The first signs of ADD are usually recognized at age 4 and 5 years, a time when children are expected to begin to attend to tasks for increasing amounts of time. Children with ADD combined with hyperactivity disorder (HD) move excessively, are difficult to contain, and refuse to attend to tasks for more than a few seconds. As they reach adolescence, their excessive gross movements decrease, but they demonstrate restlessness and fidgeting. During the teenage years their impulsive behaviors lead to breaking of school and family rules; thus they are usually in trouble with someone. In adulthood these individuals avoid sedentary activities and occupations that limit their opportunity for spontaneous movement (e.g., desk jobs).

Three distinct forms of ADD have been identified: (1) attention deficit disorder with hyperactivity (ADHD), (2) attention deficit disorder without hyperactivity (ADD-WO), and (3) attention deficit disorder–residual (ADD-R).

Behaviors common to all three forms of the disorder are short attention span, distractibility, and incompleted tasks. Specific behaviors demonstrated in each form include:

- *ADHD:* Short attention span, easy distractibility, poor listening skills, incompleted tasks, impulsiveness, restlessness, and inappropriate excessive motor activity.[28]
- *ADD-WO:* Loss of thought patterns, shifts from initial impressions, delays in delivering responses, delays in recalling names and descriptions.[28]
- *ADD-R:* Identifies the adolescent child or young adult who has not outgrown the syndrome. Ap-

proximately 30% to 60% of all ADD/HD individuals do not outgrow the problem.[7]

Estimates of prevalence of all forms of the disorder are difficult to locate because some authors include various forms of learning disabilities and/or conduct disorders in their counts. Others, particularly those in the medical profession, focus specifically on the ADHD population. It is probably safe to estimate that 10% to 20% of the school-age population experience some form of ADD, with or without concomitant problems.[37] Approximately 80% of individuals with specific learning disabilities are estimated to also have ADD/HD.[8]

Drug Therapy

Drug therapy is a common medical intervention technique used in the treatment of behavioral, emotional, and attention deficits associated with the education of children who are learning disabled.[20] Although the reported use of drug treatment with children with specific learning disabilities varies, Aman and Rojahn[1] suggest that 10% of these children may be taking prescribed psychotropic drugs.

Because of the numerous behavioral and cognitive symptoms associated with specific learning disabilities, there are a variety of drugs used with this population. These include (1) neuroleptics (antipsychotics, "major tranquilizers"), (2) anticonvulsants, (3) sedative-hypnotics, (4) antidepressant/antimanic drugs, (5) central nervous system stimulants, and (6) miscellaneous drugs.[2] Drug treatment of a child with a specific learning disability will depend on his or her physician's assessment. However, by far, the most frequent drugs prescribed are methylphenidate (Ritalin) and dextroamphetamine (Dexedrine), both of which are central nervous stimulants. Because of the increasing use of stimulant drugs by these populations,[39] physical educators should be aware of the major effects of drug treatment.

Effects of Drug Treatment

Chandler, Gualtieri, and Fahs[13] suggest that most drugs produce substantial behavioral changes in ADD children with specific learning disabilities when the drugs are properly prescribed and managed. The same improvement has been documented in ADHD adults with childhood onset.[7] Stimulant drugs that lessen hyperactivity and improve short-term memory improve learning performance. Much of the literature does not, however, support long-term academic gains due to the use of stimulants.[1]

Assessment and Management of Drug Treatment

Observations made at home and school are extremely helpful in assessing the value of drug treatment. Because single observation of the behavior of children taking drugs is rarely sufficient, Atkins and Pelham[4] suggest that multiple classroom measures involving formal teacher ratings, peer ratings, and direct observations should be made. With such assessments it is easier to determine how the drugs affect learning and social behaviors. Direct observations in the gymnasium and on the playground are helpful in determining the effects of drug treatment and management of behavior.

The side effects of drug treatment vary depending on the individual, the nature or type of drug, the length of time the student has been taking the medication, the strength of the dose, and other variables. Negative side effects from drugs that should be reported immediately are nausea, vomiting, rapid breathing, hearing problems, drowsiness, increased appetite, increased euphoria, weight loss, anemia, menstrual irregularities, insomnia, psychic disturbances, sweating, visual disturbances, weakness, fatigue, reduced heart rate, headaches, coma, convulsions, skin rashes, feeling of urinary urgency, dehydration, loss of balance, hyperactivity, fainting, and inability to concentrate.[35]

Medication Policies

It is reported that slightly less than one half of the public schools have medication policies.[20] Even when there are policies, there is little consistency across schools. Epstein et al.[20] suggest that schools should organize a multidisciplinary team to develop procedures for labeling, storing, administering, monitoring, and reporting medication.

Teaching Strategies

Regardless of what type of program a physical educator favors, tests should be administered to determine the motor-functioning level of the child with a specific learning disability. After areas of deficiency have been identified, activities can be selected to promote development in these problem areas. If appropriate activities are selected and carefully taught, the prognosis for the motor

A teenager prepares for the challenge of an above-the-ground (30 feet) ropes course. (Courtesy Wisconsin Lions Camp, Rosholt, Wis.)

development of these students is quite good. At least one study reported that once perceptual and motor deficiencies of children with learning disabilities were resolved through a well-designed bottom, up motor development program, the children continued to develop motor ability along age-expected levels.[30]

Specific activities to use with students with specific learning disabilities can be found in Chapters 4 and 5. General points to keep in mind when working with these students follow:

1. To reduce interference from hyperactive (hyperkinetic) tendencies, select a larger number of different activities and spend less time on each than you would with other children the same age.

2. Use a positive behavior modification program to get these students to finish tasks (e.g., use tokens or let them select their favorite activity once each day if they stay on task).

3. Incorporate 3 to 5 minutes of conscious relaxation instruction or practice into each class period (preferably at the end of the lesson).

4. Give brief instructions and ask the children to repeat those instructions before starting an activity. By doing this, you prevent problems that arise from the limited memory some of the children demonstrate.

5. To enhance the children's opportunities for success and willingness to persist at tasks, break tasks into small learning steps and praise every legitimate effort they make.

The Physical Education Program

Whenever possible the physical educator should limit these students' participation in group activities that are beyond their capabilities. Such practices only reinforce their feelings of inferiority. When these students are included with the regular physical education class, the more activities that use an individualized approach that enables each student to work at his or her own level without being compared with peers, the better these students' opportunity to realize some success. At the elementary school level, activities should be used that promote sensory input functioning before perceptual-motor integration or motor output behaviors are concentrated on. The greatest amount of carryover will occur if one "fills in the blanks" of missing sensory and perceptual components before teaching motor output behaviors. Several activities that can be used with elementary children of all ability levels are included in the handbook *Gross Motor Activities for Young Children with Special Needs*, which accompanies this text. At the middle and high school levels programs should be provided that encourage and reward individual effort. Examples are changing the way games are played to accommodate a variety of performance capabilities and personal fitness programs that are specifically patterned to impact the individual's present level of performance.

When small-group or whole-class programs are provided for students with specific learning disabilities, it is easier to focus on their particular needs. However, there is controversy among physical educators as to whether a bottom, up developmental approach or a task-

A paraprofessional leads a class in rhythm activity to develop body part identification skills. (Courtesy Dallas Independent School District.)

specific top, down approach should be used in the instruction of motor skills for the learning disabled. A bottom, up approach to facilitate movement efficiency would begin with sensory stimulation activities to provide prerequisite components for meaningful culturally relevant skills. With such an approach there would be extended periods during which students would be engaging in specific activities to facilitate basic sensory and reflex systems. Proponents of this approach believe that once the basic sensory and reflex systems are functioning and those stimuli are integrated, perceptual-motor development, as well as learning of specific motor skills, will occur. Admittedly, the number of components of sensory input systems, as well as perceptual-motor functions, is considerable. All of the senses, the integration of each of the senses, the perceptual-motor characteristics of the individual, the way in which information is processed, and associative and organizational structures of perceptual skills that can be linked with each of the sensory modes are taken into consideration. Effective utilization of this approach requires extensive knowledge on the part of the teacher and the willingness to delay instruction in what many consider culturally relevant skills.

The top, down approach to facilitating movement efficiency would start with the culturally relevant skills and work down toward prerequisite components when it became apparent that a learner was not benefiting from direct instruction regarding a specific task. Which approach to use can be determined through thorough evaluation and interpretation of results. When evaluation results clearly indicate no sensory or reflex deficits, the most economical method would be the top, down approach. Also, the older the learner, the less appealing the bottom, up approach becomes.

Modifications

Teaching and program modifications that are helpful for students with specific learning disabilities include the following:

1. *Controlling attention:* One of the methods for controlling attention is to establish routines that are repeated day after day. This enables the child to develop a pattern of activities. The teaching techniques, behavior modification program, and organizational patterns should be kept as structured and consistent as possible.

2. *Controlling extraneous stimuli in the environment:* In addition to stable routines, the environment should appear relatively the same from one day to the next. Positioning of equipment and systematic procedures to store equipment should be established and maintained.

3. *Controlling desired behaviors:* There should be in-

structionally relevant stimuli to focus the attention of the students (e.g., designate specific spots on the floor where students are to begin class each day). Visual cues can be used that indicate where the hands are to be placed for a push-up or for a forward roll. Specific visual or auditory information can be introduced that indicates to the individual specifically what to do with body parts to enhance motor control.

4. *Controlling methodology:* If the learner has a tendency to disassociate visually or auditorially, use the whole-part-whole method of teaching. Later, attention to details of performance can be emphasized.

5. *Using more than one sensory modality:* In addition to verbally describing the task to be performed, visual stimuli (e.g., a picture, drawing, or demonstration) should be used. In this way, if the student with a learning disability has either visual or verbal deficits, another sensory avenue can be used to comprehend the instruction. Kinesthetic aids such as manually moving a child through sequences also can be used.

Community-Based Opportunities

Individuals who grow into adulthood with specific learning disabilities must be taught compensation skills to enable them to recreate in the community. Too frequently, middle school and high school students with specific learning disabilities who have not had their condition properly identified and attended to develop all types of anxiety, guilt, and feelings of inadequacy.[34] Because they have IQs within the normal range, they are bright enough to realize that no matter how much effort they exert, as the school material becomes increasingly complex and demanding, their peers are going to outperform them academically. It is no wonder that these youngsters balk at continuing in school, demonstrate significant conduct problems, and frequently become alchohol dependent.[7] Professionals must make every effort to ensure that those students who are not performing to adequate academic standards are properly assessed so that intervention that will match their needs can be implemented. Their transition program should match their needs to the opportunities available in the community.

Probably the most significant knowledge these young adults require is that they are not to blame for their learning difficulties. The next most important piece of information they need is an understanding of their specific information-processing deficits. With that knowledge, maturing individuals can make informed decisions that will enable them to participate successfully in work and social activities.

Knowing there is a reason for the academic and social struggles they have experienced reduces the guilt, acting out and avoidance behaviors, and feelings of alienation from society. As a result, their self-confidence increases and they become more motivated to attempt and persist at difficult tasks. With knowledge about the nature of their limitations, they can then either determine the types of assistance needed to realize success or select activities that circumvent their problem areas. Frequently, selecting an activity partner to assist with decision making is sufficient. For example, if determining distances is a problem, a golfer should select a partner or caddy who is willing and able to read the layout of the course and make club recommendations. When the individual is canoeing or kayaking for any distance or on an unfamiliar body of water, a partner versed in orienteering is essential. Adults with learning disabilities should be discouraged from attempting to participate in activities requiring skills for which they are unable to compensate.

SUMMARY

Specific learning disability is a condition that is manifested through disabilities in listening, thinking, writing, speaking, spelling, and mathematical calculations. The majority of children with this disability also demonstrate sensory-perceptual-motor problems. There is widespread disagreement about the relationship between the cognitive and psychomotor problems demonstrated by children with specific learning disabilities. The controversy does not dismiss the reality of poor perceptual and motor coordination displayed by many of these children. To determine what types of delays these students are experiencing, testing must be done. Selected parts of the long form of the Bruininks Oseretsky Test of Motor Proficiency can be used to identify areas of concern.

When including this type of student in the regular physical education class, one should either select activities that will be of benefit to these students and to their classmates or allow for individualized programs for all students. There are two types of programs that will benefit students with specific learning disabilities: (1) a bottom, up approach that focuses on facilitating deficit sensory input and reflex systems is appropriate for younger children, and (2) a top, down skill development approach that focuses on instruction in specific performance tasks that are available in the community is critical for the middle school and high school student. During the school years every effort should be made to determine the reasons students are failing to benefit from their academic experiences. These knowledges are critical for developing the attitudinal and coping skills needed to participate fully in society.

Review Questions

1. What are some possible reasons why Miguel frequently demonstrates off-task behaviors?
2. What things could the physical education teacher do to reduce Miguel's off-task behavior?
3. What is the relationship between perceptual-motor abilities and cognitive functioning?
4. What are some psychomotor, cognitive, and behavioral characteristics of children with specific learning disabilities?
5. What are some positive effects of drug therapy?
6. What types of motor development delays would you expect these students to demonstrate during the assessment process?
7. What are some teaching strategies that can make learning more effective for children with specific learning disabilities?

Student Activities

1. Identify three behaviors Miguel demonstrates that must be extinguished to improve his chances of benefiting from his physical education experience. Develop one long-range behavioral goal and three short-term objectives leading to each goal that address Miguel's problem areas.
2. Select three ways to modify/alter the physical education class setting to reduce or limit Miguel's opportunities to act out.
3. Observe a class that includes students with learning disabilities. List some of the characteristics of these students as they participate in physical activity. Describe their social interactions.

References

1. Aman MJ, Rojahn J: Pharmacological intervention. In Singh NN, Beale LL, editors: *Learning disabilities: nature, theory and treatment,* New York, 1992, Springer-Verlag.
2. Aman MJ, Singh NN: *Psychopharmacology of the developmental disabilities,* New York, 1988, Springer-Verlag.
3. American Psychiatric Association: *Diagnostic and statistical manual of mental disorders DSM-IV,* Washington, DC, 1994.
4. Atkins MS, Pelham WE: School based assessment of attention-deficit hyperactivity disorder, *J Learning Disabil* 24:197-204, 1991.
5. Ayres AJ: *Sensory integration and learning disorders,* Los Angeles, 1972, Western Psychological Services.
6. Ayres AJ: *Sensory integration and the child,* Los Angeles, 1980, Western Psychological Services.
7. Biederman J et al: Gender differences in a sample of adults with attention deficit hyperactivity disorder, *Psychiatry Res* 53:13-29, 1994.
8. Blau M: A.D.D.: the scarlet letters in the alphabet, *New York Magazine,* pp 44-51 Dec 1993.
9. Bradley C: The behavior of children receiving benzedrine, *J Psychiatry* 94:577-585, 1987.
10. Brunt D, Magill R, Eason R: Distinctions in variability of motor output between learning disabled and normal children, *Percept Mot Skills* 57:731-734, 1983.
11. Cammisa K: Educational kinesiology with learning disabled children: an efficacy study, *Percept Mot Skills* 78:105-106, 1994.
12. Cermak LS: Information processing deficits in children with learning disabilities, *J Learning Disabil* 16:599-605, 1983.
13. Chandler M, Gualtieri CT, Fahs JJ: Other psychotropic drugs: stimulants, antidepressants, and anxiolytics, and lithium carbonate. In Aman MJ, Singh NN, editors: *Psychopharmacology of the developmental disabilities,* New York, 1988, Springer-Verlag.
14. Dennison P, Hargrove G: *Personalized whole brain integration,* Glendale, Calif, 1985, Edu-Kinesthetics.
15. deQuiros JB, Schrager OL: *Neuropsychological fundamentals in learning disabilities,* Novato, Calif, 1979, Academic Therapy Publications.
16. Duane D, Gray B, editors: *The reading brain: the biological basis of dyslexia,* Parkton, Md, 1991, York Press.
17. Dunn JM, Fait H: *Special physical education,* Dubuque, Iowa, 1989, Wm C Brown.
18. EDLAW, Inc: *Individuals with disabilities education act,* Potomac, Md, 1991.
19. Eichstaedt CB, Kalakian LH: *Developmental/adapted physical education,* New York, 1987, Macmillan.
20. Epstein MH et al: Psychopharmacological intervention. II. Teacher perceptions of psychotropic medication for students with learning disability, *J Learning Disabil* 24:477-483, 1991.

21. Frostig M, Maslow P: *Movement education: theory and practice,* Chicago, 1970, Follett Publishing.

22. Grant D: *Brainstem level auditory function in specific dyslexics and normal readers,* Ann Arbor, 1980, University of Michigan, DAI 3376-B.

23. Haubenstricker JL: Motor development of children with learning disabilities, *J Phys Educ Rec Dance* 53(5):41-43, 1983.

24. Hoehn T, Baumeister A: A critique of the application of sensory integration theory to children with learning disabilities, *J Learning Disabil* 27:338-350, 1994.

25. Johns ER: *Neurometric evaluation of brain function in normal and learning disabled children,* Ann Arbor, Mich, 1991, University of Michigan Press.

26. Karr R, Hughes K: Movement difficulty and learning disabled children, *Adapt Phys Act Q* 5:72-79, 1987.

27. Kephart N: *The slow learner in the classroom,* Columbus, Ohio, 1971, Charles E Merrill Publishing.

28. King KJ: The attention deficit disorder (ADD) child, *KAPPAN,* Dec 22-26, 1989.

29. Leary PM, Batho K: The role of the EEG in the investigation of the child with learning disability, *S Afr Med J,* pp 867-868, June 1981.

30. McLaughlin E: *Followup study on children remediated for perceptual-motor dysfunction at the University of Kansas perceptual-motor clinic,* Eugene, 1980, University of Oregon.

31. Menkes M, Rowe J, Menkes J: A twenty-five year follow-up study on the hyperkinetic child with minimal brain dysfunction, *Pediatrics* 39:393-399, 1967.

32. Millay K, Grant D, Pyfer J: *Structural and functional differences in brain organization in developmental dyslexics,* Unpublished paper, Denton, Tex, 1991, Texas Woman's University.

33. Morrison D, Hinshaw S, Corte E: Signs of neurobehavioral dysfunction in a sample of learning disabled children: stability and concurrent validity, *Percept Mot Skills* 61:863-872, 1985.

34. Naylor MW et al: Language disorders and learning disabilities in school-refusing adolescents, *J Am Acad Child Adolesc Psychiatry* 33:1331-1337, 1994.

35. Patton JR et al: *Exceptional children in focus,* New York, 1990, Macmillan.

36. Pyfer JL: *Sensory-perceptual-motor characteristics of learning disabled children: a validation study,* Unpublished paper, Denton, Tex, 1983, Texas Woman's University.

37. Schacher R: Childhood hyperactivity, *J Child Psychol Psychiatry* 32:155-191, 1991.

38. Shaywitz SE, Shaywitz BA: Attention deficit disorder: current perspectives, *Pediatr Neurol* 3:129-135, 1987.

39. Shaywitz SE, Shaywitz BA: Introduction to the special series on attention deficit disorder, *J Learning Disabil* 24:68-74, 1991.

40. Stewart M et al: The hyperactive child syndrome, *Am J Orthopsychiatry* 35:861-867, 1966.

41. Szklut SE, Cermak S, Henderson A: Learning disabilities. In Umphred D, editor: *Neurological rehabilitation,* ed 3, St Louis, 1995, Mosby.

Suggested Readings

Hallahan DP, Kaufman JM, Lloyd JW: *Introduction to learning disabilities,* ed 2, Englewood Cliffs, NJ, 1985, Prentice Hall.

Seaman JA, DePauw K: *The new adapted physical education: a developmental approach,* Palo Alto, Calif, 1989, Mayfield Publishing.

chapter fourteen

Emotional Disturbances

Courtesy Dallas Independent School District.

Objectives

Identify the interpersonal relationship characteristics of persons who are emotionally disturbed.

Describe the techniques used for conducting programs of physical education for students who are emotionally disturbed.

Explain the physical education teacher's role in the individual education program (IEP) process.

Describe a process for making appropriate decisions to control excessive behavior displayed by students who are emotionally disturbed.

Select appropriate activities for students who are emotionally disturbed.

Scenario

Daniel is 13 years of age. Since entering school at age 6 years, he has been receiving his educational services in a self-contained classroom for students with emotional disturbance. Because Daniel's gross motor skills are one of his strengths, he has been included in the regular physical education program since entering school. From the time he entered the program, his behavior has been difficult to manage; however, within the last few months it has been deteriorating. The physical education teacher reports the following behavior as typical of Daniel during class:

- Verbally aggressive behavior, particularly swearing, directed at his classmates and the teacher
- Physically aggressive behavior, including pushing, shoving, and tripping his classmates, throwing and kicking balls at others, and swinging bats and racquets at other children
- Destroying equipment
- Violent mood swings with no apparent trigger
- Refusal to obey teacher requests and rules
- Self-abuse behaviors, including "tattooing" self by

rubbing an eraser on his skin until the skin breaks, peeling off the scab as soon as it appears, and repeating the process so that eventually a scar develops

Task

As you read this chapter, think about Daniel's acting-out behavior. Using the information in this chapter and the behavior modification techniques described in Chapter 6, make a note of at least six ways the teacher could and should deal with Daniel's undesirable behaviors. Explain how each of the techniques you have selected will positively impact the educational setting for both Daniel and his classmates.

There are several terms in the literature that have parallel meaning to the term *emotionally disturbed.* Some of these terms are *emotionally disordered, behaviorally disordered, behaviorally disabled, emotionally handicapped, psychologically disordered,* and *mentally ill.* For the purposes of this discussion, the term *emotionally disturbed* incorporates all of these terms.

Definition

The identification of behavior disorders demonstrated by learners in special education is controversial. Emotional or behavioral disorder refers to a condition in which behavioral or emotional responses of an individual in school are so different from the generally accepted, age-appropriate, ethnic, or cultural norms as to result in significant impairment in self-care, social relationships, educational progress, classroom behavior, work adjustment,[58] or personal happiness.[37] However, in a pluralistic society, behavior that is acceptable in some groups is unacceptable in others.[37] Thus some of the elements defining behavior disorder may be (1) a description of the problem behavior, (2) the setting in which the behavior occurs, and (3) who regards the behavior as a problem.

According to the Education of the Handicapped Act, Section 121a.5(b)(8), **serious emotional disturbance** is defined as follows[63]:

1. The term means a condition exhibiting one or more of the following characteristics over a long period of time and to a marked degree, which adversely affects educational performance.
   a. Inability to learn, which cannot be explained by intellectual, sensory, or health factors.
   b. An inability to build or maintain satisfactory interpersonal relationships with peers and teachers.
   c. Inappropriate types of behavior or feelings under normal circumstances.
   d. A general pervasive mood of unhappiness or depression.
   e. A tendency to develop physical symptoms or fears associated with personal or school problems.
2. The definition includes children who are schizophrenic. The term does not include children who are socially maladjusted, unless it is determined that they are seriously emotionally disturbed.

Continuum

Emotional functioning may be viewed as a continuum of demonstrated behavior from normal to abnormal and socially unacceptable. Usually, the greater the deviance from the norm, the greater the need for resources to maintain or provide remedial services. French and Jansma[27] describe a continuum of emotional disturbance based on the percentage of inappropriate behavior.

The severity of the emotional disturbance is another important variable that reflects placement on a continuum. When acts that result from an emotional disturbance present a danger to self and to others, such behavior is said to reflect deep-seated emotional problems.

Kalakian and Eichstaedt[34] make a distinction between having an emotional disturbance and being emotionally disturbed. Having an emotional disturbance in response to frustration is expected and normal. The state of being emotionally disturbed is characterized by behavior that is disordered to a marked degree and that occurs over a protracted period.

Incidence

There is disagreement among authorities as to the incidence of emotional disturbance. In general, estimates are that 7% to 8% of all school-age children and youth may have an emotional or behavioral disorder severe enough to require treatment.[26] During the 1991 to 1992 school year, 402,668 children and youth were officially classified as emotionally disturbed. This represented less than 1% of schoolchildren who were receiving special education services for behavior disorders. The disparity between prevalence figures of emotional disturbance and the number of children receiving treatment may result from administrators who do not want to identify more children than they can treat or afford to treat with their limited resources.[37]

The data from 1984 to 1990 indicate that increasingly fewer students were being included in regular programs in spite of major inclusion initiatives.[54] During those years 16% of the students identified as emotionally disturbed were placed in regular classes, 64% were placed in resource rooms or special classes, and 20% were placed in separate schools or residential facilities, or were homebound.[62]

More than 75% of individuals in the schools who are identified as emotionally disturbed are male.[45] In the opinion of some, girls who qualify for special education services for emotional disturbance are underrepresented.[10]

Causes

The cause of emotional disturbance is believed to be a result of an interaction of environmental and genetic factors.[30] *Environmental* or *functional* causes are behavioral disorders caused by real or imagined pressures from peers, parents, teachers, or other authority figures, as well as child abuse, poverty, discrimination, peer pressure, breakdown in the family unit, perception of self as being of limited value, and/or inability to adapt to a change in surroundings. *Genetic* causes include biological bases such as chemical imbalances, glandular dysfunctions, or other inherited conditions, such as Rett syndrome.

There are differing points of view regarding the predominant cause of the more severe emotional disturbances of childhood. Many authorities trace the cause of emotional disturbance to environmental circumstances that occur early in life. Faulty parental relationships, in particular, are believed by some authorities to account for a great portion of emotional disturbance in children. Some authorities estimate that 75% of the children who are disruptive in school come from "broken" homes.[38] Grossman[29] indicates that teachers may contribute to emotional disturbance in schools by discriminating against the students by criticizing them in a harsh manner. Another factor that may contribute to problem behavior is that some students from different cultures may have trouble adjusting to authoritarian practices used in some schools.

Establishing a friendship with an animal may be the first step in trusting. (Courtesy Recreation Services, Division of Care and Treatment Facilities, Department of Health and Social Services, Northern Wisconsin Center for the Developmentally Delayed.)

Characteristics

Medical and educational models differ in their perception of characteristics of disorders. The medical model stresses symptoms that can be traced to a specific pathological factor. The symptoms are used to identify an underlying disorder but do not lead to suggested solutions to the problem. Therefore medical diagnoses alone usually are not very useful to educators.[31]

The educational model is more concerned with managing the behavior of children so that learning can occur.[11] The individual is evaluated, and an educational intervention program is designed so that the child can benefit from his or her school experience regardless of the disability. Because it is important that educators and the medical profession understand each other's language and can communicate with one another,[21] characteristics of persons with emotional disturbance according to both the medical and educational models follow.

Medical Model

The medical model puts emotional disturbance into the following disorder categories: (1) schizophrenia and other psychotic disorders, (2) mood, (3) anxiety, (4) somatoform, (5) factitious, (6) dissociative, or (7) sexual.[2] Because schizophrenia and other psychotic disorders are the most prevalent type of personality disorders demonstrated by school-age children and youth, those are the only categories described in this chapter.

Schizophrenia

Schizophrenia and other psychotic disorders are disorders that involve abnormal behavior patterns with personality disorganization. There is usually less than adequate contact with reality. Diagnostic criteria for schizophrenia as defined by the American Psychiatric Association[2] are as follows:

A. Characteristic symptoms: Two (or more) of the following, each present for a significant portion of time during a 1-month period (or less, if successfully treated): delusions, hallucinations, disorganized speech, grossly disorganized or catatonic behavior, negative symptoms.
B. Social/occupational dysfunction: For a significant portion of the time since the onset of the disturbance, one or more major areas of functioning such as work, interpersonal relations, or self-care are markedly below the expected level of interpersonal, academic, or occupational achievement for the person's age.
C. Duration: Continuous signs of the disturbance persist for at least 6 months. This 6-month period must include at least 1 month of symptoms that meet criterion A and may include periods of lessened symptoms such as manifestation of odd beliefs and/or a report of unusual perceptual experiences.
D. Schizoaffective disorder and mood disorder with psychotic features have been ruled out because no major depressive, manic, or mixed episodes have occurred concurrently with the active-phase symptoms; their total duration has been brief relative to the duration of the active and residual periods.
E. Substance/general medical condition exclusion: The disturbance is not due to the direct physiological effects of a substance (e.g., a drug of abuse, a medication) or a general medical condition.
F. Relationship to a pervasive developmental disorder: If there is a history of autistic disorder or another pervasive developmental disorder, the additional diagnosis of schizophrenia is made only if prominent delusions or hallucinations are also present for at least a month (or less if successfully treated).

Five types of schizophrenia have been identified. Diagnostic criteria for each follow.[2]

Paranoid type. Paranoid schizophrenia is a type of schizophrenia in which the following criteria are met:

1. Preoccupation with one or more delusions or with frequent auditory hallucinations

2. None of the following: disorganized speech, disorganized or catatonic behavior, or flat or inappropriate affect

Disorganized type. Disorganized schizophrenia is a type of schizophrenia in which the following criteria are met:

1. All of the following are prominent:
   a. Disorganized speech
   b. Disorganized behavior
   c. Flat or grossly inappropriate affect
2. Does not meet the criteria for catatonic type

Catatonic type. Catatonic schizophrenia is a type of schizophrenia in which the clinical picture is dominated by at least two of the following:

1. Motoric immobility as evidenced by catalepsy (including waxy flexibility) or stupor
2. Excessive motor activity (that is apparently purposeless and not influenced by external stimuli)
3. Extreme negativism (an apparently motiveless resistance to all instructions or maintenance of a rigid posture against attempts to be moved) or mutism
4. Peculiarities of voluntary movement as evidenced by posturing (voluntary assumption of inappropriate or bizarre postures), stereotyped movements, prominent mannerisms, or prominent grimacing
5. Echolalia or echopraxia

Undifferentiated type. Undifferentiated schizophrenia is a type of schizophrenia in which symptoms that meet criterion A for schizophrenia are present, but the criteria are not met for paranoid, disorganized, or catatonic type.

Residual type. Residual schizophrenia is a type of schizophrenia in which the following criteria are met:

1. Absence of prominent delusions, hallucinations, disorganized speech, and grossly disorganized or catatonic behavior
2. Continuing evidence of the disturbance, as indicated by the presence of negative symptoms or two or more of the symptoms listed in criterion A, present in an attenuated form (e.g., odd beliefs, unusual perceptual experiences)

Other psychotic disorders

Other psychotic disorders include the following:

■ *Schizophreniform disorder* is characterized by a symptomatic presentation that is equivalent to

schizophrenia except for its duration (the disturbance lasts from 1 to 6 months) and the absence of
a requirement that there be a decline in functioning.

- *Schizoaffective disorder* is characterized by a mood
episode and the active-phase symptoms of schizophrenia occurring together and being preceded or
followed by at least 2 weeks of delusions or hallucinations without prominent mood symptoms.
- *Delusional disorder* is characterized by at least 1
month of nonbizarre delusions without other active-
phase symptoms of schizophrenia.
- *Brief psychotic disorder* is a psychotic disturbance
that lasts more than 1 day and remits by 1 month.
- *Shared psychotic disorder* is a disturbance that develops in an individual who is influenced by someone else who has an established delusion with similar content.
- *Psychotic disorder due to a general medical condition* results in symptoms that are a direct physiological consequence of a general medical condition.
- *Substance-induced psychotic disorder* results in
symptoms that are a direct physiological consequence of drug abuse, a medication, or toxin exposure.
- *Psychotic disorder not otherwise specified* is included for classifying psychotic presentations that
do not meet the criteria for any of the specific psychotic disorders defined in this section or psychotic
symptomatology about which there is inadequate or
contradictory information.[2]

Educational Model

A list of characteristics that can be observed by physical
education teachers and that can be used to assist with
early identification of emotional disturbance follows. A
child is considered emotionally disturbed if he or she exhibits one or more of the following characteristics over
a long period of time to a marked degree[64]:

- An inability to learn that cannot be explained by intellectual, sensory, or health factors.
- An inability to build and maintain satisfactory interpersonal relationships with peers and teachers.
- Inappropriate types of behavior or feelings under normal
circumstances. Children who are emotionally disturbed
may act aggressively or totally withdraw from activity.

A child demonstrates solitary play skills. (Courtesy Dallas
Independent School District.)

- A general and pervasive mood of unhappiness or depression.
- A tendency to develop physical symptoms or fears associated with personal and school problems. This may be
due to long-term anxiety, excessive or unrealistic fears,
or anxieties stemming from perceived stress.

Other parts of the definition that are critical are:

Over a long period of time: Means the behavior must
be chronic. Many symptoms must be observed for
at least 6 months; however, other symptoms may
be of considerably less duration.[2] For instance,
school phobia may be apparent for only 2 weeks.

To a marked degree: Refers to the level of serious-
ness and interference with the child's total life. To
qualify as a serious behavioral problem, the behavior must impair the child's ability to function in
different environments rather than just isolated
situations.

Which adversely affects educational performance:
Means that the condition results in lowered educational achievement. Applied to performance in
physical education, this means the emotionally disturbed child fails to make reasonable progress in
sport skills or physical fitness development.

Emotionally disturbed children constitute a heterogeneous group. This becomes apparent when the behavior of an emotionally disturbed child who is hyperactive is compared with the behavior of an emotionally disturbed child who is withdrawn. There are many behavioral characteristics that are prevalent among the emotionally disturbed; however, all emotionally disturbed children do not possess all of these characteristics.

There is considerable evidence that children and youth with emotional disturbance have educational difficulties. Some of those difficulties follow:

- Only 33% of children and youth who are emotionally disturbed are receiving appropriate educational services[22]; as a result, families make tremendous financial sacrifices to secure needed services for their children.[13,39]
- Most students who are emotionally disturbed have lower grade point averages than their classmates.[40]
- Thirty-seven percent have learning disabilities.[37]
- Forty-six percent fail at least one high school course.[17,64]
- Twenty percent are arrested once before they drop out of school.[64]
- Fifty-eight percent leave school without graduating (most by the tenth grade).[62]

When children and youth are experiencing serious emotional turmoil, the teacher may be the first to notice the signals that a student is in trouble.[52,53] Symptoms that may interfere with the learning of motor skills and management of physical education classes follow:

1. Learning
   a. Poor work habits in practicing and developing motor skills and aspects of physical fitness
   b. Lack of motivation in achieving goals not of an immediate nature
   c. Disruptive class behavior on the part of students who are hyperactive
   d. Lack of involvement on the part of students who are withdrawn
   e. Inability to follow directions or seek help despite demands for constant attention
   f. Short attention span
   g. Poor coordination
   h. Development of physical symptoms (stomachache, headache, etc.) when confronted with physical activities with which the person is not secure
   i. Overactivity
   j. Restlessness
   k. Distractibility
   l. Amnesia
   m. Forgetfulness
   n. Impaired memory span
   o. General and specific disability
   p. Daydreaming
   q. Fear of teacher
   r. Resistance of authority
   s. Fear of criticism
2. Interpersonal relationships
   a. Lack of conscience
   b. Loss of emotional control
   c. Formation of superficial relationships
   d. Shyness
   e. Sensitivity
   f. Detachment
   g. Unsocialized aggressiveness
   h. Hostility
   i. Quarrelsomeness
   j. Destructiveness
   k. Temper tantrums
   l. Hostile disobedience
   m. Physical and verbal aggressiveness
   n. Holding group values of delinquency
   o. Fear
   p. Flight reaction
   q. Apprehension
   r. Anxiety
   s. Tension habits[42]
   t. Feeling of inferiority
   u. Feeling of inadequacy
   v. Disrespect of others
3. Inappropriate behavior under normal conditions
   a. Unhappiness or depression
   b. Inconsistencies in responses
   c. Rigid expectations of everyday life
   d. Carelessness, irresponsibility, and apathy
   e. Immaturity
   f. Timidity
   g. Feelings of rejection
   h. Feelings for restitution and retribution
   i. Aggressive behavior
   j. Withdrawal and self-isolation
   k. Negativism
   l. Noncooperation and contrariness

     m. Undisciplined
     n. Incorrigible
     o. Impulsive
     p. Repetitious behavior
     q. Aimless behavior
     r. Disorderly
     s. Unplanful
     t. Change of modes
     u. Physically and verbally abusive
  4. Physical and motor characteristics
     a. Poor physical condition caused by withdrawal from activity
     b. Retardation of motor skill development caused by withdrawal from activity
     c. Disorientation in space and time

Testing

Because the student who is emotionally disturbed may be poorly coordinated, a general motor test such as the Test of Gross Motor Development, as well as physical fitness testing, would be appropriate. No special modifications are required for a student who is emotionally disturbed; however, if it is suspected that a learning disability exists, additional testing using the balance and bilateral coordination subtests of the Bruininks-Oseretsky Test of Motor Proficiency may be warranted. When testing students who are emotionally disturbed, the teacher must be alerted to the fact that these individuals may feel extremely threatened by test situations. When they are placed in threatening situations, more acting-out behavior can be expected. Aggressive or withdrawing behaviors can be avoided if the student does not have to perform in the presence of peers and if the teacher is supportive of the student's efforts.

Special Considerations

The early identification of children who are emotionally disturbed is extremely important. It is recognized that the earlier educators and mental health specialists can attack this problem, the greater the prospect for ameliorating or remedying it. In many instances the treatment and education of emotionally disturbed persons involve the unlearning of behavioral patterns. If identification is made early, less unlearning is necessary.

Psychological tests are required to establish the presence of emotional disturbance. However, the psychological data and the label associated with the data do not provide specific information to assist the physical education teacher in planning instruction. Without a behavioral assessment and programming relevant to skills that are a part of the physical education program, the label is of limited value. Once a pupil is identified as emotionally disturbed, the physical education teacher should observe the student during class participation to determine which situations are most comfortable and which produce negative behaviors.

The physical educator should also be aware of other intervention programs in which the student may be participating. The four most frequent types of intervention approaches that are used with children and youth who are emotionally disturbed are (1) insight-oriented therapy, (2) play types of interventions, (3) behavioral interventions, and (4) the use of drugs to control behavior.[30]

Insight-Oriented Therapy

Insight-oriented therapy involves relieving symptoms by treating causes of behavior. A therapist, psychologist, or psychiatrist uses a nondirective, client-centered approach or a psychoanalytical approach to relieve symptoms.

Play Therapy

Development of the individual through play is the central mission of **play therapy.** Development of social relationships with others and playing out emotional problems, as well as developing positive peer relationships, are important. Through the play process, the child who is emotionally disturbed becomes aware of his or her own unconscious thoughts and the behaviors that result from these thoughts. In group play, the development of problem-solving skills can occur and be used to resolve problems in social situations. Small play groups may be formed to assist in developing social and problem-solving skills. Structured situations that involve (1) modeling, (2) role playing, (3) performance feedback, and (4) transfer of training have proved to be successful.[48]

Behavior Therapy

The purpose of **behavior therapy** is to eliminate disruptive behavior that interferes with management of classes and learning of the individual. It is useful for the control of excessive and unusual behavior, as well as for control of aggressive behavior. Behavioral interventions are usually designed to decrease undesirable behavior and increase desirable behavior. Contingency contracting and other motivational systems are used to encourage children to engage in normal behavior (see Chapter 6). This type of intervention is most effective when it is coordinated both in the home and in the school. During the 1990s many school systems adopted a system of behavioral intervention that, when used throughout the district, is extremely effective.

Drug Therapy

Drugs to relieve symptoms and to control unusual aggressive behaviors or other types of behaviors that interfere with learning are frequently prescribed for active, inattentive, and impulsive children. **Drug therapy** also may be used to control disorganized or highly erratic behavior. The decision of whether to prescribe drugs usually depends on several factors, including the severity of the disorder, the type of disorder, and the side effects of the drug. A balance between the side effects that interfere with learning and the control of the behavior must be weighed by professionals.

Medication

It is estimated that 25% of students with disabilities are receiving medication for school-related problems.[55] Estimates of the incidence of drug use for children who are in need of medication to control behavior are high. Safer and Krager[55] estimate that in the elementary school, the duration of drug treatment is an average of 2 years; in the middle school, it is an average of 4 years; and in the high school, it is an average of 7 years. The Drug Enforcement Administration[19] reports a doubling of the rate of medication for hyperactive students every 4 to 7 years. Therefore knowledge of the effects of drugs may be helpful to the physical educator in planning and conducting programs for this group of children.

Types of drugs

Psychoactive drugs produce behavioral, emotional, and/or cognitive changes. Amen and Singh[1] list 100 psychoactive drugs that are prescribed in this country. They classify these drugs as:

1. Neuroleptics (antipsychotic "major" tranquilizers)
2. Anticonvulsants
3. Sedative-hypnotics
4. Antidepressant/antimanic drugs
5. Central nervous system stimulants
6. Antiparkinson drugs
7. Miscellaneous drugs

The categories of drugs most commonly used with emotionally disturbed children are antipsychotic, sedative-hypnotic, antidepressant, and stimulant drugs.

Drug treatment

Emotionally disturbed children who are under medication often present behavioral problems that interfere with the learning of motor and physical skills, as well as with social interaction with others. It may be of interest to the physical educator to understand the effects of medication on specific behaviors that have an impact on the physical education class. Thus once the target behaviors that interfere with learning in the classroom are observed and there is knowledge of a drug intervention, the physical educator is in a position to assess the effectiveness of the drug on that behavior and the accommodations that need to be made in the physical education class for a specific child. However, antipsychotic, antidepressant, antianxiety, antimanic, and stimulant drugs often are not therapeutically specific,[1] but often have a generalizing effect or a side effect. Thus the physical educator may not be able to evaluate the total effectiveness of a drug but may be able to observe specific behaviors relevant to instruction.

Evaluation of drug treatment programs

Despite the prevalent use of psychoactive drugs to treat individuals who are emotionally disturbed, there are several problems in the administration of such drugs to students who may take part in physical education classes.[43] First, the doses may be high and thus may produce side effects; medical supervision has been less than exemplary.[1] Second, there is a need for more attention to defining specific clinical requirements and therapeutic goals. Third, the efficacy of certain drugs to modify specific behaviors that disrupt learning or the class needs further examination. Fourth, Schroeder[57] indicates that there is tremendous variability in the use of drugs from one setting to another. This may indicate the need for uniform practices in the profession for managing behavior through drug treatment programs. Fifth, the percentage of emotionally disturbed students who are responders to the drugs as compared with those who do not respond needs to be clarified.

Medical reduction

Inasmuch as there are often side effects associated with medication, it is desirable that those prescribing the medication reduce it to a minimum to lessen the side effects. Briggs et al.[5] call for medication reduction programs that involve objective identification of the student's undesirable behaviors, the collection of baseline data of the behaviors, and regular multidisciplinary assessment of the effectiveness of the medication. The physical educator could contribute to such a program in the event that the target behaviors were displayed in a particular class. The behaviors that disrupt learning of the student or other members of the class could be documented.

Whereas some drugs may control the behavior and conditions for which the medication is targeted, there are occasions where drugs that are effective in decreasing behavioral symptoms may have adverse effects on cognition and learning.[61] The majority of studies indicate that drug treatment by itself does not result in maintaining long-term academic achievement gains, even though such drugs may control undesirable behavior and improve attention.[24] It is reasonable to suggest that the prescription of medication be guided by clinical experience and the collective wisdom of colleagues in practice with subsequent feedback to those who prescribe medication.[12] There is currently a strong movement to reduce the use of psychoactive drugs.[1] This has, in part, been facilitated by court decisions that restrict the use of antipsychotic medications[6] until there is evidence that the particular drugs are effective in treating specific problems demonstrated by an individual.

Treatment uncertainties

Werry[65] suggests that attention to the overall quality of life should be the most important measure of the effects of drugs. He further states that the quality of life of the patient is too important to be left solely to the medical profession. Perhaps through observation of emotionally disturbed individuals involved in physical activity, the physical educator may contribute to such decisions.

Specific ways the physical educator can collaborate

with other professionals who work with the student, as well as with the student's IEP team, are as follows[18]:

1. Share information about the student's physical and motor needs.
2. Listen and act on relevant suggestions made by parents and other professionals.
3. Share materials and ideas with individuals working with the student.
4. Solicit support from parents and colleagues that contribute to the physical education program's effectiveness.
5. Use resource personnel effectively.

Teaching Strategies

The teacher of a child who is emotionally disturbed bears great responsibility. The teacher organizes physical activities, directs play, and, what is more critical, provides patterns of behavior for the child to emulate. It is from the teacher that immature children learn how the environment works and how persons cope.

The teacher of a child who is emotionally disturbed must be stable, flexible, and understanding toward atypical behavior and must be able to perceive what the child is experiencing. Such a teacher provides a medium through which the child may better understand his or her own behavior and modify it. This is no easy task. Being in contact with anxiety-provoking persons often stretches a teacher's emotional capacities. Some of the child's behaviors that the teacher often must tolerate are implied rejection; conflicting demands ranging from demands that immediate needs be met to severe withdrawal; aggressive tactics; and immature behaviors. Regular classroom teachers may be unaccustomed to these behaviors, but to succeed in working with these children, teachers must understand and accept their atypical behavior patterns and be able to establish a good working relationship with these students. Because of the stresses associated with working with this population, teachers of students who are emotionally disturbed are more likely to seek reassignment or leave their positions.[62] Therefore it is necessary for teachers of these students to receive special guidance and support to prevent reaching an emotional breaking point. Consultation with other personnel involved with the child, including those in psychological services, should be on a regular basis.

Trust in others is difficult for individuals who are emotionally disturbed. (Courtesy Wisconsin Lions Camp, Rosholt, Wis.)

The principles of good teaching of emotionally disturbed children in physical education are as follows:

1. Provide appropriate stimulation. Many emotionally disturbed children need a strong prompt to focus their attention on the activity at hand. Use tactile stimulation in teaching if the child does not attend to the task. However, avoid overstimulation of the child who is both hyperactive and emotionally disturbed.

2. Remove distracting objects. The attention span can be increased if seductive objects are removed from the environment because the possibilities of involvement in other activity are reduced. Bats, balls, and other play equipment should be kept out of sight until the time of use, if possible.

3. Provide manual guidance when teaching basic skills to some emotionally disturbed children. This is not necessarily a good procedure for all children. A rapport must first be built between the child and the instructor before use of manual guidance or the kinesthetic method of teaching motor skills becomes effective. Manual guidance is less effective with hyperactive children than with those who are withdrawn.

4. Do not necessarily strive for control in all situations. One major goal of education for persons who are emotionally disturbed is to effect adequate social adjustment. This does not imply strict obedience to authority but the ability of the individual to adjust to situations independently of supervision. Control should be of such a nature that the preconceived goals of the IEP are being achieved.

5. Discourage inappropriate interaction among the children. Such interaction may result in conflicts that disrupt the whole class. It may be necessary to separate children who interact in a disruptive manner.

6. Identify specific disruptive behaviors that can be brought under control. If disruptive behaviors can be identified and defined, intervention strategies from applied behavioral analysis can be used to control the disruptions (see Chapter 6 for the application of these principles).

7. Expect aggressive behavior during specific periods. Depending on specific conditions, aggressive and disruptive behaviors may fluctuate. It is important that trends of the strength and frequency of the aggressive or disruptive behavior be monitored and linked with specific behavioral techniques and strategies.

8. Do not stress elimination of neurotic behavior but build positive behavior.[16] It may be difficult to build positive behavior and extinguish neurotic behavior at the same time. Careful strategies must be developed to ensure that attempts are not made to bring too much behavior under control at one time. Eventually, neurotic behavior can be reduced within the context of a carefully thought out plan and strategies.

9. Impose reasonable limits with regard to conduct and use of equipment and facilities. Undue ex-

pectations with regard to the developmental level of emotions should not be made. However, each child should adhere to behavioral limits within his or her capabilities.

10. Students with behavior problems usually need to be taught to "own" their behavior. That is, they need to learn to discriminate between unacceptable and acceptable behaviors. In the well-managed educational environment, the behaviors that will be permitted and those that are inappropriate are clear and available.[49] That is, the teacher and, when appropriate, the students determine what the rules of conduct will be. Examples of rules appropriate for a physical education setting include:

   a. No swearing.
   b. Keep hands to yourself.
   c. Take your turn when it is your turn.
   d. No talking while the teacher is talking.
   e. Follow the rules of the sport.
   f. No arguing with the official.
   g. Take care of the equipment.
   h. Pay attention when being given instructions.
   i. No running in the shower.
   j. Arrive before the roll is taken.
   k. Participate in all class activities unless excused by the teacher.
   l. Promptly report any injuries to the teacher.

   The rules of conduct and consequences for not following these rules should be explained at the beginning of the year and whenever a new student joins the class. The rules should also be posted where they can be seen by all of the students. Noncompliance to rules and requests is one of the most commonly cited behavior problems in schools.[33] When students repeatedly defy the rules, a program of positive reinforcement, time-out, and/or guided compliance should be initiated[20,32] (see Chapter 6).

The Physical Education Program

Sport and physical activities are important for persons who are emotionally disturbed because there is the potential for the development and restoration of positive physical and emotional characteristics. Sport and physical activities provide a wide variety of opportunities to meet the interests of these students. Some of the ben-

efits of programs of sport and physical activities for the emotionally disturbed are as follows:

- The program may provide incentive for acceptable modes of conduct during sport activity.
- Aggressive tendencies may be expressed in socially acceptable ways because of controlled rules.
- Games and activities may provide opportunities for the development of social characteristics such as cooperation and competition.
- Activities requiring continuous movement tend to dissipate pent-up emotions.
- Exercise programs have been effective in reducing both stereotypical and self-injurious behavior of severely emotionally disturbed persons.[3,36,47]

The objectives of a physical education program for children who are emotionally disturbed are the same as those for children without disabilities. The program for this population should stress the development of motor skills and physical fitness, social competence, and personal adequacy. The objectives should be to develop personal and social competencies that will make the students aware of their own resources and potential for self-development. Physical activities fostering desirable relationships between self and both peers and persons in authority should be provided. Physical activities should also provide constructive and positive new experiences that enhance the concept of self and provide a feeling of worth.

The physical and motor capabilities of emotionally disturbed individuals and their ability to adapt to instructional procedures vary widely. For this reason, it is difficult to suggest specific activities that will benefit all students who are emotionally disturbed. However, children with emotional disturbances may demonstrate similar problems with learning that can be alleviated through the application of behavioral strategies and, as a result, benefit from participation in physical activity. The very nature of physical activities must be carefully studied to determine which behavioral control strategies can be most beneficial. Some general suggestions that may assist with the selection and implementation of activities can be found in the box on p. 364.

Modifications, Adaptations, and Inclusion Techniques

Although there has been considerable emphasis in the past on identifying causes before alleviating disruptive

Assistive Activities to Help Implement Physical Activity When Working with Emotionally Disturbed Individuals

1. Ensure that games of social interaction are at the social level and skill level of the child who is emotionally disturbed (see Chapter 5). However, if support systems for integrating students into the activity are used, then the individual's social abilities can be slightly below the level normally expected for participation.
2. Ensure that there is immediate feedback, provided either intrinsically from the task or extrinsically by the instructor or peers. Positive reinforcement tends to motivate the emotionally disturbed student to participate in tasks more readily. The more attention that is provided for the successful outcome of a task, the more apt the behavior is to be controlled. Tasks that provide intrinsic, immediate knowledge of results as to the correctness of the task should be provided (i.e., hitting a ball, catching a ball, hitting a target with a ball).
3. Select activities for the learner who is emotionally disturbed that are at the present level of performance. Select activities that can be modified so that the demands of the task match the ability level of the learner.
4. Individualize the activity according to the assessed needs of the child. In the event that there is little opportunity for individualized instruction, you should teach at the level that will reach all of the students in the group, even though using this "common denominator" approach may be detrimental to some students (e.g., below the level that would benefit them most).
5. Use peer tutors to provide the support system for emotionally disturbed students, and understand that successful activities are often those that can be easily learned by these tutors. Use of peer tutors is one of the best ways to really individualize physical education programs to benefit the physical and social development of students who are emotionally disturbed.
6. Use activities and a variety of games that will accommodate the students' different physical, social, and emotional developmental levels. The short attention span of these children makes it necessary to have several games on hand so that their interest can be recaptured when an initial activity is no longer productive. Novelty in activities is a great aid in holding attention.
7. Work with motor skills and games that allow some degree of success. Every satisfying experience makes for decreased anxiety and increased confidence.
8. Know when to encourage a child to approach, explore, and try a new activity or experience. A new experience is often met with resistance. In such instances it is wise to build guarantees of success into the new experience. Subsequent involvement becomes much easier for the emotionally disturbed child. The child who witnesses peers participating successfully in activities sometimes receives impetus to participate with them.
9. Discourage stereotyped play activities that develop rigid behavioral patterns. Children who are emotionally disturbed often tend to respond to the same objects or activities day after day. After a skill has been mastered, it may deter initiation of other activities.
10. Use activities that provide immediate consequences of the child's performance. The child should receive some feedback as to the limit of capability and the degree of success that was achieved on the task.

behavior, Kauffman[35] states that "the first or ultimate cause of behavior disorders almost always remains unknown . . . the focus of the educator should be on those contributing factors that can be altered by the teacher." Under most conditions, the physical education teacher cannot control the cause of abnormal behavior even if it is known. Thus it is essential that the adapted physical education teacher plan for developing skills included on the individual education program (IEP) through the use of appropriate behavioral strategies.[51]

There are very few school systems that engage in systematic screening of behavior disorders.[60] It is not easy to determine which children have problems that require special educational services. Usually, a problem in physical education class is manifested by disruption of the student's work, lack of desirable cooperation of the group, or the individual's inability to function adequately. Buhler, Smitter, and Richardson[7] describe the following sequence of behavioral patterns that lead to a severe disturbance, which may assist educators in identifying the severity of a disturbance:

1. Trivial, everyday disturbances such as giggling or the lack of concentration that teachers cannot study in detail (Action can be met with counteraction to eliminate this form of disturbance.)
2. Repetitious behavior that must be interpreted as a sign of deeper, underlying tension
3. Repetitious behavior accompanied by a serious single disturbance, a tantrum, or breaking into tears
4. A succession of different disturbances on different days, such as talking when roll is taken, poking the person standing nearby, and staring into space; indicates deep-seated tension and requires the experience of a psychologist or a psychiatrist

When the adapted physical educator encounters a student who demonstrates disruptive behavior, several questions need to be answered before an appropriate intervention program can be planned. A list of important questions that may prove to be useful when analyzing the need to change specific behaviors follows[56]:

1. *Intensity:* Is intensity of the behavior such that it disrupts the activity of the child or others?
2. *Appropriateness:* Is the behavior a reasonable response that is acceptable to others in the same environment?
3. *Duration:* Does the behavior last only a short time, or does it generalize to other activities or environments?
4. *Acceptance by peers:* Is the behavior accepted or rejected by peers?
5. *Concomitant behavior:* Are there other behavioral problems associated with the central behavior?
6. *Comparison with the norm:* Is the behavior below normative expectations for the group?
7. *Behavioral circumstances:* Is the event that triggers the behavior identifiable?
8. *Manageability:* Can the behavior be readily managed so that the outcomes are identifiable?

The information provided by answering these questions may assist the teacher in making judgments as to whether intervention should be used. This information may also assist in making judgments as to whether the behavior can be managed by the physical education teacher or whether someone with specialized training in modifying behavior should be brought in to control the student's behavior.

Developing Socialization Skills

There are specific techniques and procedures that physical education teachers can use to develop socialization skills of students who are emotionally disturbed. Persons with severe emotional disturbance may have impaired ability to relate to other persons and may choose, instead, to relate to inanimate objects. To facilitate interpersonal relationships during play, another person can be paired with the inanimate object that is the focus of the emotionally disturbed pupil's attention. A positive transfer from the inanimate object to the person paired with the object frequently occurs. Such a transfer constitutes the beginning of an interpersonal contact for the emotionally disturbed person. The teacher should follow through with practices to facilitate additional psychosocial development (see Chapter 9).

It should also be noted that team membership in sports may place social controls on behavior to such an extent that unsocialized behavior is curbed. However, the composition of the membership of the team is important. When emotionally disturbed children are grouped together, it is extremely difficult to predict group behavior. In fact, it is not uncommon to see that emotionally disturbed children who have been grouped together contribute to one another's problems as they infect one another with inappropriate behavior.[8] If children who are emotionally disturbed are placed in groups of persons with emotional maturity, group behavior becomes more predictable, especially if the students without disabilities are sensitive regarding accommodation of the emotionally disturbed students in the play environment. Also, good role models may be of value for social development of the emotionally disturbed children. Thus social development through games for disturbed children can best be accomplished in play with nondisabled peers wherein strategies planned by the teacher and nondisabled peers occur. It is important to foster sport skill development and basic levels of social skills because they are prerequisites for play in organized sport activity.

Development of Self-Concept

Emotionally disturbed persons often possess poor self-concepts. This may be due to previous failure on physical education tasks, which creates anxiety. Levels of anxiety and failure can be lessened through individualization of instruction and provision of activity in small steps that slightly extend (shape) present levels of performance (see Chapter 6). Through this procedure, failure can be controlled and learning measured. Such successful experiences may alleviate anxiety and improve the self-concept.

Peer Relationships

Peer acceptance and peer friendships play an important and distinct role in children's emotional adjustment and social development.[41] Most children begin forming social networks as soon as they enter school. Because students with disruptive behaviors have difficulty interacting with others,[14] they tend to gravitate toward, and eventually affiliate with, peers who support such behavior.[25] These students can be taught positive social skills through games and physical activities[44] if a conscious effort is made to do so. Cooperative games that require coordinated efforts of all the participants for a successful outcome contribute to self-esteem and peer acceptance[59] because cooperation is fundamental to social adjustment and provides the basis of friendship.[4] Teachers should model positive social behaviors and provide students with the opportunity to cooperate in games of physical activity.[9]

Decisions for Controlling Behavioral Disorders

To control excessive behavior of students who are emotionally disturbed, adapted physical education teachers must make decisions based on many factors. Commercial materials and teacher-training approaches that deemphasize the decision-making processes of the teacher have been developed. Examples include computerized models for making curriculum decisions for disabled students, lists of published interventions, all-inclusive packages that classify behaviors with descriptive deficits paired with interventions, and even individualized physical education programs. In the last analysis, a specific teacher needs to make a specific decision based on the behavior of a specific learner in a specific environment performing a specific task at a specific time. Thus the all-inclusive packages and other such predetermined approaches leave a great deal to be desired. Dependence of teachers on packages and general suggestions may be detrimental to the development of generalized principles involved in the decision-making process that all teachers must follow.

There are at least two decisions that need to be made to control excessive inappropriate behavior of students who are emotionally disturbed. These decisions are based on (1) assessment as to whether intervention is appropriate and (2) strategies for controlling disruptive and excessive behavior if a decision is made to intervene.

Appropriateness of the Need to Intervene

There are several considerations that must be taken into account before a decision is made to develop a strategy to control the disruptive or excessive behavior of an emotionally disturbed student. Some of the questions that need to be answered before making such a decision are as follows:

1. Is the excessive behavior a danger to other students in the class?
2. Is the excessive behavior a danger to the student (i.e., does the student engage in self-abusive behavior or risk taking that may lead to injury)?
3. Has the problem existed over a period of time? There often is a remission of many behaviors without an intervention.
4. Is the behavior such that it is acceptable in the community? If the behavior is unacceptable, its existence may stigmatize the individual and interfere with social development.
5. Would learning of instructional behaviors be improved if the excessive behaviors were reduced? Many excessive behaviors do not interfere with the learning of curriculum objectives.
6. Is the excessive behavior a concern to the teacher and other personnel who interact with the child?
7. Would the intervention be in the child's best interest? The intervention should not be a deterrent to the acquisition of the goals and objectives of the individual physical education program.

To enable successful classroom participation of the student who is emotionally disturbed, a primary consideration is that of managing behavior during instruction. To manage behavior efficiently, it is often necessary to highly structure environments. Such structure, in and of itself, may control hyperactive and aggressive behaviors. When students who are emotionally disturbed are "on task," disruptive behavior is incompatible with the activity. However, when these youth and children are not performing tasks, there is opportunity for behavior that may disrupt instruction.

The management of a classroom can be improved if there are designated spots on the floor or specific lo-

table 14-1

table 14-1

Application of Task Signals to Specific Activities to Facilitate Effective Instruction

Principles	Instructional Conditions	Task Signals
Secure a signal	Group or individualized instruction	Clap hands for attention, "ready go," "listen"
Short command	Guarding a nonmoving person in basketball	"Hand up"
	Preparation for catching a ball	"Watch the ball"
Signals no stronger than needed	Instruction on a task individualized to needs of the child	Tone of voice from a whisper to loud enthusiasm
Feedback signals	After successful catch of a ball	"Nice catch"
	Error correction in catching	"Watch the ball into your hands"

cations where the children are to be when they are not performing a learning task. Such an arrangement enables greater behavior control during the slack times when the occurrence of disruptive behavior is probable. Pupils may be placed so that they are spread over an area or are close together.

Signals that indicate the beginning and end of activity and movement of the children from one part of the play area to another part increase the structure of the play environment (Table 14-1). The characteristics of signals for providing structure to the instructional environment are as follows:

1. The command signals should be short and concise.
2. The signals should be no stronger than needed to elicit the response.
3. Signals may be needed to secure attention (such commands as "listen" and "look" may be needed to secure the attention of the more severely emotionally disturbed persons).
4. Feedback signals about task mastery are needed to provide information to the learner; through the use of these signals, the teacher should indicate to the student the level of success he or she is experiencing.

Undesirable behavior can sometimes be reduced through the use of time-out from reinforcement, which involves taking away reinforcement opportunities. This approach is used when some feature of the instructional environment is reinforcing (appealing) to the student. There is a considerable difference between time-out from reinforcement and removal from an instructional setting solely for the purpose of enabling scheduled activity to continue without interruption. Using time-out from reinforcement usually involves restricting the environment in which learning occurs. Examples of time-out procedures ranging from the least restrictive to the most restrictive for use in controlling inappropriate behavior while playing an instructional game where the game is a reinforcer are as follows (see also Table 14-2):

1. Nonexclusionary time-out from reinforcement would result by removing the student from the game for very brief periods. When removal is used, the student should be able to observe and acquire information through observing peers as the game unfolds. Under these conditions, there may still be a beneficial educational outcome. More se-

table 14-2

Application of Time-Out from Reinforcement to Control Inappropriate Behavior While Playing an Instructional Game

Technique for Inappropriate Behavior	Consequences for Inappropriate Behavior
Nonexclusionary time-out	The student is removed from the game but allowed to observe the game. The student is required to turn away from the game and not observe it (i.e., no contact with peers).
Exclusionary time-out	The child is completely removed from his or her peers at the game.

vere forms of restrictiveness in timing an individual out from reinforcement would be taking the individual farther away from the activity without total separation from his or her peers or prohibiting observation of play.

2. Exclusionary time-out, the most severe form of time-out, involves actual removal from the instructional setting for sequentially longer periods.

Analytical techniques for applying tentative principles of behavior to improve behavior are well understood and widely practiced. The application of applied behavioral analysis requires objective definition of the behavior to be changed, an intervention procedure, and a design or schedule to follow during the intervention. Treatment decisions are based on observable behavior that is to be changed, not on medical data.

Conscious Decision Making

Teachers must be taught to make transitions from theory to practice. Conscious decision making should be practiced in all pedagogy courses so that when new teachers are faced with unique situations, they have the critical thinking skills to effect change. The need for a teacher to make conscious decisions continues to heighten because of the increasing variety of student needs that must be served in the inclusive setting.[23]

Integration Processes

When children and youth with emotional disturbance are transferred from one physical education setting to another, careful preparations are recommended. Rock, Rosenberg, and Carran[54] suggest the following actions:

1. Set transition goals for the student that indicate how success in the new setting can be judged.
2. Establish the length of a trial period to determine whether or not the new setting meets the personal, social, and physical needs of the student.
3. Provide written information for the new teacher that provides suggestions for facilitating the transfer.
4. Provide technical assistance to the new teacher on request.

Community-Based Opportunities

Usually, children who are emotionally disturbed must be taught how to play and enjoy physical activity. Once constructive play is learned, it provides a medium through which the children may experiment with self-control and with the control of the environment. Play also offers opportunity for social learning and tension release. Because these children strain the educational program, they are often left out of the extracurricular and intramural activities of a regular school. This works to their detriment when they are being prepared for community living. To compound the problem, their opportunities for healthy physical activity outside the school setting are limited.

There are a considerable number of national organizations designed to facilitate community-based sports and physical activity of persons with disabilities. These national organizations serve persons who are deaf or hearing impaired, blind or visually impaired, mentally retarded, and orthopedically disabled. However, there are few, if any, national organizations that have as their sole mission the participation of persons with emotional disturbance in physical activity. Because of this lack, it is critical that persons with emotional disturbance be able to participate in integrated community physical activity.

In the past, many services for students with emotional disturbance were provided in isolation, which resulted in a disjointed program. The current literature on "best practices" in dealing with students with severe emotional disturbance urges collaborative planning and detailed program design.[28,46,50] As a result, programs are more interactive than in the past[53] and focus increasingly on providing services and assistance for the student in natural settings. The purpose of assisting the student in natural settings is to improve the possibility of successful transition from the school to the community.

In the determination of which community activities are best suited for a person with emotional disturbance, social and skill levels are primary factors to consider. In addition to determining what types of community events and situations evoke behavioral problems,[15] an analysis of required levels of skills is necessary. For instance, personal fitness activities are simple to perform and take place in less complex social environments than team sports, such as soccer, basketball, and volleyball. It is important that the social complexity of community environments and the level of skill required of the physical activity be commensurate with the developmental level of the person who is emotionally disturbed.

SUMMARY

Children and youth who are emotionally disturbed may exhibit unsatisfactory relationships with teachers and peers, inappropriate types of behavior, or a pervasive mood of depression, or they may develop physical symptoms or fears associated with school problems. These characteristics interfere with their ability to learn.

An understanding of the medical and educational models used to categorize individuals with emotional disturbance will facilitate communication among professionals who serve this population.

The central problem that needs to be addressed by physical educators working with persons who are emotionally disturbed is management of abnormal behavior in the classroom. There are several techniques and procedures that can be used to manage fear, withdrawal, aggressiveness, and hyperactivity. Among these are accepted principles of classroom management, desensitization to alleviate fears, and shaping, which may build self-concept and counter withdrawal from activity caused by previous failure.

Appropriate selection of activities may decrease excessive behaviors that interfere with learning. The use of cooperative games will help students develop the trust and sharing necessary to function more effectively in society.

To facilitate the transition from the school to the community setting, a program should be designed to match the social and skill level of the student.

Review Questions

1. What are some causes of emotional disturbance?
2. What are the personal-social and physical-motor characteristics of persons with emotional disturbance?
3. What are some behavioral patterns of children that may indicate the severity of emotional disturbance?
4. When is it important to identify persons who are emotionally disturbed?
5. What are some characteristics of a physical education teacher of students who are emotionally disturbed?
6. What are some benefits of sport activities for students who are emotionally disturbed?
7. What are the objectives of a physical education program for persons with emotional disturbance?
8. What are some teaching principles for instructing students who are emotionally disturbed?
9. What are some principles for selecting activities for students who are emotionally disturbed that may facilitate learning in physical education?

10. What decisions should be made by the adapted physical education teacher to control excessive behavior?
11. How can the physical education teacher facilitate the student's transition from the school to the community setting?

Student Activities

1. Working in small groups, discuss strategies to improve the environment in Daniel's physical education class. Report to the rest of the class on the three intervention strategies your group believes would be most effective in Daniel's class, and defend your choices.
2. Read the article by Horner et al.[32] Determine whether any of the techniques they describe might be effective in reducing any of Daniel's acting-out behaviors.
3. Observe a physical education teacher who conducts programs for students with emotional disturbance. Describe the following:
   a. The nature of the class (special or integrated class).
   b. The manner of instruction (individual, small groups, or as a total class).
   c. The ways in which the physical and motor needs were met.
   d. Strategies the teacher employed during instruction.
   e. Disruptive pupil behaviors.
4. There are several organizations designed to serve persons who are emotionally disturbed. Identify the local chapters of such groups in your area. Contact the local or national office of such an organization. Inquire about the services they render for specific clientele.
5. Articles about physical education for students with emotional disturbance can be found in the *Adapted Physical Activity Quarterly* and *Palaestra: The Forum of Sport, Physical Education and Recreation for the Disabled.* Read two articles that discuss techniques for working with students with emotional disturbance, and write a report summarizing one of the articles.
6. Interview a person from psychological services or a school counselor. Determine whether a school-wide or district-wide behavioral management system is used and why. If a system is used, describe the system.

References

1. Amen MG, Singh NN: *Psychopharmacology of developmental disabilities,* New York, 1988, Springer-Verlag.
2. American Psychiatric Association: *Diagnostic and statistical manual DSM IV,* Washington, DC, 1994, The Association.
3. Baumeister AA, MacLean WE: Deceleration of self-injurious behavior and stereotypic responding by exercise, *Appl Res Ment Retard* 5:385-393, 1982.

4. Bay-Hinitz J, Peterson RF, Quiltch RH: Cooperative games: a way to modify aggressive and cooperative behaviors in young children, *J Appl Behav Anal* 27:435-446, 1994.

5. Briggs R et al: A model for evaluating psychoactive medication with mentally retarded persons. In Mulick J, Mallany B, editors: *Transition in mental retardation: advocacy, technology and science,* Norwood, NJ, 1985, Ablex.

6. Brooks AD: The right to refuse antipsychotic medication: law and policy, 1987, *Rutgers Law Rev* 39:339-376, 1987.

7. Buhler C, Smitter F, Richardson S: What is a problem? In Long HJ, editor: *Conflict in the classroom,* Belmont, Calif, 1965, Wadsworth Publishing.

8. Carr EG: Emerging themes in the functional analysis of problem behavior, *J Appl Behav Anal* 27:393-399, 1994.

9. Cartlege G, Milburn JF: *Teaching social skills to children and youth: innovative approaches,* ed 3, Needham Heights, Mass, 1995, Allyn & Bacon.

10. Caseau D, Luckasson R, Kroth RL: Special education services for girls with serious emotional disturbance: a case of gender bias? *Behav Disord* 20:51-60, 1994.

11. Center DB: *Curriculum and teaching strategies for students with behavioral disorders,* Englewood Cliffs, NJ, 1989, Prentice Hall.

12. Chandler M, Gualtieri CT, Fahs JJ: Other psychotropic drugs: stimulants, antidepressants, anxiolytics, and lithium carbonate. In Amen MG, Singh NN, editors: *Psychopharmacology of developmental disabilities,* New York, 1988, Springer-Verlag.

13. Cohen R et al: States' use of transfer of custody as a requirement for providing services to emotionally disturbed children, *Hosp Community Psychiatry* 42:526-530, 1991.

14. Coie JD: Toward a theory of peer rejection. In Asher SR, Coie JD, editors: *Peer rejection in childhood,* Cambridge, 1990, Cambridge University Press.

15. Colbert RS: Team approach: involving parents in the treatment and education of youths with severe emotional disturbance, *BC J Spec Educ* 18:54-61, 1994.

16. Cratty BJ: *Adapted physical education for handicapped children and youth,* Denver, 1980, Love Publishing.

17. Craven RS, Ferdinand TM: *Juvenile delinquency,* ed 3, New York, 1975, Harper & Row.

18. Dettmer P, Thruston LP, Dyck N: *Consultation, collaboration and teamwork for students with special needs,* Boston, 1993, Allyn & Bacon.

19. Drug Enforcement Administration: In the matter of methylphenidate production quotas—1986, decision of the administrative law judge, Docket No 86-52, 1987, p 29.

20. Ducharme JM, Worling DE: Behavioral momentum and stimulus fading in the acquisition of and maintenance of child compliance in the home, *J Appl Behav Anal* 27:639-647, 1994.

21. Dunn JM, Fait H: *Special physical education,* Dubuque, Iowa, 1989, Wm C Brown Group.

22. Ervin CE: Parents forced to surrender custody of children with neurological disorders, *New Dir Mental Health Serv* 54:111-116, 1992.

23. Evans IM, Meyer PL: *An educative approach to behavioral problems—a practical decision model for intervention with severely handicapped learners,* Baltimore, 1985, Paul H Brookes Publishing.

24. Famularo R, Fenton T: Effect of methylphenidate on school grades in children with attention deficit disorder without hyperactivity: a preliminary report, *J Clin Psychiatry* 48:112-114, 1987.

25. Farmer TW, Hollowell JH: Social networks in mainstream classrooms: social affiliations and behavioral characteristics of students with emotional and behavioral disorders, *J Emot Behav Disord* 1:223-234, 1994.

26. Forness SR, Kavale KA, Lopez M: Conduct disorders in school: special education eligibility and comorbidity, *J Emot Behav Disord* 1:101-108, 1994.

27. French RW, Jansma P: *Special physical education,* Columbus, Ohio, 1982, Charles E Merrill Publishing.

28. Gable RA et al: Reintegration of behaviorally disordered students through behavioral consultation. In Rutherford RB Jr, Digangi S, editors: *Severe behavior disorders of children and youth, Monographs in Behavior Disorders* 12:118-131, 1989, Reston, Va, The Council for Children with Behavior Disorders.

29. Grossman H: *Special education in a diverse society,* Boston, 1995, Allyn & Bacon.

30. Hardman ML, Drew CJ, Egan MW: *Human exceptionality,* Boston, 1987, Allyn & Bacon.

31. Heward WL, Orlansky MD: *Exceptional children,* Columbus, Ohio, 1988, Charles E Merrill Publishing.

32. Horner RH et al: Interspersed requests: a non-aversive procedure for reducing aggression and self-injury during instruction, *J Appl Behav Analy* 24:265-278, 1991.

33. Houlihan D, Sloane HN, Jones RN: A review of behavioral conceptualizations and treatments of child noncompliance, *Educ Treat Child* 15:56-77, 1992.

34. Kalakian LH, Eichstaedt CB: *Developmental/adapted physical education,* Minneapolis, 1993, Burgess Publishing.

35. Kauffman JN: *Characteristics of behavior disorders of children and youth,* ed 4, Columbus, Ohio, 1989, Charles E Merrill Publishing.

36. Kern L et al: The effects of exercise on self stimulation and appropriate responding in autistic children, *J Autism Behav Disord* 12:399-419, 1982.

37. Kirk S, Gallagher J, Anastasio NJ: *Educating exceptional children,* ed 7, Boston, 1993, Houghton Mifflin.

38. Klein C: A summary of remarks at the House-Senate Education Committee hearing, Senator Reibman, chairperson, Senate Bill 1214, Harrisburg, Pa, 1978.

39. Knitzer J, Steinberg Z, Fleisch B: Schools, mental health

and the advocacy challenge, *J Clin Child Psychol* 20:102-111, 1990.

40. Koyangi C, Gaines S: *All systems failure: an examination of the results of neglecting the needs of children with serious emotional disturbance,* Washington, DC, 1993, National Mental Health Association.

41. LaGreca AM: Social skills training with children: where do we go from here? *J Clin Child Psychol* 22:288-298, 1993.

42. Langone J: *Teaching students with mild and moderate learning problems,* Boston, 1990, Allyn & Bacon.

43. Lewis MH, Mailman RB: Psychotropic drug blood levels: measurement and relation to behavioral outcomes in mentally retarded persons. In Amen MG, Singh NN, editors: *Psychopharmacology of developmental disabilities,* New York, 1988, Springer-Verlag.

44. Mace CF: The significance and future of functional analysis methodologies, *J Appl Behav Anal* 27:385-392, 1994.

45. Marder C, Cox R: More than a label: characteristics of youth with disabilities. In Wagner M et al, editors: *Youth with disabilities: how are they doing? The first comprehensive report from the National Longitudinal Transition Study of Special Education Students,* Menlo Park, Calif, 1991, SRI International.

46. Maroney SA, Smith CR: Teacher responsibilities in providing instruction for students with behavioral disorders. In Gable RA et al, editors: *Preparing to integrate students with behavior disorders,* Reston, Va, 1991, Council for Exceptional Children.

47. McGimsey JF, Favell JE: The effects of increased physical exercise on disruptive behavior in retarded persons, *J Autism Dev Disord* 18:167-179, 1988.

48. McGinnis E et al: *Skill streaming the elementary school child: a guide for teaching pro-social skills,* Champaign, Ill, 1984, Research Press.

49. Morgan SR, Reinhart JA: *Interventions for students with emotional disorders,* Austin, Tex, 1990, PRO-ED.

50. Morse WC: The helping teacher/crisis teacher concept, *Focus Except Child* 8:1-11, 1976.

51. Paine SC, Belamy GT, Wilcox B: *Human services that work,* Baltimore, 1984, Paul H Brookes Publishing.

52. Pierangelo R: *A survival kit for the special education teacher,* West Nyack, NY, 1994, Center for Applied Research in Education.

53. Rainsworth B, York J, MacDonald C: *Collaborating teams for students with severe disabilities: integrating therapy and educational services,* Baltimore, 1992, Paul H Brooks Publishing.

54. Rock EE, Rosenberg MS, Carran DT: Variables affecting the reintegration of students with severe emotional disturbance, *Except Child* 61:254-268, 1994.

55. Safer DJ, Krager JM: A survey of medication treatment for hyperactive inattentive students, *JAMA* 260:2256-2258, 1988.

56. Sailor W, Wilcox B, Brown L: *Methods of instruction for severely handicapped students,* Baltimore, 1985, Paul H Brookes Publishing.

57. Schroeder SR: Neuroleptic medications for persons with developmental disabilities. In Amen MG, Singh NN, editors: *Psychopharmacology of developmental disabilities,* New York, 1988, Springer-Verlag.

58. Shea TM, Bauer AM: *Learners with disabilities: a social system perspective in special education,* Boston, 1994, Allyn & Bacon.

59. Slavin RE: *Cooperative learning: theory, research and practice,* Englewood Cliffs, NJ, 1990, Prentice Hall.

60. Smith CR: Identification of handicapped children and youth: a state agency perspective on behavior disorders, *Remed Spec Educ* 6:34-41, 1985.

61. Sokol MS, Campbell M: Novel psychoactive agents in the treatment of developmental disorders. In Amen MG, Singh NN, editors: *Psychopharmacology of developmental disabilities,* New York, 1988, Springer-Verlag.

62. US Department of Education: *To assure the free appropriate public education of all children with disabilities. Sixteenth annual report to Congress on the implementation of the Individuals with Disabilities Education Act,* Washington, DC, 1994.

63. US Department of Health, Education, and Welfare: Regulations for the Education for All Handicapped Children Act of 1975, *Fed Reg* 4, Aug 23, 1977.

64. Wagner M, Blackorby J, Hebbeler K: *Beyond the report card: the multiple dimensions of secondary school performance for students with disabilities,* Menlo Park, Calif, 1993, SRI International.

65. Werry JS: Conclusions. In Amen MG, Singh NN, editors: *Psychopharmacology of developmental disabilities,* New York, 1988, Springer-Verlag.

chapter fifteen

Physically Disabling Conditions

Objectives

Describe a variety of physical disabilities.

List which physical activities are recommended for individuals with specific types of disabilities.

Explain variations of physical characteristics among persons with neurological and orthopedic disabilities.

Adapt activity to maximize participation in sports and games.

Introduce sports organizations that serve individuals with physical disabilities.

Scenario

Josue is a first grader with spina bifida myelomeningocele. His parents divorced in the first year after Josue's birth. His mother is having serious difficulty dealing with Josue's disability. She is in denial to the extent that she believes and tells Josue every day that he will not have spina bifida as an adult. She admitted in an individual education program (IEP) meeting that she is severely depressed and suicidal. As a result, Josue is developing behavior problems at home and at school. Though a bright little boy, he often engages in refusal behavior when asked to work.

Josue is very mobile in his chair. He is able to wheel in a straight line and in a circle, can stop and start with ease, can move backward, and is learning to do a "wheelie." He is able to get in and out of his wheelchair independently. At a recent IEP meeting, it was recommended that Josue participate in the regular physical education class and in community-based sports programs; however, his mother was very reluctant to agree.

Courtesy Iron Horse Productions, Inc.

Task

Identify strategies for convincing Josue's mother to permit him to participate in the regular physical education class and in community-based sports programs for young children with disabilities. Modify the warm-up regimen the regular class uses, and develop a cardiovascular program so Josue can participate in the warm-up and heart-healthy portion of the curriculum. Identify the types of wheelchair maneuvers and skills he should practice in class in order to be successful in a sports program. Identify types of physical education activities where the use of a wheelchair may endanger the other children, and suggest alternative activities Josue could do with a peer on the sidelines. Develop a behavior management plan that should be implemented when he refuses to participate in classroom activities.

There are many different types of physically disabling conditions. Afflictions can occur at more than 500 anatomical sites. Each person who has a disabling condition has different physical and motor capabilities. Thus each person must be treated in such a manner that his or her unique educational needs are met.

In this chapter we suggest a procedure to accomplish this task. The processes involved in this procedure are to (1) identify the specific clinical condition, (2) identify which activities are contraindicated on the basis of medical recommendations, (3) determine needed functional physical fitness and motor skills, (4) determine the activities that will assist the development of the desired fitness and motor skills, and (5) determine aids and devices that will enable the individual to function in the most normal environment.

More than 20 different disabilities are presented in this chapter. Many of these conditions, though differing in cause, result in similar movement limitations. To aid the reader in focusing on the commonalities across physically disabling conditions, the format of this chapter is slightly different from that of the other chapters dealing with specific populations. Under the headings of Neurological Disorders, Orthopedic Disabilities, and Traumatic Injuries, specific conditions are identified and defined, the incidence and cause of each condition are

given, characteristics are delineated, special considerations are discussed, and suggestions for programming and teaching are presented. Following the unique aspects of all of the specific conditions, common testing suggestions; modifications, adaptations, and inclusion techniques; and community-based opportunities are presented. It is our hope that this approach will aid the reader in organizing all of the information covered herein.

Definition and Scope

Physical disabilities affect the use of the body as a result of deficiencies of the nerves, muscles, bones, and/or joints. The three main sources of disabilities are neurological impairments, orthopedic (musculoskeletal) conditions, and trauma. Neurological disabilities are chronic debilitating conditions that result from impairments of the central nervous system. Neurological conditions discussed in this chapter include amyotrophic lateral sclerosis, cerebral palsy, epilepsy, multiple sclerosis, muscular dystrophy, Parkinson's disease, poliomyelitis, and spina bifida.

Orthopedic conditions are deformities, diseases, and injuries of the bones and joints. Orthopedic conditions discussed in this chapter include arthritis; arthrogryposis; hip disorders, including congenital dislocations, coxa plana, coxa vara, and coxa valga; Osgood-Schlatter condition; osteogenesis imperfecta; osteomyelitis; and spondylolysis and spondylolisthesis.

Traumatic conditions are the result of damage to muscles, ligaments, tendons, or the nervous system as a result of a blow to the body. Spinal cord injuries and amputations are discussed in this section (see Chapter 18 for traumatic head injuries).

Neurological Disorders
Amyotrophic Lateral Sclerosis

Amyotrophic lateral sclerosis (ALS) is a progressive neurological disorder of unknown cause that results in degeneration of the muscular system.[46] The disease is infrequent in school-age populations and is more common in adulthood, with the median age of onset being 55 years.[3] It affects men two to three times as often as women. Lou Gehrig, the hall-of-fame first baseman of the New York Yankees, who finally missed a game after more than 2000 successive starts, was forced to retire as a result of the disease. It has since been named the "Lou Gehrig" disease.

Characteristics and testing

The central feature of the disease is atrophy and muscle wasting resulting in marked weakness in the hands, arms, shoulders, and legs and in generalized weakness as well. The site of onset is random, and it progresses asymmetrically.[3] Cramps are common, and muscular weakness may cause problems with swallowing, talking, and respiration. Concomitant spinal conditions may include ruptured intervertebral disks, spinal cord tumors, and spinal malformations. Manual muscle testing is used to determine the amount of functional strength.

Special considerations

There is no specific medical treatment for ALS. Although there may be periods of remission, the disease usually progresses rapidly, with death ensuing within an average of 2 to 5 years.[46]

The physical education program and teaching strategies

The major goals of the ALS physical education program are to maintain physical capability as long as possible. It may be desirable to focus attention on activities that would maintain efficient movement of the body for activities of daily living. Leisure skills should be taught that have functional use at present or in the near future. The nature of the physical activities will depend on the physical capabilities of the individual at each point in time. The teacher should be supportive and understanding. Consultation with an occupational therapist should be sought for advice about assistive devices to enable activities of daily living.

Cerebral Palsy

Cerebral palsy is a condition rather than a disease. The term **cerebral palsy** is defined as a nonprogressive lesion of the brain before, during, or soon after birth (before age 5 years). The condition impairs voluntary movement and is a lifelong condition.

The incidence of cerebral palsy is 1 to 2 per 1000 live births.[3] Although the older studies indicated that the vast majority of cerebral palsy cases were caused by external factors such as prolonged labor, instrumental deliveries, and breech births, it is now believed that only 15% of the cases result from these causes.[3] The most recent studies indicate that central nervous system abnormalities, such as enlarged ventricles in the brain and decreased brain hemisphere size, are probably critical factors that impair function.[38]

Certain groups of infants, including those with prolonged birth anoxia, very low birth weight, and abnormal neurological symptoms, are possible candidates for cerebral palsy.[9] Many children with cerebral palsy possess poor postural adjustment. As a result, simple gross motor movements (e.g., kicking, throwing, and jumping) are difficult to perform effectively.[58]

Characteristics and types

The degree of motor impairment of children with cerebral palsy may range from serious physical disability to little physical disability. The limbs affected are identified with specific titles. **Hemiplegia** indicates involvement of both limbs on one side, with the arm being more affected than the leg. **Paraplegia** indicates involvement of both legs with little or no involvement of the arms. **Quadriplegia** or **tetraplegia** denotes involvement of all the limbs to a similar degree. **Diplegia** is an intermediate form between paraplegia and quadriplegia, with most involvement being in the legs.

Since the extent of the brain damage that results in neuromotor dysfunction varies greatly, diagnosis is related to the amount of dysfunction and associated motor involvement. Severe brain injury may be evident shortly after birth. However, cases of children with cerebral palsy who have slight brain damage and little motor impairment may be difficult to diagnose. In the milder cases, developmental lag in the motor and intellectual tasks required to meet environmental demands may not be detected until the children are 3 or 4 years old. As a rule, the clinical signs and symptoms of cerebral palsy reach maximum severity when the children reach the age of 2 to 4 years.

Individuals with cerebral palsy usually demonstrate persistence of primitive reflexes and frequently are slow to develop equilibrium (postural) reflexes. It is difficult for most performers to execute simple gross motor movements effectively unless appropriate postural adjustments occur to support such movements[58] and the individual is given additional time to plan and execute the movements.

Some of the secondary impairments that may accompany cerebral palsy are mental retardation, hearing and vision loss, emotional disturbance, hyperactivity, learning disabilities, loss of perceptual ability, and inability to make psychological adjustments. Healy[28] reports that 60% of all children with cerebral palsy have seizures.

Various authors agree that more than 50% of children with cerebral palsy have oculomotor defects. In other words, children with brain injury often have difficulty in coordinating their eye movements. The implications of this for physical activities that involve a great deal of oculomotor tracking of projectiles point to a need for programs that train for ocular control.

The different clinical types of cerebral dysfunction involve various obvious motor patterns, commonly known as hard signs. There are four clinical classifications: spasticity, athetosis, ataxia, and mixed. Of persons with cerebral palsy, 70% are clinically classified as spastic, 20% as athetoid, and 10% as ataxic; the remaining are mixed conditions (usually spasticity and athetosis).[3]

Spasticity. Muscular **spasticity** is the most prevalent type of hard sign among persons with cerebral palsy. One characteristic of spasticity is that muscle contractures that restrict muscular movement and hypertonicity give the appearance of stiffness to affected limbs. This makes muscle movement jerky and uncertain. Children with spasticity have exaggerated stretch reflexes that cause them to respond to rapid passive stimulation with vigorous muscle contractions. Tendon reflexes are also hyperactive in the involved part. When the spastic condition involves the lower extremities, the legs may be rotated inward and flexed at the hips, the knees may be flexed, and a contracted gastrocnemius muscle holds the heel off the ground. Lower leg deficiency contributes to a scissors gait that is common among persons with this type of cerebral palsy. When the upper extremities are involved, the characteristic forms of physical deviation in persons with spastic cerebral palsy include flexion at the elbows, forearm pronation, and wrist and finger flexion. Spasticity is most common in the antigravity muscles of the body. Contractures are more common in children with spastic cerebral palsy than in children with

any of the other types of cerebral palsy. In the event that contractures are not remedied or addressed, permanent contractures may result. Consequently, good posture is extremely difficult to maintain. Because of poor balance among reciprocal muscle groups, innervation of muscles for functional motor patterns is often difficult, which frequently results in a decreased physical work capacity.[22] Individuals with spastic hemiplegia or paraplegia usually have normal intelligence; however, they may demonstrate some learning disabilities. Mental retardation is more frequently seen in individuals with spastic quadriplegia and mixed forms of cerebral palsy.[3]

Athetosis. **Athetosis,** which results from basal ganglia involvement, is the second most prevalent clinical type of cerebral palsy. The distinguishing characteristic of the individual with athetosis is recognizable incoordinate movements of voluntary muscles. These movements take the form of wormlike motions that involve the trunk, arms, and legs, as well as the tongue or muscle twitches of the face. The unrhythmical, uncontrollable, involuntary movements increase with voluntary motion and emotional or environmental stimuli, and disappear during sleep. Because of the athetoid individual's inability to control muscles and the presence of primitive reflexes, posture is unpredictable and poses a problem. Impairment in the muscular control of hands, speech, and swallowing often accompanies athetosis.

Ataxia. **Ataxia,** a primary characteristic of the ataxic type of cerebral palsy, is a disturbance of equilibrium that results from involvement of the cerebellum or its pathways.[3] The resulting impairment in balance becomes evident in the walking gait. The gait of the person with ataxic cerebral palsy is wide and unstable, which causes weaving about during locomotion. Standing is often a problem. Kinesthetic awareness seems to be lacking in the individual with ataxia. Weakness, incoordination, and intention tremor create difficulties with rapid or fine movements.[3]

Mixed forms. Mixed forms are the least common of all types of cerebral palsy. Spasticity and athetosis are the most frequent characteristics, with ataxia and athetosis demonstrated less frequently.[3]

Special considerations

Increasingly, the medical community and society at large have come to understand that the focus of medical intervention should be on the prevention of disabilities through appropriate prenatal care and early intervention with at-risk children. The five procedures prevalent in the medical treatment of individuals with cerebral palsy are early intervention to minimize primitive reflex control, bracing, drug therapy, surgical correction, and rehabilitation. Braces are important as an aid in teaching joint function, as well as in assisting in the locomotion of patients who are severely disabled. Another use for bracing is the prevention of deforming contractures. Drug administration usually serves two functions: aiding in relaxation of muscle groups when neuromuscular exercise therapy is attempted and controlling epileptic seizures through the use of anticonvulsant drugs.

There are various opinions as to the value of orthopedic surgery for persons with cerebral palsy. Certain types of operative procedures have met with consider-

able success, especially with particular types of cerebral palsy. The physical growth of children affects the efficiency of muscle and tendon surgery; however, surgical operation, for the most part, is not curative but rather assists the functional activities of daily living. **Tenotomy** (tendon cutting) of the hip adductor and hamstring muscles seems to be the most valuable surgical procedure for adults with cerebral palsy.

Recently the use of electrical stimulation on the anterial tibial muscles of children with spastic hemiplegia proved to be useful in increasing the range of passive dorsiflexion of the ankle; however, the gait pattern was not significantly improved.[27] This type of intervention does hold promise as an alternative to surgery for reducing contractures.

The physical education program and teaching strategies

There is no treatment for the repair of a damaged brain. However, the portion of the nervous system that remains intact can be made functional through a well-managed training program. Intervention by the physical educator and other personnel is needed to build functional developmental motor patterns with the operative parts of the body. Each child should be evaluated closely, and programs that foster those functional abilities should be formulated. Developmental programs should be constructed to correct deficiencies that respond to treatment. The specific child should be considered when the exercise regimen is being determined. Because of their numerous involuntary muscular activities, children with athetosis are much more active than children with spasticity and ataxia.

There is growing evidence that some of the sensory and perceptual delays can be improved through training. Sensorimotor and perceptual motor training programs are designed to reduce primitive reflex involvement and develop locomotor patterns, balance, rhythm, and ocular control. All of these activities are inherent in most elementary physical education programs; however, the quality of physical education programs could be improved by consciously selecting activities of this nature for classes that include students with spastic cerebral palsy. The handbook *Gross Motor Activities for Young Children with Special Needs,* which accompanies this text, has several games that would be appropriate for the elementary school–age child.

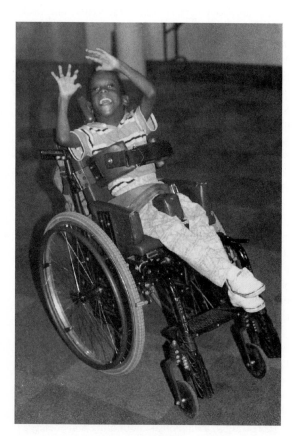

A 5-year-old boy participates in creative dance. (Courtesy Dallas Independent School District.)

The individual education program (IEP) of the student with cerebral palsy should include activities to address the individual's unique needs. Some of the therapeutic activities and techniques that could be recommended follow:

1. Muscle stretching to relieve muscle contractures, prevent deformities, and permit fuller range of purposeful motion
2. Gravity exercises that involve lifting the weight of the body or body part against gravity
3. Muscle awareness exercises to control specific muscles or muscle groups
4. **Neuromuscular reeducation** exercises that are performed through the muscles' current range to stimulate the proprioceptors and return the muscles to greater functional use
5. **Reciprocal exercises** to stimulate and strengthen the action of the protagonist
6. **Tonic exercises** to prevent atrophy or maintain organic efficiency
7. Relaxation training to assist in reducing muscle contractures, rigidity, and spasms
8. Postural alignments to maintain proper alignment of musculature
9. **Gait training** to teach or reteach walking patterns
10. Body mechanics and lifting techniques to obtain maximum use of the large muscle groups of the body
11. **Proprioceptive facilitation** exercises to bring about maximum excitation of the motor units of a muscle with each voluntary effort to overcome motor-functioning paralysis
12. Ramp climbing to improve ambulation and balance
13. **Progressive, resistive exercise** to develop muscle strength

Failure to provide children with cerebral palsy the opportunity to participate in progressive exercise may leave them short of their potential development. The opportunities for adapted physical education to maximize the physical development of these children are great. Furthermore, children with cerebral palsy frequently do not develop adequate basic motor skills because of their limited play experiences.

When a child with cerebral palsy participates in a group activity, it may be necessary to adapt the activity to the child's abilities or modify the rules or environment. A child with quadriplegic spastic cerebral palsy may be given the opportunity to play the bells during a rhythm activity, instead of being asked to dance with his or her feet. A wheelchair-enabled child with rigid cerebral palsy may "hold" one handle on the parachute with the edge of his or her chair. A child with ataxia may play a sitting circle game with classmates while propped in the teacher's lap or propped against a wall.

In addition to adaptation of activity, the capabilities of each individual must be considered. Children with spasticity, those with athetosis, and those with ataxia differ greatly in function. For instance, the child with spasticity finds it easier to engage in activities in which motion is continuous. However, in the case of the child with athetosis, relaxation between movements is extremely important to prevent involuntary muscular contractions that may thwart the development of skills.

Children with ataxia have different motor problems—they are usually severely limited in all activities that require balance. The motor characteristics of the basic types of cerebral palsy, as well as of each individual child, are important variables in the selection of activities. Rest periods should be frequent for children with cerebral palsy. The length and frequency of the rest periods should vary with the nature of the activity and the severity of the disability. The development of a sequence of activities varying in degree of difficulty is important. This sequencing provides an opportunity to place each child in an activity that is commensurate with his or her ability and proposes a subsequent goal to work toward.

Physical activities described under the definition of physical education in the Education of the Handicapped Act are appropriate for children with cerebral palsy. At the early elementary level, the focus should be on the development of sensory-motor function, body image, and rhythmicity. Appropriate motor activities might include fundamental motor patterns such as walking, running, and jumping, and fundamental motor skills such as throwing, kicking, and catching. Aquatics is a vital part of the curriculum for children with cerebral palsy. The buoyancy of the water frees the child from gravity-imposed restrictions encountered on dry land. Rhythm activities are also a vital part of the quality physical education program for children with cerebral palsy; expressive dance may prove to be vital in the development of language and communication, as well as motor skills. If possible, the physical education program for children with cerebral palsy at the elementary school level should include age-appropriate, geographically appropriate leisure and recreation skills. Horseback riding is a particularly effective intervention activity for even the most severely involved child. Other leisure and recreation skills are also an important part of the total program. The child should be introduced, for example, to skills needed to participate in bowling, including the use of automatic grip release balls and ramps, if necessary. If geographically appropriate, the child should learn the skills necessary to sled with family and friends.

The middle school curriculum should focus on the development of physical fitness, body mechanics, and relaxation techniques. Once again, aquatics is a vital component of the curriculum. Increased focus should be placed on exposing the student to community-based leisure and recreation activities and, where appropriate, competitive sports programs.

In the high school program, it is important that students with cerebral palsy maintain adequate levels of

An athlete goes for the strike. (Courtesy American Wheelchair Bowling Association, Inc.)

physical fitness, practice body mechanics, and develop more sophisticated relaxation techniques. There is impressive evidence that motor skills, muscular endurance, and strength can be developed in individuals with cerebral palsy through progressive exercise. Fernandez and Pitetti[22] indicate that individuals with cerebral palsy who exercised regularly demonstrated improvement in functional capacity. Holland and Steadward[32] have identified Nautilus weight-lifting exercises that develop the neck, chest, and arms. These authors conclude that persons with cerebral palsy can participate in intense strength training programs without sacrificing flexibility or increasing spasticity.

The secondary student's IEP must address techniques that will allow the student to make the transition from school-based to community-based leisure and recreation programs. For example, the IEP may address the skills necessary for the student to register for and participate in an adult bowling or archery league. These skills may include independent management of a ramp, for example. In addition, these students should be made familiar with the activities and programs of the U.S. Cerebral Palsy Athletic Association (see Appendix C for address).

Epilepsy

Epilepsy is a disturbance resulting from abnormal electrical activity of the brain. It is not a specific disease, but a group of symptoms that may be associated with several conditions. It is defined as a "recurrent disorder of cerebral function characterized by sudden, brief attacks of altered consciousness, motor activity, sensory phenomena, or inappropriate behavior caused by abnormal excessive discharge of cerebral neurons."[3] The estimated incidence of epilepsy is 2% of the population. Many persons with epilepsy experience their first attack during childhood. No cause can be found in 75% of the young adults who have epilepsy; however, some forms of epilepsy are due to a microscopic scar in the brain as a result of birth trauma or other head injury.[3]

Characteristics and types

There are several types of epilepsy, and each type has a particular set of characteristics. Although there are several methods of classifying various types of epilepsy, the one most commonly used includes four categories: grand mal, petit mal, focal, and psychomotor seizures.

Grand mal seizure. The **grand mal,** French for "big illness," is the most severe type of seizure. The individual often has an "aura" that immediately precedes the seizure and may give the individual some warning of the imminence of the seizure. The aura is usually a somatosensory flash—a particular smell, a blur of colors, or an itching sensation, for example. The seizure itself usually begins with bilateral jerks of the extremities, followed by convulsions and loss of consciousness. The student may be incontinent during the seizure, losing control of the bowels and bladder. After the seizure, the individual is usually confused, often embarrassed, and exhausted. Approximately 90% of individuals with epilepsy experience grand mal seizures.[3]

Petit mal seizure. The onset of the **petit** (little) **mal seizure** is sudden and may last for only a few seconds or for several minutes. Usually the individual appears to simply stare into space and have a lapse in attention. It is often characterized by twitching around the eyes or mouth. There is a loss of consciousness but no collapse. The individual remains sitting or standing. Seizures of this type usually affect children between the ages of 5 and 12 years and may disappear during puberty.

The student with petit mal seizures may experience serious learning difficulties. It is not uncommon for a child to have hundreds of petit mal seizures a day. If a child has 100 seizures and each lasts only 30 seconds, the child will have lost a full 50 minutes of learning time. Approximately 25% of individuals who have epilepsy experience petit mal attacks.[3]

Focal seizure. The **focal seizure** is similar to the grand mal seizure. It is characterized by a loss of body tone and collapse. The student usually remains conscious during the attack, but speech may be impaired. In **jacksonian focal seizures** there is a localized twitching of muscles in the extremities, which move up the arm or leg. If the seizure spreads to other parts of the brain, generalized convulsions and loss of consciousness result.

Psychomotor seizure. A **psychomotor seizure** is characterized by atypical social-motor behavior for 1 or 2 minutes. The behaviors may include uncontrollable temper tantrums, hand clapping, spitting, swearing, or shouting. The individual is unaware of the activity during and after the seizure. Psychomotor seizures may occur at any age.

There are several factors that may cause seizures. Some of these factors are (1) emotional stress such as fear, anger, or frustration; (2) excessive amounts of alcohol; and (3) menstruation.

Special considerations

Teachers should be cognizant of which students have epilepsy and whether they are taking drugs to control their seizures. Anticonvulsant drugs are the preferred medical treatment for approximately 95% of individuals with epilepsy. Drug therapy can completely control grand mal seizures in 50% of the cases and greatly reduce seizures in another 35%. In the case of petit mal seizures, drug therapy will completely control the condition in 40% of the cases and reduce the number of seizures in 35% of the cases.[3] The major antiepileptic drugs are phenytoin (Dilantin), usually the drug of choice, phenobarbital, and primidone (Mysoline) for complex partial and general seizures, and ethosuximide (Zarontin) and clonazepam (Klonopin) for petit mal seizures. Which type of drug should be given and the optimum dosage are difficult to determine and highly individualized. Teachers should be sensitive to the side effects of these drugs that may impair motor performance. Dilantin, for example, may produce lethargy, dizziness, and mental confusion in some students. Phenobarbital sometimes contributes to drowsiness and learning difficulties.[3] Drugs taken to control petit mal seizures lead to drowsiness and nausea.[3] These side effects may be detrimental to the student's performance and safety in certain activities. Information about the student's drug treatment program should be discussed during the IEP meeting.

Physical education teachers should be familiar with procedures for handling seizures. Perhaps the most significant procedure for handling a seizure is to educate the student's class members regarding the nature of epilepsy. If the child's classmates are knowledgeable about seizures, the child will not have to suffer from postseizure embarrassment.

In the event a child has a grand mal seizure, the physical educator should do the following[21]:

1. Place the student on the floor in a back-lying position.
2. Move all objects away from the student so that he or she will not bang the head or limbs against objects.
3. Loosen all restraining clothing, such as a belt or shirt collar.

4. If the student is experiencing breathing difficulty, tilt the student's head back to open the airway.
5. Once the convulsion has stopped, place a blanket or towel over the student to eliminate embarrassment if the student lost bowel or bladder control.
6. Allow the student to rest.
7. Report the seizure to the appropriate school official.

A grand mal seizure is not a life-threatening event and should be treated as a routine event. The seizure process is dangerous only if the student moves into **status epilepticus**—has a series of grand mal seizures without a break. If this happens, emergency medical personnel must be contacted immediately.

If the student experiences a focal or psychomotor seizure, the child should be removed to an isolated part of the gymnasium, if possible. If the student experiences a petit mal seizure and the teacher is aware of it, the teacher should repeat any instructions given previously.

The physical education program and teaching strategies

If medication is effective and the child's seizures are under control, the student should be able to participate in an unrestricted physical education program. However, activities that involve direct blows to the head should be avoided. Boxing or heading a soccer ball, for example, is contraindicated. Activities that are performed while a considerable height from the floor should be avoided. Rope climbing, diving, horizontal and uneven parallel bar activities, and high balance beam activities are contraindicated. Swimming should be carefully supervised. Underwater swimming, snorkeling, and scuba diving are contraindicated, as is swimming in cold water.

Multiple Sclerosis

Multiple sclerosis is a chronic and degenerative neurological disease primarily affecting older adolescents and adults. It is a slowly progressive disease of the central nervous system, leading to the disintegration of the myelin coverings of nerve fibers in the brain and spinal cord, which results in hardening or scarring of the tissue that replaces the disintegrated protective myelin sheath.[3] The cause of multiple sclerosis is unknown, but immunologic abnormality is suspected.[3] Multiple scle-

rosis occurs in 1 out of 2000 births in temperate climates and in 1 out of 10,000 births in tropical climates.[3]

Characteristics

The symptoms of multiple sclerosis include sensory problems, such as visual disturbances, tremors, muscle weakness, spasticity, speech difficulties, dizziness, mild emotional disturbances, partial paralysis, fatigue, and motor difficulties. Multiple sclerosis generally appears when the person is between the ages of 20 and 40 years and results in several periods of remissions and recurring exacerbations. Some persons have frequent attacks, whereas others have remissions that last as long as 25 years.[3]

The physical education program and teaching strategies

There is no treatment that can repair the damage to the nervous system caused by degeneration. However, each person should be evaluated individually, and programs of resistive exercise should be administered to maintain maximum functioning. In addition, **Jacobson relaxation techniques** and active and passive range-of-motion exercises should be employed to counter contractures in the lower extremities. The goal of these programs is to maintain functional skills, strength of muscles, and range of motion. It is particularly important to teach the skills necessary for functional use of walkers, crutches, and/or wheelchairs. In addition, the individual should be given the opportunity to develop compensatory skills—skills needed to function because of changes in central nervous system function. These include skills to compensate, for example, for disequilibrium. Braces may be introduced at the later stages of the disorder to assist with locomotion.

Inactivity may contribute to the progressive weakening of the muscles needed for daily activity. Instructors should constantly encourage as active a lifestyle as possible. Individuals should be urged to participate in an exercise program that maintains cardiovascular respiratory functioning and sufficient muscle strength to allow participation in activities of daily living. Interval training is recommended to reduce the possibility of fatigue and overheating.[39] Swimming[39] and aquatic aerobic exercises are recommended because they require less effort than activities on land. Individuals who enjoy competition should be encouraged to participate in wheelchair sports when their condition is in remission.

Muscular Dystrophy

Muscular dystrophy is a disease of the muscular system characterized by weakness and atrophy of the muscles of the body. The rate of progressive degeneration is different for each set of muscles.[43] Weakness often afflicts the muscles that enable breathing and results in major complications, including congestive heart failure and pneumonia.[33] Although the exact incidence of muscular dystrophy is unknown, estimates place the number of persons with the disorder in excess of 200,000 in the United States. It is estimated that in more than half of the known cases, the age of onset falls within the range of 3 to 13 years.

Speculation regarding the exact cause includes faulty metabolism (related to inability to utilize vitamin E), endocrine disorders, and deficiencies in the peripheral nerves. There is some indication that an inherited abnormality causes the body's chemistry to be unable to carry on proper muscle metabolism.

Characteristics and types

The physical characteristics of persons with muscular dystrophy are relevant to the degenerative stage as well as to the type of muscular dystrophy. In the late stages of the disease, connective tissue replaces most of the muscle tissue. In some cases deposits of fat give the appearance of well-developed muscles. Despite the muscle atrophy, there is no apparent central nervous system impairment.

The age of onset of muscular dystrophy is of importance to the total development of the children. Persons who contract the disease after having had an opportunity to secure an education, or part of an education, and develop social and psychological strengths are better able to cope with their environment than are those who are afflicted with the disease before the acquisition of basic skills.

Although the characteristics of patients with muscular dystrophy vary according to the stage of the disease, some general characteristics are as follows:

1. There is a tendency to tire quickly.
2. There may be a tendency to lose fine manual dexterity.

3. There is sometimes a lack of motivation to learn because of isolation from social contacts and limited educational opportunities.
4. Progressive weakness tends to produce adverse postural changes.
5. Emotional disturbance may be prevalent because of the progressive nature of the illness and the resulting restrictions placed on opportunities for socialization.

There are numerous classifications of muscular dystrophy based on the muscle groups affected and the age of onset. However, three main clinical types of muscular dystrophy have been identified: Duchenne (pseudohypertrophic), Becker, and facioscapulohumeral (Landouzy-Dejerine).[3]

Duchenne type. The **Duchenne (pseudohypertrophic) type** is an X-linked recessive disorder that usually presents itself during the ages of 3 to 7 years. It occurs primarily in males. It affects the pelvic girdle first, followed by the shoulder girdle.[3] Symptoms that give an indication of the disease are the following:

1. Decreased physical activity as compared with activity of children of commensurate age
2. Delay in the age at which the child walks
3. Poor motor development in walking and stair climbing
4. Little muscular endurance
5. A waddling gait with the legs carried far apart
6. Walking on tiptoe
7. Moving to all fours and then "climbing up the legs" when changing from a prone to a standing position (**Gowers' sign**)
8. Weakness in anterior abdominal muscles
9. Weakness in neck muscles, which makes it difficult to hold the head in alignment
10. Pseudohypertrophy of muscles, particularly in the calves of the leg, which are enlarged and firm on palpation
11. Pronounced lordosis and gradual weakness of the lower extremities

The progressive nature of muscular dystrophy is perhaps best illustrated by the stages of functional ability[61] outlined in the box on p. 382. As the disease progresses, imbalance of muscle strength in various parts of the body occurs. Deformities develop in flexion at the hips and knees. The spine, pelvis, and shoulder girdle also eventually become atrophied. Contractures and involvement of the heart may develop with the progressive degeneration of the disease.

The advent of the motorized wheelchair has increased independence of children in the advanced stages of muscular dystrophy. Though unable to perform activities of daily living, the child using a motorized wheelchair retains a measure of mobility that promotes independence and allows integration into many school-based and community-based programs.

Becker type. Becker muscular dystrophy is also an X-linked disorder; however, it is less severe than the Duchenne type. The advancement of this type of dystrophy mimics the Duchenne type, but this type progresses more slowly. As a result, few individuals are required to use wheelchairs by age 16 years, and 90% are still alive at age 20.[3] Active exercise is recommended to prolong ambulation. Corrective surgery is sometimes used to restore function.[3]

Facioscapulohumeral type. The **facioscapulohumeral (Landouzy-Dejerine) type of muscular dystrophy,** which is the third most common type, is characterized by weakness of the facial muscles and shoulder girdles. The onset of symptoms or signs of the facioscap-

ulohumeral type is usually recognized when the person is between the ages of 3 and 20 years, with the most common age of onset between 7 and 15 years. Both genders are equally subject to the condition.

Persons with this form of muscular dystrophy have trouble raising the arms above the head, whistling, drinking through a straw, and closing their eyes. A child with this type of disease often appears to have a masklike face that lacks expression. Later, involvement of the muscles that move the humerus and scapula will be noticed. Weakness usually appears later in the abdominal, pelvic, and hip musculature. The progressive weakness and muscle deterioration often lead to scoliosis and lordosis. This type of muscular dystrophy is often milder than the Duchenne type, and life expectancy is normal.[3] Facioscapulohumeral muscular dystrophy usually progresses slowly, ambulation is seldom lost, and pseudohypertrophy of the muscles is rare.[3]

Special considerations

Duchenne muscular dystrophy is one of the most serious disabling conditions that can occur in childhood. Although not fatal in itself, the disease contributes to premature death in most known cases because of its progressive nature. The progress of the condition is cruel and relentless as the child loses function and moves toward inevitable death. However, it is worth noting that scientific research may be close to solving unanswered questions regarding the disease, and eventually the progressive deterioration may be halted.

The physical education program and teaching strategies

An individually designed activity program may significantly contribute to the quality of life of the individual affected by muscular dystrophy. Inactivity seems to contribute to the progressive weakening of the muscles of persons with muscular dystrophy. Exercise of muscles involved in the activities of daily living to increase strength may permit greater functional use of the body. Furthermore, exercise may assist in reducing excessive weight, which is a burden to those who have muscular dystrophy. Movement in warm water—aquatic therapy—may be particularly beneficial for the child with muscular dystrophy. It aids in the maintenance of muscle tonus and flexibility, and encourages circulation.

The child's diet should be closely monitored. Prevention of excess weight is essential to the success of the rehabilitation program of persons with progressive muscular dystrophy. For individuals whose strength is marginal, any extra weight is an added burden on ambulation and on activities of daily living.

A great deal can be done to prevent deformities and loss of muscle strength from inactivity. If a specific strengthening and stretching program is outlined during each stage of the disease, it is possible that the child may extend the ability to care for most daily needs for many additional years. In addition to the administration of specific developmental exercises for the involved muscles, exercises should include development of walking patterns, posture control, muscle coordination, and stretching of contractures involved in disuse atrophy. However, it should be noted that all exercises should be selected after study of contraindications specified by a physician. It may be desirable to select activities that use the remaining strengths so that enjoyment and success can be achieved.

One must recognize that all the types of muscular dystrophy cannot be considered the same; therefore the physical and social benefits that children can derive from physical education and recreation programs are different. However, all children with muscular dystrophy can profit from a well-designed program to enhance the quality of life. The focus of the program, particularly for children with the Duchenne form of muscular dystrophy, is on the development of leisure and recreation skills that will be appropriate as the child progressively loses function. For example, a child with Duchenne dystrophy should be taught to fish and to play bocci because those are skills that can be enjoyed throughout the life span. Also, the child should be given the opportunity to learn board and video games that will provide entertainment and joy.

One focus of the program should also be the development of relaxation techniques. The progressive loss of functional skills causes a great deal of stress, as does facing the inevitability of an early death; and the quality of the child's life can be enhanced if the child has learned conscious relaxation skills.

Perhaps more important, a significant dance, music, and art therapy program should be a part of the child's total program. Movement and dance, even dance done in a motorized wheelchair, can help the child or adolescent express emotions—grief, rage, frustration and, we

hope, love and joy. Music and art therapy provide vital avenues of expression as the child loses motor capabilities. In addition, a trained therapist can be of value as the child moves through the stages of grief. The intent of the program is to enhance the quality of the child's life and, with professional support, allow the process of dying to be as humane, caring, and ennobling as possible.

Parkinson's Disease

Parkinson's disease is a slow, progressive disorder that results in physical debilitation. The disease usually appears gradually and progresses slowly. It may progress to a stage where there is difficulty with routine activities of daily living. The condition may be aggravated by emotional tension or fatigue. It affects about 1% of the population over 65 years of age, with a mean age of onset of 57 years.[3] A juvenile form of parkinsonism, which has its onset in childhood or adolescence, has also been identified.

Characteristics

The observable characteristics of Parkinson's disease are tremor of the resting muscles, a slowing of voluntary movements, muscular weakness, abnormal gait, and postural instability. These motor characteristics become more pronounced as the disease progresses. For instance, a minor feeling of sluggishness may progress until the individual is unable to get up from a chair. The walking gait becomes less efficient and can be characterized by shuffling of the feet for the purpose of postural stability. In addition, voluntary movements, particularly those performed by the small muscles, become slow, and spontaneous movements diminish.

In general, most persons require lifelong management consisting of physical therapy and drug therapy. Physical therapy consists of heat and massage to alleviate muscle cramps and relieve tension headaches that often accompany rigidity of the muscles of the neck.

The physical activity program

Because of the degenerative nature of the disease, the goals of physical activity programs are to preserve muscular functioning for purposive movement involved in the activities of daily living and required for the performance of leisure and recreation skills. The general types of physical activities that may be of value are general coordination exercises to retard the slow deterioration of movement, as well as relaxation exercises that may reduce muscular incoordination and tremors.[46] In addition, balance activities and those that teach compensation for lack of balance should be included. Exercises directed at maintaining postural strength and flexibility should be a part of the program plan.

Poliomyelitis

Poliomyelitis (polio) is an acute viral infection with a wide range of manifestations.[3] In the serious cases (nonparalytic and paralytic) an inflammation affects the anterior motor cells in the spinal cord, which in turn affects the muscles. Vaccines virtually eradicated polio during the 1960s in this country; however, an increasing number of children are now being afflicted because they have not been immunized.[60]

Characteristics and types

There are three prevalent classifications of poliomyelitis: abortive, nonparalytic, and paralytic. **Abortive poliomyelitis** accounts for 80% to 90% of the clinical infections and occurs chiefly in children.[3] This form does not involve the central nervous system. The symptoms are headache, sore throat, mild fever, and nausea.

Nonparalytic poliomyelitis involves the central nervous system but does not damage the motor cells permanently. In addition to the symptoms of abortive poliomyelitis, the victim might experience general and specific pain and acute contractions of one or more muscle groups located in the upper and lower extremities, neck, and back. Recovery is complete.[3]

Paralytic poliomyelitis includes three afflictions: spinal poliomyelitis, which may involve upper limbs, lower limbs, respiratory muscles, and/or trunk muscles; bulbar poliomyelitis, which affects the muscles of the respiratory center; and, spinal-bulbar poliomyelitis, which involves a combination of voluntary and involuntary muscles (the most serious of the three paralytic forms). In paralytic poliomyelitis 1% to 4% die. Of those who survive, approximately 25% suffer severe permanent disability, about 25% have mild disabilities, and the remaining recover completely.[3]

Recently a postpoliomyelitis syndrome has been identified that occurs many years after a paralytic poliomyelitis attack. The characteristics include muscle fatigue and decreased endurance, accompanied by weakness, and atrophy in selected muscles.[3]

The physical education program and teaching strategies

Exercise programs should focus on motor tasks that develop strength, endurance, flexibility, and coordination. Orthopedic deformities do not totally restrict movement. Children learn quickly to compensate for the inconvenience of an impaired foot or arm. At the elementary school level, many children with polio can achieve considerable athletic success. However, as they progress through school life, accumulated developmental lags as a rule influence skill development. Wheelchair sports are popular for polio victims who cannot walk.

Spina Bifida

Spina bifida is the most common congenital spinal defect. The condition is a result of defective closure of the vertebral column (Figure 15-1). The severity ranges from **spina bifida occulta,** with no findings, to a completely open spine **(spina bifida cystica).**[3] The National Information Center for Handicapped Children and Youth[45] estimates that approximately 40% of all people in the United States have spina bifida occulta, but few even know it. The incidence of spina bifida is estimated at 2 per 100 live births, making it one of the most common birth defects that can lead to physical disability.

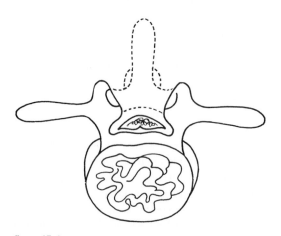

figure 15-1
Spina bifida occulta.

Characteristics

In spina bifida occulta the vertebral arches fail to fuse; however, there is no distension of the spinal cord lining or of the cord itself. In spina bifida cystica, the protruding sac can contain the lining of the spinal column, which is known as the meninges **(meningocele),** the spinal cord itself **(myelocele),** or both **(myelomeningocele).**[3] Resulting spinal cord defects may produce varying degrees of neurological impairment ranging from mild muscle imbalance and sensory loss in the lower limbs to paralysis of one or both legs. Paralysis usually affects bladder and rectal function,[3] and bladder and kidney infections are frequent. In almost half the children with spina bifida cystica, a **hydrocephalic** condition also exists. In these cases, usually a **shunt** is inserted to drain off cerebrospinal fluid that is not being reabsorbed properly. Removing the excess cerebrospinal fluid protects the child against brain damage resulting from pressure on the brain. Children who are paraplegic from spina bifida are often able to move about with the aid of braces and crutches.

Special considerations

Activities that could distress placement of any shunts or put pressure on sensitive areas of the spine must be avoided. Of considerable concern is the prevention of contractures and associated foot deformities (e.g., equinovarus) through daily passive flexibility exercises.

Many social problems result from spina bifida. In addition to the physical disability, there are often problems associated with control of bowels and bladder, which draw further attention to the children as they function in a social environment. In many cases, this has a negative social impact on the children. Often, children with spina bifida need catheterization. If someone must do it for them, the attention of others is drawn to these circumstances. However, in many cases older children may be taught to catheterize themselves. The physical disability and the associated physiological problems result in stressful social situations because groups must adapt to the child with spina bifida's physical disabilities and associated physiological problems. Social circumstances can be made more favorable if these children are integrated into regular classes in the early grades and if social integration strategies are employed (see Chapter 9).

The physical education program and teaching strategies

No particular program of physical education or therapy can be directly assigned to the student with spina bifida. Some students have no physical reaction and discover the condition only by chance through x-ray examination for another problem. On the other hand, a person may have extensive neuromuscular involvement requiring constant medical care. A program of physical education or therapeutic exercise based on the individual needs of the person should be planned.

Often children with spina bifida occulta or with a meningocele that has been repaired early in life do not require special programming. However, frequently children with myelomeningocele need programs that are modified to their needs and that stress intensive development.

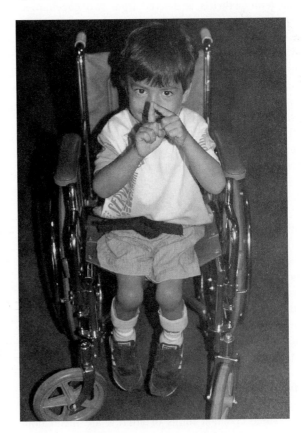

A child participates in creative story telling at camp. (Courtesy Dallas Independent School District.)

The child with spina bifida myelomeningocele is often able to participate in a regular physical education program more effectively in a wheelchair than with the use of a walker or crutches and braces. While the child with spina bifida should be encouraged to walk whenever possible, it may be difficult for the child to participate in activities safely in a crowded gymnasium.

Simple modifications can be made to allow the child using a wheelchair to participate actively in regular physical education. Specific suggestions for including young children in wheelchairs in a regular physical education program are presented later in this chapter in the section on spinal cord injuries.

Orthopedic Disabilities
Arthritis

The term **arthritis** is derived from two Greek roots: *arthro-,* meaning joint, and *-itis,* meaning inflammation. It has been estimated that more than 12 million people in the United States are afflicted with some form of arthritic disease. Since arthritis inflicts a low mortality and high morbidity, the potential for increasing numbers of those afflicted and disabled is great. It is assumed that a great many factors may predispose one to arthritis. Major contributors could be infection, hereditary factors, environmental stress, dietary deficiencies, trauma, and organic or emotional disturbances.

Types, causes, incidence, and characteristics

In most cases arthritis is progressive, gradually resulting in general fatigue, weight loss, and muscular stiffness. Joint impairment is symmetrical, and characteristically, the small joints of the hands and feet are affected in the earliest stages. Tenderness and pain may occur in tendons and muscular tissue near inflamed joints. As the inflammation in the joints becomes progressively chronic, degenerative and proliferative changes occur to the synovial tendons, ligaments, and articular cartilages. If the inflammation is not arrested in its early stages, joints become **ankylosed** and muscles **atrophy** and contract, eventually causing a twisted and deformed limb.

Three common forms of arthritis are rheumatoid, osteoarthritis, and anklyosing spondylitis.

Rheumatoid arthritis. **Rheumatoid arthritis** represents the nation's number one crippling disease, afflicting more than 3 million persons. It is a systemic disease of unknown cause. Seventy-five percent of the cases occur between the ages of 25 and 50 years and in a ratio of 3 to 1, women to men. A type of rheumatoid arthritis called **Still's disease,** or juvenile arthritis, attacks children before the age of 7 years. Approximately 250,000 children in the United States are afflicted with rheumatoid arthritis, making it a major crippler among young children.[53] The most significant physical sign is the thickening of the synovial tissue in joints that are actively involved (inflamed). Inflamed joints are sensitive to the touch. Individuals with rheumatoid arthritis are stiff for an hour or so after rising in the morning or after a period of inactivity.[3]

Osteoarthritis, the second most frequent type of arthritis, is a disorder of the hyaline cartilage primarily in the weight-bearing joints. It is a result of mechanical destruction of the coverings of the bone at the joints because of trauma or repeated use. Although evidence of the breakdown can be documented during the 20s, discomfort usually does not occur until individuals are in their 40s. Initially the condition is noninflammatory, and it impacts only one or a few joints. Pain is the earliest symptom, and it increases initially with exercise.

Ankylosing spondylitis affects the axial skeleton and large peripheral joints of the body and is most prevalent in males.[3] It usually begins between the ages of 20 and 40 years, and is the most common type experienced by persons under 35 years of age.[39] Common symptoms are recurrent back pain, particularly at night, and early morning stiffness that is relieved by activity.

Special considerations

Interventions for these types of arthritis include proper diet, rest, drug therapy, reduction of stress, and exercise. Because of its debilitating effect, prolonged bed rest is discouraged, although daily rest sessions are required to avoid undue fatigue. A number of drugs may be given to the patient, depending on individual needs; for example, salicylates such as aspirin relieve pain, gold compounds may be used for arresting the acute inflammatory stage, and adrenocortical steroids may be employed for control of the degenerative process. Drugless techniques of controlling arthritis pain, such as biofeedback, self-hypnosis, behavior modification, and transcutaneous nerve stimulation, are often used as an adjunct to other more traditional types of treatment.

A quality athletic experience can enhance life throughout the life span. (Courtesy Texas Special Olympics.)

The physical activity program and teaching strategies

Physical exercise is critical to reduce pain and increase function. The exercises required by patients with arthritis fall into three major categories: exercises to improve and maintain range of motion, exercises that strengthen muscles that surround and support affected joints, and aerobic exercises to improve cardiovascular endurance.[39] The physical educator should encourage gradual or static stretching, isometric muscle contraction, and reduced weight-bearing aerobic exercise daily.

Maintenance of normal joint range of movement is of prime importance for establishing a functional joint. Stretching may first be employed passively; however, active stretching is of greater benefit because muscle tone is maintained in the process. Joints should be moved through pain-free range of motion several times daily.[39]

Isometric exercises that strengthen muscles that support affected joints should be practiced during the day when the pain and stiffness are at a minimum. Weight-bearing isotonic exercises that cause compression of joints should be avoided.

Aerobic exercises that require a minimum of weight bearing should be used. Bicycling, swimming, and aquatic aerobics are highly recommended. Whenever possible, water activities should take place in a heated pool because the warmth will enhance circulation and reduce muscle tightness.

An individual with arthritis may need rest periods during the day. These should be combined with a well-planned exercise program. Activity should never increase pain or so tire an individual that normal recovery is not obtained by the next day.

Arthrogryposis (Curved Joints)

Arthrogryposis is a condition of flexure or contracture of joints (joints of the lower limbs more often than joints of the upper limbs). When several limbs are in contracture, the condition is referred to as multiple congenital contracture. Incidence and cause are unknown; however, the contractures may be observed relatively early in fetal life because of either a primary muscle disease or a spinal cord disease of cells controlling muscle contraction.

Characteristics

The limbs may be fixed in any position. However, the usual forms are with the shoulders turned in, the elbows straightened and extended, the forearms turned with the palms outward (pronated), and the wrists flexed and deviated upward with the fingers curled into the palms. The hips may be bent in a flexed position and turned outward (externally rotated), and the feet are usually turned inward and downward. The spine often evidences scoliosis, the limbs are small in circumference, and the joints appear large and have lost their range of motion.

Several physical conditions are associated with arthrogryposis, including congenital heart disease, urinary tract abnormalities, respiratory problems, abdominal hernias, and cleft palate. Intelligence is usually normal. Children with arthrogryposis may walk independently but with an abnormal gait, or they may depend on a wheelchair.

The deformities are at their worst at birth. Active physical therapy early in life can produce reduced contracture and improved range of motion. The literature states that articular surfaces do deteriorate with age. Therefore, developmental exercises may assist in amelioration of deficient motor ability.

Special considerations

Surgery often is used to correct hip conditions, as well as knee and foot deformities, and is sometimes used to permit limited flexion of the elbow joint, as well as greater wrist mobility.

The physical education program and teaching strategies

The awkwardness of joint positions and mechanics cause no pain, and therefore children with arthrogryposis are free to engage in most types of activity.

Congenital Hip Dislocation

Congenital hip dislocation, which is also known as developmental hip dislocation, refers to a partially or completely displaced femoral head in relation to the acetabulum (Figure 15-2). It is estimated that it occurs six times more often in females than in males; it may be bilateral or unilateral, occurring most often in the left hip.

The cause of congenital hip dislocation is unknown, with various reasons proposed. Heredity seems to be a primary causative factor in faulty hip development and subsequent **dysplasia.** Actually, only about 2% of developmental hip dislocations are congenital.

Characteristics

Generally, the acetabulum is shallower on the affected side than on the nonaffected side, and the femoral head is displaced upward and backward in relation to the ilium. Ligaments and muscles become deranged, resulting in a shortening of the rectus femoris, hamstring, and adductor thigh muscles and affecting the small intrinsic muscles of the hip. Prolonged malpositioning of the femoral head produces a chronic weakness of the gluteus medius and minimus muscles. A primary factor in stabilizing one hip in the upright posture is the iliopsoas muscle. In developmental hip dislocation, the iliopsoas muscle serves to displace the femoral head upward; this will eventually cause the lumbar vertebrae to become lordotic and scoliotic.

Detection of the hip dislocation may not occur until the child begins to bear weight or walk. Early recognition of this condition may be accomplished by observing asymmetrical fat folds on the infant's legs and restricted hip adduction on the affected side. The **Trendelenburg test** (Figure 15-3) will reveal that the child is unable to maintain the pelvic level while standing on the affected leg. In such cases, weak abductor muscles of the affected leg allow the pelvis to tilt downward on

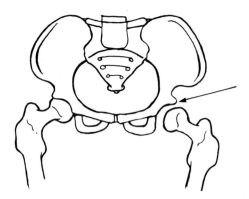

figure 15-2
Developmental hip dislocation.

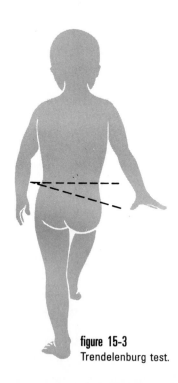

figure 15-3
Trendelenburg test.

the nonaffected side. The child walks with a decided limp in unilateral cases and with a waddle in bilateral cases. No discomfort or pain is normally experienced by the child, but fatigue tolerance to physical activity is very low. Pain and discomfort become more apparent as the individual becomes older and as postural deformities become more structural.

Special considerations

Medical treatment depends on the age of the child and the extent of displacement. Young babies with a mild involvement may have the condition remedied through gradual adduction of the femur by a pillow splint, whereas more complicated cases may require traction, casting, or surgery to restore proper hip continuity. The thigh is slowly returned to a normal position.

The physical education program and teaching strategies

Active exercise is suggested, along with passive stretching to contracted tissue. Primary concern is paid to reconditioning the movement of hip extension and abduction. When adequate muscle strength has been gained in the hip region, a program of ambulation is conducted, with particular attention paid to walking without a lateral pelvic tilt.

A child in the adapted physical education or therapeutic recreation program with a history of developmental hip dislocation will, in most instances, require specific postural training, conditioning of the hip region, continual gait training, and general body mechanics training. Swimming is an excellent activity for general conditioning of the hip, and it is highly recommended. Activities should not be engaged in to the point of discomfort or fatigue.

Coxa Plana (Legg-Calvé-Perthes Disease)

Coxa plana is the result of osteochrondritis dissecans, or abnormal softening, of the femoral head. It is a condition identified early in the twentieth century independently by Legg of Boston, Calvé of France, and Perthes of Germany. Its gross signs reflect a flattening of the head of the femur (Figure 15-4), and it is found predominantly in boys between the ages of 5 and 10 years.[3] It has been variously termed *osteochondritis deformans juvenilis, pseudocoxalgia,* and *Legg-Calvé-Perthes disease.* The exact cause of coxa plana is not known;

trauma, infection, and endocrine imbalance have been suggested as possible causes.

Characteristics

Coxa plana is characterized by degeneration of the capital epiphysis of the femoral head. Osteoporosis, or bone rarefaction, results in a flattened and deformed femoral head. Later developments may also include widening of the femoral head and thickening of the femoral neck. The last stage of coxa plana may be reflected by a self-limiting course in which there is a regeneration and an almost complete return of the normal epiphysis within 2 to 3 years.[3] However, recovery is not always complete, and there is often some residual deformity present. The younger child with coxa plana has the best prognosis for complete recovery.

The first outward sign of this condition is often a limp favoring the affected leg, with pain in the hip or referred to the knee region. Further investigation by the physician may show pain on passive movement and restricted motion on internal rotation and abduction. X-ray examination will provide the definitive signs of degeneration. The physical educator may be the first person to observe the gross signs of coxa plana and bring it to the attention of the parents or physician.

Whatever the mechanism of injury, the individual with coxa plana experiences progressive fatigue and pain on weight bearing, progressive stiffness, and a limited range of movement. A limp is apparent, which reflects weakness in the hip abductor muscles and pain referred to the region of the knee. With displacement of the epiphyseal plate, the affected limb tends to rotate externally and to abduct when flexed.

Treatment of coxa plana primarily entails the removal of stress placed on the femoral head by weight

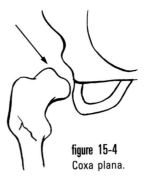

figure 15-4
Coxa plana.

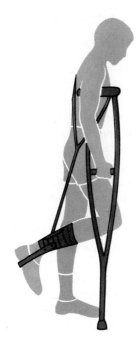

figure 15-5
Sling and crutch for hip conditions.

bearing. Bed rest is often employed in the acute stages, with ambulation and non-weight-bearing devices used for the remaining period of incapacitation. The sling and crutch method for non-weight bearing is widely used for this condition (Figure 15-5). Weight-bearing exercise is contraindicated until the physician discounts the possibility of a pathological joint condition.

The physical education program and teaching strategies

The individual with an epiphyseal affection of the hip presents a problem of muscular and skeletal stability and joint range of movement. Stability of the hip region requires skeletal continuity and a balance of muscle strength, primarily in the muscles of hip extension and abduction. Prolonged limited motion and non-weight bearing may result in contractures of tissues surrounding the hip joint and an inability to walk or run with ease. Abnormal weakness of the hip extensors and abductors may cause shortening of the hip flexors and adductors and lead the individual to display the Trendelenburg sign (see Figure 15-3).

A program of exercise must be carried out to prevent muscle atrophy and general deconditioning. When movement is prohibited, muscle-tensing exercises for muscles of the hip region are conducted, together with isotonic exercises for the upper extremities, trunk, ankles, and feet.

When the hip becomes free of symptoms, a progressive, isotonic, non-weight-bearing program is initiated for the hip region. Active movement emphasizing hip extension and abduction is recommended. Swimming is an excellent adjunct to the regular exercise program.

The program of exercise should never exceed the point of pain or fatigue until full recovery is accomplished. A general physical fitness program emphasizing weight control and body mechanics will aid the student in preparing for a return to a full program of physical education and recreation activities.

Coxa Vara and Coxa Valga

In adults the normal angle of inclination of the femoral head, or neck of the femur, is about 128 degrees. An abnormal increase in this angle is called coxa valga, and a decrease is called coxa vara (Figure 15-6). The acquired type of **coxa vara** is, by far, the most prevalent and occurs most often in adolescent boys between 10 and 16 years of age. It is commonly termed *adolescent coxa vara*.

The pathological mechanics of coxa vara and **coxa valga** result from the combined stresses of an abnormal increase or decrease in weight bearing. A variation of more than 10 to 15 degrees can produce significant shortening or lengthening of an extremity.

Coxa valga and coxa vara can be caused by many etiological factors—for example, hip injury, paralysis, non-weight bearing, or congenital malformation. Coxa vara and coxa valga are described according to where the structural changes have occurred in the femur (i.e., neck [cervical], head [epiphyseal], or combined head and neck [cervicoepiphyseal]).

Adolescent coxa vara is found in boys who have displacement of the upper femoral epiphysis. Boys who are most prone to adolescent coxa vara have been found to be obese and sexually immature, or tall and lanky, having experienced a rapid growing phase. Trauma such as hip fracture or dislocation may result in acute coxa vara. More often, through constant stress, a gradual displacement may take place.

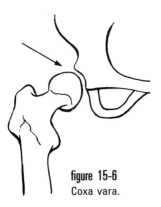

figure 15-6
Coxa vara.

Characteristics and types

Coxa vara and coxa valga are disturbances in the proximal cartilage or epiphyseal plate of the femur that result in alteration in the angle of the shaft as it relates to the neck of the femur. Two types of conditions have been recognized: the congenital type and the acquired type. The congenital type may be associated with developmental hip dislocation.

Special considerations

Management in the early stages of coxa vara involves use of crutches and the prevention of weight bearing to allow revascularization of the epiphyseal plate. Where deformity, displacement, and limb shortening are apparent, corrective surgery may be elected by the physician.

Physical education program and teaching strategies

The severity of the condition of the hip will determine the nature of the physical activity program. In many cases, the degree of involvement is such that the student with coxa vara or coxa valgus can participate in an unrestricted regular physical education program. However, if modification in the program is needed, attention should be given to modifying the amount of stress on the hip. When the condition is severe, walking and running will be limited, and strength and cardiovascular endurance may suffer. If this is the case, other ways should be found to improve the student's physical fitness levels. Swimming is an excellent activity for students with coxa vara and coxa valgus.

Osgood-Schlatter Condition

Many terms have been applied to the **Osgood-Schlatter condition;** the most prevalent are *apophysitis, osteochondritis,* and *epiphysitis of the tibial tubercle.* It is not considered a disease entity, but rather the result of a separation of the tibial tubercle at the epiphyseal junction.

The cause of this condition is unknown, but direct injury and long-term irritation are thought to be the main inciting factors. Direct trauma (as in a blow), osteochondritis, or an excessive strain of the patellar tendon as it attaches to the tibial tubercle may result in evulsion at the epiphyseal cartilage junction.

The Osgood-Schlatter condition usually occurs in active adolescent boys and girls between the ages of 10 and 15 years who are in a rapid growth period. Antich and Lombaro[2] indicate that 72% of the patients diagnosed in their study were males. Furthermore, the condition occurred more frequently in the left knee (twice as frequently) than in the right knee. Basketball was cited as a sport in which the condition was most likely to occur.

Characteristics

Disruption of the blood supply to the epiphysis results in enlargement of the tibial tubercle, joint tenderness, and pain on contraction of the quadriceps muscle. The physical educator may be the person who detects this condition based on complaints of the student. When this happens, the student should be immediately referred to a physician.

Special considerations

If the Osgood-Schlatter condition is not properly cared for, deformity and a defective extensor mechanism may result; however, it may not necessarily be associated with pain or discomfort. In most cases, the Osgood-Schlatter condition is acute, is self-limiting, and does not exceed a few months' duration. However, even after arrest of symptoms, the Osgood-Schlatter condition tends to recur after irritation.

Local inflammation is accentuated by leg activity and ameliorated by rest. The individual may be unable to kneel or engage in flexion and extension movements without pain. The knee joint must be kept completely immobilized when the inflammatory state persists. Forced inactivity, provided by a plaster cast, may be the only answer to keeping the overactive adolescent from using the affected leg.

The physical education program and teaching strategies

Early detection may reveal a slight condition in which the individual can continue a normal activity routine, excluding overexposure to sport participation, excessive exercise, strenuous running, jumping, deep knee bending, and falling on the affected leg. All physical education activities must be modified to avoid quadriceps muscle strain while preparing for general physical fitness.

While the limb is immobilized in a cast, the individual is greatly restricted; weight bearing may be held to a minimum, with signs of pain at the affected part closely watched by the physician. Although the Osgood-Schlatter condition is self-limiting and temporary, exercise is an important factor in full recovery. Physical education activities should emphasize the capabilities of the upper body and nonaffected leg to prevent their deconditioning.

After arrest of the condition and removal of the cast (or relief from immobilization), the patient is given a graduated reconditioning program. The major objectives at this time are reeducation in proper walking patterns and restoration of normal strength and flexibility of the knee joint. Strenuous knee movement is avoided for at least 5 weeks, and the demanding requirements of regular physical education classes may be postponed for extended periods depending on the physician's recommendations. Although emphasis is placed on the affected leg during the period of rehabilitation, a program also must be provided for the entire body.

The criteria for the individual to return to a regular physical education program would be as follows:

1. Normal range of movement of the knee
2. Quadriceps muscle strength equal to that of the unaffected leg
3. Evidence that the Osgood-Schlatter condition has become asymptomatic
4. Ability to move freely without favoring the affected part

After recovery, the student should avoid all activities that would tend to contuse, or in any way irritate again, the tibial tuberosity.

Osteogenesis Imperfecta (Brittle Bone Disease)

Osteogenesis imperfecta is a condition marked by both weak bones and elasticity of the joints, ligaments, and skin. It is apparently inherited, although at times it seems to be caused by spontaneous changes in the genes (mutation). There are two main types. One is evident at birth (congenital), and the other occurs after birth. Children with the congenital type are born with short, deformed limbs; numerous broken bones; and a soft skull, which if they live, tends to grow in a triangular shape, broad at the forehead and narrow at the chin. Many babies with this condition die at birth, however.

Characteristics

The bones of children with this defect are in many ways like those of the developing fetus, and the immaturity is caused by reduction in bone salts (calcium and phosphorus) rather than by any defect in the calcification mechanism. The underlying layer of the eyeball (choroid) shows through as a blue discoloration.

As growth occurs in individuals with either type of the disease, the limbs tend to become bowed. The bones are not dense, and the spine is rounded backward and often evidences scoliosis. The teeth are in poor condition, easily broken, discolored, and prone to cavities. The joints are excessively mobile, and the positions that the children may take show great flexibility.

Special considerations

No known chemical or nutrient has been shown to correct osteogenesis imperfecta, and the most satisfactory treatment is the surgical insertion of a steel rod between the ends of the long bones. This treatment, plus bracing, permits some youths to walk. Many persons with brittle bone disease need a wheelchair at least part of the time, and those with severe cases require a wheelchair exclusively.

The physical education program and teaching strategies

Some authorities have suggested that physical activities are to be ruled out for this population, whereas others suggest that persons who have undergone surgical insertion of the steel rods may participate in specialized programs of aquatics and activities taking place in special facilities. The condition of children who have undergone surgery tends to stabilize as the children grow older; they incur fewer fractures, and they may attend a regular school.

Mild activity, or even attempts to stand or walk, can cause fractures throughout the bony framework. Many children with osteogenesis imperfecta are unable to walk. Pillows are kept around both sides of the bed as well as at the head and foot. Heavy books and toys are not allowed.

Physical education teachers should be sensitive to the presence of children in their classes whose bones may be highly susceptible to injury, trauma, or breakage because of this and related conditions. These children, who approach normalcy in other areas, continue to require a highly adapted physical education program that is limited to range-of-motion exercises. Although the diagnosis of osteogenesis imperfecta is assigned only to severe cases, many children seem to have a propensity for broken bones. Physical educators should take softness of bones into consideration when developing physical education programs for children.

Osteomyelitis

Osteomyelitis is an inflammation of a bone and its medullary (marrow) cavity. Occasionally referred to as *myelitis,* this condition is caused by *Staphylococcus, Streptococcus,* or *Pneumococcus* organisms. In its early stages osteomyelitis is described as acute. If the infection persists or recurs periodically, it is called chronic. Since chronic osteomyelitis may linger on for years, the physical educator should confer with the physician about the nature of an adapted program.

Characteristics

The bones most often affected in osteomyelitis are the tibia, femur, and humerus. Pain, tenderness, and soft tissue swelling are present, and heat is felt through the overlying skin. There are limited effects on range of joint movement. The child may limp because of the acute pain.

Special considerations

If medical treatment is delayed, abscesses work outward, causing a sinus (hole) in the skin over the affected bone from which pus is discharged. This sinus is covered with a dressing that must be changed several times daily. The medical treatment is rest and intensive antibiotic therapy. Through surgery, the infected bone may be scraped to evacuate the pus.

The physical education program and teaching strategies

Rehabilitation activity can restore motor functions so that normal activity can be resumed. However, under certain conditions the child with osteomyelitis can participate in most developmental and recreational activities that allow the affected limb to be mobilized.[53] Exercise is always contraindicated when infection is active in the body.

Spondylolysis and Spondylolisthesis

Spondylolysis and **spondylolisthesis** result from a congenital malformation of one or both of the neural arches of the fifth lumbar vertebra or, less frequently, the fourth lumbar vertebra. Spondylolisthesis is distinguished from spondylolysis by anterior displacement of the fifth lumbar vertebra on the sacrum. Both conditions may be accompanied by pain in the lower back.

Forward displacement may occur as a result of sudden trauma to the lumbar region. The vertebrae are moved anteriorly because of an absence of bony continuity of the neural arch, and the main support is derived from its ligamentous arrangement. In such cases, individuals often appear to have severe lordosis.

Characteristics

Many individuals have spondylolysis, or even spondylolisthesis, without symptoms of any kind, but a mild twist or blow may set off a whole series of low back complaints and localized discomfort or pain radiating down one or both sides.

Special considerations

The pathological condition eventually may become so extensive as to require surgical intervention.

The physical education program and teaching strategies

Proper therapy may involve a graduated exercise program that may help prevent further aggravation and, in some cases, remove many symptoms characteristic of the condition. A program should be initiated that includes stretching of the lower back, the strengthening of abdominal muscles, walking to stimulate blood flow, and a general conditioning program. Games and sports that overextend, fatigue, or severely twist and bend the lower back should be avoided. In most cases, the physician will advise against contact sports and heavy weight lifting.

Traumatic Injuries
Spinal Cord Injuries

Spinal cord injuries usually result in paralysis or partial paralysis of the arms, trunk, legs, or any particular combination thereof, depending on the locus of the damage. The spinal cord is housed in the spinal or vertebral column. Nerves from the spinal cord pass down into the segments of the spinal column. Injury to the spinal cord affects innervation of muscle. The higher up the vertebral column the level of injury, the greater the restriction of body movement. Persons with spinal cord injuries are usually referred to as *paraplegics* or *quadriplegics*. A paraplegic is one whose legs are paralyzed. In the quadriplegic both the arms and legs are affected. There are 7000 to 10,000 new cases of spinal cord injury in the United States every year.[45]

Characteristics

Spinal cord injuries are classified according to the region of the vertebrae affected. The regions affected are cervical, thoracic, lumbar, and sacral. A description of the movement capability at each level of the lesion follows:

Fourth cervical level: There is use of only the neck muscles and the diaphragm. Upper limb function is possible only with electrically powered assistive devices. The student needs complete assistance moving to and from the wheelchair.

Fifth cervical level: There is use of the deltoid muscles of the shoulder and the biceps muscles of the arm. The arms can be raised; however, it is difficult to engage in manipulative tasks. Persons with this level of involvement can perform many activities with their arms. However, they need assistance with transfer to and from the wheelchair.

Sixth cervical level: There is use of the wrist extensors, and the student can push the wheelchair and make use of an overhead trapeze (a bar hung overhead to be grasped). Some persons afflicted at this level can transfer the body to and from the wheelchair.

Seventh cervical level: There is use of the elbow and

Archers who are physically challenged participate in community-sponsored activities. (Courtesy City of San Diego Parks and Recreation.)

wrist extensors. Movement of the hand is impaired. However, the person afflicted at this level may be able to perform pull-ups and push-ups, and participate in activities that involve the grasp release mechanism.

Upper thoracic levels: There is total movement capability in the arms, but none in the legs. There is some control in the muscles of the upper back. The student can control a wheelchair and may be able to stand with the use of long leg braces.

Lower thoracic levels: There is control of the abdominal musculature that rights the trunk. The use of the abdominal muscles makes it possible to walk with the support of long leg braces.

Lumbar levels: There is control of the hip joint, and there is a good possibility of walking with controlled movement.

Sacral level: There is muscular functioning for efficient ambulation. The functional level of the bladder, anal sphincters, and external genitals may be impaired.

In general, spinal cord injury results in motor and sensory loss below the level of injury, autonomic nervous system dysfunction if the injury is at T3 or lower (e.g., bowel/bladder, cardiovascular, and temperature regulation), spasticity, and contractures.[15] Specific physical characteristics are as follows:

1. Inappropriate control of the bladder and digestive organs
2. Contractures (abnormal shortening of muscles)
3. Heterotopic bone formation, or laying down of new bone in soft tissue around joints (during this process the area may become inflamed and swollen)
4. Urinary infections
5. Difficulty in defecation
6. Decubitus ulcers on the back and buttocks (caused by pressure of the body weight on specific areas)
7. Spasms of the muscles
8. Spasticity of muscles that prevent effective movement
9. Overweight because of low energy expenditures
10. Scoliosis
11. Respiratory disorders

Persons with spinal cord injury may have impaired aerobic work capacity because of fewer remaining func-

Dick Traum, Ph.D., above-knee amputee, running the 100K; time 25 hours, 16 minutes, Achilles Track Club. (Photo by Leszek Sibiski, October 1988, Kalish, Poland.)

tional muscles and impaired blood flow. If the injury is above T3, the heart rate may be impacted (120 beats per minute is high). Athletes with spinal cord injuries between C6 and T7 have maximal heart rates of 110 to 130 beats per minute.[14] Thermal regulation may also be impaired because of a loss of normal blood flow regulation and the inability to sweat below the level of injury.[14] For this reason, individuals with quadriplegia should not be left in the sun or cold for any length of time. Individuals with quadriplegia who exercise are encouraged to wear support hose and use abdominal strapping to promote venous blood flow to the heart.[15]

Special considerations

Athletes with disabilities frequently experience injuries. The most frequent types of injuries suffered by wheelchair athletes, prevention techniques, and treatment are summarized in Table 15-1.

table 15-1

Most Common Injuries Suffered by Wheelchair Athletes		
Injury	Prevention	Treatment
Soft tissue damage (overuse syndromes: tendonitis, bursitis)	Taping, splinting, protective padding; proper wheelchair positioning	Rest; selective strengthening, muscle balancing
Blisters	Taping, gloves, padding, cushioning, and callous formation	Be aware of areas that lack sensation; treat blister
Lacerations/abrasions	Check equipment for sharp surfaces, wear padding, use cushions and towels for transfers; camber wheels	Treat injury; be aware of areas that lack sensation
Decubitus/pressure areas	Adequate cushioning; proper weight shifting; dry clothing, skin inspection; good nutrition and hygiene	Bed rest to remove all pressure from weight-bearing surface; treat open wounds
Sprains/contusions	Equipment safety; appropriate padding; sport-specific spotting	Treat injury; check for signs of fracture in athletes without movement or sensation

Data from Curtis KA: *Injuries and disability-specific medical conditions of athletes with disabilities,* Unpublished paper, Coral Gables, Fla, 1993, University of Miami.

The physical education program and teaching strategies

The physical education program for persons with spinal cord injury should be based on a well-rounded program of exercises for all the usable body parts, including activities to develop strength, flexibility, muscular endurance, cardiovascular endurance, and coordination. Young children need to be taught ways to use their wheelchairs in a variety of environments and should be encouraged to interact with their ambulatory peers. The middle school and high school student should develop the physical fitness necessary to participate in the sports of their choice.

Movement and dance therapies have been used successfully in rehabilitation programs for persons who have spinal cord injuries. Berrol and Katz[4] indicate that the focus of outcomes is goal oriented and that there is considerable similarity between dance therapy, movement therapy, and those activities that are traditionally taught in a school setting. The box on p. 397 is an example of modifications that can be made in a typical warm-up session for a kindergarten or first grade class.

The emphasis in the physical education program should be on functional movement skills. The child, if wheelchair enabled, should be given every opportunity to move in the chair. Individuals with upper body func-

tion can perform most physical education activities from a wheelchair. The physical education program should include wheelchair mobility training. Project C.R.E.O.L.E. is an excellent curriculum that promotes functional training in wheelchair use.[62] The child should practice moving in the chair with activities that modify the movement variables of time, space, force, and flow. For example, the child should be able to do the following:

1. Time
   a. Wheel fast, then slow.
   b. Wheel to a 4/4 beat.
2. Space
   a. Wheel up and down inclines.
   b. Wheel on cement, linoleum, grass, a gymnasium floor, etc.
   c. Wheel around obstacles.
   d. Wheel over sticks.
   e. Wheel, holding a glass of water.
   f. Wheel, holding a ball on lap.
3. Force
   a. Wheel with buddy sitting on lap.
   b. Wheel while pulling partner on scooterboard.
   c. Push hard and see how far the chair will roll.
4. Flow
   a. Roll forward, spin in a circle, roll forward.
   b. Roll forward, stop, roll backward, stop.

Warm-Up Session with Modifications for Children in Wheelchairs

Class Activity (Song/Dance)	Modifications
"Warm-up Time"	
Clap hands	None
Swing arms	None
Bend knees	Child lifts knees with hands
Stamp feet	Child slaps feet with hands
"What a Miracle"	
Clap hands	None
Stamp feet	Child slaps feet with hands
Swing arms	None
Bend and stretch legs	Child lifts knees with hands
Twist and bend spine	None
One foot balance	Child pushes into push-up position
"Swing, Shake, Twist, Stretch"	
Swing	Child swings arms or head
Shake	Child shakes hands, elbows, or head
Twist	Child twists trunk
Stretch	Child stretches arms
"Bendable, Stretchable"	
Stretch to sky, touch floor	Child stretches to sky, touches toes
"Run, Run, Run in Place"	
Run in place	Child spins chair in circle
"Simon Says Jog Along"	
Jog	Child rolls chair in time to music
Walk	Child rolls chair in time to music

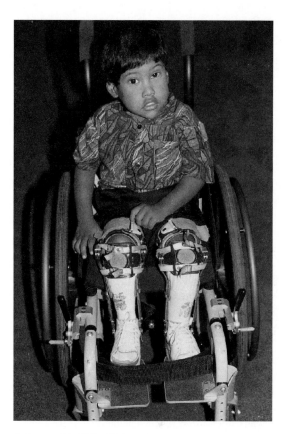

A 3-year-old child with long leg braces. (Courtesy Dallas Independent School District.)

The same type of movement activities should be made available to the child using crutches and braces.

In addition to wheelchair mobility, younger children should be taught fundamental motor skills such as throwing, hitting, and catching. Once these skills are mastered, games that incorporate these skills may be played. Modifications of games that have been described previously are appropriate for children in wheelchairs. Children in wheelchairs can participate in parachute games and target games without accommodation. They can maintain fitness of the upper body through the same type of regimens as do the nondisabled. Strengthening of the arms and shoulder girdle is important for propulsion of the wheelchair and for changing body positions when moving in and out of the wheelchair. Swimming is a particularly good activity for the development of total physical fitness. The emphasis should be on the development of functional movement skills.

It is possible to increase the heart rate response, blood pressure response, stroke volume and cardiac output, and respiration rate and depth through the use of arm exercises.[15] Development may be attained through arm pedaling of a bicycle ergometer, pushing of a wheelchair over considerable distances, and agility maneuvers with the wheelchair. DiCarlo[19] reported that males with quadriplegia with lesions at the fifth to seventh cervical level were able to increase their wheelchair propulsion endurance and cardiopulmonary function by engaging in arm cycle ergometry exercises three times a week for 8 weeks. Hardison, Isreal, and Somes[26] demonstrated the same types of gains with quadriplegic males with lesion levels ranging from T4 to T12. They demonstrated improved oxygen utilization with a training program consisting of a 70 rpm ergometer cranking rate at 60% of the subject's maximum Vo_2. Curtis[15] cautions that there are several physiological response differences between upper and lower extremity exercise. During upper body exercise: (1) maximum value of oxygen utilization is 70% of that of lower body exercise; (2) heart rate is approximately 20% higher; (3) stroke volume is 10% to 18% less; and (4) lactic acid concentrations are higher.

Stretching exercises should always be used to improve flexibility and enable an individual to achieve full joint range of motion. They are also critical for reducing the chance of stress injuries to muscles, tendons, and ligaments. Curtis[12] recommends that stretching be done both before exercise and following cooldown. The following stretches should be executed for 15 to 30 seconds each, while sitting in a wheelchair.

TRUNK STRETCHING

1. Exhale and lean forward to touch the ground; hold and return to sitting position.
2. Inhale. Bend over at waist and reach out, keeping arms and head parallel to the ground; hold and return to sitting position.
3. Arch left arm over the head and lean to the right; repeat to other side.

SHOULDER STRETCHING

1. Intertwine fingers from both hands, inhale, and lift hands overhead, pushing palms upward.
2. Intertwine fingers from both hands behind back, exhale, lean forward, and lift hands high behind back.
3. Clasp hands behind head and push elbows backward.

SHOULDER-ELBOW STRETCHING

1. Raise arms to shoulder height with palms facing forward; push arms backward while keeping elbows straight.
2. Bend arm across chest, reaching for opposite shoulder blade; push on elbow. Repeat with other arm.
3. Raise arm up next to head; reach down the back with the hand; push against elbow with other hand. Repeat with other arm.

ELBOW-WRIST STRETCHING

1. Raise left arm out in front of body keeping elbow straight; with right hand, pull left hand and fingers into extension (fingers toward the sky). Repeat with other hand.
2. Raise left arm out in front of body, keeping elbow straight; with right hand, pull left hand and fingers into flexion (fingers toward the ground).

When developing strength exercise regimens to enhance sport performance, specificity of training is critical. Manually propelling a wheelchair tends to develop the flexor muscles in front of the body; thus attention must be paid to developing unused muscle groups located in the back of the body. As a general rule, for all exercises executed in front of the body, do twice as many in the opposite direction.[15] Include backward wheelchair pushing to develop the muscles that work in opposition to the pectorals.[15] Because of the need to lift the arms to propel the wheelchair, arm abductors tend to be stronger than the adductors; thus exercises to strengthen the adductors are indicated.[15] Coordination training should also be sport specific. General power and endurance training is recommended for rounding out the exercise program.

Power training could include throwing and catching a medicine ball thrown against a small trampoline, and wind sprints in the wheelchair. Endurance training should involve wheelchair pushing for 20 minutes and longer three times a week at the target heart rate (220 minus age if the injury is below T3).

Routine exercise programs are critical for the individual who uses a wheelchair for ambulation, because the act of manually wheeling the chair produces imbalances in muscle strength. Imbalances in muscle strength lead to postural deviations that if left unaddressed will eventually become structural and further impair the individual's health. The physical educator who helps the individual in a wheelchair to develop a realistic exercise program that can be continued throughout life will, indeed, contribute to the quality of that person's life.

Amputations

Amputation is missing part or all of a limb. Amputation may be performed to arrest a malignant condition caused by trauma, tumors, infection, vascular impairment, diabetes, or arteriosclerosis. Amputees in the United States exceed 500,000 in number.[37]

Characteristics and types

Amputations can be classified into two categories: acquired amputation and congenital amputation. The amputation is acquired if one has a limb removed by operation; it is congenital if the child is born without a limb. Congenital amputations are classified according to the site and level of limb absence. When an amputation is performed through a joint, it is referred to as a disarticulation.

Special considerations

Frequently, individuals with an amputation elect to use a prosthetic appliance to replace the missing limb. The purpose of the prosthetic device is to enable the individual to function as normally as possible. The application of a prosthetic device may be preceded by surgery to produce a stump. After the operation the stump is dressed and bandaged to aid shrinkage of the stump. After the fitting of the prosthesis, the stump must be continually cared for. It should be checked periodically and cleaned to prevent infection, abrasion, and skin disorder. The attachment of a false limb early in a child's development will encourage the incorporation of the append-

figure 15-7
Mark Pietranski, a double amputee, participates in football with his classmates. (Courtesy *Denton Record Chronicle*.)

age into natural body activity more than if the prosthesis is introduced later in life.

It is not practical to fit a prothesis on some forms of amputations. Consider the case of Mark Pietranski (Figure 15-7), who was born with two small appendages where the legs should have been. One appendage had to be removed early in life; the other is not strong enough for functional use. Mark does not let his lack of legs interfere with his activities. In Figure 15-7 Mark is shown as a member of his middle school football team—despite the fact that he uses only his hands and arms to propel himself. He also swims regularly.

The physical education program and teaching strategies

The ultimate goal of a person with an amputation is to perform physical activity safely. Amputees must develop skills to use prostheses; effective use demands much effort. The remaining muscles needed for prosthetic use must be strengthened, and standing and walking must be practiced until they become automatic. To regain adequate postural equilibrium, individuals with lower limb amputations have to learn to link altered sensory input to movement patterns.[24] Practice in walking, turning, sitting, and standing is needed.

Amputees are often exposed to beneficial exercise through the use of the prosthesis. Exercises should be initiated to strengthen muscles after a stump heals. Training also enhances ambulation, inhibits atrophy and contractures, improves or maintains mechanical alignment of body parts, and develops general physical fitness.

There are several adaptations of physical activity that can be made for children with impaired ambulation. For these children the major disadvantages are speed of locomotion and fatigue to sustained activity. Some accommodations that can be made are shortening the distance the player must travel and decreasing the speed needed to move from one place to another.

Most gait deviations result from problems with the alignment of the lower limb prosthesis. Deviations may include rotations of the foot at heel strike, unequal timing, side-walking base, abducted gait, excessive heel ride, instability of the knee, excessive knee flexion, hyperextension of the knees, excessive pronation of the foot, foot slap, and rotation of the foot with continuing whip.[17]

Persons with amputations below the knee can learn

ambulation skills well with a prosthesis and training. Persons with amputation above the knee but below the hip may have difficulty in developing efficient walking gaits. Amputations at this level require alteration of the gait pattern. Steps are usually shortened to circumvent lack of knee function.

Authorities agree that children with properly fitted prostheses should engage in regular physical education activities. Amputees have considerable potential for participation in adapted sports and games. The National Amputee Golf Association, for example, provides clinics nationwide to introduce children and adults with disabilities to the sport of golf and to train teachers and coaches to adapt methods and instruction to meet the needs of amputees. There are opportunities for persons with prostheses to participate in official sports competition. Persons with above-knee amputations can walk well and engage in swimming, skiing, and other activities with the proper aids. Persons with arm amputations who have use of their feet can participate in activities that require foot action, such as soccer and running

A prosthesis enables active play. (Courtesy MAUCH Laboratories, Inc., Dayton, Ohio.)

events, as well as other activities that involve the feet exclusively.

Physical fitness of amputees should be an important part of a physical education program. Strength and flexibility and power of the unafflicted limbs are important. Furthermore, Lasko-McCarthey and Knopf[39] stress the importance of developing and maintaining the amputee's level of cardiovascular efficiency.

Testing

The type of test used depends on the functioning level of the individual, as well as the purpose for the assessment. Several different types of tests and the populations they can be used with are presented in Chapter 2. Persons who are ambulatory, including those with cerebral palsy who have spastic hemiplegia, can usually be tested using standard equipment. Fernandez and Pitetti[22] used a bicycle ergometer, a Schwinn Air Dyne ergometer, a treadmill, and an arm-crank ergometer to determine the physical work capacity of individuals with cerebral palsy. They recommended using an ergometer rather than a treadmill to avoid discriminating against persons with gait anomalies or those who are nonambulatory for whatever reason. Ponichtera-Mulcare et al.[52] recommend that a combination leg and arm ergometer be used to assess maximal power output and peak aerobic power, as well as for training. Project UNIQUE, Project M.O.B.I.L.T.E.E., and the *Physical Best and Individuals with Disabilities Handbook* by the American Alliance for Health, Physical Education, Recreation and Dance (AAHPERD) all suggest accommodations for ambulatory and nonambulatory individuals.

In addition to formal testing, it is frequently just as important to appraise individuals' functional movement capabilities. Motor programs can then be developed to meet their unique needs. The assessment should provide information about the potential for movement of each action of the body. This would involve knowledge of the strength, power, flexibility, and endurance of specific muscle groups. In addition, there should be information about which movement actions can be coordinated to attain specific motor outcomes. For instance, several throwing patterns that children with severe impairments use when participating in the Special Olympics can help circumvent movement problems of the arms and hands. The desired throwing pattern is one of extension of the arm and elbow and flexion of the wrist. If either of these actions is impaired, alternate throwing patterns need to be found. Some throwing patterns developed to circumvent extreme disability of the arm, elbow, and wrist are underhand movement, horizontal abduction of the arm and shoulder, flexion of the arm and elbow (over the shoulder), horizontal abduction of the arm (side arm), and overhand movement with most of the force generated from a rocking motion of the trunk. To maximize the potential of each of these types of throwing patterns, it is necessary to conduct training programs that will consider each child's assets and develop them fully. However, another option is to provide therapeutic exercise for each of the desired actions and then teach it as a functional, normalized movement pattern.

The ability prerequisites of strength, flexibility, endurance, power, and coordination can be applied to many wheelchair activities. Some of these activities involve (1) basic mobility skills, (2) transfer skills from and to the wheelchair, (3) performance on mats, (4) performance on gymnastics apparatus, (5) ability to maneuver vehicles, (6) motor capabilities in a swimming pool, (7) walking with aids, and (8) the ability to push and pull objects. The ability prerequisites for each fundamental movement pattern should be studied to identify specific problems so that appropriate intervention can be undertaken. Examples of the categories of activities or abilities follow:

1. Basic mobility skills[62]
   a. Moving up and down ramps
   b. Moving from a wheelchair to another chair
   c. Transporting objects
2. Transfer skills
   a. Standing from a wheelchair
   b. Moving from a wheelchair to another chair
   c. Moving from a wheelchair to mats
   d. Moving from a wheelchair to different pieces of equipment
3. Performance on mats
   a. Forward and backward rolls
   b. Partner activity
   c. Climbing on low obstacles and elevated mats
4. Performance on gymnastics apparatus
   a. Rings
   b. High bar
   c. Parallel bars
5. Ability to maneuver vehicles
   a. Floor scooters
   b. Hand-propelled carts
   c. Tricycles
   d. Upright scooters with three wheels
6. Swimming pool activity
   a. Getting into and out of the pool
   b. Use of the railing for resting
   c. Swimming
7. Walking with aids
   a. Different types of canes
   b. Crutches
   c. Walkers
8. Ability to push and pull objects
   a. Throwing a ball or pushing a ball
   b. Propelling scooters with the hands
   c. Pushing a cage ball

Each of the above-mentioned activities should be analyzed to see if the student's strength, flexibility, endurance, power, and coordination are sufficient for acquisition and proficiency of the activity. In the case of Duchenne dystrophy, **manual muscle testing**[17] (determining how much resistance is left in a muscle group by having the student flex or extend each limb) can give the evaluator some indication of the remaining strength. Students with other types of muscular dystrophy can be tested with standard tests.

Another group of persons in wheelchairs have severe impairment of the upper appendages. They may have spasticity or contractures. It is not uncommon for these children to adopt unique throwing patterns to maximize performance. Their physical structure rules out the use of standard testing techniques and teaching of mechanically sound sport skill patterns. Specific techniques must be determined for each child.

Modifications, Adaptations, and Inclusion Techniques

Many physically challenged children who participate in physical education programs use a wheelchair for locomotion, wear braces, and/or use some other assistive device. Assistive devices are used to enable fuller use of the upper limbs or aid locomotion when the legs are debilitated. Some assistive devices are hooks, canes, and crutches.

Although it is difficult to substitute for the human hand and fingers, it is possible to achieve dexterity with the use of a utility arm and split hook. These aids enable the use of racquets for paddle games if both arms are amputated. Persons who have lost a single arm can play most basic skill games and participate in more advanced sport activity without modifications. Special devices can be built by an orthotist to fit into the arm prosthesis to hold sports equipment such as gloves.

A major problem for students who use canes and crutches is the need to learn balance to free one hand for participation in activity. Use of the Lofstrand crutches, which are anchored to the forearms, enables balance to be maintained by one crutch. This frees one arm and enables participation in throwing and striking activities.

The physical educator should have a working knowledge of the care and maintenance of lower extremity braces and wheelchairs. One of the teacher's responsibilities is daily observation of the student's use and care of ambulation equipment. In conjunction with related services, the child's classroom teacher, family, and physical educator should develop a program to maximize the use of ambulation devices in the physical education setting and beyond the school boundaries. In addition, any problems that arise with the ambulation devices should be communicated to the special or regular class teacher or the parents.

Leg Braces

Leg braces are metal or plastic support frames that are strapped to the body above and below specific joints to assist with ambulation. The main purposes of lower extremity braces are to support the weight for ambulation, control involuntary movements, and prevent or correct deformities. In general, there are three classifications of lower leg braces: short leg braces, long leg braces, and hip braces.

Short leg brace

A short leg brace is appropriate when the disabling condition occurs at the ankle joint. Although there are several different types of short leg braces, the simplest form consists of a single metal upright bar attached to the shoe with a cuff around the calf of the leg (Figure 15-8). When more stability is needed, double upright bars are used. The design of this type of brace should facilitate the control of four movements of the ankle joint. Leather straps attached to the metal uprights and strapped around the ankle assist with control of the ankle joint.

Long leg brace

The long leg (knee-ankle-foot) brace assists with control of the ankle and knee joint (Figure 15-9). The fundamental purpose of the long leg brace is to prevent hyperextension of the knee caused by weak extensor

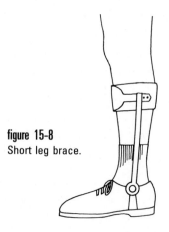

figure 15-8
Short leg brace.

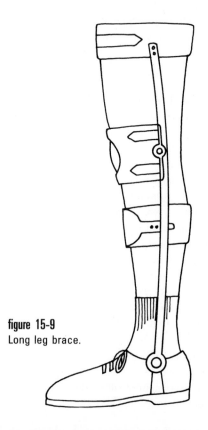

figure 15-9
Long leg brace.

muscles. The brace must be in different positions when the student is sitting as compared with standing. To accommodate the different positions of the knee, various types of locks are placed at the knee joints, the most common of which is a sliding metal lock that is easily locked and unlocked by hand. The knee joint of the long leg brace is locked when the individual is sitting in a chair. Locking devices also may be used to control the ankle when this type of brace is used.

Long leg brace with pelvic band

The long leg brace may extend from below the ankle to above the hip. Such a brace is called a hip-knee-ankle-foot long leg brace. The purpose of such a brace is to control movements of the hip joint, as well as of the knee and the ankle. To assist with control of the hip joint, a pelvic band is attached to the top of the upright bar.

The physical education teacher should have a working knowledge of the functions of leg braces. Some of the characteristics that can be observed are as follows: (1) brace joints work easily; (2) brace and anatomical joints coincide; (3) upright conforms to the leg; (4) brace is of correct length; and (5) upright coincides with the midline of the leg.

Wheelchairs

The purpose of wheelchairs is to provide a means of locomotion for persons who lack strength, endurance, or flexibility of muscles prerequisite for ambulation. Persons who can walk but cannot rise from a seated position to a standing position or those who need to transport objects but cannot do so may also need a wheelchair.

The technology is available to provide almost every person who has a severe physical disability with mobility.[44] The primary goals when designing wheelchairs are to maximize the function, comfort, and independence of those who use the technology. More specifically, the goals and objectives of wheelchair seating are to (1) maximize safety and functional independence, (2) maximize independent mobility through the ability to control the direction and speed of the chair, and (3) maximize functional communication with others in all life environments, including leisure physical activity.[57]

There are many different types of wheelchairs. Some of the types identified by Wilson[59] follow:

- *Standard*—Wheelchairs that have a folding frame with large driving wheels in the rear and small caster wheels in the front
- *Manual*—Wheelchairs propelled by the occupant
- *Attendant*—Manual wheelchairs that are propelled by another person because the occupant cannot or should not use either a manual or powered chair
- *Powered*—Wheelchairs driven by electric motors that run on batteries
- *Lightweight*—Standard wheelchairs refined to reduce overall weight
- *Sport*—Light standard wheelchairs that are easily disassembled
- *Racing*—Wheelchairs designed solely for competitive racing

Nonstandard vehicles that have been developed specifically for children with orthopedic disabilities include the following[42]:

- Hand-driven tricycle that includes a lever system that transmits arm power into the rear wheel axles

Innovative equipment designs enable a person who uses a wheelchair to move in a standing position. (Courtesy Stand-N-Go, Inc.)

Checklist for Braces and Wheelchairs

Short Leg (Ankle-Foot) Brace

A. With the brace off the student
   1. Do joints work easily?
   2. Can shoes be easily removed?
   3. Is the workmanship good?
      a. No rough edges
      b. Straps secure
      c. Leather work stitched properly
B. Student standing with brace on
   1. Are the sole and heel flat on the floor?
   2. Are the ankle joints aligned so that they coincide with the anatomical joints?
   3. Is there ample clearance between the leg and the brace (one finger width)?
   4. Does the T strap exert enough force for correction without causing deformity?
   5. Do the uprights conform to the contour of the leg?
   6. Do the uprights coincide with the midline of the leg when viewed from the side?
   7. Is the brace long enough?
      a. It should be below the bend of the knee so the student can bend the knee comfortably to 120°.
      b. It should not be lower than the bulky part of the calf muscle.
C. Student walking with brace on
   1. Is there clearance between the uprights and the leg?
   2. Are there any gait deviations?
   3. Is the brace quiet?

Long Leg (Knee-Ankle-Foot) Brace

A. With the brace off the student
   1. Do joints work easily?
   2. Can shoes be easily removed?
   3. Is the workmanship good?
      a. No rough edges
      b. Straps secure
      c. Leather work stitched properly
B. Student standing with brace on
   1. Are the knee joints aligned at the approximate anatomical joints?
      a. There should be no pressure from the thigh band when knee is bent (if so joints are too high).
      b. There should be no pressure from calf band when knee is bent (if so joints are too low).
      c. There should be no pressure on calf (if so joints are too far forward).
      d. There should be no pressure on shin or knee cap (if so joints are too far backward).
   2. Are locks secure and easy to work?
   3. Is the brace long enough?
      a. Medial upright should be up into groin region but should not cause pain.
      b. Lateral upright should be 1 inch longer.
   4. Are the thigh bands and calf bands about equal distance from the knee?

Long Leg Brace with Pelvic Band (Hip-Knee-Ankle-Foot Orthosis)

A. With the brace off the student
   1. Do joints work easily?
   2. Can shoes be easily removed?
   3. Is the workmanship good?
      a. No rough edges
      b. Straps secure
      c. Leather work stitched properly
B. Student with brace on
   1. Is the pelvic band located below the waist?
   2. Is the student comfortable sitting and standing?
   3. Are the hip joints in the right place and do the locks work easily?

Other Points to Check

A. Do the shoes fit and are they in good repair?
B. Do reddened areas go away after the brace has been off 20 minutes?
C. Is the student comfortable?
D. Is the brace helping the student?

Plastic Braces

A. Does the brace conform to and contact the extremity?
B. Is the student wearing a sock between foot and brace?
C. Does the brace pull away from the leg excessively when the student walks?
D. Do reddened areas go away after the brace has been off 20 minutes?

From Venn J, Morganstern C, Dykes MK: *Teach Except Child*, pp 51-56, winter 1979.

Checklist for Braces and Wheelchairs—cont'd

Lower Extremity Prosthetics

A. Is the student wearing the prosthesis (frequency)?
B. Does the student use assistive devices with prosthesis (crutches, canes, one cane, other)? If so, what does he or she use and how often?
C. Is the prosthesis on correctly?
  1. Is the toe turned out about the same as the other foot?
  2. When the student sits is the knee in alignment?
D. Does the leg appear the same length as the normal leg?
  1. Does the student stand straight when bearing weight on the prothesis?
  2. Are the shoulders even when leg is bearing weight (one shoulder does not drop)?
  3. When the student walks does the knee stay straight without turning out or in?

Gait Deviations

A. Does the student stand straight when bearing weight on the prosthesis?
B. Does the artificial leg swing forward without turning in or out?
C. Does the student swing the artificial leg through without rising up on the foot of the normal leg?
D. When the student walks does the leg swing straight forward? (It should not swing out in an arc.)
E. When the student stands are the feet a normal distance apart? (The stance should not be too wide.)
F. Does the knee bend and straighten like a normal leg?

Condition of the Prosthesis

A. Do the suspension joints appear to be in good condition (leather, joint, band)?
B. Does the leg stay in place when the student is standing and sitting?
C. Does the knee bend appropriately?
D. Are the joints quiet when moved?
E. Do the foot and ankle appear to be in one piece?
F. Is the shoe in good condition (heel, sole)?

Wheelchair

A. Arms
  1. Are the armrests and side panels secure and free of sharp edges and cracks?
  2. Do the arm locks function properly?
B. Back
  1. Is the upholstery free of rips and tears?
  2. Is the back taut from top to bottom?
  3. Is the safety belt attached tightly and not frayed?
C. Seat and frame
  1. Is the upholstery free of rips and tears?
  2. Does the chair fold easily without sticking?
  3. When the chair is folded fully are the front post slides straight and round?
D. Wheel locks
  1. Do the wheel locks securely engage the tire surfaces and prevent the wheel from turning?
E. Large wheels
  1. Are the wheels free from wobble or sideplay when spun?
  2. Are the spokes equally right and without any missing spokes?
  3. Are the tires free from excessive wear and gaps at the joined section?
F. Casters
  1. Is the stem firmly attached to the fork?
  2. Are the forks straight on sides and stem so that the caster swivels easily?
  3. Is the caster assembly free of excessive play both upward and downward as well as backward and forward?
  4. Are the wheels free of excessive play and wobble?
  5. Are the tires in good condition?
G. Footrest/legrest
  1. Does the lock mechanism fit securely?
  2. Are the heel loops secure and correctly installed?
  3. Do the foot plates fold easily and hold in any position?
  4. Are the legrest panels free of cracks and sharp edges?

Continued.

Checklist for Braces and Wheelchairs—cont'd

With Student Sitting in Wheelchair

A. Seat width
  1. When your palms are placed between the patient's hip and the side of the chair (skirtguard), do the hands contact the hip and the skirtguard at the same time without pressure?
  2. Or, is the clearance between the patient's widest point of either hips or thigh and the skirtguard approximately 1 inch on either side?

B. Seat depth
  1. Can you place your hand, with fingers extended, between the front edge of the seat upholstery and to the rear of the knee with a clearance of three or four fingers?
  2. Or, is the seat upholstery approximately 2 to 3 inches less than the student's thigh measurement?

C. Seat height and footrest
  1. Is the lowest part of the stepplates no closer than 2 inches from the floor?
  2. Or, is the student's thigh elevated slightly above the front edge of the seat upholstery?

D. Arm height
  1. Does the arm height not force the shoulders up or allow them to drop significantly when the student is in a normal sitting position?
  2. Is the elbow positioned slightly forward of the trunk midline when the student is in a normal sitting position?

E. Back height
  1. Can you insert four or five fingers between the patient's armpit area and the top of the back upholstery touching both at the same time?
  2. Is the top of the back upholstery approximately 4 inches below the armpit for the student who needs only minimum trunk support?

With Student Pushing or Riding in Wheelchair

A. Is the wheelchair free from squeaks or rattles?
B. Does the chair roll easily without pulling to either side?
C. Are the large wheels and casters free of play and wobble?

- Tricycle foot attachments that strap a child's feet to the pedals and allow the child with muscle weakness or spasticity to ride a tricycle
- Modified tricycle that includes a back support and a seat belt to stabilize the child's body
- Castor carts (large scooter boards) that enable a child to participate in activity at the floor level

There have been many advances in recent years in upgrading wheelchairs to facilitate the mobility of youth and adults.[42] Platform motorized wheelchairs that can be driven at moderately high speeds are popular. Options for controlling powered wheelchairs include joysticks, single switches, and voice controls.[40]

Wheelchair design is a continuous process, the goal of which is to make the wheelchair more functional. Many special features can be added to make a wheelchair more functional or comfortable, including armrests, footrests, legrests, and headrests, all of which can be removed. Leg spreaders have also been incorporated into some wheelchairs to prevent the scissoring of legs.

Analog devices for aligning the rear wheels have been developed to maximize efficiency in propelling the wheelchair.[10] Many wheelchairs can be folded for easy storage. Some other features of a wheelchair are unique folding mechanisms that allow it to double as a stroller or car seat, adjustable Velcro fasteners, pads, and attachable trays. The box on pp. 404-406 contains a checklist that will enable physical education teachers to assess wheelchairs and braces as they relate to optimum functioning and comfort of the individual.[55]

Specialized adapted seating

Adapted seating for individuals who are severely disabled has been a subject of increasing concern. Inappropriate seating of severely afflicted individuals can result in severe scoliosis with vertebral rotation. Severe contractures may result from fixed postures in a wheelchair. To avoid this, extensive adaptations of the chair may be necessary. Hundertmark[36] indicates that the anterior and posterior tilt of the pelvis and the vertical angle of the backrest are important considerations in achieving therapeutic seating for the person who is severely multihandicapped.

Adaptations for wheelchair sports competition

Wheelchair competitive sports are becoming more and more popular. Competitive wheelchair users are faced with an array of decisions when designing, building, buying, and racing wheelchairs. The ability to propel the wheelchair safely and quickly is an important factor for effective wheelchair sports competition. That capability is dependent on the user's ability, the design of the chair, and the suitability of the chair to the user. Interest in improving performance has spurred researchers to study ways to increase the efficiency of wheelchairs. Modifications in seat position,[35] number of wheels, and positioning of the body during propulsion all impact the speed at which the chair can be propelled.

The seat of a wheelchair should be adjusted to fit the width of the athlete's hips; the seat height should be altered to maximize use of forces generated at the shoulder; and lowering the height of the back of the chair will increase mobility. The number of wheels is also an important competitive factor.

Three- and four-wheeled chairs are available for competition. Higgs[30] studied the comparative advantages of both of these chairs and reported the following: The advantages of three-wheeled chairs are that they have less rolling resistance, are lighter, and have less aerodynamic drag. The disadvantages of the three-wheeled chairs are that they have less stability and more skill is required to safely handle the chair. The position of the body in the chair, use of hand pads, and strapping also impact speed and efficiency.

Gehlsen, Davis, and Bahamonde[23] indicate that a forward lean of the trunk may allow the individual to increase the range of hand-handrim contact. Hedrick et al.[29] indicate that a wheelchair racer's speed can be increased when he or she rotates the upper torso sideways or maintain a flexed position while coasting. Alexander[1] describes a technique to increase propulsion of the wheelchair in which the backs of the hands propel the wheelchair by drawing the hands up and over the wheel and finishing the power stroke with the lower arms in supination. Pads are used to increase friction between the hands and the wheelchair and allow the student a longer power phase. In addition, Burd and Grass[8] describe pro-

Ross Davis, a silver medal winner in the Barcelona Paralympics. (Courtesy Disabled Sports Association of North Texas, Dallas.)

cedures for strapping students in wheelchairs to correct posture deviations that diminish the full propulsive stroke on the handrim of the wheelchair.

In addition to improved techniques for wheelchair propulsion, research has been conducted on motivational variables that may facilitate competition in wheelchairs. Dummer et al.[20] suggest that teaching students the right strategies that are compatible with their abilities and helping them enjoy the activity and competition enhance their desire to compete. Brasile and Hedrick[7] suggest that intrinsic task-related reasons for participation are important motivators for success in physical activity for students with orthopedic and neurological disabilities.

Assistive technology

Every effort should be made to involve individuals with physical disabilities in play and games. To facilitate that participation, it may be necessary to adapt equipment to bridge an individual's functional limitations with the demands of the activity. Some devices that may improve functional movement include:

- Chest straps that improve functional reach[16]
- Elasticized abdominal binders[16]
- Seat inserts or molded cushions that improve trunk stability[16]
- Chair anchors that stabilize the wheelchair and facilitate throwing activity[48] (Figure 15-10)
- Wheelchair designs that enable propulsion with the legs rather than arms for athletes with functional leg strength[48]
- Wheelchair seats that can be rotated 180 degrees to allow participants to sit backward, which enables a strong push-off for propelling the chair[48]
- Carbon spoke wheels that offer less resistance and facilitate faster acceleration than traditional chairs[48]

However, individuals who use specialized devices

figure 15-10
A shot putter hurls from an anchored wheelchair. (Courtesy Ron Davis, Ball State University, Muncie, Ind.)

must anticipate and guard against the following problems: failure of the device, incorrect fit with the individual's need, lack of appropriate instruction in use of the device, awkwardness of the device, and denial of the disability.[25]

There are several commercially available pieces of equipment that enable persons with physical disabilities to participate in bowling. Some of the adaptations are a bowling ball with handles, a fork that allows the person to push the bowling ball as in shuffleboard, and a ramp that enables gravity to act on the ball in place of the force provided by movement. Each of these adaptations in equipment accommodates for a specific physical problem related to bowling. The adapted equipment for bowling is paired with the nature of the physical problem.

Equipment	Accommodation of Disability
Handles	Needs assistance with the grip but has use of the arm and wrist
Fork	Has use of the arm but has limited ability to control the wrist and an underhand throwing pattern
Ramp	Has limited use of the arm, wrist, and fingers as they apply to an underhand movement pattern

Computer-Controlled Movement of Paralyzed Muscles

In the past it was thought that paralyzed muscles could not contract to produce purposeful movement. The development of procedures to stimulate muscles electrically and computer technology have opened a new era for the prospect of functional movement for persons who are paralyzed.[51] Computer-controlled electrical stimulation for controlling movement is called functional electrical stimulation (FES), which involves placing electrodes made of conductive rubber over the motor point of a muscle. Small electrical currents are then conducted through the electrodes and the skin. The currents cause underlying motor nerves to discharge, which results in precise movement of muscle groups. Movement of whole limbs can be facilitated in this manner.[50] The use of computers to control functional movement of paralyzed muscles continues to be researched. These types of technology hold great promise for restoring and maintaining muscular tone until procedures for restoring damaged nerve tissue in the central nervous system can be developed.

Modifications

Many games and sports in which students regularly participate in physical education classes can, with minor modification, be made safe and interesting for persons with physical disabilities. In general, the rules, techniques, and equipment of a game or activity should be changed as little as possible when they are modified for students with disabilities. Following is a suggested procedure for adapting a sport or game for a student with a disability:

1. Select and analyze the play, game, or sport.
2. Identify the problems the individual will have in participating in the play, game, or sport.
3. Make the adaptations.
4. Select principles of adaptation that may apply to the specific situation. Specific ways that regular physical education and sport activities can be modified are the following:
   a. The size of the playing area can be made smaller, with proportionate reduction of the amount of activity.
   b. Larger balls or larger pieces of equipment can be introduced to make the game easier or to slow down the tempo so physical accommodations can be made.
   c. Smaller, lighter balls or striking implements (plastic or styrofoam balls and plastic bats) or objects that are easier to handle (a beanbag) can be substituted.
   d. More players can be added to a team, which reduces the amount of activity and the responsibility of individuals.
   e. Minor rule changes can be made in the contest or game while as many of the basic rules as possible are retained.
   f. The amount of time allowed for play can be reduced via shorter quarters, or the total time for a game can be reduced to allow for the onset of fatigue.
   g. The number of points required to win a contest can be reduced.
   h. Free substitutions can be made, which allows the students to alternately participate and then rest while the contest continues.

These modifications can be made in a game or contest whether the student participates in a segregated or integrated physical education class. If the child with a disability participates in a segregated class, it is possible to provide activities similar to those of regular physical education classes by practicing many of the culturally accepted sport skills in drill types of activities. An example would be playing basketball games such as "twenty-one" and "around the world" or taking free throws as lead-up activities to the sport. Pitching, batting, throwing, catching, and games such as "over the line" can be played as lead-up activities for softball. Serving, stroking, and volleying can be practiced as lead-up activities for tennis. Such activities can be designed to accommodate physical limitations (Table 15-2). Students with temporary injuries may become more skillful in various activities so that when they return to an unrestricted class, they may participate in the whole game or sport with a reasonable degree of success.

Students with disabilities do not always need to be involved in competitive activities. Individuals in wheel-

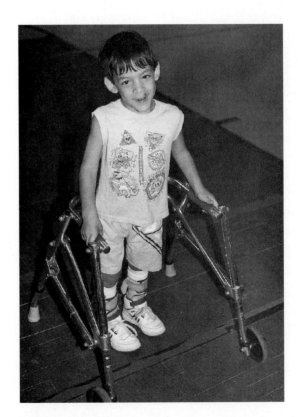

A child ambulates with a walker. (Courtesy Dallas Independent School District.)

table 15-2

Principles for Adapting Physical Activity

Activity	Modification	Consequence
Reduce Size of Playing Area		
Soccer	Reduce size of field	Less distance to cover; ball moves from one end of field to other faster
Soccer	Reduce size of goal commensurate with student's movement ability	Less distance to cover
Badminton	Reduce size of court	Less distance to cover; accommodation can be made to equate movement capability of disabled student with that of nondisabled student
Softball	Shorten distance between bases when disabled person bats	Disabled student has equitable amount of time to reach base
Introduce Larger Pieces of Equipment		
Softball	Use balloon or beach ball	Speed of the object and tempo of game are reduced
Softball	Use larger ball	Chance of success is enhanced and tempo of game is reduced
Soccer	Use larger ball	Area where ball can be propelled successfully is increased
Volleyball	Use beach ball	Area of contact is increased, enhancing success and requiring less finger strength to control ball
Introduce Lighter Equipment		
Softball	Use lighter bat	Bat can be moved more quickly so there is greater opportunity to strike ball
Soccer	Use lighter ball	Speed is reduced and successful contact is more likely
Bowling	Use lighter ball	Weaker person has greater control of ball
Archery	Use lighter bow	Weaker person can draw bow
Tennis	Use aluminum racquet	Weaker person can control racquet
Modify Size of Team		
Volleyball	Add more players	Less area for each person to cover
Soccer	Add more players	Distance each person must cover in team play is reduced
Softball	Add more players	Less area for each person to cover
Handball/tennis	Play triples	Less area for each person to cover
Make Minor Rule Changes		
Wrestling	Use physical contact on takedown for blind persons	Blind person will always be in physical contact with opponent, enables him or her to know where opponent is at all times
Volleyball	Allow person with affliction in arms/hands to carry on a volleyball hit	Opportunity for success is greater
Soccer	Reduce size of goal	Opportunity for success is greater
Gymnastics	Strap legs of paraplegic together	Strap controls legs when body moves

table 15-2		
Principles for Adapting Physical Activity—cont'd		
Activity	Modification	Consequence
Reduce Playing Time		
Basketball/soccer	Substitute every 3 or 4 minutes	Accommodation is made for fatigue
Swimming	Swim beside pool edge and rest at prescribed distances of travel or time intervals	Accommodation is made for fatigue
Reduce Number of Points Required to Win Contest		
Handball/paddleball/tennis	Lessen number to fatigue level of individual	Physical endurance will not be factor in outcome of game
Basketball	Play until specified number of points are made	

chairs should be taught to dance and to participate in water activities. The ability to move to music can be very satisfying; water activities frequently enable a freedom of movement not possible in a chair.[41]

The physical educator who is attempting to accommodate a student with a disability for participation in physical activity should work closely with school nurses and physicians. Some children with orthopedic and neurological conditions will be taking medication that may affect their attention span or level of alertness. Peck and McKeag[49] recommend that youngsters be carefully observed during activity, with any side effects noted. Also, students with bladder problems (e.g., infections, ruptures, incontinence) need to be given special attention to help them avoid the embarrassment of wetting themselves.[49]

Inclusion Techniques

There are several ways to accommodate students with limited movement in the regular class setting with their peers. First, activities and games may be selected that circumvent the inability to move. However, it is obvious that such activity will constitute but a small part of the activity, games, and sports of the total physical education program. Second, in team sports it is not uncommon for specific positions of a sport to require different degrees of movement; thus students who have limited movement capability may be assigned to positions that require less movement. Third, the rules of the game can be modified, enabling equitable competition between persons with and without disabilities. Fourth, aids can be introduced that accommodate inability so that adjustments can be made to the game. Any one or a combination of these principles of adaptation may be employed to enable children with disabilities to participate in regular classes.

Community-Based Opportunities

Persons with physical disabilities should develop skills that can be expressed in leisure and recreational activity in the community. One of the desired outcomes of the acquisition of sport skills is participation in competitive sports. Therefore the instruction in the physical education program should match opportunities for sports participation in the community. The generalization of the sport skills acquired by the student who is physically challenged in the instructional phase of the physical education program requires close study of several variables. Some considerations might be the nature of the specific disability, the equipment required for participation (wheelchairs and ancillary equipment), and ways of structuring competition to maximize fulfillment for the individual.

Opportunities for Participation

Persons with physical disabilities need opportunities to express attained sport skills in competition. Many public schools have limited numbers of students of similar ages and ability who are physically challenged. This makes organized competition among those with specific disabilities difficult. Therefore cooperative efforts need to be made among schools to provide opportunities for competition among the athletes. Wheelchair sports events are sponsored by sports associations for persons with disabilities and are staged for competition in most states in the country. Several colleges and universities also have intercollegiate wheelchair sports programs. The University of Illinois has developed one of the best intercollegiate wheelchair sports programs. Several other universities also have well-developed intercollegiate athletic programs.

The missions of sports organizations for individuals with disabilities are to provide training opportunities and promote competition. These organizations provide a forum and incentive to maximize proficiency in sports for competition. Wheelchair sports competitions are held at the local, national, and international levels. There is a movement for the organization of games for individuals with generic disabilities at the state level. Project GUMBO in Louisiana is a good example of games organized for the physically challenged at the state level.[11] More sophisticated competition is held by the International Sports Organization for the Disabled. Over 5000 athletes with a variety of physical disabilities will compete in the Paralympics in Atlanta in 1996. Competitions are intense. As a result, training camps have been developed to improve performance at international games.[18] International games have developed not only in the intensity of competition, but also in the magnitude of participation. Thus opportunities exist for many individuals with physical disabilities to participate in competitive sports at their ability level with incentive to increase skills to a world-class level. A current list of sports organizations for individuals with physical disabilities is included in Appendix C.

Nature and scope of the program

Sport activity programs involve sports that can be performed while wearing protheses or while seated in a wheelchair. Some of the sport activities that are available to individuals include archery, basketball, billiards, bowling, flying, golf, hockey, tennis, racquetball, rugby, road racing, shooting, skiing, softball, table tennis, track and field, water sports, and weight lifting. There is also a movement to enable persons with disabilities to participate with nondisabled athletes in major sporting events. For example, wheelchair athletes participate at the classic running event, the Boston Marathon.[34]

A woman with quadriplegia participates in sea kayaking. (Courtesy American Canoe Association, Inc.)

Differences in abilities

Clearly, individuals in wheelchairs do not have equal abilities. Therefore to provide equitable competition in school-based activities for persons with physical disabilities, it may be necessary to test skill performances and group the participants according to ability in the individual sports.

Official wheelchair sports competition is based on a medically designed neurological functioning classification system (Table 15-3). As will be noted when reviewing Table 15-3, sports organizations for athletes with disabilities use slightly different systems for classifying athletes for competitive purposes. In Table 15-3 three classification systems are described in relation to muscular involvement and spinal level of impairment.

The National Wheelchair Basketball Association (NWBA) uses three categories for competition purposes: I, which encompasses impairments of the cervical and thoracic spine through T7 (seventh thoracic vertebra); II, which includes impairments from T8 (eighth thoracic vertebra) through L2 (second lumbar vertebra); and III,

which includes all impairments to vertebrae below the second lumbar area.[54] Wheelchair Sports, U.S.A., and the International Stoke-Mandeville Games Federation (ISMGF) use similar classification systems. These two organizations categorize athletes with cervical level impairments as IA, IB, or IC, depending on the level of impairment: category II includes T1 through T6 impairments; category III encompasses T7 through T10 vertebral impairments; category IV includes T11 through L2 impairments; and category V includes all impairments from the third lumbar vertebra down.

The purpose of the classification system is to allow for fair competition. Tests are administered to determine the level of muscular function. Such tests do not take into account the proficiency of the athletes in competition. Several writers have questioned the validity of existing medically designed classification systems because proficiency is not taken into account.[5,6,31] Those concerns have led to the development of several functional, sport-specific classification systems.

Functional classification systems allow for observation and rating of the actual movement patterns used during sport performance. According to Curtis,[13] an ideal functional classification system should reflect the differences in movement seen during performance of the sport by athletes who either have or lack the function of key muscle groups. Typical functional classification systems include evaluation of the following areas:

- Arm function (example: triceps strength for wheelchair push)
- Hand function (example: finger flexion adequate for grasp of a field implement such as a discus)
- Trunk function for rotation (example: rotating the trunk during the release of the discus)
- Trunk stability to maintain balance in an upright position (example: ability to leave the back of the wheelchair while serving in table tennis without losing balance)
- Trunk function for forward-and-backward movement or upward-and-downward movement (example: recovery for the next wheelchair stroke by lifting the upper back and shoulders)
- Pelvic stability from side to side (example: increasing the reach to the side for a two-handed rebound in basketball)[13]

It is predicted that functional classification systems that are based on the movements inherent in the sport

Swimmers with amputations participate in community-sponsored competition. (Courtesy City of San Diego Parks and Recreation.)

table 15-3

Comparison of Wheelchair Classification Systems Based on Medical Model

Level	NWBA	Class	Wheelchair Sports U.S.A.	Class	ISMGF (except basketball)
C-5		IA	Triceps 0-3	IA	
C-6		IB	Triceps 4-5	IB	
C-7			Wrist flexion/extension present		
		IC	Finger flexion/extension 4-5	IC	
C-8			No useful hand intrinsics		
			No useful abdominals		
T-1	I	II	No lower intercostals	II	
T-2	Motor loss at T7 or above				
T-3					
T-4	Sitting balance poor				
T-5					
T-6			Upper abdominals good. No use-		
T-7		III	ful lower abdominals. No useful	III	
			lower trunk extensors.		
T-8	II				
T-9	Abdominal and spinal extensor		Poor to fair sitting balance		
T-10	muscle strength 3-5				
T-11	Sitting balance fair to good	IV	Good abdominals and spinal ex-	IV	
T-12			tensors. Some hip flexors/		
			adductors.		
L-1	Hip flexors ≤4		Fair to good balance		Good balance
	Hip adductors ≤3		Quad strength <3		1-20 points traumatic
	Quadriceps ≤2		Includes bilateral hip disarticula-		1-15 points postpolio
L-2	Includes bilateral hip disarticula-		tion amputees		Amputees not included
	tions				
L-3	III	V			
	Trunk control, pelvic control		Normal balance		
			Quad strength ≥3		
L-4	Sitting balance good to normal		<40 points		V
			Most amputees AK and BK		Normal balance
L-5	Quads 3-5		In V/VI		21-40 points traumatic
S-1	All other amputees		VI (Swimming only)		16-35 points polio
			≥40 points		Amputees not included
					VI (Swimming only)
					41-60 points traumatic
					36-50 points polio
					Not eligible >61 points traumatic
					>51 points polio

Modified from Weiss M, Curtis KA: Controversies in medical classification of wheelchair athletes. In Sherrill C: *Sport and disabled athletes—the 1984 Olympic Scientific Congress proceedings,* vol 9, Champaign, Ill, 1986, Human Kinetics.

will replace the neurologically based systems within the next few years. Information about classification systems used in competition for specific sports can be obtained directly from sport associations that have been listed in Appendix C.

Amputees are considered to possess a lesser disability when compared with other athletes confined to wheelchairs. In some instances they play sports such as volleyball standing up.[56] There are also occasions when they play volleyball sitting down (Figure 15-11). In ef-

figure 15-11
Volleyball players with amputations compete in sitting volleyball at the 1992 Paralympics. (Courtesy Ron Davis, Ball State University, Muncie, Ind.).

Ocean Escapes, a pioneer in aqua therapy for wheelchair-enabled individuals, offers weightlessness through scuba diving to individuals who, on land, are trapped by gravity. (Courtesy Ocean Escapes.)

forts to equalize competition, they are classified according to the number of amputations and the location and length of the stumps. Amputations may occur on one or both sides of the body, above or below the knee.

SUMMARY

The three types of physical disabilities discussed in this chapter are neurological conditions, orthopedic disabilities, and conditions caused by trauma. Afflictions can occur at more than 500 anatomical sites. Each student with a disability has different physical and motor capabilities and is to be provided with special accommodations that enable participation in modified games and sport activity. Contraindicated activity as identified by medical personnel must be avoided.

Physical educators should address two types of program considerations to meet the physical education needs of persons with physical disabilities. One is to implement developmental programs that enhance prerequisite motor patterns, sport skills, and physical and motor fitness. The other is to structure the environment so that students with disabilities can derive physical benefits through participation in competitive sporting activities (this may be facilitated by the use of aids for specific types of activities and disabilities).

The physical educator should be ready to accommodate the individual program needs of physically disabled persons by identifying unique needs through formal and functional assessment, using adaptive devices to permit active involvement, and modifying activities to enable the student to participate in a variety of settings.

There are many national organizations that have been developed to enable persons with disabilities to participate in sports competition. Functional classification systems are being developed to replace the older medical models to equalize competition among individuals with varying levels of function.

Review Questions

1. What are some principles for adapting physical activity for students with physical disabilities?
2. Apply these principles for adapting physical activity for a specific disability in a specific activity.
3. What are some motor and nonmotor characteristics of individuals with cerebral palsy?
4. What are the clinical classifications of cerebral palsy?
5. What are the physical characteristics of persons with muscular dystrophy?
6. Describe different types of muscular dystrophy.
7. What are the physical characteristics of developmental hip dislocations? Describe physical activity concerns.
8. What are some orthopedic conditions of the lower extremity? Describe the physical characteristics, medical prognosis, contraindications, and application of principles for adapting physical activity.
9. Explain the controversy about sports participation classification systems.
10. Name some organizations that may assist individuals with physical disabilities with participation in sport activity.

Student Activities

1. Working in small groups, share the programs you developed for Josue, and come to an agreement on the exercises/activities to include in his warm-up routine, his cardiovascular program, and his alternative activity program.
2. Working in small groups, determine what sports programs would be appropriate for Josue and develop a list of skills/abilities Josue will need to participate in those sports.
3. Write a paper on strategies to use to convince Josue's mother that participation in the regular physical education class and a community sports program will improve the quality of his life.
4. Discuss with the rest of the class the type of behavior management program that might be successful with Josue.
5. Select one or two major journals in the field of physical or special education. Some of these journals are *Journal of Health, Physical Education, and Recreation; Exceptional Children; Adapted Physical Activity Quarterly; Palaestra: The Forum of Sport, Physical Education and Recreation for the Disabled;* and *Sports n' Spokes.* Look through the issues from the past few years for articles that present useful suggestions for adapting instruction for students with physical disabilities. Make a file of these suggestions.
6. Visit a school, shopping center, or municipal building and identify architectural barriers that would deny access/use to individuals with disabilities. Evaluate the accessibility of drinking fountains, phones, different floors, eating facilities, playing areas, and emergency exits. What types of activities might enable persons with physical disabilities to gain access to these facilities?

7. Discuss with the rest of the class what you learn from a demonstration put on at your school by athletes from a sports association for persons with disabilities.
8. Discuss the pros and cons of conducting separate sports programs for individuals with physical disabilities. When are separate sports programs appropriate and under what conditions?

References

1. Alexander MJ: New techniques in quadriplegic wheelchair marathon racing, *Palaestra* 3:13-16, 1987.
2. Antich TJ, Lombaro SJ: Clinical presentation of Osgood-Schlatter disease in the adolescent population, *J Orthop Sports Phys Ther* 7:1-4, 1985.
3. Berkow R: *The Merck manual of diagnosis and therapy,* Rahway, NJ, 1992, Merck Sharpe Dohme Research Laboratories.
4. Berrol CF, Katz SS: Dance-movement therapy in the rehabilitation of individuals surviving severe head injuries, *Am J Dance Ther* 8:46-66, 1985.
5. Brasile F: Wheelchair basketball proficiencies versus disability classification, *Adapt Phys Act Q* 3:6-13, 1986.
6. Brasile F: Performance evaluation of wheelchair athletes more than a disability classification level issue, *Adapt Phys Act Q* 7:289-297, 1990.
7. Brasile F, Hedrick BN: A comparison of participation incentives between adult and youth wheelchair basketball players, *Palaestra* 7:40-46, 1991.
8. Burd R, Grass K: Strapping to enhance athletic performance of wheelchair competitors with cerebral palsy, *Palaestra* 3:28-32, 1987.
9. Cambell SK, Wilhelm IJ: Development from birth to three years of age of 15 children at high risk for central nervous system dysfunction, *Phys Ther* 65:463-469, 1985.
10. Cooper RA: A new racing wheelchair rear wheel alignment device, *Palaestra* 4:8-11, 1988.
11. Cowden JE: Project GUMBO . . . games uniting mind and body, *Palaestra* 4:13-27, 1988.
12. Curtis KA: Stretching routines, *Sports 'n Spokes* 7(5):1-3, 1981.
13. Curtis KA: Sport-specific functional classification for wheelchair athletes, *Sports 'n Spokes* 17:45-48, 1991.
14. Curtis KA, editor: *Guide to sports medicine needs of athletes with disabilities,* Coral Gables, Fla, 1993, University of Miami School of Medicine.
15. Curtis KA: *Injuries and disability-specific medical conditions of athletes with disabilities,* Unpublished paper, Coral Gables, Fla, 1993, University of Miami.
16. Curtis KA et al: Functional reach in wheelchair users: the effects of trunk and lower extremity stabilization, *Arch Phys Med Rehabil* 76:360-372, 1995.
17. Daniels L, Worthingham C: *Muscle testing,* ed 4, Philadelphia, 1980, WB Saunders.
18. Davis RW: Elite wheelchair training camp, *Palaestra* 4:48-52, 1988.
19. DiCarlo S: Effect of arm ergometry training on wheelchair propulsion endurance of individuals with quadriplegia, *Phys Ther* 68:40-44, 1988.
20. Dummer GM et al: Attributions of athletes with cerebral palsy, *Adapt Phys Act Q* 4:278-292, 1987.
21. Dunn JM, Fait H: *Special physical education,* Dubuque, Iowa, 1989, Wm C Brown Group.
22. Fernandez JE, Pitetti KH: Training of ambulatory individuals with cerebral palsy, *Arch Phys Med Rehabil* 74:468-472, 1993.
23. Gehlsen GM, Davis RW, Bahamonde R: Intermittent velocity and wheelchair performance characteristics, *Adapt Phys Act Q* 7:219-230, 1990.
24. Geurts ACH et al: Dual-tasks assessment of reorganization of postural control in persons with lower limb amputation, *Arch Phys Med Rehabil* 72:1059-1064, 1995.
25. Gitlin LN, Levine R, Geiger C: Adaptive device use by older adults with mixed disabilities, *Arch Phys Med Rehabil* 74:149-152, 1993.
26. Hardison GT, Isreal RG, Somes G: Physiological responses to different cranking rates during submaximal arm ergometry in paraplegic males, *Adapt Phys Act Q* 4:94-105, 1987.
27. Hazelwood ME et al: The use of therapeutic electrical stimulation in the treatment of hemiplegic cerebral palsy, *Dev Med Child Neurol* 36:661-673, 1994.
28. Healy A: *Cerebral palsy in medical aspects of developmental disabilities in children birth to three,* Rockville, Md, 1984, Aspen.
29. Hedrick B et al: Aerodynamic positioning and performance in wheelchair racing, *Adapt Phys Act Q* 7:41-51, 1990.
30. Higgs C: A comparison of three- and four-wheeled designs, *Palaestra* 8:29-35, 1992.
31. Higgs C et al: Wheelchair classification for track and field events: a performance approach, *Adapt Phys Act Q* 7:22-40, 1990.
32. Holland LJ, Steadward RD: Effects of resistance and flexibility training on strength, spasticity/muscle tone and range of motion of elite athletes with cerebral palsy, *Palaestra* 6:27-31, 1990.
33. Hopkins LC: Muscular dystrophies. In Conn RB, editor: *Current diagnosis,* ed 7, Philadelphia, 1985, WB Saunders.
34. Huber JH: Wheelchair division of the 93rd Boston Marathon: new world records, issues, trends, *Palaestra* 5:44-46, 1989.
35. Hughes CJ et al: Biomechanics of wheelchair propulsion as a function of seat position and user-to-chair interface, *Arch Phys Med Rehabil* 73:263-269, 1992.
36. Hundertmark LH: Evaluating the adult with cerebral palsy for specialized adapted seating, *Phys Ther* 65:209-212, 1985.
37. Hunter D et al: Energy expenditure of below-knee ampu-

tees during harness-supported treadmill ambulation, *J Orthop Sport Phys Ther* 21:268-276, 1995.

38. Khaw CWH, Tidemann AJ, Stern LM: Study of hemiplegic cerebral palsy with a review of the literature, *J Paediatr Child Health* 30:224-229, 1994.

39. Lasko-McCarthey P, Knopf KG: *Adapted physical education for adults with disabilities,* ed 3, Dubuque, Iowa, 1992, Eddie Bowers Publishing.

40. Lee K, Thomas D: *Control of computer-based technology for people with physical disabilities: an assessment manual,* Toronto, 1990, University of Toronto Press.

41. Levin S, Aquatic therapy, *Physician Sportsmed* 19:119-126, 1995.

42. Letts RM, *Principles of seating the disabled,* Boston, 1991, CRC Press.

43. Liu M, Chino N, Ishihara T: Muscle damage in Duchenne muscular dystrophy evaluated by a new quantitative computed tomography method, *Arch Phys Med Rehabil* 74:507-514, 1991.

44. Mayall JK, Desharnais G: *Positioning in a wheelchair, a guide for professional caregivers of the disabled adult,* ed 2, Thorofare, NJ, 1995, Slack.

45. McLean KP, Skinner JS: Effect of body training position on outcomes of an aerobic training study on individuals with quadriplegia, *Arch Phys Med Rehabil* 76:139-150, 1995.

46. Miller BF, Keane CB: *Encyclopedia and dictionary of medicine nursing and allied health,* Philadelphia, 1987, WB Saunders.

47. National Information Center for Handicapped Children and Youth: *Spina bifida,* Washington, DC, 1983, Department of Education.

48. Paciorek MJ: Technology only a part of the story as world records fall, *Palaestra* 10:14, 42, 1993.

49. Peck DM, McKeag DB: Athletes with disabilities: removing medical barriers, *Physician Sportsmed* 22:59-63, 1994.

50. Petrofsky JS, Brown SW, Cerrel B: Active physical therapy and its benefits in rehabilitation, *Palaestra* 9:23-27, 61, 1992.

51. Petrofsky JS, Phillips CA: Computer controlled walking in the paralyzed individual, *IEEE NAECON Rec* 2:1162-1165, 1983.

52. Ponichtera-Mulcare JA et al: Maximal aerobic exercise of individuals with multiple sclerosis using three modes of ergometry, *Clin Kines* 49:4-13, 1995.

53. Spencer CH: Juvenile rheumatoid arthritis. In Conn RB, editor: *Current Diagnosis,* ed 7, Philadelphia, 1985, WB Saunders.

54. Strohkendl H: The new classification system for wheelchair basketball. In Sherrill C, editor: *Sports and disabled athletes,* Champaign, Ill, 1986, Human Kinetics.

55. Venn J, Morganstern L, Dykes MK: Checklist for evaluating the fit and function of orthoses, prostheses, and wheelchairs in the classroom, *Teach Except Child,* pp 51-56, winter 1979.

56. Vodola T: *Motor disabilities or limitations,* Oakmont, NJ, 1976, Project Active.

57. Ward E: *Prescriptive seating for wheelchair mobility,* Kansas City, Mo, 1994, Health Wealth International.

58. Williams HG, McClenaghan B, Ward DS: Duration of muscle activity during standing in normally and slowly developing children, *Am J Phys Med* 64:171-189, 1985.

59. Wilson AB: *How to select and use manual wheelchairs,* Topping, Va, 1992, Rehabilitation Press.

60. Wiseman DC: *Physical education and exceptional students: theory and practice,* Plymouth, Mass, 1994, Delmar.

61. Worden DK, Vignos PJ: Intellectual function in childhood progressive muscular dystrophy, *Pediatrics* 29:968-977, 1962.

62. Wright J: *Project C.R.E.O.L.E.: wheelchair sports and mobility curriculum,* Harvey, La, 1989, Jefferson Parish Public School System.

Suggested Reading

Kirk S, Gallagher J, Anatasio NJ: *Educating exceptional children,* ed 7, Boston, 1993, Houghton Mifflin.

chapter **s i x t e e n**

Hearing Impairments

Objectives

List three motor characteristics of individuals who are deaf.

Demonstrate five specific signs that can be used to communicate with students in physical education who are deaf or hard-of-hearing.

List seven techniques a teacher can use for enhancing communication with students who are deaf or hard-of-hearing.

Describe the two most widely accepted communication systems used by deaf persons in this country.

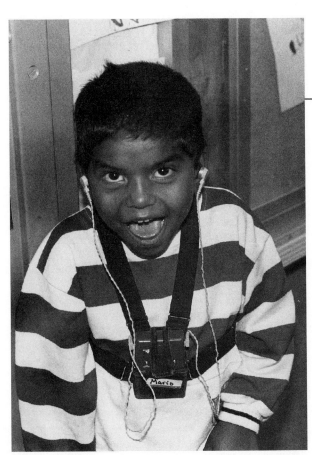

Courtesy Callier Center for Communicative Disorders, Dallas.

Scenario

Sharonda is a 16-year-old deaf student who is presently receiving educational services in a self-contained class for hard-of-hearing/deaf students in a vocational preparation program in a large southern city. Although her recent 3-year assessment indicated an IQ score of 70, her teachers believe she is much brighter and that her deafness compromised her performance during the assessment.

Sharonda is able to do some lipreading and uses American Sign Language beautifully. She is able to speak, but until one gets to know her and becomes accustomed to her speech, she is difficult to understand.

Her gross and fine motor skills are excellent, and she performs to age level on physical fitness tests.

Sharonda is the youngest of five daughters and spends the majority of her time when she is away from school baby-sitting for her sisters' children. Although she would be employable in a work setting with an interpreter and/or another employee who was able to use sign language, her mother, who is not hearing impaired, has indicated that when Sharonda graduates, she will assume the role of full-time baby-sitter for the family.

Task

It is time to develop Sharonda's transitional physical education plan. As you read through this chapter, think about the types of community activities that Sharonda should be given the opportunity to choose from that would maximize her participation outside the home.

H earing is one of the strongest lines of communication between persons and the world in which they live. Children who have permanent hearing losses often have delays in language comprehension, personal and social adjustments, and motor development. The purpose of this chapter is to provide a background into the nature of hearing loss and the needs of persons who are deaf and hard-of-hearing, and to discuss the role of physical education in meeting those needs as part of the total educational process. The designations **deaf** and **hard-of-hearing** are used because they are preferred by organizations that serve these populations. Classifications of hearing loss, characteristics of individuals who are hearing impaired, types of communication systems, teaching techniques, and ways to serve these students in the most inclusive environment are discussed.

Definition

According to The Education of the Handicapped Act[27]:

> "Deaf" means a hearing impairment which is so severe that the child is impaired in processing linguistic information through hearing, with or without amplification, which adversely affects educational performance (Section a.5.b.3). . . . "Hard of hearing" means a hearing impairment whether permanent or fluctuating, which adversely affects a child's educational performance but which is not included under deaf in this section (Section 121a.5.b.3).

This definition is useful to physical educators because it requires focus on the child as he or she participates in tasks in physical education. If there is performance deficiency, the question can be asked, "Is the deficiency the result of hearing loss?" If the answer is yes, special accommodation for the child should be made.

The continuum of degree of hearing loss and ability to understand speech ranges from that of little significance to that of extreme disability. The degree of an individual's deafness is determined according to the

table 16-1

Hearing Loss Categories		
Label	Decibel Loss	Ability to Hear Speech and Speak
Mild	20-49	May have trouble hearing distant speech; speech and language not affected
Moderate	50-69	Can understand loud speech; language usage and comprehension deficiencies
Severe	70-90	May hear loud voice 1 foot from ear; speech and language affected
Profound	>90	Cannot hear conversational speech at all; may be aware of vibrations; speech and language are defective

amount of decibel loss and the individual's ability to perceive conversation.[18] Four categories of hearing loss based on decibel loss, ability to understand speech, and quality of speech are presented in Table 16-1.

Incidence

There are approximately 76,000 to 90,000 students between the ages of 5 and 17 years in the United States who are classified as hearing impaired.[7] Furthermore, one out of eight hearing-impaired students is classified as deaf (a 91-decibel loss or more).

Causes

The acquisition of speech and language skills is basic to the subsequent development of the individual. Therefore the time of onset of deafness is a critical factor in determining the effects that it may have on the learning situation. Persons whose sense of hearing is nonfunctional for the ordinary purposes of life may be grouped into two distinct classes according to time of onset. They are the **congenitally** deaf and the **adventitiously** deaf. Congenitally deaf persons are born deaf; adventitiously deaf persons experience hearing loss after birth. According to Meyen,[14] if hearing loss occurs before or at birth, there is no chance for language to be heard normally or for incidental learning to occur. In some literature these individuals are also referred to as having a prelingual hearing impairment. A child who is afflicted with a hearing loss early in development progresses more slowly than does one who is afflicted with a loss later in the developmental process.

Proper diagnosis of hearing disabilities may provide assistance for development of physical education programs. Each type of deafness, accompanied by the uniqueness of each deaf child, requires individualized treatment by teachers. Categories of hearing loss that should be considered in the educational planning for the student are the following:

- **Conductive hearing impairments:** Typically, a condition in which the intensity of sound is reduced before reaching the inner ear, where the auditory nerve begins. A conductive hearing loss can also result when the membranes in the inner ear undergo physical changes that reduce the transfer of energy to the hair cells. The most prevalent cause of conductive hearing loss is infection of the middle ear, which is called **otitis media.** Another infection that may cause conductive hearing loss is **mastoiditis.** Mastoiditis occurs when there is chronic inflammation of the middle ear that spreads into the air cells of the mastoid process within the temporal bone. Other causes of conductive hearing loss include perforation of the eardrum from a blow to the head, allergies that make the eustachian tube swell, tumors of the external auditory canal, the presence of foreign objects in the external ear, and excessive buildup of ear wax.
- **Sensorineural hearing impairments:** A condition caused by an absence or malfunction of a sensory unit. The damage may be present in the cochlea or the eighth cranial nerve. If the dysfunction is in the inner ear, the individual has difficulty discriminating among speech sounds. Sound can be heard, but persons often cannot derive meaning from high-frequency sounds. Causes include recessive genetic sources, the mother's having had rubella (German measles) or venereal disease during the pregnancy, lesions or tumors in the inner ear or on the eighth cranial nerve, and infections of the child, such as mumps, inner ear infection, meningitis, or encephalitis.
- **Central auditory processing problems:** Deafness resulting from damage at the brainstem level or in the cortex itself. This type of deafness can occur concurrently with sensorineural impairments.[20]

Clues That Indicate Hearing Loss

The sooner a hearing loss is identified, the sooner correctable defects can be treated adequately so that interference with the child's development will be reduced. Teachers and parents should be alert to signs of hearing loss, which include:

1. Hearing and comprehension of speech
   a. General indifference to sound
   b. Lack of response to the spoken word
   c. Response to noises as opposed to words[11]
   d. Leaning toward the source of sound[10]
   e. Requests to repeat statements[10]
2. Vocalization and sound production
   a. Monotonal quality
   b. Indistinct speech
   c. Lessened laughter
   d. Meager experimental sound play
   e. Vocal play for vibratory sensation
   f. Head banging, foot stamping for vibratory sensation
   g. Yelling or screeching to express pleasure or need
3. Visual attention
   a. Augmental visual vigilance and attentiveness
   b. Alertness to gesture and movement
   c. Marked imitativeness in play
   d. Vehement gestures
4. Social rapport and adaptation
   a. Subnormal rapport in vocal games
   b. Intensified preoccupation with things rather than persons
   c. Puzzling and unhappy episodes in social situations
   d. Suspiciousness and alertness, alternating with cooperation
   e. Marked reaction to praise and affection
5. Emotional behavior
   a. Tantrums to call attention to self or need
   b. Tensions, tantrums, or resistance caused by lack of comprehension
   c. Frequent obstinance; irritability at not making self understood[11]

Psychological and Behavioral Characteristics

Hearing loss can have profound consequences on a person's behavior. Hearing loss affects language and speech development, learning, and social adjustment. The areas most affected by hearing impairment are those of comprehension and production of the English language. Obviously, the degree of hearing loss has a great impact on language development. It is reported that 86% of students with less than severe hearing loss have intelligible speech; however, 75% of students with profound hearing loss have unintelligible speech.[29]

The intellectual ability of children who are deaf or hard-of-hearing has been a subject of controversy over the years. The once-popular view that these individuals are somewhat deficient intellectually has been challenged. Several intelligence tests rely heavily on verbal skills, which obviously discriminates against individuals who are deaf or hard-of-hearing. Many professionals hold the view that IQ tests do not assess the hearing-impaired child's true capability. Estimates of the incidence of specific learning disabilities range from 1% to 75%; however, the actual prevalence is probably just over 3%.[7] Because of hearing limitations, frequently students who are deaf do not graduate from high school until they are about 20 years of age. At that time their average reading skills are about at grade 4.5, and their overall academic skills are behind those of their hearing peers.[29]

Friends at play. (Courtesy Callier Center for Communicative Disorders, Dallas.)

Social and personality development in the general population are dependent on communication. Social interaction is the communication between two or more persons, and language is a very important means of communication. Therefore the personality and social characteristics of persons who are deaf or hard-of-hearing may differ from those of persons who have normal hearing ability. Frequently a person's behavioral development is based on how well or poorly others in the environment accept them. Deaf children who are raised by deaf parents who understand and accept them are generally better adjusted than deaf children reared by hearing parents. The rates of psychoses and hospitalization for mental illness among deaf adults equal those of the hearing population.[26]

Developmental Factors

Hearing loss that afflicts youngsters in the early phases of development impairs the total developmental process. One of the effects of deafness is to limit the children's play experience with other children. Play in the preschool years is important for learning of social skills and for development of motor skills. In play situations deaf children are often uncertain as to the part they should play in the game, and therefore they often withdraw from participation. Thus the role of play, which is important to the social, psychological, and motor aspects of development in typical children, is usually limited for children who are deaf.

The social benefits of play experienced by typical children are not experienced to the same degree by children who are deaf. Consequently, social development occurs more slowly in deaf children. It is in social maturation that the disability of deafness is most apparent. This retardation is probably partially caused by language inadequacy that results from the hearing loss.

Because of their impaired ability to function socially with their peers and because of their restricted developmental experiences, children who are deaf are likely to be subjected to more strain than hearing children. Thus young children who are deaf may be less emotionally mature than hearing children of the same age.

Motor Characteristics of Individuals Who Are Hearing Impaired

Impairment of the semicircular canals, vestibule of the inner ear, and/or vestibular portion of the eighth cranial nerve has a negative effect on balance. Siegel, Marchetti, and Tecclin[24] reported significantly depressed balance performance by children with sensorineural hearing loss of below 65 decibels. Another study that did not examine etiological factors evaluated motor performance and vestibular function of a group of hearing-impaired children. The vast majority (65%) of the studied group demonstrated abnormal vestibular function, but normal motor proficiency except for balance, whereas 24% had normal vestibular function and motor proficiency, including balance. Eleven percent had normal vestibular function but poor motor proficiency and balance.[4] Butterfield and Ersing[3] found that the cause of hearing impairment may have an impact on balance proficiency. In their study, a group of hearing-impaired persons with acquired deafness performed significantly better than a group with congenital deafness. Thus it is important to point out that the balancing deficit associated with some hearing-impaired children cannot be generalized. The individual education program (IEP) must be based on the needs of each child.

One characteristic that may be negatively affected by a hearing impairment is motor speed (i.e., the time it takes the child to process information and complete a motor act).[2] Beyond that characteristic, there is disagreement about the physical abilities of individuals who are hearing impaired.

Fait and Dunn[6] have suggested that physical fitness of persons with auditory impairments may be lower than that of their hearing peers. However, according to Winnick and Short,[28] on only one test item did hearing subjects surpass the performance of auditorially impaired adolescents. Although Minter and Wolk[16] indicated that deaf children may appear hyperactive, Hattin[9] reported that deafness does not stimulate hyperactivity and that deaf children could profit from more endurance exercise to raise their levels of fitness. It appears that further research is needed to resolve these issues.

Deaf-Blind Children

Deaf-blind children have loss of both vision and hearing. They are considered to have less than 20/20 vision for a field of 20 degrees or less. In addition, they have a loss of hearing of 25 decibels or more. Thus they are often unable to be educated in classes for the deaf or the blind.

Deaf-blind children have problems similar to those of the blind child and the deaf child. However, their problems are exponential rather than additive. There is practically no foundation for communicative skills. Residual sight and/or hearing can be the basis of communication. If there is no residual sight or hearing, communication is then made kinesthetically through the hands.

Testing

Any evaluation instrument that allows the evaluator to demonstrate can be used with students who are deaf or hard-of-hearing. The Test of Gross Motor Development (TGMD) would be appropriate for the elementary and middle school–age child. In addition, the balance subtest from the Bruininks-Oseretsky Test of Motor Proficiency could be used to determine whether there is a possibility of vestibular delay. Comparison of static balance ability with eyes open and eyes closed will provide clues to vestibular delay or damage (see Chapter 13). If poor vestibular functioning is interfering with the student's ability to balance with eyes closed, it may not be possible to correct the condition. If the deafness is caused by damage to the portion of the eighth cranial nerve that also carries the vestibular impulse, activities to stimulate the vestibular system will not help the balance problem. In these cases it is best to simply teach the child to execute the balance moves needed to be successful in motor activities. Any standardized physical fitness test may be used with this population.

Special Considerations

For optimum learning to occur, a teacher must be able to effectively communicate with the students. Students with hearing losses have the greatest opportunity to learn when they have maximum hearing correction and a teacher who has mastery of the communication system the student has elected to use. New technological advances continue to improve methodology for maximizing hearing capability; however, teacher training has not kept pace with requiring all teachers to learn to communicate with students who have special hearing needs.

Technological Hearing Assistance

Hearing aids amplify sound and are effective for conductive and sensorineural hearing losses that are greater than 30 decibels. They can also be helpful for individuals whose sensorineural hearing losses are in the high-

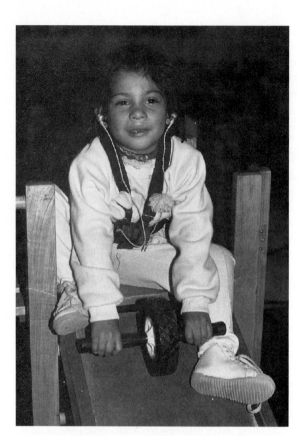

A child develops play skills. (Courtesy Callier Center for Communicative Disorders, Dallas.)

frequency range. There are two primary types of hearing aids: air conduction and bone conduction. **Air conduction hearing aids** are worn on the body, behind the ear, on the temple bars of eyeglasses, or in the ear and are hooked to the receiver located in the ear canal by an open tube or airtight seal. For profound hearing losses, the most powerful hearing aid is the body type that is worn in a shirt pocket or in front of the body in a harness and is connected to a receiver located in the ear canal. For moderate to severe hearing losses, an ear-level aid is fitted behind the pinna. Eyeglass aids that are built into the temple bar of a person's eyeglasses and in-the-ear aids are appropriate for mild and moderate hearing losses.[1]

Bone conduction hearing aids are used when a person cannot wear an ear mold. The generator is placed

in contact with the mastoid bone (behind the ear) and held in place with a spring. The sound is conducted through the bone to the cochlea.[1]

Cochlear implants are available for surgical implantation in profoundly deaf persons who cannot be helped with hearing aids. These implants enable the profoundly deaf individual to distinguish when a word begins and ends, the rhythm of the speech, and intonations.[1]

Communication Systems

The two prevalent philosophies in the education of persons in this country who are deaf or hard-of-hearing are known as the **oral communication method** and the **total communication method.** With the oral method (also known as the oral-aural method), children are provided amplification of their residual hearing and are taught through speechreading (lipreading). They express themselves through speech. The use of signs and fingerspelling is prohibited. The total communication method combines the oral method with the use of signs and fingerspelling. Children are provided amplification of sound and are taught through speechreading, fingerspelling, and signs. They express themselves through speech, fingerspelling, and signs.[17]

The term *total communication* refers to both a method of instruction and a philosophy of education. As a philosophy, it refers to the right of every person who is deaf or hard-of-hearing to select whatever form of communication is preferred. That is, depending on the circumstances, the person should have the right to choose to communicate through speech, signs, gestures, or writing. If taught through a total communication system, the person has the option to communicate in the way that best suits his or her needs.[23] Since 1975, classroom instruction of the deaf in this country has been predominantly through the total communication method.[17] A variety of forms of manual communication systems may be incorporated into the total communication method.

Manual Communication Systems

The **manual communication systems** range from simple, homemade gestures to fingerspelling. Signing systems between these two extremes include Pidgin Sign Language, American Sign Language, Manually Coded English, and fingerspelling. A description of each follows:

- *Homemade gestures:* A primitive gestural system developed to communicate between individuals or among small groups.
- *Pidgin Sign Language:* A mixture of English and American Sign Language. Key words and phrases are signed in correct order; prepositions and articles are usually omitted.[23]
- *American Sign Language:* A visual-gestural language that is governed by rules. The visual-gestural language involves executing systematic manual and nonmanual body movements simultaneously. Manual movements involve shapes, positions, and movements of the hands; nonmanual gestures involve the shoulders, cheeks, lips, tongue, eyes, and eyebrows. The rules that govern this language relate to how the language works (e.g., functions of the language, meaning, structure and organization of sentences, and the sound or phonetic system).[20]
- *Manually Coded English:* Signs are produced in English order, and fingerspelling is used for words and concepts that do not have a sign equivalent. Forms of Manually Coded English include Seeing Essential English, Signing Exact English, and Signed English. All are variations of American Sign Language that attempt to model the vocabulary and syntax of the English language.[20]
- *Fingerspelling:* Spelling each word letter by letter using a manual alphabet that consists of 26 letters. The hand is held in front of the chest, and letters are formed by using different single hand configurations.[17] Fingerspelling is also known as the Rochester method because it originated at the Rochester School for the Deaf in the late nineteenth century.[20]

Although many educators of deaf and hard-of-hearing students argue that it is in the best interest of these students to be educated using some form of Manually Coded English,[20] the most widely used signing system used by deaf adults in this country is American Sign Language.[17]

Effective and efficient communication with deaf students is a great challenge to teachers. Physical education teachers can and should improve their instructional ability by learning to communicate in a variety of ways to accommodate a wide range of pupils. Communication through hand signals will assist in communication with students who are deaf and those who are hard-of-hearing. Some of the basic survival signs needed by

physical education teachers to communicate with hearing-impaired persons are presented in Figure 16-1.

Most signs are for concepts and ideas rather than for words. Pointing, motioning, demonstrating, and signaling are perfectly acceptable.[5] A foundation for communication with hearing-impaired individuals can be developed through study of *The ABC's of Signing*.[19] Some specific signs for physical education appear in Figure 16-2.

Parent Involvement

Parent participation is important in the education of a child who has a hearing loss. Whereas deaf parents who have a deaf child are very clear about how to communicate with their child, most hearing parents who face rearing a child with a severe hearing impairment have little knowledge of what they can do. After the child is in school, it is important for the parents to be kept informed about their child's progress and what aspects of the school program can be reinforced at home.

Teaching Strategies

The ability to communicate effectively is important in instructional settings, as well as while participating in sporting events. When there is effective communication and the learning environment is properly managed, there may be little need to modify the demands of the physical activity.[3] However, when communication impairments are present, the student may perform motor and social skills less well, solely because of the communication problem. The physical educator who works with deaf and hard-of-hearing students must do everything possible to ensure effective communication.

Students who wear hearing aids are easily identifiable and should be given special consideration. One adjustment that can be made easily is to place the child close to the instructor so that greater amplification of speech is received. A second adjustment that may help is for the instructor to keep the face in view of the child who is hard-of-hearing. Visual aids can also be used to communicate. Visual demonstrations, blackboard work, films, and slides are important instructional aids for the deaf. To get the attention of the hearing-impaired child, waving the hands or turning lights off and on has proved to be effective in some instances.

Deaf persons, because of an inability to comprehend information through auditory means, must rely mainly

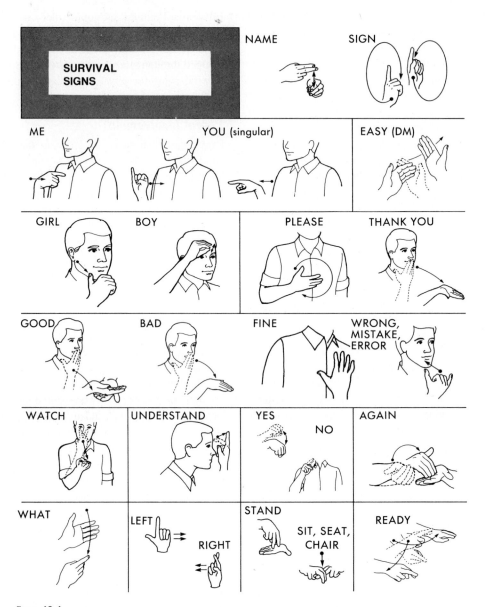

figure 16-1
Survival signs. (Reprinted with permission from the *Journal of Physical Education, Recreation, and Dance.*)

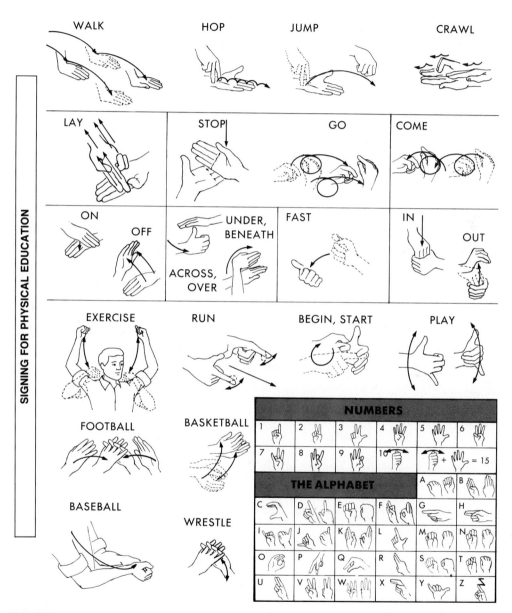

figure 16-2

Specific signs for physical education. (Reprinted with permission from the *Journal of Physical Education, Recreation, and Dance.*)

on visual and kinesthetic information during physical education instruction. Therefore, when residual hearing is insufficient for communication, these sensory media should be used. According to Ling,[12] no single method can meet the individual needs of all children with hearing disorders, and whenever possible a total communication system should be used. Verbal instructions that describe movements are ineffective for deaf individuals who cannot read lips. It is critical that precise visual models be presented to deaf individuals. To promote kinesthetic feedback, it is also helpful to move a child through the desired movement pattern. Moving the child in this fashion helps the student feel the temporal-spatial

relationship of movements associated with a skill. Using both visual and kinesthetic instruction provides opportunities for two avenues of sensory information. A quick visual model followed by a physical prompting of the behavior may facilitate learning.

Some deaf children can read lips and thus receive directions through verbal means. If the child has residual hearing or is skilled at lipreading, the physical educator should make the environment conducive to reception of the spoken word. Instruction must be given close enough to the child so that precise movement of the lips and tongue can be deciphered. The instructor should be in front and in clear view of the deaf student. When move-

Techniques for Enhancing Communication with Students Who Are Hearing Impaired

1. Position yourself where the deaf child can see your lips and maintain eye contact; do not turn your back on the child and talk (e.g., writing on the blackboard).
2. When out of doors, position yourself so that you, rather than the deaf child, face the sun.
3. Use only essential words or actions to transmit messages.
4. Use visual attention getters.
5. Make sure that the teaching environment has adequate lighting.
6. Allow the child to move freely in the gymnasium in order to be within hearing and sight range.
7. Encourage the use of residual hearing.
8. Coordinate the method (oral, total communication) that your school uses.
9. Present games with straightforward rules and strategies.
10. Familiarize the hearing-impaired student with the rules and strategies of a game before introducing the activity.
11. Learn some basic signs and use them during instruction (e.g., good, bad, okay, better, worse, line up, start, go, finish, stop, help, thank you, please, stand, sit, walk, run).
12. Use visual materials to communicate body movements (e.g., lay out footprints to indicate the foot placements required of a skill).
13. Refrain from having long lines and circle formations when presenting information to the class. This facilitates interpretation of lip movements.
14. Keep objects out of your mouth when speaking.[15]

15. Use body language, facial expression, and gestures to get an idea across.[15]
16. Avoid verbal cues during the game or activity. It is important that the deaf student fully understands his or her role before the beginning of the game or activity and that the role does not change.[15]
17. Inside facilities should be equipped with special lighting systems easily turned on and off by the instructor to get the students' attention.[15]
18. Flags or bright objects can be useful in getting the attention of students out-of-doors. However, it must be made clear to the student that it is his or her responsibility to be aware of the teacher's presence throughout the lesson. Under no circumstances should the deaf student be allowed to manipulate the teacher by ignoring attempts to gain attention.
19. Captioned videotapes, loop films, and other visual aids can be helpful in explaining strategies.
20. Demonstrate or have another student demonstrate often. It may help the student form a mental picture of how to perform a particular skill correctly.
21. Keep instructions simple and direct.[13]
22. Emphasize action rather than verbal instruction.
23. Stand still while giving directions.
24. Correct motor errors immediately.[15]
25. Select activities that allow all the children to be actively involved throughout; avoid activities that require children to spend a great deal of time sitting and waiting to participate.
26. Make use of the "buddy system" to help the student understand instructions.

ment of a game requires the child to perform an activity at a distance where lips cannot be read, it is then necessary to use some combination of signing to communicate. Eichstaedt and Seiler[5] have devised 45 signs specific to physical education to communicate with the deaf (see Figure 16-2). Use of these signs will assist the physical education teacher in communicating with the deaf student. Another source of communication to these students may come from trained hearing paraprofessionals (teacher's aides) or peers who can facilitate instruction by gaining the attention of the hearing-impaired child and then relaying instructions through visual models, signs, or tactual inputs that guide the hearing-impaired child into class activities. A number of techniques for enhancing communication with hearing-impaired students are presented in the box on p. 428.

The Physical Education Program

Considerable differences about the ways individuals respond to stimuli exist among persons who are deaf or hard-of-hearing. These differences must be taken into consideration when programming. For example, persons with **tinnitus** (ringing in the ears) are highly sensitive to noise and vibration and may not perform well in a noisy facility such as the gymnasium. Deaf children with impaired semicircular canals, which affect balance, should not climb to high places. Also, some children with hearing loss should not participate in activity where there is excessive dampness, dust, or change in temperature.

Instruction should be directed toward motor and social skills that will enable the student to participate in leisure, recreation, and sport activity in the community.[21] To encourage maximum participation, the skills and attitudes of the instructor are important.

The objectives of a physical education program for hard-of-hearing children are the same as those for non-hearing-impaired children. At the preschool and early elementary school levels, the focus should be on developing basic motor skills through games and rhythm activities. Percussion instruments such as cymbals, triangles, drums, and tambourines are valuable for rhythm activities, because they are capable of producing vibrations to which the deaf child can respond. An important area of concern for this population is balance. If vestibular functioning appears to be delayed and damage to the eighth cranial nerve can be ruled out, activities suggested in

Chapter 4 and in the handbook *Gross Motor Activities for Young Children with Special Needs,* which accompanies this text, would be appropriate. Should eighth cranial nerve damage be suspected, balance should be taught directly. Balance activities that may be included in a program are (1) standing on one foot so that the other foot can be used for kicking and trapping; (2) walking a balance beam to develop leg, hip, and trunk strength; and (3) drills that build balance skills for chasing, stopping, starting, and dodging.

At the middle and secondary school levels these students can participate in the same activities as their hearing peers. Care should be taken to ensure that they develop skills that will enable them to participate in physical fitness and leisure time activities available in their community.

Activities that enhance kinesthetic development and that are popular among hearing-impaired populations include handball and wrestling. The physical education program may focus primarily on prerequisites for performance, such as vestibular, kinesthetic, and visual stimulation, or it may use specific activities that will carry over to community involvement.

Integrating the Student Who Is Hearing Impaired

It should no longer be assumed that all deaf persons should, or want to, fit into and function in the hearing world. In some large cities there are whole communities of deaf citizens. This has occurred because deaf individuals have their own culture, which they value.[17] Requiring deaf and hard-of-hearing individuals to meet the demands of the hearing population's culture may not always be in their best interest.[17] For example, Grimes and Prickett[8] argued that insisting that deaf children use only what hearing people consider "proper" English (or Spanish, Vietnamese, or Thai) may lead to feelings of inferiority and inadequacy. For this and other reasons, the issue of placement of deaf children in an inclusive environment is a highly emotional and controversial issue with the deaf population. Moores[17] suggests that with the emphasis on individualized instruction there should be less concern for mainstreaming all children and a greater emphasis on identifying the proper match of program and child at each step in the child's development. Physical educators can make a major contribution to a deaf child's education by being sensitive to the child's individual needs and providing an appropriate and acceptable physical education program.

Some deaf individuals prefer to enroll in residential or day schools that provide segregated programs. These schools are preferred because they have a higher percentage of deaf teachers and workers, and the students have the opportunity to participate in an extensive array of academic and vocational courses, as well as a wide range of athletic and social programs.[26] Gallaudet University provides evidence of the success of segregated school programs. This well-known university for the deaf routinely competes successfully against hearing competitors in baseball and soccer.[15]

The Wisconsin School for the Deaf in Janesville, Wisconsin, is nationally known not only for academic excellence but for athletic excellence as well. Athletes from the Wisconsin School for the Deaf make regular appearances in the Wisconsin Interscholastic Athletic Association postseason tournament play in football, wrestling, and track and field.

For those deaf and hard-of-hearing students who choose to interact with a hearing population in leisure, recreation, sport, and physical education activities, communication, whether verbal or nonverbal, promotes unity and stability. It is in these settings that children with hearing loss and hearing children interact naturally. This is an important step in fostering social interaction skills. Physical educators are challenged to assist all students in developing effective social skills through participation in integrated settings.

There are certain physical education activities that enable the integration process to be accomplished with minimum support systems. Activities that require less social interaction and communication skill are movement exploration programs in the elementary school and individual sports such as bowling, archery, and weight lifting at the advanced levels. More complex team sports such as basketball, which requires frequent response to whistles and verbal communication involved in strategic situations among teammates, are more difficult to integrate. Organized football is perhaps the most difficult because of the need for ongoing information exchange between coaches and players while the game is in progress. The task is not, however, impossible. Kenny Walker, a deaf football player, was outstanding at the University of Nebraska and later played in the National Football League with the Denver Broncos.[22] Through his

interpreters, he was integrated into the game of football at the highest levels of competition. He is an excellent example of how a deaf person can be successfully integrated into a complex sport with the use of supplemental aids and services.

Students who are hearing impaired have differing needs for support systems. Therefore a list of activities that need support systems and a list of those that do not should be compiled for each hearing-impaired individual. Activities that best meet the student's needs and levels of functioning can be selected from this list. It is imperative that the move into the integrated setting be carefully planned.

The introduction of the hearing-impaired child into a regular class without prearranged support systems may

---

Inclusion Techniques for Integrating the Hearing-Impaired Student into a Regular Class

1. Provide immediate and enthusiastic acceptance of the deaf child, because this relationship can be observed by other students.[2]
2. Plan activities that constantly challenge the students but allow success.
3. Adjust the movement expectations for deaf students with equilibrium impairments.
4. Provide the hearing-impaired student with opportunities to participate in out-of-school activities, particularly on weekends and in the summer.
5. Facilitate peer interaction by planning activities that encourage turn-taking and allow the students to work together in pairs and in small groups.
6. Plan activities that require group cooperation to achieve a goal.
7. Place the deaf students in close proximity to one another during activity to facilitate peer interaction.
8. Since many deaf students may not have a strong command of English, or their native language, it is advisable not to assign out-of-class reading assignments.
9. Praise all students when it is deserved.[15]
10. The program should meet the needs and interests of the participants and should reflect the needs and interests of the community in which they will participate in leisure, recreation, and sport activities.

be devastating. Assistance with what is expected and required in order to be successful in the regular setting must be provided. A peer support system where hearing peers give guidance regarding the rules and routines required to successfully participate in the activities is an excellent way to ease a student into the inclusive setting. As is the case with all support systems, only the amount of assistance necessary for the individual to experience success should be provided.

The teacher has the major responsibility for assisting deaf and hard-of-hearing students in adjusting to the learning environment. Some techniques that will be beneficial to these students are presented in the box on p. 430.

Community-Based Activities

Physical activity and sports available in the community are important recreational outlets for persons with hearing impairment. Community recreational facilities and opportunities should be reviewed with high school students so that they can make informed decisions about what activities are available after the school years. Those activities should be included in the transitional programs and instruction provided to the students. There are also organized opportunities for high-level national and international competition among athletes who are hearing impaired. The criterion for participation in sports for deaf athletes is a hearing loss of 55 decibels or more in the better ear. In the United States the American Athletic Association for the Deaf (AAAD) has a membership of approximately 20,000 and promotes state, regional, and national events for basketball and softball tournaments and prepares athletes for the World Games for the Deaf. In 1993, 3000 athletes from 53 countries competed in 12 different sports in the Summer World Games for the Deaf in Sofia, Bulgaria.[25]

SUMMARY

Physical educators are concerned primarily with the extent to which the hearing loss affects the ability to participate in physical and sport activity. Classification of hearing loss is often based on the location of the problem within the hearing mechanism. Conductive losses interfere with the transferral of sound. Sensorineural problems result from damage to the inner ear and/or the eighth cranial nerve. Central hearing impairments occur at the brainstem or the auditory cortex.

Hearing aids and cochlear implants are used to amplify sound and enhance the communication capability of persons who are deaf or hard-of-hearing. Types of communication systems used to communicate with deaf and hard-of-hearing individuals are the oral method and the total communication method. Considerations for effective communication by teachers of the deaf during instruction are teacher-learner position, visual feedback, intensity of the commands, and special attention to the environment. Few changes are required in the physical education program. Athletic opportunities should be provided for students who are deaf or hard-of-hearing so that they have the opportunity to participate in activities that will provide enjoyment and help maintain a healthy lifestyle after their school years.

Review Questions

1. What are the different categories of deafness?
2. What are the indicators of hearing loss that can be observed by the physical education teacher while teaching a class?
3. Discuss two different methods of communicating with deaf persons.
4. What are some teaching strategies that can be used with deaf persons?
5. What competitive sport opportunities for hard-of-hearing and deaf individuals are available in your community?

Student Activities

1. Survey your community and state to locate agencies that provide services to persons who are deaf or hard-of-hearing. What types of services are available? How do these differ from services provided by the public schools? What is the address of the nearest chapter of the American Athletic Association for the Deaf?
2. List three activities in each of the following categories that could be suggested to Sharonda for inclusion in her transitional plan that would increase her opportunities to interact in the community after she graduates from school: (1) leisure time activities, (2) social activities, (3) physical fitness maintenance.
3. Simulate an interaction with a deaf person. Communicate to the person, through signs, the method of performing a physical education task.
4. Talk to a teacher of the deaf to determine the preferred method of communication. Has the teacher used more

than one method? Which method has been most effective with specific groups of deaf persons?

5. Prepare a list of points you could share with Sharonda's mother to convince her of the need and value of encouraging her daughter to participate in community activities.

6. Observe deaf and hard-of-hearing students participating in a physical education class. What teaching strategies were employed by the teacher? What adaptations were made to accommodate the children in activity? What were the behavioral characteristics of the children?

7. Simulate a hearing loss by using ear plugs. Attempt to learn a new physical activity under these conditions.

8. Research the different types of hearing aids that are available today, and write a paper describing the aids and special precautions that should be taken in the physical education class by students wearing those types of hearing aids.

References

1. Berkow R, Fletcher A, editors: *The Merck manual* of diagnosis and therapy, ed 15, Rahway, NJ, 1992, Merck.

2. Butterfield SA: Deaf children in physical education, *Palaestra* 4:28-30, 1988.

3. Butterfield SA, Ersing WF: Influence of age, sex, etiology and hearing loss on balance performance by deaf children, *Percept Mot Skills* 62:659-663, 1986.

4. Crowe T, Horak F: Motor proficiency associated with vestibular deficits in children with hearing impairments, *Phys Ther* 68:1493-1499, 1988.

5. Eichstaedt CB, Seiler P: Communicating with hearing impaired individuals in a physical education setting, *J Health Phys Educ Rec Dance*, pp 19-21, May 1978.

6. Fait HF, Dunn JM: *Special physical education*, Philadelphia, 1984, WB Saunders.

7. Gallaudet Research Institute: *Annual survey of deaf and hard-of-hearing children and youth*, Washington, DC, 1992, Center for Assessment and Demographic Studies.

8. Grimes UK, Prickett HT: Developing and enhancing a positive self-concept in deaf children, *Am Ann Deaf* 133:4, 1988.

9. Hattin H: Are deaf children usually fit? A comparison of fitness between deaf and blind children, *Adapt Phys Act Q* 3:268-275, 1986.

10. Jansma P, French R: *Special physical education*, Columbus, Ohio, 1994, Charles E Merrill Publishing.

11. Knobloch H, Pasamanick B: *Developmental diagnosis*, New York, 1974, Harper & Row.

12. Ling D: *Early total communication intervention: an introduction in early intervention for hearing-impaired children: total communication options*, San Diego, Calif, 1984, College Hill Press.

13. Luckner JL: Outdoor adventure and the hearing impaired . . . consideration for program development, *Palaestra* 4:40-43, 1988.

14. Meyen EL: *Exceptional children and youth*, Denver, 1978, Love Publishing.

15. Minter MG: Factors which may prevent full self-expression of deaf athletes in sports, *Palaestra* 5:36-38, 1989.

16. Minter M, Wolk S: Knowledge and demonstration of physical fitness among a hearing-impaired postsecondary population: preliminary implications for curriculum, *Phys Ed* 44:363-367, 1987.

17. Moores D: *Educating the deaf: psychology, principles and practices*, ed 3, Boston, 1987, Houghton Mifflin.

18. Nowell R, Marshak L: An orientation for professionals working with deaf clients. In Nowell R, Marshak L, editors: *Understanding deafness and the rehabilitation process*, Boston, 1994, Allyn & Bacon.

19. O'Rourke IJ: *ABC's of signing*, Silver Spring, Md, 1987, National Association of the Deaf.

20. Paul P, Quigley S: *Education and deafness*, New York, 1990, Longman.

21. Reagan T: Cultural considerations in the education of deaf children. In Moores DF, Meadow-Orlans KP, editors: *Education and development of aspects of deafness*, Washington, DC, 1990, Gallaudet University Press.

22. Reed WF: Kenny Walker, *Sports Illustrated* 73:10, 110, 1990.

23. Scott P: Personal communication, Certified Educator of the Deaf, Texas Woman's University, Denton, Tex, Oct 1991.

24. Siegel J, Marchetti M, Tecclin J: Age-related balance changes in hearing-impaired children, *Phys Ther* 71:183-189, 1991.

25. Stewart D, Ammons D: Awakenings: the 1993 World Games for the deaf, *Palaestra* 3:26-31, 1994.

26. Stinson M: Affective and social development. In Nowell R, Marshak L, editors: *Understanding deafness and the rehabilitation process*, Boston, 1994, Allyn & Bacon.

27. US Department of Health, Education, and Welfare: Regulations for the Education for All Handicapped Children Act of 1975, *Fed Reg* 4:42476, Aug 23, 1977.

28. Winnick JP, Short FX: *Physical fitness testing of the disabled*, Champaign, Ill, 1985, Human Kinetics.

29. Wolk S, Schildroth A: Deaf children and speech intelligibility: a national study. In Schildroth A, Karchner M: *Deaf children in America*, San Diego, Calif, 1986, College Hill Press.

Suggested Reading

Nowell R, Marshak L, editors: *Understanding deafness and the rehabilitation process*, Boston, 1994, Allyn & Bacon.

chapter **s e v e n t e e n**

Visual Impairments

Courtesy USA Blind Athletes.

Objectives

Identify and describe the types of visual impairments students may demonstrate.

List the general characteristics of children who are congenitally blind.

List five ways to modify the play environment to make it safe for students who are blind.

List eight ways to modify activities to accommodate a sightless learner.

Describe devices specially designed to enable sport participation by individuals with limited or no sight.

Describe a process for integrating individuals with and without sight into a sporting activity.

Scenario

Hosea is a 12-year-old Hispanic boy who lives in a small town in a southwestern state. He was diagnosed as blind as a result of retinopathy of prematurity (born prematurely and placed on high concentrations of oxygen during the first few months of life). He is an only child who has an identified learning disability and a mild seizure disorder that is controlled with medication. He received educational intervention by a vision specialist from the age of 6 months to 2 years. Currently he is in the fifth grade, 2 years behind his peers of the same age.

Although it is reported that Hosea did not walk until age 2 years and exhibits poor self-help and social skills, his motor skills are quite good. Even though he is totally blind, his balance and most locomotor skills are excellent; however, he has not yet developed cross-lateral integration (e.g., he has a midline problem). His

433

cardiovascular endurance, body composition, and abdominal and upper body strength are all within the average range; however, his flexibility as measured by the sit-and-reach test is below the 25th% percentile for his age group.

Task

As you read the chapter, think about ways to include Hosea in an inclusive physical education class and eventually in community recreation settings with sighted participants.

V isual disorders include both permanent and functional conditions. Children with visual disorders represent a unique challenge to the physical educator, because in addition to their visual impairments they usually demonstrate developmental lags. Many of these children have not had opportunities to physically explore the environment during their early years. As a result, intact sensorimotor systems are not stimulated adequately and motor development suffers. Low vitality and perceptual-motor development lags can prevent the children from participating in activities not contraindicated by the primary visual disorder.

Definition

There are varying degrees of blindness. Individuals at one end of the continuum have little residual vision and are unable to perceive motion and discriminate light. If a person is not totally blind, it is possible to make functional use of whatever vision remains. Some persons who are blind are capable of perceiving distance and motion but do not have enough residual vision to travel; others, although classified as legally blind, can perceive distance and motion and have enough usable residual vision to move about with a minimal amount of assistance.

Children with loss of vision are, for educational purposes, classified as blind (those who are educated through channels other than visual) or partially sighted (those who are able to be educated, with special aids, through the medium of vision, with consideration given to the useful vision they retain). Blindness is determined by visual acuity, which is expressed in a ratio with normal vision in the numerator and actual measured vision in the denominator; for example, 20/30 vision means that the eye can see at a distance of 20 feet what a normal eye can see at 30 feet. Individuals who are **legally blind** have a visual acuity of 20/200 or less in the better eye after maximum correction or have a visual field that subtends an angle of 20 degrees or less in the widest diameter.

The term **partially sighted** refers to persons who have less than 20/70 visual acuity in the better eye after correction, have a progressive eye disorder that will probably reduce vision below 20/70, or have peripheral vision that subtends an angle of less than 20 degrees.

For a child to qualify under the law for special services in physical education, the visual disability must adversely affect the child's physical education performance. Children with visual disorders who qualify for adapted/developmental physical education programs demonstrate one or both of the following:

1. A visual disability that, even with correction, adversely affects the child's educational performance; the term **visual disability** includes both partially sighted and blind children.
2. Concomitant hearing and visual impairments, the combination of which causes such severe communication and other developmental and educational problems that the child cannot be accommodated in special education programs solely for deaf or blind children.

Functional conditions not covered under the law that have an impact on motor performance efficiency are depth perception, eye-hand coordination, visual form perception, visual memory, visual-spatial development, and visual-spatial integration. Children who have any of these conditions may experience movement problems even though they are not classified as visually impaired.

Incidence

It is difficult to assess the incidence of blindness and partial vision because of the differing definitions of blindness and the problems that exist in identification. Consequently, dependable statistics on the incidence of blindness in the United States are lacking, although there is a growing awareness that a greater incidence of blindness and vision impairment exists than had been believed previously. It is estimated that 0.1% of the population can be classified as visually impaired. However, the percentage of school-age children with visual dysfunctions who are not categorized as either blind or partially sighted could be as high as 20% to 30%.

Causes

The underlying causes for visual loss are existing conditions, structural anomalies, or inefficient extraocular muscle control. Existing conditions impact the integrity of the visual impulse either in the eye, on the optic nerve, or in the visual cortex. These include diabetes, accidents and injuries, poisoning, tumors, excessive oxygen at birth, and prenatal influences such as rubella and syphilis. Structural anomalies include deviations of the eye structure. Functional causes that compromise visual efficiency are extraocular muscle imbalances caused by postural deviations, poor reading habits, and/or visual acuity problems.

Visual Conditions

Visual conditions that affect visual acuity include albinism, cataracts, glaucoma, retinitis pigmentosa, and retinopathy of prematurity. **Albinism** is a hereditary condition in which there is a lack of pigment in the eyes. Extreme light sensitivity may require the use of dark glasses. **Cataracts** cause an opacity of the normally transparent lens. **Glaucoma** creates increased pressure inside of the eye that results in visual loss and decreased peripheral vision. **Retinitis pigmentosa** is degeneration of the retina that produces gradual loss of peripheral vision. **Retinopathy of prematurity** is a visual impairment caused by excess oxygen during incubation of premature babies.

Structural Anomalies

Structural abnormalities of the eye alter the way light waves are bent (refracted) as they move into or through the eye. Visual problems that result are called refractive errors. They include hyperopia, myopia, and astigmatism. **Hyperopia,** or farsightedness, is a condition in which the light rays focus behind the retina, causing an unclear image of objects closer than 20 feet from the eye. The term implies that distant objects can be seen with less strain than near objects. **Myopia,** or nearsightedness, is a refractive error in which the rays of light focus in front of the retina when a person views an object 20 feet or more away. **Astigmatism** is a refractive error caused by an irregularity in the curvature of the cornea, so that

portions of the light rays from a given object fall behind or in front of the retina. As a result, vision may be blurry.

Inefficient Extraocular Muscle Control

Singular binocular vision involves coordinating the separate images that enter each eye into a single image in the visual cortex of the brain. When the two eyes function in unison and are coordinated, the images entering each eye are matched in the visual cortex and binocular fusion results. If, however, the supply of energy to one or more of the six extraocular muscles attached to the outside of each eyeball is out of balance, the eyes do not function in unison. When this occurs, the images from one eye deviate from those of the other eye, and the images do not match in the visual cortex. The amount of visual distress experienced because of mismatched images (**strabismus**) depends on the degree of deviation of the eyes and the ability of the central nervous system to correct the imbalance. **Amblyopia** results when the image from an eye has been suppressed by the brain for a long time because a conflict exists between the two eyes. The eye with amblyopia does not function, because the brain will not accept the deviant image. Individuals who use each eye independently of the other, suppressing first one eye and then the other, are known as **alternators.** When a person has visual suppression problems with one or both eyes, depth perception is always compromised.

The two most prevalent dysfunctions resulting from lack of extraocular muscle balance are heterotropias and heterophorias. **Heterotropias** are manifest malalignments of the eyes during which one or both eyes consistently deviate from the central axis. As a consequence, the eyes do not fixate at the same point on the object of visual attention. When the eyes turn inward, such as with crossed eyes, the condition is called **esotropia;** when one or both eyes turn outward, it is called **exotropia. Hypertropia** is the name given to the condition when one or both eyes swing upward; the term **hypotropia** is used when one or both eyes turn downward. Tropias always create depth perception difficulties.

Heterophorias are tendencies toward visual malalignments. They usually do not cause serious visual distress, because when slight variations in binocular fusion occur in the visual cortex, the central nervous system tends to correct the imbalance between the pull of the extraocular muscles. However, after prolonged use of the eyes, such as after reading for several hours, the stronger set of muscles overcomes the correction and the eyes swing out of alignment. An individual becomes aware of the malalignment when the vision of the printed page begins to blur. Phorias, like tropias, are named for the direction the eye tends to swing (*eso-* means in, toward the nose; *exo-* is a lateral drift; *hyper-* means up; and *hypo-* refers to down). Phorias create depth perception difficulties only after the correction is lost.

Nystagmus involves rapid movement of the eyes from side to side, up and down, in a rotatory motion, or a combination of these.

A number of terms and definitions of specific visual conditions, as well as clarification of the roles of specialists involved in treating a range of visual problems, are included in Table 17-1.

Characteristics

Vision loss has serious implications for the general development of motor, academic, intellectual, psychological, and social characteristics. There are widespread individual differences among persons with limited vision. However, certain characteristics appear more often than in sighted persons. Some of the characteristics that have implications for physical education are described here.

Motor Development

Limited vision restricts physical motor activity, which in turn limits the range and variety of experiences the children may encounter. Infants who are blind have little motivation to hold the head up because of lack of visual stimulation; as a result, all postural development, including trunk control, sitting, and standing, is delayed. Be-

table 17-1

Visual Impairment Conditions and Specialists

Term	Description
Alternator	Uses each eye independently of the other (e.g., one eye may be used for near-point activities, and the other for distance activities)
Amblyopia	A type of strabismus that causes the affected eye to be nonfunctional
Astigmatism	Refractive error caused by an irregularity in the curvature of the cornea of the lens; vision may be blurred
Esophoria	A tendency for an eye to deviate medially toward the nose
Esotropia	A condition in which the eye(s) turns inward (cross-eyed)
Exophoria	A tendency for an eye to deviate laterally away from the nose
Exotropia	A condition in which the eye(s) turns outward
Hyperopia	A condition in which the light rays focus behind the retina causing an unclear image of objects closer than 20 feet from the eye (farsighted)
Hyperphoria	A tendency for an eye to deviate in an upward direction
Hypertropia	A condition in which one or both eyes swing upward
Hypophoria	A tendency for an eye to deviate in a downward direction
Hypotropia	A condition in which one or both eyes swing downward
Myopia	A condition in which the light rays focus in front of the retina when a person views an object 20 feet or more away from the eye (nearsighted)
Nystagmus	Rapid movement of the eyes from side to side, up and down, in a rotatory motion, or in a combination of these motions
Ophthalmologist	Licensed physician specializing in the treatment of eye diseases and optical defects
Optometrist	A specialist in examining the eyes for optical defects and fitting glasses to correct those defects
Optician	Technician who grinds lenses and makes glasses
Orthoptic vision	The ability to use the extraocular muscles of the eyes in unison
Orthoptician	Person who provides eye exercises to refine control of the eye (e.g., visual development specialist)
Refractive vision	The process by which light rays bend as they enter or pass through the eyes
Strabismus	Any orthoptic condition interfering with the ability to use the extraocular muscles of the eyes in unison
Visual development specialist	An optometrist or ophthalmologist with specialized training in evaluating and correcting orthoptic visual problems

cause postural control precedes development of gross and fine motor development, these children are slow to walk, run, skip, reach, grasp, and develop other gross and fine motor skills.

The child with normal sight makes judgments as to where objects are in space by pairing sensory information from vision with movement information received when moving to and from objects. Because persons with severe visual impairments cannot visually compare objects at varying distances in the environment, they are unable to formulate visual judgments.

The child who is blind is often unaware of the movement potential of body parts. The lack of awareness of potential may restrict movements, which in turn retards the development of muscles and balancing mechanisms needed for the development of complex motor skills.

Studies have validated these delays. Ribadi, Rider, and Toole[14] indicate that congenitally blind individuals are less capable on static and dynamic balance tasks than are their sighted peers. Ways that delayed balance im-

pacts movement patterns are described by Gordon and Gavron.[5] They studied 28 running parameters of sighted and blind runners and found that as a group, blind runners do not have sufficient forward lean while running. They demonstrated insufficient hip, knee, and ankle extension at takeoff, which limited their power, and range of motion of the hip and the ankle was limited.

Physical Fitness

This population may demonstrate a wide range of physical fitness. Those individuals who adopt a passive lifestyle can be expected to demonstrate poor physical fitness; however, when appropriate activity programs are available, individuals who are blind can develop excellent levels of physical fitness.[11] Kleeman and Rimmer[7] tested 30 adults with visual impairments and reported that over 70% scored in the average range on cardiovascular endurance, body mass index, and flexibility. Their scores for sit-ups were slightly below average, and 23% were categorized as overweight.

Psychological and Social Adjustment

The emotional and social characteristics of persons who are visually limited vary according to the individual. Depending on early life experiences, students who are blind may have personality problems, as well as physical incapacities. Research available regarding the social maturity of children who are blind reveals that, in general, they receive significantly lower social maturity scores than do sighted children.[6]

Psychological and social adjustment of individuals with severe visual impairments depends a great deal on the extent and success of interactions with others.[9] Sighted persons acquire social habits by observing and imitating people they esteem. Individuals with severe visual impairments do not have the same opportunity to develop those skills, because they are unable to observe social interactions. Any limitation in observing and interpreting gestures of individuals as they talk results in less information about what a person is attempting to communicate. Lack of opportunity to read body language and assess the social surroundings in terms of what is appropriate may limit the social development of individuals who are blind.

Some individuals who are blind may exhibit self-stimulatory behavior, or **blindisms,** such as rocking the body or head, placing fingers or fists into the eyes, flick-

A totally blind child explores the deck before entering the water. (Courtesy Wisconsin Lions Camp, Rosholt, Wis.)

ing the fingers in front of the face, and spinning the body around repetitiously. The cause of these self-stimulatory behaviors is unknown; however, it is suspected that the individuals are attempting to access vestibular, kinesthetic, and tactile stimuli to substitute for loss of visual stimulation. Efforts to eliminate these behaviors seldom are successful for any length of time.[11]

Testing

Children with visual disabilities must be approached in accordance with their own unique educational needs. A child who has a loss of vision also may be impaired in the function of mobility and may be less able than sighted children in motor abilities. There is a great need for children with visual impairments to be provided with opportunities, through physical education, that will compensate for their movement deficiencies. All children who are blind or partially sighted should have a full evaluation as to the degree of visual loss.

Physical fitness and motor proficiency and skill tests should be administered to all students regardless of visual status. Physical fitness tests that might be used include MOBILITEE, Physical Best, and Project Unique. To determine motor proficiency, the balance and bilateral coordination portions of the Bruininks-Oseretsky Motor Proficiency Test are recommended. Motor skills can be assessed using the Test of Gross Motor Development. Regardless of what tests are used, modifications must be made to accommodate the lack of vision. Verbal instructions followed by manually moving the student through the desired pattern should be used. Also use a hitting tee or cone, rather than throwing the ball; place a ball to be kicked in front of the person's foot; and run with the individual during the cardiovascular endurance test.

Vision tests are extremely important to identify and remedy vision disorders and to facilitate the education of visually disabled persons. A widely used test of vision is the Snellen test, which is a measure of visual acuity. This test can be administered with expediency to a child by nonprofessional personnel and is applicable to young children. The Snellen chart primarily is used to detect myopia (nearsightedness). It does not give indications of far-point vision, peripheral vision, convergence ability, binocular fusion ability, or oculomotor dysfunctions. A thorough vision screening program must include tests supplementary to the Snellen test. Other vi-

sual screening tests that may provide additional information are the Keystone Telebinocular test, which measures depth perception, and the Orthoptor test, which measures acuity, phoria, central fusion, and color blindness.

Limitations in peripheral vision constitute a visual disability, particularly in some activities involving motor skills. Consequently, knowledge of this aspect of vision may assist the physical educator in determining methods of teaching and types of activities for the visually impaired child. Peripheral vision is usually assessed in terms of degrees of visual arc and is measured by the extent to which a standard visual stimulus can be seen on a black background viewed from a distance of about 39 inches when the eye is fixed on a central point.[8]

It is difficult to develop an intervention program based on results from a given test of vision, because two persons with similar vision characteristics on a screening test may display different physical, social, and psychological behaviors. Although objective screening tests of vision are important, it is suggested that daily observations be made to supplement the screening tests. Daily observation for symptoms of eye trouble has particular importance in the early primary years. Detection of visual disabilities early in development enables early intervention, which maximizes skill development. Symptoms that might indicate eye disorders and might be observed by educators are listed in the box on p. 439.

New techniques for evaluating vision and assisting individuals with visual disorders are available through low-vision clinics. Generally, people whose best corrected vision is 20/70 or less or whose visual field is restricted to 30 degrees or less are considered to have low vision and are most likely to benefit from low-vision services. This training helps persons with visual impairment to use what vision they have to the maximum extent.

Functional visual problems related to misalignment of the eyes are frequently treated using vision training. Vision therapy, or vision training, is defined as "the teaching and training process for the improvement of visual perception and/or the coordination of the two eyes for efficient and comfortable binocular vision."[16] The purpose of vision therapy is to treat functional deficiencies in order for the person to achieve optimum efficiency and comfort.[1] Although the value of this type of therapy has long been debated, when it is carried out by

Symptoms Indicative of Common Disorders of the Eye

- Eyelids that are crusted and red, and on which swelling or sties appear
- Discharge from the eyes
- Lack of coordination in directing vision of both eyes
- Frequent rubbing of the eyes
- Inattention when sustained visual activity is required or when looking at distant objects
- Body tension
- Squinting
- Forward thrust of the head
- Walking overcautiously
- Faltering or stumbling
- Running into objects not directly in the line of vision
- Failure to see objects readily visible to others
- Sensitivity to normal light levels
- Failure to visually track a moving object
- Difficulty in estimating distances
- Bloodshot eyes
- Going down steps one at a time
- Avoidance of climbing apparatus
- Holding the head close to the desk during paper-and-pencil tasks
- Turning the head and using only one eye while moving

well-trained visual behavior specialists, there is strong scientific support for its efficacy in modifying and improving oculomotor, accommodative, and binocular system disorders.[1]

Special Considerations

Differences Between Acquired and Congenital Visual Disorders

There are two basic types of visual disorders: (1) congenital, or present at birth, and (2) adventitious, or acquired after birth. The time of onset of blindness will have an impact on the development of the child. The child with congenital blindness will lack visual information on which motor responses may be built. Also, overprotection may hamper the development of the individual who is congenitally blind. Frequently, parents and teachers tend to restrict the activity of children who are blind. The overprotection complicates development because the child is not permitted to explore environments necessary for the development of motor responses. It is obvious that, depending on when blindness occurred, the child who is blinded after birth will have had some opportunities to explore the environment and receive environmental information through the visual senses for development. Previous sight experience impacts favorably on the physical and motor development of adventitiously blind persons. However, they are usually despondent over their loss of sight and need assistance in adjusting and coping. The sooner intervention counseling can begin, the better.

Mobility training

Mobility refers to the ability to move from one point to another. **Orientation** refers to the ability to relate body position to other objects in space. Obviously, these abilities are related and required for efficient movement in a variety of environments.

Mobility training is an adaptive technique that applies to blind children and children with limited vision. It enables them to learn about their physical play areas. Mobility training increases their confidence in moving with greater authority and provides greater safety while they are participating. It is a valuable way to enhance participation in the physical education program.

There are several prerequisites to efficient mobility training, including (1) sound discrimination, (2) sound location, (3) concentration, (4) memorization, (5) retention of information, and (6) physical skill. These prerequisite skills provide environmental awareness needed for travel. Deficits in these prerequisites may be a deterrent to proficient performance.

Although specific techniques are employed by professionals for mobility training, physical educators may reinforce many of the concepts that are a part of sophisticated mobility training programs. Goodman[4] suggests that routes be learned for both indoors and outdoors. Routes are organized in units and are purposely chosen courses from a starting point to a finish point for which a strategy is developed. Routes are selected according to the blind student's skills, interest, and needs. Usually routes progress in difficulty from simple, straightforward routes to more complicated ones. Activities in the physical education class that would reinforce professional mobility training programs are (1) practicing walking in straight lines while maintaining good posture, (2) locating sounds in the environment, (3) following instructions where movements have to be made that conform to instruction (memory), (4) practicing reproduction of specific walking distances with respect to time, (5) finding one's way back to starting points on different surfaces, and (6) practicing changing body positions.

Orientation and training programs should help visually impaired persons cope with physical surroundings effectively.[4] Training programs should also assist successful interaction with peers, as well as with the physical facilities and equipment. The teacher should be aware of the fact that some blind persons have **travel vision.** The individual capabilities of each child should be assessed to determine the extent of the mobility training program.

Teaching Strategies

The Teacher

The effective physical education teacher is one who respects all students regardless of their ability level, is a skilled observer of motor performance, recognizes and accommodates for individual differences, and uses teaching methods and curricula appropriate for the students they teach. These professionals establish educational environments conducive to optimum growth. They assess the needs, abilities, and limitations of all of their students and design a program to meet those needs. These are challenging tasks for all teachers; however, those who instruct students with visual impairments have an added dimension to their work. Rather than using the old standby, demonstration, as their main form of communicating a desired movement, they must be prepared to substitute a variety of other forms of sensory experiences that are meaningful to the student with a visual impairment. Adults with visual impairments who attended public school reported that their experience could have been improved if their physical educators had more knowledge about visual impairments and had provided more information about health, wellness, and the benefits of exercise.[7]

Teaching Modifications

The child who has visual limitations must depend on receiving information through sensory media other than vision. Audition is a very important sensory medium of instruction. Another sensory medium that can be used is kinesthesis. The correct feel of the movement can be communicated through manual guidance administered by an instructor or another student. Also, because the child with visual limitations has little or no understanding of spatial concepts such as location, position, direction, and distance, skin and muscular sensations that arise when the student is moved through the activity area provide the information needed to participate. The manual guidance method accompanied by verbal corrections is often effective in the correction of faulty motor skills because two senses are used for instruction. A technique that has met with some success in the integrated class is for the teacher to use the child who has a visual impairment in presenting a demonstration to the rest of the class by manually manipulating the child through the desired movements. This enables the child who is being used to demonstrate to get the tactual feel of movement, and instruction to the sighted class members is not deterred. Providing information, rules, and tests in braille for advance study of a class presentation may enable the visually limited child to better understand the presentation.

Persons with visual limitations need concrete experiences with objects and events for learning to occur. To promote participation with sighted players, Richardson and Mastro[15] suggest that audible balls be used for relay and to play such games as Steal the Bacon. With the audible ball, blind players can know where the ball is most of the time. For bowling, Stanley and Kindig[18] suggest that improvised rope guide rails can be used in conjunction with a carefully placed carpet to identify foot positions and distance traveled during instruction of a four-step approach. The carpet may replace the permanence of a guide rail and enable lesser restricted participation in bowling alleys; also, the carpet can be rolled and transported conveniently. Visually disabled individuals can participate in alpine skiing with the help of a guide who stays within 5 to 8 feet of the blind skier. The guide and the skier ski independently; however, the guide keeps an eye on both the course and on the visually impaired skier.

Both guide wires and guide runners have been shown to be effective for runners. Guide wires are ropes or heavy string stretched 36 inches above the lane markers; they help runners feel the perimeters of the lane. Figure 17-1 depicts a blind athlete using a guide wire. A

figure 17-1
This athlete uses a guide wire to participate in a 25-meter dash. (Courtesy Texas Special Olympics.)

figure 17-2
Blind runner Winford Hayes accompanied by his sighted guide. (Courtesy USA Blind Athletes.)

guide runner is a person who runs alongside the visually impaired runner and verbally describes the distance to the finish. In competition the guide runner is also permitted to touch the visually impaired runner's elbow to indicate any off-step laterally.[10] Figure 17-2 shows champion runner Winford Hayes, who is blind, running with his sighted guide.

Because of the great visual content included in the components of certain games, some skill activities are more difficult to adapt for persons with visual limitations than are others. In the case of total blindness, participation in the more complex activities may be extremely difficult to modify. However, the skills involved in a game can be taught, and lead-up games with appropriate modifications are usually within the child's grasp.

There are several adaptations that physical educators must make to effectively accommodate blind chil-

dren in the diverse activities and environments where instruction takes place. It is beyond the scope of this book to compile all these adaptations. The application of principles of accommodation may help the physical educator teach a wide variety of activities. A number of practical guidelines are presented in the box on p. 442.

Cognitive Instruction

Communication of information and testing of knowledge are part of physical education instruction. Accommodations must be made for the visually impaired during the communication of the physical education program:

1. Use large-print letters and numbers (which can be perceived by many partially sighted persons).
2. Use braille, a shorthand for tactile reading. Dots

Physical Education Principles for Working with the Visually Impaired

1. Design the instructional environment to accommodate the individual.
2. Introduce special devices, aids, and equipment to assist the individual.
3. Use special instructional techniques to accommodate the individual.
4. Introduce precautionary safety measures to meet the individual's needs.
5. Provide special feedback for tasks to facilitate learning.
6. Use sighted peers to provide individual attention and maximize participation.
7. Train the individual for mobility and understanding of the environment.
8. Allow the person with the visual impairment to decide if assistance is needed or wanted.[9]
9. Keep equipment and objects in the same place. Moving objects without telling the person with a visual impairment can be frustrating.
10. Assist with the initiation of social interactions with peers.

in a cell are raised on paper to indicate letters, numbers, punctuation, and other special signs.

3. Make better use of listening skills and position visually impaired students where they can hear instructional information best. This may be directly in front of the instructor.
4. Substitute kinesthetic (manual) guidance for vision when components of skills are to be integrated in space and time.
5. Encourage the use of residual vision during the cognitive communication process between instructor and visually impaired student.
6. Arrange seats to accommodate the range of vision.
7. Design appropriate light contrasts between figure and ground when presenting instructional materials.
8. Be alert to behavioral signs and physical symptoms of visual difficulty in all children.

Control of the Environment—Safety First

The instructional environment for individuals who are blind should be safe and familiar and possess distinguishing landmarks. As a safety precaution, play areas should be uncluttered and free from unnecessary obstructions. Children with visual impairments should be thoroughly introduced to unfamiliar areas by being walked around the play environment before they are allowed to play.

Environmental characteristics can be amplified. For instance, gymnasiums can be well lighted to assist those who possess residual vision. Boundaries for games can have various compositions, such as a base or path of dirt and concrete or grass for other areas. Brightly colored objects are easier to identify. Also, equipment may be designed and appropriately placed to prevent possible injuries. For instance, two swings on a stand are safer than three. A third swing in the center is difficult to reach without danger when the other two swings are occupied. Attention to the safety and familiarity of the environment specifically designed for the blind represents some degree of accommodation.

There are two parts to the management of safe environments. One is the structure of the environment, and the other is the teacher's control of the children as they participate in the environment. The box on p. 443 contains suggestions to ensure safe play.

The following material indicates the application of safety principles:

Principle	Safety Measure
Protection of aids	Protect all body parts; spotting in gymnastics
Protection of eyeglasses	Use a restraining strap to hold glasses in place
Safe equipment	Use sponge ball for softball, volleyball, many projectile activities
Safe environment	Check play areas for obstacles and holes in ground
Activity according to ability	Avoid activities that require children to pass each other at high speeds
Close supervision of all potentially dangerous activity	Teacher positions self close to the blind student during activity and anticipates dangerous situations and helps students avoid them

Safety Measures to Prevent Injury

1. Alter the playing surface texture (sand, dirt, asphalt); increase or decrease the grade to indicate play area boundaries.
2. Use padded walls, bushes, or other soft, safe restrainers around play areas.
3. Use brightly colored objects as boundaries to assist those with residual vision.
4. Limit the play area.
5. Limit the number of participants in the play area.
6. Play in slow motion when introducing a new game.
7. Protect the eyes.
8. Structure activities commensurate with the blind child's ability.
9. Protect visual aids such as eyeglasses.
10. Select safe equipment.
11. Structure a safe environment.
12. Instruct children to use the environment safely.

Special Instructional Methods

The application of special methods requires astute observation of the characteristics of each blind student. A list of special methods follows:

1. Give clear auditory signals with a whistle or megaphone.
2. Instruct through manual guidance.
3. Use braille to teach cognitive materials before class.
4. Encourage tactual exploration of objects to determine texture, size, and shape.
5. Address the child by name.
6. Individualize instruction and build on existing capabilities. Do not let the child exploit visual limitations to the extent of withdrawing from activity or underachieving in motor performance.
7. Use the sensory mode that is most effective for specific learners (tactile, kinesthetic, haptic, auditory).
8. Manage the instructional environment to minimize the need of vision. Use human chains where children remain in touch with one another. Participate from stationary positions. Establish reference points where all persons return for instruction.

Special Task Feedback

Children who are blind need to know the effects of their performance on physical tasks because they receive little or no visual feedback. Task feedback must come from other sensory modes. For example, buzzers or bells can be inserted inside a basketball hoop to inform the person when a basket is made. Gravel can be placed around the stake for horseshoes to indicate accuracy of the toss. Peers can also give specific verbal feedback on tasks that involve projectiles. Effective feedback is an important reinforcing property to be incorporated into physical activity for the blind.[3]

Peer Assistance

Peers without disabilities can assist children with disabilities in integrated settings. The nature of the assistance depends on the nature of the task. Peer assistance in providing feedback of task success is one example. Blind persons may choose to have sighted guides. According to Kalakian and Eichstaedt,[6] for safety in travel skills, a blind person should grasp the guide's upper arm, above the elbow, with the thumb on the outside and the fingers on the inside of the guide's arm. Both student and guide hold upper arms close to the body. When approaching doorways or objects, the guide moves the entire arm behind the back so blind students understand to walk directly behind the guide. Verbal cues inform the blind student when there are stairways and curbs. When sighted children provide such assistance, it is necessary to manage their time so as not to impede their own education.

Physical education teachers working with children who are visually disabled should attempt to minimize the stereotyped manner in which the child with visual limitations receives an education and should encourage sighted children to accept their peers on a personal basis.

The Physical Education Program
Physical Education Needs

Loss of vision, by itself, is not a limiting condition for physical exercise. A considerable amount of developmental exercises of muscular strength and endurance can be administered to such children. Through developmental exercise the child with visual limitations develops qualities such as good posture, graceful body movement, and good walking and sitting positions. Furthermore, physical education programs develop and maintain a healthy, vigorous body with physical vitality and good neuromuscular coordination. In addition to physical benefits, the physical education program contributes to social-emotional outcomes such as security and confidence and acceptance of children who are blind by their sighted peers.

The ultimate goal of the class atmosphere for children with vision losses is to provide experiences that will help them adjust to the sighted society in which they live. The selection and method of experiences in the physical education program are critical. These experiences should not be overprotective to the extent that growth is inhibited; rather, the experiences should provide challenge yet remain within the range of the children's capabilities for achieving skill objectives.

figure 17-3
A bicycle-built-for-two is a great way for a person who is blind to participate in an outdoor cardiorespiratory endurance activity. (Courtesy Wisconsin Lions Camp, Rosholt, Wis.)

Children with limited vision are capable of participating in numerous activities; however, the degree of participation possible depends on each child's particular abilities. Broad curriculum areas should be available at appropriate levels of development to accommodate each child. Children with visual impairments may represent a cross-section of any school population with regard to motor abilities, physical fitness characteristics, and social and emotional traits. The purpose of adapting methods and activities for the student with visual limitations is to provide many experiences that sighted children learn primarily through visual observation. A goal of group activity in which a child with limited vision participates is to assign a role to the child that can be carried out successfully. It is undesirable for the child to be placed in the position of a bystander. Figure 17-3 is an example of one way to enable a person who is blind to participate in a cardiorespiratory endurance activity.

Adaptation of the physical education program for individuals with visual limitations should promote their confidence to cope with their environment by increasing their physical and motor abilities. It should also produce in them a feeling of acceptance as individuals in their own right. To achieve these goals, the program should include adaptation of the general program of activities, when needed; additional or specialized activities, depending on the needs of the child; and special equipment, if needed.

Perceptual Development

Children with limited vision use other sensory abilities better as a result of increased attention to them in attempts to learn about and cope with the environment. A sighted person might be unaware of particular auditory stimuli, whereas a person who is blind might attach great significance to them.

These children need to use full kinesthetic, auditory, tactile, and space perception. Each form of perception contributes to the ability of the blind child to adapt to the environment. The kinesthetic and vestibular systems can enable a person with limited vision to maintain balance. Balance experience is acquired through participation in activities that require quick changes of direction. The kinesthetic receptors are stimulated if the tasks increase the amount of pressure applied to the joints, such as weight lifting or pushing and pulling movements.

Interrelationship of sensory systems in movement

The role of vision as it relates to movement has been the focus of much research. Visual information that assists with performing specific motor skills is integrated with information from the vestibular apparatus and kinesthetic signals resulting from reflex and voluntary movements. Organization of these sensory inputs plays a central role in successfully maintaining posture and executing movement. Sensory organization is responsible for determining the timing, direction, and amplitude of movement based on information from vision, kinesthesis, and the vestibular sense. Nashner and McCollum[13] maintain that the information necessary to control movement is provided by visual images, as well as by kinesthetic information about the specific positions of the eyes. Thus the execution of static and dynamic balance frequently requires a combination of several senses, one of which is vision. When vision is compromised, other senses must be used more fully.

Space perception

Early visual experience of spatial relations establishes a method for processing information that affects cognitive and motor learning. Persons who are blind often cannot perceive the relationship of objects to each other in space. They also have an impaired ability to relate themselves to objects in space. Therefore the auditory, vestibular, kinesthetic, and tactile senses are used to establish spatial relationships.

Physical Education Activities

A sound physical education curriculum is one that includes a wide variety of activities selected to meet the needs of the students. Obviously, student needs vary depending on their developmental level, age, and interests. Fundamental motor skills and patterns are essential prerequisites for successful and enjoyable participation in recreational sport activities, including running, jumping, throwing, and striking, all of which involve coordinated movements.

Games of low organization are an important part of elementary school physical education programs. The games that require the least modification for persons with visual impairments are those in which there is continuous contact with the participants, such as tug of war, parachute activity, end man tag, Ring Around the Rosy, Hot Potato, over-and-under relay, and wheelbarrow races.

Activities that require minimum amounts of vision for participation are (1) wrestling (the only modification is contact with an opponent at a takedown), (2) individual fitness exercises, and (3) gymnastics or tumbling. Team sports that are highly loaded with visual information require considerable accommodation. Such games include basketball, soccer, and football because the ball, as well as the offensive and defensive players, continually moves.

Variable Adaptation

Physical activities need varying amounts of adaptation for participants who are blind. Considerations for selection of activities for players who have visual impairments are as follows:

1. Activities that require a considerable amount of vision are most difficult.
2. Activities that require great amounts of movement in the environment are usually the most difficult to adapt.
3. The greater the number of visual cues required for participation, the more difficult the accommodation.
4. Environments in which there is continual change of visual cues, rather than stable visual cues, are the most difficult (e.g., team games such as basketball, football, and soccer).
5. The more modifications that have to be made in the environment, the more difficult the accommodation for the blind player.
6. The more equipment that needs to be modified, the more complex the accommodation of the motor task for the learner.

Safety Precautions

The physical educator who administers activities to children with limited vision should take special safety precautions. Some considerations that may enhance the safety factor in physical education programs for the visually limited are:

1. To secure knowledge, through medical records and observation, of the child's limitations and capabilities
2. To orient the child to facilities and equipment
3. To provide special equipment indicating direction,

such as guide lines in swimming and running events, as well as deflated softballs

Educational Settings

The physical education teacher may be requested to instruct a class in which visually limited children are integrated with the regular class, to instruct a class composed solely of visually limited children, or to instruct classes of multidisabled children.

There is a growing awareness that similarities are greater than differences when children with visual limitations are compared with sighted children. Therefore inclusion of children with visual limitation in classes with their sighted peers should take place whenever possible. Such placement emphasizes the positive aspects of the children and minimizes differences.

In the past it was not uncommon for children with limited vision to be referred to and placed in residential schools. However, with the implementation of The Education of the Handicapped Act, a countertrend has grown to bring instructional aids into resource rooms and regular classrooms of community schools. This practice has created a number of service delivery alternatives for least restrictive placement. It has been customary to provide the following cascade system for placement of children with visual disabilities:

1. Regular class
2. Regular class with assistance by vision consultant
3. Regular class with consultation and itinerant instruction (orientation and mobility training)
4. Adapted physical education conducted by specialist; children attend part time
5. Self-contained adapted physical education class
6. Residential schools for the blind

The itinerant teacher is a specialist who possesses specific skills to work with children of limited vision. This teacher teams with the regular classroom teacher on behalf of visually disabled children. For more information concerning the duties of this type of teacher, refer to the work by Moore and Peabody.[12]

Modifications, Adaptations, and Inclusion Techniques

Special Devices, Aids, and Equipment

Distance in space for the visually limited is structured by auditory cues. Therefore it is desirable to structure space with these cues. Equipment, aids, and devices that enhance participation of the blind in physical activity should provide information about the environment. Examples of auditory aids can be built into equipment as follows:

- *Audible balls* emit beeping sounds for easy location. They may be the size of a softball, soccer ball, or playground ball. The beep softball is a regular softball with a battery-operated electronic beeping sound device. This special equipment tells the blind person where the ball is at all times because of continuous sound. A goal ball is constructed with bells inside it. When the ball moves, the bells help the players locate the ball. One of the skills of the game is to roll the ball smoothly to reduce auditory information (less sound from the bells) to make it more difficult for blind players to locate it.
- *Audible goal locators* are motor-driven noisemakers. They indicate the position of backboards in basketball, targets in archery, pins in bowling, and stakes in horseshoes. Audible bases that are plastic cones 60 inches tall with a speaker and that make continuous sounds are used in the game of beep baseball. Audible locators can also be used as boundaries or to identify dangerous objects in the environment.

Activities that can be conducted to develop space perception through the use of auditory aids in the environment are as follows:

1. Walk a straight line. Measure the distance of deviations over a specific distance. Use an audible device to provide initial assistance for direction and then fade the device.
2. Face sounds made at different positions. The intensity and duration of the sound can make the task more or less difficult.
3. Reproduce pathways and specific distances just taken with a partner.

Modifications

Some modifications that can be made to enable participation of persons with visual limitations are detailed in Table 17-2.

Inclusion Techniques

The mission of physical education programs for blind persons is to enable these pupils to engage in independent recreational sport and physical activity in the community. To achieve this, it is usually necessary to move individuals from more restrictive to lesser restrictive training environments. Restrictiveness of an environment is determined by the amount of special support systems that are needed for an individual to participate or learn. Movement to lesser restrictive environments usually involves withdrawal of support systems so the indi-

table 17-2

Activity Modifications for the Visually Impaired

Activity	Modification
Aerobic dance	Include verbal description of movement with demonstration
Archery	Beeper affixed to center of target
Bicycling	Child assumes rear seat position on tandem bicycle with sighted partner in front seat
Bowling	Beeper attached above pins at end of lane
Canoeing	Child assumes bow position, with sighted partner in stern
Frisbee	Frisbee with beeper attached
Horseshoes	Beeper affixed to stake
	Path to horseshoe pit made of wood chips or sand
Running	Ropes for guidance (guide wire)
Swimming	Lane lines that designate the swimming lanes
	Swimming pool with nonslip bottom
	Pool decks with nonslip surface
	A constant sound source for orientation
	Small bells suspended near gutters, activated by waves as person approaches end of pool
Softball	Sand or wood chips for base paths
	T-stand for batting, instead of batting from pitcher
	Different texture of ground or floor when near a surface that could result in serious collision
Weight training	Equipment and weights in the same place
Class management	Environment that is ordered and consistent
	Reference points that indicate the location of the child in the play area
	Auditory cues to identify obstacles in the environment
	Tactile markings on the floor
	Boundaries of different texture

vidual gradually learns to function with greater independence. At least two considerations need to be studied for the placement of persons who are blind in integrated sport activity: (1) whether it is possible to integrate an activity and (2) the need for support systems to enable integration.

Support systems for integration of disabled individuals have been suggested by Fait and Dunn.[3] These involve (1) design of the game in which the nonsighted and sighted players play together (e.g., in beep ball the pitcher and the catcher need to be sighted), (2) the use of peer tutors for activity play, and (3) a variety of environments where support for integrated activity is gradually withdrawn so that the individual eventually can participate independently in recreational skills in the community. There are currently many educational integration models; however, in the last analysis, blind individuals must participate in the lesser restricted environment in the community. What is needed are educational models that match activities available in the community. Songster and Doherty[17] have identified a formal process for integration of disabled individuals, including blind players, into sport activity. The process involves (1) selection of the activity around which the integration process will take place, (2) development of a system of sequential supports in environments that enable greater independent functioning of the athletes among their normal peers, (3) placement of the individuals in appropriate environments commensurate with their social and physical abilities, (4) provision of needed supports to the individual, and (5) fading of the support systems of the individual through the lesser restrictive environments. It is to be emphasized that before the integration process is attempted, the sequential environments and support systems must be fully designed.

One of the purposes of physical education for students who have visual impairments is development of skills that can be used in interscholastic athletics or intramurals, or for leisure in the community after formal schooling. Therefore activity should be community based. Clearly, according to the laws, there are to be equal opportunities for participation in extracurricular activities for individuals with and without disabilities. Therefore opportunities for sports participation outside the schools should be integrally linked with the physical education program in the public schools. Such considerations for extension of extracurricular activities to the blind involve identification of activities that are available in the community.

Community-Based Activities

Adults with visual impairments who have had a positive physical education experience remain active after leaving school.[7] Activities and equipment that can be used to maintain the adult's physical and motor fitness include weight lifting, Universal gym equipment, isometric exercises, stationary running, the exercise bicycle, and the rowing machine. Instruction in proper technique and familiarity with community facilities that provide these types of equipment as part of the transition program will enhance the probability of continued participation after the school years. A growing number of sport activities are also available to persons with visual impairments. Instruction goal ball and beep baseball are two popular competitive sports for persons with visual impairments, and each can be modified to include players with sight.

Goal Ball

Goal ball is a game that originated in Germany for blind veterans of World War II to provide gross motor movement cued by auditory stimuli (a bell ball). It is now played under the rules of the International Sports Organization for the Disabled.

The purpose of the game is for each team of three persons to roll the ball across the opponent's goal, which is 8.5 m (9¼ yards) wide for men and 7.5 m (about 8 yards) wide for women. A ball is rolled toward the opponent's goal. The entire team attempts to stop the ball before it reaches the goal by throwing the body into an elongated position. The ball is warded off with any part of the body. Games are divided into two 5-minute halves with a 5-minute halftime. All players are blindfolded.

Many of the principles of accommodating persons with visual impairments have been incorporated into this game. The following are examples:

Instructional environment to accommodate the individual	The boundaries are made of rope so they can be detected by the players.
Special aids and equipment	Elbow and knee pads are provided to the players so they are not hurt when the body hits the floor or lunges to stop the ball. Bells are placed in the ball so the rolling ball can be heard en route to the goal.
Special instructional techniques	Kinesthetic movement of the body is required to instruct the players on how to lunge to block the ball.
Precautionary safety measures	Pads and mats can be placed at the end of the gym where the goals are. The sidelines should be clear of objects.
Special feedback to facilitate learning	A piece of tin or materials that make sounds can be placed at the goal so players know when a goal has been scored rather than successfully defended.
Nondisabled peers to assist instruction	Nondisabled persons can provide feedback as to whether the movements of the game have been successfully achieved.
Train the players to understand the environment	The players should be trained to know where the goal ball training area is within the gym and how to enter and leave the gymnasium.

Beep Ball

Beep ball is a game played throughout the United States that is designed to encourage blind and sighted players to compete in softball. Each team has its own sighted pitcher and catcher. The catcher sets the target where the batter normally swings the bat, and the pitcher attempts to hit the target with the ball. Equipment required to play beep ball is available through the Telephone Pioneers of America. Equipment includes a buzzing base and a ball 16 inches in circumference with a battery-operated electronic sound device inside. Specifications of the equipment and playing area are (1) a regulation bat, (2) a beep ball, (3) bases that are 48-inch, pliable plastic cones with a 36-inch bottom and a 10-inch-long cylinder of foam-rubber top, (4) bases placed 90 feet down respective lines and 5 feet off of the lines, and (5) sounding units that give off a buzzing sound when activated and that are fixed 20 feet from the bases.

Specific rules of beep ball are as follows: (1) the umpire activates one of the bases when a ball is hit; (2) the runner must identify the correct base and run to it before a play is made by the defense; (3) a run is scored if the runner reaches the base before the fielder plays the ball and the beeper is turned off (there is no running from one base to another); (4) the batter is allowed five rather than the traditional three strikes (the fifth strike must be a total miss); (5) a hit ball must travel at least 40 feet to be considered fair (otherwise, it is considered foul); and (6) games are six innings in duration with three outs per inning. There is only a first and third base, which are 90 feet apart.[1] Teams are usually coed.

USABA Activities

The U.S. Association for Blind Athletes (USABA) sponsors national championships in several sports every year. Such high-level competition is an incentive for blind persons to engage in training regimens from which there are personal and physical benefits. Persons with visual impairments who participate in competitive activities such as those sponsored by the USABA may reach both sport and personal development goals.

To provide equity in competition, classification of these competitors is based on the amount of sight. The USABA classification system of legally blind athletes is as follows:

1. *Class A:* Totally blind; possess light perception only, have no visual acuity or see less than 3 degrees in the visual field
2. *Class B:* Visual acuity no better than 20/400 or those with 3 to 10 degrees in the visual field; can see hand movement
3. *Class C:* Visual acuity 20/399 through 20/299 or those with 10+ to 20 degrees in the visual field

table 17-3

USABA Athletic Competition and Leisure Activities

Activity	Skill
Track running event	Physical fitness program
Cycling	Physical fitness and recreational program
Weight lifting	Physical fitness programs and body building
Sailing	Recreational aquatics
Crew rowing	Rowing a boat for fishing and boat safety
Competitive diving	Recreational swimming and diving
Archery	Recreational shooting at archery ranges
Swimming	Recreational swimming in community pools
Downhill and cross-country skiing	Recreational skiing in selected communities where the resources are appropriate

Several activities sponsored by USABA are related to leisure activities. Thus the competition can serve participants in two ways: for athletic competition and for participation in leisure activities in the community. Some of the activities that are a part of international competition and that can be expressed as a recreational skill in the community are listed in Table 17-3.

Other activities that are less community-based recreational activities but that provide opportunities to develop personal and social skills through participation are field events in track, wrestling, and gymnastics. Specific events in gymnastics and track and field are the floor exercise; balance beam; uneven bars; vaulting; all-around competition; 60- or 100-meter dash; and 200-, 400-, 800-, 1500-, 3000-, and 10,000-meter runs.

SUMMARY

Children with visual disorders vary in functional ability to participate in physical activity. Persons classified as partially sighted have less than 20/70 acuity, and individuals are classified as blind if their acuity is 20/200 or less. There are two basic causes of blindness: congenital blindness means that the person was born blind; adventitious blindness means the person was blinded after birth.

There are several types of functional visual problems that interfere with an individual's ability to see. Those associated with curvature of the light rays as they enter or pass through the eye are myopia, hyperopia, and astigmatism. Suppression, and tropias are associated with difficulties in depth perception. Phorias are tendencies for the eyes to misalign.

Functional visual impairments may be identified by the Snellen test or with telebiopter visual screening tests. They also may be identified by observing abnormal eye conditions, movement patterns and preferences, and visual discrimination. Low-vision clinics offer evaluations and assistance to individuals with visual disorders.

Vision loss has serious implications for motor, intellectual, psychological, and social development. Vision loss early in life may delay mastery of motor responses, which can affect other areas of development. Planned physical experiences will enhance physical and motor fitness and may counter maldevelopment in other areas.

Training programs in mobility increase the degree of independence of persons who are blind. Accompany-

ing direct instruction to develop travel vision and motor skills are techniques for adaptation. This may be accomplished by modifying activity and instructional environments and introducing special aids, devices, or equipment.

Persons with visual disorders should be trained with self-help or recreational skills that can be used in the community. This may enable participation in some of the community sports programs for the blind and visually limited.

A process that will integrate players who are blind into inclusive physical activities involves assessment of the social and physical skill level of the individual to ensure success in the activity, appropriate placement in a continuum of environments with the appropriate sighted support systems, and sequential withdrawal of support systems and movement to lesser restrictive participation environments that are commensurate with improved motor and social skills.

Review Questions

1. Compare the movement capabilities of a child with slight loss of vision with those of a child who is totally blind.
2. List the classification system for severity of blindness used by the U.S. Association for Blind Athletes.
3. List some causes for loss of vision.
4. List some general characteristics of persons with limited vision that impair physical performance of skills.
5. Discuss problems and solutions for the social adjustment of students who are blind and who are integrated into inclusive physical education settings.
6. List five ways in which the physical education environment could be modified to include a student who is visually impaired.
7. Discuss the essential components for integrating players who are blind with sighted players in physical activity.

Student Activities

1. Working in small groups, devise a plan that would eventually enable Hosea to participate independently in community recreational activities.
2. There are several ways of adapting instruction and the environment to accommodate persons like Hosea. Select eight activities and indicate how you might modify the activity, environment, or equipment to enable him to participate with his sighted peers.
3. There are organizations designed to serve parents of children who are blind. Contact a local or a national organization to learn the purpose of these groups. What in-

formation do they provide? Do they serve as advocates for parents? What should physical education teachers know about these organizations?
4. Blindfold half of the class so that they can experience the problems associated with moving without sight. Assign the other half of the class to teach a unique movement to a blindfolded partner. Afterward have the students discuss the problems, frustrations, and successes they experienced.

References

1. American Foundation for the Blind: *Creative recreation,* New York, 1988.
2. American Optometric Association: The efficacy of optometric vision therapy; special report, *Am Optom* 59:95-105, 1988.
3. Fait H, Dunn J: *Special physical education,* Philadelphia, 1984, WB Saunders.
4. Goodman W: *Mobility training for people with disabilities,* Springfield, Ill, 1989, Charles C Thomas.
5. Gordon B, Gavron SJ: A biomechanical analysis of the running pattern of blind athletes in the 100 meter dash, *Adapt Phys Act Q* 4:192-203, 1987.
6. Kalakian LH, Eichstaedt CB: *Developmental adapted physical education,* Minneapolis, 1982, Burgess Publishing.
7. Kleeman M, Rimmer JH: Relationship between fitness levels and attitudes toward physical education in a visually impaired population, *Clin Kines,* pp 29-32, summer 1994.
8. Luria A: *Higher cortical functions in man,* ed 2, New York, 1980, Basic Books.
9. Mastro JV, Canabal MY, French R: Psychological mood profiles of sighted and unsighted beep baseball players, *Res Q Exerc Sport* 59:262-264, 1988.
10. McGuffin K, French R, Mastro J: Comparison of three techniques for sprinting by visually impaired adults, *Clin Kines* 44:97-99, 1990.
11. McHugh BE: *The development of stereotypic rocking behavior among individuals who are blind: a qualitative study,* Unpublished dissertation, Denton, 1995, Texas Woman's University.
12. Moore MW, Peabody RL: *A functional description of the itinerant teacher of visually disabled children in the Commonwealth of Pennsylvania,* Pittsburgh, 1976, School of Education, University of Pittsburgh.
13. Nashner LM, McCollum G: The organization of human postural movements: a formal basis and experimental synthesis, *Behav Brain Sci* 8:135-172, 1985.
14. Ribadi H, Rider RA, Toole T: A comparison of static and dynamic balance and congenitally blind and sighted blindfolded adolescents, *Adapt Phys Act Q* 4:220-225, 1987.
15. Richardson MJ, Mastro JV: So I can't see, I can play and I can learn, *Palaestra* 3:23-32, 1987.

16. Rouse M: Management of binocular anomalies: efficiency of visual therapy, *Am J Optom Physio Optics* 64:391-392, 1987.

17. Songster T, Doherty B: The Special Olympics integration process, Washington, DC, 1990, *Special Olympics International Research Monograph.*

18. Stanley SM, Kindig EE: Improvisations for blind bowlers, *Palaestra* 2:38-39, 1986.

Suggested Readings

Buell C: *Physical education for blind children,* ed 2, Springfield, Ill, 1984, Charles C Thomas.

Dunn J, Fait H: *Special physical education,* Philadelphia, 1996, WB Saunders.

chapter **e i g h t e e n**

Other Conditions

Courtesy Dallas Independent School District.

Objectives

Explain the nature of AIDS and its impact on children.

Describe the characteristics of a person with anemia.

Describe the role of exercise in asthma.

List the signs and symptoms of physical abuse, sexual abuse, neglect, and psychological abuse.

Describe the role of exercise in the child with cystic fibrosis.

Explain the value of exercise for individuals with diabetes.

List emergency procedures for treating a diabetic attack brought on by hyperglycemia or hypoglycemia.

Explain the effect of diet and activity on dysmenorrhea.

Describe the primary characteristic of students with Prader-Willi syndrome.

List the characteristics of Tourette syndrome.

Describe the guidelines for the management of concussion in sports.

Task

As you read this chapter, identify three conditions you know little about. Develop an individual education program (IEP) for each condition based on what you learned from the chapter. Each IEP should include the type of test used to evaluate the student, the test results you would expect based on the characteristics presented in the chapter, appropriate annual goals and short-term objectives based on the test results, and suggestions for community-based leisure and recreational activities.

The federal laws that have been passed in the United States during the last 20 years virtually ensure a free and appropriate public education to every individual who has a real or perceived impairment that limits major life activities. Conditions that may qualify students for a modified physical education program that are included in this chapter are acquired immunodeficiency syndrome (AIDS), anemia, asthma, child abuse, childhood cancer, cystic fibrosis, diabetes, Prader-Willi syndrome, premenstrual syndrome and dysmenorrhea, Tourette syndrome, and traumatic head injury.

It is believed that when children with health impairments improve their motor performance, they also benefit socially and psychologically. Physical education programs that increase exercise tolerance and recreational sport skills may also improve self-care and social competence. Improved physical performance capability usually gives the student a great psychological boost. Involving students in skill and physical development activity programs often helps break a cycle of passive, debilitating physical and social lifestyles.

AIDS

Acquired immunodeficiency syndrome (AIDS) has swept a deadly path throughout the world. Although AIDS was not recognized as a disease entity until 1981, it is estimated that worldwide 40 million individuals will be infected by the virus that causes AIDS by the year 2000.[61]

Definition

AIDS is the development of opportunistic infections and/or certain secondary cancers known to be associated with human immunodeficiency virus (HIV) infection, such as Kaposi's sarcoma and non-Hodgkin's lymphoma, especially primary lymphoma of the brain.[8] AIDS is the final stage of a series of diseases caused by HIV infection. The term "HIV disease" describes all manifestations of infection before the development of AIDS.

Incidence

As of 1995, there were approximately 250,000 cases of AIDS reported in the United States, and 60% of those patients had died. Of this number, approximately 5000 were younger than 13 years.[55] AIDS is clearly one of the most serious health problems that is confronting the United States. More than 1.5 million Americans are believed to be infected with HIV, which causes AIDS. Approximately 50% of HIV-infected patients develop AIDS within 8 years of infection. Their survival rates are 50%, 30% and 15% for 1, 2, and 3 years, respectively. It is believed that unless a cure is found, all persons who develop AIDS will eventually die.[61]

Causes

Infection is caused by one of several retroviruses that cause both malignant and nonmalignant diseases.[8] Once the virus enters a person, it becomes integrated into the host's DNA and is then able to duplicate itself. The HIV is spread from one person to another via body fluids. The primary transmission fluids are blood and blood products, semen, vaginal secretion, breast milk, and amniotic fluid.[61] In this country the high-risk categories for receiving and transmitting the viruses are homosexual or bisexual males (58% of cases), intravenous drug abusers (23% of cases), prostitutes and those who frequent them, transfusion recipients and hemophiliacs (particularly those who received transfusions before 1985), and sexual contact with any of those groups. Worldwide, 75% of AIDS cases are a result of heterosexual transmission.[61] A child can get the HIV virus from the mother during pregnancy, childbirth, or breastfeeding.

Characteristics

HIV infection causes a wide range of symptoms ranging from flulike symptoms to full-blown AIDS. Symptoms of HIV infection include severe weight loss and wasting, chronic diarrhea, nonproductive cough with shortness of breath, dementia, fevers of unknown origin, chronic fatigue, and swollen lymph glands.[61] In a 1993 study of children and adolescents ages 9 to 16 years who had perinatally acquired HIV infection, 24% were reported to be asymptomatic (no symptoms), but 66% demonstrated significant HIV-related symptoms.[30]

Individuals who develop AIDS can demonstrate a number of neurologic symptoms and/or AIDS-related conditions. The most common treatable neurological illness demonstrated is **toxoplasmic encephalitis,** which results in headaches, lethargy, confusion, seizures, and ring-enhancing lesions.[8] AIDS-related conditions that frequently are the cause of death because the individual's immune system has been severely compromised include:

- **Pneumocystis carinii pneumonia,** a life-threatening form of pneumonia caused by reactivation of chronic latent infections
- **Kaposi's sarcoma,** a malignant tumor that may be present in the gastrointestinal tract, lymph nodes, brain, liver, spleen, or heart
- **Mycobacterial infections** that cause severe disease localized to the lung or lymph nodes
- Other disorders, such as cytomegalovirus, herpes simplex, disseminated toxoplasmosis, and cryptococcal meningitis (see *The Merck Manual*[8])

Special Considerations

Because of the manner in which the virus is spread, caution should be exercised if the child with AIDS becomes injured and there is blood loss. Although the risk of contracting AIDS through providing first-aid assistance is minimal, the Universal Precautions to protect against all infectious diseases should be followed. Those precautions state that staff must routinely use appropriate barrier precautions to prevent skin and mucous membrane exposure to blood and body fluids containing visible blood in the following ways[56]:

1. Whenever possible, wear disposable plastic or latex gloves. Use towels or cloth between yourself and blood or body fluids when gloves are not available.
2. Gloves must always be worn whenever you are in contact with blood, body fluids, diapering, or invasive procedures if you have an open wound or lesion.
3. Toys should be cleansed by immersing in a germicidal solution and rinsed thoroughly after use each day.
4. Cleaning up spills of body fluids requires the use of gloves. All surfaces should be cleansed with a germicide solution and rinsed, then air dried.
5. Soiled cloths and diapers should be placed in a plastic bag and given to the parent to clean at home.
6. Trash should be placed in a plastic bag and tied securely for removal.

7. All staff must use hand-washing technique between handling each child during feeding, diapers, and nose cleaning.

In recent years athletic governing bodies are becoming more aware of the risks associated with the HIV virus. Rather than ban players known to be HIV positive from competition, caution should be exercised.[49] Commonsense techniques that can prevent transmission include covering open wounds before competition and removing bleeding players from competition until wounds can be covered. In sports carrying a high risk for bleeding, such as wrestling and hockey, athletes should be encouraged to submit to voluntary testing to determine their HIV status.[61] It is not permissible to exclude individuals who are HIV positive from activities, even high-risk ones, without supporting medical justification.[49]

Teaching Strategies

Hopefully, all schools will require that HIV infection, HIV diseases, and AIDS information be included in the school curriculum; however, increasingly in this country, sex-related topics are being removed from health education content. To deny a teacher the right to share information critical to a student's health and welfare seems shortsighted and contrary to good educational practice; however, teachers must follow administration policies or risk dismissal. In schools where these topics cannot be included in the curriculum, the school administration should be encouraged to allow medical resources in the community to provide this vital information, and to solicit parental support for accessing those professionals.

A student who is HIV positive can be included in the physical education program without the teacher being aware of the condition. A physician may not disclose the status of a child's health to a third party without parental consent; however, in many states public health laws require the reporting of HIV cases to a state agency.[49] This information may, or may not, be shared with the school. If the teacher is aware of a student with an HIV condition, precaution should be taken to ensure the avoidance of injury that leads to bleeding. Most schools have developed policies to follow should such injuries occur. Ways to prevent the possibility of contamination through contact with blood should be part of those policies, and should be followed to the letter.

If the other students in the class are aware of the

presence of a student who is HIV positive *and* the school administration and the student approve, a frank discussion with the class should allay fears of the infection being spread to classmates. Students should understand the condition, as well as the necessary precautions.

As is always the case, a sensitive, knowledgeable teacher who treats all students with respect and courtesy can make a tremendous difference in the quality of interaction that occurs in a class. Teachers must set the pace for the class by always presenting themselves as accepting, caring individuals who value all students. McHugh[45] provides several suggestions of ways teachers can address student's social needs in the physical education setting. The ideas she presents could be incorporated into any physical education class but would be particularly effective in a class where one or more students were differently abled.

The Physical Education Program

Children who are HIV positive and who are in the public school should have an individual education program (IEP) commensurate with their needs. The physical education teacher should consult with the student's physician to determine activity levels. Because of the progressive nature of HIV diseases, students' levels of physical and motor performance should be assessed frequently and their program modified to accommodate their levels of function. Surburg[64] has suggested that procedures to follow when implementing physical education programs for high school students with AIDS should include providing appropriate rest periods, monitoring pulse rate, generally increasing the intensity level of exercise, and reducing activity in hot and/or humid conditions. However, for children who are rapidly deteriorating physically, it may be realistic to develop a program that will promote maintenance of existing skills and capabilities. Each child with AIDS will be different because of the many different forms of the illness; however, the ultimate goal should always be to include the student in as many activities as possible.

Modifications, Adaptations, and Inclusion Techniques

Although some lower federal courts have ordered HIV-positive youth not to participate in school-sponsored contact sports, that position conflicts with U.S. Supreme Court authority.[49] The teacher cannot arbitrarily exclude a student from an activity without supporting medical justification. Rather, if the student who is HIV positive has been identified, and his or her physician contacted for program suggestions, modifications, and limitations, the teacher should discuss the content of the student's physical education program with the student. It is critical that the student understand the potential for injury in the various activities included in the program and be given the option to participate or select an alternative. Should the student decide to engage in all the class activities, the teacher has the responsibility for keeping the potential for injury to a minimum.

Community-Based Opportunities

The Americans with Disabilities Act of 1990 prohibits unjustified discrimination against all persons with disabling conditions.[49] All members of the community should have an opportunity to select the types of leisure activities they enjoy and can afford. It should be no different for the individual who is HIV positive. In most of the larger communities in this country, support groups for individuals who are HIV positive have been formed and are available for the asking. Individuals who make up these support groups should encourage the person who is HIV positive to enjoy those activities for which he or she has the interest and strength. As is always the case, precautions should be taken should an injury that results in bleeding occur.

Anemia
Definition

Anemia is a condition of the blood in which there is a deficiency of hemoglobin, which delivers oxygen to body tissues. This deficiency of hemoglobin may be a result of the quantity contained in the red corpuscles of the blood or a reduction in the number of red corpuscles.

There are several forms of anemia. **Chlorosis,** or iron deficiency anemia, is characterized by a reduced amount of hemoglobin in the corpuscles and usually occurs in young women at about the time of puberty. Occurring less often than chlorosis, **pernicious anemia** is characterized by a decrease in the number of red corpuscles. It can cause changes in the nervous system, along with loss of sensation in the hands and feet. In **aplastic anemia,** the red bone marrow that forms blood cells is replaced by fatty marrow. This form of anemia can be caused by radiation, radioactive isotopes, and atomic fallout. Certain antibiotics also may be causative factors. One prevalent type of anemia among African-Americans is sickle cell anemia.

Sickle cell anemia, one of the most well-known forms of anemia, is an inherited disorder. Specific sites of the body that are most commonly affected by sickle cell anemia are the bones (usually the hands and feet in young children), intestines, spleen, gallbladder, brain, and lungs. Chronic ankle ulcers are a recurrent problem. Episodes of severe abdominal pain with vomiting may simulate severe abdominal disorders. Such painful crises usually are associated with back and joint pain.

Another form of anemia is referred to as **sports anemia.** It apparently afflicts athletes with low values of red blood cells or hemoglobin. These athletes may range from fit individuals performing daily submaximum exercise to individuals participating in prolonged severe exercise and strenuous endurance training. Persons who have anemia because of a disease process have different medical needs than do athletes with sports anemia who are apparently healthy. Sports anemia is a consequence of physical activity and is only marginal.[12]

Incidence

The prevalence of iron deficiency anemia for adolescent girls and adult women in the United States is 6%; the reported incidence in high school and college female athletes ranges as high as 19%. Estimates of nonanemic iron deficiency that can, if uncorrected, lead to iron deficiency anemia are 30% for adult women and 39% for adolescent girls in this country.[32] It is estimated that the sickle cell anemia trait is carried by about 8% of American blacks and over 17% of black Africans.[21] Over 100,000 babies are born each year with sickle cell disease.[8]

Causes

There are many causes of anemia that can be categorized as either congenital or acquired. The congenital form is present at birth. An example of this form is sickle cell anemia. The acquired form may occur at any time during one's life and persist or move into remission. Some of the specific causes of anemia are as follows:

- Iron deficiencies in the diet
- Inadequate or abnormal utilization of iron in the blood

- Menstrual loss (primary source of iron loss in females)
- Chronic posthemorrhaging when there is prolonged moderate blood loss, such as that caused by a peptic ulcer
- Acute posthemorrhaging caused by a massive hemorrhage such as a ruptured artery
- Decreased production of bone marrow
- Vitamin B_{12} deficiency
- Deficiency in folic acid, which is destroyed in long-term cooking
- Mechanical injury or trauma that impacts blood circulation
- Gastrointestinal loss, common in runners
- Urinary loss in the presence of urinary tract trauma
- Sweat loss when exercise is prolonged
- Disorders of red blood cell metabolism
- Defective hemoglobin synthesis[8,32,47]

Primary diseases that give rise to anemia as a secondary condition include malaria, septic infections, and cirrhosis. In addition, poisons such as lead, insecticides, intestinal parasites, and arsenobenzene may contribute to anemia. Diseases associated with endocrine and vitamin deficiencies, such as chronic dysentery and intestinal parasites, may also cause anemia.

Characteristics

The physical education teacher should be aware of the characteristics that anemic persons display. Some of the symptoms that signify anemia are an increased rate of breathing, a bluish tinge of the lips and nails (because the blood is not as red), headache, nausea, faintness, weakness, and fatigue. Severe anemia results in vertigo (dizziness), tinnitus (ringing in the ears), spots before the eyes, drowsiness, irritability, and bizarre behavior.[8]

Performance effects of iron deficiency anemia include[32]:

- Diminished $V_{O_{2max}}$
- Decreased physical work capacity
- Lowered endurance
- Increased lactic acidosis
- Increased fatigue

Testing

The student with anemia should be tested to determine the present level of physical fitness. Any standardized test may be used, as long as the teacher carefully monitors the student's performance during cardiovascular endurance activities. Motor skills can be evaluated using the TGMD for elementary children and the OSU-Sigma for middle and high school students.

Special Considerations

Anemia is symptomatic of a disturbance that in many cases can be remedied. The school nurse should be alerted if a student is suspected of being anemic. The nurse will be able to recommend specific medical intervention to enable treatment to be determined and initiated. Inasmuch as there are several varieties of anemia, the method of treatment depends on the type of anemia present. Treatment of iron deficiency anemia usually involves physician-directed iron supplementation. Physicians usually prescribe several months of iron therapy coupled with supplements of vitamin C for individuals who are nonanemic iron deficient.[32] Aplastic anemia may be corrected by transplantation of bone marrow from healthy persons and by use of the male hormone testosterone, which is known to stimulate the production of cells by the bone marrow if enough red marrow is present for the hormone to act on. Vitamin B_{12} is stored in the liver and released as required for the formation of red blood cells in the bone marrow.

There is no drug therapy for sickle cell anemia. The symptoms are treated as they appear. The initial symptoms of overexertion are headache or dizziness, leg cramps, chest pain, and/or left upper quadrant pain.[21] Continuing exercise under those conditions can lead to coma and/or death. Individuals with sickle cell anemia should avoid maximum effort exercise when unconditioned, in hot weather, or when new to a high altitude.[21] Coaches are advised that during preseason conditioning all athletes should train wisely, stay hydrated, heed environmental stress, and be alert to reactions to heat.[21]

Teaching Strategies

The alert physical educator should be able to assist in the identification of anemia and thus refer the student to medical authorities. Undiagnosed anemia may curtail motor skill and physical development and thus may set the child apart from peers in social experiences. The student who has been identified as having anemia should be evaluated to determine physical fitness and motor skill development levels so that an appropriate intervention program can be started.

The primary difficulty the student will experience is lowered stamina. Both the teacher and the student must be sensitive to the need to curtail activity levels so that the student does not overexert during the physical education class period. Indications that the student is reaching a point of fatigue include loss of body control (e.g., running into other players, stumbling and/or falling frequently), irritability, loss of temper, breathlessness, and/or an unwillingness to continue to participate. Should any of these behaviors appear, if the student does not ask to sit out, the teacher should insist on an immediate rest period. The student will be the best judge of when to return to activity. In the meantime, the teacher should offer encouragement and be supportive.

The Physical Education Program

The final decision regarding the nature of physical education activities for a student with anemia should be made by medical personnel. A well-conceived and supervised physical education program can be of great value because exercise stimulates the production of red blood cells through the increased demand for oxygen. However, to be beneficial, an activity must be planned qualitatively with regard to the specific anemic condition. It is not uncommon for children who have anemia to be delayed in the development of physical strength and endurance.

Modifications, Adaptations, and Inclusion Techniques

For the most part, students with anemia can participate in physical activities in the regular program; however, they should be closely monitored. Appropriate activities include modified (if needed) activities and prerequisite activities such as balance, eye-hand coordination, gross body coordination, and agility, as well as physical fitness components such as strength, endurance, and flexibility. Experiences that minimize access to a ready supply of oxygen, such as underwater swimming where students may be required to hold their breath for prolonged periods, should be avoided.[20]

Community-Based Opportunities

Individuals who have been provided with information about the impact of anemia on physical performance and stamina while in school will be alert to signs and symptoms that emerge after the school years. Medical advice should always be sought because most types of anemia can be treated and physical fitness levels restored. However, adults with anemia should only participate in physically demanding activities under the supervision of a physician or physical therapist.

Asthma
Definition

Asthma is a chronic lung disease characterized by airway obstruction that is reversible (but not always completely so), airway inflammation (edema or swelling in the lining of the bronchial tubes), and increased airway responsiveness to a variety of stimuli.[53]

Incidence

There are approximately 12 million persons with asthma in the United States,[9] 13% of whom are under the age of 17 years.[50] It is more common in males than in females (3:2 ratio).

Causes

The disease is a result of the body's reaction to an allergen such as animal dander, mold spores, pollens, or house dust mites, or to a nonallergenic stimulus such as cold air or exercise. The airways become obstructed because of a combination of factors, including spasm of smooth muscle in the airways, edema of mucosa in the airways, increased mucus secretion, infiltration of the cells in the airway walls, and eventual permanent damage to the lining of the airways.[8]

Characteristics

The symptoms of asthma vary widely. Some asthmatics just wheeze and have a dry cough. Others have a tight chest, wheeze and cough frequently, and have increased difficulty breathing following exposure to allergens, viral infections, and exercise.[8] An attack usually begins with an irritating cough, and the student complains of a tightness in the chest and difficulty breathing, especially during inspiration. The severity of the attack can be measured by the symptoms[8] (Table 18-1).

Exercise-induced asthma

Exercise-induced asthma (EIA) causes a muscular constriction of the bronchial tubes resulting in wheezing, shortness of breath, chest tightness, cough, and in-

table 18-1	
Levels of Severity of an Asthma Attack	
Stage	Symptoms and Signs
I: Mild	Adequate air exchange, mild shortness of breath, diffuse wheezing
II: Moderate	Respiratory distress at rest, marked wheezing, use of accessory muscles to breathe, difficulty breathing
III: Severe	Marked respiratory distress, cyanosis, unable to speak more than a few words, marked wheezing, and use of accessory muscles to breathe
IV: Respiratory failure	Severe respiratory distress, lethargy, confusion, marked use of accessory muscles to breathe

creased production of mucus during and/or after exercise. The bronchodilation may last for a few minutes or for as long as 60 minutes beyond the exercise period.[50] Also, some children may have a second reaction 3 to 4 hours after exercising, which may last as long as 9 hours. About 50% of asthmatics have a refractory period of 2 to 4 hours after ceasing to exercise. During the refractory period their airways respond to a second bout of exercise 50% better than during the initial exercise period.[62] It is estimated that 60% to 90% of all asthmatics develop EIA.[6]

Testing

The medical history of the student with asthma should always be reviewed before testing. Particular attention should be paid to whether the student has EIA, what medications are being taken, and the student's normal activity level. No modifications of test procedures are necessary unless indicated in the medical history; however, cardiovascular endurance tests should not be given when the student is experiencing any upper respiratory distress, either as a result of a cold or in response to pollen, mold, dust, or dry, cold air. The student with asthma should be monitored during testing for signs of distress and allowed to determine the need to discontinue. If a fitness test is being used to measure cardiovascular endurance, the usual warm-up should take place. The test should start slowly until the target heart rate is reached, and then continue for 5 minutes. Strength testing or training that involves lifting heavy weights while holding the breath or sustaining forced expiration should be avoided.[50]

Special Considerations

Most individuals with asthma who are under a physician's care take either oral or inhaled medication to control their condition. The use of medication before exercise will allow most individuals with asthma to perform to the level of their nonasthmatic peers. Two categories of medications are used to reverse or prevent airflow obstruction for both acute and chronic asthma: antiinflammatory agents and bronchodilators.[9] Corticosteroids (taken orally, intravenously, or as an inhalant) and nonsteroidal inhalants such as cromolyn sodium are used to control inflammation. Bronchodilators include beta$_2$-agonists and methylxanthines such as theophylline.[9] Beta$_2$-agonists are the most effective bronchodilators to prevent and reverse EIA. One or two doses just before exercise will greatly enhance the student's ability to persist with an exercise bout. Those who do not benefit from beta$_2$-agonist inhalants frequently use the nonsteroidal inhalant cromolyn sodium because it blocks postexercise bronchoconstriction that occurs several hours after exercise.[4] The usual respiratory medications are not effective in preventing or reducing ozone-induced pulmonary effects.[28]

Teaching Strategies

It is important for individuals with asthma to participate in the regular physical education class because of the physical and psychological benefits of exercise and the opportunities to socialize with classmates. Individual attention should be provided when needed to give the student the opportunity to develop sport skills to gain greater status and recognition by others.[50] As is always the case, an understanding and sensitive teacher can make the difference between an outstanding experience or a devastating one. The teacher must be aware of the student's condition, limitations, and anxieties in order to adjust the activity demands on the student and foster understanding among other students in the class. A moderate or severe asthma attack can be very frightening to the child who is having the attack, as well as to the classmates who observe it. The teacher should request permission from the parents and the child who has asthma to provide information about asthma to the entire class.

The Physical Education Program

Inasmuch as children with asthma vary in their capabilities to participate in activity that is intense, each student's physical education program should be individualized as much as possible. This is not to say the program should be watered down for these students. Clearly, many persons with asthma are world class athletes. In the 1984 Olympics, approximately 11% of the U.S. Olympians had EIA. Forty-one of these athletes won medals. Therefore assumptions should not be made about the physical capabilities of students with asthma. For the most part, students with asthma can participate in the regular program without modification; however, environmental controls, special instruction in breathing and conscious relaxation, and a carefully controlled progressive exercise program are critical for these students.

The person with asthma must be selective about when and where to exercise. Gong and Krishnareddy[27] recommend limiting outdoor exercise to early morning or in the evening to avoid peak airborne allergen levels. Also, whenever possible, exercising in cold and dry environments, as well as outside on high–ozone and/or allergen level days, should be avoided. Swimming in a heated pool and walking indoors are the least reaction-provoking activities; however, scuba diving is contraindicated for this population.[50]

All students should be taught to breathe through the nose and be given training in abdominal breathing. Breathing through the nose allows the air to warm as it enters the body and controls the rate of expiration. Conscious relaxation and abdominal breathing are recommended as part of the cooldown to reduce postexercise reactions.[50] Abdominal (deep) breathing can be accomplished by having the students lie on their back on the floor and place one or both hands on their abdomen as they proceed with the following instructions:

1. Inhale slowly and naturally through your nose deep enough to push the diaphragm down (which will cause the hands on the abdomen to rise).
2. Exhale slowly against pursed lips to keep the small airways open.
3. Pause without holding your breath and count to yourself, one thousand one, one thousand two.

During this pause, allow your exhalation to come to a natural, unforced conclusion.

4. Repeat the first three steps for several minutes.

Abdominal breathing exercises will increase the strength and endurance of the respiratory muscles and allow greater amounts of air to be inhaled and made available for exercise. Students with asthma should be cautioned that breathing in this manner may initially increase their phlegm and cause them to cough and wheeze. After extended training, those reactions will be greatly reduced.

At the elementary school level, every class should end with 3 to 4 minutes of relaxation techniques. At the middle and high school levels, relaxation sessions should be included at the end of any class using high–cardiovascular endurance activities. Training in relaxation is particularly critical for the individual with asthma because the practice can be used to lower the impact of anxiety on the body. When an individual's anxiety level is lowered, the tendency to cough and wheeze is also reduced. Several different relaxation techniques are described in Appendix A.

Progressive exercise programs are a must for the individual with compromised endurance, whether it be a result of asthma, a sedentary lifestyle, or some other reason. Regular exercise that is gradually increased in frequency and intensity will improve both respiration and circulation. Training outcomes for the student with asthma will include (1) increased physical exercise capacity at which one can exercise before lactate begins to accumulate in the blood, (2) reduced residual volume of the lungs due to less air being trapped in the lungs, (3) a more efficient pattern of respiration due to slower and deeper breathing, and (4) increased maximal attainable rate of ventilation due to less air being needed to perform submaximal work.[50] Elementary school children will benefit from a movement education program that is essentially self-paced; older students require an ongoing physical fitness program that is designed to meet their specific needs. Specific exercise guidelines are presented in the box above. See Chapter 8 for information on developing physical fitness programs.

Modifications, Adaptations, and Inclusion Techniques

Unless a physician indicates otherwise, no special modifications other than allowing the student to reduce his

---

Exercise Guidelines for Individuals with Asthma

1. Choose exercises that can be performed in a warm, humid environment, such as a pool.
2. If exercising outside in cold weather, wear a scarf or mask over the mouth to limit exposure to cold and pollutants.
3. Breathe through the nose whenever possible to warm and humidify inspired air.
4. Work out inside when pollutant or allergen levels are high outside.
5. Do 5 to 10 minutes of stretching and breathing exercises before a high-intensity workout.
6. Work out slowly for the first few minutes after warm-up.
7. Do a 10- to 20-minute cooldown after a workout

From Gong H, Krishnareddy S: *Physician Sportsmed* 23(7):35-42, 1995.

---

or her activity level and/or rest when needed are required for the student with asthma. However, until the student has developed skills and fitness levels commensurate with peers, the student's progress should be carefully monitored to ensure ease of participation and continual improvement. The student should be given responsibility for taking the appropriate dosage of medication before exercise and regulating his or her exercise pace. To keep the student's anxiety about the possibility of an asthma attack to a minimum, the teacher should ensure that the appropriate program is followed, be attentive to the status of the student, and provide needed encouragement.

Community-Based Opportunities

Adults with asthma should be given every opportunity to participate in ongoing exercise programs of their choice. Students who have been carefully taught about healthful exercise practices will continue to accrue benefits from regular exercise during their adult years. Adults who have not received appropriate instruction during their school years should seek out a health club or a university that employs a certified exercise physiologist who will provide the needed testing and exercising information.

Child Abuse and Neglect

The physical educator must be aware of the nature of child abuse and neglect and be alert for its signs and indications. Not only does the teacher have a moral imperative to report suspected child abuse and neglect, but teachers are among a large group of professionals required by law to report suspected child abuse and neglect.

The types of child abuse and mistreatment considered in this chapter include physical abuse, sexual abuse, psychological abuse, and physical neglect. In most cases it is difficult to separate the different types of abuse. It is unusual, for example, for a child to be a victim of physical abuse and not suffer from neglect and psychological abuse as well.

Definition

Child abuse and neglect is defined as physical or mental injury, sexual abuse, negligent treatment, or maltreatment of a child under 18 years of age by a person who is responsible for the child's welfare, resulting in harm to the child's health or welfare.[8] Generally, the breakdown of impulse control in the parent or guardian leads to abuse. Neglect is a result of families with poorly organized lifestyles and multiple problems, such as depression, desertion of a parent, drug abuse, and/or homelessness.

Incidence

The incidence of child abuse and neglect has escalated in this society. More than 1½ million children are abused and neglected in this country annually, with as many as 20% of those who are physically abused being permanently injured.[8] Neglect occurs 10 to 15 times more frequently than abuse.[8] These incidents occur in all social classes, but poor children suffer neglect 12 times more frequently than others. (Refer to Chapter 9 for a discussion of abuse as it relates to children with disabilities.)

Causes

In essence, child abuse (and any other form of abuse) is a function of lack of empowerment. An individual who feels helpless, hopeless, and unempowered may need to demonstrate control or mastery. That person may choose to abuse another to feel power. A child is often a victim of this need for power—since the child is unable to fight back.

In at least one large city in this country, 50% of the cases of serious child abuse or neglect were a result of parental abuse of alcohol, cocaine, or heroin.[52] Maternal drug abuse appears to be a more significant factor than paternal drug abuse in the abuse of children.[52]

Poverty and homelessness are also significant factors in child abuse and neglect.[39,52] Severe poverty and homelessness particularly contribute to the neglect of children. Growing unemployment is significantly related to increasing levels of poverty and homelessness and is a major factor in the increased incidence of abuse. Inadequate education is a factor in child abuse and neglect as well.[37,58] This is particularly true of young, teenage mothers who do not have the skills or knowledge to raise a baby or young child.

Child abuse also tends to be part of a vicious family cycle.[37,39] An individual who was abused as a child is more likely to be an abuser as an adult. Indeed, the abusive behavior is the only parental "model" the individual has had and, subsequently, the only parenting behavior the individual ever learned.

Characteristics

Physical abuse

Physical abuse is injury to a child caused by a caretaker that results in skin lesions, abrasions, traumatic injury to any part of the body, and fractures.[8] The injury may be caused by a blow to the body with a body part (hand, fist, foot) or instrument or be caused by impact, penetration, heat, a caustic, a chemical, or a drug.[14]

Indicators of possible physical child abuse include[1,37-39,44,71]:

1. Affective disturbances
   a. Lowered self-esteem
   b. Hopelessness
   c. Depression
   d. Nonresponsiveness
   e. Flat affect
2. Soft tissue damage (most common site—buttocks, hips)
   a. Soft tissue bruises, particularly multiple bruises
   b. Bruises in different stages of healing (day 1 to 2: red/blue; day 3 to 5: blue/purple; day 6 to 7: green; day 8 to 10: yellow/brown)
   c. Bruises that occur before a child can walk
   d. Bruises with shapes of objects used for abuse

(hand, knuckles [fist], belt, belt buckle, looped electrical cord, stick/whip, fly swatter, coat hanger, board or spatula, paddles, hairbrush, spoon, saucepan)

3. Burns
   a. Burns in areas child could not reach
   b. Burns shaped in patterns of objects used to inflict burn (hot plate, light bulb, curling or steam iron, cigarette lighter, immersion)
4. Head trauma from blows or shaking the child
   a. Cephalohematoma
   b. Intercranial soft tissue damage
   c. Skull fracture
5. Sternum or scapula fracture
6. Transverse or spiral fractures
7. Joint dislocation
8. Abdominal trauma

Sexual abuse

Sexual acts of adults on children include exposure, genital manipulation, sodomy, fellatio, and coitus. If the adult is biologically related to the child, the offense is termed **incest.** If the perpetrating adult is unrelated and penetration occurred, the abuse is considered **rape.**[8]

The signs of sexual abuse may include[22,37,38]:

1. Pregnancy
2. Sexually transmitted disease
3. Affective disturbances
   a. Deficit in age-appropriate social skills
   b. Fearfulness of adults
   c. Feelings of hopelessness and despair
   d. Age-inappropriate preoccupation with issues of sexuality
   e. Deficit in age-appropriate play skills
4. Physical indicators
   a. Genital, urethral, or anal injuries
   b. Genital, urethral, or anal lesions
   c. Genital, urethral, or anal discharge
   d. Soft tissue injuries on or around the mouth and breasts
   e. Rope burns about the wrists and ankles
   f. Difficulty sitting
   g. Pain and irritation during urination

Psychological abuse

Emotional manifestations of abuse are not as easily identified as are physical and sexual abuse. In general,

inadequate parental stimulation and interaction with a small child for whatever reason often delays the child's development.[8]

Psychological abuse and maltreatment can result from acts of omission (neglect) or commission (abuse),[24,25,33] including rejecting, threatening, terrorizing, teasing, isolating, and/or exploiting the child. For example, the parent who sells a child's food to buy drugs is exploiting the child. The parent who keeps a child chained in the basement is abusing the child by isolating the child. In addition, psychological abuse may include degrading and corrupting the child. For example, the parent who forces a child into prostitution is guilty of corrupting and degrading the child. Forcing the child to deny his or her emotions also may be psychologically abusive.

Claussen and Crittenden[15] have noted that psychological damage is not usually done in one isolated incident, but in repeated omissions or commissions. Long-term psychological deprivation, the absence of appropriate nurturing, can have long-term effects on the mental, social, and emotional health of the child.

Psychological abuse indicators include[15,24,25,33,37]:

1. Affective disturbances
   a. Flat affect
   b. Volatility or "acting out" behaviors
   c. Inability to maintain significant relationships or friendships
   d. Inability to participate in age-appropriate play
2. Physical indicators
   a. Failure to thrive
   b. Malnutrition

Physical neglect

Neglect includes failure to meet a child's basic physical needs (e.g., food, clothing, shelter) and health needs (e.g., adequate medical intervention, regular physical examinations, and needed inoculations against childhood disease). The increased incidence of physical neglect appears to be tied to increased unemployment, poverty, and homelessness (see Chapter 9). Caregivers who may really care about their children are often forced by their circumstances into patterns of neglect.

The indicators of physical neglect include:

1. Failure to thrive
   a. Below-average height for age
   b. Underweight for age

2. Malnutrition
3. Poor physical fitness levels
4. Low energy levels
5. Complaints of hunger
6. Inappropriate clothing for weather

Testing

No special types of testing are recommended, because child abuse cases differ. Routine physical fitness assessments may give evidence of a child who is failing to develop normally according to height and weight measurements. Observations of children at play will give evidence of those who have difficulty demonstrating age-appropriate play and personal-social interaction skills.

Special Considerations

Child abuse and neglect must be considered within the context of the child's total ecosystem. Child abuse is not usually "something" done to a child by an unknown stranger. Child abusers are most often parents, siblings, other relatives, or people entrusted with the care of the child—baby-sitters, child care workers, and youth group leaders, for example. Indeed, one of the most tragic issues surrounding child abuse and neglect is that the abuser is almost always someone the child trusts and/or someone on whom the child is dependent.

Child abuse is difficult to consider within the context of a society that endorses the notion that children are the property of the parent. The courts typically have supported the notion that the best possible place for a child to be raised is with the natural parents. The efforts of professionals involved in child protection are often thwarted by the interpretation of laws that continue to support the notion that a parent "owns" his or her child and subsequently has the right to treat the child, the "property," as he or she sees fit. Teachers who report suspected cases of child abuse are often dismayed to learn that an abused child is returned to the home, or place where the abuse occurs, after investigation. The issue of child abuse is also difficult to address in a society that endorses corporal punishment and assumes that parents have the right to spank, slap, and in other ways physically punish their children. If a woman hits another person's child on the street, that woman is prosecuted for assault and battery. If that same woman strikes her own child on the street, passersby are fearful to intervene. Corporal punishment as a technique for child rearing is

still endorsed in some states and allowed by some school districts.

Teaching Strategies

The physical educator is in a unique position to see the signs and indications of child abuse. In addition, the physical educator is more likely than other school personnel to see children or adolescents who are not fully clothed. A child with legs badly bruised from being kicked may be able to hide them in the regular classroom but may have difficulty hiding the bruises if the required dress for physical education is shorts, for example. A child in a swimming suit may find it difficult to hide vaginal or anal discharge.

If a physical educator suspects abuse, it must be reported. Most school districts have policies that outline the steps the teacher should take to report it. Referrals are usually made to child protective service agencies or the police through principals, school nurses, and/or school counselors; however, if those responsible for reporting do not do so, the teacher must take the responsibility to ensure that the child's rights are protected.

The Physical Education Program

The physical education program should be adjusted to accommodate the abused child's physical, social, and motor needs. Children who cannot keep up with their classmates because of underdevelopment, malnourishment, or behavioral problems should be placed in a setting where it is possible for them to succeed. Whenever possible, the middle and high school physical education programs should be used to help these students to develop self-responsibility. (See article by D. Hellison in the suggested readings at the end of this chapter.)

Modifications, Adaptations, and Inclusion Techniques

Because the young child who has been abused may be delayed socially, as well as physically, placement in a physical education setting with younger children might allow the child to function best. That placement should never deviate more than two grades from the child's age-appropriate placement.

Community-Based Opportunities

Too frequently, the child who is abused grows up to feel like a social outcast. While he or she is in school, every effort should be made to engage the child who has been abused in activities that are readily available in community recreation programs. If youngsters can be taught to invest their aggressive urges in sporting and leisure activities, their emotions can be expressed in a positive rather than a destructive manner.

Childhood Cancer
Definition

Cancer is a cellular malignancy whose unique characteristic is a loss of normal cell control. The body literally loses control of its cells' growth and the distribution of cells by function. Uncontrolled cell growth is common. There is also a lack of differentiation of cells. The cells tend not to assume a particular function in the body. In addition, these unique, apparently random cells have the ability to invade local, healthy tissues and metastasize (spread), destroying the healthy cells.[8]

Incidence

Childhood cancer, a devastating childhood disease, is the major cause of death by disease in children between the ages of 1 and 15 years.[73] Between 6000 and 7000 chil-

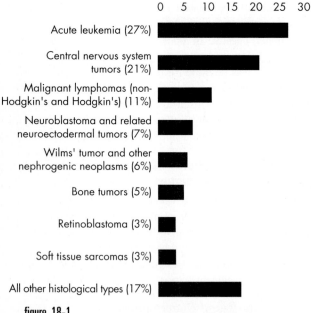

figure 18-1
Types of childhood cancers by percentages. (Data from Gurney GG et al: *Cancer* 75:2186-2195, 1995.)

dren under the age of 15 are diagnosed with cancer each year in the United States. The distribution of cancers of childhood is reported in Figure 18-1. Leukemia and lymphomas account for 38% and central nervous system tumors and tumors of the sympathetic nervous system account for 28% of all childhood cancers in children under the age of 15 years.[31]

Causes of Cancer

The onset of childhood cancer appears to be related to the relationship between the child's genetic/familial endowment and the child's environment. If the child has a chromosomal aberration, as is seen in Down syndrome, trisomy G, or Klinefelter's syndrome, for example, the child is more likely than another to develop childhood cancer. In fact, children with Down syndrome are 15 times more likely than other children to develop acute lymphoblastic leukemia.[58] Chromosomal instability is also related to the development of childhood cancers, as are inherited traits for immunodeficiency. The best example of this is the child born with AIDS; that child is highly likely to develop AIDS-related cancers.

It has been discovered that there are cellular proto-oncogenes, normal cells that have a latent capability to transform into malignant cells. In addition, there appear to be genes that suppress the tendency for a cell to become malignant. These tumor-suppressor genes are growth-regulating genes with encoding proteins that suppress the tumor formation.[17] The formation of cancerous, malignant cells in the body appears to be a function of the relationship between the two. Many malignant cells appear to be a function of a body with activated proto-oncogenes and inactive or ineffectual tumor suppressor genes.[17]

The transformation of a cell from normalcy to malignancy is thought to occur in one cell through a series of two or more steps. The development of cancer cells or malignancies is initiated by a cell that is affected by an event. This cell then becomes an "initiated" cell. If this cell is further stimulated by an event, the cell may become precancerous. Any subsequent conversion or modification of this cell causes it to become malignant. Then the malignant cell "clones" itself. It appears that most tumors are "clonal" expansions of cells that grow unchecked because of acquired changes or alterations in the genes that regularly control the growth and development of cells.[70]

Pratt[59] suggested the following environmental factors may be related to the development of childhood cancer: ultraviolet light, ionizing radiation, asbestos, viruses, and chemical agents. For example, if an infant is exposed to a large dose of radiation, one of the child's cells may become an "initiated" cell. If that cell is, subsequently, exposed to additional large doses of radiation, precancerous cell growth may be promoted. Any further modification of the cell may cause it to become malignant and then "clone" itself, metastasizing into other healthy tissues.[34] Chronic phenytoin (Dilantin) use is an example of a chemical agent that has been found to be related to lymphoma.[51]

Characteristics

The general symptoms of childhood cancer include the following[8]:

- Fatigue
- Weight loss
- Cough
- Changes in blood composition
- Changes in bowel activity
- Persistent pain
- Skeletal pain
- Fever
- Sweating

Types of Childhood Cancers

Leukemia

Leukemia is a condition in which malignant neoplasms (tumors) have a significant negative impact on the blood-forming tissues of the body.[8] The factors that predispose a child to the development of leukemia are the same as those that predispose a child to the development of other forms of childhood cancer. These include the Epstein-Barr virus, human T-cell lymphotrophic virus, exposure to ionizing radiation, genetic defects (such as Down syndrome), and familial disorders (Fanconi's anemia).[8]

Acute leukemia is the most common form of malignancy in childhood.[58] There are two major forms: acute lymphoblastic leukemia (ALL) and acute nonlymphoblastic leukemia (ANLL). ALL accounts for 75% of the 2000 cases of leukemia diagnosed each year.[58] The peak incidence is between the ages of 2 and 6 years. ALL is twice as likely to affect children of Anglo heritage than children of African heritage. Like other forms of childhood cancer, it is more common in boys than in girls.[58]

The signs and symptoms of ALL include[58]:

- Anemia
- Pallor
- Extreme fatigue
- Bleeding
- Bone and joint pain
- Enlargement of the spleen
- Enlargement of the liver
- Significantly elevated white blood cell count
- Lymph node pathology

Acute nonlymphoblastic leukemia represents less than 25% of the cases of acute leukemia.[29] The incidence of ANLL is constant from birth through 10 years, and then there is a slight peak in adolescence. Children predisposed to ANLL include those treated with alkylating agents for solid tumors, such as Hodgkin's disease, and those with genetic or chromosomal disorders, such as Fanconi's anemia or Bloom's syndrome.[34] The cancerous cells eventually dominate the bone marrow and make it impossible for the production of blood cells to occur.

Central nervous system tumors

The most common primary childhood brain tumors are medulloblastomas, astrocytomas, and brainstem gliomas.[2,17,23] These primary childhood tumors tend to remain confined to tissues within the central nervous system but are devastating in their impact on the total human being.

Most of the general signs and symptoms of brain tumors are significantly related to elevated levels of intracranial pressure caused by the presence of abnormal tissue growth. These include[8,17]:

- Headaches
- Nausea and vomiting
- Swelling and distention of the head
- Convulsive and focal seizures
- Visual disturbances
- Ataxia

Depending on the site of the tumor, the following mental/emotional indicators may be present[8]:

- Drowsiness
- Lethargy
- Obtuseness
- Personality changes

- Conduct disorders
- Impaired mental faculty, including impaired short- and long-term memory
- Psychotic symptoms

Hodgkin's disease

Hodgkin's disease in childhood is similar to Hodgkin's disease that affects adults. About 15% of those affected by Hodgkin's disease are younger than 15 years of age. It is a chronic condition in which large multinucleated reticulum cells (Reed-Sternberg cells) are present in lymph node tissue or in other nonreticular formation sites. The presence of these cells causes lesions. The primary lesions are located in the lymph nodes, spleen, and bone marrow.

The most common signs and symptoms include:

- Enlarged lymph nodes
- Enlarged spleen
- Changes in the composition of blood
- Anemia
- Fever[19]

Late effects of Hodgkin's disease include skeletal and bone growth abnormalities, sterility, and a tendency to develop subsequent malignant tumors.[59] In fact, the survivors of childhood cancers are 20 times more likely than the general population to experience a second malignant neoplasm.[59]

Neuroblastoma

A **neuroblastoma** is a common solid tumor of childhood of the embryonal neural crest of the sympathetic nervous system. One in 7000 children under the age of 5 years is affected. Approximately 75% of the cases are found in children under the age of 5 years.[8,68]

Wilms' tumor

Wilms' tumor is a form of nephroblastoma or renal embryoma. It is a very aggressive, commonly lethal tumor.[8] It is important to note that Wilms' tumor can be accounted for by heredity in 100% of the cases where tumors exist on both sides of the body.[5]

Soft tissue tumors

One of the more common forms of soft tissue tumors in children is rhabdomyosarcoma, representing approximately 65% of childhood soft tissue sarcomas.[17] This malignancy affects the muscle tissue. In fact, the malignant cells arise from progenitor cells of the striated muscles.

Bone tumors

The two best known childhood bone malignancies are Ewing's sarcoma and osteosarcoma. **Ewing's sarcoma** is the second most common form of malignant primary bone tumor of childhood.[36] It is a round cell bone tumor of childhood, the primary symptoms of which are pain and swelling, fever, and a mass. The primary bone tumor usually appears in the extremities and most commonly metastasizes to the lungs and bone marrow. **Osteosarcoma** is a form of childhood bone cancer that appears between the ages of 10 and 20 years. Pain and a noticeable mass are the usual symptoms. It is most common in the knee joint and is highly malignant.

Retinoblastoma

A **retinoblastoma** is a malignant tumor that arises from the immature retina. The disease may be inherited and has been traced to an autosomal dominant trait.[8] It has a significant negative impact on the child's vision.

Testing

The young child who is just beginning school may be developmentally delayed because of limited opportunities to run and play. An evaluation of basic locomotor and object control skills, such as the Test of Gross Motor Development, should be administered to identify the level of development. Also, if structural deviations such as functional scoliosis are suspected, a postural examination should be conducted.

No special testing modifications are required for students who have or are recovering from cancer; however, their tolerance for exercise may be considerably lower than that of their classmates. Pihkala et al.[57] report compromised cardiopulmonary status of postcancer individuals from 2 to 13 years after they received radiation and chemotherapy. The deterioration was mild in most cases; however, the authors raise the questions as to whether these individuals will become victims of premature coronary heart disease or myocardial failure before middle age.[57]

When the cardiorespiratory endurance of students who have had cancer is being evaluated, it is recommended that a test requiring minimal endurance be used.

A walk/run or a step test should be administered, and the student should be permitted to cease exercising should fatigue set in.

Special Considerations

New and innovative treatments of childhood cancer have increased the likelihood that children who are diagnosed early will have a chance of survival. The remarkable advances in medicine have made it possible for so many to survive that by the turn of the century, 1 in every 1000 young adults will be a survivor of childhood cancer. Many of these survivors return to school and attempt to restore relative normalcy to their lives. The teacher must be aware of the side effects of the cancer and its treatment and be sensitive to the psychosocial needs of the student.

The side effects of the childhood cancers and their treatments include[42,46,59]:

- Retardation of growth
- Impaired fertility
- Scoliosis or other skeletal impairments
- Impaired renal, pulmonary, hepatic, and/or cardiac function
- Neuropsychological deficits
- Psychosocial deficits, including vastly affected peer relationships

Teaching Strategies

The teacher needs to be sensitive to the physical deficits and needs of the child survivor of cancer and work in close cooperation with the child's physician, rehabilitation therapist, and parents in the development of a program that addresses the unique health needs of the student. In addition, the teacher must be aware of the significant psychosocial effects that a life-threatening illness has on the child, the parents and siblings, members of the extended family, and friends. The child who is able to return to school, able to move from the more restricted hospital/homebound education program to the less restricted public school program, will face peers with a history of markedly different experiences. It is often difficult for the child to find and make friends who are not fearful of cancer. It is frequently difficult for the child to make the difficult transition from a life-and-death situation to a life of play and games and sports. However, play, games, and sports often serve as a vital link to normalcy for the child.

The Physical Education Program

The physical education program for students recovering from cancer should be designed to meet demonstrated specific needs. If the child's physical development lags behind his or her peers, opportunities should be provided to promote development in the needed area. In elementary schools where a movement education program is in place, it is relatively easy to provide for individual differences. In more structured educational settings, care must be taken not to place the child in a game or play situation beyond his or her capabilities. These children should be assigned less active roles that will enable them to participate as they gain the needed skills and performance levels of their classmates. Highly competitive activities should be avoided so that these students are not placed in a situation where the level of play creates a potential for injury, or where their need to restrict their all-out efforts results in negative reactions from teammates. Physical fitness regimens should begin at the student's present level of performance and slowly build toward higher levels of fitness. Also, if a postural deviation is identified during testing, a corrective program should be initiated (see Appendix A).

Modifications, Adaptations, and Inclusion Techniques

When a child returns to school after an extended absence because of cancer, special efforts should be made to help the child feel as one with his or her peers. Integration into educational settings could be aided by assigning special buddies to interact with the student in various settings (e.g., lunch, physical education, art, field trips). The activity level the student is capable of maintaining is usually low because of the period of inactivity, as well as the therapeutic intervention. Regardless of the student's age, he or she must always be given the responsibility for self-regulating involvement in activity and determining when a rest period is needed.

Community-Based Opportunities

The student who has been given appropriate instruction in developing and maintaining a healthy lifestyle should continue to do so after leaving the school setting. The student who has been instructed in a variety of activities that are available in most communities will have the skills he or she needs to select from a variety of options.

Cystic Fibrosis
Definition

Cystic fibrosis is a disease of the exocrine glands primarily affecting the gastrointestinal and respiratory systems.[8] The primary organs affected are the lungs, pancreas, intestines, and sweat glands.[13]

Incidence

The disease affects 1 in every 2400 Caucasian births, and 1 in every 17,000 African-American births.[8] During the last 40 years the median life span of individuals with cystic fibrosis has improved from 4.5 to 28 years, with some living into their 30s.[8]

Causes

Cystic fibrosis is an inherited disorder that is generally fatal. It is the most common inherited life-shortening disease in America.

Characteristics

The disease is characterized by the production of abnormally thick mucus, impaired absorption of fat and protein, a high concentration of sodium and chloride in the sweat, and progressive lung damage. The more rapid the progression of lung damage, the faster the debilitation of the individual.[63]

The symptoms and severity of cystic fibrosis vary from apparently "normal" to markedly impaired health. Although in young school-age children there are often chronic problems with the lungs and with malnutrition, in about 10% of the cases the diagnosis of cystic fibrosis is not made until the student is in the late teens.[63] There is usually continuing destruction of pancreatic tissue. The proportion of children with residual pancreatic function is less than 20%.[47] Older children may also have diabetes. Thus the varied impact of the disorder on the functioning of the individual accounts for considerable variance in the physical capabilities of children with cystic fibrosis.

Testing

Each program should be tailored to the individual's physical capability. Any standard motor development or motor proficiency test can be administered to students with cystic fibrosis. However, if a cardiovascular endurance test is going to be administered to determine exercise tolerance and maximum heart rate, the student's physician must be contacted to provide pulmonary function advice and clearance. Regardless of how the cardiovascular endurance measure is made, the initial pace should be slow and the increment gradual. Heart rate should be constantly monitored. Because individuals with cystic fibrosis may have limited ventilation capacity, they may have to cease exercise before their maximum heart rate is reached.[13] If a treadmill or bicycle ergometer protocol is used, steady state can be assumed to have been reached between 4 and 5 minutes after the start of the exercise.[13] Should the individual show signs of pallor and/or breathlessness at any time, testing should be discontinued.

Special Considerations

Increased understanding about cystic fibrosis and the value of aggressive intervention programs has resulted in improved prognosis over the last 40 years. Successful intervention includes a special diet, salt supplements, control of infection, pulmonary therapy, and physical exercise.

Diet

To offset the undernourishment that results from underabsorption of fat and protein, additions to the diet and supplements are used. The recommended special diet includes an intake of calories and protein that exceeds the Recommended Dietary Allowance (RDA) by 50%, and includes a high fat intake. Twice the recommended daily allowance of multivitamins and supplemental vitamin E in water-miscible form are used to strengthen the immune system. Salt supplements during periods of exposure to high temperature and sweating reduces the chances of heat-associated illnesses.[18]

Control of infection

A high incidence of pulmonary infections requires intermediate- to long-term use of antibiotics, depending on the individual. Vitamin K supplements are recommended for individuals receiving long-term antibiotic therapy and/or those individuals with liver involvement.[8] Immunizations against whooping cough, measles, and flu are routine.

Pulmonary therapy

Progressive bronchiolar and bronchial obstruction leads to infection of the bronchi and breakdown of lung tissue. Every effort is made to clear the bronchi of thick mucus that continually accumulates. Pulmonary involvement leads to death in over 90% of individuals with cystic fibrosis. Pulmonary therapy to lessen the accumulation of mucus consists of postural drainage, percussion, vibration, and assistance with coughing on indication of pulmonary involvement. Oral and/or aerosol bronchodilators are also used to reverse airway obstruction.[8] In severe cases constant use of supplemental oxygen is necessary.

Teaching Strategies

It may be helpful for physical education teachers to understand behavior and medical treatments of individuals with cystic fibrosis. Some common behaviors and/or needs they demonstrate include:

- They need to cough out the mucus in their lungs. Therefore they should be encouraged to do so. Other students in the class need to understand that cystic fibrosis is not a communicable disease.
- The diet of the student may be different from the norm; as such, the child may need to make frequent trips to the restroom.
- Although individuals with cystic fibrosis may have less stamina than others, it is important that they participate in modified physical activity commensurate with their abilities.
- Some may be on medication for both pancreatic and lung involvement and may subsequently need to take medication during physical education class.
- Aerosol administration of bronchiodilator drugs is helpful in some cases and may need to be taken in class.
- Precautions should be taken to minimize the probability of respiratory infections.
- Teenagers frequently demonstrate a declining tolerance for exercise. Their physical education activity should be modified accordingly.

The Physical Education Program

Studies have demonstrated that individuals who have cystic fibrosis can benefit greatly from participating in regular exercise. Ongoing exercise programs have been shown to improve the flow of mucus from the lungs, build endurance of the breathing muscles,[18] and improve the clinical status, sense of well-being, overall morale, and independence.[11]

The physical education program for young children with cystic fibrosis should not differ from that of their classmates. Students at the middle and high school levels should be encouraged to participate within their own limitations. They should be discouraged from engaging in highly competitive sports where there are pressures to exercise beyond what is a safe level for the individual.[13] Their individual physical fitness program should begin with low-intensity exercise and gradually increase to a target intensity of 50% to 70% of maximum rate for 20 to 30 minutes per session.[13] Three to five times weekly is recommended unless the person has severe dysfunction, in which case days of rest must be interspersed with exercise days.[13] The types of exercise programs that have been shown to benefit the individual with cystic fibrosis include running, swimming, bicycling, and active play. Neither sky diving nor water diving is recommended for the person who has cystic fibrosis.[13]

Modifications, Adaptations, and Inclusion Techniques

To offset the boredom that can come from participating in repetitious activities involving large groups, it is recommended that individuals be given the opportunity to select from a variety of activities that interest and appeal to them. The greater the amount of selection available to the high school student, the greater their interest and compliance over time.

Community-Based Opportunities

Exercising with others should be promoted. Individuals are more inclined to exercise regularly if they have a friend or family member to share an activity they enjoy. Public and private health clubs in the community can increase interest and participation by offering special exercise opportunities in addition to their usual exercise fare.

Diabetes
Definition

Diabetes is a general term referring to a variety of disorders that are primarily divided into two groups: **diabetes mellitus** and **diabetes insipidus.**[8] Diabetes mellitus is a group of metabolic disorders resulting from insufficiency of insulin, and diabetes insipidus results from an inability to concentrate urine in the kidneys. Diabetes mellitus, which is the most common type, includes four classifications:

Type I	Insulin-dependent diabetes
Type II	Non-insulin-dependent diabetes
Type III	Gestational diabetes
Type IV	Secondary diabetes

There are two types of diabetes insipidus: pituitary and nephrogenic.

Incidence

Diabetes is reported to be the most complicated disease managed in primary care in this country.[40] About 15 million Americans are estimated to have diabetes mellitus.[43] The incidence of diabetes insipidus is much less prevalent.

Causes

Diabetes mellitus has diverse genetic, environmental, and pathogenic origins.[8] Type I, insulin-dependent diabetes, is a genetically conditioned disease that results in destruction of more than 90% of the insulin-secreting cells in the pancreas. Type II, non-insulin-dependent diabetes, is a heterogeneous group of disorders in which hyperglycemia results from impaired insulin secretion and decreased insulin effectiveness; most of these disorders have a genetic basis but do not emerge until after age 30 years. Type III, gestational carbohydrate intolerance diabetes, is a form of diabetes mellitus that is brought on by the metabolic stress of pregnancy; a genetic basis has not been validated. Type IV, secondary diabetes, results from other conditions that impact glucose tolerance.[8]

Both pituitary and nephrogenic diabetes insipidus have genetic bases. Pituitary diabetes insipidus results from damage to the pituitary and/or hypothalamus, which leads to a deficiency of the antidiuretic hormone (ADH); it can be inherited or acquired. This form may be complete or partial, permanent or temporary, and occur at any age. It is characterized by excessive thirst and excessive need to urinate. If it is not treated with the appropriate hormone or drug therapy, permanent renal damage may occur.[8] Nephrogenic diabetes insipidus is a genetic disorder that is caused by a lack of response of resorption of the renal tubules. Because fluids are not resorbed in the kidneys, urine is excreted frequently in a nonconcentrated form. The recommended treatment is adequate and ongoing water intake.[8]

Characteristics

In diabetes mellitus the body is unable to burn up its intake of carbohydrates because of a lack of production of insulin by the pancreas. The lack of insulin in the blood prevents storage of glucose in the cells of the liver. Consequently, blood sugar accumulates in the bloodstream in greater than usual amounts (hyperglycemia). Every tissue in the body that metabolizes glucose is affected by diabetes mellitus. Long-term effects include loss of elasticity of the skin, ligaments, and joint capsules, and loss of bone density.[16]

The most common complications for the vast majority of persons who have diabetes over a long period of time (e.g., 10 to 20 years) is neuropathy, peripheral vascular disease, and retinopathy.[16] Sensory and motor neuropathy diminish motor strength, balance, coordination, and proprioception. **Sensory neuropathy** results in loss of pain, light touch, and thermal sensitivity, which causes the loss of protective sensation, particularly in the feet. **Motor neuropathy** results in an inbalance between the intrinsic and extrinsic muscles, particularly those in the feet. This loss contributes to deformities of the foot, change in gait pattern, and ulceration. **Autonomic neuropathy** leads to poor vascular supply and lack of sweating of the feet. The skin becomes dry and cracks, which leads to infection. **Peripheral vascular disease** results in insufficient blood flow to all the blood vessels.[16] **Retinopathy** is the major cause of blindness of individuals who have type I or II diabetes mellitus. Visual symptoms include blurred vision, sudden loss of vision in one or both eyes, and/or black spots or flashing lights in the field of vision. Yearly retinal examinations are strongly recommended because venous dilation and small red dots on the retina are the first signs of onset. These signs can be identified only through retinal examination.[8]

Type I, insulin-dependent diabetes mellitus, which accounts for 10% to 15% of all diabetes mellitus, is characterized by hyperglycemia and must be controlled with insulin. The amount of insulin needed by these individuals varies widely. The biggest risk with this group is to take in more insulin than can be utilized, which will result in a hypoglycemic coma. Although insulin-dependent mellitus can occur at any age, it is usually acquired before age 30.[8] It is the form that is most prevalent in school-age children. The onset is acute (sudden), and early symptoms include weight loss despite normal or increased dietary intake, frequent urination, and fatigue.[8] Persons with type I diabetes may lower their need for insulin by exercising; however, they must monitor their carbohydrate intake before exercise and their blood sugar before, during, and after exercise and modify their short-acting insulin injections accordingly.[66]

Type II, non-insulin-dependent diabetes mellitus, is also characterized by hyperglycemia, but because individuals with this disease usually retain some insulin secretion capability, ongoing insulin therapy is usually not necessary. Its onset is gradual and frequently does not occur until after age 30 years; however, it can occur in children and adolescents.[8] Obesity usually accompanies type II diabetes mellitus. Like type I, common symptoms include fatigue, weakness, thirst, and frequent urination. For individuals with type II diabetes mellitus, long-term exercise can help reduce weight, lower insulin levels, improve serum lipid levels, and reduce the frequency of heart and circulation disease, as well as other complications resulting from diabetes.[66]

Type III, gestational carbohydrate intolerance diabetes mellitus, is usually not identified until a woman becomes pregnant. All pregnant women should be screened for this type of diabetes because untreated gestational carbohydrate intolerance results in increased fetal and neonatal loss. The problem occurs in 1% to 3% of all pregnancies; however, the incidence is higher in Mexican-Americans, Indians, Orientals, and Pacific Islanders.[8] Pregnant women with type III diabetes frequently must take insulin during their pregnancy; however, diet modification, moderate exercise, maintaining normal body weight, and weekly monitoring of glucose levels will also aid in controlling the condition.

Type IV, secondary diabetes, results from conditions and syndromes that impact glucose tolerance, such as cystic fibrosis, organ transplants, acromegaly, renal dialysis, and drugs and chemical agents.[8] Care of the person with type IV diabetes is tied directly to the primary condition or syndrome.

Testing

In general, no testing modifications are needed for the student with diabetes mellitus. However, because of the impact exercise has on the level of blood glucose lev-

els, the student's physician should be contacted before stressful testing, particularly cardiovascular endurance and/or resistive exercise testing. The testing demands should be discussed with the physician to ensure that the exercise stress levels are within the student's workload capacity. In addition to medical guidance, the physical educator should discuss the type of testing that will be administered with the student before the testing sessions. Every effort should be made to balance the type of testing being done so that the workload is consistent from one period to the next. Equalizing the workload demands will enable the student to determine appropriate levels of carbohydrate intake, blood glucose levels, and insulin dosage before the exercise period. Adequate amounts of water, and in some cases carbohydrates, must always be available for the student.

Special Considerations

Individuals with diabetes mellitus should be encouraged to exercise because regular, long-term exercise provides many benefits that contribute to control of the disease. However, unless strict food and insulin guidelines are followed, a single exercise bout can lead to negative reactions. Three negative exercise reactions that can occur but are avoidable are hypoglycemia, hyperglycemia, and ketoacidosis.

Hypoglycemia is the greatest concern of the individual who has type I diabetes mellitus. Signs of hypoglycemia (abnormally low blood sugar level) include double vision, fatigue, excessive hunger, an increased heart rate, nervousness, headache, numbness, palpitations, slurred speech, excessive sweating, and tremor.[66] Taunton and McCargar[65] caution that hypoglycemia can occur during exercise because of the following:

- A greater and often unpredictable amount of glucose is used during exercise.
- Insulin efficiency is enhanced with exercise, also to an unpredictable extent.
- Counterregulatory hormonal mechanisms are often somewhat impaired during exercise, which may limit glucose release from the liver.
- People often exercise to lose or control weight and are hesitant to eat extra food before exercising.

Because school-age children who are diabetic most frequently have type I diabetes, if they have a negative reaction to exercise, it will probably be in the form of hypoglycemia. Hypoglycemic reactions can occur because of an error in insulin dosage, a missed meal, unplanned exercise, or without apparent cause.[8] A hypoglycemic reaction should be suspected when a student who has type I diabetes mellitus demonstrates any or all of the following symptoms:

- Confusion
- Inappropriate behavior
- Visual disturbance
- Stupor
- Seizures

Should a student have a hypoglycemic reaction in class, the following intervention should be followed:

1. Give some form of sugar immediately (improvement should be evident within a few minutes).
2. When improvement occurs, give additional food and then have the child resume normal activities.
3. If the child does not improve after sugar intake, call parents, the physician, and emergency medical assistance.
4. If the student becomes unconscious or is unable to take the sugar, immediately call for medical assistance.

Hypoglycemic reactions can be prevented by decreasing insulin or increasing carbohydrate consumption before, during, and after exercise. There are formulas for determining how much short-acting insulin can be reduced (never change the dosage of long-acting insulin); also, alternate injection sites should be selected (e.g., inject into the abdomen or a limb not used during exercise).

Hyperglycemia (an excess amount of blood sugar) is also a problem for the active individual with either type I or type II diabetes mellitus. Hyperglycemia results when daily exercise volume is suddenly reduced without increasing insulin or any oral agents being used to control glucose levels.[65] Symptoms of hyperglycemia are:

- Increased thirst
- Increased urination

Ketoacidosis is a violent reaction to lack of circulating insulin. It is caused by failure to take an appropriate dose of insulin or by an acute infection or trauma that requires additional insulin.[8] Students who forget to take their insulin or experience an acute infection or trauma may have a ketoacidotic reaction. Symptoms include:

- Abdominal pain

- Dehydration caused by excessive urination
- Drowsiness
- Fruity-smelling breath
- Nausea
- Glucose and ketones in the urine

This condition requires immediate treatment with insulin, fluids, and electrolytes.[65] Delayed intervention can cause lethargy, which may lead to a coma.[8]

Teaching Strategies

The physical educator should be aware of students' individual needs. The school nurse can be very helpful in providing information about students who have existing medical conditions. After students with medical conditions are identified, programs of exercise should be established (with medical counsel) according to the needs of each student. The limits to the activity each diabetic child can perform vary; therefore it is important that the physical educator be clear about the status of each child.

Information should be gathered from the primary physician, the student, and the student's caregivers. Awareness of the knowledge and attitudes of the student and his or her parents concerning the benefits of physical activity, the extent to which the student is able to monitor his or her own blood sugar levels, and the student's understanding of the condition all impact the type of physical education program the teacher recommends for the student. In addition, once a program of activity is initiated, the teacher has the responsibility for carefully monitoring the student's progress.

Every year more studies validate the roles of exercise and proper diet in the management of diabetes. As this knowledge reaches primary care physicians, they are better able to counsel individuals with diabetes and their caregivers about the importance of maintaining ongoing regimens of appropriate exercise and diet. The knowledgeable physician is the conscientious physical educator's best ally. The physical educator should seek both cooperation and advice from the physician. Information gathered should include the type of diabetes, including the type of diet and therapeutic intervention, knowledge level of the student and the student's parents or caregivers, recommendations of desirable activity levels, and contraindications.

Successful management of diabetes requires that the student participate in a regimen of care. Noncompliance with health practices related to diabetes can have seri-

Required Practices of Students with Type I or Type II Diabetes Mellitus

1. Blood sugar levels should be monitored before, during, and after workouts, and the diet should be adjusted to make up for energy lost during exercise. If the blood sugar is less than 100 mg/dl, a snack should be eaten that contains at least 15 to 30 grams of carbohydrate (e.g., a slice of bread or 60 to 120 calories of fruit or crackers).
2. Always eat something 2 to 3 hours before and after exercise.
3. Prevent dehydration by drinking 2 cups of water 2 hours before exercise, 1 to 2 cups 30 minutes before, ½ a cup every 15 minutes during exercise, and enough afterward to regain any weight lost during the workout.
4. Spend 5 to 10 minutes warming up before exercising and cooling down after exercising with stretching and slow large muscle activity (e.g., walking, jogging).
5. Exercise with a buddy who knows the signs of hypoglycemia, hyperglycemia, and ketoacidosis.
6. Wear appropriate, well-fitting shoes for the activity (soft leather with few seams are best), and check feet regularly for infected blisters, scratches, or open wounds. Don't ever burst a blister.
7. Carry insulin, oral drugs, or hard candy with you.
8. Wear identification that gives your name, address, parents' home and work phone numbers, physician's name and phone number, and type of diabetes.
9. In addition, individuals with type I diabetes should:
   a. Keep a logbook to record levels of blood sugar, dosage of insulin, amount and type of food eaten, and type and intensity of exercise. That information will help the student establish the relationship among those factors and be better able to adjust for low and high levels of blood sugar.
   b. Review the effect frequent use of short-acting insulin has on blood sugar levels before, during, and after exercise.
   c. Not exercise if the blood sugar reading is less than 60 mg/dl.
   d. Time exercise to miss the peak period of administered insulin. Begin exercising no earlier than 1 hour after taking the insulin.
   e. Choose insulin administration sites away from actively exercising muscle groups.
   f. Take a high-carbohydrate snack, such as fruit juice, bread, or plain cookies, before exercise. Eat about 15 grams of carbohydrate or more if needed.
   g. For moderate bouts of exercise, reduce the dose of short-acting insulin by 10%. For vigorous bouts of exercise, reduce the dose of short-acting insulin by up to 50%.
   h. If only using intermediate-acting insulin, reduce the morning dose by 30% to 40% for moderate to vigorous exercise in the morning, midday, or early afternoon.
   i. Prevent nighttime hypoglycemia by exercising earlier in the day and by reducing insulin dosages in the evening after exercising. If hypoglycemia persists, monitor blood sugar levels at night and take additional carbohydrates before sleep.

   The teacher may want to develop a checklist with all of this information for the student. Until the routine becomes habitual, the student can refer to the checklist daily and occasionally share the results with the teacher.

Data from Taunton JE, McCargar L: *Physician Sportsmed* 23(3):55-56, 1995.

ous short- and long-term effects. In general, a student with type I or type II diabetes should have the information presented in the box above.

The Physical Education Program

Regular exercise programs are of value to all individuals with diabetes, and it is particularly important that the child with diabetes be provided proper instruction that can be used throughout life. Leon[43] has indicated

that exercise is an essential component of an effective treatment program for many diabetics. He reports that an exercise program may be helpful in the following ways:

1. It may improve diabetic control by decreasing the insulin requirements for insulin-dependent diabetics.
2. Strengthening of skeletal muscles can make a significant contribution to the control of diabetes.

3. It reduces the risk of coronary heart disease by controlling risk factors such as overweight.
4. It provides increased stamina and physical functioning to improve work capacity.
5. The benefits of exercise provide a sense of well-being and self-confidence.

The child with diabetes can and should participate, in general, in the activities of the unrestricted class. However, in many cases diabetic patients are more susceptible to fatigue than their nondiabetic peers. Therefore the physical educator should be understanding in the event that the diabetic student cannot withstand prolonged bouts of more strenuous exercise.

The intensity of aerobic activities will be determined by the present levels of performance determined through testing. Individuals who have been sedentary and have not been able to develop adequate physical fitness levels should begin slowly and progress at a rate commensurate with their capability. The student's reactions during and after exercise will dictate the intensity, duration, and frequency levels. Individuals with either type I or type II diabetes mellitus should eventually participate in aerobic activity three to five times weekly for 30 minutes at 50% to 70% of maximal oxygen uptake.[65] To sustain that percentage, a heart rate between 100 to 160 should be maintained.

Modifications, Adaptations, and Inclusion Techniques

As indicated earlier in this section, it is recommended that the student with diabetes mellitus be included in the regular physical education program, but be given the opportunity to rest when needed. To aid the teacher in monitoring student status, a buddy who has been trained to recognize the adverse reactions to exercise described previously should be assigned to exercise with the student with diabetes.

In developing an exercise program, it is desirable to provide activity that meets the student's interests and needs and still uses the large muscles of the body. Sport activity and aerobic exercise, such as walking, jogging, cycling, swimming, and cross-country skiing, are particularly desirable. Adults with type I or type II diabetes mellitus should avoid activities that would place them or others at significant risk of injury, such as scuba diving, hang gliding, parachuting, and automobile racing. Also, individuals with diabetes who develop autonomic

neuropathy (discussed earlier) may bicycle and swim but should probably avoid running and hiking. Should retinopathy develop, activities that cause sudden increases in blood pressure, such as weight lifting, sprints, and other intense exercise, should be avoided.[65]

Community-Based Opportunities

Individuals who have grown up with diabetes and have been provided an appropriate physical education should reach adulthood with all the information necessary to maintain a healthy lifestyle. They should use the public and private recreation facilities of their choice with proper precautions, including alerting supervisory personnel of their condition and wearing identification with diabetic information and the emergency procedure that should be followed if a negative reaction to exercise should occur. If they decide to participate in training regimens for participation in sports, athletes with either type I or type II diabetes should maintain a diet similar to that of nondiabetic athletes. Their diets should be 55% to 65% carbohydrate, 10% to 15% protein, and 25% to 30% fat. Energy and water requirements of these athletes are greater than those of nonaffected athletes.[66]

Prader-Willi Syndrome
Definition

Prader-Willi syndrome is a neonatal hypotonia and feeding difficulty that is followed by excessive appetite, pica behavior (eating indiscriminately—dirt, crayons, paste, paper, etc.), and obesity starting in early childhood.

Incidence

The incidence of the condition is reported to be 1 in every 10,000 live births.[35]

Causes

The cause of Prader-Willi syndrome is a deletion of portions of, or absence of, the paternally contributed chromosome 15.[67]

Characteristics

Children and adults are short and have small hands and feet, almond-shaped eyes, a triangular-shaped mouth, a prominent nasal bridge, and underdeveloped gonads. As a group, individuals with Prader-Willi syndrome are very heterogeneous, with IQs ranging from less than 20 to 100. Individuals with intelligence in the normal range frequently have learning disabilities but do demonstrate strong visual-spatial perception.[69]

Testing

A self-testing program in which the learner is actively involved in the evaluation process is best for the student with Prader-Willi syndrome. As with any obese learner, he or she will experience considerable failure and embarrassment if asked to participate, for example, in mass fitness testing. A time should be selected when the teacher can work one-on-one with the student, or the student's movements should be observed during routine class activities.

Special Considerations

The physical educator or adapted physical educator must work closely with the learner's parents. In addition to the physical education program at school, it is vital that the parents engage the child in regular exercise in the home. The physical educator can help the parents develop a home walking program, for example, that includes all family members. In addition to ongoing communication with the parents, it is vital that the school nurse be involved in the development of the IEP and be an active participant in the IEP meeting. The school nurse should schedule regular "check-ups" in which the learner's height/weight, heart rate, and blood pressure are monitored.

Teaching Strategies

Developing strategies for externally motivating the student with Prader-Willi syndrome is a vital and integral part of teaching. As is typical of most obese children, the student with Prader-Willi syndrome tends to fall into a vicious cycle in which he or she avoids activity because of a history of failure—tends to gain more weight and fatty tissue—which makes movement yet more difficult and increases the likelihood of failure—and avoids activity all the more. To provide motivation so that the child with Prader-Willi syndrome will persist, the use of a reward/encouragement system is usually critical. Rewards that may be particularly helpful in reinforcing interest in play, games, and leisure, recreation, and sport activities include:

- Baseball cards

- Five minutes to "shoot hoops" one-on-one with the teacher before or after school
- Passes to sporting events

It should be noted that when behavior modification programs are used to motivate students with Prader-Willi syndrome, food should never be used as a reinforcer.

The Physical Education Program

Because of the characteristic obesity, precautions must be taken to avoid overtaxing the cardiovascular system. It is crucial that these individuals participate in calorie-burning activities—activities that will elevate the body's metabolism. These individuals should participate in activities commensurate with their abilities; however, heart rate and blood pressure should be routinely monitored. In addition, it is vital that these individuals learn the skills necessary to participate in leisure and recreation activities. This is a better alternative than sedentary activities, which tend to be the choice of obese individuals.

A program with a wide range of activities, particularly individual leisure and recreation activities in which the learner has some choice in selection, is useful for the learner with Prader-Willi syndrome. Having the opportunity to select Frisbee golf, rather than vaulting in a gymnastics unit, will free the learner to develop a sense of competency in activity. In programs in which such choices are limited by necessity because of staff and facility limitations, a station approach to intervention may be helpful. For example, in a physical fitness unit, the learner may be given the opportunity to move to a station in which he or she plays catch with a medicine ball rather than trying to climb a suspended rope. Once again, if the learner is given a choice, he or she may experience success—and then be more likely to seek, rather than avoid, movement.

Modifications, Adaptations, and Inclusion Techniques

Children and young adults with Prader-Willi syndrome are discriminated against more because of their obesity than because of their potentially limited intelligence. Under no circumstances should a learner with Prader-Willi syndrome be required to use a group shower; this is particularly crucial for an adolescent because embarrassment about the reduced size of genitalia may be devastating at this vulnerable developmental stage. In addition, if aquatics are part of the curriculum, the learner and the parents should discuss participation, and the learner should be given the opportunity to choose not to participate. If the learner chooses to participate, an individual dressing area is crucial, and the learner should be allowed to wear a T-shirt over his or her swimming suit.

A buddy system may be particularly helpful for the learner with Prader-Willi syndrome. The teacher must enlist the help of a caring and nurturing peer who will be a "buddy" to the learner during class and who will interact with the learner at lunch, during recess, and before/after school.

Community-Based Opportunities

The learner with Prader-Willi syndrome may experience success in a number of leisure and recreation activities. These community-based opportunities include, but are not limited to:

- Bowling
- Frisbee and Frisbee golf
- Miniature golf
- Archery
- Riflery
- Camping
- Walking/hiking

It is important for the physical educator or adapted physical educator to discuss neighborhood leisure and recreation choices with the student and his or her family to identify common interests. The student with Prader-Willi syndrome, for example, may experience great success in bowling, but if no one in the family and/or neighborhood bowls, it is unlikely the learner will use the skills within the community. Selecting activities that some or all of the family enjoy will increase the likelihood that the student will pursue opportunities to participate in the activity after the school years.

Premenstrual Syndrome and Dysmenorrhea

Menstruation is a complex process that involves the endocrine glands, uterus, and ovaries. The average menstrual cycle lasts for 28 days. However, each girl or woman has her own rhythmic cycle of menstrual function. The cycle periods usually range from 21 to 35 days, but they occasionally may be longer or shorter and still fall within the range of normal.

The average total amount of blood lost during the normal menstrual period is 3 ounces; however, from 1½ to 5 ounces may be lost. This blood is replaced by the active formation of blood cells in bone marrow and consequently does not cause anemia. On occasion, some girls or women may have excessive menstrual flow, and in this event a physician should be consulted. The average menstrual period lasts 3 to 5 days, but 2 to 7 days may be considered normal. The average age of onset of menstruation is 12.5 years, although the range of onset may be from 9 to 18 years. **Premenstrual syndrome (PMS)** and/or **dysmenorrhea** may be associated with the menstrual cycle.

Definitions

PMS is a condition that occurs during the 7 to 10 days before menstruation and usually disappears a few hours after the onset of menstrual flow; however, it may persist throughout the menses.[8] Dysmenorrhea is cyclic pain that usually starts just before or with menses, peaks in 24 hours, and subsides after 2 days.[8]

Incidence

Significant functional dysmenorrhea is more common in the teenage years and tends to diminish with maturity, whereas PMS frequently begins in the 20s and increases with age.[8]

Causes

PMS seems to be related to estrogen and progesterone imbalances; however, carbohydrate metabolism changes, retention of sodium and water by the kidneys, and psychogenic factors have also been implicated. Most dysmenorrhea is functional, meaning it results from passage of tissue through the cervix, malposition of the uterus, lack of exercise, or anxiety. However, approximately 30% of the cases are acquired as a result of organic causes such as ovarian cysts, endocrine imbalance, or infections.[8]

Characteristics

PMS is characterized by nervousness, irritability, emotional instability, depression, and possibly headaches and edema. Dysmenorrhea is low abdominal pain that may be crampy or a dull constant ache that frequently radiates to the lower back and down the legs. Headache, nausea, constipation or diarrhea, and urinary frequency may accompany both conditions.[8]

Testing

These two conditions have a significant impact on a teenager's attitude. It is difficult to concentrate and put forth one's best effort when one is not feeling well. Thus when motor or fitness testing is being conducted, it is recommended that the teenager who is experiencing PMS or dysmenorrhea be given the option of being tested during the scheduled time or delaying until she feels better.

Special Considerations

Many girls and women are unaware of the effects dietary habits can have on their degree of comfort before and during their menstrual flow. During this age of fast foods saturated with salt, the modern girl or woman needs to understand how her diet choices can influence her comfort during the menstrual cycle. With such knowledge, it is possible to reduce the painful discomfort of functional dysmenorrhea. Reduction of pain is directly associated with the amount of salt stored in the body.

Approximately 1 week before the onset of the menstrual period, the body begins storing sodium chloride. When this storing process begins, the girl or woman craves salt. If she yields to the craving for salt at that time in her cycle, a whole series of events occur that result in abdominal bloating, which increases the pain associated with the first 2 days of the menstrual flow.

What occurs is that when salt intake is increased, the salt tends to move into and be held by the body tissues. The salt stored in the body tissues draws water toward those tissues, thereby upsetting the osmotic balance in the body. Much of the water that is drawn into the tissues is pulled from fecal matter moving through the large intestine. When large amounts of water are removed from the fecal mass, the mass begins to harden and its progress is slowed. Thus the net result of increasing salt intake 1 week before the onset of the menstrual period is bloating from stored water and accumulating fecal material. This increased congestion presses against nerves in the abdominal and lower back area and causes pain.

The entire chain of events can be avoided (or markedly reduced) if, 1 week before the onset of her menstrual flow, the girl or woman decreases (or at least does not increase) salt intake and, at the same time, increases water and roughage (raw celery, carrots, apples) intake.

By following these simple guidelines, she can preserve the osmotic balance of water in the body, and softness and progression of the fecal mass through the large intestine can be maintained. Regular movement of the fecal mass results in reduction of the amount of bloating associated with the menstrual period. Reduced bloating and faithful adherence to the exercises described later in this chapter will relieve most of the pain associated with menstruation.

Teaching Strategies

The sensitive teacher will recognize the signs of PMS and/or dysmenorrhea. When normally high-spirited or easy-going teenage girls become irritable and moody, the menstrual cycle is frequently at fault. Encouraging the student to dress out, but allowing her to sit and observe the class if she chooses to do so, is recommended. Requiring that the student dress for class sends the message that the girl is experiencing a condition, not a sickness. Giving permission to sit out implies that the person experiencing the discomfort is in the best position to determine whether or not she should participate. In these cases, when the person who is not participating observes her classmates enjoying class activities, it is not uncommon for her to choose to join in some parts of the activity.

The Physical Education Program

There have been questions raised about the desirability of young women participating in physical education and exercise during the menstrual period. There is a perception among some that exercise during a period of discomfort is undesirable and that young women during this period should be excused from physical education classes. Young women have varying experiences as they pass through the menstrual cycle. Thus judgments about physical exercise during menstruation should be made on an individual basis. However, there is evidence that there are benefits from physical exercise as it relates to physical fitness and postural efficiency in lessening the pain associated with menstruation.

The consensus among physicians and gynecologists is that restriction from participation in vigorous physical activity, intensive sports competition, and swimming during all phases of the menstrual period is unwarranted for those who are free of menstrual disturbances. However, with regard to the first half of the menstrual period, some physicians advise moderation with limited participation in intensive sports competition. The reason for moderation during the first half of the menstrual period is that the flow is heavier during the first 2 or 3 days and some girls and women experience cramps during this time.

Modifications, Adaptations, and Inclusion Techniques

Regular exercise has been shown to relieve the symptoms of PMS and functional dysmenorrhea. Exercise reduces stress and provides relief of congestion in the abdominal cavity caused by gravity, poor posture, poor circulation, and/or poor abdominal muscle tone. Physical activity also helps relieve leg and back pain by stretching lumbar and pelvic ligaments in the fascia to minimize pressure on spinal nerves. Undue muscular tension also may have a bearing on painful menstruation; therefore relaxation techniques and positioning of the body, accompanied by heat from a heating pad on the lower back area, may relax tensions and consequently lessen the pain. Other relaxation techniques and exercises also may be used to reduce tension in the body (see Appendix B).

Girls and women who suffer from dysmenorrhea may benefit from a daily exercise program designed to alleviate this condition. The exercises should provide for improvement of posture (especially lordosis), stimulation of circulation, and stretching of tight fascia and ligaments. The exercises discussed here are suggested to alleviate the symptoms of dysmenorrhea.

Fascial stretch

The purpose of fascial exercise is to stretch the shortened fascial ligamentous bands that extend between the lower back and the anterior aspect of the pelvis and legs. These shortened bands may result in increased pelvic tilt, which may irritate peripheral nerves passing through or near the fascia. The irritation of these nerves may be the cause of the pain. This exercise produces a stretching effect on the hip flexors and increases mobility of the hip joint (Figure 18-2). To perform the exercise, the girl or woman should stand erect, with the left side of her body about the distance of the bent elbow from a wall; the feet should be together, with the left forearm and palm against the wall, the elbow at shoulder height, and the heel of the other hand placed against

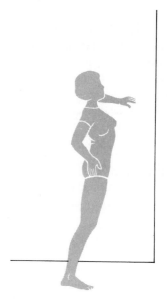

figure 18-2
Fascial stretch.

the posterior aspect of the hollow portion of the right hip. From this position, abdominal and gluteal muscles should be contracted strongly to tilt the pelvis backward. The hips should slowly be pushed forward and diagonally toward the wall, and pressure should be applied with the right hand. This position should be held for a few counts; then a slow return should be made to the starting position. The stretch should be performed three times on each side of the body. The exercise should be continued even after relief has been obtained from dysmenorrhea. It has been suggested that the exercise be performed three times daily. To increase motivation, the girl or woman should record the number of days and times she performs the exercise.

Abdominal pumping

The purpose of abdominal pumping is to increase circulation of the blood throughout the pelvic region. The exercise is performed by assuming a hook-lying position, placing the hands lightly on the abdomen, slowly and smoothly distending the abdomen on the count of one, then retracting the abdomen on the count of two, and relaxing (Figure 18-3). The exercise should be repeated 8 to 10 times.

figure 18-3
Abdominal pumping.

figure 18-4
Pelvic tilt with abdominal pumping.

figure 18-5
Knee-chest position.

Pelvic tilt with abdominal pumping

The purpose of the pelvic tilt with abdominal pumping is to increase the tone of the abdominal muscles. In a hook-lying position, with the feet and knees together, heels 1 inch apart, and hands on the abdomen, the abdominal and gluteal muscles are contracted. The pelvis is rotated so that the tip of the coccyx comes forward and upward and the hips are slightly raised from the floor. The abdomen is distended and retracted. The hips are lowered slowly, vertebra by vertebra, until the original starting position is attained (Figure 18-4). The exercise should be repeated 8 to 10 times.

Knee-chest position

The purpose of the knee-chest exercise is to stretch the extensors of the lumbar spine and strengthen the abdominal muscles. The exercise is performed by bending forward at the hips and placing the hands and arms on a mat. The chest is lowered toward the mat, in a knee-chest position, and held as close to the mat as possible for 3 to 5 minutes (Figure 18-5). This exercise should be performed once or twice a day.

Community-Based Opportunities

The teenager who has been taught how to control PMS and functional dysmenorrhea through diet and exercise will have the knowledge she needs to continue to maintain a healthy and active lifestyle into her adult years.

Tourette Syndrome
Definition

Tourette syndrome (TS) is a disorder that results in multiple motor tics and one or more vocal tics.[3] The age of onset may be as early as 2 years and is usually during childhood or early adolescence.[4] The duration of the disorder is usually lifelong, although the symptoms may go into remission for months to years.[4]

Incidence

The prevalence rate is estimated to be 4 to 5 cases per 10,000 births[4] and is three times more common in males than in females.[8]

Causes

TS is an inherited neurological disorder with some associated symptoms that affect behavior.

Characteristics

Characteristics of individuals with this syndrome include involuntary motor and vocal tics and symptoms that come and go and change over time.[10] A tic is a sudden, rapid, recurrent, nonrhythmic, stereotyped movement or vocalization.[3] The **motor tics** that may be seen include sudden twitches of the entire body, shoulders, and/or head; eyeblinks or rolling of the head; repetitive tapping, drumming, or touching behaviors; or grimacing. The **vocal tics** are involuntary utterings of noises, words, or phrases, including sniffing, throat clearing, or repeated coughing, coprolalia (saying socially inappropriate words), laughing involuntarily, uttering a variety of sounds or yells, barking, grunting, and echolalia (repeating what others or oneself has just said).[10] Sometimes the symptoms are very frequent, and sometimes the child does not demonstrate them at all. Also, they change from one year to the next.

A high percentage of children with TS also have problems with attention, activity, and impulse control; learning disabilities; and visual-motor integration problems.[10] Some also demonstrate obsessive-compulsive behaviors.

Diagnostic criteria developed by the American Psychiatric Association[3] are:

- Both multiple motor tics and one or more vocal tics have been present for some time during the illness, although not necessarily concurrently.
- The tics occur many times a day (usually in bouts) nearly every day or have occurred intermittently throughout a period of more than 1 year, and during this period there was never a tic-free period of more than 3 consecutive months.
- The disturbance causes marked distress or significant impairment in social, occupational, or other important areas of functioning.
- The onset is before age 18.
- The disturbance is not due to the direct physiological effects of a substance (e.g., stimulants) or a general medical condition (e.g., Huntington's chorea or postviral encephalitis).

Testing

No adjustments in testing are required for the student with TS; however, allowances must be made for motor tics that are severe enough to interfere with voluntary motor control. If the student also has a specific learning disability, the teacher is referred to the testing procedures and interpretations provided in Chapter 13 of this text.

Special Considerations

Students with learning disabilities and those with impulse control difficulties represent a special challenge to a teacher. When a learning disability is present, the mode of presenting information to the student may have to be altered to accommodate his or her method of processing information. Some students learn better visually, others learn better auditorily, and some need a combination of techniques to comprehend new information. To determine how the student learns best, the teacher is advised to consult with the school counselor or other resource personnel who have access to the student's academic and cognitive test results.

When impulse control creates acting-out problems in class, the teacher must have a strategy for intervening, always keeping in mind that the student's behavior is involuntary. When possible and feasible, the teacher and the student should discuss anticipated

problems early in the school year and agree on a procedure to follow should impulse control become a major problem.

The student may wish to have the option to time himself or herself out or may prefer that the teacher intervene if the behavior interferes with other students' benefits from the class. Also, with the student and the student's parents' permission, the teacher or another representative of the school should share information about the condition with the student's classmates so they will understand that the unusual behaviors are not under voluntary control.

Teaching Strategy

Because the median age of onset for motor tics is 7 years,[3] the teacher of the child with TS may be the first to become aware of the emergence of the symptoms. Other than learning to tolerate the student's involuntary tics, the physical educator's primary concerns will probably be with fostering acceptance in the class and addressing the student's learning disabilities, impulse control, and visual-motor problems.

The Physical Education Program

Individuals with TS have a variety of visual-motor integration problems. These range from alternating visual suppression (using each eye independently of the other), to one or both eyes sitting in misalignment, to mild depth perception difficulties. If an individual is suppressing one eye or if the eyes are misaligned, the individual's motor performance will suffer. Performance clues include poor striking success, inability to catch a thrown ball, avoidance of climbing apparatus, and/or descending stairs one step at a time. Should a student demonstrate any of these difficulties, the child should be referred for an orthoptic visual examination and remediation (see Chapter 17) before a physical education program is designed. If the student does not have visual-motor integration problems that interfere with movement efficiency, no modifications in the activity program are needed except for those addressed under Special Considerations.

Modifications, Adaptations, and Inclusion Techniques

As the individual in charge, it is the teacher's responsibility to establish and maintain a learning environment that will provide all students with the opportunity to learn and grow. A teacher is expected to make needed modifications and adaptations to enhance a student's potential to learn. Teachers can offer alternative strategies to individual students when they possess the needed information and have a class size that permits individual attention. The presence of a student with a potentially disabling condition provides a special learning opportunity for everyone in the class. Knowledge about an existing condition, acceptance of the situation, realistic expectations, and cooperation are prerequisites for a positive learning environment for all members of the class. Students with TS can easily become alienated from other students in the class because of their uncontrollable, unique behaviors. However, when the teacher and other students in the class understand the condition, know what to expect, and what outcomes will result, opportunities will be enhanced and difficulties reduced to a minimum for the student with TS. The sensitive teacher will take the responsibility for ensuring that all members of the class are treated with fairness and respect.

Community-Based Opportunities

Adults with TS can participate in any public or private recreational activities where they feel comfortable. Their involuntary tics may, however, be met with ridicule, fear, and/or hostility by individuals who do not know them or understand the condition. As noted earlier in this section, an identifying characteristic of TS is that it "causes marked distress or significant impairment in social, occupational, or other important areas of functioning."[3] Attempts must be made to educate individuals who work and play in settings that the person with TS may frequent. A support group of friends and family members who are willing to "run interference" can provide others with information about the condition and perhaps facilitate understanding and acceptance.

Traumatic Head Injuries
Definition

A **traumatic head injury** is an injury to the head that results in minor to serious brain damage. The effects of head injuries on school behavior depend on the extent of the insult to the brain tissue. Although no classification system exists, a commonly used system for grading severity of brain damage is[41]:

Severity	Description
Minor	Common bumps to the head with no evidence of concussion; generally, not seen by a physician
Mild	Only brief loss of consciousness, if any, with accompanying symptoms of concussion, such as vomiting, lethargy, or lack of recall of the injury
Moderate	Evidence of concussion; loss of consciousness for less than 5 minutes
Severe	Concussion or skull fracture; loss of consciousness for 5 to 30 minutes
Serious	Loss of consciousness for more than 30 minutes; concussion or skull fracture and notable neurological sequelae

Incidence

Approximately 500,000 head injuries occur in the United States each year, with 10% resulting from recreational sports.[26] The number of school-age children with head injuries is significant; 1 in 500 school-age children are hospitalized with head injuries each year, and by age 15, 3% of the school population will have sustained a head injury.[48]

Causes

Causes of head injuries include motor vehicle accidents (most common in adolescence), falls, bicycle accidents, child abuse, assaults, and sport injuries.

Characteristics

The location and severity of brain damage greatly affect the characteristic behaviors of the child and the speed of recovery. Generally, cognitive, motor, behavior, and language functions are impaired to some extent. These posttrauma reactions frequently lead to a misdiagnosis of learning disabled, mentally retarded, or emotionally disturbed.[54] Although rapid recovery of most functions occurs during the first 2 or 3 years after injury, problems frequently persist for longer periods. Cognitive problems include difficulty with organization of sensory input, concept formation, understanding complex instructions, coherent organization of verbal and written reports, and flexible thinking.[60] Motor impairments include speed of execution of refined and complex movements.[7] Difficulty processing and integrating information, as well as abnormal brain activity, contribute to negative behaviors, including low tolerance for frustration, aggression, impulsiveness, and noncompliance.[54] Ongoing language problems include difficulty finding words, organizing sequences of words, and comprehension of complex instructions.[72] The extent and frequency of these problems should be addressed in the student's IEP.

Testing

The type of test administered will depend on the extent and severity of the student's brain damage. If an individual is having difficulty organizing sensory input, decision and movement time will be compromised, as well as movement efficiency. The type of teaching approach (bottom, up or top, down) a teacher uses will dictate the assessment instrument used. The teacher who uses the bottom, up approach will elect to sample sensory input function, whereas the teacher who uses the top, down approach will want to measure motor performance more directly. To determine what types of sensory input problems exist, the physical educator may wish to administer a sensory input screening instrument similar to the one presented in Chapter 7.

If the evaluator is more interested in simply pinpointing the areas of motor functioning that have been affected, a motor development or motor proficiency test such as the Test of Gross Motor Development or the Bruininks-Oserestsky Test of Motor Proficiency (balance, strength, and bilateral coordination subtests) should be administered.

Special Considerations

The extent of the brain damage will determine the number of special considerations that must be made. The person who suffers from brain damage as a result of traumatic head injury will have good days and bad days. On a good day it is relatively easy to attend, follow directions, and tolerate minor frustrations. On a bad day everything is blown out of proportion—it is hard to sit still, listen to instructions, overlook minor problems, and comply with rules. The sensitive teacher will attend carefully to clues that indicate the type of day the student with brain damage is experiencing and adjust expectations for the student accordingly. Allowance must always be made for basic organizational problems and learning difficulties that have resulted from the insult to the brain tissue. The more positive and user-friendly the educational environment, the better.

Guidelines for Management of Concussion in Sports

Grade 1: Confusion Without Amnesia or Loss of Consciousness

Remove from event and evaluate on site. If no symptoms are present at rest or on exertion, return to the event may be permitted after 20 minutes of observation.

Grade 2: Confusion with Amnesia but No Loss of Consciousness

Remove from event, evaluate, and observe over the next 24 hours. Return to participation may be allowed after 1 week without symptoms at rest or on exertion.

Grade 3: Any Loss of Consciousness

Transport for immediate medical evaluation, with admission indicated if any abnormalities are detected. After 1 month, if the athlete has been asymptomatic at rest and on exertion during the last 2 weeks, return to participation may be permitted.

Data from Genuardi FJ, King WD: *Pediatrics* 95(2):216-218, 1995.

It is critical that students who have suffered a traumatic head injury, no matter how mild, be carefully monitored before returning to participation in sports. The reason for this is that the effects of repeated concussions are cumulative in nature. Because of the increasing number of reports of death following what appears to be a minor second impact after a previous concussion, the American Academy of Pediatrics endorsed concussion guidelines that are presented in the box above.

Teaching Strategies

Physical education personnel should be particularly attentive to the posttrauma student's ongoing psychomotor, cognitive, and behavior problems. Care must be exercised in sequencing motor tasks, providing instructions, and simplifying motor demands. Tasks should be reduced to their simplest components without making the student feel babied; instructions should be brief and to the point; and game strategies should be simple rather than complex. The student should be given the option of timing himself or herself out when the demands of the class prove to be too frustrating to handle on a given day. Any adjustments that will reduce the student's frustration to a minimum and increase his or her capability of cooperating in a group setting will contribute to the possibility of the student's success in physical education.

The Physical Education Program

The type of physical education provided for the student with a traumatic head injury will depend on the test results and the teacher's judgment of the student's capability. The more individualized the program, the less frustration the student will experience. Being required to contribute to a competitive team effort where winning is highly valued will create significant problems for the individual who is slow to make critical playing decisions and moves. Should the student be given opportunities to pursue his or her own exercise program, a buddy system should prove to be effective in keeping the student with brain damage on task and following appropriate safety procedures.

Modifications, Adaptations, and Inclusion Techniques

Depending on the extent and severity of brain damage, educational modifications that may need to be included in the IEP are[48]:
- Reduced course load
- Scheduling the most demanding courses in the morning when the student is fresh
- Resource room with the assistance of an aide
- Rest breaks as needed
- Adapted physical education or a modified regular physical education program
- Peer tutoring
- Counseling
- Provisions for taping lectures and extra time for completing written work and examinations

Community-Based Opportunities

The individual with a strong support system made up of friends and family will have greater opportunities to be active in community settings than will the individual who has little or no outside support. Persons with a traumatic brain injury who understand the components of a healthy lifestyle and have been taught to select activities that will promote that lifestyle will seek out opportunities to stay active on their good days. On their bad days their support group will provide them with the encouragement and motivation they need to expend the extra effort to stay active. Caution should be exercised when selecting activities. Highly competitive sports, particularly those that involve contact, can easily provoke a sensitive individual and result in undesirable impulsive, aggressive behaviors. Less competitive games and exercise routines will provide the same level of benefit without the potential negative emotional and physical outcomes.

SUMMARY

Some other conditions in the laws that qualify a student for special programming consideration are AIDS, anemia, asthma, child abuse, childhood cancer, cystic fibrosis, diabetes, Prader-Willi syndrome, Tourette syndrome, and traumatic head injury. Additional conditions that may limit a student's strength, vitality, or alertness are premenstrual syndrome and dysmenorrhea. The physical educator should understand the nature of each of these conditions, how the condition can affect a student's performance capabilities, and the types of program modifications that best meet the needs of each student.

Most of the conditions discussed in this chapter require medical attention. When this is the case, it is advisable to consult with the student's physician to ensure that the type of exercises and activities selected for the student will not aggravate the condition. In most situations mild exercise will benefit the student. However, in the case of the diabetic student, the type of diabetes must be known before specific exercise programs can be developed.

Review Questions

1. What are four symptoms of diabetes?
2. In what ways should persons with type I diabetes adjust their insulin levels to accommodate increased exercise levels?
3. How should physical education be modified for students with asthma?
4. Summarize the Universal Precautions to protect against all infectious disease. Identify those that are most pertinent to physical education.
5. What are some of the physical characteristics of a child with AIDS?
6. Describe the similarities and differences between each of the types of child abuse and neglect.

7. Explain precautions that must be used in developing an individual exercise program for a child with cystic fibrosis.

8. What are three characteristics of an anemic person?

9. How do the emergency treatment procedures for hypoglycemia and hyperglycemia differ?

10. What modifications may be needed in the physical education program of an individual returning to school after being in a coma as a result of a traumatic brain injury?

11. What is the primary characteristic of the child with Tourette syndrome? How does this interfere with the child's psychosocial development?

12. What are some precautions the physical educator should take with children who have asthma?

13. What is the major characteristic of a child with Prader-Willi syndrome? What precautions must be taken in the development of an exercise program for children with Prader-Willi syndrome?

14. What are the three guidelines for determining whether a person whose head is injured during activity should return to the activity?

Student Activities

1. Present an IEP that you developed on one of the conditions covered in the chapter to the rest of the class and provide your rationale for the tests, goals, objectives, and community-based leisure and recreational activities you selected.

2. Look through six recent issues of the *Journal of the American Medical Association*. List the articles that relate to the conditions described in this chapter. Read through some of the articles to see if exercise is mentioned as a possible way to relieve the condition.

3. Interview a person with diabetes. Find out what type of medication the person takes and how often it must be taken. Ask if the person ever failed to take the medication and how he or she felt because of missing the dosage.

4. Interview a school nurse. Find out what percentage of the students in the nurse's school have the conditions discussed in this chapter.

5. Contact an organization that advocates for children with the health impairments discussed in this chapter and study their literature. Identify the information that is relevant to conducting a physical education program for individuals with these health impairments.

6. Identify an athlete who is or was afflicted with one of the health impairments discussed in this chapter. Write a paper on accommodations that had to be made for the athlete.

References

1. Allen DM, Tarnowski KJ: Depressive characteristics of physically abused children, *J Abnorm Child Psychol* 17:1-11, 1989.

2. Allen JC: Childhood brain tumors: current status of clinical trials in newly diagnosed and recurrent disease, *Pediatr Clin North Am* 32:633-651, 1985.

3. American Psychiatric Association: *DSM-IV Diagnostic and statistical manual of mental disorders,* Washington, DC, 1994, The Association.

4. Anderson SD: Exercise-induced asthma. In Middleton E et al, editors: *Allergy: principles and practice,* ed 4, St Louis, 1993, Mosby.

5. Arthur DC: Genetics and cytogenetics of pediatric cancers, *Cancer* 58:534, 1986.

6. Asthma and Allergy Foundation of America, *Allergy Asthma Adv* 2:9-10, 1984.

7. Bawden H, Knights R, Winogron H: Speeded performance following head injury in children, *J Clin Exp Neuropsychol* 7:30-54, 1985.

8. Berkow R, Fletcher AJ, editors: *The Merck manual of diagnosis and therapy,* ed 15, Rahway, NJ, 1992, Merck.

9. Borkgren MW, Gronkiewicz CA: Update your asthma care from hospital to home, *Am J Nurs,* pp 26-34, Jan 1995.

10. Bronheim S: *An educator's guide to Tourette syndrome,* Bayside, NY, 1990, Tourette Syndrome Association.

11. Canny GJ, Levison H: Exercise response and rehabilitation in cystic fibrosis, *Sports Med* 4:143-152, 1987.

12. Carlson DL, Mawdsley RH: Sports anemia: a review of the literature, *Am J Sports Med* 14:109-122, 1986.

13. Cerny F, Orenstein D: Cystic fibrosis. In Skinner JS, editor: *Exercise testing and exercise prescription for special cases,* Philadelphia, 1993, Lea & Febiger.

14. Child Abuse Program: Annual report, Children's Hospital, Columbus, Ohio, 1986-1987.

15. Claussen AH, Crittenden PM: Physical and psychological maltreatment: relations among types of maltreatment, *Child Abuse Negl* 15:5-18, 1991.

16. Conti SF, Chaytor ER: Foot care for active patients who have diabetes, *Physician Sportsmed* 23(6):53-68, 1995.

17. Crist WM, Kun LE: Common solid tumors of childhood, *N Engl J Med* 324:461-471, 1991.

18. Cystic Fibrosis Foundation: *Cystic fibrosis and exercise: a beginner's guide,* Rockville, Md, 1984, The Foundation.

19. Donaldson SS, Link MP: Hodgkin's disease: treatment of the young child, *Pediatr Clin North Am* 38:457-473, 1991.

20. Dunn JM, Fait H: *Special physical education,* Dubuque, Iowa, 1989, Wm C Brown.

21. Eichner ER: Sickle cell trait, heroic exercise, and fatal collapse, *Physician Sportsmed* 21(7):51-61, 1993.

22. Elliott DJ, Tarnowski KJ: Depressive characteristics of sexually abused children, *Child Psychiatry Hum Dev* 21:37-47, 1989.

23. Friedman HS, Horowitz M, Oakes WJ: Tumors of the central nervous system: improvement in outcome through a multimodality approach, *Pediatr Clin North Am* 38:381-391, 1991.

24. Garbarino J, Garbarino AC: *Emotional maltreatment of children,* Chicago, 1986, National Committee for Prevention of Child Abuse.

25. Garbarino J, Guttman E, Seely JW: *The psychologically battered child,* San Francisco, 1986, Jossey-Bass.

26. Genuardi FJ, King WD: Inappropriate discharge instructions for young athletes hospitalized for concussions, *Pediatrics* 95(2):216-218, 1995.

27. Gong H, Krishnareddy S: How pollution and airborne allergens affect exercise, *Physician Sportsmed* 23(7):35-42, 1995.

28. Gong H, Linn W: Health effects of criteria air pollutants. In Tierney DF, editor: *Current pulmonology,* vol 15, St Louis, 1994, Mosby.

29. Grier HE, Weinstein HJ: Acute nonlymphocytic leukemia, *Pediatr Clin North Am* 32:653-668, 1985.

30. Grubman S et al: Older children and adolescents living with perinatally acquired human immunodeficiency virus infection, *Pediatrics* 95:657-663, 1995.

31. Gurney GG et al: Incidence of cancer in children in the United States, *Cancer* 75:2186-2195, 1995.

32. Harris SS, Tanner S: Helping active women avoid anemia, *Physician Sportsmed* 23(5):35-47, 1995.

33. Hart SN, Grassard MR: A major threat to children's mental health: psychological maltreatment, *Am Psychol* 42:160-165, 1987.

34. Helman LJ, Thiele CJ: New insights into the causes of cancer, *Pediatr Clin North Am* 38:201-221, 1991.

35. Holm VA: The diagnosis of Prader-Willi syndrome. In Holm VA, Salzbacher S, Pipes PL, editors: *The Prader-Willi syndrome,* Baltimore, 1981, University Park Press.

36. Horowitz ME, Neff JR, Kun LE: Ewing's sarcoma: radiotherapy versus surgery for local control, *Pediatr Clin North Am* 38:365-380, 1991.

37. Huettig C, DiBrezzo R: *Factors in abuse and neglect of handicapped children.* Paper presented at American Alliance of Health, Physical Education, Recreation and Dance National Convention, Las Vegas, April 1987.

38. Jason J: Child abuse or maltreatment. In Conn RB, editor: *Current diagnosis,* ed 7, Philadelphia, 1985, WB Saunders.

39. Johnson CF: Inflicted injury versus accidental injury, *Pediatr Clin North Am* 37:791-814, 1990.

40. Kerr CP: Improving outcomes in diabetes: a review of the outpatient care of NIDDM patients, *J Fam Pract* 40(1):63-75, 1995.

41. Klonoff H, Low M, Clark C: Head injuries in children: a prospective five year follow-up, *J Neurol Neurosurg Psychiatry* 40:1211-1219, 1977.

42. Lansky SB: Management of stressful periods in childhood cancer, *Pediatr Clin North Am* 32:625-632, 1985.

43. Leon AS: Diabetes. In Skinner JS, editor: *Exercise testing and exercise prescription for special cases,* Philadelphia, 1993, Lea & Febiger.

44. McClelland CQ, Kingsbury GH: Fractures in the first year of life: a diagnostic dilemma, *Am J Dis Child* 136:26-29, 1982.

45. McHugh E: Going "beyond the physical": social skills and physical education, *J Phys Educ Rec Dance* 66(4):18-21, 1995.

46. Meadows AT, Krejimas NL, Belasco JB: The medical cost of cure: sequelae in survivors of childhood cancer. In van Eys J, Sullivan MP, editors: *Status of curability of childhood cancers,* New York, 1980, Raven Press.

47. Miller J, Keane RR: *Encyclopedia and dictionary of medicine, nursing, and allied health,* Philadelphia, 1987, WB Saunders.

48. Mira M, Tyler J: Students with traumatic brain injury: making the transition from hospital to school, *Focus Except Child* 23:1-12, 1991.

49. Mitten MJ: HIV-positive athletes: when medicine meets the law, *Physician Sportsmed* 22 (10):63-68, 1994.

50. Morton AR, Fitch KD: Asthma. In Skinner JS, editor: *Exercise testing and exercise prescription for special cases,* Philadelphia, 1993, Lea & Febiger.

51. Mulvihill JJ: Ecogenetic origins of cancer in the young: environmental and genetic determinants. In Levine AS, editor: *Cancer in the young,* Paris, 1981, Masson.

52. Murphy JM et al: Substance abuse and serious child mistreatment: prevalence, risk, and outcome in a court sample, *Child Abuse Negl* 15:197-211, 1991.

53. National Institutes of Health, National Asthma Education Program: *Expert panel, guidelines for the diagnosis and management of asthma,* NIH Pub No 91-3042, Washington, DC, Aug 1991, US Government Printing Office.

54. New Medico Head Injury System: Emotionally charged: why do head injuries make some people seem out of control? *Headlines* 1:2-9, 1990.

55. Nozyce M et al: Effect of perinatally acquired human immunodeficiency virus infection on the neurodevelopment in children during the first two years of life, *Pediatrics* 94:883-891, 1994.

56. Payton B: *Health and safety,* Dallas, 1994, Dallas Independent School District.

57. Pihkala J et al: Cardiopulmonary evaluation of exercise tolerance after chest irradiation and anticancer chemotherapy in children and adolescents, *Pediatrics* 95:772-726, 1995.

58. Poplack DG: Acute lymphoblastic leukemia in childhood, *Pediatr Clin North Am* 32:669-681, 1985.

59. Pratt CB: Some aspects of childhood cancer epidemiology, *Pediatr Clin North Am* 32:541-556, 1985.

60. Routke B, Fisk J, Strong J: *Neuropsychological assessment of children: a treatment-oriented approach,* New York, 1986, Guilford Press.

61. Seltzer, DG: Educating athletes on HIV disease and AIDS, *Physician Sportsmed* 21(1):109-115, 1993.

62. Shoeffel RE et al: Multiple exercise and histamine challenge in asthmatic patients, *Thorax* 3:164, 1990.

63. Shor DP: Cystic fibrosis. In Blackman JA, editor: *Medical aspects of developmental disabilities in children birth to three,* Rockville, Md, 1984, Aspen.

64. Surburg PR: Are adapted physical educators ready for the students with AIDS? *Adapt Phys Ed Q* 5:259-263, 1988.

65. Taunton JE, McCargar L: Managing activity in patients who have diabetes, *Physician Sportsmed* 23(3):41-52, 1995.

66. Taunton JE, McCargar L: Staying active with diabetes, *Physician Sportsmed* 23(3):55-56, 1995.

67. Trembath RC: Genetic mechanisms and mental retardation, *J R Coll Physicians Lond* 28(2):121-125, March/April 1994.

68. Tuchman M et al: Screening for neuroblastoma at 3 weeks of age: methods and preliminary results from the Quebec Neuroblastoma Screening Project, *Pediatrics* 86:765-773, 1990.

69. Waters J, Clarke DJ, Corbett JA: Educational and occupational outcome in Prader-Willi syndrome, *Child Care Health Dev* 16:271-282, 1990.

70. Weinberg RA: Oncogenes, antioncogenes and the molecular bases of multistep carcinogenesis, *Cancer Res* 49:3713-3721, 1989.

71. Wilson EF: Estimation of the age of cutaneous contusions in child abuse, *Pediatrics* 60:750-752, 1977.

72. Ylvisaker M: Language and communication disorders following pediatric head injury, *J Head Trauma Rehabil* 1:48-56, 1986.

73. Young C et al: Cancer incidence, survival and mortality for children younger than age 15 years, *Cancer* 58(suppl 2):598-602, 1986.

Suggested Readings

Conti SF, Chaytor ER: Steps to healthy feet for active people with diabetes, *Physician Sportsmed* 23(6):71-72, 1995.

Harris SS, Tanner S: Give yourself the iron advantage, *Physician Sportsmed* 23(5):44, 1995.

Hellison D: Teaching physical education to at-risk youth in Chicago—a model, *J Phys Educ Rec Dance* 61(6):38-39, 1989.

part *five*

Organization and Administration

The varied roles and responsibilities of adapted physical educators are identified and discussed in this section. Also discussed are ways to use site-based management, multiculturalism, and family involvement to enhance the physical education program for students with disabilities.

chapter nineteen

Program Organization and Administration

Objectives

In general, describe the hierarchical structure within the U.S. educational system.

Describe the personnel involved and function of a quality motor development team.

List school reform initiatives.

Explain how the "total quality" philosophy applies to adapted physical education.

Describe the six levels of involvement in a parent/school/community partnership and give examples of each.

Explain teaching strategies for honoring and validating students representing diverse cultures.

Describe the factors that cause stress in families with children with disabilities.

List inexpensive equipment that can be used in the physical education program for children with and without disabilities.

Courtesy Zipp, Inc.

The essence of effective organization and administration in adapted physical education, or in any other program for that matter, is communication. To serve students with disabilities, the adapted physical education program must be designed to allow a flow of communication between those with responsibilities for the education of the student (most important, the parents of the student). In this chapter, organization and administration strategies to enhance communication between personnel are discussed. Communication strategies for interaction with administrators, other special education personnel, physical education teachers, parents, and students are considered.

The Education System

The individual physical education teacher with a commitment to children and young adults with disabilities is but one small "cog" in a huge "machine" designed to provide educational services to *all* children. Federal education policy is set by the U.S. Department of Education. A state education agency is responsible for implementing federal policy at the state level and interpreting federal legislation to meet the needs of learners within the given state. A local education agency or education cooperative, a cluster of small school districts without sufficient resources to provide education for their children independently, is responsible for implementing state policy and interpreting that policy to meet the needs of learners within the district or cooperative. It is the responsibility of the school to contribute to the fullest possible development of each individual student entrusted to its care. This is a basic tenet of our democratic structure.

In most school districts the responsibility for educating the district's children is placed in the hands of the members of a school board. In most communities the individuals who serve on this school board are elected officials, responsible to the voters for their performance. The school board is responsible for implementing state policy and interpreting that policy to meet the needs of learners within the school district.

The primary administrator within the school district is usually called the "superintendent of schools." Recently there has been a trend toward naming this individual the "chief executive officer" of the district. The responsibilities of the superintendent or chief executive officer include the assurance of a quality education for all children. This individual, particularly in a large district, often has associate superintendents who help with quality control and assist with decisions regarding student services, budget, personnel, and facilities and equipment.

Within that structure, historically, an individual has been designated as the "director of special education" or the "operations executive." That person is responsible for implementing school board policy as it relates to students who are in need of special education services in order to be successful learners, and, ultimately, productive and capable citizens.

Adapted Physical Education and the Administrative Hierarchy

Adapted physical education is usually, but not always, aligned administratively with the special education, rather than the physical education, department. This is expedient because of the unique requirements of the law regarding specially designed physical education programs for children with disabilities. This is also administratively effective because of federal and state funding protocols for students with disabilities.

In a small school district or small special education cooperative, the adapted physical educator or adapted physical education consultant may be directly responsible to the director of special education. Regardless of who has the responsibility for overseeing physical education services for students with disabilities, the adapted physical educator is accountable to the director of special education for the provision of quality adapted physical education services, which include:

- Assessment and prescription within the psychomotor domain
- Development of the individual physical education plan (IPEP)
- Implementation of the IPEP
- Representing adapted physical education at individual education program (IEP) or multidisciplinary team meetings
- Provision of direct services to children with disabilities, when appropriate
- Consultation with regular special education and regular physical education personnel
- Consultation with community-based leisure, recreation, and sport facilities managers regarding program and facility accessibility
- Curriculum development and/or revision
- Communication with parents
- Management of budget
- Purchase and maintenance of equipment

The responsibilities of the adapted physical educator in a large school district or large special cooperative are the same as those in a smaller district. The levels of bureaucracy are simply more complex. In a large school district or large special service cooperative, one member of the adapted physical education staff may be designated as the "lead teacher" or "department chair." This person is directly accountable for the activities of the

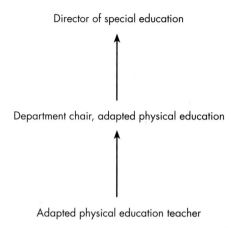

figure 19-1
Adapted physical education administrative hierarchy.

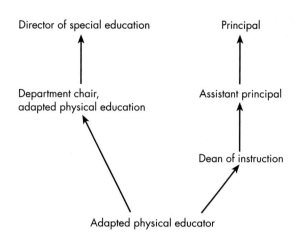

figure 19-2
Administrative hierarchy in a school district with site-based management.

staff and must report to his or her immediate supervisor. The responsibilities of the staff members are the same as those of educators in smaller districts. The layers of bureaucracy may simply be more complex.

For example, the adapted physical education teacher may be responsible within the administrative hierarchy shown in Figure 19-1. This administrative hierarchy may be more complex in school districts that also have **site-based management** (Figure 19-2). In a school district with site-based management, the adapted physical education teacher may be accountable to the local campus administrator, or principal, as well as to the director of special education.

One of the major responsibilities of the adapted physical educator is to communicate regularly and effectively with his or her direct supervisor. Frequently neither the director of special education nor the building principal understands the specific requirements of the law as it applies to adapted physical education. The teacher should inform these persons about the requirements of the law and share legal updates and current articles describing state-of-the-art practices in adapted physical education. The single most effective way to communicate the worth of the program is through demonstrated student results, based on assessment data, and through student and parent testimony regarding the effectiveness of the program.

Unfortunately, many administrators simply do not understand the nature or scope of the field of adapted physical education. As a student, the administrator may have had a bad experience in "PE" and, as such, does not understand the benefits of quality physical education instruction. Timely information that clarifies the goals and objectives of the program and describes the "before and after" status of students served in adapted physical education may help the administrator understand the value of the program. If possible, the administrator should be invited to attend a class or activity that demonstrates quality programming to meet individual student needs and highlights the accomplishments of the students.

It is vital that the adapted physical educator secure the support of the administrator if the program is to receive its share of district and school resources and if the adapted physical educator is to be considered a vital and integral part of the instructional team within the district. The administrator can help by:

- Giving enthusiastic support to the total program
- Providing an adequate budget
- Hiring adequately trained teachers
- Supporting necessary student schedule changes
- Maintaining a low student-teacher ratio
- Providing auxiliary services such as medical aid, nursing, transportation, and maintenance

Basic Components of the Adapted Physical Education Program

The director of the adapted physical education program and its teacher(s) are responsible for meeting federal, state, and local mandates regarding the provision of a quality physical education program for *all* children with disabilities who need a specially designed program in order to learn and grow.

The components of a quality adapted physical education program are as follows:

- Philosophy
- Definition of adapted physical education
- Goals and objectives
- Criteria for eligibility
- Referral process
- Assessment procedures
- IEP
- Continuum of services, placement, and personnel
- Accountability

Philosophy

The philosophy of the program must reflect that of the school board and be consistent with state and federal policy regarding the provision of services to children with disabilities. The Denton (Texas) Independent School District has developed a philosophy statement that indicates it will "provide all students, including those with disabilities, with an appropriate physical education program . . . and ensure that students with disabilities have access to a program that enables them to acquire the same essential elements of physical education as their nondisabled peers."[6]

Definition of Adapted Physical Education

The definition of adapted physical education discussed in Chapter 1, the definition in P.L. 94-142, is appropriate for all districts:

1. The term means the development of:
   a. Physical and motor fitness
   b. Fundamental motor skills and patterns
   c. Skills in aquatics, dance, and individual and group games and sports (including intramural and lifetime sports)
2. The term includes special physical education, adapted physical education, movement education, and motor development.

Goals and Objectives

The goals and objectives of the adapted physical education program should be consistent with those established by the state education agency for every learner who participates in physical education. This is particularly true if children with disabilities are to be included in "regular" physical education programs.

The Denton (Texas) Independent School District included these objectives in their program manual[6]:

1. Psychomotor
   a. Develop sensory integration and perceptual motor function.
   b. Develop and maintain efficient fundamental motor skills and patterns.
   c. Develop and maintain an adequate level of physical and motor fitness.
   d. Develop the ability to relax.
   e. Develop skills in rhythmical movements.
   f. Develop skills in gymnastics and tumbling.
   g. Develop skills in individual and group games and sports.
2. Cognitive
   a. Develop knowledge and understanding for rhythmical movement.
   b. Develop knowledge and understanding required for gymnastics and tumbling skills.
   c. Develop knowledge and understanding of rules and strategies of individual and group games and sports.
   d. Develop knowledge of safety practices required for a variety of physical activities.
3. Affective
   a. Develop appropriate social interaction skills.
   b. Develop respect for rules, authority figures, and others.
   c. Develop a positive self-concept, body image, and confidence.
   d. Develop and demonstrate cooperative and competitive skills through physical activity.
   e. Accept limitations that cannot be changed and learn to adapt to the environment to make the most of strengths.

Criteria for Eligibility

Eligibility for special education services is mandated by federal law. In addition, those individuals who may sign the eligibility statement are specified. For example, for a student to meet eligibility requirements for the category "other health impaired" a licensed physician must sign the statement.

Those students who are eligible for special education services may also be eligible for adapted physical education. That is, if the learner cannot make adequate progress toward the successful acquisition of the "essential elements" of physical education in the regular physical education setting, he or she is eligible for adapted physical education services.

Referral Process

Referral, assessment, and placement procedures are the crux of the adapted physical education program and are vital in the process of ensuring that each eligible student receives the appropriate intervention, an individualized education program.

The instructional model for adapted physical education follows these steps:

1. Accumulation of information about the student
2. Screening and, if necessary, assessment
3. Prescribing a program to meet the student's individual needs
4. Determining the least restrictive environment placement to meet those needs
5. Implementation of the program
6. Monitoring progress

See Figure 2-1 for the Denton Independent School District prereferral and referral form.

Assessment Procedures

It is vital that the adapted physical education assessment be completed by a trained professional who has vast experience in assessment in the psychomotor domain. Because it is unusual for a regular physical educator to have specific training in a comprehensive assessment that identifies sensory-motor delays, many school districts hire individuals specifically for assessing and recommending an appropriate instructional program. For more information regarding assessment procedures, refer to Chapter 2.

IEP

The IEP is the cornerstone of the educational process that ties together data from the comprehensive assessment

and information from the child's classroom and physical education teacher with a specific plan to intervene to meet goals and objectives specially designed for the student. For more information on the IEP process, refer to Chapter 3.

Continuum of Services, Placement, and Personnel

A continuum of service and placement options is the basis of a district's ability to provide physical education services within the least restrictive environment. Infor-

table 19-1			
Sample Daily Service Log			
Date	Service	Student(s) Served/School	Time
2/10	Direct service— teaching*	EC Class/Adams	8:00-9:00
	Direct service— teaching*	S/Ph Class/Adams	9:00-10:00
	Travel to Cabell		10:00-10:15
	Motor/fitness assessment	J. Flores/Cabell	10:15-12:00
	Lunch/travel to White		12:00-12:45
	Consultation—PE teacher	K. Black/White	12:45-1:30
	Travel to office		1:30-1:45
	Written report*	J. Flores/Cabell	1:45-3:15
	Prepare for IEP meeting		3:15-3:45
2/11	Direct service— teaching*	EC Class/Foster	8:00-8:45
	Direct service— teaching*	HI Class/Foster	9:00-9:45
	Travel to Cabell		9:50-10:00
	IEP meeting	J. Flores/Cabell	10:30-12:00
	Travel/lunch		12:00-12:45
	Direct service— teaching	S/Ph Class/Grant	1:00-1:45
	Travel to community pool		1:45-2:00
	Direct service	MD students/ district	2:15-3:30
	Swimming instruction*		

*See attached lesson plans.

mation regarding the continuum of services and placement options is included in Chapter 5. The ways in which a multidisciplinary motor team can contribute to program development and delivery are discussed later in this chapter. Related service personnel roles are described in Chapter 3.

Accountability

The adapted physical educator *must be accountable* for the delivery of appropriate education services. In some states, federal and state funding of the local special education program is based on the numbers of documented contact hours between the professional and the student. Contact hours are usually documented with a service log. Service logs are used to record daily involvement in the adapted physical education program. Those logs are routinely checked by the adapted physical educator's supervisor. A sample of such a log is provided in Table 19-1.

In addition to a daily log that accounts for time and student contact, the adapted physical educator, like other teachers in the district, may be responsible for lesson plans that may have to be submitted to a building principal. Adapted physical education teachers with large caseloads (more than 50 students) will find it impossible to manage the paperwork, including daily lesson plans, without the use of computer technology. The teacher who can generate daily lesson plans using a basic word-processing system and a prepared template will save hours daily. The procedure greatly simplifies the process of writing plans because basic information required on every plan does not have to be written by hand. In addition, generating the plans on the computer allows the teacher to readily trace the progress of each student within each class. A sample lesson plan, which corresponds to one class listed in Table 19-1, is included below:

Sample	Daily Lesson Plan
Teacher:	Buddy Nelson
Class:	Early childhood/Paul Dunbar Learning Center
Date:	December 7, 1996
Warm-up:	"If You're Happy and You Know It"
Rhythms:	"What a Miracle"; "Swing, Shake, Twist, Stretch"; "Flick a Fly"
Equilibrium activities:	Magic Carpet Ride; Crazy Sidewalk; Freeze
Relaxation:	Pretend to be a rag doll and a sleepy kitten

Interaction with Other Special Education Personnel

Within the larger structure of the school district and local campus, the effective adapted physical education teacher works in close cooperation with other direct service providers and with related service personnel as well. The most crucial interactions are with the special education teacher(s), related service personnel serving a given child, and the child's regular physical educator.

The relationship between the adapted physical educator and the physical therapist, occupational therapist, and recreation therapist is particularly crucial given the direct concern of each professional regarding the child's motor efficiency. Related service personnel play an important role in physical education programs for children with disabilities. In addition to providing services that will help the children benefit from the program, they may also enhance the program by:

- Interpreting the program to medical personnel in the district, to parents, and to the total school population
- Handling or making referrals of students with special problems
- Recommending exercises and activities

The intent of the Education of the Handicapped Act was for professionals involved in the education of a learner with a disability to share their knowledge, expertise, and technical skill not only with the learner, but with each other as well. The most efficient way to ensure cooperation among the adapted physical educator and related service personnel is to formalize the relationship by forming a **multidisciplinary motor team.**

The use of a multidisciplinary team to provide services is an excellent way to ensure communication among service providers. The members of the interdisciplinary motor development team often include the adapted physical educator, the physical therapist, the occupational therapist, and the recreation therapist. The regular physical educator and the speech therapist may also function as part of the motor development team. Common functions of members of motor development teams made up of adapted physical educators, physical therapists, occupational therapists, and recreation therapists can include:

1. To screen and evaluate students with functional and/or educational problems to determine needs for special services.

A modification of a screening form developed for an Oregon school district is presented in the box on pp. 496-497. This screening instrument gives direction to classroom educators, special educators, and physical educators who may need to refer children to the motor development team. Once the members of the motor development team receive the information, they decide which specialist should serve as the lead member of the evaluation process. That lead person initiates and organizes a subsequent full-scale gross motor evaluation, which reduces the amount of duplicated effort. For example, both the occupational therapist and the adapted physical educator routinely use the Bruininks-Oseretsky Test of Motor Proficiency. As a member of the motor development team, either the adapted physical educator or the occupational therapist may administer the test and share results with other professionals on the team.

2. To develop an IEP, as part of the total multidisciplinary team, to address the child's motor needs.

Members of the motor development team develop an IEP that addresses the needs of the child. In some school districts and special service cooperatives the members of the motor development team actually create an **individual motor education plan** (**IMEP**) (see Chapter 3).

3. To implement an intervention program that facilitates learning.

Once the IMEP is approved by the entire IEP committee, the members of the motor development team implement the intervention program. Like the evaluation/assessment, the intervention program is cooperative in nature. Each member of the team addresses the child's motor needs. Instead of limiting focus to one specific component of motor development, all professionals on the team share responsibility for implementing the program or designate one service provider to represent the team.

4. To manage and supervise motor programs.

Each member of the motor development team assumes a specific responsibility for the management and supervision of the program. If a team leader has been designated, each member of the motor development team will communicate directly with that person regarding the student's progress.

5. To document service delivery.

Careful documentation of services delivered is a vital part of the process. Each member of the team must

table 19-2

Sample Motor Development Team Service Provider Log

Date	Service Provider	IMEP Goal	Child's Performance
10/1	C. Jones, OTR	10 sit-ups	3 reverse sit-ups
10/2	J. Hernandez, LPT	10 sit-ups	4 reverse sit-ups
10/4	J. Smith, APE Spec	10 sit-ups	3 minutes supine scooter play; 5 minutes supine cageball kick
10/5	G. Meza, RTR	10 sit-ups	25 minutes horse-back riding
10/8	C. Jones, OTR	10 sit-ups	5 reverse sit-ups

be accountable not only to the child served, but to each other as well. The motor development team, if it is to function effectively, demands professional accountability. This is often done by using a service provider log. Table 19-2 is a sample of a motor development team log that may reflect service delivery to a child lacking abdominal strength and whose IMEP included this annual goal: The child will be able to perform 10 bent-knee sit-ups independently. This type of log is vital for communication among professional members of the motor development team and may serve as crucial documentation of services provided during the annual review of the child's progress.

6. To cooperatively provide or create resources that help other professionals meet the motor needs of students.

Members of the motor development team have specialized knowledge that should be shared with educators who are in daily contact with the learners. In some school districts or special service cooperatives, the members of the motor development team have created motor development handbooks for use by teachers in early childhood classrooms or physical education programs. In others, the members of the motor development team have developed curricula for use by special educators in prevocational preparation programs. Those resources provide vital information for each student's educational program.

7. To conduct cooperative in-service motor development training for other school personnel, parents, and volunteers.

District 19 Motor Team Screening Form

Name: _____ DOB _____

Date of referral: _____ Grade: _____ Teacher: _____

School: _____

Specialist: _____ Physician _____

Was student retained? ___ Yes ___ No

PE time: _____ Recess time: _____

Current disabling conditions: _____

_____

Does the student use adaptive equipment (braces, crutches, etc.)? _____

_____

Please check those items that have been observed.

Gross Motor

___ Lacks age-appropriate strength and endurance

___ Difficulty with run, jump, hop, or skip compared with others his or her age

___ Stiff and awkward in his or her movements

___ Clumsy, seems not to know how to move body, bumps into things, falls out of chair

___ Demonstrates mixed dominance

___ Reluctant to participate in playground activities

___ Play pattern is inappropriate for age group (does not play, plays by self, plays beside but not with, stereotypical) (Circle one)

___ Has postural deviations

___ Complains of pain during physical activities

___ Demonstrates unusual wear patterns on shoes and/or clothing

Fine Motor

___ Poor desk posture (slumps, leans on arm, head too close to work) (Circle)

___ Difficulty drawing, coloring, copying, cutting

___ Poor pencil grasp and/or drops pencil frequently

___ Lines drawn are light, wobbly, too faint, or too dark

___ Breaks pencil often

___ Lack of well-established dominance after 6 years of age

___ Student has difficulty using both hands together (stabilization of paper during cutting and paper activities)

Self-Care Skills

___ Difficulty with fasteners (buttons, zippers, snaps, shoe tying, lacing) (Circle)

___ Wears clothes backward or inside out; appears messy

___ Has difficulty putting clothes on or taking them off

___ Difficulty with the eating process (opening packages, feeding self, spilling, using utensils) (Circle)

___ Oral-motor problems (drools, difficulty chewing, swallowing, difficulty drinking from straws) (Circle)

___ Needs assistance with toileting (wiping, flushing, replacing underwear/clothes) (Circle)

Academic (Check Those Areas Presenting Problems)

___ Distractibility

___ Following directions

___ Hyperactivity

___ Memory deficit

___ Difficulty naming body parts

___ Slow work

___ Restlessness

___ Organizing work

___ Finishing tasks

___ Attention deficit

District 19 Motor Team Screening Form—cont'd

Tactile Sensation

___ Seems to withdraw from touch
___ Craves touch
___ Tends to wear coat when not needed; will not allow shirtsleeves pulled up
___ Has trouble keeping hands to self, will poke or push other children
___ Apt to touch everything he or she sees ("learns through fingers")

___ Dislikes being hugged or cuddled
___ Avoids certain textures of foods
___ Dislikes arts-and-crafts activities involving different textures (clay, finger paints)
___ Complains of numbness, tingling, and other abnormal sensations

Auditory Perception

___ Appears overly sensitive to sounds
___ Talks excessively
___ Likes to make loud noises
___ Has difficulty making self understood

___ Appears to have difficulty understanding teacher/para-professionals/peers
___ Tends to repeat directions to self

Visual Perception

___ Difficulty discriminating colors and shapes doing puzzles
___ Letter and/or number reversals after first grade
___ Difficulty with eye-tracking (following objects with eyes, eyes and head move together)
___ Difficulty copying designs, numbers, or letters

___ Has and wears/doesn't wear glasses
___ Difficulty transcribing from blackboard or book to paper
___ Difficulty with eye-hand or eye-foot coordination (catching, striking, kicking)

Emotional

___ Does not accept changes in routine easily
___ Becomes easily frustrated
___ Acts out behaviorally; difficulty getting along with others
___ Tends to be impulsive, heedless, accident prone
___ Easier to handle in large group, small group, or individually (Circle)

___ Marked mood variations, outbursts or tantrums
___ Marked out-of-seat behavior
___ Noncompliant
___ Unstable home situation
___ Notable self-stimulatory behaviors

Additional Concerns

Assigned to: _____

Date received: _____   Evaluation date: _____

Professionals on the motor development team share common functions yet retain professional integrity and responsibility for the motor development and motor proficiency of the child served.[24] Each has a unique contribution to offer to students and professionals who provide direct services to students with disabilities. The traditional emphasis by each professional who may function as a member of a motor development team is illustrated in Figure 19-3. It is important to note that this model is not restrictive. The intent of the motor development team is to share professional competency, judgment, and expertise. For example, members of the adapted physical education staff of the Jefferson Parish, Louisiana, Project Creole are actively involved in in-

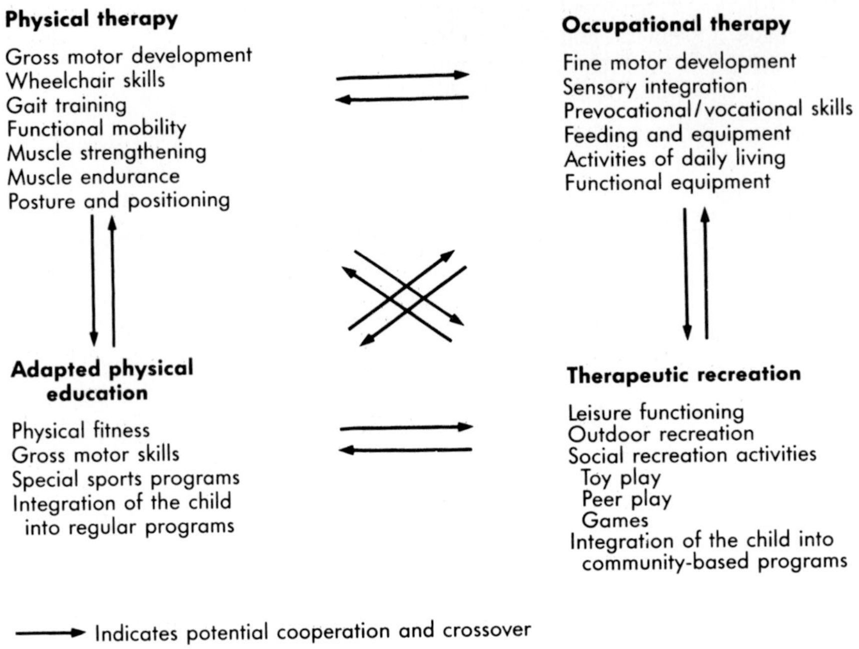

Physical therapy

Gross motor development
Wheelchair skills
Gait training
Functional mobility
Muscle strengthening
Muscle endurance
Posture and positioning

Occupational therapy

Fine motor development
Sensory integration
Prevocational/vocational skills
Feeding and equipment
Activities of daily living
Functional equipment

**Adapted physical
education**

Physical fitness
Gross motor skills
Special sports programs
Integration of the child
  into regular programs

Therapeutic recreation

Leisure functioning
Outdoor recreation
Social recreation activities
  Toy play
  Peer play
  Games
Integration of the child into
  community-based programs

⟶ Indicates potential cooperation and crossover

figure 19-3
Motor development team. (From Sugars A: *The adapted physical educator as a member of the motor development team.* TAHPERD State Convention, Lubbock, Tex, 1990.

service and preservice education of physical and occupational therapists to train those professionals to teach orthopedically disabled children to use their wheelchairs in sport, leisure, recreation, and functional mobility skills. In contrast, an occupational therapist member of a multidisciplinary team may provide sensory integration in-service to physical educators to ensure that the students receive ongoing, appropriate intervention services.

This type of model for the delivery of services to children with motor deficits is particularly important in school districts and cooperatives unable to locate sufficient numbers of certified, trained professional staff. For example, if a school district is unable to hire and retain a licensed physical therapist as part of the staff, it may be necessary for other professionals to implement the program designed by a contracted therapist. In school districts with limited adapted physical education specialists, it is vital that the regular physical educator who provides direct services be provided information necessary

for appropriate services. When he or she is included as part of the motor development team, the therapist can provide needed direction.

Physical education services must be provided to students with disabilities enrolled in public education. The quality of those services will be dependent on the availability, training, and knowledge of the service providers. In best-case scenarios, all direct service providers will be equipped to determine and provide the needed services. However, in the vast majority of schools, personnel knowledgeable about the physical and motor development needs of students with disabilities are limited. Those who are designated to provide those services frequently work under the supervision of the director of special education and have responsibility for assessing, defining goals and objectives, recommending placement, and providing or directing direct services to the student. Those individuals must be accountable to their supervisors through record keeping and the filing of daily lesson plans with their supervisors. Because of the limited number of professionals trained in physical and motor development of individuals with disabilities, motor development teams that share responsibilities are formed. These teams, through direct teaching, consulting, and resource development, allow greater continuity of services to learners with special needs.

Once the adapted physical education program has been established, its success will depend on the quality of services provided, the ability of the personnel to communicate effectively, and the flexibility of the program. Flexibility to function within a school district is crucial because of the number of changes public education is undergoing in this country. In the following section a number of initiatives that have surfaced during the 1990s are presented. The adapted physical educator is challenged to explore ways to participate and contribute to these new frontiers.

School Reform Initiatives

The public schools in this country, and the students they serve, are in the midst of a crisis that is undermining the very fabric of the nation. The schools are failing to prepare students for informed participation in our democracy, for full and vital participation in careers and vocations, for parenting, for active volunteerism and social service, and for creative use of leisure and recreation time. This is occurring at a time in which the vast inequality between the "haves" and "have nots" continues to escalate and entitlement programs are being slashed.

As a result, the structures of schools in the United States are changing, as is the nature of the students and parents who are being served. These changes, known collectively as school reform initiatives, impact the role and the responsibility of the physical educator and the adapted physical educator. The initiatives have great potential for improving the quality of education for every student. As professionals who take our responsibility seriously, physical educators should be on the cutting edge of these changes.

School reform and school restructuring initiatives are occurring in many districts in response to heightened public concern regarding the quality of public education. These reform initiatives include the following:

- Site-based management[9]
- Restructuring of curriculum and instruction[9]
- Restructuring of school calendars/time[9]

- School choice options[9]
- Implementation of total quality management in the schools[4]
- Community-school-parent education partnerships[8]
- Embracing of multiculturalism[16,19,22]
- Inclusion (see Chapter 5)

Site-Based Management

Site-based management is a strategy to increase school effectiveness by allowing the major players (i.e., the principal, teachers, parents, students, and community members) more control over policies and procedures that affect *their* school. It is an attempt to increase participation and interest in learning within the community surrounding the school and to empower those responsible for learning to make decisions regarding what is best for their children.

When 170 principals from 12 suburban school districts in the Indianapolis and Minneapolis/St. Paul areas were surveyed, they found[9]:

. . . (a) meaningful change is most likely to occur at the school level rather than the school district level (87.9% agreement); (b) for change to occur, individual schools need flexibility with regard to regulations (83.2% agreement); and (c) broad representation of the school community in the decision making process produces a level of commitment necessary to bring about change (86.6% agreement).

The beauty of site-based management is that the very people responsible for the quality of learning are held directly accountable for that learning and are given greater decision-making authority in that process. Now in many districts it is virtually impossible for the instructional leader on the local campus to get rid of low-performing and, sometimes, abusive teachers. However, that will change when the school principal is given more authority to hire and fire. In addition, the school principal is often limited by district policies that limit the authority of teachers and parents. Site-based management gives teachers more responsibility for decision making in and through campus-based committees. It gives parents and students the opportunity to provide input and to serve on **campus-based decision-making committees.** In addition, it gives members of the community the opportunity to serve its constituents and to help train those students who will eventually be part of the workforce.

The physical educator can and *must* be a part of the

school-based team. When the physical educator is involved in decision making, the program can be recognized as a vital and integral part of the total educational process.

Restructuring of Curriculum and Instruction

Gaul, Underwood, and Fortune[9] reported that the restructuring of curriculum and instruction occurring in the following areas is making a difference in the quality of education:

- Computer instruction programs
- Programs for at-risk students
- Foreign language instruction
- Adoption of a common core curriculum
- Dropout prevention programs
- Whole-language instruction

Restructuring of School Calendars and Time

Most reform initiatives have included lengthening the school year and expansion of extended-year services (summer school). Additional initiatives include before- and after-school programs, such as tutorials, and block scheduling.

School Choice Options

In some states and local school districts, parents will be given the option of which school in the district their children may attend, including magnet or charter schools. The use of payment vouchers that enable parents to send their children to private schools is a growing practice in this country.

Implementation of Total Quality Management in the Schools

As Glasser[11] pointed out, the recommendations in *A Nation At Risk* focused on lengthening the school day and year and implementing stiffer graduation requirements; however, no suggestions were made as to how teachers might better teach and manage student behavior. Simply increasing the time spent in an ineffective educational environment will not improve the quality of learning.

A philosophy for enabling teachers to provide more effective instruction, manage behavior better, and inspire excellence is called **total quality management.** This movement is based on the work of Dr. W. Edwards Deming, a philosopher, Rennaissance man, visionary, and world leader who provided the impetus for radical change in the way that Americans do business. This change agent helped transform many American businesses from top-down, authoritarian, unempowering organizations into vital, energy-based, enabling organizations in which the contributions of individuals are respected, honored, and valued. The emphasis in Dr. Deming's philosophy of life and business is that individuals must be given the opportunity to do quality work.

Dr. Deming summarized his philosophy in 14 tenets,[3] which are discussed here as they apply to the total quality management movement that is impacting education. Their potential impact on physical education for individuals with disabilities is also addressed.

1. Create constancy of purpose for improvement of product and service.

The emphasis in education would be on the learning process, not on the product. A lifelong excitement and interest in learning would be encouraged. In the adapted physical education program, the emphasis would be on a deep and abiding commitment to individual wellness and to the continuous exploration of individual potential in play, games, and leisure, recreation, and sport activities.

2. Adopt the new philosophy.

The primary tenet of Deming's philosophy is that every individual and every organization must seek continued improvement. The physical educator must be committed to the continuous improvement of his or her program. This requires an ongoing evaluation (plan-do-review) process. In the adapted physical education program, every student would be recognized for his or her abilities and encouraged in every possible way to seek continual improvement.

3. Cease dependence on mass inspection.

If education is to evolve to really meet the learning needs of the students it serves, the emphasis must shift from ridiculous, often invalid, mass state- and district-mandated testing of students to individual consideration of student needs. In this, special education and adapted physical education have the potential to be on the cutting edge with the implementation of the IEP. If Deming's principles were truly embraced, every student (with or without disabilities) would have an IEP. Also as important, every student would be given the opportunity to learn to evaluate his or her own progress.

4. End the practice of doing business on the basis of price tag alone.

In the development of a quality school, the emphasis would be on the student and the student's family as customers. To that end, the school's program and curricula would be specially designed to meet the needs of the student *and* the family. To ensure that this happened, the school would be involved in an effort to be a vital part of the community. The physical education program would be designed to be sensitive to the needs of the student and the student's family within the community. For example, in Wisconsin part of the program would address activities such as showshoeing, cross-country skiing, ice skating, and sledding—activities that would hardly be appropriate for students growing up in the South. If the students served in the school represent a largely Hispanic community, rhythms and dance activities that represent their culture would be infinitely more significant to them than the "Hokey Pokey."

5. Improve constantly and forever the system of production and service.

School administrators committed to the notion of quality would empower their faculty and staff to grow and learn and experiment with teaching techniques and strategies in order to constantly improve the existing system. Faculty and staff would be encouraged to engage in the constant cycle of "plan-do-review" to keep program evaluation ongoing. The physical educator would be involved in the constant process of evaluating the quality of services given to students with disabilities; the teacher would conduct ongoing needs assessments of students with disabilities and their parents.

6. Institute programs of training.

In-service education programs would be designed by the faculty and staff to meet their needs—not the needs of an administrator.

7. Institute leadership.

In a system of true quality, only those leaders who were capable of managing in a system of trust, in which the faculty/staff and students were empowered to grow and change, would be allowed to remain in a position of leadership. Those with a top-down and autocratic management style would be encouraged to seek employment elsewhere. Only those physical educators able to encourage students to learn, grow, and change in an environment sensitive to their needs would be allowed to remain in a position of leadership. Those whose classes resembled a quasi-military setting would be asked to seek employment elsewhere. Students would be taught

to learn to set and measure personal goals in relation to play, games, and leisure, recreation, and sport activities. In addition, students would be given the skills necessary to evaluate personal fitness levels.

8. Drive out fear.

According to Bonstingl,[3] "Fear is counterproductive. . . . Fear is destructive of the school culture and everything good that is intended to take place within it." The verbally or physically abusive teacher has no place in our schools.

9. Break down barriers between staff areas.

Multidisciplinary school teams, multi-age groupings of students, community-parent-faculty collaborative efforts, and cooperative learning would be the focus of the school.

10. Eliminate slogans, exhortations, and targets for the workplace.

Catchy phrases and slogans may be fun, but they should not replace a fundamental and basic commitment to quality within the school.

11. Eliminate numerical quotas.

In the school setting, this means that the focus of learning would be on learning as a process and not on arbitrarily determined state standards. Teachers would not teach for "test success" but would help students learn how to learn. The physical educator would eliminate mass physical fitness tests, for example, in favor of individual self-testing of health-related fitness.

12. Remove barriers to pride and joy of workmanship.

The instructional leader would develop an environment where his or her teachers would feel pride in their work. The teachers would create a learning environment in which the students could take pride in their performance, learning, and accomplishments. The joy in learning would return to the schools. The schools would cease being empty shells in which children are treated disrespectfully and would become joyous places in which children are revered and held in a place of honor.

13. Institute a vigorous program of education and retraining.

Everyone in the school would be excited about learning and would be given every opportunity to seek new learning and new joy in the process.

14. Take action to accomplish the transformation.

The responsibility for change lies with the professional educator who cares about students. Those individuals who favor protecting the status quo should leave. Dr. Deming would shake his head in disgust at educators who claim that such a transformation could not occur. He would simply tell them to "make it happen . . . now."

Community/School/Family Partnerships

A vital and integral part of any school reform movement involves the child, the child's family, and the community and school as partners in educating and embracing the child. A wonderful African saying that should be the watchword for education in the twenty-first century is, "It takes a whole village to raise a child."

Epstein wrote[8]:

> The way schools care about children is reflected in the way schools care about the children's families. If educators view children simply as *students,* they are likely to see the family as separate from the school. That is, the family is expected to do its job and leave the education of children to the schools. If educators view students as *children,* they are likely to see both the family and the community as partners with the school in children's education and development. Partners recognize their shared interests in and responsibilities for children, and they work together to create better programs and opportunities for students.

Epstein[8] has developed a model for the development of family/community/school partnerships to best serve the children within any given community. She has identified the following six types of involvement of families and community members within the schools:

Type 1   Parenting: Help all families establish home environments to support children as students.

Type 2   Communicating: Design effective forms of school-to-home communications about school programs and children's progress.

Type 3   Volunteering: Recruit and organize parent help and support.

Type 4   Learning at home: Provide information and ideas to families about how to help students at home with homework and other curriculum-related activities, decisions, and planning.

Type 5   Decision making: Include parents in school decisions, developing parent leaders and representatives.

Type 6   Collaborating with community. Identify and integrate resources and services from the community to strengthen school programs, family practices, and student learning and development.

Suggestions for the regular physical educator and adapted physical educator for increasing involvement in each of the six types are considered here.

TYPE 1   PARENTING

1. Provide parents and members of the learner's extended family with information that will help them develop reasonable expectations regarding the motor development of a student with a developmental delay or disability.
2. Provide parents and members of the learner's extended family with information regarding developmentally appropriate play (e.g., the child needs to learn to engage in cooperative play before he or she can engage in competitive experiences with success).
3. Model appropriate play and motor intervention strategies for parents (e.g., toss the ball in a horizontal path when a student is learning to catch so that the child is not overwhelmed by trying to track an object moving through horizontal and vertical planes).
4. Share information with parents about strategies for making inexpensive equipment for the student to play with in the home (e.g., an old mattress or an old tire covered with a secured piece of carpeting makes a wonderful trampoline).
5. Share information about community resources and opportunities for students with disabilities to participate in play, games, and leisure, recreation, and sport activities.
6. Provide family support and information regarding securing health services for the student.

TYPE 2   COMMUNICATING

1. Use your computer to generate a physical education and/or adapted physical education newsletter or ask for a column or space in the school newspaper.
2. Send home brief notes to communicate with the student's family, such as the computer-generated certificate shown in Figure 19-4.

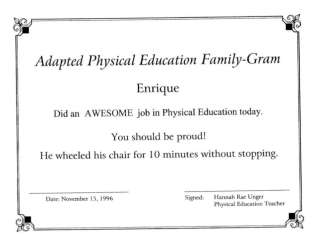

Adapted Physical Education Family-Gram

Enrique

Did an AWESOME job in Physical Education today.

You should be proud!

He wheeled his chair for 10 minutes without stopping.

Date: November 15, 1996   Signed: Hannah Rae Unger
                                                    Physical Education Teacher

figure 19-4
A customized certificate is an excellent way to communicate with a student's family.

2. Videotape a class activity and make the video available for parent checkout.
3. Call a parent to discuss student progress. This is particularly effective if the physical educator or adapted physical educator calls to praise a child. Much too often, teachers only communicate with parents when there is a problem.
4. Be an active participant in regularly scheduled parent-teacher conferences. Communicate with parents a willingness to meet at other times as well.
5. Write positive comments on student report cards.

TYPE 3 VOLUNTEERING

1. Enlist parent support to teach dances and games that reflect their culture.
2. Encourage parents to serve:
   a. As an assistant in classes
   b. As a director or assistant in before- and after-school recreation, intramural, or sports programs
   c. As an assistant coach
   d. As a director or assistant in school play day
   e. As the editor or publisher of the newsletter
   f. As a parent-to-parent trainer
   g. As a raffle organizer to raise money for equipment
   h. As an assistant playground supervisor
   i. As a clerical assistant to generate certificates, progress charts, etc.

TYPE 4 LEARNING AT HOME

1. Provide information to parents regarding curriculum and activities required at each grade level.
2. Provide information to parents with strategies for helping the learner develop motor skills necessary to participate in play, games, and leisure, recreation, and sport activities; include information regarding the development and maintenance of physical fitness.
3. Demonstrate age-appropriate activities that parents can use with groups of children at a park or in an open area within their apartment or project complex, for example.
4. Provide a calendar for parents that helps them follow unit themes and special activities.
5. Recommend television shows or videotapes that reflect the philosophy of your program. For example, suggest that the family share together:
   a. Television coverage of the Olympics
   b. Television coverage of the Paralympics
   c. Television coverage of the Special Olympics
   d. A videotape of "The Jim Thorpe Story"
   e. A videotape of "The Babe Didrickson Story"

TYPE 5 DECISION MAKING

1. Invite parent participation in a subcommittee of the Parent-Teacher Association/Organization (PTA/PTO) that addresses the physical education/adapted physical education program.
2. In districts where there is a special education advisory committee, ensure that a parent with a commitment to physical education/adapted physical education is on that committee.
3. Encourage parents to serve as advocates for adapted physical education programs and services.

TYPE 6 COLLABORATING WITH COMMUNITY

1. As the physical educator or adapted physical educator, ask to serve on boards or committees of community recreation and/or sports organizations.
2. Develop a collaborative physical education or recreation program to meet the needs of learners within the community, using shared facilities, shared equipment, and, if possible, shared personnel.
3. Recruit community personnel to help develop and build playgrounds for the schools. Particularly in large urban districts, playgrounds are often nonexistent or antiquated.
4. Encourage older learners to provide service within the community as coaches and recreation leaders.

Embracing of Multiculturalism

According to Manning[15]:

> Schools have long based expectations, perceptions of motivations and success, learning methodologies, and selection of curricular materials on middle-class, Anglo-American perceptions. This decision may have resulted from the belief that culturally diverse learners should acculturate toward middle-class Anglo-American perspectives, the belief that the schools should cater to the majority social class and culture, or the belief that culturally diverse learners did not deserve the advantages of the dominant culture. Regardless of the reason, the decision resulted in inequitable treatment of culturally different learners; and in the process, schools may have perpetuated racism, prejudice, and discrimination.

The demographics within the United States and our schools have changed remarkably within the past decade. As Markowitz[16] points out, "For the first time in U.S. history, the mainstream is about to become the minority, and the group that has held the power, made the laws, set the policies, controlled the money and dictated to everyone else is on the verge of being outnumbered." Educators must seize every opportunity to embrace *each child* they serve—without regard to race, culture, socioeconomic status, religion (or lack thereof), gender, gender preference, and ability or disability. We have the responsibility to ensure that all public schools have equitable resources, all cultures are represented in the curriculum, and students representing all socioeconomic levels, as well as each gender and gender preference, are fairly treated.

To ensure educational equity, it has become increasingly obvious that the schools must be prepared to honor students representing diverse cultures. If students are to be empowered as learners and as people, their families and their cultures must be respected. According to Markowitz[16]:

> Multiculturalists argue that the price of cutting off a significant cultural legacy is internalized shame and diminished self-esteem. This is even more pronounced for those who come from cultures already in a one-down economic position, like refugees or people from developing nations, or those whose cultures include a history of colonization or persecution, like descendants of African slaves.

This respect for the student's culture is particularly important because minority students are much more likely to be in high-poverty schools and face discrimination and stereotypes; also, a much greater concentration of health, social, and neighborhood problems is found in high-poverty schools.[22]

Creating a school environment in which each child and the child's "culture," in its broadest sense, are represented requires a serious commitment to understanding. It requires educators to seriously examine their values and their own cultural identity and to be willing to try new approaches in their classrooms in order to make their coursework relevant.[19]

The teacher must be able to engage in an honest and open dialogue with his or her learners, their parents, members of their extended families, and individuals within the communities in which the students live. Many dedicated educators choose to be involved in an experience known as a cultural plunge, in which they choose to live in or visit a setting that represents a culture very different from their own.[19] For example, a Hispanic teacher may choose to attend a church service attended primarily by African-Americans. Or, an Anglo-American teacher may attend a Cinco de Mayo celebration. While this is only one step, it is the beginning of a process in which the teacher begins to develop empathy and appreciation of the unique heritages and beliefs of his or her students.

According to Markowitz,[16] "Ultimately, multiculturalism is a movement to make society a place in which people from all cultures have equal respect and equal voice and equal influence in shaping larger community values." The physical educator or adapted physical educator can have an impact on the process of enabling all students to learn within the public schools and still retain dignity.

The notion of culture is diverse and is not limited to one facet of the life of human beings. When educators consider "culture," it must be considered within a broad perspective because we all carry several cultures at once—our inherited cultures, the generation in which we were born, our gender, and our socioeconomic class.[16] Each of these cultural facets impacts our perceptions and actions, and may significantly affect our choices and options.

It is helpful to understand the impact culture has on behavior, because the teacher who is knowledgeable about and sensitive to cultural differences is capable of modifying instruction to fit the characteristics of the individual and group.[12] With a reminder that these "cultural characteristics" are basic and may not be true of all individuals representing a particular culture, teaching strategies that may maximize the performance of students representing those cultures are presented here.

HISPANIC CULTURES

- Emphasize the importance of the extended family.
- Celebrate cultural awareness by celebrating cultural holidays.
- Emphasize respect for Hispanic cultural beliefs.
- Expect moral and ethical behavior.
- Encourage respect for Spanish as a living language.
- Emphasize the primary role of family and family loyalty.
- Learn best in real-life situations and contexts.
- Value quality interpersonal relationships.
- May be awed by persons considered to be in a position of authority.

Specific teaching strategies:
1. Use demonstrations and rely on gestures and body language for communication.
2. Avoid competition and emphasize collaborative learning.
3. Use sequential learning.

AFRICAN-AMERICAN CULTURES

- Emphasize the importance of the extended family and kinship within the community.
- Celebrate an awareness of African-American history.
- Emphasize the priority of the church as the central force within the community.
- Emphasize a community responsibility for raising children.
- Encourage respect for the elderly.
- Learn best in real-life situations and simulations.
- Recognize and embrace oral language and storytelling.
- Place a real value on interpersonal relationships.
- May distrust the public school system, and its teachers, as part of the larger "system" that has betrayed them.

Specific teaching strategies:
1. Emphasize collaborative learning and cooperative play.

2. Encourage individual expression.
3. Vary tasks frequently.
4. Help students develop personal goals and assist them by providing positive feedback.

ASIAN-AMERICAN CULTURES

- Emphasize respect for individuals with authority.
- Encourage respectful, quiet, cooperative behavior.
- Establish and maintain very high academic and behavior standards.
- Place an emphasis on the integrity of the family as a unit.
- Teach children to avoid behavior that might embarrass the family.
- Teach respect for the elderly.
- Respect and value the complexity of language.
- Emphasize the work ethic.

Specific teaching strategies:
1. Provide opportunity for individual and independent work.
2. Provide a hierarchy of challenges so that each child can seek improvement.
3. Use overhead projectors and provide extra-credit reading assignments.

INDIAN-AMERICAN CULTURES

- Emphasize respect for all individuals.
- Emphasize respect for nature and the environment.
- Encourage the group welfare of the tribe and the family.
- Put an emphasis on self-sufficiency and on providing children the skills needed to learn and grow early in life.
- May distrust the public school system, and its teachers, as part of the larger "system" that has betrayed them.
- Tend to learn best by participating in active learning.
- Value personal and cultural dignity.

Specific teaching strategies:
1. Link the past to the present; emphasize the historical context of play, games, and sports.
2. Avoid competition and emphasize cooperative learning.
3. Analyze tasks to create a hierarchy of objectives.

ANGLO-AMERICAN CULTURES

- Emphasize individual initiative.
- View history from a limited European perspective.
- Emphasize respect for one's individual family.
- Rely heavily on verbal rather than nonverbal communication.
- Encourage increasing independence as children get older.

Specific teaching strategies:
1. Help students develop personal goals and develop skills to evaluate their own progress.
2. Provide a great deal of variety in the program.

Other basic strategies that may be used by the physical educator are:
1. Know and use each child's name. This is a funda-

mental requirement if the teacher is to communicate the fact that the child is valued.
2. Do not jump to quick conclusions regarding a child's behavior, particularly if the child represents a different culture. For example, children from many Asian cultures have been taught to lower their heads and their eyes to show respect to adults. A teacher insisting that the child, "Look at me when I'm talking to you" is literally asking the child to show disrespect.
3. Ensure that there is someone available to translate if the teacher does not understand the language or dialect of the student. Often, another student can help communicate. While it would be wonderful for the teacher to be familiar with basic phrases in the native language or mode of communication of each child in his or her classes, it is not unusual in a large urban district for children to use more than 90 different languages and dialects.
4. Minimize the use of verbal language and rely heavily on demonstrations.
5. Use posters that reflect a diverse community.
6. Learn to read the student. Body language, gestures, and facial expressions can often communicate intent and feelings better than verbal language.
7. The teacher should select and use music that represents a variety of cultures.
8. Invite parents and members of the community to teach games and other activities that represent the cultures of the children served.
9. Honor diverse religious and cultural celebrations. Ask parents and other members of the community to share that diversity to celebrate, for example, Juneteenth, Cinco de Mayo, Rosh Hashanah, and the Chinese New Year.

Communication with Parents

Increasingly, the parent(s) and members of the learner's extended family are being encouraged to be active participants in the learner's education and are increasingly part of the education system at all levels—as members of the state board of education, as members of a local school board, as members of site-based management committees, and as active participants in the day-to-day operation of the school, as tutors, for example.[10]

In many situations, the parents may be effective participants in the total assessment/evaluation process, providing evaluators with information about the learner's behavior in the home and on the neighborhood playground.[23] Many parents are becoming increasingly involved in the IEP process.

One of the most challenging aspects of the role of the adapted physical educator is effective communication with the parents. This vital communication, which can and should lead to an effective partnership between the teacher and the parent and between the school and the home, is often challenging because of cultural, ethnic, and socioeconomic differences. According to Olson,[21] "As the two major forces entrusted with educating and socializing children in society, parents and teachers should be natural allies. But far too often, they find themselves on opposite sides of an exceedingly high fence."

To communicate effectively with the parents and families of learners with disabilities, the physical educator or adapted physical educator must be aware of the comprehensive effects of a child's disability on the total ecology of the family. There are three major theories regarding the impact of a child's disability on the child's parents, siblings, and extended family: chronic sorrow syndrome, dominant stage theory, and nonsequential stage theory. **Chronic sorrow syndrome** describes the reactions of parents or siblings when faced with the constant reminder of "loss" associated with disability. The parent or sibling with chronic sorrow syndrome may cope relatively well with the day-to-day requirements of providing support for the child with a disability, but the individual's underlying emotions include sadness, fear, anger, and guilt.[20]

The **dominant stage theory** suggests that the parent or sibling of a child with a disability experiences emotions and reactions that are identical to those that are experienced by an individual facing the death of a loved one or facing a terminal illness. These stages of grief—denial, bargaining, anger, depression, and acceptance—were first described in the teachings of Dr. Elisabeth Kübler-Ross.[14] It is important to note that these emotional stages also parallel those experienced by a child or adult with an adventitious disability (a condition acquired after a history of "normal" development).

The **nonsequential stage theory** suggests that the parents, siblings, or extended family members may experience some or all of the stages of grief described by Kübler-Ross, but not necessarily in predictable stages. The nonsequential stage theory suggests that a response to the child's disability may be the result of facing particular milestones.[4] The initial diagnosis of disability may cause denial, anger, and depression. These emotions may resurface when the parents are faced with the fact that their child needs to receive special education services; again as the child reaches adolescence and the parents must deal with the realities of sexuality; and/or as the parents deal with their own aging and the inevitability of providing alternate care for their offspring.

Parent support groups have acknowledged the serious need for parent(s) of learners with disabilities to deal, proactively, with their grief in order to continue to function not only as parents but also as human beings. Blanchard[2] suggests that a parent needs to actively release the "dream" that accompanies the loss of the child imagined during pregnancy—a child with the physical skills of Michael Jordan, the cognitive/language skills of Barbara Jordan, the artistic ability of Picasso, the musical ability of Joan Baez, the looks of Robert Redford or Christie Brinkley, and the altruism of Mother Theresa. A grieving ritual allows parents to identify all the characteristics they hoped their child would have and gives them permission to release that. Blanchard describes that extremely painful process[2]:

> I began by leafing through magazines to find pictures of my "dream child"—the child I didn't get. I cut out any picture that moved me. I especially looked for pictures of the ideal birth where everyone is smiling and the wet, shining baby is laid on the mother's chest. I found pictures of babies sitting up and crawling, of young girls running and playing. I cut out a paper doll from a large piece of blank paper and was amazed that holding this piece of paper to my chest caused me to cry. I glued my dream child pictures all over the paper doll. I decorated her with glitter, paint and colorful markers. I cut out a back for her, and stuffed her with more of my "dreams" . . . I had decided to burn this dream child to transform her energy and let her float away. So after discussing my dreams with my friends, I put the paper doll in the fireplace, lit a match and let her go.

Understanding the response to a child with a disability is further complicated by the fact that there appear to be sociocultural differences in parent reactions. Mary[17] studied the reactions of black, Hispanic, and white mothers toward their child with a disability and found that Hispanic mothers reported an attitude of self-sacrifice more often than the other mothers. In addition,

Hispanic mothers noted greater spousal denial of the disability than other mothers.

Willoughby and Glidden[26] studied 48 married, middle-class, predominantly Anglo-European parents and found that when fathers participated actively in the care of the child with a disability, both parents expressed greater satisfaction in the marriage. Sharing time and stress demands appeared to lessen stresses associated with coping in both spouses.

The adapted physical educator hoping to work successfully in the home must not only recognize the emotional responses of family members to a child with a disability, but must also be sensitive to the forces that affect the family. The family is often overwhelmed by the need to interact with the huge, often impersonal, medical bureaucracy. The sense of despair is often heightened by the sense of feeling helpless and unempowered when facing the barrage of medical personnel, hostile medical insurance representatives, and incomprehensible medical bills. New HMO and other insurance reforms have heightened the sense of helplessness experienced by the family of a learner with a disability. The family may experience a sense of isolation as friends and others in the community respond in fear. The family may be frustrated by huge time constraints involved in the care of a child with a disability. According to Bratlinger,[4] "Parenting is always demanding, but having a child with a handicapping condition usually adds to the complexity of the task." Parents of children with disabilities are more likely than others to experience significant stress, and Blacher[1] reported that these parents are more likely to develop emotional and personality disorders. Dyson[7] found that such stress is persistent even in the absence of other socioeconomic disadvantages.

Weiss[25] and McConachie[18] reported that parents of children with significant developmental delays experience a great deal of stress, including:

- Dealing with professional and other support services
- Family strains
- Stigmatization
- The child's aberrant behavior
- Broken, sleepless nights
- Concerns regarding their own future mental/emotional health
- Fears regarding the child's future, including financial planning, residential versus community living,

and vocational and social integration (It is interesting to note that in a study of 57 adult caregivers and their adult children with mental retardation, over half had not made any long-term plans for their children.[13])

These stressors are not uncommon to the parents of any child with a disability. The nature of the disability and its severity have a direct bearing on the extent and type of stress. In addition, the nature of the support resources offered to parents and siblings has a direct impact on the stress and coping ability of the family members.[18]

Equipment

In addition to possessing proper attitudes, knowledge, skills, and sensitivity to individual and group needs, as well as participating in new school initiatives, the physical educator is responsible for securing equipment and managing facilities. As the practice of the art and science of adapted physical education responds to the changing school structure and the ever-changing sociocultural environment, the methods and environments in which children are served have changed dramatically.

We have eliminated the section of the previous edition that described ideal segregated facilities for adapted physical education. This decision was made for several reasons: (1) the trend toward inclusionary practices virtually eliminates the need for every school/school district to have separate facilities for the provision of adapted physical education; and (2) budget cuts at the federal, state, and local levels have significantly reduced the likelihood that a school/school district can afford separate, state-of-the art facilities, even if that were deemed appropriate. The emphasis in this section is on equipment that can be used by the physical educator and adapted physical educator to better meet the needs of his or her students.

Equipment for Elementary School Physical Education for Children with Disabilities

As mentioned earlier, if children with disabilities are able to receive physical education instruction in the regular physical education program, they generally share equipment with the other children. The physical education teacher who serves children with disabilities in the regular elementary physical education program may wish to supplement basic equipment needed for quality elementary physical education instruction with additional equipment. The basic equipment needed for such a program is listed below. This list also represents the basic requirements for an adapted physical education program in a more restricted environment.

1. Locomotor skills
   a. Wide balance beams or balance boards (6, 8, 10, and 12 inches wide)
   b. Oversize scooter boards
   c. Colorful plastic tape for marking floors
   d. Plastic hoops
   e. Jump ropes
2. Manipulative skills
   a. Balloons
   b. Punch balls
   c. Assorted Nerf-type balls for catching and kicking
   d. Assorted balls, including large playground balls
   e. Velcro paddles and Velcro balls for catching
   f. Wands with ribbons attached
   g. Small balls with ribbons attached
   h. Beanbags
3. Low-organized group games
   a. Huge group parachutes
   b. Cage balls
   c. Tug-of-war rope
4. Lead-up games for individual and team sports
   a. Oversize tennis and badminton racquets
   b. Oversize bats
   c. Nerf-type soccer balls, footballs, and volleyballs
   d. Junior-size basketballs
   e. Adjustable basketball hoop that can be lowered
5. Tumbling and developmental gymnastics
   a. Floor mats
   b. Incline mats
   c. Carpeted barrels
   d. Inner tubes (covered for jumping)
6. Rhythms and dance
   a. Portable "boom box"
   b. Assorted tapes and records
   c. Music-making equipment (bells, drums, maracas, etc.)

See Table 19-3 for sources of adapted physical education equipment.

With some ingenuity, the teacher can provide an excellent adapted physical education program for students at the elementary school level with minimum equipment. Play equipment can be made inexpensively. Following are suggestions for inexpensive equipment for use in the physical education program:

- Rope for skipping, making shapes, jumping over, or climbing under
- Cardboard boxes to climb in and through, to catch with, or to use as targets (particularly empty refrigerator, television, or washer/dryer boxes)
- Tape to make shapes on the floor for moving on, around, and in
- Chalk for making "own body" shapes or puzzles
- Half-gallon or gallon plastic jugs for catching, throwing, knocking over, etc.
- Scrap lumber for balance beams
- Yarn for yarn balls
- Carpet squares to skate on, slide on, sit on, or use as targets
- Cardboard barrels to roll in or throw objects into
- Old garden hoses to make hula hoops
- Old ladders to walk on or through
- Traffic cones for obstacle courses
- Balloons
- Wire clothes hangers and old nylons (nylons suspended around the clothes hangers make inexpensive racquets)
- Butcher paper
- Paper bags filled with sand for "barbells"
- Tin cans filled with cement and held together with pipe for "barbells"
- Dowel rods cut into sections for lumni sticks
- Rags tied into knots to make balls

Play equipment for adapted physical education students at the elementary school level usually may be borrowed from the regular physical education teacher. Also, a wide variety of excellent specialized equipment for use by persons of all ages and with most types of disabilities has been developed by numerous manufacturers.

Equipment for Middle and Secondary School Physical Education for Children with Disabilities

Equipment for a fitness program, as well as leisure, recreation, and sports, at the middle and secondary school levels should allow the participation of all students, with different levels of ability. Basic equipment needs for a physical fitness program are listed on pp. 512-513.

| table 19-3 |

Equipment for the Disabled

Equipment/Modification	Brand Name	Corporation
Sport wheelchairs	Quickie's	Sunrise Medical 2842 Business Park Avenue Fresno, CA 93727
Sport wheelchairs	Fortress Edge	Fortress P.O. Box 489 Clovis, CA 93613
Sport wheelchairs	Action's	Action Technology 34655 Mills Road North Ridgeville, OH 44039
Sport wheelchairs		SOPUR WEST, Inc. 601 East Sola Street Santa Barbara, CA 93103
Sport wheelchairs	Max	Kuschall of America 753 Calle Plano Camarillo, CA 93012
Sport wheelchairs	Heat The Predator (hand-crank)	Top End 6551 44th Street N., #5002 Pinellas Park, FL 33565
Sport wheelchairs	Avatar	Wheel Ring, Inc. 199 Forest Street Manchester, CT 06040
Sport wheelchairs	Screaming Eagle	Eagle Sportschairs 2351 Parkwood Road Snellville, GA 30278
Sport wheelchairs for children	Hall's Wheels	Bob Hall P.O. Box 784 Cambridge, MA 02238
Sport wheelchairs Electric wheelchairs Three-wheeled scooters	Action Pro-T The Arrow	Invacare Corporation 34655 Mills Road North Ridgeville, OH 44039
Suspension wheelchairs	The Iron Horse	Iron Horse Productions, Inc. 2624 Conner Street Port Huron, MI 48060
Off-road wheelchairs	Cobra	Up and Over Engineering 1509 Liberty Street El Cerrito, CA 94530
Sport wheelchairs Easy-Stands	ALTimate	ALT, Inc. 913 S. Washington Redwood Falls, MN 56283
Wheelchairs/walkers	Stand-N-Go	Stand-N-Go Route 5, Box 22A Fergus Falls, MN 56537
All-terrain vehicles Hand-controlled (motor)		Recreative Industries 60 Depot Street Buffalo, NY 14206

Continued.

table 19-3

Equipment for the Disabled—cont'd		
Equipment/Modification	**Brand Name**	**Corporation**
All-terrain hand cycles	Quantum Leap	Quantum Leap 974 Pinson Blvd. Rockledge, FL 32955
Electric scooters Wheelchair van lifts	Tri-Wheeler	Braun Corporation 1014 S. Monticello Winamac, IN 46996
Wheelchairs/standing boxes	Lifestand	IDC Medical Equipment 20 Independence Court Folcroft, PA 19032
Transfer machines	EasyPivot	Rand-Scot, Inc. 401 Linden Center Drive Fort Collins, CO 30524
Wheelchair treadmills	The Bug Roller	McLain Cycle Products 1718 106th Avenue Otsego, MI 49078

Stationary aerobic hand cycles with:
    Limited-grasp handgrips
    Adjustable-loop handgrips
    Gripp Cuffs
	Saratoga cycle	Saratoga Access & Fitness
		P.O. Box 2346
		Clifton Park, NY 12065

Weight-training machines	Versatrainer	Pro-Max Bowflex of America, Inc. 2200 NE 65th Ave., Suite C Vancouver, WA 98661
Weight-training machines	Equalizer Home Gym	Helm Distributing, Inc. 911 Kings Point Road Polson, MT 59860
Weight-training machines	Freedom Machine	Freedom Machine 2323 W. Encanto Blvd. Phoenix, AZ 85009
Weight-training machines	FreeForm ProLink	James Design Co., Inc. 412 S. Wade Blvd. Millville, NJ 08332
Weight-training machines		Moto's Custom Iron Works 3787 Shasta Dam Blvd. Central Valley, CA 96019
Weight-training machines	The Activator	Magic Industries 11906 Northeast Halsey Portland, OR 97220
Muscle stimulators/exercisers	Power Trainer	Sinties Scientific, Inc. 1216 N. Lansing Ave., Suite B Tulsa, OK 74106
Prosthetic foot development	Seattle Lightfoot	Model & Instrument 861 Poplar Place S. Seattle, WA 98144

table 19-3

Equipment for the Disabled—cont'd

Equipment/Modification	Brand Name	Corporation
Prosthetic feet	Quantum Foot	Hosmer Dorrance Corp. 561 Division Street Campbell, CA 95008
Prosthetic feet Knee/ankle prostheses	Natural Toes Endolite	Kingsley Mfg. Co. Costa Mesa, CA 1-800-LITE-LEG
Lower leg prostheses	Flex-Foot and Flex-Walk II	Flex-Foot, Inc. 27071 Cabot, Suite 106 Laguna Hills, CA 92653
Lower leg prostheses	Swing-N-Stance	Mauch Laboratories 3035 Dryden Road Dayton, OH 45439
Para golf/golf carts for wheelchair users		Para Golf P.O. Box 24303 Houston, TX 77229
Three-wheeled racers Mono-skis (snow) Mono-ski boots (snow)	Shadow Racer Shadow Mono-Ski	Magic in Motion, Inc. 20604 84th Avenue S. Kent, WA 98032
Hand-cycle attachments for wheelchair Mono-skis (snow)	Shadow Cycl-One Yetti	Radventure, Inc. 20755 SW 238th Place Sherwood, OR 97140
Sit-skis (water)	Kan Ski	Kan Ski 2704 Hwy 99E Biggs, CA 95917
Ski picks (snow)		Innovator of Disability Equipment & Adaptations 1393 Meadowcreek Drive, Suite 2 Pewaukee, WI 53072
Fishing rod holders	Strong-Arm	Strong Arm Fishing Products 2046A Pharmacy Avenue Scarborough, Ontario Canada M1T 1H8
Single rowing shell Double rowing shells Rowing pontoons	Pocock Pocock Double Wherry Rowcat	U.S. Rowing Association 201 S. Capitol Avenue, Suite 400 Indianapolis, IN 46225
Adjustable basketball hoops	Rim Ball	Snitz Manufacturing 2096 S. Church Street East Troy, WI 53120
Automatic return basketball hoops		Jayfro Corporation P.O. Box 400 Waterford, CT 06385
Bowling ramps		Flaghouse, Inc. 150 N. MacQuesten Pkwy. Mt. Vernon, NY 10550

Continued.

table 19-3		
Equipment for the Disabled—cont'd		
Equipment/Modification	Brand Name	Corporation
Automatic grip release bowling balls		Flaghouse, Inc. 150 N. MacQuesten Pkwy. Mt. Vernon, NY 10550
Custom-seat kayaks		Gopher Sports Equipment 220 24th Avenue N.W. Owatonna, MN 55060
Sports gloves for wheelchair athletes		Mega Bike 916 N. Western Avenue #226 San Pedro, CA 90732
Racing rims for sport wheelchairs	Mistral M19A II	Sun Metal Products, Inc. P.O. Box 1508 Warsaw, IN 46581
Snow chains for wheelchairs	Sno-Traks	Handi-Trak, Inc. 1521 S. 85th Street Milwaukee, WI 53214
Wheelchair accessible motor homes	Freedom Edition	Rehabilitation Equipment and Supply 311 N. Western Avenue Peoria, IL 61604

1. Mirrors
2. Wide, padded benches
3. Multistation, heavy resistance machine on which students can exercise a number of different areas of the body. Nautilus equipment or other isokinetic machines should be used.
4. Stationary bicycle
5. Stationary rowing machine
6. Stationary cross-country skiing simulator
7. Stair stepper
8. Treadmill

Equipment for leisure, recreation, and sports should include the following:

1. Archery
    a. Lightweight bows
    b. Large, fluorescent target faces
    c. Beepers to attach to target
2. Badminton
    a. Oversize racquets
    b. Oversize shuttlecocks
3. Basketball
    a. Adjustable-height basketball standards
    b. Basketball standards with return nets
    c. Junior-size basketballs
4. Bowling
    a. Bowling ball with retractable handle
    b. Portable bowling ramp
    c. Wooden shuffleboard sticks for pushing the ball down the floor
    d. Lightweight balls with appropriate holes (4- to 6-inch balls)
    e. Beepers for target at end of lane
5. Goal ball
    a. Goal ball with beeper
    b. Goal ball nets
6. Golf
    a. Clubs with enlarged head size
    b. Fluorescent golf balls
    c. Fluorescent golf-size wiffle balls
7. Rhythms and dance
    a. "Boom box" with excellent bass adjustment
    b. Percussion instruments

8. Snow skiing
   a. Sit-skis
   b. Pulk skis
9. Softball
   a. Adjustable T-ball stands
   b. Beeper softballs
   c. Large, *soft* softballs
   d. Oversize bats
   e. Fluorescent bases
10. Tennis
    a. Oversize racquets
    b. Fluorescent balls
11. Track and field
    a. Beep cones
    b. Guide ropes with movable plastic holder
12. Volleyball
    a. Beach balls, brightly colored
13. Waterskiing
    a. Sit-skis

Modification of Equipment

Modification of equipment frequently enables individuals with disabilities to participate in leisure, recreation, sport, and physical fitness activities from which they would otherwise be excluded. Entrepreneurs have come to understand that individuals with disabilities are as serious about quality leisure, recreation, sport, and physical fitness activities as individuals without disabilities. Within the past few years, there has been a remarkable growth in equipment that enhances athletic performance for individuals with and without disabilities. There are hundreds of types of shoes that can be selected specifically to improve performance in a given activity. There are also a wide variety of sport wheelchairs and modified equipment designed to improve performance in a given activity. There are now, for example, specific wheelchairs designed for sprint racing, distance road racing, basketball, tennis, rugby, football, and wilderness trekking (see Table 19-3).

SUMMARY

The nature of the education system—both the structure and the nature of the students and parents served—is changing rapidly. The physical educator must respond to these changes in order to ensure a valid place within the education community.

The physical educator is one of the many professionals who has a vested interest in students' growth, development, and maturation. The adapted physical educator has the specific responsibility for ensuring that each student with a disability is provided an appropriate physical education experience. The teacher must inform the administration of the school's obligations, and provide and document the appropriateness of the services provided to students.

The quality adapted physical education program requires excellent communication among all involved. Adapted physical educators and regular physical educators serving learners with disabilities may serve a vital role as a member of a motor development team made up of professionals with a particular commitment to motor performance.

A number of educational reform initiatives are in place in many schools/districts as educators, administrators, parents, and members of the community seek excellence in the public schools. One of the most important initiatives is the increased involvement of parents in the lives of their children.

Changes in funding and philosophy have made separate facilities for adapted physical education a rarity. Creative uses of equipment improve program quality.

Review Questions

1. What is the role of the adapted physical educator in school reform?
2. Describe the motor development team and the roles of the professionals involved.
3. What are some of the specific strategies the physical educator can use to embrace a multicultural community?

Student Activities

1. Attend a celebration or an event that represents a culture different from your own. Ask a participant, honestly, what he or she expects of his or her child's teacher.
2. Talk with a physical therapist, occupational therapist, or dance therapist regarding his or her perceptions of the adapted physical educator as part of the motor development team.
3. Talk with parents regarding the process they went through to cope with the disability of their child.
4. Interview a principal who has gone through the process of converting to site-based management.

References

1. Blacher J: Sequential stages of parental adjustment to the birth of a child with handicaps: fact or artifact? *Ment Retard* 22:55-68, 1984.
2. Blanchard S: Grieving a dream, *Except Parent,* pp 26-30, Oct 1994.
3. Bonstingl J: *Schools of quality: an introduction to total quality management in education,* Alexandria, Va, 1992, Association for Supervision and Curriculum Development.
4. Bratlinger E: Home-school partnerships that benefit children with special needs, *Elementary School J* 91:249-259, 1991.
5. Delgado-Gaitan C: School matters in the Mexican-American home: socializing children to education, *Am Educ Res J* 29(3):495-513, fall 1992.
6. *Denton Independent School District, Adapted Physical Education Program Guide,* Feb 1995.
7. Dyson L: Families of young children with handicaps: parental stress and functioning, *Am J Mental Retard* 95:623-629, 1991.
8. Epstein J: School/family/community partnerships: caring for the children we share, *Phi Delta Kappan,* May 1995.
9. Gaul T, Underwood K, Fortune J: Reform at the grass roots, *Am School Board J,* Jan 1994.
10. Giroux H: Educational leadership and the crisis of democratic government, *Educ Res* 21(4):4-11, 1992.
11. Glasser W: *The quality school: managing students without coercion,* New York, 1992, HarperCollins.
12. Jensen E: *Turning point for teachers,* Del Mar, Calif, 1992.
13. Kaufman A et al: Permanency planning by older parents who care for adult children with mental retardation, *Ment Retard* 29:293-300, 1991.
14. Kübler-Ross E: *On death and dying,* New York, 1969, Macmillan Publishing.
15. Manning M: Understanding culturally diverse parents and families, *Equity Excel Educ* 28(1):52-57, 1995.
16. Markowitz L: The cross-currents of multiculturalism, *Networker,* pp 20-28, June/Aug 1994.
17. Mary N: Reactions of black, Hispanic, and white mothers to having a child with handicaps, *Ment Retard* 28:1-5, 1990.
18. McConachie H: Implications of a model of stress and coping for services to families of young disabled children, *Child Care Health Dev* 20:37-46, 1994.
19. Nieto J et al: Passionate commitment to a multicultural society, *Equity Excel Educ* 27(1):51-57, 1994.
20. Olshansky S: Chronic sorrow: a response to having a mentally retarded child, *Soc Casework* 43:190-193, 1962.
21. Olson L: Parents as partners: redefining the social contract between families and schools, *Educ Week,* pp 17-24, April 1990.
22. Orfield G et al: The growth of segregation in American schools: changing patterns of separation and poverty since 1968, *Equity Excel Educ* 27(1):5-8, 1994.
23. Simeonsson R: Family involvement in multidisciplinary team evaluations: professional and parent perspectives, *Child Care Health Dev* 21(3):199-213, 1995.
24. Sugars A: *The adapted physical educator as a member of the motor development team.* TAHPERD State Convention, Lubbock, Tex, 1990.
25. Weiss S: Stressors experienced by family caregivers of children with pervasive developmental disorders, *Child Psychiatry Hum Dev* 21:203-215, 1991.
26. Willoughby J, Glidden L: Fathers helping out: shared child care and marital satisfaction of parents of children with disabilities, *Am J Ment Retard* 99(4):399-406, 1995.

Appendixes

appendix A

Posture and Body Mechanics

Postural disorders impair the health and quality of life of millions of people in the United States. Low back pain has reached epidemic proportions.[14] It has been estimated that 8 out of 10 persons will suffer from low back pain at one time or another in their lives.[23] It is the main cause of absence from work and is the leading musculoskeletal cause of disability in this country.[16] The cost of medical care and lost job time is estimated to be 12 billion dollars per year.[6] Furthermore, a significant number of students from the public schools are reaching colleges or universities with postural asymmetries[7]; nearly half are unaware of these problems.[1] There is compelling evidence that postural disorders can be prevented through activity programs.

Movement and exercise are essential for developing and maintaining physical fitness and adequate levels of bone mass and density.[43] Physical activity programs that include exercises to strengthen and stretch postural muscles should help prevent problems in later life. However, for maximum benefit, individuals need to continue those exercises throughout the life span. When back pain does occur, function can be restored through intensive aggressive physical therapy followed by adherence to a daily exercise regimen. The inability to maintain an ongoing exercise program is the major reason why individuals suffer recurrences of ongoing problems associated with back and joint pain.[17] The differences between those who achieve their program goals and those who do not are (1) level of self-motivation, (2) tolerance of pain, and (3) ability to adapt their schedules to include regular exercise sessions. Achieving and maintaining good posture can be beneficial in many ways.

Good posture might be defined as a position that enables the body to function to the best advantage with regard to work, health, and appearance. An individual's posture, in large measure, determines the impression that he or she makes on other persons. Good posture gives the impression of enthusiasm, initiative, and self-confidence, whereas poor posture often gives the impression of dejection, lack of confidence, and fatigue. We know that faulty posture does not necessarily indicate illness; however, we also know that good posture and body mechanics help the internal organs assume a position in the body that is favorable to their proper function and that allows the body to function most efficiently. Good posture should not be confused with the ability to assume static positions in which the body is held straight and stiff and during which good alignment is achieved at the sacrifice of the ability to move and to function properly. Possibly, good *body mechanics* would be a better term to use in describing the proper alignment and use of the body during both static and active postures.

Body mechanics is the proper alignment of body segments and a balance of forces so as to provide maximum support with the least amount of strain and the greatest mechanical efficiency.[18] There is general agreement that the human body operates best when its parts are in good alignment while sitting, standing, walking, or participating in a variety of occupational and recreational types of activities. There is no such thing as a normal posture for an individual. Certain anatomical and mechanical principles have been developed over the years that aid physicians, therapists, and physical educators in the identification of faulty body mechanics and posture.[15] Application of these principles helps individuals keep their bodies in proper balance with as small an expenditure of energy as possible and with the minimum amount of strain.

The **center of gravity** of the human body is located at a point where the pull of gravity on one side is equal to the pull of gravity on the other side. This center of gravity (higher in men than in women) falls in front of the sacrum at a point ranging from approximately 54%

to 56% of the individual's height when standing. The center of gravity is changed any time the body or its segments change position.

In the upright standing position, the human body is relatively unstable. Its base of support (the feet) is small, whereas its center of gravity is high; and it consists of a number of bony segments superimposed on one another, bound together by muscles and ligaments at a large number of movable joints. Any time the body assumes a static or dynamic posture, these muscles and ligaments must act on the bony levers of the body to offset the continuous downward pull of gravity.

Whenever the center of gravity of the body falls within its base of support, a state of balance exists. The closer the center of gravity is to the center of the base of support, the better will be the balance, or equilibrium. This has important implications for the individual both in terms of good posture and as it relates to good balance for all types of body movement. The body is kept well balanced for activities in which stability is important, whereas it may be purposely thrown out of equilibrium when movement is desired, speed is to be increased, or force is to be exerted on another object.[13,18] As the human being matures, balance for both static and dynamic positions becomes more automatic. An individual develops a feel for a correct position in space so that little or no conscious effort is needed to regulate it and attention can be devoted to other factors involved in movement patterns. This feeling for basic postural positions, as well as for dynamic movement, is controlled by certain sensory organs located throughout the body. The eyes furnish visual cues relative to body position. The semicircular canals of the inner ear furnish information on body equilibrium. Receptors in the tendons, joints, and muscles also contribute to the individual's ability to feel the body's position in space. The loss or malfunction of any of these sense organs requires that major adjustments be made by the individual to compensate for its loss.

Some individuals with disabilities develop poor posture because they are unable to integrate sensory impulses critical to achieving and maintaining good posture.[47] Persons who do not have the ability to provide their muscles with information necessary for good posture frequently experience balance problems. Lack of appropriate information interferes with both their automatic balance reactions and their voluntary balance adjustments.[38] In addition to the physical and sensory prerequisites that enable the disabled to maintain and facilitate appropriate movement, posture is the ability to integrate the sensory and motor aspects of motor patterns. There is evidence that some individuals may have breakdowns in correlation of the amplitude of muscular responses during postural movement.[47] These movement breakdowns may jeopardize balance as a result of lack of speed and adroitness necessary to ensure recovery of stability. Inappropriate use of visual and/or somatosensory input may have a negative effect on balance, which relates to moving posture. Persons who have movement problems involving postural efficiency may have slower voluntary, as opposed to reflexive, mechanisms for correcting postural disturbances.[38]

Causes of Poor Posture

There are many causes of poor posture and poor body mechanics, including environmental influences, psychological conditions, pathological conditions, growth handicaps, congenital defects, reduced muscular strength, and nutritional problems. Any of these may have an adverse effect on the posture of the growing child, the adolescent, or the adult. Extended periods are needed to establish good body mechanics.[27] The habits of poor posture cannot be overcome with a few minutes of daily exercise. The neuromuscular system must be reeducated so that positions and movements become conscious and subconscious routines.

Poor posture that contributes to incorrect muscle development, tension, spinal deviations, lower back disorder, poor circulation, and unattractive appearance can be overcome through specific muscle training and reorientation of postural habits.

Pathological conditions often lead to functional and structural posture deviations. Some of these conditions are faulty vision and hearing, various cardiovascular conditions, tuberculosis, arthritis, and neuromuscular conditions resulting in atrophy, dystrophy, and spasticity. Disabilities related to growth include weaknesses in the skeletal structure and in the muscular system, growth divergencies, fatigue, and glandular malfunctions. Congenital defects include amputations, joint and bone deformities, spina bifida, and clubfoot. Nutritional problems include underweight, overweight, and poor nourishment. Some children with disabilities, such as those with cerebral palsy, have persisting primitive reflexes and delayed postural responses.[46] Associated with delay in postural reflex development are slower response time and sensory organization capability deficits. Physical educators should consider these delays and deficits when programming for these students.

Postural Development

Growing children do not demonstrate the same posture that adults do. Children who are in the early stages of development have insufficient muscular strength to enable the anatomical parts of the body to be appropriately aligned. Body parts most frequently malaligned in young children are the legs and the spine.

Children between the ages of 18 months and 24 months often appear to have mild cases of bowlegs.[6] However, the condition usually corrects itself by 2 years of age. Furthermore, during the preschool years, the knees may not be properly aligned, and some children may have severely pronated feet. This is not considered a major problem unless it persists beyond the age of 8 years.[9] Treatment of **pronated feet** as prescribed by a physician usually consists of an inner-wedge support worn in the shoes. Stretching exercises and isometric strengthening activities may be employed to correct leg and foot positions.

As a result of improper alignment of the knees during the preschool years, children may develop deficient walking patterns. One of the walking patterns identified in children 12 to 16 months of age is the pronated foot accompanied by external rotation at the hip. A study in which a young child was required to walk faster and at sequentially greater degrees of incline on a treadmill resulted in proper alignment of the feet and legs.[3] Having the young child walk fast on a gradual incline increased muscle activity at the ankle, knee, and hip. Apparently, the need to generate additional force to keep pace with the speed of the treadmill caused the child to properly align the legs and feet.

Typically, young children under the age of 5 years have a protruding abdomen ("pot belly"). Their appearance may be one of postural abnormality, but in reality there is not maldevelopment. Normal play activities usually firm the abdominal muscles eventually; such activities also allow the pelvis to assume its correct position.

Scoliosis is a prevalent postural disorder. One out of every 10 persons has some degree of scoliosis and 3 in every 100 have a progressive condition.[32] Scoliosis is

an abnormal condition that can develop at any age. If the curvature develops during the first 3 years of life, it is termed **infantile scoliosis.** If it develops between the third and twelfth years in girls and after age 14 (but before maturity) in boys, it is called **adolescent scoliosis.** It is desirable for the physical educator to know not only deficiencies in posture in children, but also whether the deficiency of a given child is a function of normal development or an abnormality that will affect future alignment of the body.

Postural Conditions Among Persons with Disabilities

There are many prerequisites for efficient posture. Among these are strength of the postural muscles, flexibility of the joints, vitality and muscular endurance to maintain appropriate positioning of anatomical parts, and kinesthetic and visual orientations that enable proper alignment and sufficient balance to erect the body and stabilize it over its base of support. If any one of these prerequisites is not fulfilled, postural disorders may result. Children with disabilities may have poor posture because of deficient prerequisites. For instance, an individual with an orthopedic impairment may have muscle imbalances due to muscular weakness or lack of joint flexibility. Individuals who are mentally retarded often do not generalize their postural mechanism through varying positions. The person who is blind may lack the necessary visual orientation to maintain efficient upright posture. Persons with other health impairments may lack the strength and vitality to maintain adequate efficient posture over extended periods.

Orthopedic Disabilities

Because of the nature of their disability, individuals with orthopedic problems often lack postural muscle strength and joint flexibility. There may be differences in muscle strength on the two sides of the body because of an impairment on one side of the body (e.g., one leg may be shorter than the other). Orthopedically disabled individuals who use wheelchairs may have weak trunk muscles that cause them to lean to one side of the wheelchair. When this condition occurs, the possibility of developing scoliosis is increased. Therefore, precautions should be taken to ensure that children in wheelchairs have enough strength and endurance of the musculature of the abdominal and postural muscles to maintain upright sitting postures so that they do not tilt sideways or forward. Some persons in the later stages of muscular dystrophy may have weakened abdominal and hip muscles. When this happens, excessive tightening of the lumbar extensors frequently causes lordosis. Some children with orthopedic disabilities walk on their toes. This tends to tighten the heel cords. If the condition is a result of habit, strengthening the dorsal flexors and stretching the reciprocal plantar flexors should alleviate the condition. If the toe walking is a result of persisting extensor thrust or

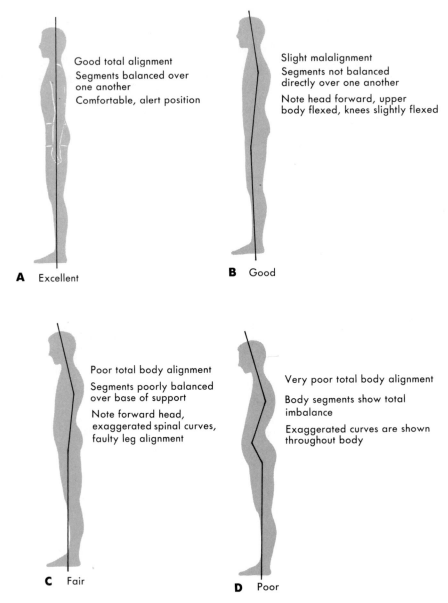

A   Excellent

Good total alignment
Segments balanced over one another
Comfortable, alert position

B   Good

Slight malalignment
Segments not balanced directly over one another
Note head forward, upper body flexed, knees slightly flexed

C   Fair

Poor total body alignment
Segments poorly balanced over base of support
Note forward head, exaggerated spinal curves, faulty leg alignment

D   Poor

Very poor total body alignment
Body segments show total imbalance
Exaggerated curves are shown throughout body

figure A-1
Four-figure system for rough assessment of posture is used to identify students in need of a more discriminating type of posture examination.

positive support primitive reflexes, activities to promote integration of the reflexes should be used.

Mental Retardation

Many individuals who are mentally retarded have poor posture. Although there are few studies that describe the postural alignment of these populations, observation would suggest that the more severe the retardation, the greater the possibility of postural problems. If an individual with mental retardation does not generalize locomotor patterns to gait, has poorly developed vestibular and/or kinesthetic systems, or has a depth perception problem, he or she will walk with the head down. Thus over time an abnormal posture may develop. The abnormalities of locomotion may be transferred to posture in a general sense. Individuals with deficient balance and/or depth perception problems walk with a wide, shuffling gait and descend stairs one step at a time. In addition to specific strengthening and stretching activities of postural muscle groups, kinesthetic awareness of head and trunk alignment, along with improvement in balance and depth perception, may contribute to more efficient postures.

Blind

Persons who are blind frequently have postural abnormalities. Visual cues in the environment provide information to the body as to where parts should be aligned. Blind individuals are without external visual aids and must rely more on the kinesthetic awareness of where the body parts are in relationship to one another. These individuals should receive specific instruction in the proper alignment of the body to enable them to develop the "feel" of good posture.

Postural Development Procedures

There are specific procedures that can be employed to improve posture. The six components involved in a program designed for postural development are[2]:

1. Introduction and explanation of the use of the postural analysis form
2. Posture screening
3. Explanation of the screening results
4. Referral to persons who will individualize instruction
5. Practice time for postural exercises
6. Evaluation of progress after 8 weeks

Postural Assessment

After the postural analysis form has been introduced and explained, the next step in development of a postural education program is to assess each person to determine whether there is a need for postural programs. There are two major types of screening. One is group screening, and the other involves individual assessment. Group screening may be done by observing students as they move throughout the gymnasium or as they sit at their desks. The other major type of screening involves individual assessment of each child by the teacher. There are several types of individual postural assessment (Figure A-1). The focus of our discussion is on individual assessment techniques.

Plumb Line Test

The **plumb line test** is used to assess posture because it allows comparison of body landmarks with a gravity line (Figure A-2). The plumb line can be hung so that it falls between the person being examined and the instructor. The vertical line is used as a reference to check the student's anteroposterior and lateral body alignment. Certain surface landmarks on the body that align with a gravity line of the human body have been located by ki-

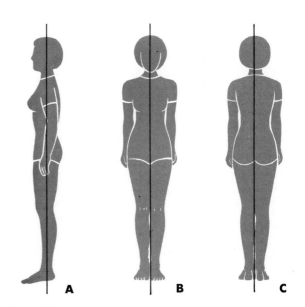

figure A-2
Plumb line tests. **A**, Lateral examination. **B**, Anterior examination. **C**, Posterior examination.

nesiologists and engineers. These surface landmarks can be used as points of reference in conducting examinations designed to see how well the body is balanced and how well its segments are aligned in the upright position.

Lateral view

From the lateral view (showing anteroposterior deviations), starting at the base of support and working up the body, the gravity line should fall at a point about 1 to 1½ inches anterior to the external **malleolus** of the ankle, just posterior to the **patella,** through the center of the hip at the approximate center of the greater trochanter of the femur, midway between the chest and back, through the center of the shoulder (acromial process), and through or just behind the earlobe.

Viewed from the front or rear, the spinal column should be straight. However, when the spine is viewed from the side, or lateral view (Figure A-3), curves normally exist in various vertebral segments. The cervical spine is slightly hyperextended, stretching from the base of the skull to about the top of the thoracic vertebrae. The spine is flexed throughout the area of the thoracic

vertebrae and hyperextended throughout the area of the lumbar vertebrae, and the sacral curve is flexed. These curves are present in the spinal column to help the individual maintain balance and to absorb shock, and they should be considered normal unless they are exaggerated (Figure A-4).

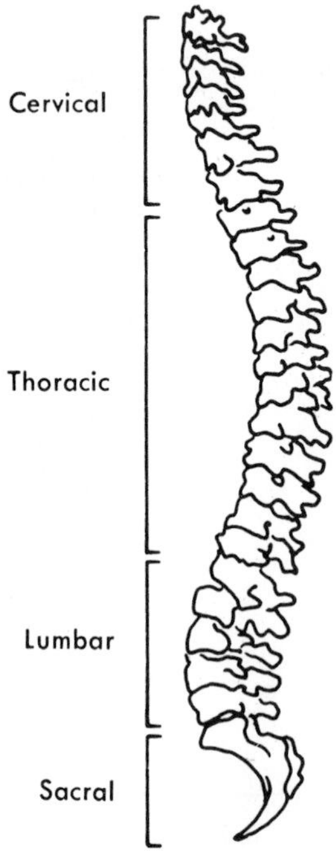

Anterior view

From the anterior view (showing lateral deviations), the gravity line should fall an equal distance between the internal malleoli and between the knees; it should pass through the center of the symphysis pubis, the center of the umbilicus, the center of the linea alba, the center of the chin, and the center of the nose; and it should bisect the center of the upper portion of the head.

Posterior view

The landmarks to be checked in the posterior examination (showing lateral deviations) would include the same points as those checked in the anterior examination in the region of the ankle and knee, the cleft of the buttocks, the center of the spinous processes of the spinal column, and the center of the head.

Recording data

There are several ways in which data from a plumb line test can be recorded. A widely accepted assessment system has been adopted in the New York State Physical Fitness Test. Three sets of pictures represent three different and sequential levels of postural fitness. One sequence of pictures represents model posture, a second sequence represents deviant posture, and a third sequence represents marked discrepancies from normal posture. The observer views the student according to plumb line testing procedures and for each picture on the evaluation sheet asks the question, "Which picture does the person being tested most look like?" The posture profile has various numbering systems. Some are ranked on a 10, 5, 1 scale, with 10 being good/model, 5 deficiency, and 1 marked deficiency. Other grading scales are 5, 3, 1 and 7, 5, 3. The scoring system is used to assign a number to the postural condition of the person observed. These numbers can be totaled for a postural index. However, the treatment plan must be derived from an evaluation of the specific anatomical parts of the body that are malaligned. Usually, diagnosed deficiencies reflect a clinical postural disorder that is caused

figure A-3
Normal spine.

Cervical

Thoracic

Lumbar

Sacral

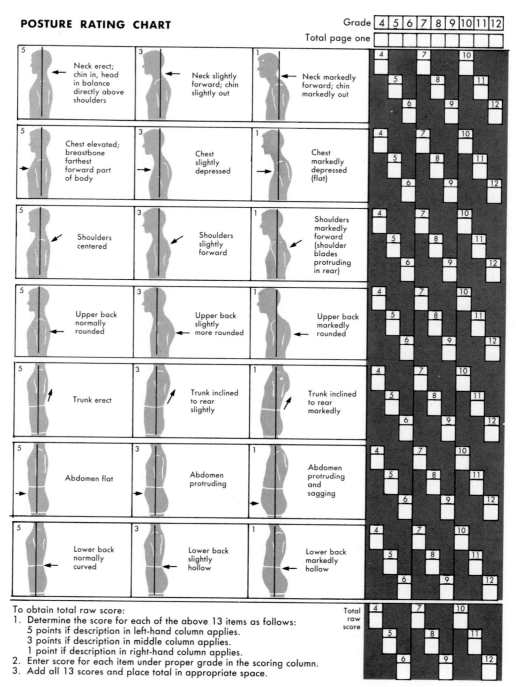

POSTURE RATING CHART

Grade | 4 | 5 | 6 | 7 | 8 | 9 | 10 | 11 | 12

Total page one

To obtain total raw score:
1. Determine the score for each of the above 13 items as follows:
   5 points if description in left-hand column applies.
   3 points if description in middle column applies.
   1 point if description in right-hand column applies.
2. Enter score for each item under proper grade in the scoring column.
3. Add all 13 scores and place total in appropriate space.

figure A-4

Lateral postural survey chart. (Courtesy New York State Education Department.)

by tight or weak muscles. The target muscle groups must be identified, and specific types of activity must be assigned to meet the unique problem of the specific postural deficiency.

A posture examination is much more meaningful to the student and far more useful to the teacher if the findings are carefully recorded by the examiner (especially during review of the material obtained in the examination before setting up an exercise or activity program or when doing a reevaluation of the pupil several months after the original examination). The examination form must provide space for the instructor to record the findings of the examination quickly and accurately. Provisions should be made for recording the severity of each of the conditions identified in the examination. The findings of successive examinations also can be recorded on the same form.

Posture Screen

Another form of posture testing may be done with a **posture screen.** The posture screen is a grid of vertical and horizontal lines that can be used as reference points to evaluate all segments of the body in relationship to each other. It consists of a rectangular frame mounted on legs so that it stands upright and laced with string so that a 2-inch-square grid pattern (4- and 6-inch squares are recommended by some) crosses the frame. The vertical lines are parallel to a center (gravity) line, and the horizontal lines are exactly at right angles to the gravity line (Figure A-5). The color of the center line usually differs from that of the other strings. This makes the center line

easy to identify and to use in comparison with the landmarks described previously.

The posture screen should be checked for proper alignment with a plumb line to be sure that the gravity line is true and that the screen is also plumb when viewed from the side. It is then necessary to locate a point about 18 inches from the posture screen where the student will be centered properly behind the gravity line. The instructor determines this point by moving to a position 10 to 15 feet away from the posture screen and standing in alignment with the center string while holding a plumb line out in front. Sighting through the plumb line and the center line of the screen, the examiner then marks a point on the floor 18 inches behind the screen. This point is in alignment with the instructor and the center line itself. Thus when the student stands behind the screen, it is possible to evaluate the posture from the anterior, posterior, and lateral views in relation to the center line of the screen.

A posture screen may be used to give quick, superficial screening examinations to identify students in need of special postural correction programs, or it may be used to give very thorough examinations to students who have already been identified as requiring such programs. An example showing a three-way figure with the proper labels and with numbers to indicate the severity of the conditions discovered is shown in Figure A-6. With this kind of prepared examination form, the instructor can quickly identify deviations observed through the posture grid and can record them by drawing a diagonal line through the number that indicates the severity of the con-

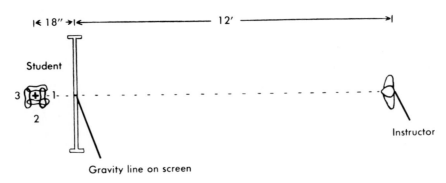

figure A-5
Alignment of posture as viewed from above. *1,* Anterior; *2,* lateral; *3,* posterior.

POSTURE EXAMINATION USING POSTURE SCREEN WITH 2-INCH GRIDS

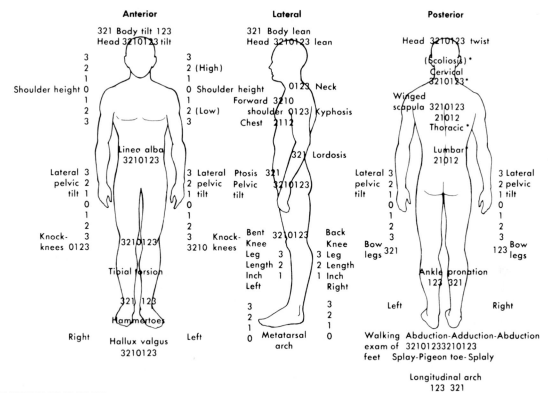

Anterior

321 Body tilt 123
Head 321 0 123 tilt

```
3
2
1
Shoulder height 0
1
2
3
```

Lineo alba
3210123

Lateral 3
pelvic   2
tilt   1
         0
         1
         2
Knock-   3
knees 0123

3210123

Tibial torsion

321 123

Hammertoes

Right   Hallux valgus
               3210123

Lateral

321 Body lean
Head 321 0 123 lean

```
3
2 (High)
1
0  Shoulder height
1
2 (Low)
3
```

0123 Neck

Forward 3210
shoulder 0123 Kyphosis
Chest 2112

32 Lordosis

3 Lateral   Ptosis 321
2 pelvic   Pelvic 321 0 123
1 tilt   tilt
0
1
2
3
Knock-   Bent 32 0123
3210 knees Knee
            Leg   3
            Length 2
            Inch 1
            Left

Back
Knee
Leg   3
Length 2
Inch 1
Right

```
3       3
2       2
1       1
0 Metatarsal 0
  arch
```

Left

Posterior

Head 321 0 123 twist

(Scoliosis) *
Cervical
3210123*

Winged
scapula 3210123
21012
Thoracic *

Lumbar
21012

Lateral 3   3 Lateral
pelvic   2   2 pelvic
tilt   1   1 tilt
         0   0
         1   1
         2   2
         3   3
Bow   Bow
legs 321   123 legs

Ankle pronation
123 321

Left   Right

Walking Abduction-Adduction-Abduction
exam of 32101233210123
feet   Splay-Pigeon toe- Splaly

Longitudinal arch
123 321

SUMMARY OF FINDINGS
Medical 123 Injuries 123 Posture 123 Feet 123 Nutrition 123

REMARKS:
Recommendations:

A. Student's interest toward improvement:

B. Corrective exercises: (indicate nos. assigned)
1 2 3 4 5 6 7 8 9 10 11 12 13 14 15 16
17 18 19 20 21 22 23 24 25 26 27 28 29
30 31 32 33 34 35 36 37 38 39 40

C. Other exercises assigned:

D. Remarks and disposition of student:

figure A-6
Data-recording sheet for use with posture grid.

dition (first degree, slight; second degree, moderate; and third degree, severe). No other writing is necessary unless the instructor identifies a problem that does not appear on the chart or wishes to record special information. The same posture form can be used for successive examinations with different-colored pencils used to indicate second, third, or fourth examinations. In this way,

improvement can be shown through the use of the cumulative record.

Anterior view

The student is instructed to stand directly behind the posture screen with the internal malleoli of the ankles an equal distance from the mark on the floor. This will place the student in the proper position so that the surface landmarks of the body will fall in correct alignment in relation to the center (gravity) line of the screen. The student is then instructed to stand as he or she would normally. The instructor should take a position about 10 to 15 feet away from the posture screen and in direct line with the center line. The posture examination record can be mounted on a clipboard held by the examiner, or a lectern can be used to hold the forms to facilitate recording the findings. Since the feet serve as the base of support, it is important to examine the student from the feet upward in checking for proper body alignment. Specific examinations for the foot, ankle, and leg are covered in later sections of the chapter.

The feet should be checked to see if they are pointed straight forward or are toeing-in or toeing-out. The longitudinal arch should be higher on its medial side than on its lateral side. The inner and outer malleoli should be about equal in prominence. The ankles and knees should be straight, with the kneecaps facing directly forward when the feet are held in the straight forward position. The height of the kneecaps should be even. The gravity line passes midway between the ankle bones, between the knees, and directly through the umbilicus, the linea alba, the center of the chin, and the center of the nose.

The symmetry of the sides of the body must then be checked. Any abnormal curvature or creasing on one side of the trunk (not found on the other side) should lead to more careful examination to determine whether a lateral sway or tilt of the body or a lateral curvature of the spine exists. Lateral spine curvature must be checked if any deviations in the position of the umbilicus exist or if there are any apparent differences in the depth of the sides of the chest (Figure A-7). With boys the nipple levels are compared, and with both boys and girls the heights of the creases made where the arms join the body should be checked to be sure that the two creases on either side are symmetrical. It is also necessary to check to see if one arm hangs closer to the trunk than the other (Figure A-8). The shoulder height must be checked to see if the shoulders are level. If the pelvis is found to have a lateral tilt, or if a high or low shoulder is noted, the student is then checked for lateral curvature of the spine. Although lateral curvatures do not occur with all the previously noted conditions, these types of conditions may serve as possible indicators of such a problem. The examiner next checks the head position to be sure that it aligns with the gravity line and to determine if there is any twisting of the head and neck. Finally, the total body should be viewed to determine whether it is being held in good alignment and balance and whether any lateral tilts of the total body exist.

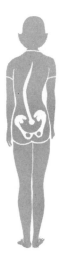

figure A-7
Lateral pelvic tilt.

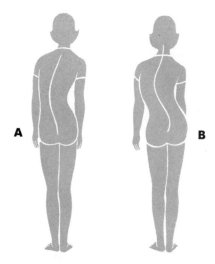

figure A-8
Scoliosis. **A,** Total left C curve. **B,** Regular S curve.

Posterior view

For posterior examination, the student is instructed to assume the same position in relation to the posture screen as in the anterior examination, except that the back is now turned to the screen (i.e., with the inner ankle bones over the marker on the floor). The posterior examination gives the instructor an opportunity to double-check many of the conditions noted from the anterior view and to make an evaluation of certain other conditions that cannot be checked during the anterior view examination.

The gravity line passes directly up through the center of the spinous processes of each of the vertebrae, bisecting the head through its center. The posterior view is the best view for detecting scoliosis (rotolateral curvature). If a lateral curvature exists, further examinations should be made to see if there is any rotation or torque in the pelvic girdle. The degree of lateral deviation and the amount of rotation should be checked. The posture card indicates all the areas where lateral deviation of the spine could be present and provides a place to record the degree of severity. If scoliosis is suspected, the examiner can make the evaluation of the spinal column more meaningful by marking the posterior surfaces of the spinous processes of the vertebrae with a skin pencil so that the curves can be observed more accurately. The sides of the trunk also are checked as they were in the anterior view for any abnormal unilateral curvatures and for any creases or bulges on one side only, which would indicate the presence of a tilt or of a lateral spinal curve.

The shoulder blades (or scapulae) are viewed from the posterior aspect to determine whether they are flat against the rib cage, whether the medial borders have been pulled laterally in abduction, and whether the medial borders and the inferior angles project outward from the back of the rib cage (this condition is called **winged scapula**).

Lateral view

For the lateral (side) view, the student stands with the left side to the screen (the side facing the screen is the one shown on the posture examination form). One foot is placed on either side of the mark on the floor, with the inner malleolus about 1½ inches behind its center. Deviations in alignment and posture can readily be observed through the screen. Abnormalities in flexion and extension of the toes may be easier to see from the side than they were from the front. The lateral examination is used to verify conditions noted in other phases of the examination.

If the student has a total forward or backward lean of the body, alignment is basically correct at all joints except the ankle, where he or she is leaning too far forward or backward. In this case, the examiner will find that the reference points become progressively farther out of alignment with each segment from the foot to the head. If the alignment is correct at the ankle and at the shoulder, but the center of the hip is too far forward, the individual has a total body sway. If the hips are too far back, the individual has a distorted position of the low back and buttocks. If the alignment is correct at the ankle, knee, and hip but the shoulder and the head are positioned too far back, the student has what is called a posterior overhang (Figure A-9). It is quite easy to identify these various conditions when the body landmarks are viewed in relation to the gravity line of the posture screen. The amount of deviation is ascertained by judging the distance the affected body parts are out of alignment against one of the vertical lines. It is usually easier to evaluate these landmarks if the student places a finger on each of them so that the examiner can see them more easily.

The vertebral spine should then be checked throughout its length for what would be termed its normal cur-

figure A-9
Posterior overhang.

vatures. The two conditions that are noted in the region of the lower back are excessive hyperextension in the lumbar spine, a condition called **lordosis,** and too little curve in the lumbar spine, known as flat low back. When the lumbar spine goes into a flexion curve, it is called lumbar **kyphosis.** This is not observed frequently, however. Usually associated with these lower back conditions are a forward pelvic tilt (with lordosis) and a backward pelvic tilt (with a flat low back). Abdominal **ptosis** is often associated with these conditions, especially lordosis. Ptosis refers to a relaxation of the lower abdominal muscles with forward sagging of the abdomen often accompanied by misplacement of the pelvic organs. The degree of severity of this deviation must be judged subjectively.

In the region of the chest and shoulders, the normal curvature of the spine is one of mild flexion. The abnormal condition that would be looked for in the thoracic spine is an excessive amount of flexion, which in its severest form is called humpback. Any abnormal increase in flexion is known as kyphosis. Kyphosis is often associated with flattening of the chest and rib cage and, frequently, with deviations in the alignment of the shoulder girdle, called forward shoulders and winged scapula. Although these four conditions are often found in the same individual, they do not necessarily occur together. The winged scapula, mentioned in the discussion of the posterior examination, should be checked again from the lateral position to determine whether the inner border projects to the rear and whether the inferior angle projects outward from the rib cage. The degree of deviation in forward (round) shoulders is judged subjectively and is related to how far forward of the gravity line the center of the shoulder falls.

The most common condition found in the region of the neck is a forward position of the cervical vertebrae accompanying a forward head. An abnormal amount of hyperextension in the cervical or neck vertebrae exists when the individual has attempted to correct a faulty head position by bringing the head back and the chin up.

In all the examinations described previously, the instructor must be alert to the possibility that one postural deviation often leads to or is the result of another. It is a pattern of the human body to attempt to keep itself in some semblance of a state of balance **(homeostasis).** Therefore, when one segment or various segments of the body become malaligned, it is customary for the body to attempt to compensate for this by throwing other segments out of alignment, thus obtaining a balanced position. An example of this would be the individual with lordosis who compensates with kyphosis and forward head. The individual with a simple C-shaped scoliosis curve in the spine may compensate for this with a complex S-shaped curve (an effort to return the spine and thus the body to a state of balance).

Tests for Functional or Structural Conditions

There are two types of postural conditions. One is functional, and the other is structural. **Functional postural deficiencies** result from muscular imbalances. They can be corrected by strengthening the antigravity postural muscles and stretching out the opposing muscle groups. On the other hand, **structural postural deficiencies** involve abnormalities in the bones and joints and are usually not responsive to exercise programs. When the condition is structural, procedures usually are required to alter the postural alignment.

Several tests may be used to determine whether spinal curvatures are functional (involving the muscles and soft tissue) or structural (involving the bones). Postural deviations that are the result of muscle and soft tissue imbalance often disappear when the force of gravity is removed. Structural postural deviations, which have gone beyond the soft tissue stage, with involvement of the supportive bones and connective tissue, are not eliminated by the removal of gravitational influences.

Prone lying test

The **prone lying test** is designed to check anteroposterior or lateral curves of the spine. Functional curves disappear or decrease when the student assumes the prone position on a bench, a table, or the floor.

Hanging test

The **hanging test** has the same uses as the prone lying test. The individual hangs by the hands from a horizontal support. Functional curves disappear or are decreased in this position (Figure A-10, *B*).

Adam test

The **Adam test** is used to determine whether a lateral deviation of the spine (scoliosis) is functional or structural. The student assumes a normal standing posi-

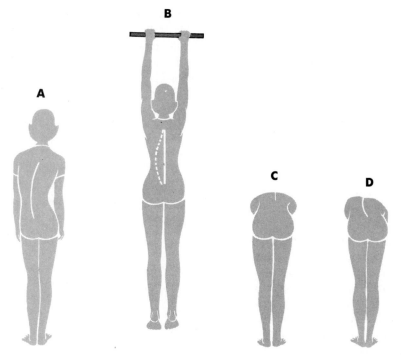

figure A-10
Test for functional versus structural scoliosis. **A,** Left C-curve scoliosis. **B,** Hanging test for scoliosis. Note straight line indicates spinal position during hanging test. **C,** Adam test showing functional scoliosis. **D,** Adam test showing structural scoliosis.

tion, then gradually bends the head forward, continuing with the trunk until the hands hang close to the toes. The instructor stands a short distance behind the student and observes the student's spine and the sides of the back as the student slowly bends forward. If the spine straightens, and if the sides of the back are symmetrical in shape and height, the scoliosis is considered functional (Figure A-10, *C*). Corrective procedures should be started under the direction of a physician.

If the spine does not straighten, and if one side of the back (especially in the thoracic region) is more prominent (sticks up higher) than the other as the student bends forward, the scoliosis is judged to be structural (Figure A-10, *D*). In structural cases the rotation of the vertebrae accompanying the lateral bend of the spine causes the attached ribs to assume a greater posterior prominence on the convex side of the curve. This curve does not disappear in the Adam test after changes occur

in the bones of the spinal column. Structural cases must be cared for by an orthopedist.

Sitting Posture

The position of the body while sitting is similar to the position of the body while standing (i.e., the head is held erect, the chin is kept in, normal anteroposterior curves are maintained in the upper and lower back, and the abdomen is flat). The hips should be pushed firmly against the back of the chair. The thighs should rest on the chair and help support and balance the body. The feet should be flat on the floor, or the legs should be comfortably crossed at the ankles. The shoulders should be relaxed and level, with the chest kept comfortably high.

There is sophisticated, expensive equipment available to assess posture. The instruments that measure functional capability include three-dimensional digitizers, vector stereography, and photographic methods.[11]

Moving Posture Tests

Many persons have been critical of static posture evaluations for the following reasons:

1. Students are likely to pose in this type of examination.
2. Students may use it to obtain visual cues to correct faulty posture.
3. It does not indicate the student's habitual standing posture.
4. No attention is given to dynamic posture and alignment as they would relate to student's movements in activities.

For these reasons, it is wise to include, as a part of the total posture examination, certain phases in which the students are actually in motion and during which they may or may not know that they are being examined. This may be accomplished in several different ways. One is to observe a class as they perform during an exercise session and when they are standing or sitting between exercises. To enable the examining teacher to identify students with major deviations and to record this, either the instructor must know all the students by name or by a number, or the students must be removed from the group as posture deviations are noted. Their names should then be taken so that the posture deviations noted are recorded for the proper students.

Another technique that can be used to evaluate posture and body mechanics during movement is to have the students gather in a large circle (with the teacher standing at the center or periphery of the circle) and then walk, run, or do various kinds of activities as they move continuously around the circle. The teacher or therapist identifies the children who are in special need of postural correction and records their names along with the appropriate information regarding their postural deviations. As a part of each of these two types of examinations, especially if they are given in lieu of any type of static examination, the students should also assume a normal standing position, with the teacher evaluating posture from the front, lateral, and rear views.

Walking posture

The basic position of the body in walking is similar to that of the standing posture, but all parts of the body are also involved in moving through space. The toes face straight ahead or toe out very slightly as the leg swings straight forward. The heel strikes the ground first, with the weight being transferred along the lateral side of the bottom of the foot. The weight is then shifted to the forward part of the foot and balanced across the entire ball of the foot. The step is completed with a strong push from all the toes. The upper body should be held erect, with the arms swinging comfortably in opposition to the movement of the legs. The head is held erect, with the chin tucked in a comfortable position. The

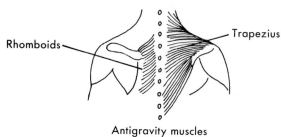

Antigravity muscles

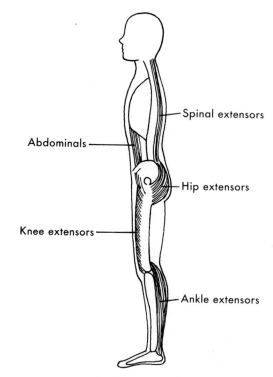

Antigravity muscles

figure A-11
Antigravity muscles involved in maintaining erect posture.

chest is held high, the shoulder blades are flat against the rib cage, and the shoulders are held even in height (Figure A-11).

Persons with deviations in their sitting, standing, or moving posture and body mechanics should receive special attention so that programs may be designed for correction of these problems. Suggestions for correction and prevention, for measurement, and for program adaptations are presented in this chapter as a part of the discussion of each deviation.

Guidelines for Testing Posture

Gathering information on the postural characteristics of students requires many decisions. Some guidelines for testing posture follow:

1. Determine the method of postural evaluation (group or single subject).
2. Select a feasible assessment instrument (posture screen, comparative checklist, plumb line).
3. Determine a data collection procedure (notes, numerical scoring system).
4. Require children to wear as little clothing as possible during the examination.
5. Keep posture assessment equipment in correct working condition.
6. Use the correct testing procedures.
7. Have the same person administer the test on successive occasions.
8. Record all information accurately and indicate the date the test was given.
9. Determine accurately the location of landmarks used in measurement if they are included in the evaluation process.
10. Standardize evaluation procedures and provide a written description of these procedures so that they can be followed on each occasion by any examiner.
11. Determine whether disorders are functional or structural.

Beattie, Rothstein, and Lamb[4] have listed advantages and disadvantages of commonly used postural assessment tools. An important aspect of a measuring tool is its validity (e.g., how truthful is the tool). For instance, frequently the sit-and-reach test is used to measure low back functioning. However, the results should be interpreted with caution,[36] because that test actually measures flexibility of multiple joints (e.g., the entire back and

hips). Excessive flexibility in one area may mask inflexibility in another area. Other things to consider when selecting postural assessment tools are (1) expense of the equipment, (2) reliability (constancy) of the measure, (3) requirements of the student, (4) limitations in the movement capability or intelligence of the students, and (5) precision of the instrument.

The postural assessment methods described in the previous sections are well established and widely used by professionals. However, modifications to assessment procedures and the evaluation of impact of service delivery, particularly in the area of low back pain, are continually being developed. Functional status questionnaires for this purpose include the Sickness Impact Profile (SIP), the Roland Morris Survey, the Jan Van Breeman Institute Survey, and the Oswestry Scale (Stratford).[39] There is disagreement as to whether these questionnaires measure pain or disability.[12]

Postural Deviations: Causes and Corrections

The first step for conducting a postural education program is assessment of the present level of postural functioning. If there is need of intervention, activities need to be selected to remedy specific postural disorders. Usually weakening or tightening of specific muscle groups contributes to a specific postural disorder. Correction then involves strengthening the weak muscles and stretching the tight muscles. Daniels and Worthingham[13] have provided detailed procedures for assessing the functional level of muscles that may contribute to poor posture. Exercise regimens for strengthening weak muscles are described in Chapter 8. Levels of exercise from the least taxing to the most demanding are performance of the movement with gravity, without gravitational pull, against gravity, and against gravity with resistance. Garrison and Read[18] have suggested that stretching for tight muscles is enhanced under the following conditions:

1. The stretch is carried out to the point of moderate pain.
2. There is application of increased effort at regular intervals.
3. The stretch is done slowly and under control without development of momentum.
4. Movement of the body part proceeds through the full range.

Techniques that could be used to improve the effectiveness of postural education programs include the following:

1. Increased training and education before beginning physical activities that could injure the musculoskeletal system have been successful in elimination of inhibitory factors such as pain and fear of injury.[24]

2. Specialized equipment that provides auditory and somatosensory feedback facilitates effective postural education.[20]

3. Quantitative feedback improves both accuracy and consistency of performance in mobilization of the spine.[20]

4. Self-help books for persons with ongoing spinal problems provide valuable information about effective exercise programs and techniques for dealing with chronic pain.[19]

5. Graded activity programs combined with operant conditioning are successful in developing function and reducing sick leave time.[25]

6. Ability to eccentrically contract postural muscles should be developed to stabilize muscles needed for daily living activities.[37]

The following sections include discussions of specific conditions, as well as exercises to assist with the remediation of each condition. This information will prove useful for teachers and therapists as they program for participants (with and without disabilities).

Foot and Ankle

Postural deviations of the foot and ankle can be observed while the student is standing, walking, or running. The evaluation of the foot should be made by observation from the anterior, lateral, and posterior views and should involve examination of both walking and static positions. The number of persons with deviations of the foot is large at all age levels, and the number of persons who

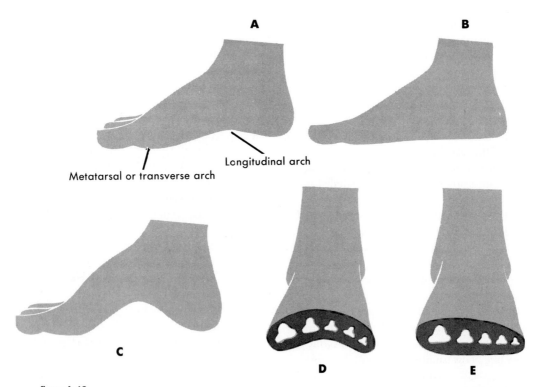

figure A-12
Arches of foot. **A,** Normal foot. **B,** Pes planus. **C,** Pes cavus. **D,** Cross section of normal metatarsal arch. **E,** Flat metatarsal arch.

have foot pain increases with increasing age. Muscles and joints of the foot and ankle become weakened from age and misuse. Pain associated with faulty mechanics in the use of the feet also begins to occur with increased age. The good mechanical use of the feet throughout life plus other factors such as good basic health, maintenance of a satisfactory level of physical fitness, proper choice of shoes and socks, and proper attention to any injury or accident to the foot should serve as preventive measures to the onset of weakness of the ankles and feet in later life.

The foot consists of a longitudinal arch that extends from the anterior portion of the calcaneus bone to the heads of the five metatarsal bones. The medial side of the longitudinal arch is usually considerably higher than the lateral side, which, as a general rule, makes contact throughout its length with the surface on which it is resting (Figure A-12, *A* to *C*). This is particularly true when the body weight is being supported on the foot. The longitudinal arch is sometimes described as two arches—a medial arch and a lateral arch—extending from the anterior aspects of the heel to the heads of the metatarsal bones. However, it is most frequently described as one long arch that is dome shaped and higher on the medial side than on the lateral side. On the forepart of the foot, in the region of the metatarsal bones, a second arch can be distinguished that runs across the forepart (ball) of the foot. This arch, called the transverse or **metatarsal arch,** is slightly dome shaped, being higher at the proximal ends of the metatarsal bones than at the distal ends. It often is considered a continuation of the dome-shaped long arch described previously, and thus we have just one dome-shaped arch of the foot (Figure A-12, *D* and *E*).

There is substantial agreement about the need for correct structures and placement of the bones, the importance of the strong ligamentous bands that help hold the bones in place to form the arches of the foot, and the need for good muscular balance among the antagonist muscles that support the foot. All these factors have an important effect on the position of the foot under both weight-bearing and non-weight-bearing conditions. A foot is considered strong and functional when it has adequate muscle strength (especially the anterior tibial muscle and the long flexor muscles of the toes) to support the longitudinal arch, when the bones have strong ligamentous and fascial bindings, and when the small intrinsic muscles are developed sufficiently to maintain proper strength of the arch in the metatarsal region.

In addition to considering the structure of the foot and ankle, it also is necessary to consider other factors such as the range of movement in the foot and ankle, the support of the body by the foot and ankle, and the effect that various positions of the foot, ankle, knee, and hip have on the mechanics of the foot itself. A consideration of the various movements possible in the foot and ankle, together with a description of the terms used to describe these movements, should help clarify the discussion of deviations of the foot and ankle.

The ankle joint is a hinge joint; therefore only dorsiflexion and plantar flexion are possible. The numerous articulations between the individual tarsal bones and between the tarsal and metatarsal bones allow for inversion, eversion, abduction, and adduction of the foot (Figure A-13).

Movements of the foot are as follows:

- **Dorsiflexion:** Movement of the top of the foot in the direction of the knee

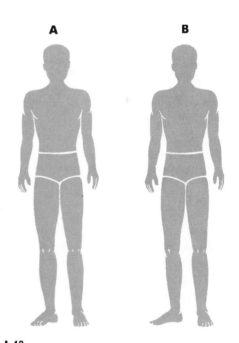

figure A-13
Abduction of foot and leg. **A,** Abduction of foot. **B,** Toeing-out resulting from outward rotation of hip joint. Note difference in position of patella.

- **Plantar flexion:** Movement of the foot downward, in the direction of the sole
- **Inversion:** Tipping of the medial edge of the foot upward, or varus (walking on the outer border of the foot)
- **Eversion:** Tipping of the lateral edge of the foot upward, or valgus (walking on the inner border of the foot)
- **Adduction:** Turning of the whole forepart of the foot in a medial direction (toeing-in)
- **Abduction:** Turning of the forepart of the foot in a lateral direction (toeing-out)
- **Pronation:** Combination of tipping of the outer border of the foot and toeing-out (eversion with abduction)
- **Supination:** Combination of tipping of the inner edge of the foot upward and toeing-in (inversion with adduction)

It also should be remembered that it is possible to turn the foot into toed-in and toed-out positions by rotating the lower leg when the knee is bent and by rotating the whole leg at the hip when the knee is straight. Thus when an individual toes-in or toes-out while walking or standing, the examiner must determine whether this is the result of a foot deviation or a rotation of the leg. Many foot and ankle deviations are closely linked to alignment problems occurring in the leg above the ankle.

On many occasions physicians will prescribe orthotic longitudinal arch supports to improve proper foot positionings. In addition, appropriate exercises are needed to build muscle strength and increase joint flexibility for optimum functioning.[40] Exercises should be progressive to build on the present levels of specific muscle group function.

Pes planus

Pes planus, or flatfoot, is a lowering of the medial border of the longitudinal arch of the foot. The height of this side of the longitudinal arch may range from the extremely high arch known as pes cavus to a position in which the medial border lies flat against the surface on which the individual is standing. When this side of the foot is completely flat, the medial border of the foot may even assume a rather convex appearance (see Figure A-12, A to C). Pes planus may be a result of faulty bony framework, faulty ligamentous pull across the articula-

tions of the foot, an imbalance in the pull of the muscles responsible for helping hold the longitudinal arch in its proper position, or racial traits. The specific cause often may be linked to improper alignment of the foot and leg and to faulty mechanics in the use of the foot and ankle.

When the foot is held in a toed-out (abducted) position while standing and walking, there is a tendency to throw a disproportionate amount of body weight onto the medial side of the foot, thus causing stress on the medial side of this arch. Over a period of time, this stress may cause both a gradual stretching of the muscles, tendons, and ligaments on the medial aspect of the foot and a tightening of like structures on the lateral side. When the individual walks with the foot in the abducted position, these factors are again accentuated and there is a tendency for the individual to rotate the leg medially in

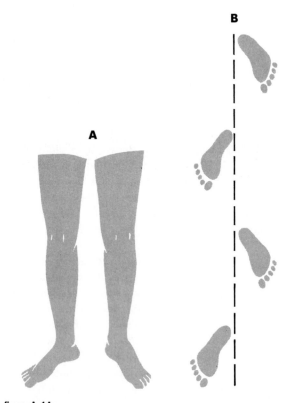

figure A-14

Improper walking. **A,** Toeing-out and walking across medial border of foot. **B,** Footprints show outward rotation, or splayfoot position, while walking.

order to have it swing in alignment with the forward direction of the step. When the leg is swung straight in line with the direction of travel and with the foot toed-out, the individual walks across the medial side of the foot with each step (Figure A-14). This not only weakens the foot but also predisposes the individual to a condition called tibial torsion. Since the individual is walking with the leg in basically correct alignment but with the foot abducted, malalignment results. Thus it will be found that when the legs and kneecaps face straight forward, the feet are in the abducted position, and when the feet are parallel to one another, the kneecaps are facing in a slightly medial direction (tibial torsion). This may produce strain and possibly cause a lowering of the medial side of the longitudinal arch.

Correction of pes planus must involve a reversal of the factors and conditions just described. The total leg from the hip through the foot must be properly realigned so that the weight is balanced over the hip, the knee, the ankle, and the foot itself. The antagonist muscles involved must be reoriented so that those that have become stretched (tibial muscles) are developed and tightened and those that have become short and tight (peroneal muscles) are stretched; thus the foot is allowed to assume its proper position. The muscles on the lateral side of the foot must be stretched (peroneal group). The gas-

trocnemius and soleus muscles, which sometimes become shortened in the case of flatfoot, exert an upward pull on the back of the calcaneus bone, thus adding to the flattening of the arch. These muscles must also be stretched whenever tightness is indicated. The major muscle group that must be shortened and strengthened is the anterior tibial muscle group, which is extremely important in terms of supporting the longitudinal arch, along with help from the long and short flexor muscles of the toes. The individual also must be given foot and leg alignment exercise in front of a mirror to observe the correct mechanical position of the foot while exercising, standing, walking, and otherwise using the feet (Figures A-15 to A-17).

Such activities as walking in soft dirt, on grass, or in sand with the foot held in the proper position can do much to help strengthen the foot and realign it with the ankle and hip. Emphasis here should be on walking straight over the length of the foot and placing the heel down first, with the weight being transferred along the

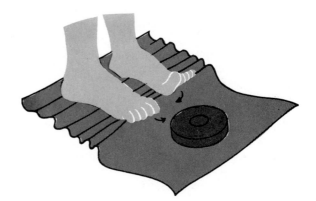

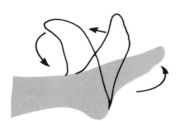

figure A-15
Foot circling.
Specific for: Metatarsal arch and toe flexors
Beneficial in: Flexibility and strength of foot and ankle and longitudinal arch
Starting position: Sitting on bench with knees extended, shoes off, and toes pointed
Actions:
1. Circle foot inward; toes extended.
2. Circle foot upward; toes extended.
3. Circle foot outward; toes extended.
4. Circle foot downward; toes flexed.
5. Repeat actions 1 to 4.

figure A-16
Building mounds.
Specific for: Metatarsal arch and toe flexors
Beneficial in: Strength of intrinsic muscles of feet
Starting position: Sitting on a bench, feet directly under knees, toes placed on end of a towel
Actions:
1. Grip towel with toes.
2. Pull toward body; both feet work together and build mounds; heels remain on floor.
3. Repeat movements until end of towel is reached.
Measurement: Amount of weight that is placed on towel and distance over time the weight travels

figure A-17
Foot curling.
Specific for: Metatarsal arch and toe flexors
Beneficial in: Flexibility and strength of foot and ankle and
   longitudinal arch
Starting position: With no shoes or socks, sitting on a bench,
   knees straight, heels rest on bench, mat, or floor
Actions:
   1. Circle foot inward with toes flexed.
   2. Circle foot upward with toes extended.
   3. Circle foot outward; extend toes.
   4. Circle foot downward while flexing toes.
   5. Repeat, making full circles with feet.
Contraindications: Should never be used for students with
   hammer toes
Measurement: Circumference of circle and repetitions over
   time

outer border of the foot and with an even and equal push-off from the forepart of the foot and the five toes. In actual practice, the great toe should be the last toe to leave the surface on the push-off.

Pes cavus

Pes cavus is a condition of the foot in which the longitudinal arch is abnormally high. This condition is not found as frequently in the general population as is pes planus. If the condition is extreme, the student is usually under the care of an orthopedic physician. Special

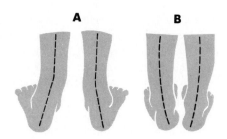

figure A-18
Faulty foot and ankle positions. **A,** Foot and ankle pronation.
B, Supinated foot.

exercises are not usually given for the high arch unless the person has considerable associated pain, requiring special corrective procedures recommended by the physician (see Figure A-12, *C*).

Pronation of the foot

Since the ankle joint is a hinge joint allowing only plantar flexion and dorsiflexion, pronation of the ankle—as it is sometimes called—is actually a condition of pronation of the foot (Figure A-18). As described previously, this is a combination of abduction and eversion of the foot. Since pronation involves eversion, the medial border of the foot is lowered because it is in the flat longitudinal arch. The forward part of the foot is also abducted, a condition caused by a shifting of the calcaneus bone downward and inward. (The reverse of this condition, one that involves inversion and adduction of the forepart of the foot, is called supination of the foot.) Correction of pronation of the foot is similar to that described for pes planus or flatfoot.

Metatarsalgia

Two types of metatarsalgia may be recognized in a thorough foot examination. The first is a general condition involving the transverse (metatarsal) arch, in which considerable pain is caused by the pressure of the heads of the metatarsal bones on the plantar nerves. The second type, Morton's toe, is more specific.

General metatarsalgia. **General metatarsalgia** may be caused by undue pressure exerted on the plantar surface of the foot. This pressure ultimately causes inflammation and therefore pain and discomfort. Its causes relate to such factors as wearing shoes or socks that are too short or too tight, wearing high-heeled shoes for long periods, and participating in activities that place great stress on the ball of the foot. The mechanism of injury may result in stretching of the ligaments that bind the metatarsophalangeal joints together, therefore exerting pressure on the nerves in this area. Correction involves the removal of the cause, if this is possible, and the assignment of special exercises to increase flexibility of the forepart of the foot. Exercises are then assigned to strengthen and shorten the muscles on the plantar surface, which may aid in maintaining a normal position in the metatarsal region. The physician may prescribe special shoes or suggest that an arch support or metatarsal bar be worn to support the metatarsal region of the foot to help reduce pain.

Morton's toe. **Morton's toe,** often called true metatarsalgia, is more specific than the general breakdown of the metatarsal arch described previously. The onset of true metatarsalgia is often abrupt, and the pain associated with it may be more intense than that found in general metatarsal weakness. In true metatarsalgia the fourth metatarsal head is severely depressed, sometimes resulting in a partial dislocation of the fourth metatarsophalangeal joint. The abnormal pressure on the plantar nerve often produces a neuritis in the area, which in turn causes intense pain and disability. Treatment consists first of the removal of the cause of the condition. The orthopedic physician will advise which procedure will follow this. Another type of Morton's toe is characterized by the presence of a second metatarsal bone that is longer than the first metatarsal bone.

Hammer toe

In **hammer toe** the proximal phalanx of the toe is hyperextended, the second phalanx is flexed, and the distal phalanx is either flexed or extended. The condition

often results from congenital causes or from having worn socks or shoes that are too short or too tight over a prolonged period (Figure A-19). Tests must be made to determine whether the condition has become structural. If the condition is functional in nature and the affected joints can be stretched and loosened, corrective measures may be taken to reorient the antagonist muscle pull involved in this deviation. The first step, however, must be the removal of the cause, and in severe cases an orthopedic physician should be consulted relative to special bracing, splinting, or surgery for correction of this condition.

Hallux valgus

A faulty metatarsal bone or shoes or socks that are too short, too narrow, or too pointed can cause a deviation of the toe known as **hallux valgus.** In this condition the great toe is deflected toward the other four toes at the metatarsophalangeal joint (Figure A-20). Correction of this condition must involve consultation with a physician. If the foot is not properly aligned and is toeing-out excessively, remedial measures should be taken to correct this alignment and prevent a further aggravation of hallux valgus.

Knee and Leg

Three conditions involving the knee and the upper and lower leg may be noted when a student is examined from the anterior or posterior view. Bowlegs and knock-knees are recognized from either of these two views, whereas tibial torsion is more easily identified from the anterior view.

figure A-19
Hammer toe.

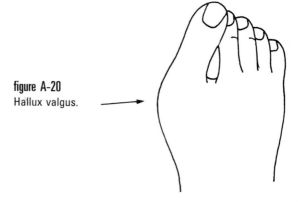
figure A-20
Hallux valgus.

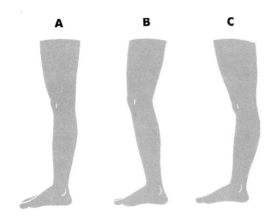

figure A-21
The knee. **A,** Normal. **B,** Bent (flexed). **C,** Hyperextended.

Other common deviations of the knee consist of hyperextension (genu recurvatum) and hyperflexion. The normal position of the knee is straight but not stiff. The student can correct a forward or backward knee by realigning the pull of the muscles that control its flexion or extension and by readjusting to the proper position of the leg (Figure A-21). A bent knee and backward knee are often associated with a flat lower back and lordosis of the lumbar spine, respectively.

Bowlegs (genu varum)

Bowlegs **(genu varum)** can be identified by examining a student with a plumb line, by comparing alignment of the leg with one of the vertical lines of the posture screen, or by having the student stand with the internal malleoli of the ankles touching and the legs held comfortably straight. In the last of these three tests, if a space exists between the knees when the malleoli are touching, the individual may be considered to have bowlegs. Unless this is either a functional condition in the young child (which may be outgrown) or a condition related to hyperextension of the knees and rotation of the thighs in order to separate the knees, corrective measures ordinarily must be prescribed by an orthopedic physician. The student can correct hyperextension and rotation of the knees by assuming the correct standing position and developing proper balance in the pull of the antagonist muscles of the hip and leg (Figure A-22, *C*).

Knock-knees (genu valgum)

Knock-knees **(genu valgum)** can be identified as described in the section on bowlegs; however, in this case, when the inner borders (medial femoral condyles) of the knees are brought together, a space exists between the internal malleoli of the ankles. Knock-knees may be related to pronation of the ankle and weakness in the lon-

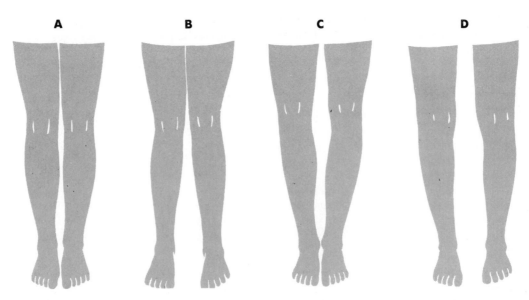

figure A-22
Leg alignment. **A,** Normal. **B,** Knock-knees. **C,** Bowlegs. **D,** Tibial torsion.

gitudinal arch. Correction involves realignment of the antagonist muscles of the leg and foot, which control proper alignment (Figure A-22, *B*). This usually involves development of the outward rotators of the thigh and stretching of the internal rotators of the thigh. Correction of this condition also involves realignment of the foot, ankle, and hip. Knock-knees also may be related to tibial torsion.

Tibial torsion

Tibial torsion, or twisting of the tibia, is identified by examination of the student from the anterior view. When the feet are pointed straight ahead, one or both of the kneecaps face in a medial direction; or when the kneecaps are facing straight forward, the feet are rotated in a toed-out position (Figure A-22, *D*). Correction of this condition involves realignment of the total leg, with emphasis being placed on the regions of the ankle, knee,

and hip. The outward rotators of the hip and the thigh must be developed, whereas muscles on the medial and lateral sides of the foot and ankle must be stretched to obtain proper alignment (Figures A-23 to A-25).

Trunk, Head, and Body
Pelvic tilt

The normal pelvis is inclined forward and downward at approximately a 60-degree angle when a line is drawn from the lumbosacral junction to the symphysis pubis. Any variation in this angle with the pelvis tipping (tilting) downward and forward usually results in a greater curve of the lumbar spine; by the same token, a variation in the angle with the pelvis tipping upward and backward tends to produce a flatness in the lumbar area. Since the sacroiliac joint is basically an immovable joint and only a minimum amount of motion takes place at

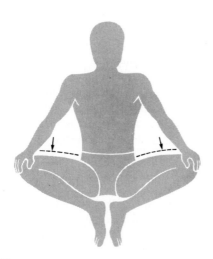

figure A-23
Hip stretching.
Specific for: Hip adductors
Beneficial in: Knock-knees
Starting position: Sitting, soles together, hands on inner surface of abducted knees
Actions:
1. Push knees toward floor.
2. Release pressure.
3. Repeat 1 and 2.
Measurement: Distance between outer portion of knee and floor

figure A-24
Hip stretching.
Specific for: Hip adductors
Beneficial in: Knock-knees
Starting position: Lying on back, legs at right angle to trunk, and resting against a wall, arms reverse T
Actions:
1. Lower (abduct) legs as far as possible with knees straight.
2. Return legs to original position.
Measurement: Distance between inner portion of heels

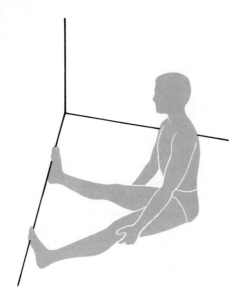

figure A-25
Hip stretching.
Specific for: Hip adductors
Beneficial in: Knock-knees
Starting position: Sitting, facing a wall, legs adducted, feet
    propped against wall at right angle, hands beneath knees,
    knees straight
Actions:
1. Bend forward with spine extended; pull trunk with
   arms.
2. Relax and return to starting position.
3. Repeat 1 and 2.

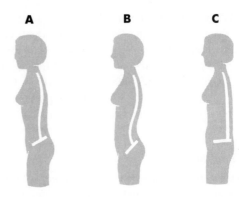

figure A-26
Pelvic positions. Note position of spine as pelvic position changes. **A,** Normal. **B,** Forward (downward) pelvic tilt. **C,** Backward (upward) pelvic tilt.

the lumbosacral joint, pelvic inclination and lumbar spinal curves are closely linked (Figure A-26). Since exaggerated spinal curves may limit normal motion in the lower back, both lordosis and a flat low back require special attention.

A lateral pelvic tilt, in which one side of the pelvis is higher or lower than the other side, can be observed during anterior and posterior postural examinations. The examiner can evaluate these conditions by marking either the anterosuperior iliac spines or the posterosuperior iliac spines of the ilium and then observing their relative height through the grids of a posture screen. The examiner can also evaluate the height of the pelvis by placing his or her fingers on the uppermost portion of the crest of the ilium and by observing the relative height

of the two sides of the pelvis. A lateral pelvic tilt may result from such things as unilateral **ankle pronation,** knock-knees, bowlegs, a shorter long bone in either the lower or upper portion of one leg, structural anomalies of the knee and hip joint, and deviations in the pelvic girdle, or scoliosis. Before an exercise program for lateral pelvic tilt is initiated, the cause of the condition must be determined by a physician, who may then suggest either symmetrical or asymmetrical exercises to realign the pelvic level. The position of the pelvic girdle as viewed from the anterior or posterior view has definite implications for the position of the spinal column as it extends upward from the sacrum. A lateral tilt of the pelvis will be reflected in the spinal column above it, since the sacroiliac and the lumbosacral joints are semi-immovable. The resulting lateral spinal curvatures are discussed in the following section. A lateral tilt of the pelvis may also be related to a twisting of the pelvic girdle itself. This is a complicated orthopedic problem involving both hip joints, the legs, and the vertebral column. Such cases should be referred to an orthopedic physician for treatment and for advice relative to a special exercise program.

Lordosis

Lordosis is an exaggeration of the normal hyperextension in the lumbar spine. It is usually associated with tightness in the lower erector spinae (sacrospina-

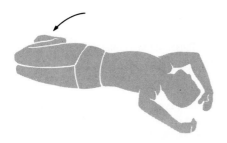

figure A-27

Spine mobilization.

Specific for: Mobilize lower spinal area

Beneficial in: Lordosis

Starting position: Hook-lying, arms reverse T, knees flexed
fully

Actions:

1. Raise both knees until thighs are vertical; shoulders
   are flat.
2. Lower knees to one side until they touch floor.
3. Repeat actions 1 and 2; legs do not fall but are
   controlled throughout movement.

Measurement: Repetitions over time

Sequence: Increase the distance below the hip where knees
are to touch floor/mat; the closer to the hips, the more
difficult

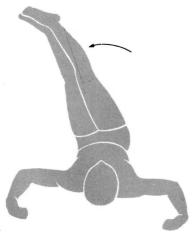

figure A-28

Spine mobilization.

Specific for: Mobilize lower spinal area

Beneficial in: Lordosis

Starting position: Lying on back

Actions:

1. Flex knees to chest.
2. Straighten knees, extending legs as high as possible.
3. Return knees to chest

Measurement: Repetitions over time

lis), iliopsoas, or rectus femoris muscle group and with
either weakness or stretching of the abdominal muscles.
Correction of this condition would therefore necessitate
stretching and loosening of the lower erector spinae (Figures A-27 to A-32), the iliopsoas (Figures A-33 to A-35),
and the rectus femoris muscles, together with assignment
of exercises designed to shorten and tighten the abdominal muscle group (Figures A-36 to A-40). It also may
be important to develop control of the gluteal and hamstring muscle groups, which can exert a downward pull
on the back of the pelvis. The development of the gluteal and hamstring muscle groups can help the individual
assume a correct position while stretching and exercising, and even while in the static standing position, but
these muscles must be relaxed when the individual
wishes to walk, move, or run. It is then necessary for
the abdominal muscles to hold the front of the pelvis up
and to maintain the desired curvature in the lower back.

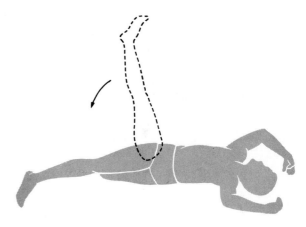

figure A-29

Spine mobilization (single leg).

Specific for: Mobilize lower spinal area

Beneficial in: Lordosis

Starting position: Lying on back, arms reverse T

Actions:

1. Flex one leg to a right angle.
2. Move flexed leg so foot touches floor on opposite side
   of body at *hip level.*
3. Return leg to a vertical position; keep thorax as flat as
   possible.
4. Lower leg to original position.

Measurement: Repetitions over time

Sequence: Foot hits floor at lower levels down the leg

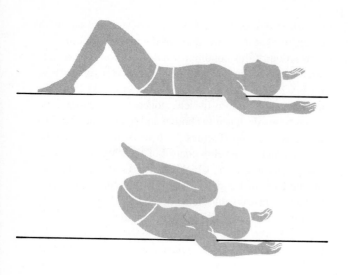

figure A-30
Knee-chest curl.

Specific for: Ptosis, lordosis, and developing abdominal strength

Beneficial in: Development of hip flexors and stretch of spinal extensors

Starting position: Lying on back with knees bent at right angles, feet flat on floor, arms straight out from shoulders, elbows bent 90 degrees, palms up

Actions:
1. Bring knees toward chest by pulling with abdominals. Curl spine, segment by segment, off the mat; knees touch chest or shoulders.
2. Return to starting position, keeping legs as close to floor as possible.
3. Repeat 1 and 2.

Measurement: Number of repetitions and distance knees are from chin

figure A-31
Mad cat.

Specific for: Lordosis and abdominal muscles

Beneficial in: Dysmenorrhea, arms, shoulders, shoulder girdle, and low back stretch

Starting position: Kneeling on all fours

Actions:
1. Hump low back by tightening abdominal and buttocks muscles.
2. Lean forward by bending arms until forehead touches floor.
3. Repeat 1 and 2.

Measurement: Number of repetitions and height of middle of lumbar region of spine from floor

figure A-32
Arm windmill.

Specific for: Mobilizing spine

Beneficial in: Lordosis

Starting position: Sitting position, arms out

Actions:
1. Rotate trunk at lumbar region.
2. Rotate trunk in opposite direction

Measurement: Number of degrees of rotation.

figure A-33

Hip and knee flexion (single leg).

Specific for: Hip flexors

Beneficial in: Lordosis

Starting position: Hook-lying, arms reverse T

Actions:

1. Flex one knee to chest; maximal flexion.
2. Extend opposite leg so it rests on floor.

Measurement: Distance back of knee is from floor

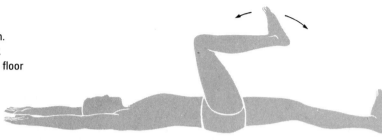

figure A-34

Stretch hip flexors.

Specific for: Hip flexors

Beneficial in: Lordosis

Starting position: Back-lying diagonal position on table, outside leg hangs over edge of table

Action: Hold flexed knee to chest.

Measurement: Distance heel is from floor; program should be built with a table specified distance from floor

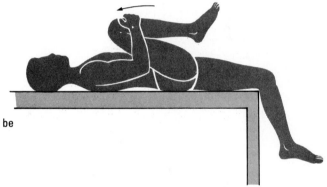

figure A-35

Lunges.

Specific for: Hip flexors

Beneficial in: Lordosis

Starting position: Kneeling, hip and knee of one leg flexed

Actions:

1. Lean trunk forward against thigh.
2. Slide resting knee back as far as possible.

Measurement: Distance between heel of flexed leg and knee of rear leg; height of hip from floor

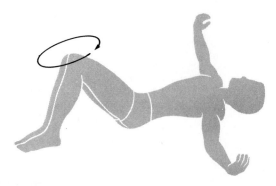

figure A-36
Knee circles.
Specific for: Abdominals
Beneficial in: Lordosis
Starting position: Hook-lying, arms reverse T
Actions:
1. Flex knees until thighs are vertical; shoulders are flat.
2. Make circles with knees, keeping heels close to thighs.
Measurement: Repetitions
Sequence: Increase radius of circle to make task more difficult.

figure A-37
Abdominal curl.
Specific for: Ptosis (protruding abdomen), lordosis, and developing and shortening abdominals
Beneficial in: Forward pelvic tilt
Starting position: Lying on back, elbows at side of body and bent at 90 degrees, knees flexed, feet flat on floor
Actions:
1. Curl body forward: back flat on mat, elbows at side bent 90 degrees.
2. Uncurl slowly and with control.
Measurement: Repetitions; height of nose from floor on sit-up
Note: In all leg raising or trunk raising from backward lying position, student should exhale or count aloud as legs or trunk is raised to relieve intraabdominal pressure and strain.

figure A-38
One-legged curl.
Specific for: Abdominals
Beneficial in: Lordosis
Starting position: Hook-lying, hands behind neck
Actions:
1. Simultaneously flex one thigh toward chest and touch knee with opposite elbow so they contact at waist level.
2. Repeat to other side.
Sequence: Reach farther with elbow and less with opposite knee.
Measurement: Repetitions over time

figure A-39
Bicycle.
Specific for: Abdominals and lumbar extensors
Beneficial in: Lordosis
Starting position: Hook-lying, arms in reverse T
Actions:
1. Move knees to chest with low back and neck flat.
2. Extend legs upward with knees straight.
3. Alternately flex knees and move to chest.
4. Lower flexed knees to table.
Increase difficulty: Abduct and adduct legs when they are in extended positions.
Measurement: Repetitions over time

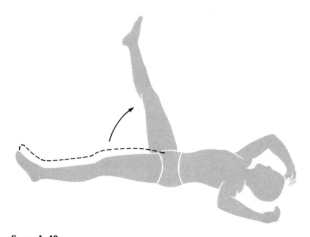

figure A-40
Leg raise (straight).
Specific for: Abdominals
Beneficial in: Lordosis
Starting position: Hook lying, back flat on floor
Actions:
1. Raise leg with knee straight to a height of 6 inches.
2. Lower raised leg to floor 10 times.
3. Repeat with other leg.
Measurement: Number of repetitions

A condition called ptosis (visceroptosis) is often associated with a forward pelvic tilt and lordosis. This condition is characterized by sagging of the lower abdominal muscles and protrusion of the lower abdominal area. It can also be corrected by shortening, tightening, and strengthening of the abdominal muscle groups. Clinically it has been assumed that there is a relationship among abdominal muscle strength, pelvic tilt, and lordosis. Strengthening the abdominal musculature and stretching the lumbar extensors are presumed to assist in controlling the position of the pelvis and relieving the lordotic condition. However, recent research is challenging the assumed relationships of these muscle groups to lordosis.[45]

Flat lower back

A flat lower back condition can develop when the pelvic girdle is inclined upward at the front, thereby decreasing the normal curvature of the lumbar spine. Often associated with this condition are tightness in the hamstring and gluteus maximus muscles, stretching of the iliopsoas and rectus femoris muscles, and weakness in the lumbar section of the erector spinae muscle group. The student can correct a flat back by stretching and increasing the length of the hamstring (Figures A-41 and

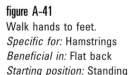

figure A-41
Walk hands to feet.
Specific for: Hamstrings
Beneficial in: Flat back
Starting position: Standing
Movement to desired position: Lean forward and rest weight on hands with knees straight.
Action: Move hands toward feet; keep heels of hands on floor/ground and knees straight; keep heels on floor.
Measurement: Distance between heel of hands and toes

A　　　**B**

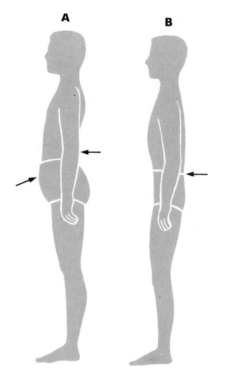

figure A-42
A, Ptosis and lordosis. **B,** Flat back.

A-42) and gluteal muscles and by developing, shortening, and tightening the iliopsoas, rectus femoris, and erector spinae muscle groups.

In the correction of both lordosis and a flat low back, the individual student must learn to feel what it is like to stand with the body in the correctly aligned position. It is helpful for the student to stand sideways to a regular or three-way mirror and observe the body in the correct mechanical position. A gravity line painted on the mirror or a plumb line hung down the length of the mirror will assist the student in realigning the body.

Lower back pain

Participation in physical activity may result in injury to the low back. About 10% of the injuries from strenuous physical activity involve the spine. When there is an injury to the back, pain should not be ignored or treated lightly,[28] because if severe pain persists for more than 3 weeks, structural anomalies may result.[22] Within

the last 10 years there has been an increase in the prevention, treatment, and management of low back pain, primarily because of its high cost to the health care system. Even though it is estimated that 90% of normal individuals with low back pain will improve within 6 weeks with[38] or without intervention,[8] there is a need for physical educators to understand low back pain prevention and treatment techniques. Low back pain is generally not a common cause for activity limitations during the school years, and therefore physical educators might easily overlook the importance of this concern for their disabled students.[36]

From a medical perspective, low back pain has long been a difficult problem. A major reason for this difficulty has been the inability of medical practitioners to accurately diagnose the specific cause of the condition.[41] Nachemson[31] reported an inability to find an objective cause for pain in 18% of his patients with low back pain. However, others propose that the very structure of the joints and surrounding musculature in the back could be major factors in the cause of low back pain.[42] The argument is made that programs designed to strengthen and therefore stabilize the lower back will prevent future low back problems. As a result, "healthy back schools" for the prevention and management of low back problems are growing in popularity in this country.[44]

Programs advocated by healthy back schools vary in nature; however, all provide information and exercises believed to activate muscles related to low back problems. Such exercises have been shown to enhance the strength of muscles related to posture (e.g., lumbar extensors).[34] In addition to providing exercises to strengthen specific groups of muscles, most programs include postural reorientation exercises.[5]

The growing number of back schools has resulted in empirical studies of their effectiveness. Linton and Kamwendo[26] reviewed a number of these studies and concluded that there is limited evidence that low back schools have a positive impact on the number of health care contacts, amount of sick leave, work status, pain intensity or duration, activity level, or medication consumption. They believe that critical issues that need to be examined to demonstrate effectiveness are the extent to which patients comprehend the instructions and comply with the exercise regimen.

Perhaps what is critical for the physical educator is sensitivity to the growing problem of low back pain.

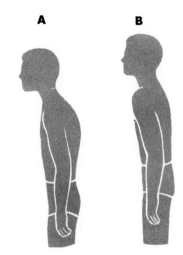

figure A-43
A, Kyphosis. **B,** Forward (round) shoulders.

Awareness of the magnitude of the problem should lead to instruction of students in proper lifting and carrying techniques, as well as inclusion of general posture-enhancing exercises in the physical education program.

Kyphosis

Kyphosis (Figure A-43, *A*) is an abnormal amount of flexion in the dorsal or thoracic spine. An extreme amount of kyphosis is called humpback. This condition ordinarily involves weakening and stretching of the erector spinae and other extensor muscle groups in the dorsal or thoracic regions, along with shortening and tightening of the antagonist (pectoral) muscles on the anterior side of the chest and shoulder girdle. Its correction is effected primarily through stretching of the anterior muscles of the chest and shoulders, which allows the spinal extensor and shoulder girdle adductor muscle groups to be developed, strengthened, and shortened and thus pull the spine back into a more desirable position. Forward (round) shoulders, a flat chest, and winged scapula are often associated with kyphosis. Exercises for correcting kyphosis are presented in Figures A-44 to A-50.

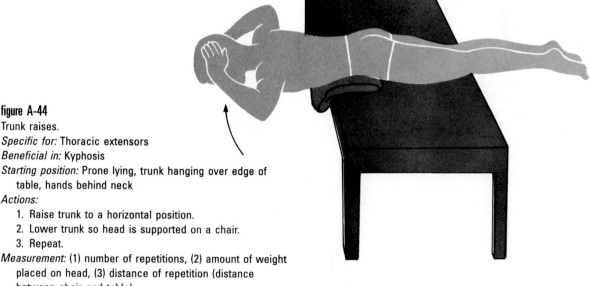

figure A-44
Trunk raises.
Specific for: Thoracic extensors
Beneficial in: Kyphosis
Starting position: Prone lying, trunk hanging over edge of table, hands behind neck
Actions:
  1. Raise trunk to a horizontal position.
  2. Lower trunk so head is supported on a chair.
  3. Repeat.
Measurement: (1) number of repetitions, (2) amount of weight placed on head, (3) distance of repetition (distance between chair and table)

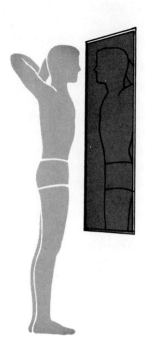

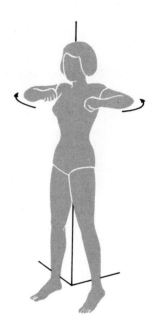

figure A-45

Neck flattener at mirror.

Specific for: Forward head, kyphosis, forward shoulders, lordosis, and shoulder development

Beneficial in: Total anteroposterior postural deviations

Starting position: Standing tall in front of mirror, head up, chin in, elbows extended sideways at shoulder level, fingertips behind base of head

Actions:

1. Draw head and neck backward vigorously as fingers are pressed forward for resistance and elbows are forced backward (flattening upper back). Inhale.
2. Flatten low back by tucking pelvis by tightening abdominals and hip extensors.
3. Hold; exhale; return to starting position. (Student can stand facing mirror or with side of body toward mirror to check body position and to correct either anteroposterior or lateral posture deviations.)

figure A-46

Breaking chains.

Specific for: Forward shoulders

Beneficial in: Kyphosis, flat chest, forward head, lordosis, and shoulder development

Starting position: Standing with back against corner of post or sharp edge of corner of room, feet 6 inches apart; place fists together in front of chest with elbows at shoulder level

Actions:

1. Pull fists apart, keeping elbows at shoulder level; pinch shoulder blades together.
2. Inhale.
3. Tuck pelvis and press low back to wall as close as possible.
4. Hold position for 10 seconds.
5. Repeat.

Measurement: Repetitions

Caution: Keep abdomen and buttocks tight and maintain body in starting plane during exercise; when lordosis is present, exercise may be done in sitting position with legs crossed in tailor's position.

figure A-47

Neck, back, and shoulder flattener.

Specific for: Forward head, cervical lordosis, kyphosis, forward shoulders, and lordosis

Beneficial in: Pelvic tilt

Starting position: Lying on back, knees drawn up, arms at sides with palms down

Actions:

1. Inhale and expand chest as nape of neck is forced to mat by stretching tall and pulling chin toward chest.
2. Flatten small of back to mat by tightening abdominal and buttocks muscles.
3. Neck and back are flat on mat. Fingers cannot pass under neck. As it becomes easier to flatten back, the exercise may be made more difficult and more beneficial by gradually extending legs until low back cannot be maintained in a flattened position.

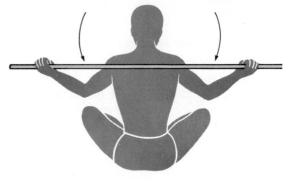

figure A-48

Pectoral stretch (wand).

Specific for: Pectorals

Beneficial in: Round shoulders

Starting position: Sitting, grasp wand with hands, arms extended overhead

Actions:

1. Lower wand to shoulders; good extension of neck and spine by flexing arms.
2. Return wand to starting position with arms straight.

Measurement: Distance between inner portions of hands

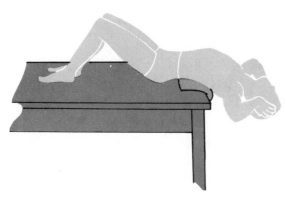

figure A-49

Pectoral stretch (lying).

Specific for: Pectorals

Beneficial in: Kyphosis

Starting position: Back-lying, hands behind neck, edge of table across base of scapula

Actions:

1. Simultaneously lean trunk back and down toward floor, adduct scapula, and extend cervical spine.
2. Relax to starting position.
3. Repeat.

Measurement: Distance elbows are from floor; program should be developed with specific measurement of height of table

figure A-50

Pectoral stretch (sitting).

Specific for: Pectorals

Beneficial in: Kyphosis

Starting position: Sitting in chair, hands behind neck (touch head)

Actions:

1. Simultaneously lean trunk backward, extend upper spine, adduct scapula, and pull arms backward.
2. Relax to starting position.

Measurement: Distance elbows are from ground/floor

Forward (round) shoulders

Forward shoulders (Figure A-43, *B*) is a condition involving an abnormal position of the shoulder girdle. This condition usually exists when the anterior muscles of the shoulder girdle (pectoral muscles) become shortened and tightened and the adductor muscles of the shoulder girdle (rhomboid and trapezius muscles) become weak and stretched. It is often associated with a flat chest and kyphosis. The basic means of correction of this condition is to stretch and loosen the anterior muscles of the chest shoulder girdle and to develop, strengthen, and shorten the adductor muscles of the shoulder girdle.

The student with kyphosis or forward shoulders should also practice standing and sitting in good alignment in front of a mirror to get the feeling of what it is like to hold the body comfortably in proper balance. When the correct position becomes easy and natural, the student will no longer have to rely on the mirror and the visual cues associated with its use.

Kypholordosis

Kypholordosis is a combination of kyphosis in the upper back and lordosis in the lower portion of the spine. Often one of these deviations is a compensation for the other and involves the body's attempt to keep itself in balance. Correction of kypholordosis consists of the same basic principles involved in correcting the individual conditions described previously; however, time often can be saved in the exercise program by assigning certain exercises that are beneficial for the correction of both conditions.

Flat upper back

A flat upper back is the opposite of a kyphotic spine and involves a decrease or absence of the normal anteroposterior spinal curve in the dorsal or thoracic region. Stretching of the posterior muscles of the upper back allows the antagonist muscles on the anterior side of the body to be developed and shortened and thus is beneficial for this condition.

Winged scapula

Winged scapula is a condition that involves the abduction or protraction of the shoulder blades (the medial border of the affected scapula being farther from the spinal column than normal). Projection of the medial

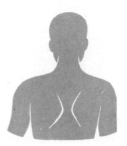

figure A-51
Winged scapula.

border of the scapula posteriorly and protrusion of the inferior angle are concomitants of this condition (Figure A-51). Winged scapula is very common among children, who exhibit it especially when their arms are raised forward to the shoulder level. This results from lack of shoulder girdle strength; ordinarily, the condition is outgrown as the children begin to participate in hanging and climbing activities for the development of the muscles of the shoulder girdle. In adolescents and young adults the condition involves unequal pull on the antagonist muscles of the shoulder girdle, and corrective measures may be necessary. In general, the procedure would be to stretch and loosen the anterior muscles of the shoulder girdle and to develop the adductors of the scapula, involving both the trapezius and the rhomboid muscles. Developmental exercises for the serratus anterior muscle also are necessary, since it has a major responsibility for keeping the scapula in the correct position flat against the rib cage.

Forward head

A forward head is one of the most common postural deviations. Chronic head placement may cause pain because of constant strain to the muscles that are being stretched or shortened.[21] It often accompanies kyphosis, forward shoulders, and lordosis. Two factors are involved in analyzing the causes of a forward head and correcting it. The extensors of the head and neck are often stretched and weakened because of the habitual malposition of the head (Figure A-52, *B*). Correcting this condition involves bringing the head into proper alignment, with the chin tucked so that the lower jaw is basically in line with the ground and so that it is not tipped up when the head is drawn back. This involves reorientation of the head and neck so that the individual knows what it feels like to hold the head in the correct posi-

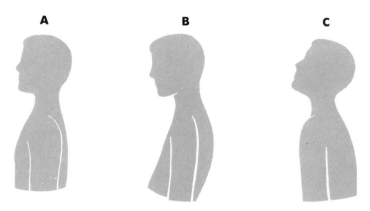

figure A-52
A, Normal head position. **B,** Forward head. **C,** Cervical lordosis.

tion. The antagonist muscles involved must be reeducated to hold the head in a position so that the lobe of the ear approximates a position in line with the center of the shoulder.

Cervical lordosis

Cervical lordosis may result from an attempt to compensate for other curves occurring at a lower level in the spinal column or from incorrect procedures in attempting to correct a forward head. The spinal extensors are often tight and contracted so that the head is tilted well back and the chin is tipped upward (Figure A-52, *C*). As in the case of a forward head, reeducation of the antagonist muscles and the proprioceptive centers involved is necessary so that the lower jaw is held in line with the ground. In the correction of cervical lordosis and a forward head, the student must learn to assume the proper position and must exercise in front of a mirror in order to recognize this position.

Posterior overhang (round swayback)

In posterior overhang, the upper body sways backward from the hips so that the center of the shoulder falls behind the gravity line of the body. To compensate for this position, the hips and thighs may move forward of the gravity line, the head may tilt forward, and the chest may be flat. Correction of posterior overhang involves reorientation of the total body so that its several parts are returned to a position of alignment. The student is instructed to work in front of a mirror and align the body with a gravity marker on the mirror. As an alternative, the instructor may check and correct the student's posture. The exercise program includes reeducation of the antagonist muscles to enable the student to return the body to a position of balance. The muscle groups needing special attention are the abdominal muscles, the antagonist muscle groups responsible for anteroposterior alignment of the tilt of the pelvis, the adductor muscles of the shoulder girdle, and the extensor muscles of the upper spine. The student must stand tall, with the chin tucked and the abdomen flat, to correct this condition.

Scoliosis

Estimates vary on the incidence of abnormal posture because of the differing criteria and assessment instruments used to determine abnormality.[29] However, there is agreement that lateral curvature beyond 10 degrees is abnormal.[10] Some available data indicate that 10% of the population has some degree of scoliosis. The initial symptoms are slight curvature of the back with no accompanying pain. Mild scoliotic curves are very common and will rarely progress.[10] However, when a small curve is identified, it should be continually monitored.[33] The curve may be aggravated during adolescence and in adulthood. Should a deviation progress beyond 10 degrees during the growth years, intervention is necessary. If the condition remains untreated, scoliosis can cause pain, arthritic symptoms, and obvious physical deformity resulting in heart and lung complications that limit activity.[32]

Scoliosis is rotolateral curvature of the spine. When viewed from the front or from the rear, a scoliotic spine has a curvature to one side; in advanced stages it may curve both to the left and to the right. A scoliotic curve is ordinarily described in relation to its position as the individual is viewed from the rear. A curvature is described as a simple C curve to the left or right. In a more advanced stage, compensation above or below the original curve may occur, and the resulting curvature is described as a regular S curve or a reverse S curve. Examples of scoliotic curves are shown in Figure A-53.

Initially, a lateral deviation of the spine may involve only a simple C curve to the left or right in any segment of the spine, depending on the cause of the problem, the resulting change in soft tissues, and the pull of the antagonist muscles. These curves are often functional in nature and thus are correctable through properly assigned stretching and developmental exercises under the guidance of a physician. Untreated spines often become progressively worse, involving permanent structural changes.

Scoliosis is often caused by asymmetry of the body. Lateral pelvic tilt, low shoulder, asymmetrical development of the rib cage, leg length discrepancy,[30] or lateral deviation of the linea alba may be a cause or effect of rotolateral curvature of the spine. Evidence of this would be found in one or more of the following body changes:

1. When the thoracic vertebral column is displaced laterally, the rotation of the vertebral bodies is in the direction of the convexity of the curve.
2. Lateral bending of the spine is accompanied by a depression and protrusion of the intervertebral disks on the concave side, with a greater separation between the sides of the vertebrae on the convex side of the lateral curve.
3. There is an imbalance in the stability and pull of the ligaments and muscles responsible for holding the vertebral column in its normal position. Muscles and ligaments on the concave side become tight and contracted, whereas those on the convex side become stretched and weak. Muscle atrophy may occur.

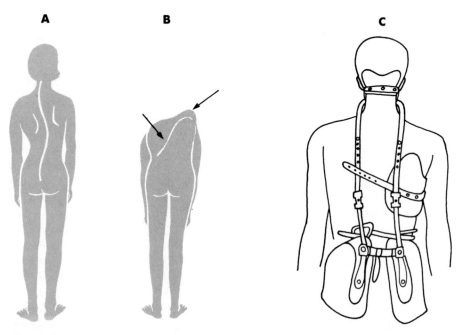

figure A-53
Scoliosis. **A,** Rotolateral curve. **B,** Rotation viewed from Adam's position. **C,** Milwaukee brace.

4. Changes in the rib cage involve flattening and depression of the posterior aspects of the ribs on the concave side, with a posterior bulging of the ribs on the side of the convex spinal curve. The opposite is true of the anterior aspect of the chest. There the ribs on the concave side are prominent, whereas they are flattened or depressed on the convex side.

During the past several years, orthopedic physicians have stressed the importance of identifying and treating scoliosis in young children between the ages of 9 and 14 years. Early detection by physical education teachers, therapists, and nurses and immediate referral to a physician who specializes in scoliosis treatment may prevent permanent deformity in many of these young persons.

The treatment of scoliosis is rather specific, depending on the cause of the condition and the resulting changes in the spinal column. Students with scoliosis must be referred to an orthopedist for examination and recommendations relative to stretching and developmental exercises, which may be either symmetrical or asymmetrical in nature. Some orthopedic physicians believe that the treatment of scoliosis should be very specific and indicate the types of asymmetrical exercises to be performed by the student. Others subscribe to the theory that the cause of scoliosis should be eliminated if possible, but that only symmetrical types of exercise should be assigned for this condition.

Since scoliosis is complicated and difficult to diagnose and treat, it is necessary for the adapted teacher or therapist to rely on the advice of the physician concerning the types of activities and exercises that should be prescribed for the student. Since lateral spinal curves are accompanied by a certain amount of rotation of the spine, a great deal of skill is required to diagnose and treat the condition correctly. Recommendations relative to types of games, sports, and activities should therefore be made by the examining physician.

Treatment may consist of the use of casts or braces (Figure A-53, C) combined with a special exercise program assigned by the physician. Exercise programs without a cast or brace are not usually recommended. Cases that are not discovered early may require operation with spinal fusion or the insertion of rods along the vertebral column to straighten the severely curved spine (Figure A-54).

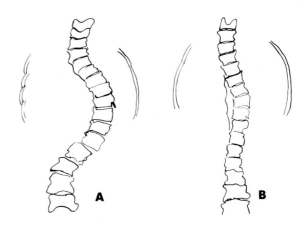

figure A-54
Severe scoliosis. **A,** Before surgery. **B,** After surgery and corrective procedures.

Treatment of patients with severe scoliosis may include any or all of the following:

1. Removal of the cause, if possible
2. Assignment of symmetrical exercises, especially for the abdomen, back, and hip regions
3. Mobilization of tightness in soft tissue in the trunk, shoulder girdle, and hip region
4. Assignment of asymmetrical exercises to strengthen muscles on the convex side of the curves on the recommendation of an orthopedic physician
5. Recommendation of traction of the spine by the physician
6. Assignment of exercises to increase the strength, anteroposterior balance, and alignment of the spine
7. Specific prescription of any derotation exercises by the physician
8. Restoration of symmetrical hip rotation[12]

Physical educators who specialize in adapted physical education and specialists in therapeutic recreation should inform those teaching regular physical education, the school nurse, and other health-related personnel of the importance of early screening of young persons to detect scoliosis and other body mechanics problems. The students can then be involved in preventive programs under the guidance of a physician who specializes in the diagnosis and care of scoliosis and other serious orthopedic problems.

Shoulder height asymmetry

It is rather common for an individual to have one shoulder higher or lower than the other. This condition usually results from asymmetrical muscle or bone development of the shoulder girdle or lateral curvature in the spinal column. Correction of an abnormal curve in the spine may result in the return of the shoulders to a level position, although special exercises may be required in the process. When the cause is faulty muscle development, correction is a relatively simple matter of developing the strength of the weaker or higher side and stretching the contracted side. This also involves a reorientation of the student's feeling for the correct shoulder and body alignment. Exercises for a low or high shoulder should be performed in front of a regular or three-way mirror to enable the student to recognize the position of the body when it is being held in proper alignment.

Head tilt or twist

When viewed from the anterior or posterior view, the head may be either tilted directly to the side or tilted to the side with a concomitant twisting of the neck. In either case, it is necessary to reorient the student to the proper position of the head. Often, deviations in the position of the head and neck are compensatory for other postural deviations located below this area. The correction of these conditions involves reorientation to the proper position of the head. This entails reeducating the antagonist muscles responsible for holding the head in a position of balance, plus reorienting the student in terms of holding the head in the correct position, which will activate the appropriate proprioceptive centers and balance organs. The exercise program for correction of the condition should be rather specific in terms of the muscle groups that are stretched and developed. Moreover, the student should practice the exercise program standing in front of a mirror so that he or she can visualize the correct position and develop the feeling of holding the head in correct alignment.

Body tilt

Another deviation that may be noted in the anterior and posterior postural examinations is a problem of body alignment in which the total body is tilted to the left or right of the gravity or plumb line (Figure A-55). Standing with the body tilted to the side causes increased

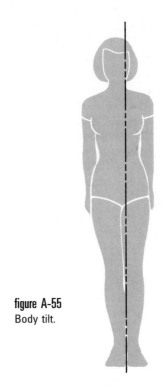

figure A-55
Body tilt.

strain on the bones, joints, and muscles and may result in compensation being made to bring the body back into a position of balance over its base of support. Often this compensation results in the hips and shoulders being thrown out of alignment, leading to the development of lateral curvature in the spine. Correction of this condition involves an analysis of the causative factors of the tilt, such as unilateral flatfoot, pronated ankle, knock-knee, or short leg. On the other hand, standing out of balanced alignment may be habitual with the student. Before correction of the lateral body tilt can be accomplished, unilateral deviations must be corrected. Specific suggestions for the correction of a weak foot, ankle, or knee are contained in another section of this chapter. Together with these specific corrective measures, exercises should be given to the student for body tilt. Exercises and activities that involve the symmetrical use of the total body and that will help the student learn to stand with the body in correct alignment and balance are needed. Exercising in front of the mirror will give the student a visual concept of the feeling of standing with the body in a balanced position, which should help effect a correction of a lateral tilt of the body.

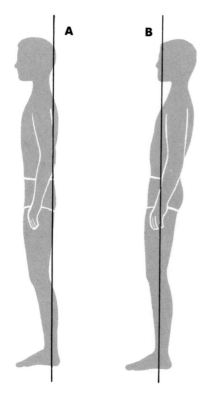

figure A-56
Total body forward (**A**) and backward (**B**) leans (plumb line test).

Postural sway

Standing balance is a dynamic process of maintaining stable, upright posture. Postural sway results when individual movements of different joints create oscillations of the body either forward and backward or side to side.[30] Control over postural sway is a desirable goal of a postural education program. Ratcliffe et al.[35] have reported the use of a therapeutic technique called approximation (compression of joints), which decreases the postural sway of healthy subjects and stabilizes standing balance.

Body lean

When viewed from the side, the total body may lean a considerable distance either forward or backward of the line of gravity. When the total body is in good alignment but leans forward or backward from the ankle so

that the lobe of the ear is positioned either anterior or posterior to the gravity line, the condition is considered to be a total body lean (Figure A-56). If the body lean is not corrected, as the individual attempts to compensate for the lean and bring the body back into a balanced standing position, the body often will be transferred into one or more of the postural conditions discussed previously. Correction of the forward or backward lean of the total body is primarily a matter of reorientation of the proprioceptive centers of the body to enable the individual to feel when the body is in correct alignment in the standing position. Checking the forward or backward deviation of the body against a gravity line or a plumb line hung vertically before a three-way mirror is an excellent way for the student to recognize the feel of standing with the body in the correct position. Symmetrical exercises can then be assigned so that the student can develop the flexibility and strength necessary to hold the body in correct alignment.

SUMMARY

Good posture contributes to the well-being of the body and gives the impression of enthusiasm and self-confidence. There are good postures for sitting, standing, and walking. Antigravity muscles that are weak and stretched and reciprocal muscles that shorten are often the functional causes of poor posture. The procedure for ameliorating poor posture is as follows: (1) know the model of good posture, (2) assess the individual against the model of normal posture for deficiency, (3) identify the specific muscles that need to be strengthened or stretched, and (4) conduct programs to develop the deficient muscles. The specific areas to be assessed for postural abnormalities are the feet, ankles, legs, hips, anteroposterior aspect of the spinal column, lateral aspect of the spinal column, shoulders, and head and neck.

Tests and measurements can be used in physical education to evaluate improvement, aid in instruction, determine whether body parts are properly aligned, and motivate students to work toward correction of body malalignment. Some of the tests and measurements traditionally used in adapted physical education programs are not highly valid or reliable but may still be of some use in identifying deviations, helping the instructor explain malalignments to students, and motivating students to work toward self-improvement. If any of these values are obtained from testing, it should be a worthwhile part of the program. The data obtained are used to formulate specific performance objectives for each person.

The physician and the physical educator may diagnose and prescribe physical activity for school-age children with postural disorders. If a physician diagnoses a postural disorder and prescribes treatment, this should be noted in the student's school health record. All activity that has been contraindicated by the physician should be noted by the physical educator. Under these conditions there should be close communication between the physical educator and the physician.

When postural conditions are of structural origin, surgical techniques can usually improve mechanical alignment. Thus remedies for postural conditions that are structural in nature are under the jurisdiction of the medical profession. On the other hand, postural conditions caused by soft tissue and functional defects may respond to physical fitness programs to increase the strength and flexibility of specific muscles as directed by physical educators. Postural education regarding functional disorders requires specially designed instruction to meet the postural needs of children. In accordance with regulations for engaging "related services," if children do not respond to or benefit from the postural education programs, they should be referred to a physician.

Although there is optimum mechanical body alignment, children at young ages may have mechanical malalignments of body parts and still have normal posture for their age. There are apparent postural deficiencies among people with orthopedic disabilities because of muscular involvement associated with the disorders. Individuals who are mentally retarded and have neurological involvement have postural problems associated with vestibular and kinesthetic delays and depth perception problems. Other disabling conditions that affect strength and vitality may also have an impact on their postural alignment. The growing incidence of low back pain in the United States should alert the physical educator to the need to provide students with low back information and stabilizing exercises.

Review Questions

1. What are the values of a postural education program?
2. What are the positions from which posture may be evaluated?

3. Can you list some deviations of the foot and the ankle? What activities might be used to ameliorate the conditions?
4. What are some disorders of the legs? How would one go about correcting the deficiencies?
5. Can you describe lordosis and identify activities that may remedy the condition?
6. Can you describe postural deviations of the upper back and scapula and indicate activities that may help correct the muscles that contribute to the deficiencies?
7. How would you treat abnormal postural conditions of the head and neck?
8. Can you describe the different scoliotic curves and suggest activities to treat the disorders?
9. Can you describe tests to determine deviations of the foot and ankle, leg, pelvis, and spine?
10. How would you determine whether a postural deviation is structural or functional?
11. Provide examples of postural malalignment in young children that may be regarded as normal with respect to their chronological age.
12. What disabling conditions have the greatest prevalence of postural deficiencies?

Student Activities

1. Examine a peer for postural deficiencies and indicate activities that may assist the individual to better his or her posture.
2. Visit a home for the aged and assess the posture of some of the clients. Analyze each segment of the body in terms of good alignment and indicate appropriate activities for the individual.
3. Teach your peers some postural exercises. Specify the manner in which the activities are to be performed and identify the muscles that are to benefit from the activity.
4. Visit a teacher who conducts a postural education program. Are there individual postural education programs and postural objectives for each child? Do the activities that children are performing match the assessment information?
5. Have three persons evaluate an individual's postural fitness. Indicate differences and agreement on the evaluation of each of the areas of the postural assessment.
6. Study young children from 1 to 4 years of age to determine postural malalignments that are considered normal for their chronological age.

References

1. Althoff SA, Heyden MS, Roberson LD: Back to basics—whatever happened to posture? *J Health Phys Educ Rec Dance* 59:20-24, 1988.

2. Althoff SA, Heyden MS, Roberson LD: Posture screening: a program that works, *J Health Phys Educ Rec Dance* 59(8):26-32, 1988.

3. Auxter DM et al: *Correcting hip retroversion in walking gait of an infant,* Final report to the US Department of Education, Project No. 029AH50223, 1986.

4. Beattie P, Rothstein JM, Lamb RL: Reliability of the attraction method for measuring lumbar spine backward bending, *Phys Ther* 67:364-369, 1987.

5. Biering-Sorenson F: Physical measurements as risk indicators for low back trouble over a one year period, *Spine* 9:106-109, 1984.

6. Binkley J et al: Diagnostic classification of patients with low back pain: report on a survey of physical therapy experts, *Phys Ther* 73:138-150, 1993.

7. Blackman JA, editor: *Medical aspects of developmental disabilities in children birth to three,* Rockville, Md, 1984, Aspen.

8. Bracker D, Gargen SR, Singer SA: Low back pain in a tennis player, *Physician Sportsmed* 16:75-83, 1988.

9. Cailliet R: *Low back pain syndrome,* Philadelphia, 1974, FA Davis.

10. Cassell CC, Hall JE: Current treatment approaches in the nonoperative and operative management of adolescent idiopathic scoliosis, *Phys Ther* 71:897-99, 1991.

11. Chiarello CM, Cavidge R: Interrater reliability of the Cybex EDI-320 and fluid goniometer in normals and patients with low back pain, *Arch Phys Med Rehabil* 74:32-37, 1993.

12. Chibulka MT: The treatment of the sacroiliac joint component to low back pain: a case report, *Phys Ther* 72:917-922, 1992.

13. Daniels L, Worthingham C: *Muscle testing: techniques of manual examination,* Philadelphia, 1982, WB Saunders.

14. DeRosa CP, Porterfield JA: A physical therapy model for the treatment of low back pain, *Phys Ther* 72:1093-1100, 1994.

15. Fairbanks BL: *Vigor and vitality,* Salt Lake City, 1982, Hawkes Publishing.

16. Feuerstein M, Beattie P: Biobehavioral factors affecting pain and disability in low back pain: mechanisms and assessment, *Phys Ther* 75:267-280, 1995.

17. Fisher AC, Domm MA, Wuest DA: Adherence to sport-injury programs, *Physician Sportsmed* 16:47-50, 1988.

18. Garrison L, Read AK: *Fitness for every body,* Palo Alto, Calif, 1980, Mayfield Publishing.

19. Hage M: *The back pain book: a self-help guide for daily relief of neck and back pain,* Atlanta, Ga, 1992, Peachtree.

20. Hamman RG et al: Training effects during repeated therapy sessions of balance training using visual feedback, *Arch Phys Med Rehabil* 73:738-751, 1992.

21. Hanten WP et al: Assessment of total head excursion and resting head posture, *Arch Phys Med Rehabil* 72:877-880, 1991.

22. Johnson RJ: Low back pain in sports, *Physician Sportsmed* 21(4):53-59, 1993.

23. Kellett KM, Kellett DA, Nordholm LA: Effects of an exercise program on sick leave due to back pain, *Phys Ther* 71:283-290, 1991.

24. Kohles S et al: Improved physical performance outcomes after functional restoration treatment in patients with chronic low back pain: early versus recent training results, *Spine* 15:1321-1324, 1990.

25. Lindsrom I et al: The effects of graded activity on patients with subacute low back pain: a randomized prospective clinical study with an operant-conditioning behavioral approach, *Phys Ther* 72:279-289, 1992.

26. Linton SJ, Kamwendo K: Low back schools: a critical review, *Phys Ther* 678:1375-1383, 1987.

27. Miller DK, Allen TE: *Fitness: a lifetime commitment,* Minneapolis, 1982, Burgess Publishing.

28. Miniaci A, Johnson PQ: Spondylolysis of the lumbar vertebrae with associated reactive sclerosis of the pedicle of the contralateral side: report of a case, *Clin J Sports Med* 3:189-191, 1993.

29. Moore S, Brunt D: Effects of trunk support and target distance on postural adjustments prior to a rapid reaching task by seated subjects, *Arch Phys Med Rehabil* 72:638-641, 1991.

30. Murrell P, Cornwall MW, Doucet SK: Leg-length discrepancy: effect on the amplitude of postural sway, *Arch Phys Med Rehabil* 72:646-648, 1991.

31. Nachemson A: Work for all, *Clin Orthop* 79:77-85, 1983.

32. The National Scoliosis Foundation: *One in every ten persons has scoliosis,* Belmont, Mass, 1985, The Foundation.

33. Pearsall DJ, Reid GJ, Hedden DM: Comparison of three noninasive methods for measuring scoliosis, *Phys Ther* 72:648-657, 1992.

34. Pollock ML et al: Effects of resistance training on lumbar extension strength, *Am J Sports Med* 17:624-628, 1989.

35. Ratcliffe KT et al: Effects of approximation on postural sway in healthy subjects, *Phys Ther* 67:502-506, 1987.

36. Sharpe GL, Liemohn WP, Snodgrasss LB: Exercise prescription and low back, *J Health Phys Educ Rec Dance* 59(9):74-78, 1988.

37. Shirado O et al: Concentric and eccentric strength of trunk muscles: influence of test postures on strength and characteristics of patients with chronic low-back pain, *Arch Phys Med Rehabil* 76:604-611, 1995.

38. Stelmach GE et al: Age related decline in postural control mechanisms, *Aging Hum Dev* 9:205-223, 1989.

39. Stratford PW et al: Assessing change over time in patients with low back pain, *Phys Ther* 74:528-533, 1994.

40. Subotnick SI: Foot orthoses: an update, *Physician Sportsmed* 11:103-109, 1983.

41. Tenhula JA, Rose SJ, Delitto A: Association between di-

rection of lateral lumbar shift, movement tests and side of symptoms in patients with low back pain syndrome, *Phys Ther* 70:480-485, 1990.

42. Tigny RL: Anterior dysfunction of the sacroiliac joint as a major factor in the etiology of idiopathic low back pain syndrome, *Phys Ther* 70:250-262, 1990.

43. Twomey LT: A rationale for the treatment of back pain and joint pain by manual therapy, *Phys Ther* 72:885-891, 1992.

44. Waddell B: A new clinical model for the treatment of low back pain, *Spine* 12:632-644, 1987.

45. Walker ML et al: Relationships between lumbar lordosis, pelvic tilt and abdominal muscle performance, *Phys Ther* 67:512-516, 1987.

46. Woolacott MH: Normal and abnormal development of posture control in children. In Yabe K, Kusano K, Nakata H, editors: *Adapted physical activity: health and fitness,* New York, 1994, Springer-Verlag.

47. Woolacott MH, Shumway-Cook A, Nashner LM: Aging and postural control: changes in sensory organization and muscular coordination, *Int Aging Hum Dev* 23:97-114, 1986.

Suggested Readings

Cailliet R: *Back pain and disability,* ed 3, Philadelphia, 1992, FA Davis.

Russell GS, Highland RR: *Care of the low back: a patient guide,* Philadelphia, 1990, FA Davis.

Weinstein JN, editor: *Clinical efficacy and outcome in the diagnosis and treatment of low back pain,* New York, 1992, Raven Press.

White LA: *Spine: state of the art reviews: back school,* Philadelphia, 1991, Hanley & Belfus.

Stress Reduction Techniques

Stress

Hans Selye[20] defined stress as "the nonspecific response of the human organism to any demand placed upon it." More generally, stress is the physiological, mental, and emotional response of the body to events that are new, threatening, frightening, or exciting.[8]

Stress is a common problem that is expensive and life-threatening. It is estimated that the annual cost of stress and stress-related diseases in the United States exceeds $100 billion.[8] There is growing evidence that chronic stress suppresses the immune system, which in turn leads to illness.

Selye[21] suggested the existence of a general adaptation syndrome that occurs in animals and humans when they are subjected to continual emotional stress. This syndrome is composed of three consecutive stages: (1) the alarm reaction, which represents normal body changes caused by emotion; (2) the resistance to stress, or one's adjustment to the alarm reaction, which requires considerable energy resources; and (3) the exhaustion stage, in which the store of energy is used up. The exhaustion stage may lead to the death of single cells, organs, organ systems, or the entire organism.

Kune[12] has expanded on Selye's model in an attempt to highlight the importance of an individual's reaction to stress. She proposes that the amount of resistance a person offers is dependent on the perceptions and emotional state of the person; the more resistance offered, the more negative the result. Her five-step model leads from an event to the disease state: Event, followed by a negative perception of the event, followed by a negative emotional response to the perception, followed by a physiological response to the perception, followed by a psychophysiological mechanism (such as suppression of the immune system) that facilitates expression of a disease. Thus it is not the event itself that causes the stress, but a person's way of thinking about and perception of the event that result in the negative outcome.

Some authorities have suggested stress as a possible cause of hypertension, rheumatism, arthritis, ulcers, allergies, cancer, and other conditions.[17] An individual with uncontrolled stress has a high level of cerebral and emotional activity, coupled with nervous muscular tension, which may eventually lead to the exhaustion stage and perhaps to psychosomatic disorders.

It is critical that the causes of stress and ways to break up the chain of events that result from a stressful event be understood. Techniques that are helpful for effectively dealing with stress are a variety of interventions that reduce negative psychological and physiological reactions. These include coping training, exercise, and conscious reduction of tension.

Stress-Coping Training

Stress-coping training requires an individual to differentiate between desirable and undesirable states of tension (e.g., having no headache versus having a headache). The learner is taught to identify relationships between situations that create tension in the body, bodily sensations of distress, emotional states, and thoughts that lead to tension. To help a person discriminate between anxiety-producing situations and nonthreatening situations, the person should keep a log of circumstances surrounding the times when he or she feels tense and when he or she feels relaxed. Once he or she learns to identify tension-producing situations, he or she can begin practicing relaxation before or when confronted with these situations. In most medical settings, relaxation techniques are used in combination with some form of drug therapy. As a person improves his or her ability to relax through self-suggestion, drug use is decreased and, hopefully, eventually terminated.[7]

Exercise

Physical activity has proved to be a powerful way to control stress. Types of activity that have proved to be beneficial include stretching, rhythmical motion, and vigorous aerobic exercise. Muscle stretching, including hatha-yoga, known as **asana,** has been shown to reduce muscular tension within the musculotendinous unit. Stretching the body helps one overcome stiffness and allows the various body segments to relax. Research indicates that a steady progressive stretch tends to decrease the myotatic reflex and reduce muscle tension, whereas the ballistic or jerky stretch increases tension. Many of the asanas of hatha-yoga tend to improve joint range of motion. Each yoga posture is executed slowly and deliberately. Devotees believe that relaxation occurs as the mind and body become harmonious.

Music and rhythm are used extensively to initiate coordinated movement and relaxation. Synchronization of specific movement patterns, as expressed through kinesthesia, is the basis for skilled activity. As early as 1969, Rathbone[18] advocated rhythmical exercise to relieve the feeling of fatigue and residual tension. Recent studies have demonstrated that rhythmic activity stimulates alpha brain wave production, the same wave patterns that are seen during meditation and conscious relaxation practice. Activities that are based on a continuous or even sequence of movement (e.g., walking, dancing, swimming, and bicycle riding) result in reduced tension.

Vigorous exercise lasting longer than 30 minutes not only dissipates tension but also results in the release of endorphins. Vigorous exercise that fatigues muscles results in relaxed muscles, as well as improved cardiovascular health and reduced blood pressure. Endorphin release induces a soothing calmness.[8]

Conscious Control of Muscular Tension

Conscious control of muscular tension is also an effective method for reducing the side effects of stress. Physiological benefits from willed relaxation include reductions in oxygen consumption, respiratory rate, heart rate, and muscle tension. Four excellent techniques for consciously reducing tension are progressive relaxation, autogenic training, differential relaxation, and meditation.

Progressive Relaxation

Edmund Jacobson, a physiologist-physician, is known as the father of **progressive relaxation.**[10] His technique emphasizes relaxation of voluntary skeletal muscles. During progressive relaxation training, an individual becomes aware of muscular tension and learns to consciously release tension in specific muscle groups. Jacobson's system starts with muscles of the left upper extremity and moves to the right upper extremity, followed by the left lower extremity, right lower extremity, abdominal muscles, respiratory muscles, back pectoral region, shoulder muscles, and facial muscles. Persons are encouraged to gradually stiffen each body part and then slowly release that tension.[16]

Progressive muscular relaxation is a standardized method that can be learned and can be practiced in the home.[6] According to Larson and Melin,[15] relaxation training can have positive effects on tension-type headaches of schoolchildren in a school setting. Moreover, reports show that a home-based relaxation approach may be as effective as a clinically delivered treatment.[11,23] The effectiveness of using audiotaped suggestions of heaviness, warmth, calmness, and regular breathing by Sorbi and Tellegen[22] further indicate the importance of extending relaxation training into the home.

Autogenic Training

Autogenic training in relaxation was developed by H.H. Schulz, a German neurologist.[19] This technique is designed to reduce exteroceptive and proprioceptive stimulation through mental activity described as passive concentration. Using this method, an individual brings to mind images that promote a relaxed state.

Autogenic training begins with phrases that suggest heaviness of the whole body and the individual parts, followed by phrases that suggest warmth or regularity to the body, heart, respiratory system, and abdominal area. A third set of phrases promotes images of colors and relaxing in warm, soft, pleasant surroundings.[19]

Differential Relaxation

Decreasing and increasing muscular tension levels at will requires varying degrees of coordination. All skilled movement requires differential relaxation. A technique that has been found to be beneficial for training individuals to selectively control specific muscles is known as **muscle tension recognition and release.**[3,4] This technique starts with the subject tensing and relaxing the entire body and then learning bilateral body control (control of both upper limbs and then of both lower limbs).

Following demonstration of bilateral limb control, the subject advances to unilateral body control, whereby muscular tension is increased on one side of the body and completely released on the other (e.g., with tensing of the right arm and leg and relaxing of the left arm and leg). From unilateral control, the subject progresses to cross-lateral body control, which involves tensing of the opposite arm and leg. The last stage of differential relaxation training involves the isolation and relaxation of specific body parts at will. In general, differential relaxation training is a useful tool for developing total body control, increasing body awareness, and reducing anxiety. However, this technique should be limited to the developmental level of the individual. These techniques, used individually and in combination, reduce nervous tension and tactile defensive responses in children.[2]

Meditation

Meditation is the art and technique of blocking out thoughts that create tension and refocusing attention and energy on soothing, quieting mental activity. Individuals who practice meditation should assume a physically relaxed position in a room or area where there will be no interruptions and then proceed to practice either Western- or Eastern-world meditation.[8] Western-world meditation techniques range from focusing or concentrating on developing rhythmical breathing patterns, to imaging energy flowing through the body from the feet to out through the top of the head, to picturing disease-fighting mechanisms conquering disease in the body, to thinking about an uplifting message read just before meditating. Eastern-world meditation techniques more frequently seek to create a void in consciousness to cleanse the mind and allow it to rest from activity. It is recommended that meditation be practiced once or twice a day for a minimum of 15 minutes.

Benefits of Relaxation

Learning to relax is a motor skill and must be considered an important part of the total education program or physical education program. As a skill, relaxation must be taught and practiced for competency. Too often, teachers of physical education are concerned with gross movement activities alone. To lie down when tired or to practice relaxation when tense or overanxious is considered a waste of time by many teachers. This narrow point of view ignores an important aspect of the field of physi-

cal education—that relaxation is of special importance to many atypical, as well as typical, students.

A number of positive benefits can be accrued by individuals who have conscious control of their tension levels. Energy can be conserved, and better control of emotions can result (fears and anxieties become less intense). Sleep comes easier, the acquisition and performance of motor skills are enhanced, pain and physical discomfort become less intense, and the ability to learn may be improved. Relaxation therefore becomes a vital tool in the total machinery of the educational process.

To the physiologist, relaxation indicates a complete absence of neuromuscular activity (zero state).[16] The relaxed body part does not resist stretch but rather reflects the lengthening of muscle fibers. An overt sign of relaxation is a limp and completely motionless body part. Through relaxation of overly tense muscles, a number of positive effects may occur in respiration, circulation, and neuromuscular coordination.

Respiration

The reduction of tension in the thorax and muscles of respiration allows for a greater capacity for inspiration and expiration and thus a more efficient exchange of oxygen and carbon dioxide within the body. For persons with breathing disorders, relaxation of the thoracic mechanism allows for a greater respiratory potential.

Circulation

Relaxation of tense skeletal muscles allows the blood to circulate unimpeded by constricted blood vessels to all the body tissues. A person with cardiovascular disease is greatly aided by the ability to reduce muscular tension at will. Blood pressure may be reduced by diminishing outside resistance, which subsequently decreases strain on the heart and blood vessels.

Neuromuscular coordination

In order for the body to move uninhibited, there must be a smooth synchronization of muscles. Differential relaxation or controlled tension attributable to the reciprocal action of agonist and antagonist muscles provides for coordinated movement without undue fatigue. Persons who exhibit poor coordination as a result of neuromuscular or cerebral problems must learn to relax tense muscles differentially in order for their purposeful movement to be smooth, accurate, and enduring.

Experiments are being done to determine whether relaxation techniques can affect physiological functioning. One such group of studies has attempted to alleviate headaches through relaxation techniques. Larson and Melin[15] report that relaxation therapy alone led to significant reductions in headaches of school-age children. They reported that children seemed to react in an "all or none" fashion (either the headache totally disappeared, or it continued with no relief whatsoever).

Much attention in clinical experimentation has been devoted to muscle contraction as an underlying cause of headaches.[5] Attempts have been made to control headaches with relaxation training of the frontalis (forehead) muscle through electromyography (EMG).[13] Cottier, Shapiro, and Julius[6] have indicated that relaxation does affect physiological measures. They found that responders to progressive muscle relaxation were characterized by faster heart rates and higher plasma norepinephrine levels. They also found that with progressive relaxation the treated group had a significant decrease in oxygen consumption compared with the control group. Furthermore, Agras[1] noted that relaxation training has a direct effect on catecholamines and results in the blocking of noradrenergic receptors. While there is evidence of physiological changes as a result of relaxation training, as yet it is difficult to apply these findings to daily living behavior. LaCroix et al.[14] concluded that the link between frontalis EMG results and "muscle contraction" headaches is a questionable one. Thus, according to these researchers, the changes brought about in headaches through biofeedback or relaxation training are most likely attributable to a generalization of feelings of mastery over the environment or an increase in self-esteem resulting from the subject's apparent success at the task.

Teaching a System of Relaxation

Relaxation therapy is a treatment that involves teaching a person to achieve a state of both muscular and mental tension reduction by the systematic use of environmental cues.[9] Relaxation training focuses primarily on promoting a balance between the sympathetic and parasympathetic subsystems. For the most part it can be learned in a short period and produces an overall feeling of well-being and relaxation.[1]

The instructor of physical education can teach a variety of relaxation techniques depending on the time and conditions available. As has been described earlier in this discussion, imagery and recognition of tension provide a convenient means of learning to relax. These methods may be combined and used with success in the typical 30-minute physical education period.

Identification of abnormal tension areas in the body requires the performance of a series of muscle contractions and relaxations. In this modified system of progressive relaxation, muscle contractions should be performed gradually and slowly for 30 seconds, and then the muscles should be relaxed for 30 seconds in an attempt to obtain a "negative" state. The student is reminded to tense only the muscles the instructor indicates and to keep all other body areas relaxed while tensing a single part. Special consideration is given to the areas of the body that are difficult to relax (e.g., the lower back and the abdominal, shoulder, neck, and eye regions). After the guided session, the student makes a record of the areas that were difficult to relax. Eventually, with diligent practice, the student will have to tense and relax only those areas that are difficult to relax. In doing so, the student can achieve at will a general decrease of muscular tonus throughout the body.

Preliminary Requirements

In order for the student to develop a keen perception of tension and to learn to relax, the instructor should consider a number of environmental and learning factors that may strongly affect the ability to reduce body tension.

Room

The room in which relaxation exercises are conducted should have a comfortable temperature (between 72° and 76° F; it should be well ventilated with no chilling drafts. The light may be dimmed or turned off, and signs may be posted outside to prevent interruption of the relaxation lesson.

Dress

The student should wear comfortable, warm, loose-fitting apparel and no shoes.

Equipment

In actuality, very little equipment is needed to teach relaxation. Ideally, five small pillows or rolled-up towels and a firm mat are useful; however, relaxation can be accomplished on any comfortable surface without the use of props. All students should have a pencil and paper nearby so that they can record personal reactions after the session.

Positioning

Although a person can learn to relax while standing or sitting, the ideal position for tension recognition is that of lying on a firm mat with each body curve comfortably supported by a pillow or towel (Figure B-1). Contour support is afforded the curves of the cervical and lumbar vertebrae; each forearm is supported, resulting in a slight bend to each elbow; and the knees, like the elbows, are maintained in a slightly flexed position with the thighs externally rotated. With minimum support given to the body curves and limbs, free muscle contraction can take place while the individual is in a comfortable, relaxed position. However, if equipment for joint support is not available, a flat mat surface will suffice.

Sound

A number of techniques using sound may be used by the teacher to aid the student in acquiring the right frame of mind for relaxation. Soft music playing in the background may be beneficial. If music is not available, the monotonous pattern of a metronome clicking at 48

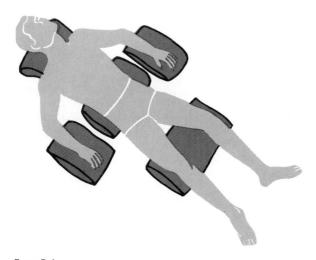

figure B-1
Basic position for tension reduction exercises (see also Figures B-2 to B-13).

or fewer beats per minute may be helpful. However, the most important sound is the voice of the instructor, which should be quiet, slow, rhythmical, and distant.

Breathing

During the relaxation session the student is instructed to take slow, deep inhalations through the nose and make long, slow exhalations through the mouth. Gradually, through breathing control, the student consciously tries to let go of all the body tension. As relaxation occurs, breathing becomes slower and more shallow.

Imagery

The tension recognition technique involves two distinct phases: a contraction phase, whereby the subject contracts a particular muscle or group of muscles to sense tension, and a "let go" phase, whereby the subject seeks a complete lack of tension, or negativeness. To aid the pupil in the second phase, the teacher encourages the use of imagery. The student is told to imagine very relaxing things. Image-inducing statements such as "your body is heavy against the floor," "your heart is beating regularly and calmly, like a clock ticking," and "listen to the sound of your breathing" may help the student relax. Children at the elementary school level have keen imaginations and respond readily to suggestions such as imagining their bodies as snowmen on a hot day or as butter in a hot pan.

Sleep

The pupil should be instructed that the main purpose of the exercise session is to develop awareness of tense body areas and the ability to relax consciously without falling asleep. However, if sleep does occur during the session, it should be considered a positive reaction.

Principles of Teaching Relaxation

There are a number of ways the instructor can proceed with relaxation guidance. The teacher can begin by having the pupils contract their facial muscles and then move downward to finish in the lower limbs or, conversely, by having them contract muscles from foot to head. If less time is available, contraction of large muscle groups with progression to the smaller muscles of the body is another alternative. Whatever the technique used, the goals are the same, and the teacher will soon develop a style that seems to work best.

Because of the limited amount of time available in the physical education period, many sessions may be required before desired results are attained. A home program should be encouraged for persons who find it difficult to let go of tension.

Directions to the student

For expediency in the physical education setting, each muscular contraction phase and each relaxation phase are conducted for approximately 30 seconds, providing a total of 1 minute for each step. During the introductory session the muscle contraction should be intense enough to cause a degree of fatigue. The tension is reduced gradually with each subsequent session, requiring a greater perceptual sensitivity. The following is a sample of a relaxation session given to a group of students in a typical school setting:

Step 1: Lie still for a minute and stare at an object on the ceiling. Do the eyes feel as though they are getting heavy? As this occurs, gradually let them close. Take five deep breaths, inhaling and exhaling slowly. Think of all the joints of the body as being very relaxed.

Step 2: Curl the toes downward and point both feet downward toward the end of the mat. Feel the tension on the bottoms of the feet and behind the legs. Keep the mouth relaxed and continue to breathe deeply and slowly. While tensing one area of the body, all other parts should be relaxed. Now release the muscle contractions slowly, letting go to a completely relaxed state. Feel the body getting extremely heavy and sinking into the mat.

Step 3: Curl the toes and both feet upward toward the head (Figure B-2). Sense the tenseness on the tops of the feet and legs. Remember not to reinforce the movement by tensing other parts of the body. Breathe easily and relax. Let go of the muscle contraction, allowing the feet and ankles to go limp slowly.

Step 4: Leaving the legs in their original position, with the knees slightly bent, press the legs down (Figure B-3). Feel the tension in the backs of the thighs and buttocks. Remember, while holding this contraction, all other parts of the body should be at ease. Relax, slowly feeling the discomfort of tension completely leave the body.

Step 5: Remain in the position as for step 4 and straighten the legs to full extension (Figure B-4). Feel the tightness in the tops of the thighs. Now let go. Breathing should be easy and relaxed, and a profound sense of heaviness should be present throughout the body.

Step 6: With the legs and thighs in the original resting position, draw the thighs upward to a bent-knee position, with the heels raised from the mat about 3 inches (Figure B-5). Tension should be felt primarily in the bend of

the hip. Try to keep all other muscle groups relaxed. Return slowly to the starting position and then let go to a negative state again.

Step 7: Forcibly rotate the thighs outward (Figure B-6). Feel the muscle tension in the outer hip region. Do not let tension creep into other parts of the body. Now slowly relax the hip rotators. Go limp.

Step 8: Rotate the thighs inward. Feel the muscle tension deep in the inner thighs. Relax slowly, let go of all tension, and let the thighs again rotate outward. Sense the body sinking deeper into the mat.

Step 9: Squeeze the buttocks (gluteal muscles) together tightly and tilt the hips backward (Figure B-7). Muscular tension should be felt only in the buttocks and lower back region. Again, be aware of other tensions that may be occurring in the body. Now let go of the contraction and try to sense the joints becoming extremely loose.

Step 10: Tighten the abdominal muscles by pressing downward on the rib cage while rolling the hips backward; at the same time, flatten the lower back (Figure B-8). Tension is felt both in the abdominal muscles and in the lower back region. Inhale slowly and let the back settle into the mat.

Step 11: Inhale and exhale slowly and as deeply as possible three times (Figure B-9). A general tension should be felt throughout the rib cage. After the last forced inspiration and expiration, return to normal quiet breathing and sense the difference in tension levels.

Step 12: Accentuating the curve of the neck (cervical spine), press the head back and lift the upper back off the mat (Figure B-10). Tension should be felt in the back of the neck and upper back. Settle slowly back to the mat.

Step 13: Pinch the shoulders back, squeezing the two shoulder blades together. Tension is felt in the back of the shoulders. Release the contraction slowly and fall easily back to the mat. Be aware of any residual tension that might remain after returning to the mat.

Step 14: Leaving the arms in the resting position, lift and roll shoulders inward so that tension is felt in the front of the chest. Do not allow the shoulders to drop back to the mat in the resting position. Feel the tension leave the chest.

Step 15: Spread and grip the fingers of both hands. Do this three times (Figure B-11). Tension is felt in the hands and forearms. As the fingers are gripped and spread, be sure not to lift the elbows from the mat. After the third series, let the hands and forearms fall limply back to their supports.

Step 16: Make a tight fist with both hands and slowly curl the wrists backward, forward, and to both sides. Tension should be felt primarily at the fist, wrist, and forearm. After these movements, allow the fingers and thumbs to open gradually.

Step 17: Make a tight fist with both hands and slowly bend (flex) the arms at the elbows until the forearms rest against the upper arms, at the same time lifting the shoulders (Figure B-12). Tension is felt in the front part of the

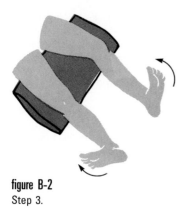

figure B-2
Step 3.

figure B-3
Step 4.

figure B-4
Step 5.

figure B-5
Step 6.

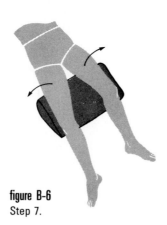

figure B-6
Step 7.

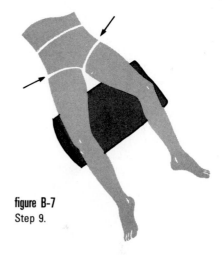

figure B-7
Step 9.

figure B-8
Step 10.

figure B-9
Step 11.

figure B-10
Step 12.

figure B-11
Step 15.

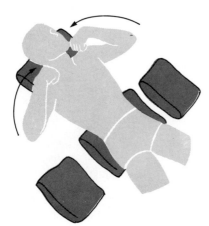

figure B-12
Step 17.

figure B-13
Step 19.

forearms, in the biceps regions, and in the front part of the shoulders. After the arms are slowly uncurled and returned to the resting position, relax each segment separately until they become limp, motionless, and negative.

Step 18: Make a tight fist with both hands, stiffen the arms, and press hard against the mat. Tension should be felt in the forearms and in the backs of the upper arms and shoulders. Hold the pressure against the mat for 30 seconds and then release slowly.

Step 19: Shrug the right shoulder and then bend the head sideways (laterally flex neck), touching the ear to the elevated shoulder (Figure B-13).

Step 20: As in step 19, shrug the left shoulder; then laterally flex the neck, touching the ear to the elevated shoulder. Tension should be felt only in the upper left shoulder and in the lateral muscles of the neck. Release the contraction, slowly returning the neck and shoulder to the resting position.

Step 21: Bend the head forward, touching the chin to the chest. Tension is felt in the front of the neck. Relax and slowly return the head to the resting position. Continue to concentrate on the body as being extremely heavy and at a zero state.

Step 22: Lift the eyebrows upward and wrinkle the forehead. Feel the tension in the forehead. Let the face go blank.

Step 23: Close the eyelids tightly and wrinkle the nose. Tension is felt in the nose and eyes. Let the face relax slowly. Concentrate on the tension leaving the face.

Step 24: Open the mouth widely as if to yawn. Feel the tension in the jaw. Now let the mouth close slowly and lightly.

Step 25: Bite down hard and then show the teeth in a forced smile. Tension should be felt in the jaw and lips. Slowly allow the face to return to a blank expression. Be sure not to tense other parts of the body when contracting the facial muscles.

Step 26: Pucker the lips hard as if to whistle. Sense the tension at the edge of the mouth. Let the tension melt away.

Step 27: Push the tongue hard against the roof of the mouth. Let go. Push the tongue against the roof of the mouth again as hard as possible. Relax. Push the tongue against the upper teeth. Relax. Sense the contraction of the tongue muscles. Try not to use any other body parts. Relax.

Step 28: Lie very still for a short while and try to be conscious of the body areas that were difficult to relax. Move slowly and take any position desired. Relax and rest.

Step 29: Try to hold the color of black or white in the mind's eye. Once you see one color, do not let any other color or picture slip into your mind.

Step 30: Roll to one side and sit up slowly.

Evaluation

Although the most accurate indication of abnormal tension is provided by electromyographic tests, subjective evaluation still has its place for the physical education instructor. Tension is easily observable through mannerisms such as extraneous movements or muscle twitches (eye twitches, finger movements, stiffness, changes of position, and playing with hands) and vocal sounds. The instructor should test muscle resistance by lifting the student's arms and legs after the relaxation session. Limbs that have residual tension do not feel limp or lifeless; they tend to feel stiff and unyielding. The instructor tells the student that he oe she will be tested for relaxation at the end of the session. The following four factors may be made apparent by the tests: (1) whether the student assists the movement, (2) whether the student resist the movement, (3) whether the student engages in posiotning body parts, or (4) whether the student ideally displays a complete lack of tension.

After the exercise session, the students are asked to answer questions about their personal reactions, writing their answers on a sheet of paper by their side. Some suggested questions include the following:

1. What was your general reaction to the session—good, bad, or indifferent?
2. Were you comfortable for the entire session? If not, what disturbed you?
3. Did you sense the tensions and relaxations at all times? If not, why not?
4. Were there areas of the body that you just could not continually relax? What were they?

Questions such as these help the student identify reactions to the relaxation session. The student may require a number of sessions before being able to identify tense body regions accurately. While learning to relax individual parts, the student will gradually be able to relax larger segments and eventually the whole body at will.

References

1. Agras WS: *Medical uses of relaxation training,* Paper presented at Grand Rounds, Madison, 1983, Department of Psychiatry, University of Wisconsin.
2. Anneberg L: *A study of the effect of different relaxation techniques on tactile deficient and tactile defensive children,* Unpublished master's thesis, Lawrence, 1977, University of Kansas.
3. Arnheim DD, Pestolisi RA: *Developing motor behavior in children: a balanced approach to elementary physical education,* St Louis, ed 2, 1978, Mosby.
4. Arnheim DD, Sinclair WW: *The clumsy child: a program of motor therapy,* ed 2, St Louis, 1979, Mosby.
5. Blanchard EB et al: Biofeedback and relaxation training with three kinds of headache: treatment effects and their prediction, *J Consult Clin Psychol* 50:562-575, 1982.
6. Cottier C, Shaprio K, Julius S: Treatment of mild hypertension with progressive muscle relaxation, *Arch Intern Med* 144:1954-1958, 1984.
7. Curb JD, Borhani NO, Blaszkowski TP: Long-term surveillance for adverse effects of antihypertensive drugs, *JAMA* 253:3263-3268, 1985.
8. Hoeger WWK, Hoeger SA: *Lifetime physical fitness and wellness,* ed 3, Colorado, 1992, Morton Publishing.
9. Jacob RS et al: Relaxation therapy for hypertension: comparison of effects with concomitant Piacaho, diuretic, and β-blocker, *Arch Intern Med* 146:2335-2391, 1986.
10. Jacobson EO: *Modern treatment of tense patients,* Springfield, Ill, 1970, Charles C Thomas.
11. Jurish SE et al: Home- versus clinic-based treatment of vascular headache, *J Consult Clin Psychol* 51:749-751, 1983.
12. Kune S: Stressful life events and cancer, *Epidemiology* 4:395-397, 1993.
13. LaCroix JM: Mechanisms of biofeedback control on the importance of verbal (conscious) processing. In Davidson RJ, Schwartz GE, Shaprio K, editors: *Consciousness and self-regulation: advances in research,* vol 4, New York, 1986, Plenum.
14. LaCroix JM et al: Physiological changes after biofeedback and relaxation training for multiple-pain tension-headache patients, *Percept Mot Skills* 63:139-153, 1986.
15. Larson B, Melin C: Chronic headaches in adolescents: treatment in a school setting with relaxation training as compared with information-contact and self-regulation, *Pain* 25:325-336, 1986.
16. Moback R: The promise of biofeedback: don't hold the party yet, *Psychology Today* 9:18-22, 80-81, 1975.
17. O'Leary A: Stress, emotion, and human immune function, *Psychol Bull* 108:363-382, 1990.
18. Rathbone JL: *Relaxation,* Philadelphia, 1969, Lea & Febiger.
19. Schulz HH, Luthe W: *Autogenic training,* New York, 1959, George A Straton.
20. Selye H: *Stress without distress,* New York, 1974, Signet.
21. Selye H: *The stress of life,* New York, 1976, McGraw-Hill.
22. Sorbi M, Tellegen B: Differential effects of training in relaxation and stress coping in patients with migraine, *Pain* 29:473-481, 1986.
23. Teders SJ et al: Relaxation training for tension headache: comparative efficacy and cost effectiveness of a minimal therapist contact versus a therapist-delivered procedure, *Behav Ther* 15:59-70, 1984.

Suggested Readings

Schaef AW: *Meditations for women who do too much,* San Francisco, 1990, Harper & Row.
Chopra D: *Ageless body, timeless mind,* New York, 1993, Harmony Books.

Sports Organizations for Persons with Disabilities

Amputee Sports

Disabled Sports USA
451 Hungerford Drive, Suite 100
Rockville, MD 20850

Eastern Amputee Athletic Association
2080 Ennabrock Road
North Bellmore, NY 11710

Archery

Wheelchair Archery, USA
5295 Highway 78, Suite D
P.O. Box 204
Stone Mountain, GA 30087

Basketball

Canadian Wheelchair Basketball Association
1600 James Naismith Drive
Gloucester, Ontario K1B 5N4
Canada
Fax 613-748-5889

National Wheelchair Basketball Association
2850 N. Garey Avenue
P.O. Box 6001
Pomona, CA 91769-6001
Fax 909-593-0153

Billiards

National Wheelchair Billiards Association
325 Hickory Drive
Cleveland, OH 44107

Bowling

American Blind Bowling Association
411 Sheriff
Mercer, PA 16137

American Wheelchair Bowling Association
5809 N.E. 21st Avenue
Ft. Lauderdale, FL 33308

National Deaf Bowling Association
9244 E. Mansfield Avenue
Denver, CO 80237

National Deaf Women's Bowling Association
33 August Road
Simsbury, CT 06070

Flying

Freedom's Wings International
1832 Lake Avenue
Scotch Plains, NJ 07076

International Wheelchair Aviators
1117 Rising Hill
Escondido, CA 92029
Fax 619-746-7714

Golf

Association of Disabled American Golfers
7700 E. Arapahoe Road, Suite 350
Englewood, CO 80112
Fax 303-843-9284

Eastern Amputee Golf Association
R.D. 7, Box 7336
Bethlehem, PA 18015

National Amputee Golf Association
P.O. Box 5801
Coralville, IA 52241-5801
Fax 319-351-5129

Hockey

American Hearing Impaired Hockey Association
1143 West Lake Street
Chicago, IL 60607

American Sled Hockey Association
10933 Johnson Avenue, S.
Bloomington, MN 55437
Fax 612-888-5331

Multisport

American Athletic Association of the Deaf
3607 Washington Blvd., Suite 4
Ogden, Utah 84403-1737
Fax 801-393-2263

Canadian Wheelchair Sports Association
1600 James Naismith Drive
Gloucester, Ontario K1B 5N4
Canada
Fax 613-748-5722

Disabled Sports Association of North Texas
3810 W. Northwest Highway, Suite 205
Dallas, TX 75220
Fax 214-352-1744

Disabled Sports USA
451 Hungerford Drive, Suite 100
Rockville, MD 20850

Dwarf Athletic Association of America
417 Willow Way
Lewisville, TX 75067

International Blind Sports Association
Hybratenveien No. 7C
Oslo 10, Norway

International Sports Organization for the Disabled
Idrottens Hus
Storforsplan 44
12387, Farsta
Sweden

International Stoke Mandeville Wheelchair Sports
  Federation
Stoke Mandeville Sports Stadium
Harvey Road
Aylesbury, Bucks HP 21 8PP
United Kingdom

Lions Blind Sport Foundation
1939 16th Avenue
San Francisco, CA 94116

Special Olympics and Special Olympics International
Kennedy Foundation
1350 New York Avenue, Suite 500
Washington, DC 20005

U.S. Association for Blind Athletes
33 N. Institute
Brown Hall, Suite 015
Colorado Springs, CO 80903
Fax 719-630-0616

U.S. Cerebral Palsy Athletic Association
Edgehill Campus
Independence Square Foundation of Rhode Island
Newport, RI 02840

U.S. Les Autres Sports Association
1475 W. Gray, Suite 165
Houston, TX 77019

Wheelchair Sports, U.S.A.
3595 E. Fountain Blvd., Suite L-1
Colorado Springs, CO 80910
Fax 719-574-9840

Quad Sports

Power Soccer
Bay Area Outreach Recreation Program
830 Bancroft Way
Berkeley, CA 94710

U.S. Quad Rugby Association
309 Stoney Ford Road
Holland, PA 18966
Fax 215-504-0445

Racquet Sports

International Wheelchair Tennis Federation
Palliser Road, Barons Court
London W14 9EN, United Kingdom
Fax 011-44-71-610-1264

National Foundation of Wheelchair Tennis
2380 McGinley Road
Monroeville, PA 15146
Fax 714-361-6603

National Wheelchair Racquetball Association
2380 McGinley Road
Monroeville, PA 15146

Recreation

American Handcycle Association
1744 Pepper Villa Drive
El Cajon, CA 92021-1214

Blind Outdoor Leisure Development (BOLD)
533 E. Main Street
Aspen, CO 81611

National Handicap Motorcyclist Association
315 W. 21st Street, Suite 6F
New York, NY 10011

North American Riding for the Handicapped Association
P.O. Box 33150
Denver, CO 80233

Paraplegics on Independent Nature Trips (POINT)
4144 N. Central Expressway, Suite 515
Dallas, TX 75204

The City of San Diego Park and Recreation Department
Disabled Services Program
War Memorial Building, M.S. 33
3325 Zoo Drive, Balboa Park
San Diego, CA 92101
Fax 619-525-8251

Road Racing

International Wheelchair Road Racers Club, Inc.
30 Myano Lane
Stamford, CT 06902

Michigan United Sports Chair League Endurance Series
  (MUSCLES)
18964 Whitby
Livonia, MI 48152

Shooting

National Wheelchair Shooting Federation
102 Park Avenue
Rockledge, PA 19046

One-Arm Dove Hunt Association
Box 582
Olney, TX 76374

Skiing

American Blind Skiing Foundation
610 S. William Street
Mt. Prospect, IL 60056

Disabled Sports USA
451 Hungerford Drive, Suite 100
Rockville, MD 20850

Ski for Light, Inc.
1400 Carole Lane
Greenbay, WI 54313

U.S. Deaf Skiers Association
8980 Rossman Highway
Diamondale, MI 48821

U.S. Disabled Ski Team
P.O. Box 100
Park City, UT 84060

Softball

National Wheelchair Softball Association
1616 Todd Ct.
Hastings, MN 55033

Table Tennis

American Wheelchair Table Tennis Association
23 Parker Street
Port Chester, NY 10573

Track and Field

Achilles Track Club
One Times Square, Tenth Floor
New York, NY 10036
Fax 212-354-3978

Wheelchair Athletics of the U.S.A.
30 Myano Lane
Stamford, CT 06902

Volleyball

American Deaf Volleyball Association
300 Roxborough Street
Rochester, NY 14619

Water Sports and Recreation

Access to Sailing
19744 Beach Blvd., Suite 340
Huntington Beach, CA 92648
Fax 714-987-4047

American Canoe Association
7432 Alban Station Blvd., Suite B-226
Springfield, VA 22150
Fax 703-451-2245

American Water Ski Association
Adaptive Aquatics, Inc.
P.O. Box 337
Bolingbroke, GA 31004

Handicapped Scuba Association
1104 El Prado
San Clemente, CA 92672-4637

National Ocean Access Project
P.O. Box 10726
Rockville, MD 20849-0726

U.S. Rowing Association
201 S. Capitol Avenue, Suite 400
Indianapolis, IN 46225
Fax 317-237-5656

U.S. Wheelchair Swimming
229 Miller Street
Middleboro, MA 02346

Weightlifting

U.S. Wheelchair Weightlifting Federation
39 Michael Place
Levittown, PA 19057

Glossary

A

abdominal strength Muscular strength of the abdominal muscles.

abduction Away from the midline of the body.

abortive poliomyelitis An acute viral infection that causes a headache, sore throat, mild fever, and nausea.

acquired immunodeficiency syndrome (AIDS) The final stage of a series of diseases caused by infection by the human immunodeficiency virus.

Adam test Position to determine the extent to which a scoliosis is structural.

adapted physical education The art and science of assessment and prescription within the psychomotor domain to ensure that an individual with a disability has access to programs designed to develop physical and motor fitness, fundamental motor skills and patterns, and skills in aquatics, dance, and individual and group games and sports so that the individual can ultimately participate in community-based leisure, recreation, and sport activities and, as such, enjoy an enhanced quality of life.

adapted physical educator A professional with specialized training in evaluating, designing, and implementing specialized physical education programs.

adaptive skill areas Communication, home living, community use, health and safety, leisure, self-care, social skills, self-direction, functional academics, and work.

adduction Toward the midline of the body.

administrative feasibility The extent to which it is practical to use a given test.

admission An indicator that a student qualifies for special services because of an identifiable disability that interferes with educational progress.

adolescent scoliosis Scoliosis that develops between the ages of 3 and 12 years in females and ages 3 to 14 years in males.

adventitious A condition acquired after birth.

affective function Emotions resulting from experiences, beliefs, values, and predispositions.

agility The ability to change direction while moving.

air conduction hearing aid A hearing aid that is hooked to receivers located in the outer ear canal.

albinism Lack of pigment in the eyes.

alternate-form reliability The degree to which scores from two different tests purported to measure the same things agree when administered to two different groups.

alternator A person who visually suppresses images received by one eye and then the other eye.

amblyopia Cortical suppression of visual images received by one or both eyes.

ambulatory Able to walk.

amputation Missing part or all of a limb.

amyotrophic lateral sclerosis (ALS) A progressive neurological disorder that results in degeneration of the muscular system; also known as Lou Gehrig disease.

anemia Condition of the blood in which there is a deficiency of hemoglobin.

ankle pronation Abnormal turning of the ankle downward and medially (eversion and abduction).

ankylosed Pertaining to the immobility of a joint resulting from pathological changes in the joint or in adjacent tissues.

ankylosing spondylitis A gradual thickening of the axial skeleton and large peripheral joints of the body that causes back pain and early morning stiffness.

annual goals Statements that describe what a specific learner with a disability should be able to accomplish in a given year.

anorexia nervosa A condition where the person stops eating.

Apgar scores Numerical indicators of an infant's status immediately after birth.

aplastic anemia A form of anemia in which the red bone marrow that forms blood cells is replaced by fatty marrow.

arthritis Inflammation of a joint.

arthrogryposis A congenital condition that results in flexure or contracture of joints.

asana Muscle-stretching exercises used in hatha-yoga.

Asperger's syndrome A condition known as "high-level autism" that shares many of the same symptoms as classic autism, but that also includes motor clumsiness and a family history of Asperger traits.

assessment A problem-solving process that involves gathering information from a variety of sources.

assistive technology A piece of equipment or product system that increases, maintains, or improves functional capabilities of children with disabilities.

assistive technology service Any service that directly assists an individual with a disability in the selection, acquisition, or use of an assistive technology device.

asthma Labored breathing associated with a sense of constriction in the chest.

astigmatism Refractive error caused by an irregularity in the curvature of the cornea of the lens; vision may become blurred.

asymmetrical tonic neck reflex A reflex that causes extension of the arm on the face side and flexion of the arm on the posterior skull side when the head is turned.

at risk Refers to individuals whose development is jeopardized by factors that include poverty, homelessness, prenatal and postnatal maternal neglect, environmental deprivation, child abuse, violence, drug abuse, and racism.

ataxia Clinical type of cerebral palsy that is characterized by a disturbance of equilibrium.

athetosis Clinical type of cerebral palsy that is characterized by uncoordinated movements of the voluntary muscles, often accompanied by impaired muscle control of the hands and impaired speech and swallowing.

atlantoaxial instability Greater than normal mobility of the two upper cervical vertebrae.

atrophy Wasting away of muscular tissue.

audiologist A specially trained professional who can provide comprehensive evaluations of individuals' hearing capabilities.

audition Pertaining to the sense of hearing and the hearing organs involved.

autogenic training Teaching a person to use mind images to promote a relaxed state.

autonomic neuropathy A complication resulting from long-standing diabetes that leads to poor vascular supply and lack of sweating of the feet.

B

backward chaining The last of a series of steps is taught first.

balance The ability to maintain equilibrium in a held (static) or moving (dynamic) position.

Becker muscular dystrophy A disease of the muscular system very similar to Duchenne muscular dystrophy except that it progresses more slowly.

behavior modification Changing of behavioral characteristics through application of learning principles.

behavior therapy See behavior modification.

behavioral management technology Techniques for structuring the environment to produce changes in behavior.

bio-underclass Infants who are destined to fail to develop normally because of physical and chemical damage to their brain as a result of the mother's use of drugs and/or malnutrition during the fetal period.

blindisms Self-stimulatory behaviors, such as rocking the body or head, placing fingers or fists into the eyes, or flicking fingers in front of the face.

body awareness How a person pictures his or her body and his or her attitude toward and knowledge of his or her bodily capabilities and limitations.

body composition The percentage of body fat in relation to lean tissue in the body.

body image System of ideas and feelings that a person has about his or her structure.

body righting reflex Reflex that enables segmental rotation of the trunk and hips when the head is turned.

body-state regulation The ability of the body to maintain homeostasis.

bone conduction hearing aid A hearing aid that is placed in contact with the mastoid bone.

bottom, up strategy Process whereby the sensory input system is evaluated and then ability tests are used to determine which deficits are in evidence.

bulimia A condition wherein the person overeats and then purges the body of the intake.

C

campus-based decision-making committees Groups of individuals who contribute to site-based management policies and procedures.

cancer A cellular malignancy resulting in loss of normal cell function and uncontrolled cell growth.

cardiovascular/cardiorespiratory endurance The ability of the heart, lungs, and blood vessels to direct needed oxygen to the muscles.

cataract A condition in which the normally transparent lens of the eye becomes opaque.

center of gravity A point in the human body where the pull of gravity on one side is equal to the pull of gravity on the other side.

central auditory processing problems Deafness resulting from damage to the brainstem or in the cortex.

cerebral palsy Condition in which damage inflicted to the brain resulted in a motor function disorder.

chaining Leading a person through a series of teachable components of a motor task.

child abuse and neglect Physical or mental injury, sexual abuse, negligent treatment, or maltreatment of a child under 18 years of age by a person who is responsible for the child, resulting in harm to the child's health or welfare.

Child Find A national effort to identify children who have developmental disabilities or are at risk for developmental delays.

chlorosis Iron deficiency anemia that is characterized by a reduced amount of hemoglobin in the corpuscles.

chronic sorrow syndrome A theory that proposes that the family of a child with a disability can cope with the day-to-day requirements of providing support for the child with a disability; however, their underlying emotions include sadness, fear, anger, and guilt.

classic autism A disorder originally known as Kanner's syndrome. Characteristics include global language disorder, abnormal (bizarre) behavior patterns, social isolation, and usually, but not always, mental retardation.

classroom conduct problems Behaviors children demonstrate that interfere with instruction, impede social interaction, or endanger others.

cognitive function Ability to organize, reorganize, and contemplate information in the brain.

community-based assessment Assessment that focuses on skills needed to live independently in the community.

community-based resources Recreation, sport, and leisure agencies and facilities located in the community.

component model of functional routines Breaking down a person's daily sport and other physical activities into a series of routines that are composed of several skills.

concentric muscular contraction The amount of tension in the muscle is greater than the amount of applied resistance, so that the muscle shortens and movement results.

condition shifting Program in which several conditions of behavioral objectives are altered to produce activities that are sequenced from lesser to greater difficulty.

conditions A description of how the learner is to perform an objective.

conductive hearing impairment Condition in which the intensity of sound is reduced before reaching the inner ear, where the auditory nerve begins.

congenital Present at birth.

construct validity The degree to which a test measures what its author claims it measures.

content-referenced assessment A process of determining which components of a task or steps in a sequence of tasks have been mastered or not mastered.

content-related validity The degree to which the contents of the test represent an identified body of knowledge.

contingency agreement An agreement between the student and the teacher that indicates what the student must do to earn a specific reward.

continuous reinforcement schedule Reinforcing a behavior every time it is demonstrated.

convergence The ability to turn the eyes inward (medially) while visually tracking an object moving toward the body.

corrective physical education Activity designed to habilitate or rehabilitate deficiencies in posture or mechanical alignment of the body.

counselor Professional trained to facilitate students' affective development.

coxa plana Avascular, necrotic flattening of the head of the femur; also known as Legg-Calvé-Perthes disease.

coxa valga Increase in the angle of the neck of the head of the femur to less than 120 degrees.

coxa vara Decrease in the angle of the neck of the head of the femur to less than 120 degrees.

criterion for mastery Stated level of performance indicating attainment of an objective.

criterion shifting Programs in which the level of mastery (number of repetitions, distance traveled, speed, or range of motion) is modified to make the task easier or more difficult.

criterion-referenced test A test that provides information about a person's level of mastery of a skill or behavior.

criterion-related validity The degree to which a test compares to another acceptable standard of the same performance.

cross-lateral Coordination of both sides of the body.

cross-pattern creep Coordinating movements of legs and arms on opposite sides of the body while supporting the body on hands and knees.

cues and correction procedures Techniques used to increase the probability that a skill learned in one setting will be demonstrated in a different setting.

cystic fibrosis An inherited disease of the exocrine glands primarily affecting the gastrointestinal and respiratory systems.

D

de facto integration Placing students in educational settings without concern for their individual needs.

deaf Nonfunctional hearing for the ordinary purposes of life.

deaf-blind Loss of both hearing and vision.

debilitating conditions Physiological situations that progressively weaken individuals.

depth perception The ability to visually determine the position of objects in space by comparing the images entering each eye with each other.

developmental delay Retarded or arrested stages of performance that hinder a child's ability to be successful at a task.

developmental disabilities A term to describe all disabilities collectively.

developmentally appropriate learning environment A learning situation that is sensitive and responsive to the unique needs of children.

developmentally appropriate movement experience Play and movement opportunities, based on individual need, that allow a child to choose to participate in play and movement activities with success.

developmentally appropriate movement/play assessment Observing and recording children's cognitive, social-emotional, communication and language, and sensorimotor development as they interact with their environment.

diabetes A chronic metabolic disorder in which the cells cannot use glucose.

diabetes insipidus A condition that results from an inability to concentrate urine in the kidneys.

diabetes mellitus A group of metabolic disorders resulting from insufficiency of insulin.

diplegia Neurological affliction of both the arms and the legs, with the most involvement in the legs.

direct appeal to value areas Controlling behavior by calling on values children have internalized.

direct services Those professions identified by law with responsibility for providing educational services to students with disabilities (e.g., classroom teachers and physical educators).

directionality Perception of direction in space.

disability An obstacle.

disabled An individual with physical, social, or psychological variations that significantly interfere with normal growth and development.

disciplinary review A meeting between parents and educational professionals to discuss a student's disruptive behavior and develop a behavior management strategy or plan.

disorder General mental, physical, or psychological malfunction of the processes.

divergence The ability to turn the eyes outward (laterally) while visually tracking an object moving away from the body.

dominant stage theory A theory that proposes that the parent or sibling of a child with a disability experiences emotions and reactions that are identical to those experienced by an individual facing the death of a loved one or facing a terminal illness.

dorsiflexion The act of bending the foot upward (flexion).

dorsoflexion of the head Extending the head toward the back of the body.

drug therapy Use of prescribed medications to relieve symptoms and to control unusual aggressive behaviors and other types of behaviors that interfere with learning.

Duchenne muscular dystrophy (pseudohypertrophic) A disease of the muscular system characterized by progressive weakness and atrophy of the pelvic girdle followed by the shoulder girdle muscles.

due process The procedure to be followed to determine the extent to which an individual's constitutional rights have been made available.

duration recording Noting the length of time a behavior occurs.

dysmenorrhea Painful menstruation.

dysplasia Separation of the hip joint.

E

early childhood intervention (ECI) Providing developmentally appropriate programs for infants and toddlers ages birth to 3 years.

early childhood intervention (ECI) natural settings initiative Educating infants and toddlers ages birth to 3 years in their most natural environments.

eccentric muscular contraction The resistance is greater than the tension in the muscle so that the muscle gradually lengthens without relaxing.

ecological inventory A checklist of behaviors one should master to become self-sufficient in the natural environment.

educational accountability A particular educational program, method, or intervention can be demonstrated to cause a significant positive change in one or more behaviors.

educational classification The educational status of a student that has been determined by testing.

educational services The curricula, programs, accommodations, placements, behavior management plans, and personnel available to students.

empathy experiences Attempting to get the "feel" of having a disability by participating in activities while having a sensory or motor limitation placed on oneself (e.g., being blindfolded, ambulating in a wheelchair, wearing ear covers).

epilepsy Disturbance in electrochemical activity of the brain that causes seizures and convulsions.

equilibrium dysfunction Inability to maintain static and/or dynamic balance.

equilibrium reflexes A reflex that helps a person maintain an upright position when the center of gravity is suddenly moved beyond the base of support.

esotropia A condition in which the eyes turn inward, such as cross-eyes.

event recording Noting the number of times a specifically defined behavior occurs within a time interval.

eversion Lifting the outer border of the foot upward.

Ewing's sarcoma A round cell bone tumor of childhood.

exclusionary time-out Removing a student from the immediate environment to eliminate the possibility of the student disrupting the class through inappropriate behavior.

exercise-induced asthma (EIA) Muscular constriction of the bronchial tubes resulting from excessive and prolonged exercise.

exertion level Amount of effort required for a task.

exotropia A condition wherein an eye deviates laterally away from the nose.

expressive language Ability to communicate feeling, emotions, needs, and thoughts through speaking and gesturing (facial or manual).

extinction Removal of reinforcers that previously followed the behavior.

extraocular muscles of the eyes The six pairs of muscles attached to the eye that permit movement of the eyes.

F

facioscapulohumeral muscular dystrophy (Landouzy-Dejerine) A disease of the muscular system characterized by weakness of the facial muscles and shoulder girdles.

fading Gradually withdrawing help from a task.

fetal alcohol syndrome Severe mental retardation because of impaired brain development as a result of maternal use of alcohol during pregnancy.

fixed-interval ratio reinforcement schedule Reinforcing the occurrence of a desirable behavior demonstrated a set number of times according to a predetermined schedule (e.g., one reinforcer for every three instances of desired behavior).

flexibility Range of motion available at any one or a combination of joints.

focal seizure A seizure that involves loss of body tone and collapse while remaining conscious.

forward chaining The first step of a series of tasks is taught first.

fragile X syndrome An abnormality of the X chromosome that results in a folic acid deficiency and leads to learning disabilities or mild to severe mental retardation.

full inclusion Educating all children in supported, heterogeneous, age-appropriate, natural, child-focused classroom, school, and community environments.

functional adaptations Modification by using assistive devices or by changing the demands of a task to permit participation.

functional postural deficiencies Postural imbalances that result from asymmetrical muscle development.

functional skills Movements that can be used for a variety of tasks.

G

gait training Teaching or reteaching an individual to ambulate by walking.

general metatarsalgia Pain in the foot caused by undue pressure exerted on the plantar surface.

generalization The transfer of abilities and skills from the training environment to nontraining environments.

genu valgum Knock-knee.

genu varum Bowleg.

glaucoma A condition in which the pressure of the fluid inside the eye is too high, causing loss of vision.

Gowers' sign Moving from a hands and knees kneeling position to an upright position by pushing the hands against the legs in a climbing pattern.

grand mal seizure Seizure that involves severe convulsions accompanied by stiffening, twisting, alternating contractions and relaxations, and unconsciousness.

H

habilitation An educational term that indicates the person with a disability is to be taught basic skills needed for independence.

hallux valgus Displacement of the great toe toward the other toes, such as occurs with a bunion.

hammer toe The proximal phalanx (first joint) of the toe is hyperextended, the second phalanx (second joint) is flexed, and the distal phalanx (third joint) is flexed or extended.

hanging (posture) test Visually assessing the alignment of the spine as the person being evaluated hangs by the hands from a horizontal support.

hard-of-hearing Conditions of hearing impairment or persons who have hearing impairments but who can function with or without a hearing aid.

health-related fitness Components of physiological functioning that are believed to offer protection against degenerative diseases.

health-related tests Assessment instruments that include measures of cardiovascular endurance, muscular strength, percentage of body fat, and flexibility.

hemiplegia Neurological affliction of both limbs on one side, with the arm being more affected than the leg.

heterogeneous groupings Amassing students with different levels of abilities together.

heterophoria Tendency toward visual malalignment.

heterotropia Malalignments of the eyes in which one or both eyes consistently deviate from the central axis.

hierarchical order A continuum of ordered activities in which a task of lower order and lesser difficulty is prerequisite to acquisition of a related task of greater difficulty.

high rates of inappropriate behavior Demonstrated behaviors that interfere with appropriate behavior and that occur frequently or for long periods of time.

Hodgkin's disease A chronic condition in which large, multinucleated reticulum cells are present in lymph node tissue or in other nonreticular formation sites.

homeostasis The human body's attempt to keep itself in a state of balance.

homogeneous grouping Amassing students with similar levels of abilities together.

hurdle lesson Structuring a task in which a child can be successful to boost self-confidence and discourage the possibility of disruptive, avoidance behaviors.

hydrocephalic Refers to an abnormal condition that results when cerebral spinal fluid is not reabsorbed properly, thus collecting around the brain.

hyperglycemia A condition that results in too much blood sugar.

hyperopia A condition in which the light rays focus behind the retina, causing an unclear image of objects closer than 20 feet from the eye.

hypertropia A condition in which one or both eyes swing upward.

hypoglycemia A condition that results in too little blood sugar.

hypotropia A condition in which one or both eyes turn downward.

I

impulse control The ability to resist an impulse, drive, or temptation to perform a harmful, disruptive, or inappropriate behavior.

inappropriate reflex behavior Persistence of primitive reflexes beyond 1 year and/or failure to demonstrate all of the equilibrium reflexes after the first year of life.

incest A sexual act on a child by an adult who is biologically related to the child.

incidental learning Learning that is unplanned.

inclusive environment An environment designed to accommodate a variety of learners regardless of functional abilities.

indirect services Services provided by related service personnel to enable a student with a disability to function more fully.

individual education program (IEP) Specially designed instruction to meet the unique needs of a person for self-sufficient living.

individual education program (IEP) document An individual student's formal IEP report that must be approved by parents/guardians and educational professionals.

individual education program (IEP) meeting A formally scheduled gathering of parents and educational professionals to discuss a student's present level of educational performance, goals, and educational alternatives.

individual education program (IEP) process The procedure followed to develop an appropriate educational experience.

individual family service plan (IFSP) A family-centered plan for assessing and prioritizing needs, programming, and providing services for at-risk children under the age of 3 years.

individual motor education plan (IMEP) A substitute name for the individual physical education plan (IPEP).

individual physical education plan (IPEP) That portion of the IEP that addresses the physical and motor needs of the student.

individual transition plan (ITP) The specific strategies needed to move a child with a disability smoothly from home to preschool, preschool to school, or school to community.

individualized physical education program An activity program developed from assessment information to meet the unique needs of an individual with a disability.

infantile scoliosis Scoliosis that developed during the first 3 years of life.

inner language process Ability to transform experience into symbols.

insight-oriented therapy Relieving symptoms by treating causes of behavior.

instructional environment A setting designed for the education of students.

integration Placement of students with disabilities in environments with nondisabled students

interest boosting Involving a child in an activity to engage his or her interest in positive behaviors.

interval recording Counting the occurrence or nonoccurrence of a behavior within a specified time interval.

intervention strategies Techniques for weakening or eliminating disruptive behaviors or reinforcing desirable behaviors or practices.

inversion Turning upward of the medial border of the foot.

isokinetic exercises Exercises that provide resistance through the entire range of movement either by pushing one limb against the other or by using an exercise machine that provides resistance equal to the amount of pull throughout the range of motion.

isometric (static) muscular contraction The amount of tension in the muscle equals the amount of applied resistance, so that no movement occurs.

isotonic exercises Exercises using progressive resistance using free weights or a machine using stacked weights.

J

jacksonian focal seizure A seizure that involves localized twitching of muscles in the extremities.

Jacobson relaxation techniques Consciously relaxing voluntary skeletal muscles by stiffening and relaxing each body part in sequence.

K

Kaposi's sarcoma An AIDS-related condition that manifests itself as a malignant tumor.

ketoacidosis A violent reaction to lack of circulating insulin.

kinesthetic guidance Manually moving a student through the correct movement pattern so that the individual can get the "feel" of the motion.

kinesthetic system Muscles, tendons, joints, and other body parts that help control and coordinate activities such as walking and talking.

kypholordosis Exaggerated thoracic and lumbar spinal curves (round swayback).

kyphosis Exaggerated thoracic spinal curve (humpback).

L

labyrinthine portion of inner ear That part of the inner ear located in the vestibule that responds to movements of the head against gravity.

labyrinthine righting reaction An equilibrium reflex that causes the head to move to an upright position when the head is suddenly tipped while the eyes are closed.

laterality An awareness of the difference between both sides of the body.

least restrictive environment The setting that enables an individual with disabilities to function to the fullest of his or her capability.

legally blind Visual acuity of 20/20 or less in the better eye after maximum correction or having a visual field that subtends an angle of 20 degrees or less.

leukemia A type of cancer that negatively affects the body's blood-forming tissues.

locus of control The extent to which behavior is determined from within oneself or is dependent on others.

lordosis Exaggerated lumbar vertebral curve (swayback).

low rates of appropriate behavior Inability to remain on task for a prolonged time in familiar or unfamiliar settings.

low vitality A generalized long-lasting feeling of lack of energy.

M

mainstreaming Placement of children with disabilities in regular class, based on an IEP.

maintenance The perpetuation of a trained behavior after all formal intervention has ceased.

malleolus Ankle bone.

malnutrition Faulty or inadequate nourishment resulting from an improper diet.

manual communication system Techniques for communicating, including Pidgin Sign Language, American Sign Language, Manually Coded English, and fingerspelling.

manual guidance Physically moving a person through a movement.

manual muscle testing Evaluating the strength of a muscle by having an individual attempt to move a limb while the evaluator physically resists the movement.

mastoiditis Infection of the air cells of the mastoid process.

medical diagnostic service personnel Medical personnel who provide diagnostic services to children with disabilities and verify the disability status of individuals.

medically fragile Children with special health management needs who require technology, special services, or some form of ongoing medical support for survival.

meditation The art and technique of blocking out thoughts that create tension and refocusing attention and energy on soothing, quieting mental activity.

meningocele A protruding sac containing the lining of the spinal column.

menstruation The monthly loss of blood in mature females in response to hormonal cues.

mental retardation Significantly subaverage general intellectual functioning existing concurrently with deficits in adaptive behavior, manifesting before age 18 years.

metatarsal arch The transverse arch of the foot that runs across the ball of the foot.

metatarsalgia Also known as Morton's toe; severe pain or cramp in the metatarsus in the region of the fourth toe.

midline problem The inability to coordinate limbs on opposite sides of the body.

mobility training An adaptive technique that is applied to the blind and enhances the ability to travel.

modeling Demonstration of a task by the teacher or reinforcement by another student who performs a desirable behavior in the presence of the targeted student.

momentary time sampling Noting whether a behavior is occurring at the end of specified time intervals.

Morton's toe See metatarsalgia.

motor coordination The ability to use the muscles of the body to efficiently produce complex movement.

motor development lag See developmental delay.

motor fitness Characteristics of movement that are essential to the efficient coordination of the body.

motor milestones Significant movement patterns and skills that emerge at predictable times during the life of a typically developing child.

motor neuropathy A complication resulting from long-standing diabetes that causes an imbalance between the intrinsic and extrinsic muscles and contributes to deformities of the foot, change in gait pattern, and ulceration.

motor tics Sudden twitches of the entire body, shoulders, and/or head; eyeblinks or rolling of the head; repetitive tapping, drumming, or touching behaviors; or grimacing.

motor-planning deficit Inability to determine and execute a sequence of tasks needed to achieve a goal.

multidisciplinary motor team A group of direct service and related service providers who cooperate to determine and provide for students' physical and movement needs.

multiple sclerosis A chronic degenerative neurological disease primarily affecting older adolescents and adults.

muscle tension recognition and release Tensing and relaxing muscle groups at will; also known as differential relaxation.

muscular dystrophy Chronic, progressive, degenerative, non-contagious disease of the muscular system, characterized by weakness and atrophy of muscles.

muscular endurance The ability of a muscle to contract repetitively.

mycobacterial infections An AIDS-related condition that causes severe diseases localized in the lung or lymph nodes.

myelocele A protruding sac that contains the spinal cord.

myelomeningocele A protruding sac that contains the spinal cord and the lining of the spinal column.

myopia A refractive condition in which the rays of light focus in front of the retina when a person views an object 20 feet away or more.

N

natural environment Community settings where individuals function.

negative practice or satiation Constantly acknowledging a behavior for the purpose of discouraging demonstration of the behavior.

negative support reflex A reflex in which there is flexion of the knees when pressure is removed from the feet.

neuroblastoma A solid tumor of the embryonal neural crest of the sympathetic nervous system.

neurological components Sensory input systems and perceptual processes that underlie movement patterns and skills, and affective and cognitive functioning.

neurological validity The extent to which a test item truly measures central nervous system function.

neuromuscular reeducation Exercises performed through a muscle's current range of motion to stimulate proprioceptors and enable greater functional use.

neurophysiological differences Pertaining to structural and/or functional changes to the central nervous system.

nonexclusionary time-out Removing the student from an activity but allowing the student to remain in the vicinity of the class.

nonparalytic poliomyelitis An acute viral infection that involves the central nervous system but does not damage the motor cells of the spinal cord.

nonsequential stage theory A theory that proposes that the parents, siblings, or extended family members of a child with a disability may experience some or all of the stages of grief described by Kübler-Ross, but not necessarily in predictable stages.

normalization Making available to disabled individuals patterns and conditions of everyday life that are as close as possible to the norms and patterns of the mainstream of society.

normative-referenced test A test that measures an individual in comparison with others of the same age. Comparison standards are reported in percentiles, age equivalencies, and/or stanines.

nystagmus Rapid movement of the eyes from side to side, up and down, in a rotary motion, or in a combination of these movements.

O

obesity Pathological overweight in which a person is 20% or more above the normal weight (compare with overweight).

occupational therapist Professional who improves functional living and employment skills.

ocular-motor control The ability to visually fixate on objects and track their movement.

optical righting reaction An equilibrium reflex that causes the head to move to the upright position when the body is suddenly tipped and the eyes are open.

oral communication method Hearing-impaired persons are provided amplification of sound and are taught through speechreading (lipreading).

orientation Obtaining the response and reinforcing the response.

orthoptic vision The ability to use the extraocular muscles of the eyes in unison.

orthoptics The science of correcting deviations of the visual axis of the eye.

Osgood-Schlatter condition Epiphysitis of the tibial tubercle.

osteoarthritis Chronic and degenerative disease of joints.

osteogenesis imperfecta (brittle bone disease) A condition marked by both weak bones and elasticity of the joints, ligaments, and skin.

osteomyelitis Inflammation of a bone and its medullary cavity.

osteosarcoma A form of childhood bone cancer.

otitis media Infection of the middle ear.

overcorrection Repeated practice of an appropriate behavior whenever an inappropriate behavior is demonstrated.

overload principle Improving muscular strength by gradually increasing the resistance used over time (days or months).

overweight Any deviation of 10% or more above the ideal weight for a person (compare with obesity).

P

paralytic poliomyelitis An acute viral infection that involves the central nervous system and interferes with voluntary and involuntary muscle function.

paraplegia Neurological affliction of both legs.

parent counselors and trainers Specially trained professionals who provide education and support services to parents of children with disabilities.

Parkinson's disease A progressive disease that results in tremor of the resting muscles, a slowing of voluntary movements, muscular weakness, abnormal gait, and postural instability.

partial-interval time sampling Noting whether a behavior was demonstrated any time during given periods of time.

partially sighted Having less than 20/70 visual acuity in the better eye after correction, having a progressive eye disorder that will probably reduce vision below 20/70, or having peripheral vision that subtends an angle less than 20 degrees.

patella Knee cap.

percentage of body fat The amount of body fat in relation to muscle, bone, and other elements in the body.

perceptual function Ability to integrate sensory input information into constructs in the central nervous system.

perceptual-motor Use of activities believed to promote the development of balance, body image, spatial awareness, laterality, and directionality.

peripheral vascular disease Insufficient blood flow to blood vessels of the extremities.

permanent product recording Counting the actual products or behaviors that are demonstrated.

pernicious anemia An anemia caused by a decrease in the number of red corpuscles in the blood.

personal futures planning (PFP) A proactive strategy for identifying resources within and without the school that will provide ongoing support to a student with a disability.

pes cavus Exaggerated height of the longitudinal arch of the foot (hollow arch).

pes planus Extreme flatness of the longitudinal arch of the foot.

petit mal seizure Nonconvulsive seizure in which consciousness is lost for a few seconds.

physical fitness A physical state of well-being that allows people to perform daily activities with vigor, reduce their risk of health problems related to lack of exercise, and establish a fitness base for participation in a variety of activities; also refers to physical properties of muscular activity, such as strength, flexibility, endurance, and cardiovascular endurance.

physical lag A deficit in physical fitness components or function of a specific body part.

physical priming Physically holding and moving the body parts of the learner through the activity.

physical restraint Holding students to prevent them from physically harming themselves or someone else.

physical therapist A professional who evaluates and treats physical impairments through the use of various physical modalities.

placement Alternative educational environments available to students with disabilities.

planned ignoring Choosing not to react to a behavior to avoid reinforcing the behavior.

plantar flexion Moving the foot toward its plantar surface at the ankle joint (extension).

play therapy A type of intervention used with emotionally disturbed children that involves using play to provide insight into emotional problems.

plumb line (posture) test Comparing body landmarks with a gravity line to assess posture.

pneumocystis carinii pneumonia An AIDS-related condition that is a form of pneumonia caused by reactivation of chronic latent infections.

poliomyelitis (polio) An acute viral infection that may or may not lead to paralysis.

poly drugs More than one type of drug.

portfolio assessment process Using a variety of techniques to gather ongoing information about a child's developmental progress.

positive reinforcement A pleasing consequence that follows an action.

positive support reflex A reflex that causes the legs to extend and the feet to plantar flex when one is standing.

posttraumatic stress syndrome A recurring intense fear, helplessness, or horror as a result of direct or indirect personal experience of an event that involves actual or threatened death, serious injury, or threat to personal integrity.

posture screen Comparing body landmarks with a grid of vertical and horizontal lines to evaluate all segments of the body in relationship to each other.

Prader-Willi syndrome A condition characterized by neonatal hyptonia and feeding difficulty followed by excessive appetite, pica behavior, and obesity starting in early childhood.

premenstrual syndrome (PMS) A condition that occurs in some females 7 to 10 days before menstruation and persists until the menstrual flow begins, and that is characterized by nervousness, irritability, emotional instability, depression, and possibly headaches and edema.

present level of educational performance The skills, behaviors, and patterns an individual can demonstrate at any given time.

primitive reflexes Automatic reactions that should appear in an infant's movement repertoire during the first 6 months of life.

principle of normalization Routines of life that are typical for individuals without disabilities.

progressive relaxation Consciously releasing tension in specific muscle groups.

progressive resistive exercise Systematically adding resistance to an exercise to place additional demand on a muscle for the purpose of increasing strength.

prompting Physically holding and moving the body parts of the learner through an activity.

pronated feet A combination of tipping of the outer border of the foot and toeing out.

pronation Rotation of the palm of the hand downward or eversion and abduction of the foot.

prone lying test Visually assessing the alignment of the spine as the person being evaluated lies prone.

proprioceptive facilitation Exercises designed to excite motor units of a muscle to overcome paralysis.

proprioceptors Sensory receptors located in the muscles, joints, tendons, deep tissues, and vestibular portion of the inner ear that respond to movement.

protective extensor thrust reflex A reflex that causes immediate extension of the arms when the head and upper body are tipped suddenly forward.

proximity control Positioning oneself close to a child to encourage on-task behavior.

psychiatrist A physician with specialized training in the study and treatment of disorders of the mind.

psychologist A licensed professional who measures the cognitive, affective, and/or social status of a child with a disability and recommends intervention strategies.

psychomotor seizure Seizure in which one may lose contact with reality and manifest bizarre psychogenic behavior.

psychosocial competence Sense of self-confidence necessary to participate in successful interpersonal relationships.

psychosocial development The level of one's psychosocial competence.

ptosis Weakness and prolapse of an organ (e.g., prominent abdomen).

Q

quadriplegia (tetraplegia) Neurological affliction of all four extremities.

R

rape A sexual act involving penetration by an adult who is unrelated to the victim.

reasonable accommodation Modification of policies, practices, and/or procedures, including provision of auxiliary aids and/or services to enable a person with disabilities to use a facility.

receptive language Ability to comprehend meaning associated with language.

reciprocal exercises Exercises to stimulate and strengthen a muscle's agonist (protagonist).

recreation therapist Professional who works with physical and adapted physical educators and who provides information for individuals with disabilities to help them in making wise decisions in the use of leisure time.

reduction of tension through humor Using amusing comments or behaviors to reduce anxiety-producing situations.

refractive vision The process by which light rays are bent as they enter the eyes.

regular education initiative (REI) A federally endorsed effort to return children with disabilities to regular education programs to receive the majority of services regardless of the child's unique needs.

regular education program Routine educational services available to students without disabilities.

rehabilitation counselor Specially trained person who helps individuals with disabilities gain the confidence and learn the skills necessary to function as normally as possible.

reinforcement of an appropriate target behavior Rewarding a student for demonstrating a prespecified target behavior.

reinforcement of behavior other than target behavior Rewarding a student for not demonstrating a prespecified misbehavior during a predetermined time limit.

reinforcement of incompatible behavior Rewarding a student for demonstrating a behavior that is incompatible with the target misbehavior (e.g., rewarding a student for assisting rather than fighting with a peer).

reinforcement schedule The frequency with which reinforcers are given.

reinforcer distribution frequencies See reinforcement schedule.

related services Services that help a person benefit from direct services.

relaxation therapy Teaching a person to achieve a state of both muscular and mental tension reduction by the systematic use of environmental cues.

remedial physical education Activity designed to habilitate or rehabilitate functional motor movements and develop physical and motor prerequisites for functional skills.

removal of seductive objects Controlling behavior by eliminating from view equipment children are attracted to.

repetition The number of times the work interval is repeated under identical conditions.

response generalization Changes in behavior that were not specifically targeted for change.

response maintenance generalization Changes in behavior that continue to be demonstrated after the reinforcement has stopped.

restructure of classroom program Modifying a class routine to control student behavior.

retinitis pigmentosa Degeneration of the retina that produces gradual loss of peripheral vision.

retinoblastoma A malignant tumor that arises from the immature retina.

retinopathy A complication resulting from long-standing diabetes that is characterized by blurred vision, sudden loss of vision in one or both eyes, and/or black spots or flashing lights in the field of vision.

retinopathy of prematurity A visual impairment caused by excess oxygen during incubation of premature infants.

Rett syndrome A neurological disorder characterized by normal development during the first 6 months of life, followed by loss of acquired fine motor skills and development of impaired language skills, gait apraxia, and stereotypical hand movements.

reverse mainstreaming The infusion of individuals without disabilities into educational and recreation settings to interact with persons with disabilities.

rheumatoid arthritis (Still's disease) A systemic disease that causes inflammation, and eventual thickening, of the synovial tissue that surrounds joints.

S

scaffolding Providing an educational environment/support system that allows a child to move forward and continue to build new competencies.

schizophrenia Abnormal behavior patterns and personality disorganization accompanied by less-than-adequate contact with reality.

school health service personnel School staff, usually registered nurses, who monitor student health records, administer medicine, and provide other prescribed medical services.

scoliosis Lateral and rotational deviation of the vertebral column.

self-correct The ability to think about and modify one's own behavior.

self-management Shifting responsibility for behavior from the teacher or parent to the student.

self-management practice The ability to control one's own behavior.

sensorineural hearing impairment A loss of hearing caused by absence or malfunction of the cochlea or eighth cranial nerve.

sensory input system dysfunction Failure of a sensory system to function because of a delay in development or neurological impairment.

sensory integration deficit Failure to process sensory information at the central nervous system level.

sensory neuropathy A complication resulting from long-standing diabetes that is characterized by loss of the senses of pain, light touch, and heat.

serious emotional disturbance A condition exhibiting one or more of the following characteristics over a long period of time and to a marked degree that adversely affects educational performance: (1) inability to learn that cannot be explained in other ways, (2) inability to maintain or build satisfactory interpersonal relationships, (3) inappropriate types of behavior or feelings, (4) general pervasive mood of unhappiness or depression, and (5) tendency to develop physical symptoms or fears associated with personal or school problems.

shaping Reinforcement of small, progressive steps that lead toward the desired behavior.

shortened gestation In utero life of less than 36 weeks. Gestations of less than 27 weeks result in at-risk infants.

short-term instructional objectives The measurable intermediate steps that lead from the present level of performance to an annual goal.

shunt A drainage tube that is inserted to drain cerebral spinal fluid that is not being reabsorbed properly.

sickle cell anemia An inherited form of anemia that affects the bones, intestines, spleen, gallbladder, brain, and lungs.

signal interference Providing the student with a visible sign that a behavior is undesirable.

simulated training environment Establishing a teaching situation with task demands similar to those in the natural environment.

site-based management Local control of a school by a committee that includes the school's principal, teachers, parents, students, and community members.

situation or setting generalization Changes in behavior that occur from one environment to another and/or from one person to another.

skill problems Behaviors that interfere with a student's motor performance learning or efficiency.

skills Utilization of abilities to perform complex tasks competently as a result of reinforced practice.

social toxins Factors such as violence, poverty, hunger, homelessness, inadequate parenting, abuse and neglect, racism, and classism that seriously compromise the quality of life of children.

social worker A professional who provides individual and group counseling/assistance to children and their families.

socially aberrant behaviors Acting-out behaviors that are contrary to societal norms.

somatosensory strip in cerebral cortex The section of the cortex just posterior to the central sulcus that serves as a repository for incoming sensory information.

spasticity Clinical type of cerebral palsy characterized by muscle contractures and jerky, uncertain movements of the muscles.

spatial awareness The ability to replicate space in the "mind's eye" without visual input.

spatial relations The position of objects in space, particularly as the objects relate to the position of the body.

special physical education Another term used to describe adapted physical education.

specific learning disability A disorder in one or more of the basic psychological processes involved in understanding or in using language, spoken or written, which may manifest itself in the imperfect ability to listen, speak, read, write, spell, or do mathematical calculations.

speech therapist A professional who evaluates children with speech and language deficits and provides intervention programs.

spina bifida Congenital separation or lack of union of the vertebral arches.

spina bifida cystica Congenital separation of the vertebral arches resulting in a completely open spine with a protruding sac.

spina bifida occulta Congenital separation of the vertebral arches with no interference with function.

splinter skill Particular perceptual or motor acts that are performed in isolation and do not generalize to other areas of performance.

split-half reliability The degree to which scores from two halves of the same test agree when administered to one group.

spondylolisthesis Congenital malformation of one or both of the neural arches of the fifth lumbar vertebra and anterior displacement on the sacrum.

spondylolysis Congenital malformation of one or both of the neural arches of the fourth (rare) or fifth lumbar vertebra.

sports anemia A form of anemia that afflicts athletes with low values of red blood cells or hemoglobin.

sport-specific skills Movements that are used to perform sport activities.

status epilepticus A continual series of grand mal seizures with no letup.

Still's disease See rheumatoid arthritis (Still's disease).

stimulus change Modifying the environment to discourage expression of an undesirable behavior.

strabismus Crossed eyes resulting from inability of the eye muscles to coordinate.

strength The ability of a muscle to contract against resistance.

stress-coping training Teaching a person to identify tension-producing situations and practice relaxation before or when confronted with those situations.

structural postural deficiencies Postural imbalances that involve abnormalities in the bones and joints.

supination Rotation of the palm of the hand upward, or abduction and inversion of the foot.

support from routine Creating a highly structured program to enable insecure and/or emotionally disturbed children to function more effectively.

support personnel Individuals who assist the direct service provider in enabling students with disabilities to function in the least restrictive environment.

symmetrical tonic neck reflex A reflex in which the upper limbs tend to flex and the lower limbs extend when ventroflexing the head. If the head is dorsiflexed, the upper limbs extend and the lower limbs flex.

T

tactile defensive An aversion to touch and other tactile stimulation.

tactile system Knowledge of where the body ends and space begins and the ability to discriminate among pressure, texture, and size.

task-specific approach Teaching a skill directly and generalizing it to a variety of environments. If the skill cannot be learned, the prerequisites are taught.

tenotomy Surgical operation on the tendons.

test objectivity Freedom from bias and subjectivity.

test reliability A measure of a test instrument's consistency.

test standardization Administering an evaluation instrument to a large group of persons under the same conditions to determine whether the instrument discriminates among the group members.

test validity How truthful a test is.

test-retest reliability The degree to which scores agree when the same test is administered twice to the same persons.

three-year comprehensive reevaluation Laws require that every student with a disability who qualifies for special education services must receive a full reevaluation at least every 3 years.

tibial torsion Medial twisting of the lower leg on its long axis.

tinnitus Ringing in one or both ears in the absence of external stimuli.

token economy A form of contingency management in which tokens are earned for desirable behavior.

tonic exercises Passive movements of a muscle group to reduce the possibility of atrophy and/or to maintain organic efficiency.

tonic labyrinthine reflexes Reflexes that are present when one maintains trunk extension when supine and trunk flexion when prone.

total communication method The hearing-impaired person elects to communicate through speech, signs, gesture, or writing.

total quality management (TQM) A philosophy that promotes the practice of helping educators view themselves as supporters rather than judges; as mentors and coaches rather than lecturers; and as partners with parents, students, administrators, teachers, businesses, and entire communities rather than isolated workers within the walls of a classroom.

Tourette syndrome An inherited neurological disorder characterized by spasmodic, involuntary motor and vocal tics.

toxoplasmic encephalitis An AIDS-related condition that results in headaches, lethargy, confusion, seizures, and ring-enhancing lesions.

transdisciplinary A team of individuals representing different professions or disciplines.

transdisciplinary, play-based assessment (TPBA) Two or more professionals sharing information about children they observed in structured and unstructured play situations for the purpose of determining levels of functioning.

transition Changing from one situation to another (e.g., from home to a school setting or from the school setting to a community environment).

transition service personnel Specially trained professionals who provide the expertise to ensure that individuals with disabilities have the skills needed to work and function in the community.

transition services Services available to facilitate the process of a child with a disability first entering public school, moving from a preschool to a school program, or preparing to move from the school setting to a community setting.

transportation specialists Individuals who assist in ensuring that disabled students are provided appropriate and timely transportation services.

traumatic head (brain) injury Blows to the head that result in insult to brain tissue.

travel vision Residual vision in the blind that enables travel.

Trendelenburg test A test for hip dislocation that is performed by standing on one leg.

type I, insulin-dependent diabetes mellitus A form of diabetes that is characterized by hyperglycemia and must be controlled with insulin therapy.

type II, non-insulin-dependent diabetes mellitus A form of diabetes that is characterized by hyperglycemia, but for which ongoing insulin therapy is usually not necessary.

type III, gestational carbohydrate intolerance diabetes mellitus A form of diabetes that occurs in some pregnant women.

type IV, secondary diabetes A form of diabetes that results from conditions and syndromes that impact glucose tolerance.

U

undernutrition Insufficient nourishment resulting in detriments to health and growth.

V

variable-interval ratio reinforcement schedule Modifying the number of behaviors reinforced according to a predetermined schedule (one reinforcer for every three instances followed by one reinforcer for every five instances of desirable behavior, etc.).

ventroflexion of the head Flexing the head toward the front of the body.

vestibular sense Response for balance; located in the nonauditory section of the inner ear.

vestibular system The inner ear structures that are associated with balance and position.

vision specialist A specially trained professional who evaluates the extent of visual disabilities and designs intervention programs that make possible a successful educational experience.

visual behavioral specialist An optometrist or ophthalmologist who has specialized training in assessing and remediating misalignments of the eyes.

visual development specialist See visual behavioral specialist.

visual disability Having a classification as partially sighted or blind.

vocal tics Involuntary uttering of noises, words, or phrases, including sniffing, throat clearing, or repeated coughing, coprolalia, laughing involuntarily, uttering a variety of sounds or yells, barking, grunting, and echolalia.

W

whole-interval time sampling Noting whether a behavior occurred throughout an entire interval.

Wilms' tumor A lethal tumor that is a form of nephroblastoma or renal embryoma.

winged scapula Vertebral borders of the scapula project outward because of weakness of the serratus anterior of the middle and lower trapezius muscles.

Z

zero tolerance A school policy to expel students from school or place them in an alternative educational environment if they engage in specified disruptive behaviors.

Index